Bangkok and the Beaches Handbook

The travel guide

Footprint

Joshua Eliot and Janie Bickersteth

with Natapon Buranakul and Sophia Buranakul

"In the Kingdom of Siam there is no trade more unprofitable than that of tailor, for the common people have no need of such a man"

Nicolas Gervaise, a French missionary, who visited Siam in 1683-1686

Bangkok and the Beaches Handbook

Published by Footprint Handbooks
6 Riverside Court
Lower Bristol Road
Bath BA2 3DZ. England
T +44 (0)1225 469141
F +44 (0)1225 469461
Email info@footprintbooks.com
Web www.footprintbooks.com

ISBN 1 900949 78 4
CIP DATA: A catalogue record for this
book is available from the British Library.

In USA, published by
NTC/Contemporary Publishing Group
4255 West Touhy Avenue, Lincolnwood
(Chicago), Illinois 60712-1975, USA
T 847 679 5500 F 847 679 24941
Email NTCPUB2@AOL.COM

ISBN 0-658-04157-9
Library of Congress Catalog Card
Number: 00-132907

Credits

Series editor
Patrick Dawson and Rachel Fielding
Editor
Felicity Laughton
Maps
Sarah Sorensen
Production
Typesetting: Emma Bryers, Leona Bailey
Maps: Kevin Feeney (colour),
Robert Lunn, Claire Benison, Angus
Dawson, Maxine Foster
Front cover: Camilla Ford

Design
Mytton Williams

Photography
Front cover: Getty One Stone.
Back cover: Robert Harding.
Inside colour section: Impact, Pictor
International Ltd and Robert Harding
Picture Library.

Print
Manufactured in Italy by LEGOPRINT

Bangkok & the Beaches

BANGKOK

Chao Phraya River

CAMBODIA

Ratchaburi

Bight of Bangkok

Chonburi

Phetburi

Koh Si Chang

Koh Phai

Pattaya

Koh Lan

Chantaburi

Hua Hin

Koh Khram Yai

Koh Samaesan

Koh Samet NP

MYANMAR
(BURMA)

Koh Chang

Koh Maak

Koh Kut

*Gulf of
Thailand*

N

Ao Bang Saphan

Chumphon

0 km   50

0 miles   50

See back of book for
colour maps 1-6

Koh Ang Tong

Koh Phangan

Surin
Islands

Koh Phaluai

Koh Samui

Ao Ban Don

Surat Thani

Altitude in metres

1000

200

100

0

Neighbouring
Country

Similan
Islands

Nakhon Si
Thammarat

*Ao
Nakhon*

Phangnga NP

Koh Wa Yai

Koh Yao Noi

Krabi

——— Expressways

Koh Phuket

Koh Yao Yai

——— Main roads
(National Highways)

Phuket

Koh Phi Phi

Koh Klang

*Thale
Luang*

——— Other roads

Koh Lanta Nai

Koh Lanta Yai

Koh Po

Trang

——— Railway

Koh Hai (Ngai)

◆ National Park

Koh Talibong

*Thale Sap
Songkhla*

Koh No &
Koh Maew

–·–·– International Border

Koh Sukon

Songkhla

Hat Yai

Koh Yo

*Andaman
Sea*

Koh Bulon-Leh

Koh Rawi

Koh
Turatao

Narathiwat

Koh Adang

Lankawi
Island

MALAYSIA

Contents

Right: *Floating market at Damnoen Saduak, near Bangkok*

A foot in the door

Top: *Wat Phra Kaeo, situated within the walls of the Grand Palace, contains the Emerald Buddha, Thailand's most revered image of the Buddha.* ***Right***: *The raw ingredients.* ***Above***: *Not exactly everyone's cup of tea, Bangkok's crocodile farm (said to be the world's oldest) is home to 50,000 of these prehistoric beasts which not only entertain tourists but are also converted into bags, boots and steaks when their showbiz days are over.*

Highlights and Bangkok

Thailand is an Asian cliché. Exotic, inscrutable, hot, Oriental, delicate, sumptuous... Take **The first step**
the first few hours of an average visitor's arrival in Bangkok. Off the plane and into a
swanky new airport terminal. Lilting Thai voices, and a strange alphabet. Into the city
along an elevated highway in the company of an apparently deranged taxi driver, with
a magic diagram inscribed on the roof of his car, a picture of a long-dead king lodged
reverently in the tachometer, a cheap gold Buddha glued to the top of the dashboard,
and a garland of plastic frangipani hanging from the rear-view mirror. Out of the taxi
and into a quiet, cool hotel with copies of the Asian *Wall Street Journal* artfully
arranged on reception and CNN in the bedrooms. Or into a small guesthouse run by a
Thai bobbing to Bob Marley and offering sweltering rooms the size of chicken coops
for the price of a dozen eggs. But aside from the delights of Thailand that can never be
planned, what has the country to offer?

As Thailand's premier city, Bangkok lies at the epicentre of political, economic, social **Bangkok swank**
and cultural life. The swankiest restaurants, the richest monasteries, the grooviest
music, the finest art, the hippest bars, and the best shopping are all to be found in
Bangkok. Enjoy the city for what it is, not for what it isn't. It is not a peaceful, elegant,
refined and sedate place. It is a vibrant cornucopia of life where over 10 million people
live and love - and battle with perhaps the worst traffic in the world.

Near the top of any list of Bangkok's attractions must be the Grand Palace, built in 1782 **The Grand**
by the founder of the current Chakri dynasty. The Palace's most important building is **Palace**
Wat Phra Kaeo, the Temple of the Emerald Buddha, housing the Kingdom's most
revered image of Buddha. Bangkok lies at the centre of the country, the Grand Palace
lies at the core of Bangkok, and the Emerald Buddha is at the heart of the Grand Palace.

Bangkok is not, though, a one-sight wonder. The Chao Phraya River, on which Bangkok **Wats and**
is built, offers an entrée into the city's alter-ego, its sister city of Thonburi. There are **markets**
hundreds of monasteries from the gauche Wat Traimitr with its five-and-a-half tonne
solid gold image of the Buddha, through to the elegant Wat Rakhang. North of the
centre is the Weekend Market where 10,000 stall holders create one of the world's
great conflagrations of buying and selling.

While most people do touch base in effervescent Bangkok, and some grow to love the **Moving on**
city, for many it is just a means to an end, a way station en route to the islands, beaches,
towns and countryside of the south. With 2,614 km of coastline, there's a lot of potential.

Beaches and islands

People have been coming to the beaches of Thailand for recreation since the 1920s. Early guidebooks to Thailand called Hua Hin, 150 miles south of Bangkok, Hua Hin-on-Sea treating it like a sort of Oriental Margate. The Railway Hotel was built here in 1923 and starred in the film *The Killing Fields* when it was reinvented as a similarly renowned hostelry in Phnom Penh. But mass beach tourism in Thailand had to await the invention of the bikini, the development of cheap air transport, the onset of the Vietnam War, and humanity's love affair with the sun-bronzed body.

Phuket and Pattaya Thailand's most developed beach resorts are Phuket and Pattaya, the latter just a 3-4-hour drive from Bangkok. Reaching Phuket, Thailand's largest island, involves a short flight or a long train and bus ride. Both resorts have thousands of hotel rooms, restaurants and bars. Entertainment is on tap but these are not really beach resorts for the thin of wallet and shallow of pocket. Backpackers head elsewhere. Pattaya's beaches and sea are second rate; Phuket's are rather better.

Koh Samui and Hua Hin Koh Samui and Hua Hin offer a wider range of accommodation, geared to people of most budgets. The latter is suffering some of the problems afflicting Pattaya – unsustainable, unplanned and rather thoughtless development. Koh Samui, with several beaches and a more dispersed pattern of development has managed to avoid most of these problems. It still has some peaceful places as well as a zingy nightlife and a great choice of restaurants and bars. Many backpackers have moved on from Koh Samui to Koh Phangan and Koh Tao, smaller and less-developed islands in the same island group. Koh Tao, within the Ang Thong Marine National Park, has become an important dive centre.

Koh Samet Koh Samet, also set within the limits of a marine national park, has been a popular weekend island getaway from Bangkok for several years. The bungalow operations here are generally low key, and the beaches and sea in reasonable shape. It couldn't be counted a lost paradise island, but it's the nearest you will come to one within a 5-hour drive and boat trip from Bangkok.

Koh Phi Phi Koh Phi Phi enjoyed its 15 minutes of fame when *The Beach*, with Leonardo DiCaprio, was filmed here. There can't be many places with a more idyllic setting. It's just a shame there hasn't been a more concerted effort to plan and limit bungalow development. Still, even the overbuilding and plastic bottles on the beach can't completely take away the beauty of the place.

Other islands There are many, many more beaches and islands, each with its own character and advantages: Koh Lanta, Cha-am, Rai Leh and Ao Nang, Trang's Andaman islands, Koh Chang, Khao Lak, Koh Similan and Koh Surin, the Turatao islands…

Top: Some areas of Phuket have developed into vibrant, buzzy tourist areas with bars, restaurants and assorted entertainments to keep easily bored visitors at their ease. **Above**: Orange robes in a row. **Left**: Koh Samui was a haven for backpackers until the 1980s when the opening of an airport encouraged the development of more up-market hotels. But stretches of serenity remain. **Next page**: More than nine out out every ten Thais are Buddhist. It is only in the far south of the country that Buddhists are outnumbered by Thais professing another religion - in this case, Islam.

Off the beach

Most visitors to the south of Thailand rarely stray more than a few hundred yards from the coast. Which is a shame, because there is life, not to mention history, culture and nature, out of the hammock and away from the sand.

Historical sights

Phetburi is one of Thailand's bestpreserved Ayutthaya period towns – largely because it was never attacked by the Burmese who, historically, have made a habit of ransacking Thailand's cities. There is a series of fine monasteries dating from the 14th century, as well as a palace built by Rama IV in the late 19th century. Around 500 km south of Phetburi is one of Thailand's holiest monasteries, Wat Phra Boromthat Chaiya, dating from the 8th-9th century. This clearly shows the influence of the Sumatra-based Srivijayan Empire in this area of southern Thailand. Another monastery which dates from the Srivijaya period is Wat Mahathat in Nakhon Si Thammarat. But even better than the monastery is the fair which is held here each year in September or October.

For something just a little different, it is possible to visit one of the former hideouts of the Communist Party of Malaya that mounted a long-running insurgency first against the British and then the Malaysian government from the end of World War II through to 1989. Tucked away in the jungle near Betong, former guerillas now make a living regaling visitors with tales of their former rebellious lives.

Southern Thailand isn't really a place that people visit for the museums, but if happenstance should find you standing outside one with nothing to do, then the National Museum in Songkhla and the Thalang National Museum in Phuket are the best of the bunch.

National park and natural sights

The Khao Sam Roi Yod National Park was one of Thailand's first national parks and is a particularly good place to see waterfowl – from painted storks to numerous species of wader. In fact, southern Thailand offers the best waterbird sanctuaries in the country. The Thale Noi Waterbird Sanctuary at the northern end of southern Thailand's great lake, the Thale Sap Songkhla, and the Khu Khut Waterfowl Park towards the southern end, are two of the best. Khao Luang National Park, not far from Nakhon Si Thammarat, is named after southern Thailand's highest mountain and while it is rare for visitors to see the tigers, leopards and elephants that are said to inhabit the park, the waterfalls aren't quite so reclusive.

While many visitors are blissfully unaware of the fact, a number of Thailand's beach resorts and islands have been gazetted as national parks. These include, Koh Chang, Koh Samet, Koh Phi Phi, Koh Tarutao, Koh Tao, Laem Son, and Koh Surin. The fact that development has continued almost unhindered is a source of considerable concern and anger.

Cultural sights

Two of Thailand's bestknown Buddhist retreats are found in southern Thailand – Wat Suan Mok, 50 km from Surat Thani and Wat Khao Tum. Both offer 10day meditation courses. Nakhon Si Thammarat is a centre of shadow puppet theatre - a tradition which was probably introduced from Java. It is possible to visit a workshop where puppets are hammered out from buffalo hide and see a short performance.

For Chinese cuisine, try the brash and crass southern city of Hat Yai, popular with Malaysian-Chinese tourists, but if you have an ounce of love for the much maligned shark, avoid the shark's fin soup. Si Racha, home of Thailand's fiery chilli sauce is a pilgrimage spot for seafood lovers.

Essentials

2

Essentials

Planning your trip

Where to go

Top of the list for many people visiting Thailand, especially if they come from a less than tropical country, is a beach. Most are concentrated in the **South**, which stretches over 1,000 km to the border with Malaysia. The Gulf of Thailand lies to the east of the southern peninsula and the waters of the Andaman Sea to the west. Pattaya, Phuket, Koh Samui, Koh Phi Phi and Hua Hin are probably the best-known beach resorts, but there are scores of lesser-known islands and stretches of sand including Koh Chang, Koh Tao, Koh Samet, Ao Nang, Khao Lak, Trang's Andaman Islands and Koh Lanta. Whether you are looking for a luxury hotel in a resort with nightlife and restaurants galore, or a quiet out-of-the-way place with just a handful of 'A' frame huts a few steps from the sea, it is here to be found.

Most visitors begin their stay in Thailand in **Bangkok**. The capital has, it must be said, a poor reputation for pollution and congestion. But it's not just an urban nightmare. The city has impressive historical sights, the canals which gave it the label (along with several other cities in Asia) Venice of the East, great food, a throbbing night life and good shopping.

A few years ago the Tourist Authority of Thailand undertook a survey to discover where tourists went in the Kingdom. The results showed that the great majority visit just a handful of places. Many areas see scarcely a tourist from one week to the next. While in some countries this might be put down to remoteness and inaccessibility, virtually all of Thailand is easily reached, even at the height of the wet season. It does not take much of a spirit of adventure to find a small town which, for a day or two, you can call your own. For some more ideas, see the colour section at the beginning of the book.

When to go

See page 448 for more details on climate and for monthly climate graphs for Bangkok (see page 76), Phuket (see page 248) and Koh Samui (see page 336). Thailand's meteorological office has a website that posts daily weather reports: metnet.tmd.go.th For Bangkok the best time to visit is November to February when the rains have ended and temperatures are at their lowest (but don't expect to be cool!). However, although the rainy season brings thoughts of torrential day-long tropical rain to many people, this is rarely the case: heavy showers interspersed with clear skies is a more accurate description, and it is perfectly sensible to visit Thailand during the monsoon. Flooding is most likely towards the end of the rainy season in September and October. On average there are five to six hours of sunshine every day, even during the rainy season. Visitors will also benefit from lower hotel room rates. Note that the seasons become less pronounced the further south you travel. Generally the best times to visit the west side of the peninsula (Phuket, Krabi, Phi Phi, etc) is between November and April, while the east coast (Koh Samui, Koh Phangan, etc) is drier between May and October.

What to take

Travellers usually tend to take too much. Almost everything is available in Thailand's main towns and cities – and often at a lower price than in the West. Even apparently remote areas will have shops that stock most things that a traveller might require from toiletries and batteries to pharmaceuticals and film.

Suitcases are not appropriate if you are intending to travel overland by bus. A backpack, or even better a travelpack (where the straps can be zipped out of sight), is recommended. Travelpacks have the advantage of being hybrid backpacks-suitcases;

they can be carried on the back for easy porterage, but they can also be taken into hotels without the owner being labelled a 'hippy'. **NB** For serious hikers, a backpack with an internal frame is still by far the better option for longer treks.

In terms of clothing, dress in Thailand is relatively casual – even at formal functions. Jackets and ties are not necessary except in a few of the most expensive hotel restaurants. However, though formal attire may be the exception, dressing tidily is the norm. This does not apply on beaches and islands where (almost) anything goes and sarongs, thongs and such like are de rigueur. Nevertheless, while dress may be casual this does not extend to undress: topless sunbathing, which does – increasingly – occur, is frowned upon by Thais who are usually too polite to say anything. This is particularly true in the Muslim areas of the south.

There is a tendency, rather than to take inappropriate articles of clothing, to pack too many of the same article. Laundry services are cheap, and the turn-around rapid.

Checklist   Bumbag; earplugs; first-aid kit; hiking boots (if intending to visit any of the national parks); insect repellent and/or electric mosquito mats, coils; International driving licence; money belt; passports (valid for at least six months); photocopies of essential documents; short wave radio; spare passport photographs; sun hat; sun protection; sunglasses; Swiss Army knife; torch; umbrella; wet wipes; zip-lock bags.

Those intending to stay in budget accommodation might also include:
Cotton sheet sleeping bag; padlock (for hotel room and pack); soap; student card; toilet paper; towel; travel wash.

Note that all of the above are available in Thailand so don't think that you have to pack six weeks' supply of toilet paper!

Money   Travellers' cheques denominated in most major currencies can be exchanged in provincial centres whether they are recognized tourist destinations or not. Keep cash separate from your TCs. Cash can be withdrawn from ATMs in most towns using a credit or Cirrus card and personal identification number (PIN). Increasingly, people are travelling without travellers' cheques and merely getting by on credit and cash cards. However, a small supply of US$ cash is always useful in an emergency.

ISIC   Anyone in full-time education is entitled to an International Student Identity Card (ISIC). These are issued by student travel offices and travel agencies across the world and offer special rates on all forms of transport and other concessions and services. The ISIC head office is: ISIC Association, Box 9048, 1000 Copenhagen, Denmark, T45-33939303.

Before you travel

Visas   All tourists must possess passports valid for at least six months longer than their intended stay in Thailand.

30-day visa exemptions Passport holders from the 56 countries listed below do not require a visa when entering Thailand for tourist purposes if their stay in the Kingdom does not exceed 30 days. If you intend to stay longer, obtain a 60-day tourist visa (see below). Visitors are fined ฿100 per day each day they exceed the 30-day limit to a maximum of ฿20,000 – or 200 days. Payment can be made at the airport before departure or at the Immigration Department (see below). While, in theory, visitors can be denied entry if they do not have an onward ticket and sufficient funds for their stay, in practice customs officials almost never check. The same is true of tourists who arrive via the Thai-Malaysian border by sea, rail or road. The 30-day exemption applies to nationals of the following countries: Algeria, Argentina, Australia, Austria, Bahrain, Belgium, Brazil, Brunei, Canada, Denmark, Djibouti, Egypt, Fiji, Finland, France, Germany, Greece, Iceland, Indonesia, Ireland, Israel, Italy, Japan, Kenya, Korea, Kuwait, Luxembourg, Malaysia, Mauritania, Mexico, Morocco, Myanmar (Burma), Netherlands, New Zealand, Norway, Oman, Papua New Guinea, Philippines, Portugal, Qatar, Saudi Arabia, Senegal, Singapore, Slovenia, South Africa, Spain, Sweden, Switzerland, Tunisia, Turkey, UAE, UK, USA, Vanuatu, Western Samoa, Yemen. Malaysian nationals arriving by road from Malaysia do not need evidence of onward journey. Visitors from Hong Kong (China) do not require a visa for visits of up to 15 days.

Visas on arrival For tourists from 99 countries not in the list above, it is possible to have a visa issued on arrival. There is a visa booth at Don Muang (Bangkok) Airport, at customs control, and even a photo booth to provide passport snaps (one photograph required). Note that these visas are valid for 15 days only (฿300). Applicants must also have an outbound (return) ticket. There are similar desks at Chiang Mai, Phuket and Hat Yai airports.

Tourist visas These are valid for 60 days from date of entry (single entry) and must be obtained from a Thai embassy before arrival in Thailand. They can be extended for a further 30 days. Multiple entry visas are also available.

90-day non-immigrant visas These are also issued and can be obtained in the applicant's home country (about US$30). A letter from the applicant's company or organization guaranteeing their repatriation should be submitted at the same time.

Re-entry permit For those who wish to leave and then re-enter Thailand before their visa expires, it is possible to apply for a re-entry permit from the Immigration Department (see below) (฿500).

Visa extensions These are obtainable from the Immigration Department in Bangkok (see below) for ฿500. The process used to be interminable, but the system is now much improved and relatively painless. Extensions can also be issued in other towns, such as Koh Samui (see page 344) and Chiang Mai. Applicants must bring two photocopies of their passport ID page and the page on which their tourist visa is stamped, together with three passport photographs. It is also advisable to dress neatly. It may be easier to leave the country and then re-enter having obtained a new tourist visa. Visas are issued by all Thai embassies and consulates. The length of time a visa is extended varies according to the office and the official. However those on a 30-day no-visa entry can usually have their stay extended by a week, sometimes 10 days; those with a 60-day tourist visa can usually expect a 30-day extension.

For latest information on visas and tourist visa exemptions see the Consular Information section of the Thai Ministry of Foreign Affairs website: www.mfa.go.th/ConsInfo/

In the UK there is now a **visa information line**, operating 24 hours a day, T0891-600150.

Australia 111 Empire Circuit, Yarralumla, ACT, 2600 Canberra, T06-62731149. *Austria* Cottaggasse 48, 1180 Vienna, T431-4783335. *Belgium* 2 Place du Val de la Cambre, Brussels, T322-6406810. *Canada* 180 Island Park Drive, Ottawa, Ontario, K1Y 0A2, T613-7224444. *Denmark* Norgesmindevej 18, 2900 Hellerup, Copenhagen, T45-39625010. *France* 8 Rue Greuze, 75116 Paris, T331-56265050. *Germany* Uberstrasse 65, 53173 Bonn, T0228-956860. *Greece* 23 Taigetou St, PO Box 65215, Paleo Psychico 15452 Athens, T301-6717969. *Italy* Via Nomantana, 132, 00162 Rome, T396-86204381. *Japan* 3-14-6, Kami-Osaki, Shinagawa-Ku, Tokyo 141,

Thai embassies worldwide

Essentials

T813-34472247. *Laos* Route Phonekheng, Vientiane, PO Box 128, T85621-214581. *Malaysia* 206 Jalan Ampang, 50450 Kuala Lumpur, T093-2488222. *Myanmar (Burma)* 45 Pyay Rd, 65 1/2 Mlie, Hlaing Township, Yangon, T951-525670. *Nepal* Ward 3, Bansbari, PO Box 3333, Kathmandu, T9771-371410. *Netherlands* Laan Copes Van Cattenburch 123, 2585 E3, The Hague, T3170-3450632. *New Zealand* 2 Cook St, Karori, PO Box 17226, Wellington, T644-4678618. *Norway* Eilert Sundts Gate 4, 0244 Oslo, T47-22128660. *Portugal* Rua de Alcolena 12, Restelo 1400 Lisbon, T3511-3015051. *Spain* Calle del Segre 29-2 A, 28002 Madrid, T3491-5632903. *Sweden* Floragatan 3, 114 31, Stockholm 100 40, T4608-7917340. *Switzerland* Kirchstrasse 56, 3097 Bern, T4131-3722281. *UK* 29-30 Queen's Gate, London, SW7 5JB, T0171-5892944. *USA* 1024 Wisconsin Avenue, NW, Suite 401, Washington, DC 20007, T202-9443600.

Foreign embassies & consulates in Bangkok
Australia 37 Sathorn Tai Rd, T2872680. *Austria* 14 Soi Nandha, off Soi Attakarnprasit (Soi 1), Sathorn Tai Rd, T2873970. *Belgium* 44 Soi Phya Pipat, off Silom Rd, T2360150. *Canada* 11th and 12th Floors, Boonmitr Building, 138 Silom Rd, PO Box 2090, T2374125. *Denmark* 10 Soi Attakarn Prasit, Sathorn Tai Rd, T2132021. *France* 35 Soi Rong Phasi Kao (Soi 36), Charoen Krung Rd, T2668250. *Germany* 9 Sathorn Tai Road, T2132331. *Greece* 79 Sukhumvit Soi 4 (Nana Tai), Sukhumvit Rd, Prakanong, T2542939. *Italy* 399 Nang Linchee Rd, Thungmahamek, T2854090. *Japan* 1674 New Petchburi Rd, T2526151. *Laos* 520, 520/1-3 Soi Ramkamhaeng 39, Bangkapi, T5383696. *Malaysia* 15th Floor, Regent House, 183 Rajdamri Rd, Pathumwan, T2541700. *Myanmar (Burma)* 132 Sathorn Nua Rd, T2332237. *Nepal* 189 Soi 71 Sukhumvit Rd, Prakanong, T3902280. *Netherlands* 106 Wireless Rd, T2547701. *New Zealand* 93 Wireless Rd, T2542530. *Norway* 1st Floor, The Bangkok of America Building, 2/2 Wireless Rd, T2530390. *Portugal* 26 Bush Lane, T2342123. *Spain* 7th Floor (701-702), Deithelm Towers (Tower A), 93/1 Wireless Rd, T2526112. *Sweden* 20th Floor, Pacific Place, 140 Sukhumvit Rd, T2544955. *Switzerland* 35 North Wireless Rd, PO Box 821, T2530156. *UK* 1031 Wireless Rd, T2530191. *USA* 120-122 Wireless Rd, T2054000.

Vaccinations

No vaccinations required, unless coming from an infected area (if visitors have been in a yellow fever infected area in the 10 days before arrival, and do not have a vaccination certificate, they will be vaccinated and kept in quarantine for six days, or deported).

Money

Plastic is increasingly used in Thailand and just about every town of any size will have a bank with an ATM. Visa and MasterCard are the most widely taken credit cards and cash cards with the Cirrus logo can also be used to withdraw cash at many banks. Generally speaking, AMEX can be used at branches of the Bangkok Bank; JCB at Siam Commercial Bank; MasterCard at Siam Commercial and Bangkok Bank; and Visa at Thai Farmers' Bank and Bangkok Bank. Most larger hotels and more expensive restaurants take credit cards as well. Because Thailand has embraced the ATM with such exuberance, many foreign visitors no longer bother with travellers' cheques and rely entirely on plastic. Even so, a small stash of US$ cash can come in handy in a sticky situation.

Credit cards **Notification of credit card loss**: American Express, IBM Bldg, Phahonyothin Rd, T2730040; Diners Club, Dusit Thani Bldg, Rama IV Rd, T2332645, 2335775, 2335644, 2383660; JCB T2561361, 2561351; Visa and MasterCard, Thai Farmers Bank Bldg, Phahonyothin Rd, T2522212, T2701801-10.

• •
Exchange rates: October 2000

Currency	Baht
US$	43.7
£	63.3
Euro	36.7
Japanese Yen	0.4
Malaysian Ringgit	11.4
Singapore $	24.9
Hong Kong $	5.6
Swiss Franc	24.5
Dutch Guilder	16.7
French Franc	5.6
Italian Lire	0.02
Australian $	23.1
New Zealand $	17.5

• •

Cost of living Visitors staying in first-class hotels and eating in hotel restaurants will probably spend a minimum of ฿1,000 per day and conceivably much more. Tourists staying in cheaper air-conditioned accommodation, and eating in local restaurants will probably spend about ฿500-750 per day. A backpacker, staying in fan-cooled guesthouses and eating cheaply, might expect to be able to live on ฿200 per day. In Bangkok, expect to pay 20-30% more.

Currency The unit of Thai currency is the **baht** (฿), which is divided into 100 **satang**. Notes in circulation include ฿20 (green), ฿50 (blue), ฿100 (red), ฿500 (purple) and new ฿1,000 (orange and grey). Coins include 25 satang and 50 satang, and ฿1, ฿5, and ฿10. The two smaller coins are gradually disappearing from circulation and the 25 satang coin, equivalent to the princely sum of US$0.003 (3 cents), is rarely encountered. The colloquial term for 25 satang is *saleng*.

Exchange rates The exchange rate can be found in the daily newspapers or on the web. Bangkok Bank's site is www.bbl.co.th/bankrates/ Another useful site is www.oanda.com/converter/classic which will provide exchange rates for any specified currencies. It is best to change money at banks or money changers which give better rates than hotels. There is no black market. First-class hotels have 24-hour money changers. There is a charge of ฿13 per cheque when changing TCs (passport required) so it works out cheaper to travel with large denomination TCs (or avoid TCs altogether). Indonesian rupiah, Nepalese rupees, Burmese kyat, Vietnamese dong, Lao kip and Cambodian riels cannot be exchanged for baht at Thai banks. (Money changers will sometimes exchange kyat, dong, kip and riel and it can be a good idea to buy the currencies in Bangkok before departure for these countries as the black-market rate often applies.)

For 13 years, until 2 July 1997, the Thai baht was pegged to the US$ and you could be sure, on arrival, that US$1 would buy you ฿25, give or take a *saleng*. Since the baht was forced from its peg and allowed to float it has fluctuated a great deal more. At the time of going to press there were around ฿44 to US$.

Getting there

Air

The majority of visitors arrive in Thailand through Bangkok's Don Muang airport. Phuket, Hat Yai and Koh Samui in the south are also international airports. More than 35 airlines and charter companies fly to Bangkok. **Thai International** or THAI is the national carrier.

From Europe The approximate flight time from London to Bangkok (non-stop) is 12 hours. There are direct flights from most major cities in Europe. From **London** Heathrow, airlines offering non-stop flights include Qantas, British Airways, Thai Airways and Eva Air. Philippine Airlines flies a two-stop service from **Gatwick**. There are non-stop flights from **Athens** on Thai and Olympic, **Amsterdam** on KLM and China Airlines, **Copenhagen** on Thai and SAS, **Frankfurt** on Thai, Lufthansa and Garuda, **Paris** on Thai and Air France and **Zurich** on Thai and Swiss Air.

Essentials

Essentials

Discount flight agents in the UK and Ireland

Council Travel, *28a Poland St, London,*
W1V 3DB, T020-74377767,
www.destinations-group.com
STA Travel, *86 Old Brompton Rd, London,*
SW7 3LH, T020-74376262, www.
statravel.co.uk They have other branches
in London, as well as in Brighton, Bristol,
Cambridge, Leeds, Manchester,
Newcastle-Upon-Tyne and Oxford and on
many university campuses. Specialists in
low-cost student/youth flights and tours,

also good for student IDs and insurance.
Trailfinders, *194 Kensington High Street,*
London, W8 7RG, T020-79383939.
Usit Campus, *52 Grosvenor Gardens,*
London, SW1 0AG, T0870 240 1010,
www.usitcampus.co.uk Student/youth
travel specialists with branches also in
Belfast, Brighton, Bristol, Cambridge,
Manchester and Oxford. The main Ireland
branch is at 19 Aston Quay, Dublin 2,
T01-602 1777.

From the USA & Canada The approximate flight time from Los Angeles to Bangkok is 21 hours. There are one-stop flights from **Los Angeles** on THAI and two-stops on Delta; one-stop flights from **San Francisco** on Northwest and United and two-stops on Delta; and one-stop flights from **Vancouver** on Canadian.

From Australasia There are flights from **Sydney** and **Melbourne** (approximately nine hours) daily with Qantas and Thai Airways. There is also a choice of other flights with British Airways, Alitalia, Lufthansa, and Lauda Air which are less frequent. There are flights from **Perth** with Thai Airways and Qantas. From **Auckland**, Air New Zealand, Thai Airways and British Airways fly to Bangkok.

From South Asia Thai Airways, Air India, Indian Airlines and Aeroflot fly from **Delhi**. Air Lanka, Thai Airways and Cathay Pacific fly from **Colombo**. From **Dhaka** there are flights with Biman Bangladesh Airlines or Thai Airways. PIA and Thai Airways fly from **Karachi**. Balkan flies from **Male**. Royal Nepal Airlines and Thai Airways fly from **Kathmandu**.

From the Middle & Far East Gulf Air fly from **Bahrain**, and Egyptair from **Cairo**. Numerous airlines fly from **Hong Kong, Tokyo** and **Manila** as well as regional destinations like **Kuala Lumpur, Singapore** and **Jakarta**.

Links to South East Asia Bangkok is a transport hub for air connections with Yangon/Rangoon (Myanmar/Burma), Vientiane (Laos), Hanoi and Ho Chi Minh City/Saigon (Vietnam), and Phnom Penh (Cambodia). Partly as a result it also has a concentration of tour companies specializing in Indochina and Myanmar and is a good place to arrange a visa.

Domestic Links It is possible to fly direct to **Phuket** from Dusseldorf and Munich as well as Hong Kong, Kuala Lumpur, Penang, Singapore, Taipei and Tokyo. **Hat Yai** has daily connections with Singapore and Kuala Lumpur, and **Koh Samui** with Singapore.

Train

Regular rail services link Singapore and Bangkok, via Kuala Lumpur, Butterworth and the major southern Thai towns. Express air-conditioned trains take two days from Singapore, 34 hours from Kuala Lumpur, 24 hours from Butterworth (road connections to Penang). The *Magic Arrow Express* leaves Singapore on Sunday, Tuesday and Thursday, Bangkok-Singapore (฿899-1,965), Bangkok-Kuala Lumpur (฿659-1,432) and to Ipoh (฿530-1,145). An additional train from Butterworth departs at 1340, arriving Bangkok 1130 the next day. The train from Bangkok to Butterworth departs 1400, arriving Butterworth 1240 (฿457-1,147). All tickets should be booked in advance.

Discount flight agents in Australia and New Zealand

Flight Centres, 82 Elizabeth St, Sydney, T13-1600; 205 Queen St, Auckland, T09-309 6171. Also branches in other towns and cities.
STA Travel, T1300-360960, www.statravelaus.com.au; 702 Harris St,

Ultimo, Sydney, and 256 Flinders St, Melbourne. In NZ: 10 High St, Auckland, T09-366 6673. Also in major towns and university campuses.
Travel.com.au, 80 Clarence St, Sydney, T02-929 01500, www.travel.com.au

Orient-Express Hotels, which operates the Venice Simplon Orient-Express also runs the luxury *Eastern & Oriental Express* between Bangkok, Kuala Lumpur and Singapore. The air-conditioned train of 22 carriages including a saloon car, dining car, bar and observation deck and carrying just 132 passengers runs once a week from Singapore to Bangkok and back. Luxurious carriages, fine wines and food designed for European rather than Asian sensibilities make this not just a mode of transport but an experience. This locomotive extravaganza departs from Bangkok on Wednesday and returns from Singapore every Sunday. The journey takes 41 hours (two nights, one day) to cover the 2,000-km one-way trip. Passengers can disembark at Hua Hin, Butterworth (Penang) and Kuala Lumpur. Reservations can be made at Orient-Express Hotels, Sea Containers House, 20 Upper Ground, London SE1 9PF, UK T020-78055100; Orient-Express Hotels also has agents in Bangkok, Singapore and Kuala Lumpur to handle reservations – in Bangkok T2168661; in Singapore contact: 32-01 Shaw Towers, Beach Road, T3923500, F3923600. Booking and information available in Australia (+61(2) 99059295), France (+33(1) 55621800), Italy (+39 55180003), Japan (+81(3) 32651200), USA (+1 630 9542944).

Road

The main road access is to and from Malaysia. The principal land border crossings into Malaysia are near Betong in Yala Province, from Sungei Golok in Narathiwat Province (see page 424) and at Padang Besar, where the railway line crosses the border.

Boat

No regular, scheduled cruise liners sail to Thailand any longer but it is sometimes possible to enter Thailand on a freighter, arriving at Khlong Toey Port in Bangkok. The *Bangkok Post* publishes a weekly shipping post with details on ships leaving the kingdom.

There are frequent passenger ferries from Pak Bara, near Satun, in southern Thailand to Perlis and Langkawi Island, both in Malaysia (see page 322). The passenger and car ferries at Ta Ba, near the town of Tak Bai, south of Narathiwat, make for a fast border crossing to Pengkalan Kubor in Malaysia (see page 417). An alternative is to hitch a lift on a yacht from Phuket (Thailand) or from Penang (Malaysia). Check at the respective yacht clubs for information.

Touching down

Immigration Department Soi Suan Plu, Thanon Sathorn Tai, Bangkok 10120, T2873101. ■ *Mon-Fri 0930-1630, Sat 0830-1200 (tourists only).*

Tax clearance All visitors who have earned income while staying in Thailand are required to pay income tax and obtain a tax clearance certificate. Contact the Revenue Department, Chakrapong Road, Bangkok, T2829899.

● ●

Discount flight agents in North America

Air Brokers International, *323 Geary St,* *air travel information and reservations.*
Suite 411, San Francisco, CA94102, *STA Travel*, *5900 Wilshire Blvd, Suite 2110,*
T01-800-883 3273, www.airbrokers.com *Los Angeles, CA 90036, T1-800-777 0112,*
Consolidator and specialist on RTW and *www.sta-travel.com Also branches in New*
Circle Pacific tickets. *York, San Francisco, Boston, Miami,*
Council Travel, *205 E 42nd St, New York,* *Chicago, Seattle and Washington DC.*
NY 10017, T1-888-COUNCIL, www. *Travel CUTS*, *187 College St, Toronto, ON,*
counciltravel.com Student/budget agency *M5T 1P7, T1-800-667 2887,*
with branches in many other US cities. *www.travelcuts.com Specialist in student*
Discount Airfares Worldwide On-Line, *discount fares, Ids and other travel*
www.etn.nl/discount.htm A hub of *services. Branches in other Canadian cities.*
consolidator and discount agent links. *Travelocity*, *www.travelocity.com Online*
International Travel Network/Airlines *consolidator.*
of the Web, *www.itn.net/airlines Online*

● ●

Airport information

Don Muang airport lies 25 km north of Bangkok. There are two international terminals (adjoining one another) and one domestic terminal. Terminal 1 serves Asia, and Terminal 2 the rest of the world. A 500 m-long covered and air-conditioned walkway links the domestic and international terminals. Facilities include: banks and currency exchange, post office, left luggage (฿70 per item per day – maximum four months, located between terminals 1 and 2), hotel booking agency, airport information, airport clinic, lost and found baggage service, duty-free shops, restaurants and bars including a whole slate of newly opened fast-food outlets – Burger King, Svensson's, Pizza Hut and Upper Crust. **NB** Food is expensive here – cheap food is available across the footbridge at the railway station. The *Amari Airport Hotel* is linked to the international terminal by a walkway. It provides a 'ministay' service for passengers who wish to 'freshen-up' and take a room for up to three hours between 0800 and 1800 (T5661020/1)

A new airport for Bangkok in 2004: In 2000 a government panel finally decided that Nong Ngu Hao – or Cobra Swamp – would become Bangkok and Thailand's new international gateway in 2004, taking over from Don Muang. Nong Ngu Hao is in Bang Phli district, Samut Prakan province, south of Bangkok (Don Muang is north). But Don Muang will remain open for two years while Nong Ngu Hao is expanded and a second runway added. Given the Thai authorities' tendency to change their minds, don't imagine that this is signed and sealed until the first aircraft hits the tarmac at Nong Ngu Hao.

T5351386 for departures, T5351301 for arrivals. Domestic flight information: **Flight** T5351253. The new domestic terminal has a hotel booking counter, post office, **information** currency exchange counters, restaurant and bookshop. An elevated a/c walkway connects the international and domestic terminals; a shuttle bus is sometimes available; but beware, taxis grossly overcharge for a drive of under 1 km.

Passport control at Don Muang Airport during peak arrival periods (usually 1200-1400) can be choked with visitors – be prepared for a wait of an hour or more before reaching the arrivals hall.

1. File a report with the local police. 2. Take the report to your local embassy or **Procedure for** consulate and apply for a new travel document or passport (if there is no **lost or stolen** representation, visit the Passport Division of the Ministry of Foreign Affairs). 3. Take **passport** the new passport plus the police report to Section 4, Subdivision 4, Immigration

Essentials

Touching down

Police: *T191, T123.* **Tourist Police:** *T195.* **Fire:** *T199.* **Ambulance:** *T2522171-5.* **Tourist Assistance Centre:** *Rachdamnern Nok Avenue, Bangkok, T2828129.* **Hours of business** *Banks: 0830-1530 Monday-Friday.* **Currency exchange services:** *0830-2200 Monday-Sunday in Bangkok and other tourist centres like Pattaya, Phuket and Chiang Mai. In other towns opening hours are usually rather shorter.* **Government offices:** *0830-1200, 1300-1630 Monday-Friday.* **Tourist offices:** *0830-1630 Monday-Sunday.* **Shops:** *0830-1700, larger shops: 1000-1900 or 2100.*

Official time *Seven hours ahead of GMT.* **Voltage** *220 volts (50 cycles) throughout Thailand. Most first and tourist class hotels have outlets for shavers and hair dryers. Adaptors are recommended, as almost all sockets are two pronged.* **Weights and measures** *Thailand uses the metric system, although there are some traditional measures still in use, in particular the rai, which equals 0.16 ha. There are four ngaan in a rai. Other local measures include the krasorp (sack) which equals 25 kg and the tang which is 10-11 kg. However, for most purchases (for example fruit) the kilogram is now the norm.*

Bureau, room 311 (third floor), Old Building, Soi Suan Plu, Sathorn Tai Road, Bangkok, T2873911, for a new visa stamp.

Airport tax Payable on departure – ฿500 for international flights. Tax on domestic departures is included in the price of the ticket. **Tax clearance:** any foreign visitor who has derived income while staying in Thailand must pay income tax. In addition, all travellers who have stayed in Thailand for 90 days or more in any one calendar year must obtain a tax clearance certificate. To avoid delay at the airport, contact the Revenue Department, Chakrapong Road, T2829899.

Visitors in transit for less than 12 hours are permitted to enter the country and not pay departure tax on leaving again.

Customs **Duty-free allowance** 250 grams of cigars or cigarettes (or 200 cigarettes) and one litre of wine or spirits. One still camera with five rolls of film or one movie camera with three rolls of 8mm or 16mm film.

Currency regulations Non-residents can bring in up to ฿2,000 per person and unlimited foreign currency although amounts exceeding US$10,000 must be declared. Maximum amount permitted to take out of the country is ฿50,000 per person.

Prohibited items All narcotics; obscene literature, pornography; fire arms (except with a permit from the Police Department or local registration office).
Some species of plants and animals are prohibited, for more information contact the Royal Forestry Department, Phahonyothin Road, Bangkok, T5792776. Permission of entry for animals by air is obtainable at the airport. An application must be made to the Department of Livestock Development, Bangkok, T2515136 for entry by sea. Vaccination certificates are required; dogs and cats need rabies certificates.

Export restrictions No Buddha or Bodhisattva images or fragments should be taken out of Thailand, except for worshipping by Buddhists, for cultural exchanges or for research. However, it is obvious that many people do – you only have to look in the antique shops to see the abundance for sale. A licence should be obtained from the Department of Fine Arts, Na Prathat Road, Bangkok, T2241370, from Chiang Mai National Museum, T221308 or from the Songkhla National Museum, Songkhla,

T311728. Five days notice is needed; take two passport photographs of the object and photocopies of your passport.

A *Amari Airport*, 333 Chert Wudthakas Rd, T5661020, F5661941, airport @mozart.inet.co.th A/c, restaurants, pool, fitness centre, connected to airport by a/c footbridge; 400-plus rooms look onto attractive gardens. Useful hotel for transit passengers with short-term stays for wash and rest available. Ladies and executive floors, several restaurants including Japanese and *Le Bel-Air* for steaks and seafood. **A** *Rama Gardens*, 9/9 Vibhavadi Rangsit Rd, Bangkaen (7 km from the airport), T5610022, F5611025. A/c, restaurants, two attractive large pools, out of town on road to airport, inconvenient for most except those merely stopping over for a few hours, but spacious grounds with fitness centre, tennis, squash, golf, putting; **A-B** *Quality Suites*, 99/401-486 Chaeng Wattana Rd, Soi Benjamitr, T9822022, F9822036. A/c, restaurant, indoor pool, 'mini' stays available (maximum eight hours), slightly cheaper than the *Amari* but 15 minutes from airport, OK for a night's stopover. **A** *Asia Airport*, 99/2 Moo 8 Phahon-Yothin Rd, T9926999, F5323193, Sale@asiahotel.co.th Huge and impersonal, but all the amenities if you can't face driving into town.

Airport accommodation

Taxi Official taxi booking service in the arrivals hall. There are two desks. One for the more expensive official airport taxis (newer, more luxurious vehicles); one for public taxis. The former cost ฿400 downtown; ฿300 to the northern and northeastern bus terminals; ฿450 to the southern bus terminal; ฿1,500 to Pattaya. Note that airport flunkies sometimes try to direct passengers to this more expensive 'limousine' service: walk through the barriers to the public taxi desk. A public taxi to downtown should cost about half these prices – roughly ฿200. Note that tolls on the expressways are paid on top of the fare on the meter. If taking a metered taxi, the coupon from the booking desk will quote no fare – ensure that the meter is used or you may find that the trip costs ฿300 instead of ฿200. Keep hold of your coupon – some taxi drivers try to pocket it – as it details the obligations of taxi drivers. Some regular Don Muang visitors recommend going up to the departures floor and flagging down a taxi that has just dropped passengers off. Again, expect to pay ฿200. **Warning** There have been cases of visitors being robbed in unofficial taxis. To tell whether your vehicle is a registered taxi, check the colour of the number plate. Official aiport limousines have green plates, public taxis have yellow plates – and a white plate means the vehicle is not registered as a taxi. The sedan service into town costs ฿500-650. Cars are newer, more comfortable and better maintained than the average city taxi. It takes 30 minutes to one hour to central Bangkok, depending on the time of day and the state of the traffic. The elevated expressway can reduce journey time to 20 minutes – ask the taxi driver to take this route if you wish to save time but note, again, that there is a toll fee. Also note that there have been some complaints about taxi drivers at the domestic terminal forming a cartel, refusing to use their meters and charging a fixed rate considerably above the meter rate.

Transport to town

Courtesy car Many up-market hotels will meet passengers and provide transport to town gratis. Check before arrival or contact the Thai Hotels Association desk in the terminal building.

Bus An air-conditioned airport bus service operates every 15 minutes, 0500-2400, ฿70 to Silom Road (service A1), Sanaam Luang (service A2) (most convenient for Khaosan Road guesthouses) and Phra Khanong (service A3). Stops are as follows: **Silom service (A1):** Don Muang Tollway, Din Daeng, Pratunam, Lumpini Park, Silom. **Sanaam Luang service (A2):** Don Muang Tollway, Din Daeng, Victory Monument, Phayathai, Phetburi, Lan Luang, Democracy Monument, Sanaam Luang. **Phra Khanong service (A3):** Don Muang Tollway, Din Daeng, Sukhumvit, Ekamai, Phra

Essentials

Essentials

Khanong. Hotel stops are: **Silom service (A1)**: *Century, Indra, Anoma, Grand Hyatt, Erawan, Regent, Dusit Thani,* and *Narai* hotels. **Sanaam Luang service (A2)**: Victory Monument, *Siam City Hotel,* Soi King Phet, Saphan Khao, *Majestic* and *Rattanakosin* hotels. **Phra Khanong service (A3)**: Amari Building, *Ambassador* and *Delta Grand Pacific* hotels, Bang Chan Glass House, *Novotel,* Soi Ekkamai (Sukhumvit). **NB** Return buses have slightly different stops.

Although many visitors will see ฿70 as money well spent (but note that for three or four passengers a taxi is as cheap or cheaper) there will still be the hardened few who will opt for the regular bus service. This is just as cheap and slow as it ever was, 1½-3 hours (depending on time of day) (฿7-15). The bus stop is 50 m north of the arrivals hall. Buses are crowded during rush-hours and there is little room for luggage. Bus 59 goes to Khaosan Road, bus 29 goes to Bangkok's Hualamphong railway station, via the Northern bus terminal and Siam Square. Air-conditioned bus 10 goes to Samsen Road and Silom Road via the Northern bus terminal; air-conditioned bus 4 goes to Silom Road, air-conditioned bus 13 goes to Sukhumvit Road and the Eastern bus terminal, air-conditioned bus 29 goes to the Northern bus terminal, Siam Square and Hualamphong railway station. **By minibus**: ฿100 to major hotels, ฿60 shuttle bus to the *Asia Hotel* on Phayathai Road. ฿50-80 to Khaosan Road, depending on the time of day. Direct buses to Pattaya at 0900, 1200 and 1700, ฿180.

Train The station is on the other side of the north-south highway from the airport. Regular trains into Bangkok's Hualamphong station, ฿5 for ordinary train, third class (the cheapest option). But only six ordinary trains per day. For 'rapid' and 'express' a supplementary charge of ฿40-60 is levied. The State Railways of Thailand runs an 'Airport Express' five times a day (but not on Saturday and Sunday), with air-conditioned shuttle bus from Don Muang station to airport terminal, 35 minutes (฿100).

Ferry A civilized way to avoid the traffic – if booked in the *Oriental, Shangri-la* or *Sheraton* hotels – is to get a minibus from the airport to the ferry terminal on the river. Then take the hour-long river crossing by long-tailed boat to the appropriate hotel.

Tourist information

The **Tourist Authority of Thailand** (TAT) is Thailand's very efficient tourism organization. The head office has moved to the 10th floor, Le Concorde Building, 202 Rachadaphisek Road, T6941222, F6941220, towards the northeastern edge of the city centre. ■ *Mon-Fri, 0830-1630.* There is a more convenient office at 4 Rachdamnern Nok Avenue, T2829773, F2829775. ■ *Mon-Sun, 0830-1630.* There is also a third minor office at the Chatuchak Weekend Market, Kamphaeng Phet 2 Road, T2724440-1. ■ *Sat and Sun only, 0900-1700.* The TAT's useful web site is www.tourismthailand.org/tat

Local offices are found in most major tourist destinations in the country and their addresses are listed in the appropriate sections. TAT offices are a useful source of local information, often providing maps of the town, listings of hotels/guesthouses and information on local tourist attractions. ■ *Mon-Sun 0830-1630.*

Special interest tours
Alternative tours *Responsible Ecological and Social Tour (REST)* Bangkok, T6910437, 6910438. *Alternative Tour* 14/1 Soi Rajatapan, Rachprarop Road, Bangkok, T2452963, F2467020 (see page 114 for more details). *Eagle House,* 'Eco' tours, where profit from tours goes to fund village projects and visitors are encouraged to be sensitive to the environment (and the people) are organized by Annette Kunigagon of Eagle House, 16 Chang Moi Gao Road, Soi 3, T874126, F216368. *Friends of Nature,* 133/1 Rachprarop Road, Bangkok, T6424426, F6424428, organizes environment-friendly treks, raft trips and other tours, mostly lasting two to four days. *Nature Travellers,* 495 Gankheha Soi 19, Sukaphiban 1 Road, Bangkapi, Bangkok,

T3777959, rafting tours in Tak province in the lower north. *Siam Society Tours*, Kamthieng House, Sukhumvit Soi Asoke (Soi 21), Bangkok, T2602930. The *Siam Society* is Thailand's premier scholarly association but they also run tours usually with an educational angle. *Sea Canoe*, PO Box 276, Phuket, T076-212252, F076-212172, www.seacanoe.com run environmentally aware trips around the limestone coastlines of Phuket, Krabi and Phangnga in the south.

Adventure tours *Wild Planet*, BT7128188 or BF7128748 (Bangkok), www.wild-planet.co.th Thai-based adventure tour company with a good reputation. Tours include bicycling trips through up-country Thailand, diving expeditions, canoeing, and so on. *T Rex Tours*, T6474750, www.wild-exotic-thailand.com Another Thai-based adventure tour company with a good reputation. It offers culturally and environmentally focused tours in the southern and northern regions. *Exodus Travels*, T020-87723822, sales@exodustravels.co.uk

Bicycling *Bike and Travel*, Thai-based tour company specialising in bicycling trips. T9900274 (Bangkok), biketravel@loxinfo.co.th

Birdwatching *Ornitholidays*, 29 Straight Mile, Romsey, Hants SO51 9BB, T01794 519445, F01794 523544, ornitholidays@compuserve.com

Cruise *Princess Cruises*, 77 New Oxford St, London WC1A 1PP, T020-78002468, F0171-2402805.

Golf *Fairway International Travel Ltd*, 3 Crown Yard, Southgate, Elland, West Yorkshire HX5 0DQ, T01422-378141, F01422-310716.

Essentials

The TAT's overseas offices are:

Australia
Level 2, National Australia Bank House, 255 George St, Sydney, T02247-7549, F02251-2465

France
90 Ave des Champs Elysées, 75008 Paris, T4562-8656, F01-4563-7888

Germany
Bethmannstr 58 D-60311 Frankfurt/ Main 1, T069-295-704, F069-281-468

Hong Kong
Room 401 Fairmont House, 8 Cotton Tree Drive, Central, T868-0732, F868-4585

Italy
Via Barberini 50, 00187 Roma, T06-487-3479, F06-487-3500

Japan
Hiranomachi Yachiyo Bldg 5F, 1-8-13 Hiranomachi Chuo-ku, Osaka 514, T06-231-4434, F06-231-4337, and Yurakucho Denki Building, South Tower 2F,

Room 259, 1-7-1, Yurakucho, Chiyoda-ku, Tokyo 100, T03-218-0337, F03-218-0655

Malaysia
c/o Royal Thai Embassy, 206 JI Ampang, Kuala Lumpur, T093-2480958, F093-2413002

Singapore
c/o Royal Thai Embassy, 370 Orchard Rd, Singapore, T2357694, F7335653

UK
49 Albemarle St, London W1X 3FE, T020-7499 7679, F020-76295519

USA
5 World Trade Center, Suite No 3443, New York, NY 10048, T212-432-0433, F212-912-0920 and 3440 Wilshire Blvd, Suite 1100, Los Angeles, CA 90010, T213-382-2353, F213-389-7544 and 303 East Wacker Drive, Suite 400, Chicago, IL 60601, T312 819 3990 F312-565-0359.

Others *NESS Thai*, PO Box 48 Amphur Muang Krabi, Thailand, T6675-622377, www.NESSThai.com A network for environmentally and socially sustainable tourism offering the possibility of volunteer work while travelling in Thailand.

Walking *Ramblers Holidays*, PO Box 43, Welwyn Garden City, Herts AL8 6PQ, T01707-331133, F01707-333276.

Note: additional local tour operators and companies are listed under individual town entries.

Essentials

Rules, customs and etiquette

This is common, except in the large department stores (although they may give a **Bargaining**
discount on expensive items of jewellery or furniture) and on items like soap, books
and most necessities. Expect to pay anything from 25-75% less than the asking price,
depending on the bargainer's skill and the shopkeeper's mood. Bargaining is viewed
as a game, so enter into it with good humour.

In towns and at religious sights, it is courteous to avoid wearing shorts and singlets (or **Clothing**
sleeveless shirts). Visitors who are inappropriately dressed may not be allowed into
temples (*wats*). Most Thais always look neat and clean. *Mai rieb-roi* means 'not neat' and
is considered a great insult. Beach resorts are a law unto themselves – casual clothes are
the norm, although nudity is still very much frowned upon by Thais. In the most
expensive restaurants in Bangkok diners may well be expected to wear a jacket and tie.

Thais are generally very understanding of the foibles and habits of foreigners (*farangs*) **Conduct**
and will forgive and forget most indiscretions. However, there are a number of 'dos and
don'ts' which are worth observing:

Among Thais, the personal characteristic of *jai yen* is very highly regarded; literally, this **Cool & hot**
means to have a 'cool heart'. It embodies calmness, having an even temper and not **hearts**
displaying emotion. Although foreigners generally receive special dispensation, and are
not expected to conform to Thai customs (all *farang* are thought to have *jai rawn* or 'hot
hearts'), it is important to try and keep calm in any disagreement – losing one's temper
leads to loss of face and subsequent loss of respect. An associated personal
characteristic which Thais try to develop is *kreng jai*; this embodies being understanding
of other people's needs, desires and feelings – in short, not imposing oneself.

Traditionally Thais greet one another with a *wai* - the equivalent of a handshake. In a **Greeting people**
wai, hands are held together as if in prayer, and the higher the *wai*, the more respectful
the greeting. By watching Thai's *wai* it is possible to ascertain their relative seniority
where a combination of class, age, wealth, power and gender all play a part. Juniors or
inferiors should initiate a *wai*, and hold it higher and for longer than the senior or
superior. Foreigners are not expected to conform to this custom – a simple *wai* at
chest to chin height is all that is required. You should not *wai* to children or to waiters,
waitresses and other people offering a service. When *farangs* and Thais do business it
is common to shake hands. The respectful term of address is *khun*, which applies to
both men and women. This is usually paired with a Thai's first name so that, for
example, Somchai Bamruang would be greeted as Khun Somchai. The closest
equivalent to the English Mr and Mrs/Miss are *Nai* and *Nang*, which are also used as
formal terms of address. Thais also invariably have nicknames like *Kai* (Chicken), *Ooy*
(Sugar) or *Kung* (Shrimp) while people from certain professions will also have
respectful titles – like *ajaan* for a teacher or lecturer.

Try not openly to point your feet at anyone – feet are viewed as spiritually the lowest **Heads & feet**
part of the body. At the same time, never touch anyone's, even a child's, head which is
the holiest, as well as the highest, part. Resting your feet on a table would be regarded
as highly disrespectful while stepping over someone sitting on the floor is also
frowned upon. If sitting on the floor, try to tuck your feet under your body – although
Westerners unused to this posture may find it uncomfortable after even a short time.

Never criticize any member of the royal family or the institution itself. The monarchy is **The monarchy**
held in very high esteem and *lèse majesté* remains an offence carrying a sentence of up
to 15 years in prison. You should treat even coins and bank notes with respect as they

Essentials

bear the image of the King, and the same goes for postage stamps which Thais will methodically moisten using a sponge rather than their tongues. In cinemas, the National Anthem is played before the show and the audience is expected to stand. At other events, take your lead from the crowd as to how to behave. A dying custom, but one which is still adhered to in smaller towns as well as certain parts of Bangkok like at Hualamphong railway station, is that everybody stops in their tracks at 0800 and 1800, when the National Anthem is relayed over loudspeaker.

Monastery (*wat*) & monk etiquette Remove shoes on entering any monastery building, do not climb over Buddha images or have your picture taken in front of one, and when sitting in a bot or *viharn* ensure that your feet are not pointing towards a Buddha image. Wear modest clothing – women should not expose their shoulders or wear dresses that are too short (see above, clothing). Ideally, they should be calf length although knee length dresses or skirts are usually acceptable. Women should never touch a monk, hand anything directly to a monk, or venture into the monks' quarters. They should also avoid climbing chedis (stupas). As in any other place of worship, visitors should not disturb the peace of a *wat*.

Open shows of affection Observant visitors will quickly notice that men and women rarely show open, public signs of affection. It is not uncommon however to see men holding hands – this is usually a sign of simple friendship, nothing more. That said, in Bangkok, traditional customs have broken down and in areas such as Siam Square it is common to see young lovers, hand-in-hand.

Sanuk A quality of *sanuk*, which can be roughly translated as 'fun' or *joie de vivre*, is important to Thais. Activities are undertaken because they are *sanuk*, others avoided because they are *mai sanuk* ('not fun'). Perhaps it is because of this apparent love of life that so many visitors returning from Thailand remark on how Thais always appear happy and smiling. However, it is worth bearing in mind that the interplay of *jai yen* and *kreng jai* means that everything may not be quite as it appears.

Smoking Prohibited on domestic flights, public buses in Bangkok, department stores and in cinemas. Many fast-food restaurants also ban smoking – except at outside tables.

Further reading A useful book delving deeper into the do's and don'ts of living in Thailand is Robert and Nanthapa Cooper's *Culture shock: Thailand*, Time Books International: Singapore (1990). It is available from most bookshops.

Safety

In general, Thailand is a safe country to visit. Physical violence against tourists, while it does occur, is rare. Confidence tricksters, touts, pick-pockets and other thieves all operate, particularly in more popular tourist centres, but care and common sense usually avoids them. On the whole police react efficiently to tourist complaints and the country's health infrastructure, especially in provincial capitals and popular tourist destinations, is good. For background information on staying healthy, see page 48.

Dealing with emergencies Calling one of the emergency numbers (see inside front cover) will not usually be very productive as few operators speak English. It is better to call the Tourist Police or have a hotel employee or other English-speaking Thai telephone for you. For more intractable problems contact your embassy or consulate.

Tourist Police In 1982 the government set up a special arm of the police to deal with the demands of the tourist industry – the Tourist Police – and in 1995 there were around 500 officers stationed in the main tourist destinations. The Thai police have come in for a great deal of scrutiny over recent years. Although most policemen are honest and only too happy to help the lost or luckless overseas visitor, it is worth being aware of some of the complaints that have reached the press or been expressed in letters to us. **Tourist Police:** T2815051 or T2216206. ■ *0800-2400*.

There have been some worrying attacks on tourists and a handful of murders. It must be emphasized that these are very few and far between. Most have occurred when visitors have become involved in local conflicts, or when they have tried to outwit thieves. Robbery is much more common; it ranges from simple pick-pocketing, to the drugging (and subsequent robbing) of bus and train passengers. As in all countries, watchfulness and simple common sense should be employed. Women travelling alone should be especially careful. Always lock hotel rooms and place valuables in a safe deposit if available (or if not, take them with you).

Personal security

The Communist Party of Thailand (CPT) which was influential in parts of the South, North and Northeast during the late 1970s and early 1980s is virtually moribund and does not pose a threat to visitors. Rather more problematic at the moment is PULO (the Pattani United Liberation Organization) which is agitating for an independent Muslim state in the far south. While it is not thought that armed PULO rebels number more than a few dozen, there were a handful of bombings during the 1990s. Travel throughout almost all of the country is safe.

Insurgency & security in border areas

Perhaps the greatest danger is from the traffic – especially if you are attempting to drive yourself. More foreign visitors are killed or injured in traffic accidents than in any other way. Thai drivers have a 'devil may care' attitude towards the highway code, and there are many quite horrific accidents. Be very careful crossing the road – just because there is a pedestrian crossing, do not expect drivers to stop. Be particularly wary when driving or riding a motorcycle (see page 36).

Traffic

Many prostitutes and drug dealers are in league with the police and may find it more profitable to report you than to take your custom (or they may try to do both). They receive a reward from the police, and the police in their turn receive a bonus for the detective work. Note that foreigners on buses may be searched for drugs. Sentences for possession of illegal drugs vary from a fine or one year's imprisonment for marijuana up to life imprisonment or execution for possession or smuggling of heroin. (The death penalty is usually commuted.)

Drugs & prostitution

Inevitably, Thailand's tourist industry has created a side-industry populated by touts and confidence tricksters. More visitors get 'stung' buying what they hope are valuable gems than in any other way (see the box on page 145 and the 'Tricksters' section under **Shopping** below). There is also a rich tradition in card scams. Along with the scammers and confidence tricksters, there are scores of touts who make their living guiding tourists towards certain shops and hotels where they are paid a commission for their pains. Ignore touts who claim that hotels have closed, are full, or are dirty or substandard. Likewise, it is best to avoid taxi or tuk-tuk drivers who are offering to drive you to a hotel or guesthouse for free.

Touts & confidence tricksters

The way to make your way in life, for some people in Thailand, is through the strategic offering of gifts. A Chulalongkorn University report recently estimated that it 'costs' ฿10 million to become Bangkok Police Chief. Apparently this can be recouped in just two years of hard graft. Although bribing officials is by no means recommended, resident *farangs* report that they often resort to such gifts to avoid the time and hassle involved in filling in the forms and making the requisite visit to a police station for a minor traffic offence. As a visitor, the best first step is to play it straight.

Bribery

Hotel classifications

L: ฿5,000+ luxury and **AL:** ฿2,500-5,000 **International:** the entire range of business services (fax, translation, seminar rooms, etc), sports facilities (gym, swimming pool, etc), Asian and Western restaurants, bars, and discotheques.

A: ฿1,250-2,500 **First class:** usually offer comprehensive business, sports and recreational facilities, with a range of restaurants and bars.

B: ฿750-1,250 **Tourist class:** these will probably have a swimming pool and all rooms will have air-conditioning and an attached bathroom. Other services include one or more restaurants and 24-hour coffee shop/room service. Some may have televisions in the rooms showing cable films.

C: ฿400-750 **Economy:** rooms should be air-conditioned and have attached bathrooms with hot water. A restaurant and room service will probably be available. Sports facilities are unlikely.

D: ฿200-400 **Budget:** rooms are unlikely to be air-conditioned although they should have an attached bathroom. Toilets may be either Western-style or of the 'squat' Asian variety, depending on whether the town is on the tourist route. Toilet paper should be provided. Many in this price range, out of

tourist areas, are 'Thai' hotels. Bed linen and towels are usually provided, and there may be a restaurant.

E: ฿100-200 **Guesthouse:** fan-cooled rooms, in some cases with shared bathroom facilities. Toilets are likely to be of the 'squat' Asian variety, with no toilet paper provided. Bed linen should be provided, although towels may not. Rooms are small, facilities few. Guesthouses popular with foreigners may be excellent sources of information and also sometimes offer cheap tours and services such as bicycle and motorcycle hire. Places in this category vary a great deal, and can change very rapidly. One year's best bargain becomes the following year's health hazard. Other travellers are the best source of up-to-the-minute reviews on whether standards have plummeted.

F: under ฿100 **Guesthouse:** fan-cooled rooms, usually with shared bathroom facilities. Toilets are likely to be of the 'squat' Asian variety with no toilet paper provided. Some of these guesthouses can be filthy, vermin-infested, places. At the same time others are superb value. As in the category above, standards change very fast and other travellers are the best source of information.

Prisons Thai prisons are very grim. Most foreigners are held in two Bangkok prisons – Khlong Prem and Bangkwang. One resident who visits overseas prisoners in jail recently wrote to us saying: "You cannot over-estimate the horrors! Khlong Prem has 7,000 prisoners, five to a cell, with not enough room to stretch out, no recreation, one meal a day (an egg on Sundays)...". 100 prisoners in a dormitory is not uncommon, and prisoners on Death Row have waist chains and ankle fetters permanently welded on.

Where to stay

As a premier tourist destination and one of the world's fastest-growing economies, Thailand has a large selection of hotels – including some of the very best in the world. However, outside the tourist centres, there is still an absence of adequate 'Western-style' accommodation. Most 'Thai' hotels are distinctly lacking in character and are poorly maintained. Due to the popularity of the country with backpackers, there are also many small guesthouses, geared to Westerners serving Western food and catering to the foibles of foreigners.

Hotels Hotels are listed under eight categories, according to the average price of a double/twin room for one night. It should be noted that many hotels will have a range of rooms, some with air-conditioning (a/c) and attached bathroom facilities, others with just a fan and shared facilities. Prices can therefore vary a great deal. If a hotel entry lists 'some a/c', then these rooms are likely to be in the upper part of the range, perhaps even in the next range. Unlike, say, Indonesia, few hotels in Thailand provide breakfast in the price of the room. A service charge of 10% and government tax of 7% will usually be added to the bill in the more expensive hotels (categories **B-L**). Ask whether the quoted price includes tax when checking in. Prices in Bangkok are inflated. **NB** During the off-season, hotels in tourist destinations may halve their room rates so it is always worthwhile bargaining or asking whether there is a special price. Given the fierce competition among hotels, it is even worth trying during the peak season. Over-building has meant that there is a glut of rooms in some towns and hotels are desperate for business.

Getting around

Air

Thai Airways is the national flag carrier and is also by far the largest domestic airline. Although it has had a turbulent few years and standards have declined since the halcyon days of the late 1980s – in 1995-96 the airline underwent a major internal review by outside consultants – it is still a good outfit. Planes are maintained to a high standard and crews are professional.

THAI flies to 22 destinations in Thailand as well as Bangkok. This includes seven towns in the south – Hat Yai, Krabi, Nakhon Si Thammarat, Narathiwat, Phuket, Surat Thani and Trang. THAI have introduced a four-stop 'Amazing Thailand Air Pass' for US$199 for internal routes. The pass must be bought prior to arrival in Thailand. **Head office for THAI** is 89 Vibhavadi Rangsit Road, T5130121 (www.thaiair.com) but it is

Domestic air routes

better to book flights through one of the local offices or a travel agent displaying the THAI logo. In April 2000 domestic fares went up for the first time for many years.

Bangkok Airways (see page 154), fly from Bangkok to Koh Samui (nearly 20 flights daily) and Ranong, and from Koh Samui to Krabi, Phuket and Pattaya (U-Tapao). There are also plans to fly direct from Bangkok to Krabi. Bangkok Airways' international connections currently only extend to flights between Bangkok and Phnom Penh and Siem Reap in Cambodia, and between Koh Samui and Singapore. However there are plans to open routes to Medan (Indonesia), Kuala Lumpur (Malaysia) and Bali (Indonesia) to their international connections. Bangkok Airways head office is at 60 Queen Sirikit National Convention Centre, Ratchadapisek Road, T2293456, F2293450, www.bkkair.co.th The airline also has domestic offices at Don Muang Airport, and in Krabi, Pattaya, Phuket, Samui, Ranong, Sukhothai and Chiang Mai.

In September 1998 **Angel Airlines** began operations. They have leased a Boeing 737-500, a 30-seat Dornier 328 and a luxury Beech jet. Head office: 3rd Floor, Benchachinda Building, Tower B, Vibhavadi Rangsit Road, Bangkok, T9532260, www.angelairlines.com. Currently their only scheduled service is between Bangkok and Chiang Rai. However, they have plans to add Udon Thani, Chiang Mai and Phuket to their list of domestic destinations. The airline also operates international connections with Kunming and Chengdu in China and are negotiating for landing rights in Laos, Myanmar, Cambodia and Singapore. The company says it intends to fly on routes not currently covered by THAI's network.

Thailand's newest commercial outfit is **PB Air**. Head office: 1001 Samsen Road, Bangkok, T2610220. The airline received permission at the beginning of 1999 to run services between Bangkok and Chumphon in the south and now also fly to Krabi as well as Chiang Mai, Roiet, Khon Kaen and Udon Thani in the North and Northeast. The airline operate 30-seat Dornier 328s.

Train

The State Railway of Thailand is efficient, clean and comfortable, with five main routes to the north, northeast, west, east and south. It is safer than bus travel but can take longer. The choice is first-class air-conditioned compartments, second-class sleepers, second-class air-conditioned sit-ups with reclining chairs and third-class sit-ups. Travelling third class is often the cheapest way to travel long distance. First and second class are more expensive than the bus but infinitely more comfortable. Express trains are known as *rot duan*, special express trains as *rot duan phiset* and rapid trains as *rot raew*. Express and rapid trains are faster as they make fewer stops; there is a surcharge for the service. Reservations for sleepers should be made in advance (up to 60 days ahead) at Bangkok's Hualamphong station (T2233762, 2247788). The Advance Booking Office is open Monday-Sunday 0700-0400. It is advisable to book the bottom sleeper, as lights are bright on top (in second-class compartments). It still may be difficult to get a seat at certain times of year, such as during festivals (like Songkran in April). Personal luggage allowance is 50 kg in first class, 40 kg in second and 30 kg in third class. Children aged 3-12 and under 150 cm in height pay half fare; those under three years old and less than 100 cm in height travel free, but do not get a seat. It is possible to pick up timetables at Hualamphong station (from the information booth in the main concourse). There are two types: the 'condensed' timetable (by region) showing all rapid routes, and complete, separate timetables for all classes. Some travel agencies book tickets. For rail information T2237010, T2237020. A queue-by-ticket arrangement works efficiently, and travellers do not have to wait long. If you change a reservation the charge is ฿10. If travelling north or south during the day, try to get a seat on the side of the carriage out of the sun.

A 'bullet train' may soon transport visitors along the eastern seaboard to Pattaya. See page 461 for fares listing.

A 20-day rail pass costs ฿1,100 for adults, ฿550 for children (blue pass), valid on all **Tourist passes** trains, second and third class, supplementary charges NOT included. A red pass includes supplementary charges, ฿2,000 for adults, ฿1,000 for children. For further details visit the Advance Booking Office at Hualamphong station in Bangkok, T2233762, 2247788 or F2256068, 2263656.

Boat

The waterways of Thailand are extensive. However, most people limit their water travel to trips around Bangkok (see page 109) or to Ayutthaya (page 111). *Hang-yaaws* (long-tailed boats) are the most common form of water-travel – they are motorized, noisy, fast, and entertaining.

The following tour operators can organize cruise holidays: *Seatran Travel*, 1091/157 **Cruise holidays** Metro Shopping Arcade, Phetburi Road, T2535307; *Songserm Travel Centre*, 121/7 Soi Chalermla, Phayathai Road, T2500768; *Phuket Travel and Tour*, 1091/159 Metro Shopping Arcade, Phetburi Road, T2535510; *Thai Yachting*, 7th Floor, Rachdamri Arcade, Rachdamri Road, T2531733; *Asia Voyage*, Ground Floor, Charn Issara Tower, 942/38 Rama IV Road, T2354100; *Yacht Charter*, 61/3 Mahadlek Luang 3, Rachdamri Road, T2519668.

An alternative to the usual overland tour of Thailand is to book a berth on the *Andaman Princess*. This large cruise ship sails to Koh Tao and back (three days/two nights). Passengers can snorkel at Koh Tao and the level of service and safety is very high. Large numbers of young, middle class Thais make the journey and there is lots of entertainment. Around ฿5,000 for a single berth. Contact: *Siam Cruise*, 33/10-11 Sukhumvit Soi Chaiyod (Soi 11), T2554563, F2558961.

Bus

Private and state-run buses leave Bangkok for every town in Thailand; it is an extensive network and an inexpensive way to travel. The government bus company is called *Bor Kor Sor* (an abbreviation of *Borisat Khon Song*), and every town in Thailand will have a BKS terminal. There are small stop-in-every-town local buses plus the faster long-distance buses (*rot duan* – express – or *rot air* – air-conditioned). Standard air-conditioned buses come in two grades: *chan nung* (first class) and *chan song* (second class). *Chan song* have more seats and less elbow and leg room. The local buses are slower and cramped but are a great experience for those wishing to sample local life. The seats at the very back are reserved for monks (why, is a mystery), so be ready to move if necessary. For longer/overnight journeys, air-conditioned deluxe (sometimes known as *rot tour*) or VIP buses, stewardess service is provided with food and drink supplied en route, and more leg room (plus constant Thai music or videos). Many fares include meals at roadside restaurants, so keep hold of your ticket. **NB** The overnight air-conditioned buses are very cold and it is a good idea to take a few extra layers of clothing.

Many tour companies operate bus services in Thailand; travel agents in Bangkok will **Private tour** supply information. These buses are normally more comfortable than the state buses but **buses** are more expensive. Overnight trips usually involve a meal stop (included in price of ticket) and stewardess service for drinks and snacks. They often leave from outside the company office which may not be located at the central bus station. (See page 461 for fares listing.)

A non-comprehensive primer to driving in Thailand

So you were thinking about hiring a self-drive car for your travels around Thailand, but now your friends all think you must be completely crazy, and after that first trip from the airport in the taxi you are beginning to think they may be right. Well, don't despair. It is possible to enjoy driving in Thailand, and you don't have to be crazy to do so. Not only that, but it does provide opportunities to see places that most tourists never get near. The key to enjoying driving in Thailand is to allow plenty of time to get from A to B. The rigidly law-abiding and the very nervous probably shouldn't attempt a self-drive holiday. But if you do take the plunge, remember:

* Bangkok isn't Thailand. While places such as Hat Yai and Chiang Mai do suffer from heavy traffic it never reaches the levels of Bangkok's infamous traffic jams. For much of the rest of the country traffic is pretty quiet, driving is enjoyable and most people are courteous.
* A combination of corrupt building contractors and overloaded trucks have left roads in parts of Thailand in a terrible state of disrepair. This is often worse the closer one gets to large cities.
* Signposting is often poor – make sure you leave ample time, have a decent map and a good sense of direction.
* Stick to driving during the day. Night time brings out the police road blocks, the heavy trucks, and the speeding pick-up trucks. It also reveals that some Thais don't believe that it is necessary to have lights – or to turn them on – when travelling at night. Other oddities to watch out for: motorcyclists travelling together in a cozy row (three lights all heading in the same direction) or two motorcyclists holding hands as they drive!
* Country driving brings its own hazards: drivers who rarely bother to look when turning onto a road, and buffaloes, dogs, goats and other assorted wildlife that have limited road sense. Slow down, honk the horn and be ultra suspicious of anyone's intentions, human or animal.
* Motorcyclists in the countryside are frequently over-burdened with passengers and other loads. Give them room when passing.

Car hire

There are two schools of thought on car hire in Thailand: one, that under no circumstances should *farangs* (foreigners) drive themselves; and second, that hiring a car is one of the best ways of seeing the country and reaching the more inaccessible sights. Increasing numbers of people *are* hiring their own cars and internationally respected car hire firms are expanding their operations (such as Hertz and Avis). Roads and service stations are generally excellent. Driving is on the left-hand side of the road. See the box here for more hot tips on driving in Thailand!

There are a few points that should be kept in mind: accidents in Thailand are often horrific. If involved in an accident, and they occur with great frequency, you – as a foreigner – are likely to be found the guilty party and expected to meet the costs. **Ensure that the cost of hire includes insurance cover**. Many local residents recommend that should foreigners be involved in an accident, they should not stop but drive on to the nearest police station – if possible, of course.

Songkran carnage 2000 There is endless hope in Thailand that the country's roads will become safer as roads are upgraded, cars are better maintained, and drivers learn to drive with a little more care and less alcohol. But there's still some way to go. During the Songkran holiday of 2000 between 12th and 17th April there was, at first, hope that things had improved on the nation's roads. On the 18th local papers were reported 'only' 142 deaths and 1,272 injuries in 813 road accidents. But a day later, as information filtered through, it became clear that things were a trifle bloodier. By the 19th it was being reported that 204 people had been killed and 1,599 injured. That's a pretty high attrition rate.

* Be aware that motorcyclists are expected to use the shoulder (in some places they are required to by law), and are not generally considered to 'equal' a car.
* You cannot depend on maps being up-to-date or completely accurate.
* Road construction projects provide little warning on approach and you should not expect logical traffic management systems to be in place. Heavy machinery is a give away that something may be just around the corner.
* Some trucks will use their indicators to let you know if it is safe to pass: flashing the right indicator means oncoming traffic; flashing the left indicator means it is clear to pass. There are variations in different parts of the country, but it is usually fairly clear what is going on.
* Oncoming traffic flashing the headlights on and off is a warning. It can mean "I'm not stopping to let you through", "don't try passing" and in some cases "get out of the way I'm coming through". It is not uncommon to move on to the shoulder to avoid oncoming traffic, particularly if that oncoming traffic is a tour bus or a truck.

* Recently, many motorists have taken to switching their hazard lights on to indicate they are going straight on when they come to an intersection. This can be very confusing if you can only see one side of the car.
* Remember that while you may be confident you know the highway code, the same does not apply to everyone else. Junctions, whether with lights or not, are frequently sites of accidents and of long pauses as each person tries to work out who can go first and who must wait.
* If you are going on a long drive through a relatively unpopulated area, fill up with petrol whenever you get the opportunity.
* Road markings make little difference to most drivers. Passing on solid yellow lines, on blind corners and over hills is common. Passing on the left on a dual carriageway or on the shoulder is also very common and adds to the fun.
* It is worth putting your hazards on if you have to brake very suddenly as most cars are not fitted with two sets of brake lights and it is not always possible to distinguish between slowing and stopping!

The average cost of hiring a car from a reputable firm is ฿1,000-1,500 per day, ฿6,000-10,000 per week, or ฿20,000-30,000 per month. Some rentals come with insurance automatically included; for others it must be specifically requested and a surcharge is added. An international driver's licence, or a UK, US, French, German, Australian, New Zealand, Singapore or Hong Kong licence is required. The lower age limit is 20 years (more for some firms). Addresses of car hire firms are included in the sections on the main tourist destinations. If the mere thought of competing with Thai drivers is terrifying, an option is to hire a chauffeur along with the car. For this service an extra ฿300-500 per day is usually charged, more at weekends and if an overnight stay is included. Note that local car hire firms are cheaper although the cars are likely to be less well maintained and will have tens of thousands of Ks on the clock.

Other land transport

Towns in Thailand will often have their own distinctive forms of transport for hire. In Chonburi and Si Racha, chariot-like seats have been attached to large motorbikes; in Prachuap Kiri Khan there are motorbikes with sidecars.

We have had a number of letters from people who have bicycled through various parts of Southeast Asia. The advice below is collated from their comments, and is meant to provide a general guideline for those intending to tour the country by bicycle (which is becoming more and more common). There may be areas, however, **Cycling** where the advice does not hold true. (Some of the letters we have received even disagree on some key points.)

Bike type Touring, hybrid or mountain bikes are fine for most roads and tracks in Thailand – take an ordinary machine; nothing fancy. Spares are readily available for most machines, and even small towns have bicycle repair shops where it is often possible to borrow larger tools such as vices. Mountain bikes have made an impact, so accessories for these are also widely available. What is less common are components made of unusual materials – such as titanium and rarer composites. It is best to use common accessories. Buses are used to taking bicycles (although the more expensive air-conditioned tour buses may prove reluctant), and most carry them free, although some drivers may ask for a surcharge. Many international airlines take bicycles free of charge, provided they are not boxed. Take the peddles off and deflate the tyres. Check your carrier's policy before checkingin. **NB** The maps in this guide are not sufficiently detailed for bicycling and a good, colour map is useful for determining contours and altitude, as well as showing minor roads.

Attitudes to bicyclists It is still comparatively rare to see foreigners bicycling in Thailand, so expect to be an object of interest. Cars and buses often travel along the hard shoulder, and few expect to give way to a bicycle. Be very wary, especially on main roads.

Useful equipment Basic tool kit – although there always seems to be help near at hand, and local workshops seem to be able to improvise a solution to just about any problem – including a puncture repair kit, spare tubes, spare tyre and pump. Also take a good map of the area, bungee cords, first-aid kit and water filter.

Unnecessary equipment A tent is generally not needed. Every small town will have a guesthouse of some description. Nor is it worth taking a stove, cooking utensils, sleeping bag or food ... it is almost always possible to get food and a place to sleep – and cheaply, too. The equipment is simply a burden. The exception to this rule of thumb are national parks where camping is common, and camping grounds exist.

In general Avoid major roads. Avoid major towns.

Hitchhiking Thai people rarely hitchhike and tourists who try could find themselves waiting a long time at the roadside. It is sometimes possible to wave down vehicles at the more popular beach resorts.

Motorbike taxi These are becoming increasingly popular, and are the cheapest, quickest and most dangerous way to get from 'A' to 'B'. Riders wear coloured vests (sometimes numbered) and tend to congregate at key intersections or outside shopping centres, for example. Agree a price before boarding – expect to pay ฿10-20.

Motorbike hire Mostly confined to holiday resorts and prices vary from place to place. ฿200-300 per day is usual for a 100-150 cc machine. Often licences do not have to be shown and insurance will not be available. Off the main roads and in quieter areas it can be an enjoyable and cheap way to see the country. Riding with shorts and flip-flops is dangerous. Borrow a helmet if at all possible and expect anything larger than you to ignore your presence on the road. Be extremely wary. Thousands of Thais are killed in motorcycle accidents each year and large numbers of tourists also suffer injuries. (Koh Samui has been said to have the highest death rate anywhere in the world!) Some travellers are now not just hiring motorbikes to explore a local area, but are touring the entire country by motorcycle. It is the cheapest way to be independent of public transport, but the risks rise accordingly.

In December 1992 the Thai government introduced a new – and long overdue – law requiring that motorcyclists wear helmets on Bangkok's 240 main roads. In April 1995 this was extended to all roads and sois (lanes) in the capital. At the end of June

Death highways

It doesn't take very long after arriving in Bangkok to realize that the city has a transport problem. But the emphasis on the capital's congestion and pollution sometimes obscures another, equally serious, issue: the country's stupendous accident rate. The Kingdom has the highest fatality rate from road accidents of any country in the Southeast Asian region. On current trends, it was estimated in November 1998 that by the year 2000 road accidents will claim a staggering 68,000 lives, or eight each hour. In 1995 the number killed was 16,727 but this has been increasing at a rate of over 30% each year. In 1997 the estimated figure was around 28,000 or three deaths every hour. (The number injured in 1995 was 50,546.) Preecha Chosap, the secretary of the Transport and Communications Ministry, announced at the end of 1998 that a new Master Plan on road safety was in the process of being set up. As he explained to the press, part of the problem is that no one takes responsibility for road safety. "If a full passenger coach overturns," he said, "killing a large number of people and you ask the police, they'll say it's nothing to do with them. If you ask the Land Transport Department or the Highways Department, they'll say the same thing." The government doesn't even know the true number of people who die in road-related accidents – the figures are collected from hospital admissions where, it is said, some 30% of beds are occupied by patients injured in road accidents.

Another piece in the explanatory puzzle is that drivers who infringe the law are dealt with extremely leniently – if they are ever caught. The fine for speeding or drunk driving is just 1,000. But in some areas of the country there are just 24 highway police patrolling 1,000 km of road, so the chances of being stopped are pretty slim in any case. Getting proof that someone is drunk is also hard when, in 1998, there were only 35 breathalysers for use throughout the country.

1995 Chiang Mai also made the wearing of helmets mandatory. However, outside Bangkok the wearing of helmets in most areas is not compulsory.

Saamlor ('three wheels') These come in the form of pedal or motorized machines. Saamlor drivers abound and will descend on travellers in any town. Fares should be bargained and agreed before setting off. Drivers are a useful source of local information and will know most places of interest, plus hotels and restaurants (and sometimes their prices). In Bangkok, and now in some other large towns, the saamlor is a motorized, gas powered, scooter known affectionately as the **tuk-tuk** (because of the noise it makes). Pedal-powered saamlors were outlawed in Bangkok a few years ago and they are now gradually being replaced by the noisier motorized version throughout the country. Always bargain and agree a price before setting out on a journey. It will not take long to discover what is a reasonable price, but don't expect to pay the same as a Thai.

Songthaew ('two rows') Songthaews are pick-up trucks fitted with two benches and can be found in many up-country towns. They normally run fixed routes, with set fares, but can often be hired and used as a taxi service (agree a price before setting out). To let the driver know you want to stop, press the electric buzzers or tap the side of the vehicle with a coin.

Taxi Standard taxis can be found in some Thai towns. This is the most expensive form of public motorized transport, and many now have the added luxury of air-conditioning. In Bangkok almost all taxis have meters. If un-metered, agree a price before setting off, and always bargain. In the south of Thailand, long-distance share taxis are common.

Essentials

Keeping in touch

Points of contact The British Council, Alliance Française and Goethe Institute all have offices in Bangkok. Most countries also have embassies in the capital. Outside Bangkok there are consulates in Pattaya, as well as Chiang Mai (in the north). These are listed in the relevant town entries.

Language The Thai language is tonal and, strictly speaking, monosyllabic. There are five tones: high, low, rising, falling and mid-tone. These are used to distinguish between words which would otherwise be identical. For example: *mai* (low tone, new), *mai* (rising, silk), *mai* (mid-tone, burn), *mai* (high tone, question indicator), and *mai* (falling tone, negative indicator). Not surprisingly, many visitors find it hard to hear the different tones, and it is difficult to make much progress during a short visit (unlike, say, with Malaysian or Indonesian). The tonal nature of the language also explains why so much of Thai humour is based around homonyms – and especially when *farangs* say what they do not mean. Although tones make Thai a challenge for foreign visitors, other aspects of the language are easier to grasp: there are no marked plurals in nouns, no marked tenses in verbs, no definite or indefinite articles, and no affixes or suffixes.

Visitors may well experience two oddities of the Thai language being reflected in the way that Thais speak English. An 'l' or 'r' at the end of a word in Thai becomes an 'n', while an 's' becomes a 't'. So some Thais refer to the 'Shell' Oil Company as 'Shen', a name like 'Les' becomes 'Let', while 'cheque bill' becomes 'cheque bin'. It is also impossible to have two consonants after one another in Thai. If it occurs, a Thai will automatically insert a vowel (even though it is not written). So the soft drink 'Sprite' becomes 'Sa-prite', and the English word 'start', 'sa-tart'.

In general, English is reasonably widely spoken on the tourist trail, and visitors should be able to find someone to help. English is taught to all school children, and competence in English is regarded as a very useful qualification. Off the tourist trail, making yourself understood becomes more difficult.

Despite Thai being a difficult language to pick up, it is worth trying to learn a few words, even if your visit to Thailand is short. Thais generally feel honoured that a *farang* is bothering to learn their language, and will be patient and helpful. If they laugh at some of your pronunciations do not be put off – it is not meant to be critical.

Post **Local postal charges** ฿1.50 (postcard) and ฿2 (letter, 20 g). **International postal charges** Europe and Australasia – ฿9 (postcard), ฿12.50 (letter, 10 g); US – ฿9 (postcard), ฿14.50 (letter, 10 g). Airletters cost ฿10. **Poste Restante** Correspondents should write the family name in capital letters and underline it, to avoid confusion.

Outside Bangkok, most post offices are open from 0800-1630 Monday-Friday and only the larger ones will be open on Saturday.

Telephone From Bangkok there is direct dialling to most countries. Outside Bangkok, it is best to go to a local telephone exchange for phoning outside the country.

Codes Local area codes vary according to province. Individual area phone codes are listed throughout the book in the margin underneath town headings; the code can also be found at the front of the telephone directory.

Directory inquiries Domestic long distance including Malaysia and Vientiane (Laos) T101, Greater Bangkok BMA T183, international calls T2350030-5, although hotel operators will invariably help make the call if asked.

Callboxes Calls cost ฿1. All telephone numbers marked in the text with a prefix 'B' mean that they are Bangkok numbers.

Fax Now widely available in most towns. Postal and telex/fax services are available in most large hotels.

Internet access and email Thailand has embraced the Web with alacrity and enthusiasm. There are internet cafés in most towns, especially in areas where there is a tourist presence. Rates clearly vary but expect to pay ฿2 per minute (often with a minimum of five minutes) in tourist centres and a figure of half this or less in internet cafés frequented by locals. For a global internet café listing, see www.netcafeguide.com.

Internet (margin)

Newspapers Until recently there were two major English-language daily papers – the *Bangkok Post* and the *The Nation*. They provide good international news coverage and are Thailand's best-known broadsheets. At times of social conflict they have also represented dissenting liberal voices. Both *The Nation* and the *Bangkok Post* have websites: www.nationgroup.com/ for the former and www.bangkokpost.net/ for the latter. Alternatively there is a site with links to 150-odd online newspapers in Asia and the Middle East – www.inesmedia.com

Media (margin) — *Essentials* (margin)

In the mid-1990s these two august institutions – which until then had the English-language newspaper market to themselves – were joined by three other dailies: the *Business Day*, *Asia Times* and *Thailand Times*. The latter two closed down during the economic slump of 1997 leaving just *Business Day* battling it out with the *Bangkok Post* and *The Nation*. *Business Day* is, as the name suggests, aimed at the business market. It is jointly owned by a group of Thai investors along with Singapore Press Holdings and Malaysia's New Straits Times group (http://bday.net).

There are a number of Thai-language dailies and weeklies as well as Chinese-language newspapers. The Thai press is one of the least controlled in Southeast Asia (although controls were imposed following the coup at the beginning of 1991 and during the demonstrations of May 1992), and the local newspapers are sometimes scandalously colourful, with gruesome annotated pictures of traffic accidents and murder victims. International newspapers and magazines are readily available in Bangkok, Chiang Mai, Pattaya and Phuket, although they are more difficult to come by up-country.

Television and radio Five TV channels, with English-language soundtrack available on FM. Channel 3 – 105.5 MHz, Channel 7 – 103.5 MHz, Channel 9 – 107 MHz and Channel 11 – 88 MHz. The *Bangkok Post* lists programmes where English soundtrack is available on FM. Short wave radio can receive the BBC World Service, Voice of America, Radio Moscow and other foreign broadcasts, see below.

The BBC World Service's *Dateline East Asia* provides probably the best news and views on Asia. Also with a strong Asia focus are the broadcasts of the ABC (Australian Broadcasting Corporation).

Short Wave Radio British Broadcasting Corporation (BBC, London), *Southeast Asian service* 3915, 6195, 9570, 9740, 11750, 11955, 15360; *Singapore service* 88.9MHz; *East Asian service* 5995, 6195, 7180, 9740, 11715, 11750, 11945, 11955, 15140, 15280, 15360, 17830, 21715. **Voice of America (VoA, Washington)**, *Southeast Asian service* 1143, 1575, 7120, 9760, 9770, 15185, 15425; *Indonesian service* 6110, 11760, 15425. **Radio Beijing**, *Southeast Asian service (English)* 11600, 11660. **Radio Japan (Tokyo)**, *Southeast Asian service (English)* 11815, 17810, 21610.

Food and drink

Food

Thai cuisine Thai food is an intermingling of Tai, Chinese, and to a lesser extent, Indian cuisines. This helps to explain why restaurants produce dishes which must be some of the (spicy) hottest in the world, as well as others which are rather bland. *Laap* (raw – now more frequently cooked – chopped beef mixed with rice, herbs and spices) is a traditional 'Tai' dish; *pla priaw waan* (whole fish with soy and ginger) is Chinese in origin; while *gaeng mussaman* (beef 'Muslim' curry) was brought to Thailand by Muslim immigrants. Even *satay*, paraded by most restaurants as a Thai dish, was introduced from Malaysia and Indonesia (which themselves adopted it from Arab traders during the Middle Ages).

Despite these various influences, Thai cooking is distinctive. Thais have managed to combine the best of each tradition, adapting elements to fit their own preferences. Remarkably, considering how ubiquitous it is in Thai cooking, the chilli pepper is a New World fruit and was not introduced into Thailand until the late 16th century (along with the pineapple and papaya).

When a Thai asks another Thai whether he has eaten he will ask, literally, whether he has 'eaten rice' (*kin khaaw*). Similarly, the accompanying dishes are referred to as food 'with the rice'. A Thai meal is based around rice, and many wealthy Bangkokians own farms up-country where they cultivate their favourite variety. There are two main types of rice – 'sticky' or glutinous (*khao niaw*) and non-glutinous (*khao jao*). Sticky rice is usually used to make sweets (desserts) although it is the staple in the northeastern region and parts of the North. *Khao jao* is standard white rice.

A meal usually consists (along with the rice) of a soup like *tom yam kung* (prawn soup), *kaeng* (a curry) and *krueng kieng* (a number of side dishes). Generally, Thai food is chilli-hot, and aromatic herbs and grasses (like lemon grass, coriander, tamarind and ginger) are used to give a distinctive flavour. *Nam pla* (fish sauce) and *nam prik* (nam pla, chillies, garlic, sugar, shrimps and lime juice) are two condiments that are taken with almost all meals. *Nam pla* is made from steeping fish, usually anchovies, in brine for long periods and then bottling the peatish-coloured liquor produced. Chillies deserve a special mention because most Thais like their food HOT! Some chillies are comparatively mild; others – like the tiny, bright red *prik khii nuu* (mouse shit pepper) – are fiendishly hot.

Due to Thailand's large Chinese population (or at least Thais with Chinese roots), there are also many Chinese-style restaurants whose cuisine is variously 'Thai-ified'. Many of the snacks available on the streets show this mixture of Thai and Chinese, not to mention Arab and Malay. *Bah jang*, for example, are small pyramids of leaves stuffed with sticky rice, Chinese sausage, salted eggs, pork and dried shrimp. They were reputedly first created for the Chinese dragon boat festival but are now available 12 months a year – for around ฿20.

To sample Thai food it is best to go in a group to a restaurant and order a range of dishes. To eat alone is regarded as slightly strange. However there are a number of 'one-dish' meals like fried rice and *phat thai* (fried noodles) and restaurants will also usually provide *raat khao* ('over rice') which is a dish like a curry served on a bed of rice for a single person.

The etiquette The Thai philosophy on eating is 'often', and most Thais will snack their way through the
of eating day. Eating is a relaxed, communal affair and it is not necessary to get too worked up about etiquette. Dishes are placed in the middle of the table where diners can help themselves. In a restaurant rice is usually spooned out by a waiter or waitress – and it is considered good manners to start a meal with a spoon of rice. While food is eaten with a spoon and fork, the fork is only used to manoeuvre food onto the spoon. Because most

Why all the spice?

People have occasionally considered the vexed question of why tropical countries tend to produce spicy food. Some people have suggested that it is because the spices disguise the taste of bad food. Others have hazarded that spices have some useful nutritional value. Still more ingenious is the argument that spices stimulate sweating and thus increase evaporational cooling in hot climates. However Jennifer Billing and Paul Sherman have, apparently, resolved the dilemma. In the March 1998 issue of the Quarterly Review of Biology *they revealed that many spices have anti-bacterial properties, particularly useful in hot climates where food spoils rapidly.*

food is prepared in bite-sized pieces it is not usually necessary to use a knife. At noodle stalls chopsticks and china soup spoons are used while in the Northeast most people – at least at home – use their fingers. Sticky rice is compressed into a ball using the ends of the fingers and then dipped in the other dishes. Thais will not pile their plates with food but take many small portions from the dishes arranged on a table. It is also considered good manners when invited out to leave some food on your plate, as well as on the serving dishes on the table. This demonstrates the generosity of the host.

Where to eat

It is possible to get a good, tasty and nutritious meal almost anywhere – and at any time – in Thailand. Thais eat out a great deal so that most towns have a range of places. Starting at the top, in pecuniary terms at any rate, are the more **sophisticated restaurants**. These are usually air-conditioned, and sometimes attached to a hotel. In places like Bangkok and Chiang Mai they may be Western in style and atmosphere. In towns less frequented by foreigners they are likely to be rather more functional – although the food will be just as good. In addition to these more up-market restaurants are a whole range of places from **noodle shops** to **curry houses** and **seafood restaurants**. Many small restaurants have no menus. But often the speciality of the house will be clear – roasted, honeyed ducks hanging in the window, crab and fish laid out on crushed ice outside. Away from the main tourist spots, 'Western' breakfasts are commonly unavailable, so be prepared to eat Thai-style (noodle or rice soup or fried rice).

Towards the bottom of the scale are **stalls and food carts**. These tend to congregate at particular places in town – often in the evening, from dusk – although they can be found just about anywhere: outside the local provincial offices, along a cul-de-sac, or under a conveniently placed shady tree. Stall holders will tend to specialize: noodles, rice dishes, fruit drinks, sweets, and so on. Hot meals are usually prepared to order. While stall food may be cheap – a meal costs only around ฿15-20 – they are frequented by people from all walks of life. A well-heeled businessman in a suit is just as likely to be seen bent over a bowl of noodles at a rickety table on a busy street corner as a construction worker.

A popular innovation over the last 10 years or so has been the *suan a-haan* or **garden restaurant**. These are often on the edge of towns, with tables set in gardens, sometimes with bamboo furniture and ponds. Another type of restaurant worth a mention is the **Thai-style coffee shop**. These are sometimes attached to hotels in provincial towns and feature hostesses dressed in Imelda-esque or sparingly spangly costumes. The hostesses, when they are not crooning to the house band, sit with customers, laugh at their jokes and assiduously make sure that their glasses are always full. They may provide other services too, but usually not at the table. In the North, **khantoke dining** is de rigueur – or so one might imagine from the number of restaurants offering it. This is traditional to the North and involves sitting on the floor, usually with cushions provided for Westerners unused to being at ground level for extended periods, and eating regional delicacies accompanied by traditional music and dance.

Essentials

Thai dishes

It is impossible to provide a comprehensive list of Thai dishes. However (and at the risk of offending connoisseurs by omitting their favourites) popular dishes include:

Soups (gaeng chud)

Tom yam kung – *hot and sour prawn soup spiced with lemon grass, coriander and chillies*

Tom ka kai – *chicken in coconut milk with laos (loas, or ka, is an exotic spice)*

Khaaw tom – *rice soup with egg and pork (a common breakfast dish) or chicken, fish or prawn. It is said that the soup can cure fevers and other illnesses. Probably best for a hangover.*

Kwaytio – *Chinese noodle soup served with a variety of additional ingredients, often available from roadside stalls and from smaller restaurants – mostly served up until lunchtime.*

Kaeng juut – *bean curd and vegetable soup, non-spicy*

Rice-based dishes

Single-dish meals served at roadside stalls and in many restaurants (especially cheaper ones).

Khaaw phat kai/mu/kung – *fried rice with chicken/pork/prawn*

Khaaw naa pet – *rice with duck*

Khaaw gaeng – *curry and rice*

Khaaw man kai – *rice with chicken*

Khaaw mu daeng – *rice with red pork*

Noodle-based dishes

Khaaw soi – *a form of Kwaytio with egg noodles in a curry broth*

Phak sii-u – *noodles fried with egg, vegetables and meat/prawns*

Kwaytio haeng – *wide noodles served with pork and vegetables*

Ba-mii haeng – *wheat noodles served with pork and vegetables*

Phat thai – *Thai fried noodles*

Mee krop – *Thai crisp-fried noodles*

Curries (gaeng)

Gaeng phet kai/nua – *hot chicken/beef curry*

Gaeng khiaw waan kai/nua/phet/pla – *green chicken/beef/duck/fish curry (the colour is due to the large number of whole green chillies pounded to make the paste that forms the base of this very hot curry)*

Gaeng phanaeng – *chicken or beef curry*

Gaeng plaa duk – *catfish curry*

Gaeng mussaman – *Muslim beef curry served with potatoes*

Meat dishes

Laap – *chopped (once raw, now more frequently cooked) meat with herbs and spices*

Kai/nua phat prik – *fried chicken/beef with chillies*

Nua priaw waan – *sweet and sour beef*

Mu waan – *sweet pork*

Kai/mu/nua phat kapow – *fried meat with basil and chillies*

Kai tort – *Thai fried chicken*

Kai tua – *chicken in peanut sauce*

Kai yang – *garlic chicken*

Priao wan – *sweet and sour pork with vegetables*

Tourist centres also provide good European, American and Japanese food at reasonable prices. Bangkok boasts some superb restaurants. Less expensive Western **fast-food** restaurants can also be found – McDonalds, Pizza Hut, Kentucky Fried Chicken and others.

Drink

Drinking water   Water in smaller restaurants can be risky, so many people recommend that visitors drink bottled water (widely available) or **hot tea**.

Soft drinks   **Coffee** is also now consumed throughout Thailand (usually served with Coffee-mate or creamer). In stalls and restaurants, coffee comes with a glass of Chinese tea. Soft drinks are widely available. Many roadside stalls prepare **fresh fruit juices** in liquidizers (*bun*) while hotels produce all the usual cocktails.

Essentials

Seafood

Plaa priaw waan – *whole fried fish with ginger sauce*
Plaa too tort – *Thai fried fish*
Haw mok – *steamed fish curry*
Plaa nerng – *steamed fish*
Plaa pao – *grilled fish*
Thotman plaa – *fried curried fish cakes*
Luuk ciin – *fishballs*

Salads *(yam)*

Yam nua – *Thai beef salad*
Som tam – *green papaya salad with tomatoes, chillies, garlic, chopped dried shrimps and lemon (can be extremely hot)*

Vegetables

Phak phat ruam mit – *mixed fried vegetables*

Sweets *(kanom)*

Khaaw niaw sankhayaa – *sticky rice and custard*
Khaaw niaw mamuang – *sticky rice and mango (a seasonal favourite)*
Kluay buat chee – *bananas in coconut milk*
Kanom mo kaeng – *baked custard squares*
Kluay tort – *Thai fried bananas*
Leenchee loi mek – *chilled lychees in custard*

Fruits *(see page 44)*

Chomphu – *rose apple*
Khanun – *jackfruit. Season: January-June*
Kluay – *banana. Season: year round*
Lamyai – *longan; thin brown shell with translucent fruit similar to lychee. Season: June-August*

Linchi – *lychee. Season: April-June*
Lamut – *sapodilla*
Makham wan – *tamarind. Season: December-February*
Malakho – *papaya. Season: year round*
Manaaw – *lime. Season: year round*
Mang khud – *mangosteen. Season: April-September*
Maprao – *coconut. Season: year round*
Majeung – *star apple*
Mamuang – *mango. Season: March-June*
Ngo – *rambutan. Season: May-September*
Noi na – *custard (or sugar) apple. Season: June-September*
Sapparot – *pineapple. Season: April-June, December-January*
Som – *orange. Season: year round*
Som o – *pomelo. Season: August-November*
Taeng mo – *watermelon. Season: October-March*
Thurian – *durian. Season: May-August.*

Cookery Courses

For those interested in taking a course in Thai cookery, contact: UFM Baking and Cooking, 593/29-39 Sukhumvit Soi 33/1, T2590620; the Thai Cooking School at the Oriental Hotel, 48 Oriental Ave, T4376211; Modern Housewife Centre, 45/6-7 Setsiri Rd, T2792831; all in Bangkok. For more details on courses in Bangkok see page 142. Courses are also available in Phuket, page 254.

Alcohol

Spirits Major brands of spirits are served in most hotels and bars, although not always off the tourist path. The most popular spirit among Thais is **Mekhong** – local cane whisky – which can be drunk straight or with mixers such as Coca-Cola. It can seem rather sweet to the Western palate but it is the cheapest form of alcohol.

Beer drinking is spreading fast. In 1987, beer consumption was 98 million litres; in 1992, 330 million litres. The most popular local beer is *Singha* beer brewed by Boon Rowd. The company commands 89% of the beer market. It is said that the beer's distinctive taste is due to the formaldehyde that it contains. When the company removed the chemical (it was no longer needed as bottling technology had been improved) there was such an outcry from Thais that they quickly reincorporated it. Whether or not the story is true, an evening drinking *Singha* can result in quite a hangover. Its alcohol content of 6% must be partly to blame.

Among expatriates, the most popular Thai beer is the more expensive *Kloster* brand (similar to a light German beer) with an alcohol content of 5.7%. *Singha* introduced a

● ●

👉 *Distinctive fruits*

Custard apple (or sugar apple) Scaly green skin, squeeze the skin to open the fruit and scoop out the flesh with a spoon. Season: June-September.

Durian (Durio zibethinus) A large prickly fruit, with yellow flesh, about the size of a football. Infamous for its pungent smell. While it is today regarded by many visitors as simply revolting, early Europeans (16th-18th centuries) raved about it, possibly because it was similar in taste to Western delicacies of the period. Borri (1744) thought it was "God himself, who had produc'd that fruit". But by 1880 Burbridge was writing: "Its odour – one scarcely feels justified in using the word 'perfume' – is so potent, so vague, but withal so insinuating, that it can scarcely be tolerated inside the house". Banned from hotel rooms throughout the region, and beloved by most Southeast Asians, it has an alluring taste – some maintain it is an addiction. Durian-flavoured chewing gum, ice cream and jams are all available. Season: May-August.

Jackfruit Similar in appearance to durian but not so spiky. Yellow flesh, tasting slightly like custard. Season: January-June.

Mango (Mangifera indica) A rainforest fruit which is now cultivated. Widely available in the West; in Southeast Asia there are hundreds of different varieties with subtle variations in flavour. Delicious eaten with sticky rice and a sweet sauce. The best mangoes in the region are considered to be those from South Thailand. Season: March-June.

Mangosteen (Garcinia mangostana) An aubergine-coloured hard shell covers this small fruit which is about the size of a tennis ball. Cut or squeeze the purple shell to reach its sweet white flesh which is prized by many visitors above all others. In 1898, an American resident of Java wrote, erotically and in obvious ecstasy: "The five white segments separate easily, and they melt on the tongue with a touch of tart and a touch of sweet; one moment a memory of the juiciest, most fragrant apple, at another a remembrance of the smoothest cream ice, the most exquisite and delicately flavoured fruit-acid known – all of the delights of nature's laboratory condensed in that ball of neige parfumée". Southeast Asians believe it should be eaten as a chaser to durian. Season: April-September.

Papaya (Carica papaya) A New-World fruit that was not introduced into Southeast Asia until the 16th century. Large, round or oval in shape, yellow or green-skinned, with bright orange flesh and a mass of round, black seeds in the middle. The flesh, in texture and taste, is somewhere between a mango and a melon. Some maintain that it tastes 'soapy'. Season: Year round.

Pomelo A large round fruit the size of anything from an ostrich egg to a football, with thick, green skin and pith, and flesh similar to a grapefruit's, but less acidic. Season: August-November.

Rambutan (Nephelium lappaceum) The bright red and hairy rambutan – rambut is the Malay word for 'hair' – with its slightly rubbery but sweet flesh is a close relative of the lychee of southern China. The Thai word for rambutan is ngoh, which is the nickname given by Thais to the fuzzy-haired Negrito aboriginals in the southern jungles. Season: May-September.

Salak (Salacca edulis) A small pear-shaped fruit about the size of a large plum with a rough, brown, scaly skin (somewhat like a miniature pangolin) and yellow-white, crisp flesh. It is related to the sago and rattan trees.

Tamarind (Tamarindus indicus) Brown seedpods with dry brittle skins and a brown tart-sweet fruit which grow on a tree introduced into Southeast Asia from India. The name is Arabic for 'Indian date'. The flesh has a high tartaric acid content and is used to flavour curries, jams, jellies and chutneys as well as for cleaning brass and copper. Elephants have a predilection for tamarind balls. Season: December-February.

● ●

light beer called *Singha Gold* a few years back which is quite similar to *Kloster. Amarit* is a third, rather less widely available, brand but popular with foreigners and brewed by the same company who produce *Kloster*. Between them, *Kloster* and *Amarit* control about 10% of the market. Two 'local' beers to enter the fray in the last 10 years are *Heineken* and *Carlsberg*. At the beginning of the 1990s Carlsberg built a brewery north of Bangkok and had clearly done their homework. The beer is sweeter and lighter than *Singha* and *Kloster* but still strong with an alcohol content of 6%. The Carlsberg brew has made considerable inroads into the markets of the established brands – although in so doing they are said to have lost many millions of baht. A little later Carlsberg introduced a new beer specifically for the Thai market, *Bier Chang* or *Elephant Beer*, which is yet more alcoholic at 7%. More recently still Heineken have opened a local brewery near Sena in the Central Plains – again producing beer with a much higher alcohol content than the equivalent in the West. These beers have now been joined by a wave of new locally produced beers – often brewed in collaboration with overseas breweries. The cheapest is *Leo* brand beer which is brewed in Khon Kaen in the Northeast. Their advertising campaign emphasises that this is a Thai beer but Bangkok's sophisticates snigger under their breath at anyone stooping to drink the stuff. In fact, *Leo Super* is quite palatable – the same can't be said of *Lao thammada*. Then there's *Amstel* (a Dutch beer) and *Mittweida*. The latter's advertising campaign, in contrast to Leo's, plays on the fact that, apparently, almost the entire population of Germany drinks the stuff for breakfast, lunch and tea. That few Germans seem to have heard of the brew doesn't seem to have tempered the ad company's enthusiasm.

Beer is relatively expensive in Thai terms as it is heavily taxed by the government. But it is a high status drink so, as Thais become wealthier, more are turning to beer in preference to traditional, local whiskies. It is the burgeoning middle class, especially the young, which explains why brewers are so keen to set up shop in this traditionally non-beer drinking country. In a café, expect to pay ฿30-50 for a small beer, in a coffee shop or bar ฿50-70, and in a hotel bar or restaurant, rather more than that. Some pubs and bars also sell beer on tap – which is known as *bier sot*, 'fresh' beer.

Wine Thais are fast developing a penchant for wines. Imported wines are expensive by international standards and Thai wines are pretty ghastly – overall. An exception is *Chateau de Loei* which is produced in the northeastern province of Loei by Chaijudh Karnasuta with the expert assistance of a French wine maker. They produce a *chenin blanc* and a *chenin rouge* and they are eminently drinkable. At the 1996 Asia-Europe meeting (ASEM), Khun Chaijudh managed to get bottles placed in all the heads of state's rooms – what President Chirac thought, and whether he even tried the wine, is not known.

Shopping

When it comes to shopping, Bangkok offers the greatest variety and choice. But it is difficult to find bargains in Bangkok any longer. The department stores and shopping malls contain high-price, high-quality merchandise (all at a fixed price), much of which is imported.

Thailand has had a reputation as being a Mecca for **pirated goods**: cassette and video tapes, Lacoste shirts, Gucci leather goods, Rolex watches, computer software, and so on. These items are still available, but pressure from the US to protect intellectual copyright is leading to more enthusiastic crackdowns by the police. In Bangkok, *genuine* cassette tapes can be bought (at what are still bargain prices compared with the West), and buying pirated videos requires, in many cases, a retreat to some back room. This clampdown on pirated goods is likely to continue – in 1994-95 Thailand brought a new copyright law onto the statute books, and for fear of trade retaliation from the US, the law is being respected to a much greater degree than ever before.

The widest selection of **Thai silk** is available in Bangkok, although cheaper silk as well as good quality cotton can be obtained in the Northeast (the traditional centre of silk weaving). **Tailor-made clothing** is available (suits, shirts and dresses), although designs are sometimes rather outdated; it might be better for the tailor to copy an article of your own clothing (see page 150). However, things change and there are now some top designers in Bangkok. **Leather goods** include custom-made crocodile skin shoes and boots (for those who aren't squeamish, after seeing the brutes in one of the crocodile farms).

Bangkok is also a good place to buy **jewellery** – gold, sapphires and rubies – as well as **antiques**, bronzeware and celadon. **NB** See section on tricksters, below. Handicrafts are best purchased up-country. In general, Bangkok has by far the best selection of goods, and by shopping around, visitors will probably be able to get just as good a price as they would further afield.

Competition Between shopkeepers competition is fierce. Do not be persuaded into buying something before having a chance to price it elsewhere – Thais can be enormously persuasive. **NB** Also, watch out for guarantees of authenticity – fake antiques abound, and even professionals find it difficult to know a 1990 Khmer sculpture from a 10th-century one.

Tips Generally unnecessary. A 10% service charge is now expected on room, food and drinks bills in the smarter hotels as well as a tip for any personal service. Increasingly, the more expensive restaurants add a 10% service charge; others expect a small tip.

Tricksters Tricksters, rip-off artists, fraudsters, less than honest salesmen – call them what you will – are likely to be far more of a problem than simple theft. People may well approach you in the street offering incredible one-off bargains, and giving what might seem to be very plausible reasons for your sudden good fortune. Be wary in all such cases and do not be pressed into making a hasty decision. Unfortunately, more often than not, the salesman is trying to pull a fast one. Favourite 'bargains' are precious stones, whose authenticity is 'demonstrated' before your very eyes (see the box on page 145). Although many Thais do like to talk to *farangs* and practice their English, in tourist areas there are also those who offer their friendship for pecuniary rather than linguistic reasons. Sad as it is to say so, it is probably a good idea to be suspicious.

Holidays and festivals

Festivals with month only are movable; a booklet of holidays and festivals is available from most TAT offices. For movable festivals, check the TAT's website, www.tourismthailand.org/tat The dates given here for movable festivals and public holidays are for 2001.

January *New Year's Day* (1st: public holiday).

February/March *Chinese New Year* (movable, end of January/beginning of February) celebrated by Thailand's large Chinese population. The festival extends over 15 days; spirits are appeased, and offerings are made to the ancestors and to the spirits. Good wishes and lucky money are exchanged, and Chinese-run shops and businesses shut down. *Magha Puja* (movable, full-moon: public holiday, 8th February 2001). Buddhist holy day, celebrates the occasion when the Buddha's disciples miraculously gathered together to hear him preach. Culminates in a candle-lit procession around the temple bot (or ordination hall). The faithful make offerings and gain merit.

April *Chakri Day* (6th: public holiday) commemorates the founding of the present Chakri Dynasty. *Songkran* (movable: public holiday, 13th April 2001) marks the beginning of the Buddhist New Year. The festival is particularly big in the North, much less so in the South and (understandably) the Muslim far south. It is a three- to five-day celebration, with parades, dancing and folk entertainment. Traditionally, the first day represents the last chance for a 'spring clean'. Rubbish is burnt, in the belief that old and dirty things will cause misfortune in the coming year. The wat is the focal point of celebrations. Revered Buddha images are carried through the streets, accompanied by singers and dancers. The second day is the main water-throwing day. The water-throwing practice was originally an act of homage to ancestors and family elders. Young people pay respect by pouring scented water over the elders heads. The older generation sprinkle water over Buddha images. Gifts are given. This uninhibited water-throwing continues for all three days (although it is now banned in Bangkok). On the third day birds, fish and turtles are all released, to gain merit and in remembrance of departed souls.

Labour Day (1st: public holiday). *Coronation Day* (5th May: public holiday) **May/June** commemorates the present King Bhumibol's crowning in 1950. *Ploughing Ceremony* (movable: public holiday, 16th May 2001) performed by the King at Sanaam Luang near the Grand Palace in Bangkok. Brahmanic in origin, it traditionally marks the auspicious date when farmers could begin preparing their riceland. Impressive bulls decorated with flowers pull a sacred gold plough. *Visakha Puja* (full-moon: public holiday, 7th May 2001) holiest of all Buddhist days, it marks the Buddha's birth, enlightenment and death. Candle-lit processions are held at most temples.

Asalha Puja and *Khao Phansa* (movable, full-moon: public holiday, 5th July 2001) – **July** commemorates the Buddha's first sermon to his disciples and marks the beginning of the Buddhist Lent. Monks reside in their monasteries for the three-month Buddhist Rains Retreat to study and meditate, and young men temporarily become monks. Ordination ceremonies all over the country and villagers give white cotton robes to the monks to wear during the Lent ritual bathing.

The Queen's Birthday (12th: public holiday). **August**

Chulalongkorn Day (23rd: public holiday) honours King Chulalongkorn (1868-1910), **October** perhaps Thailand's most beloved and revered king. *Ok Phansa* (three lunar months after Asalha Puja) marks the end of the Buddhist Lent and the beginning of Krathin, when gifts – usually a new set of cotton robes – are offered to the monks. Particularly venerated monks are sometimes given silk robes as a sign of respect and esteem. **Krathin** itself is celebrated over two days. It marks the end of the monks' retreat and the re-entry of novices into secular society. Processions and fairs are held all over the country; villagers wear their best clothes and food, money, pillows and bed linen are offered to the monks of the local wat.

Loi Krathong (full-moon, mid-November) a *krathong* is a small model boat made to **November** contain a candle, incense and flowers. The festival comes at the end of the rainy season and honours the goddess of water. The little boats are pushed out onto canals, lakes and rivers. Sadly, few *krathongs* are now made of leaves: polystyrene has taken over and the morning after Loi Krathong lakes and river banks are littered with the wrecks of the night's festivities. **NB** The 'quaint' candles in flower pots sold in many shops at this time, are in fact large firecrackers.

The King's Birthday (5th: public holiday). Flags and portraits of the King are erected all **December** over Bangkok, especially down Rachdamnern Avenue and around the Grand Palace. *Constitution Day* (10th: public holiday). *New Year's Eve* (31st: public holiday).

NB Regional and local festivals are noted in appropriate sections.

Health

Staying healthy in Thailand is straightforward. With the following advice and precautions you should keep as healthy as you do at home. Most visitors return home having experienced no problems at all beyond an upset stomach. However in Thailand the health risks, especially in the tropical areas, are different from those encountered in Europe or the USA. It also depends on how you travel and where. The country has a mainly tropical climate; nevertheless the acquisition of true tropical disease by the visitor is probably conditioned as much by the rural nature and standard of hygiene of the surroundings than by the climate. There is an obvious difference in health risks between the business traveller who tends to stay in international class hotels in the large cities and the backpacker trekking through the rural areas. There are no hard and fast rules to follow; you will often have to make your own judgement on the healthiness or otherwise of your surroundings.

Medical facilities

There are English-speaking doctors in Bangkok and other major cities who have particular experience in dealing with locally occurring diseases. Your Embassy representative will often be able to give you the name of local reputable doctors and most of the better hotels have a doctor on standby. If you do fall ill and cannot find a recommended doctor, try the outpatient department of a hospital – there are excellent private hospitals in Bangkok which, although they are not cheap, offer a very acceptable standard to foreigners. The likelihood of finding good medical care diminishes very rapidly as you move away from the big cities. Especially in the rural areas there are systems and traditions of medicine wholly different from the Western model and you will be confronted with less orthodox forms of treatment such as herbal medicines and acupuncture, not that these are unfamiliar to most Western travellers.

Before travelling

Take out medical insurance. Make sure it covers all eventualities especially evacuation to your home country by a medically equipped plane, if necessary. You should have a dental check up, obtain a spare glasses prescription, a spare oral contraceptive prescription (or enough pills to last) and, if you suffer from a chronic illness (such as diabetes, high blood pressure, ear or sinus troubles, cardio-pulmonary disease or nervous disorder) arrange for a check up with your doctor, who can at the same time provide you with a letter explaining the details of your disability in English. Check the current practice in countries you are visiting for malaria prophylaxis (prevention). If you are on regular medication, make sure you have enough to cover the period of your travel.

Medicines There is very little control on the sale of drugs and medicines in Thailand. You may be able to buy any and every drug in pharmacies without a prescription. Be wary of this because pharmacists can be poorly trained and might sell you drugs that are unsuitable, dangerous or old. Many drugs and medicines are manufactured under licence from American or European companies, so the trade names may be familiar to you. This means you do not have to carry a whole chest of medicines with you, but remember that the shelf life of some items, especially vaccines and antibiotics, is markedly reduced in hot conditions. Buy your supplies at the better outlets where there are more refrigerators, even though they are more expensive, and check the expiry date of all preparations you buy. Immigration officials occasionally confiscate scheduled drugs (Lomotil is an example) if they are not accompanied by a doctor's prescription.

More preparation is probably necessary for babies and children than for an adult and **Children** perhaps a little more care should be taken when travelling to remote areas where health services are primitive. This is because children can be become more rapidly ill than adults (on the other hand they often recover more quickly). Diarrhoea and vomiting are the most common problems, so take the usual precautions, but more intensively. Breast-feeding is the best and most convenient for babies, but powdered milk is available in the cities, as are a few baby foods. Bananas and other fruits are all nutritious and can be cleanly prepared. The treatment of diarrhoea is the same for adults, except that it should start earlier and be continued with more persistence. Children get dehydrated very quickly in hot countries and can become drowsy and uncooperative unless cajoled to drink water or juice plus salts. Upper respiratory infections, such as colds, catarrh and middle ear infections are also common and if your child suffers from these normally take some antibiotics against the possibility. Outer ear infections after swimming are also common and antibiotic eardrops will help. Wet wipes are always useful and can be found in Bangkok and the large cities as can disposable nappies.

You may like to take some of the following items with you from home: sunglasses – **Medical** ones designed for intense sunlight; earplugs – for sleeping on aeroplanes and in noisy **supplies** hotels; suntan cream – with a high protection factor; insect repellent – containing DET for preference; mosquito net – lightweight, permethrin-impregnated for choice; travel sickness tablets; tampons – can be expensive in some countries in Southeast Asia; condoms; contraceptives; water sterilizing tablets; anti-malarial tablets; anti-infective ointment, for example Cetrimide; dusting powder for feet, etc – containing fungicide; antacid tablets – for indigestion; sachets of rehydration salts plus anti-diarrhoea preparations; painkillers such as Paracetamol or Aspirin; antibiotics – for diarrhoea, etc; first aid kit – small pack containing a few sterile syringes and needles and disposable gloves. The risk of catching hepatitis, etc from a dirty needle used for injection is very low in Thailand, but some may be reassured by carrying their own supplies – available from camping shops and airport shops.

Smallpox vaccination is no longer required anywhere in the world and cholera **Vaccination &** vaccination is no longer recognized as necessary for international travel by the World **immunization** Health Organization – it is not very effective either. Yellow fever vaccination is not required either although you may be asked for a certificate if you have been in a country affected by yellow fever immediately before travelling to Southeast Asia. Vaccination against the following diseases is recommended:

Typhoid A disease spread by the insanitary preparation of food. A number of new vaccines against this condition are now available; the older TAB and monovalent typhoid vaccines are being phased out. The newer, for example Typhim Vi, cause less side effects, but are more expensive. For those who do not like injections, there are now oral vaccines.

Poliomyelitis Despite its decline in the world this remains a serious disease if caught and is easy to protect against. There are live oral vaccines and in some countries injected vaccines. Whichever one you choose it is a good idea to have a booster every three to five years if visiting developing countries regularly.

Tetanus One dose should be given with a booster at six weeks and another at six months and 10-yearly boosters thereafter are recommended. Children should already be properly protected against diphtheria, poliomyelitis and pertussis (whooping cough), measles and HIB all of which can be more serious infections in Southeast Asia than at home. Measles, mumps and rubella vaccine is also given to children

Essentials

throughout the world, but those teenage girls who have not had rubella (German measles) should be tested and vaccinated. Hepatitis B vaccination for babies is now routine in some countries. Consult your doctor for advice on tuberculosis inoculation: the disease is still widespread in Southeast Asia.

Infectious Hepatitis Is less of a problem for travellers than it used to be because of the development of two extremely effective vaccines against the A and B form of the disease. It remains common, however, in Southeast Asia. A combined hepatitis A & B vaccine is now licensed and has been available since 1997 – one jab covers both diseases.

Other vaccinations These might be considered in the case of epidemics, for example meningitis. Meningococcal meningitis and Japanese B encephalitis (JVE): there is an extremely small risk of these rather serious diseases. Both are seasonal and vary according to region. Meningitis can occur in epidemic form. JVE is a viral disease transmitted from pigs to man by mosquitoes. For details of the vaccinations consult a travel clinic.

Further information

Further information on health risks abroad, vaccinations, etc may be available from a local travel clinic. If you wish to take specific drugs with you such as antibiotics these are best prescribed by your own doctor. Beware, however, that not all doctors can be experts on the health problems of remote countries. Other sources can provide more detailed or more up-to-date information. In the UK there are hospital departments specializing in tropical diseases in London, Liverpool, Birmingham and Glasgow and the Malaria Reference Laboratory at the London School of Hygiene and Tropical Medicine provides free advice about malaria, T0891-600350. In the USA such information can be obtained from the local Public Health Services and from the Centres for Disease Control (CDC) in Atlanta, T404-3324559.

There are, in addition, computerized databases which can be accessed for destination-specific up-to-the-minute information. In the UK there is MASTA (Medical Advisory Service to Travellers Abroad), based at the London School of Hygiene and Tropical Medicine, T020-76314408, Tx8953473, F020-74365389 and Travax (Glasgow, T0141-9467120, Ext 247). Other information on medical problems overseas can be obtained from the book by Richard Dawood (Editor) – *Travellers' Health, How to Stay Healthy Abroad*, Oxford University Press 1992, £7.99 (new edition imminent). We strongly recommend this revised and updated edition, especially to the intrepid traveller heading for the more out-of-the-way places. General advice is also available in the UK in *Health Information for Overseas Travel* published by the Department of Health and available from HMSO, and *International Travel and Health* published by WHO. Handbooks on First Aid are produced by the British & American Red Cross and by St John's Ambulance (UK). The Ross Institute, London School of Hygiene and Tropical Medicine, Keppel Street, London WC1E 7HT, publishes *The Preservation of Personal Health in Warm Climates*. The Centres for Disease Control (CDC) in Atlanta, Georgia, USA will provide equivalent information (www.cdc.gov/travel). A helpful travel health website is Shoreland's Travel Health Online, www.tripprep.com. A more general publication is John Hatt's *The Tropical Traveller* (Penguin, 1993).

On the way

For most travellers a trip to Southeast Asia means a long air flight. If this crosses time zones then jetlag can be a problem where your body's biological clock gets out of synchrony with the real time at your destination. The main symptoms are tiredness and sleepiness at inconvenient times and, conversely, a tendency to wake up in the middle of the night feeling like you want your breakfast. Most find that the problem is worse when flying in an easterly direction. The best way to get over jetlag is probably to try to force yourself into the new time zone as strictly as possible which may involve, on a westward flight, trying to stay awake until your normal bedtime and on an eastward flight forgetting that you have lost some sleep on the way out and going to bed relatively early but near your normal time the evening after you arrive. The symptoms of jetlag may be helped by keeping up your fluid intake on the journey, but not with alcohol. The hormone melatonin seems to reduce the symptoms of jetlag but is not presently licensed in most of Europe although it can be obtained from health food stores in the USA.

On long-haul flights it is also important to stretch your legs at least every hour to prevent slowing of the circulation and the possible development of blood clots. Drinking plenty of non-alcoholic fluids will also help.

If travelling by boat then sea sickness can be a problem – dealt with in the usual way by taking anti-motion sickness pills.

Staying healthy

Intestinal upsets The thought of catching a stomach bug worries visitors to Southeast Asia but there have been great improvements in food hygiene and most such infections are preventable. Travellers' diarrhoea and vomiting is due, most of the time, to food poisoning, usually passed on by the insanitary habits of food handlers. As a general rule the cleaner your surroundings and the smarter the restaurant, the less likely you are to suffer.

Foods to avoid Uncooked, undercooked, partially cooked or reheated meat, fish, eggs, raw vegetables and salads, especially when they have been left out exposed to flies. Stick to fresh food that has been cooked from raw just before eating and make sure you peel fruit yourself. Wash and dry your hands before eating – disposable wet-wipe tissues are useful for this.

Shellfish Eaten raw shellfish are risky and at certain times of the year some fish and shellfish concentrate toxins from their environment and cause various kinds of food poisoning. Liver fluke can also be transmitted The local authorities notify the public not to eat these foods. Do not ignore the warning.

Heat treated milk (UHT pasteurized or sterilized) is becoming more available in Southeast Asia as is pasteurized cheese. On the whole matured or processed cheeses are safer than the fresh varieties. Fresh unpasteurized milk from whatever animal can be a source of food poisoning germs, tuberculosis and brucellosis. This applies equally to ice-cream, yoghurt and cheese made from unpasteurized milk, so avoid these home-made products – the factory-made ones are probably safer.

Tap water is rarely safe outside the major cities, especially in the rainy season. Stream water, if you are in the countryside, is often contaminated by local communities. Filtered or bottled water is usually available and safe, although you must make sure that somebody is not filling bottles from the tap and hammering on a new crown cap. If your hotel has a central hot water supply this water is safe to drink after cooling. Ice for drinks should be made from boiled water, but rarely is so stand your glass on the ice cubes, rather than putting them in the drink. The better hotels have water purifying systems.

Travellers' diarrhoea This is usually caused by eating food which has been contaminated by food poisoning germs. Drinking water is rarely the culprit. Sea water or river water is more likely to be contaminated by sewage and so swimming in such dilute effluent can also be a cause.

Infection with various organisms can give rise to travellers' diarrhoea. They may be viruses, bacteria, for example escherichia coli (probably the most common cause world-wide), protozoa (such as amoebas and giardia), salmonella and cholera. The diarrhoea may come on suddenly or rather slowly. It may or may not be accompanied by vomiting or by severe abdominal pain and the passage of blood or mucus when it is called dysentery.

How do you know which type you have caught and how to treat it? If you can time the onset of the diarrhoea to the minute ('acute') then it is probably due to a virus or a bacterium and/or the onset of dysentery. The treatment in addition to rehydration is Ciprofloxacin 500 milligrams every 12 hours; the drug is now widely available and there are many similar ones.

If the diarrhoea comes on slowly or intermittently ('sub-acute') then it is more likely to be protozoal, that is caused by an amoeba or giardia. Antibiotics such as Ciprofloxacin will have little effect. These cases are best treated by a doctor as is any outbreak of diarrhoea continuing for more than three days. Sometimes blood is passed in amoebic dysentery and for this you should certainly seek medical help. If this is not available then the best treatment is probably Tinidazole (Fasigyn), one tablet four times a day for three days. If there are severe stomach cramps, the following drugs may help but are not very useful in the management of acute diarrhoea: Loperamide (Imodium) and Diphenoxylate with Atropine (Lomotil). They should not be given to children.

Any kind of diarrhoea, whether or not accompanied by vomiting, responds well to the replacement of water and salts, taken as frequent small sips, of some kind of rehydration solution. There are proprietary preparations consisting of sachets of powder which you dissolve in boiled water or you can make your own by adding half a teaspoonful of salt (3.5 grams) and four tablespoonfuls of sugar (40 grams) to a litre of boiled water.

Thus the linchpins of treatment for diarrhoea are rest, fluid and salt replacement, antibiotics such as Ciprofloxacin for the bacterial types and special diagnostic tests and medical treatment for the Amoeba and Giardia infections. Salmonella infections and cholera, although rare, can be devastating diseases and it would be wise to get to a hospital as soon as possible if these were suspected.

Fasting, peculiar diets and the consumption of large quantities of yoghurt have not been found useful in calming travellers' diarrhoea or in rehabilitating inflamed bowels. Oral rehydration has on the other hand, especially in children, been a lifesaving technique and should always be practised, whatever other treatment you use. As there is some evidence that alcohol and milk might prolong diarrhoea they should be avoided during and immediately after an attack. So should chillies!

Diarrhoea occurring day after day for long periods of time (chronic diarrhoea) is notoriously resistant to amateur attempts at treatment and again warrants proper diagnostic tests (cities with reasonable sized hospitals have laboratories for stool samples). There are ways of preventing travellers' diarrhoea for short periods of time by taking antibiotics, but this is not a foolproof technique and should not be used other than in exceptional circumstances. Doxycycline is possibly the best drug. Some preventatives such as Enterovioform can have serious side effects if taken for long periods.

Paradoxically **constipation** is also common, probably induced by dietary change, inadequate fluid intake in hot places and long bus journeys. Simple laxatives are useful in the short term and bulky foods such as rice, beans and plenty of fruit are also useful.

Purifying water   There are a number of ways of purifying water in order to make it safe to drink. Dirty water should first be strained through a filter bag (camping shops) and then boiled or treated. Bringing water to a rolling boil at sea level is sufficient to make the water safe for drinking, but at higher altitudes you have to boil the water for longer to ensure that all the microbes are killed.

There are sterilizing methods that can be used and there are proprietary preparations containing chlorine (eg *Puritabs*) or iodine (eg *Pota Aqua*) compounds. Chlorine compounds generally do not kill protozoa (eg giardia).

There are a number of water filters now on the market available in personal and expedition size. They work either on mechanical or chemical principles, or may do both. Make sure you take the spare parts or spare chemicals with you and do not believe everything the manufacturers say.

Heat & cold

Full acclimatization to high temperatures takes about two weeks. During this period it is normal to feel a bit apathetic, especially if the relative humidity is high. Drink plenty of water (up to 15 litres a day are required when working physically hard in the tropics), use salt on your food and avoid extreme exertion. Tepid showers are more cooling than hot or cold ones. Large hats do not cool you down, but do prevent sunburn. Remember that, especially in the highlands, there can be a large and sudden drop in temperature between sun and shade and between night and day, so dress accordingly. Warm jackets or woollens are essential after dark at high altitude. Loose cotton is still the best material when the weather is hot.

Air pollution

There is serious traffic congestion and air pollution in the major cities, especially in Bangkok. Expect sore throats and itchy eyes. Sufferers from asthma or bronchitis may have to increase their regular maintenance treatment.

Insects

These are mostly more of a nuisance than a serious hazard and if you try, you can prevent yourself entirely from being bitten. Some, such as mosquitoes are, of course, carriers of potentially serious diseases, so it is sensible to avoid being bitten as much as possible. Sleep off the ground and use a mosquito net or some kind of insecticide. Preparations containing pyrethrum or synthetic pyrethroids are safe. They are available as aerosols or pumps and the best way to use these is to spray the room thoroughly in all areas (follow the instructions rather than the insects) and then shut the door for a while, re-entering when the smell has dispersed. Mosquito coils, which release insecticide as they burn slowly, are widely available and useful out of doors. Tablets of insecticide which are placed on a heated mat plugged into a wall socket are probably the most effective. They fill the room with insecticidal fumes in the same way as aerosols or coils.

You can also use insect repellents, most of which are effective against a wide range of pests. The most common and effective is diethyl metatoluamide (DET). DET liquid is best for arms and face (care around eyes and with spectacles – DET dissolves plastic). Aerosol spray is good for clothes and ankles and liquid DET can be dissolved in water and used to impregnate cotton clothes and mosquito nets. Some repellents now contain DET and permethrin, an insecticide. Impregnated wrist and ankle bands can also be useful.

If you are bitten or stung, itching may be relieved by cool baths, antihistamine tablets (care with alcohol or driving) or mild corticosteriod creams, for example hydrocortisone (great care: never use if any hint of infection). Careful scratching of all your bites once a day can be surprisingly effective. Calamine lotion and cream have limited effectiveness and antihistamine creams are not recommended – they can cause allergies themselves.

Bites which become infected should be treated with a local antiseptic or antibiotic cream such as Cetrimide, as should any infected sores or scratches.

When living rough, skin infestations with body lice (crabs) and scabies are easy to pick up. Use whatever local commercial preparation is recommended for lice and scabies.

Crotamiton cream (Eurax) alleviates itching and also kills a number of skin parasites. Malathion lotion 5% (Prioderm) kills lice effectively, but avoid the use of the toxic agricultural preparation of Malathion, more often used to commit suicide.

Ticks Usually attach themselves to the lower parts of the body often after walking in areas where cattle have grazed. They take a while to attach themselves strongly, but swell up as they start to suck blood. The important thing is to remove them gently, so that they do not leave their head parts in your skin because this can cause a nasty allergic reaction some days later. Do not use petrol, Vaseline, lighted cigarettes, etc to remove the tick, but, with a pair of tweezers remove the beast gently by gripping it at the attached (head) end and rock it out in very much the same way that a tooth is extracted. Certain tropical flies which lay their eggs under the skin of sheep and cattle also occasionally do the same thing to humans with the unpleasant result that a maggot grows under the skin and pops up as a boil or pimple. The best way to remove these is to cover the boil with oil, Vaseline or nail varnish so as to stop the maggot breathing, then to squeeze it out gently the next day.

Sunburn The burning power of the tropical sun, especially at high altitude, is phenomenal. Always wear a wide-brimmed hat and use some form of suncream or lotion on untanned skin. Normal temperate-zone suntan lotions (protection factor up to seven) are not much good; you need to use the types designed specifically for the tropics or for mountaineers or skiers with protection factors up to 15 or above. These are often not available in Thailand. Glare from the sun can cause conjunctivitis, so wear sunglasses especially on tropical beaches, where high protection factor sunscreen should also be used.

Prickly heat This very common, intensely itchy rash is avoided by frequent washing and by wearing loose clothing. It is cured by allowing skin to dry off through use of powder or by spending two nights in an air-conditioned hotel!

Athlete's foot This and other fungal skin infections are best treated with Tolnaftate or Clotrimazole.

Other risks and more serious diseases

Remember that rabies is endemic throughout Southeast Asia, so avoid dogs and cover your toes at night from vampire bats, which also carry the disease. If you are bitten by a domestic or wild animal, do not leave things to chance: scrub the wound with soap and water and/or disinfectant, try to have the animal captured (within limits) or at least determine its ownership, where possible, and seek medical assistance at once. The course of treatment depends on whether you have already been satisfactorily vaccinated against rabies. If you have (this is worthwhile if you are spending lengths of time in developing countries) then some further doses of vaccine are all that is required. Human diploid vaccine is the best, but expensive: other, older kinds of vaccine, such as that derived from duck embryos may be the only types available. These are effective, much cheaper and interchangeable generally with the human derived types. If not already vaccinated then anti-rabies serum (immunoglobulin) may be required in addition. It is important to finish the course of treatment whether the animal survives or not.

AIDS Aids is increasing its prevalence in Southeast Asia. It is not wholly confined to the well-known high-risk sections of the population, that is homosexual men, intravenous drug abusers, prostitutes and the children of infected mothers. Heterosexual transmission is now the dominant mode of infection and so the main risk to travellers is from casual sex. The same precautions should be taken as when encountering any sexually transmitted disease. The disease has had a huge impact on Thailand due to the high rates of prostitution and, in some areas, drug abuse. The AIDS virus (HIV) can be passed via unsterile needles which have been previously

Modelling AIDS in Southeast Asia

There has been a tendency to assume that there is a single AIDS 'pandemic'. However in reality it seems that there are possibly three different patterns to the spread of AIDS – one is characteristic of Europe and North America, the second of Sub-Saharan Africa, and the third of Asia. This third pattern, described by Tim Brown and Peter Xenos of the East-West Population Institute in Hawaii, is different in a number of important respects. Furthermore, they argue that these differences are likely to make the disease both more serious and more intractable. The pattern is based on the experience of Thailand, and it is assumed that the Thai experience will soon be seen reflected in other countries in Asia.

It seems that the possibility of transmission per exposure, whether that be through sexual relations or needle sharing, is higher in Asia than in Europe and North America because of the high incidence of sexually transmitted diseases, especially among sex workers. Furthermore, a significant proportion of the male population of the countries of the region visit prostitutes for sex, meaning that the population 'at risk' is also very high. Therefore, in Thailand – and by implication also soon in many other countries of Asia – AIDS quickly made the cross-over from the homosexual and drug-using populations, to the heterosexual population. Thailand's first AIDS case was reported in 1984. By the end of 1988, 30% of addicts visiting methodone treatment centres were HIV positive. Five years later, by the end of 1993, levels of infection among sex workers had similarly reached 30%. Now, nearly 2% of women visiting pre-natal clinics are testing HIV positive. Thus, in the space of less than 10 years – far faster than in Europe and North America, and even faster than in Africa – AIDS has spread from homosexuals and drug addicts to the wives and babies of heterosexual men.

In August 1994, at a major international conference on AIDS in Asia, James Allen of the American Medical Association likened (and provoking considerable anger, it should be added) AIDS to the Black Death in Europe. The costs to Asia of the disease are likely to be truly staggering: McGraw-Hill have put a figure of US$38-52bn on the social and economic costs of AIDS in the region.

Southeast Asia: potential for the spread of AIDS/HIV

Rapidly increasing: Myanmar; Cambodia; Thailand
Potential for rapid increase: Indonesia; Laos; Malaysia; Vietnam
Increasing: Singapore
Not classified: Brunei

Essentials

used to inject an HIV positive patient, but the risk of this is very small indeed. It would, however, be sensible to check that needles have been properly sterilized or disposable needles are used. The chance of picking up Hepatitis B in this way is more of a danger. Be wary of carrying disposable needles. Customs officials may find them suspicious. The risk of receiving a blood transfusion with blood infected with the HIV virus is greater than from dirty needles because of the amount of fluid exchanged. Supplies of blood for transfusion are supposed to be screened for HIV in all reputable hospitals so the risk should be small. Catching the virus which causes AIDS does not necessarily produce an illness in itself; the only way to be sure if you feel you have been put at risk is to have a blood test for HIV antibodies on your return to a place where there are reliable laboratory facilities. However the test does not become positive for many weeks.

Malaria is prevalent in Southeast Asia and remains a serious disease and you are advised to protect yourself against mosquito bites as above and to take prophylactic (preventative) drugs. Start taking the tablets a few days before exposure and continue

Malaria

to take them six weeks after leaving the malarial zone. Remember to give the drugs to babies and children; pregnant women should also take them.

The subject of malaria prevention is becoming more complex as the malaria parasite becomes immune to some of the older drugs. Nowhere is this more apparent than in Southeast Asia, especially parts of Laos and Cambodia. In particular, there has been an increase in the proportion of cases of falciparum malaria which is resistant to the normally used drugs. It would not be an exaggeration to say that we are near to the situation where some cases of malaria will be untreatable with presently available drugs.

Before you travel you must check with a reputable agency the likelihood and type of malaria in the countries which you intend to visit. Take note of advice on prophylaxis but be prepared to receive conflicting advice. Because of the rapidly changing situation in the Southeast Asian region the names and the dosage of the drugs have not been included but chloroquine and proganil may still be recommended for the areas where malaria is still fully sensitive, while Doxycycline, Mefloquine and Artemether are presently being used in resistant areas. Quinine, Halofantrine and Tetracycline drugs remain the mainstay of treatment. It is still possible to catch malaria even when taking prophylactic drugs, although it is unlikely. If you do develop symptoms (high fever, shivering, severe headache and sometimes diarrhoea) seek medical advice immediately. The risk of the disease is obviously greater the further you move from the cities into rural areas with primitive facilities and standing water.

Information regarding country-by-country malaria risk can be obtained from the **World Health Organization** (WHO) or in Britain from **The Ross Institute, London School of Hygiene and Tropical Medicine**, Keppel Street, London WC1E 7HT.

Infectious hepatitis (jaundice) The main symptoms are pains in the stomach, lack of appetite, lassitude and yellowness of the eyes and skin. Medically speaking there are two main types. The less serious, but more common is hepatitis A for which the best protection is the careful preparation of food, the avoidance of contaminated drinking water and scrupulous attention to toilet hygiene. The other, more serious, version is hepatitis B which is acquired usually as a sexually transmitted disease or by blood transfusion. It can less commonly be transmitted by injections with unclean needles and possibly by insect bites. The symptoms are the same as for hepatitis A. The incubation period is much longer (up to six months compared with six weeks) and there are more likely to be complications.

Hepatitis A can be protected against with gamma globulin. It should be obtained from a reputable source and is certainly useful for travellers who intend to live rough. You should have a shot before leaving and have it repeated every six months. The dose of gamma globulin depends on the concentration of the particular preparation used, so the manufacturer's advice should be taken. The injection should be given as close as possible to your departure and as the dose depends on the likely time you are to spend in potentially affected areas. Again, the manufacturer's instructions should be followed. Gamma globulin has really been superseded now by a proper vaccination against hepatitis A (Havrix), which gives immunity lasting up to 10 years. After that boosters are required. Havrix monodose is now widely available as is junior Havrix. The vaccination has negligible side effects and is extremely effective. Gamma globulin injection can be a bit painful, but it is cheaper than Havrix and may be more readily available in some places.

Hepatitis B can be effectively prevented by a specific vaccine (Engerix) – three shots over six months before travelling. If you have had jaundice in the past it would be worthwhile having a blood test to see if you are immune to either of these two types, because this might avoid the necessity and costs of vaccination or gamma globulin. There are other kinds of viral hepatitis (C, E, etc) which are fairly similar to A and B, but vaccines are not available as yet.

Can still occur carried by ticks. There is usually a reaction at the site of the bite and a fever. Seek medical advice. **Typhus**

These are common and the more serious ones such as hookworm can be contracted from walking barefoot on infested earth or beaches. Some cause an itchy rash on the feet – 'cutaneous larva migrans'. **Intestinal Worms**

Various other tropical diseases can be caught in jungle areas, usually transmitted by biting insects. Examples are leishmaniasis and filariasis.

Various forms of leptospirosis are transmitted by a bacterium which is excreted in rodent urine. Fresh water and moist soil harbour the organisms which enter the body through cuts and scratches. If you suffer from any form of prolonged fever consult a doctor. **Leptospirosis**

This is a very rare event indeed for travellers but if you are unlucky (or careless) enough to be bitten by a venomous snake, spider, scorpion or sea creature, try to identify the creature, without putting yourself in further danger. Snake bites in particular are very frightening, but in fact rarely poisonous – even venomous snakes bite without injecting venom. What you might expect if bitten are: fright, swelling, pain and bruising around the bite and soreness of the regional lymph glands, perhaps nausea, vomiting and a fever. Signs of serious poisoning would be the following symptoms: numbness and tingling of the face, muscular spasms, convulsions, shortness of breath or a failure of the blood to clot, causing generalized bleeding. Victims should be taken to a hospital or a doctor without delay. Commercial snake bite and scorpion kits are available, but are usually only useful for the specific types of snake or scorpion. Most serum has to be given intravenously so it is not much good equipping yourself with it unless you are used to making injections into veins. It is best to rely on local practice in these cases, because the particular creatures will be known about locally and appropriate treatment can be given. **Snake bite**

Treatment of snake bite Reassure and comfort the victim frequently. Immobilize the limb by a bandage or a splint or by getting the person to lie still. Do not slash the bite area and try to suck out the poison because this sort of heroism does more harm than good. If you know how to use a tourniquet in these circumstances, you will not need this advice. If you are not experienced, do not apply a tourniquet.

Precautions Avoid walking in snake territory in bare feet or sandals – wear proper shoes or boots. If you encounter a snake, stay put until it slithers away, and do not investigate a wounded snake. Spiders and scorpions may be found in the more basic hotels. If stung, rest and take plenty of fluids and call a doctor. The best precaution is to keep beds away from the walls and look inside your shoes and under the toilet seat every morning.

Marine bites and stings Certain tropical sea fish when trodden upon inject venom into bathers' feet. This can be exceptionally painful. Wear plastic shoes when you go bathing if such creatures are reported. The pain can be relieved by immersing the foot in extremely hot water for as long as the pain persists.

This is increasing world-wide including in Southeast Asia. It can be completely prevented by avoiding mosquito bites in the same way as for malaria. No vaccine is available. Dengue is an unpleasant and painful disease, presenting with a high temperature and body pains, but at least visitors are spared the more serious forms (haemorrhagic types) which are more of a problem for local people who have been exposed to the disease more than once. There is no specific treatment for dengue – just painkillers and rest. **Dengue fever**

When you return home Remember to take your anti-malarial tablets for six weeks after leaving the malarial area. If you have had attacks of diarrhoea it is worth having a stool specimen tested in case you have picked up amoebas. If you have been living rough, blood tests may be worthwhile to detect worms and other parasites. If you have been exposed to schistosomiasis by swimming in lakes, etc, check by means of a blood test when you get home, but leave it for six weeks because the test is slow to become positive. Report any untoward symptoms to your doctor and tell the doctor exactly where you have been and, if you know, what the likelihood of disease is to which you were exposed.

The above information has been compiled for us by Dr David Snashall, who is presently Senior Lecturer in Occupational Health at the Guy's, King's & St Thomas' Hospitals in London, and until recently Chief Medical Advisor of the British Foreign and Commonwealth Office. He has travelled extensively and keeps in close touch with developments in preventative and tropical medicine.

Travelling with children

Many people are daunted by the prospect of taking a child to Southeast Asia. Naturally, it is not something which is taken on lightly; travelling is slower and more expensive and there are additional health risks for the child or baby. But it can be a most rewarding experience, and with sufficient care and planning, it can also be safe. Children are excellent passports into a local culture. You will also receive the best service, and help from officials and members of the public when in difficulty.

Children in Thailand are given 24-hour attention by parents, grandparents and siblings. They are rarely left to cry and are carried for most of the first eight months of their lives – crawling is considered animal-like. A non-Asian child is still something of a novelty and parents may find their child frequently taken off their hands, even mobbed in more remote areas. This can be a great relief (at mealtimes, for instance) or most alarming. Some children love the attention, others react against it; it is best simply to gauge your own child's reactions.

Practicalities

Accommodation At the hottest time of year, air-conditioning may be essential for a baby or young child's comfort. This rules out many of the cheaper hotels, but air-conditioned accommodation is available in all but the most out-of-the-way spots. When the child is bathing, be aware that the water could carry parasites, so avoid letting him or her drink it.

Food & drink The advice given in the health section on food and drink (see page 51) should be applied even more stringently where young children are concerned. Be aware that expensive hotels may have squalid cooking conditions; the cheapest street stall is often more hygienic. Where possible, try to watch food being prepared. Stir-fried vegetables and rice or noodles are the best bet; meat and fish may be pre-cooked and then left out before being re-heated. Fruit can be bought cheaply: papaya, banana and avocado are all excellent sources of nutrition, and can be self-peeled ensuring cleanliness. Powdered milk is also available throughout the region, although most brands have added sugar. But if taking a baby, breast-feeding is strongly recommended. Powdered food can be bought in most towns – the quality may not be the same as equivalent foods bought in the West, but it is perfectly adequate for short periods. Bottled water and fizzy drinks are also sold widely. If your child is at the 'grab everything and put it in mouth' stage, a damp cloth and some *Dettol* (or equivalent) are useful. Frequent wiping of hands and tabletops can help to minimize the chance of infection.

Essentials

Children and babies

Younger travellers seem to be more prone to illness abroad, but that should not put you off taking them. More preparation is necessary than for an adult and perhaps a little more care should be taken when travelling to remote areas where health services are primitive. This is because children can become more rapidly ill than adults (they often recover more quickly however). For more practical advice on travelling with children and babies see page 58.

Diarrhoea and vomiting are the most common problems so take the usual precautions, but more intensively. Make sure all basic childhood *vaccinations* are up to date as well as the more exotic ones. Children should be properly protected against diphtheria, whooping cough, mumps and measles. If they have not had the disease, teenage girls should be given rubella (german measles) vaccination. Consult your doctor for advice on BCG inoculation against tuberculosis: the disease is still common in the region. Protection against mosquitos and drug prophylaxis against malaria is essential. Many children take to "foreign" food quite happily. Fresh and powdered milk is available in most towns of any size in Thailand; breast feeding for babies even better.

Upper respiratory infections such as colds, catarrh and middle ear infections are common – antibiotics could be carried against the possibility. *Outer ear infections* after swimming are also common – antibiotic ear drops will help.

The treatment of *diarrhoea* is the same as for adults except that it should start earlier and be continued with more persistence. Children get dehydrated very quickly in the tropics and can become drowsy and uncooperative unless cajoled to drink water or juice plus salts. Oral rehydration has been a lifesaving technique in children.

Protect children against the sun with a hat and high factor tanning lotion. Severe sunburn at this age may well lead to serious skin cancer in the future.

Transport Public transport may be a problem; trains are fine but long bus journeys are restrictive and uncomfortable. Hiring a car is undoubtedly the most convenient way to see a country with a small child. Back-seatbelts are rarely fitted but it is possible to buy child-seats in capital cities.

Essentials

Disposable nappies These can be bought in Thailand, but are often expensive. If you are staying any length of time in one place, it may be worth taking Terry's (cloth) nappies. All you need is a bucket and some double-strength nappy cleanse (simply soak and rinse). Cotton nappies dry quickly in the heat and are generally more comfortable for the baby or child. They also reduce rubbish – many countries are not geared to the disposal of nappies. Of course, the best way for a child to be is nappy-free – like the local children.

Baby products Many Western baby products are available in Thailand: shampoo, talcum powder, soap and lotion. Baby wipes can be difficult to find.

Health

Emergencies Babies and small children deteriorate very rapidly when ill. A travel insurance policy which has an air ambulance provision is strongly recommended. When planning a route, try to stay within 24 hours' travel of a hospital with good care and facilities. Many expatriates fly to Singapore for medical care, which has the best doctors and facilities in the region.

Sunburn **Never** allow your child to be exposed to the harsh tropical sun without protection. A child can burn in a matter of minutes. Loose cotton-clothing, with long sleeves and legs and a sunhat are best. High-factor sun-protection cream is essential.

Checklist

Baby wipes; child paracetamol; disinfectant; first-aid kit; flannel; immersion element for boiling water; decongestant for colds; instant food for under-one-year-olds; mug/bottle/bowl/spoons; nappy cleanse, double-strength; ORS (oral rehydration salts) such as *Dioralyte*, widely available in Thailand, and the most effective way to alleviate diarrhoea (it is not a cure); portable baby chair, to hook onto tables; this is not essential but can be very useful; sarong or backpack for carrying child (and/or lightweight collapsible buggy); sterilizing tablets (and container for sterilizing bottles, teats, utensils); cream for nappy rash and other skin complaints such as *Sudocrem*; sunblock, factor 15 or higher; sunhat; terry's (cloth) nappies, liners, pins and plastic pants; thermometer; zip-lock bags for carrying snacks, etc.

Further information

Suggested reading Pentes, Tina and Truelove, Adrienne (1984) *Travelling with children to Indonesia and South-East Asia,* Hale & Iremonger: Sydney. Wheeler, Maureen *Travel with children,* Lonely Planet: Hawthorne, Australia.

Further reading

Magazines *Asiaweek* (weekly). A lightweight *Far Eastern Economic Review;* rather like a regional *Time* magazine in style.
The Far Eastern Economic Review (weekly). Authoritative Hong Kong-based regional magazine; their correspondents based in each country provide knowledgeable, in-depth analysis particularly on economics and politics.
Metro (monthly). Bangkok's own *Time Out.* The best source for information on new restaurants, bands, clubs and much else.

Books on Southeast Asia

Buruma, Ian (1989) *God's dust,* Jonathan Cape: London. Enjoyable journey through Thailand, Myanmar, Malaysia and Singapore along with the Philippines, Taiwan, South Korea and Japan; journalist Buruma questions how far culture in this region has survived the intrusion of the West.
Clad, James (1989) *Behind the myth: business, money and power in Southeast Asia,* Unwin Hyman: London. Clad, formerly a journalist with the *Far Eastern Economic Review,* distilled his experiences in this book; as it turned out, rather disappointingly – it is a hotch-potch of journalistic snippets.
Dingwall, Alastair (1994) *Traveller's literary companion to Southeast Asia,* In Print: Brighton. Experts on Southeast Asian language and literature select extracts from novels and other books by Western and regional writers. The extracts are annoyingly brief, but it gives a good overview of what is available.
Dumarçay, Jacques (1991) *The palaces of South-East Asia: architecture and customs,* OUP: Singapore. A broad summary of palace art and architecture in both mainland and island Southeast Asia.
Fraser-Lu, Sylvia (1988) *Handwoven textiles of South-East Asia,* OUP: Singapore. Well-illustrated, large-format book with informative text.
Higham, Charles (1989) *The archaeology of mainland Southeast Asia from 10,000 BC to*

the fall of Angkor, Cambridge University Press: Cambridge. Best summary of changing views of the archaeology of the mainland.

Keyes, Charles F (1977) *The golden peninsula: culture and adaptation in mainland Southeast Asia*, Macmillan: New York. Academic, yet readable summary of the threads of continuity and change in Southeast Asia's culture. The volume has been recently republished by Hawaii University Press, but not updated or revised.

King, Ben F and Dickinson, EC (1975) *A field guide to the birds of South-East Asia*, Collins: London. Best regional guide to the birds of the region.

Miettinen, Jukko O (1992) *Classical dance and theatre in South-East Asia*, OUP, Singapore. Expensive, but accessible survey of dance and theatre, mostly focusing on Thailand, Myanmar and Indonesia.

Osborne, Milton (1979) *Southeast Asia: an introductory history*, Allen & Unwin: Sydney. Good introductory history, clearly written, published in a portable paperback edition. A new revised edition is now on the shelves.

Rawson, Philip (1967) *The art of Southeast Asia*, Thames & Hudson: London. Portable general art history of Myanmar, Cambodia, Vietnam, Thailand, Laos, Java and Bali; by necessity, rather superficial, but a good place to start.

Reid, Anthony (1988) *Southeast Asia in the age of commerce 1450-1680: the lands below the winds*, Yale University Press: New Haven. Perhaps the best history of everyday life in Southeast Asia, looking at such themes as physical well-being, material culture and social organization.

Reid, Anthony (1993) *Southeast Asia in the age of commerce 1450-1680: expansion and crisis*, Yale University Press: New Haven. Volume 2 in this excellent history of the region.

Rigg, Jonathan (1991) *Southeast Asia: a region in transition*, Unwin Hyman: London. A thematic geography of the ASEAN region, providing an insight into some of the major issues affecting the region today.

Rigg, Jonathan (1997) *Southeast Asia: the human landscape of modernization and development*, London: Routledge. A book which covers both the market and former command economies (ie Myanmar, Vietnam, Laos and Cambodia) of the region. It focuses on how people in the region have responded to the challenges and tensions of modernization.

SarDesai, DR (1989) *Southeast Asia: past and present*, Macmillan: London. Skilful but at times frustratingly thin history of the region from the first century to the withdrawal of US forces from Vietnam.

Savage, Victor R (1984) *Western impressions of nature and landscape in Southeast Asia*, Singapore University Press: Singapore. Based on a geography PhD thesis, the book is a mine of quotations and observations from Western travellers.

Steinberg, DJ *et al* (1987) *In search of Southeast Asia: a modern history*, University of Hawaii Press: Honolulu. The best standard history of the region; it skilfully examines and assesses general processes of change and their impacts from the arrival of the Europeans in the region.

Tarling, Nicholars (1992) (ed) *Cambridge History of Southeast Asia*, Cambridge: Cambridge University Press. Two-volume edited study, long and expensive with contributions from most of the leading historians of the region. A thematic and regional approach is taken, not a country one, although the history is fairly conventional.

Waterson, Roxana (1990) *The living house: an anthropology of architecture in Southeast Asia*, OUP: Singapore. An academic but extensively-illustrated book on Southeast Asian architecture and how it links with lives and livelihoods. Fascinating material for those interested in such things.

Essentials

Books on Thailand

Novels   Garland, Alex *The Beach*. Available just about everywhere in Thailand but while it is an easy and enjoyable read, it hardly deserves all the media hype and attention that it has received. It is most interesting to read while travelling through the beach resorts of the country where the observations on Thailand, hedonism and the power of the guidebook (but not this one!) are instructive.

Collis, Maurice (1982) *Siamese White*, DD Books: Bangkok. A story based on King Narai's court in 17th-century Ayutthaya.

Diehl, William (1989) *Thai horse*, Ballantine Books: New York. A novel about the Thai drug trade and the underworld in Thailand and the US.

Grey, Anthony (1990) *The Bangkok secret*, Pan: London. Novel of intrigue based around the murder/assassination of King Ananda; banned in Thailand.

Moore, Christopher G (1991) *Spirit house*, White Lotus: Bangkok. Novel based on life in the red-light districts of Bangkok.

History   Boulle, Pierre (1990) *The bridge over the River Kwai*, Bantam Books: New York. The story of the infamous bridge in western Thailand.

Manich Jumsai (1972) *Popular history of Thailand*, Chalermit: Bangkok. A rather second-rate history of Thailand; all fact and dates and names and no story line or analysis. Widely available in Thailand though and relatively cheap.

Terwiel, BJ (1983) *A history of modern Thailand, 1767-1942*, University of Queensland Press: St Lucia, Queensland. Reasonably solid history but not very easily found.

Wright, Joseph (1991) *The balancing act: a history of modern Thailand*, Pacific Rim Press: Oakland. Most detailed modern history (to 1991) but not as scholarly as Wyatt's volume.

Wyatt, David K (1982) *Thailand: a short history*, Yale University Press: New Haven. Simply, the best history of Thailand from the beginning of recorded Thai history to the 1980s.

Biography &   Kruger, Rayne (1964) *The devil's discus*, Cassell: London. Best investigation into the
autobiography   death of King Ananda; banned in Thailand and rather difficult to get hold of. Worth tracking down in your local library as it is a good read.

Leonowens, Anna [1870] (1988) *The English governess at the Siamese court*, Oxford University Press: Singapore. The book on which the play and film *The King and I* was based starring Yul Brynner. A travesty of history and offensive to many Thais in the manner in which it depicts one of Thailand's greatest monarchs, but entertaining nonetheless and now reprinted.

Warren, William (1970) *The legendary American: the remarkable career and strange disappearance of Jim Thompson*, Houghton Mifflin: Boston. The story of the strange life and even stranger disappearance of the so-styled 'saviour' of Thailand's silk industry.

Travel &   Bock, Carl (1884) *Temples and elephants*, White Lotus: Bangkok. An entertaining and
geography   informative account of an early European visitor's time in Siam. Reprinted by White Lotus in Bangkok in 1985 and easily available.

Bowring, Sir John (1857) *The kingdom and people of Siam*, OUP: Kuala Lumpur. An account of Bowring's visit which led to the signing of the important Bowring Treaty in 1855. A remarkable book when one considers how short a time he was in Siam. Reprinted by OUP in 1969.

Maugham, Somerset (1930) *The gentlemen in the parlour: a record of a journey from Rangoon to Haiphong*, Heinemann: London. An account of Maugham's journey through Southeast Asia, including Thailand, in classic limpid prose.

McCarthy, James (1994) *Surveying and exploring in Siam with descriptions of Las dependencies and of battles against the Chinese Haws*, White Lotus: Bangkok. Reprint of an account first published in 1900 telling of the travels of Englishman James McCarthy who was employed by the government of Siam as a surveyor and adviser; an interesting book to read when travelling, particularly, in the North and Northeast.

Shearer, Alistair (1989) *Thailand: the lotus kingdom*, John Murray: London. Good background to culture and history of Thailand, rather derivative but entertaining.

West, Richard (1991) *Thailand: the last domino*, Michael Joseph: London. An 'alternative' travel book which provides considerable historical and cultural background; entertaining and interesting, occasionally inaccurate.

Economics, politics & development

Ekachai, Sanitsuda (1990) *Behind the smile: voices of Thailand*, Thai Development Support Committee: Bangkok. Vignettes of Thai life and the strains of development by a *Bangkok Post* journalist; interesting and informative.

Keyes, Charles, F (1987) *Thailand: Buddhist kingdom as modern nation-state*, Westview Press: Boulder, Colorado. Good, clearly written background to Thailand, especially good on politics and society, widely available in cheaper DK (Duang Kamol) edition in Thailand.

Pasuk Phongpaichit and Baker, Chris (1998) *Thailand's boom ... and bust!*, Silkworm Books: Chiang Mai. A collaborative book by a well-known Thai economist and her partner, a British historian turned advertising executive. They have written a book that tries to bridge the gap between popular and academic and have been generally pretty successful although it is rather breathless in tone. This new edition analyses Thailand's economic collapse (the first edition, published in 1996, had the title *Thailand's boom!*.

Rigg, Jonathan (1995) (ed) *Counting the costs: economic growth and environmental change in Thailand*, ISEAS: Singapore. The title says it all: an edited collection of papers examining the conflicts between economic growth and the conservation of the environment.

Tapp, Nicholas (1989) *Sovereignty and rebellion: the White Hmong of Northern Thailand*, OUP: Singapore. Scholarly study of the tensions under which the Hmong are forced to live their lives.

Art & archaeology

Fickle, Dorothy (1989) *Images of the Buddha in Thailand*, OUP: Singapore. Small, portable book with background to the main periods in Thailand's plastic arts and outline of the major styles and images.

Labbe, AJ (1985) *Ban Chiang, art and prehistory of Northeast Thailand*, Bowers Museum: Santa Ana, California. Only for the truly interested – illustrated account of the discovery and significance of this important archaeological site in Northeast Thailand.

Moore, Elizabeth, Stott, Phili and Suriyavudh Sukhasvasti with photographs by Michael Freeman (1996) *Ancient capitals of Thailand*, Thames & Hudson, London (also published by River Books in Thailand). A heavyweight coffee-table book with marvellous photographs of Sukhothai, Si Satchanalai, Kamphaeng Phet, Phitsanulok and Ayutthaya and an informative text written by two art historians and a historical geographer. Expensive.

Ringis, Rita (1990) *Thai temples and temple murals*, OUP: Singapore. Good background to Thailand's *wats* and their murals; illustrated and quite widely available in Thailand.

Smitthi Siribhadra and Moore, Elizabeth (1991) *Palaces of the gods: Khmer art and architecture in Thailand*, River Books: Bangkok. Expensive but nicely illustrated coffee table book covering the Khmer monuments of Thailand, text by an art historian at London's School of Oriental and African Studies.

Stratton, Carol and Scott, Miriam M. (1981) *The art of Sukhothai: Thailand's golden age*, OUP: Kuala Lumpur.

Van Beek, S and Tettoni, LI (1991) *The arts of Thailand*, Thames & Hudson: London (revised). Glossy coffee table book with good photographs and informative text.

Essentials

Maps of Thailand and Southeast Asia

A decent map is an indispensable aid to travelling. Although maps are usually available locally, it is sometimes useful to buy a map prior to departure to plan routes and itineraries. Below is a select list of maps. Scale is provided in brackets.

Regional maps Bartholomew Southeast Asia (1:5,800,000); ITM (International Travel Maps) Southeast Asia (1:6,000,000); Nelles Southeast Asia (1:4,000,000); Hildebrand Thailand, Burma, Malaysia and Singapore (1:2,800,000).

Country maps Bartholomew Thailand (1:1,500,000); ITM (International Travel Maps) Thailand (1:1,000,000); Nelles Thailand (1:1,500,000).

City maps Nelles Bangkok.

Other maps Tactical Pilotage Charts (TPC, US Airforce) (1:500,000); Operational Navigational Charts (ONC, US Airforce) (1:500,000). Both of these are particularly good at showing relief features (useful for planning treks); less good on roads, towns and facilities.

Locally available maps are widely available in Thailand and many are given out free, although the quality of information is sometimes poor.

Map shops in London, the best selection is available from Stanfords, 12-14 Long Acre WC2E 9LP, T020-78361321; also recommended is McCarta, 15 Highbury Place, London N15 1QP, T020-73541616.

Films on and about Thailand

The Beach Filmed in Thailand and released in 2000, this celluloid version of Alex Garland's book of the same title created a mini-environmental crisis (see the box on page 306). Leonardo DiCaprio does a reasonable job but this is not a film that will be particularly remembered.

Anna and the King Yes, another version of the King and I (with Yul Brunner), released in 2000. This time a Hong Kong Chinese actor Chow Yun-Fat plays King Mongkut while Anna is portrayed as a feisty proto-feminist by Jodie Foster. Of course the historians have lambasted the film as a travesty – Anna would never have been allowed to do these things or get so close to the King – and the Thai authorities banned it (as they do with anything of this sort). The result? Pirated videos and endless letters to the Thai newspapers.

Brokedown Palace The least publicised of the three films about Thailand that have recently been released – this one opened in 1999 – and the least good of a mediocre offering. This one recounts the tale of two high school graduates who go to Thailand, get seduced into carrying drugs, are arrested and thrown in prison only to be pardoned when they get to see the King. Sure! Also banned in Thailand.

The Bridge Over the River Kwai The best of the bunch, which only goes to show that good old (1957) acting always beats slick technology. Alec Guinness stars in this Academy Award-winning account of the horror of the prison camp in Kanchanaburi province where prisoners of war (and many Chinese – who don't really feature) were used by the Japanese to build the Burma-Siam Railway and the bridge that gives the film its name.

In addition to these films there are many, many with a Vietnam War focus which were filmed in Thailand, and may have scenes in Thailand, but aren't really about Thailand. These include: **The Killing Field** (about Cambodia under Pol Pot); **The Deer Hunter** (the dark side of the conflict); and **Good Morning Vietnam** (Robin Williams in good form as a disk jockey). And lastly there's the Bond movie **The Man With the Golden Gun** which uses Bangkok and Phangnga Bay as a backdrop.

The internet

www.tourismthailand.org/tat. The Tourist Authority of Thailand's website; a useful **General** first stop and generally well regarded. www.pata.org The Pacific Asia Travel **tourism-** Association, better known simply as PATA, with a useful news section arranged by **related sites** country, links to airlines and cruise lines, and some information on educational, environmental and other initiatives. www.tourthai.com A private website with a fair amount of material on transport, national parks, hotels, restaurants and the like (much sourced from the TAT). There is also a photo library of 2,000 images. www.sabuy.com Named after two Thai cartoon characters. The Thai version is better than the English, but the latter is being improved. www.Siamguide.com Will have travel information in both Thai and English for destinations across the Kingdom but is currently under construction. www.yahoo.com/Regional Countries/[name of country] Insert name of country to access practical information including material from other travel guides.

www.lib.utexas.edu/Libs/PCL/Map_collection/asia/htm Up-to-date maps of **Maps** Asia showing relief, political boundaries and major towns. http://plasma.nationalgeographic.com/mapmachine National Geographic's cartographic division, which takes maps from their current Atlas of the World. www.expediamaps.com US biased but still pretty comprehensive. Key in a town and wait for it to magically appear.

http://metnet.tmd.go.th Thailand's meteorological department with weather **Weather &** forecasts for numerous towns. **geographical information**

www.rainorshine.com A simple but effective weather site with five-day forecasts for 800 cities worldwide.

www.travel.state.gov/travel_warnings.html The US State Department's **Travel** continually updated travel advisories on its Travel Warnings & Consular **advisories** Information Sheets page.

www.fco.gov.uk/travel The UK Foreign and Commonwealth Office's travel warning section.

www.cdc.gov/travel Managed by the Center for Disease Control and Prevention **Travel & health** (CDC) in Atlanta, this is one of the best health sites, providing detailed and authoritative information including special sections on such diseases, ailments and concerns as malaria, dengue fever, HIV/AIDS, rabies and Japanese encephalitis.

www.tripprep.com Shoreland's Travel Health Online provides health advice by country.

www.siam-travel.com The number of hotels listed on the Siam Hotel Network site is **Hotel sites** limited – online reservations possible.

www.citynet.com/asia/asia Hotel booking information for Asia.

www3.sympatico.ca/donna.mcsherry/asia.htm Stuck overnight at Don Muang airport? Then check out the Budget Traveller's Guide to Sleeping in Airports.

www.netcafeguide.com/ Around 2,000 cyber cafés in 113 countries are listed here **Cyber cafés** and it also provides discussion forums for travellers and a language section.

Transport sites	www.thaiindex.com Mainly business and cultural, but also includes bus, train and air timetables along with some other useful travel information (sometimes out of date). www.thaiair.com Thai Airways site.
	http://bkkair.com Bangkok Airways website.
Newspapers, news & the media	www.nationgroup.com/ Homepage for *The Nation,* one of Thailand's main English-language daily newspapers. www.bangkokpost.net/ Homepage for the *Bangkok Post* including back issues and main stories of the day.
	www.isop.ucla.edu/eas/web/asia-web.htm For information on Asian radio and television broadcasts. Access includes free downloadable software.
Currencies	www.oanda.com/converter/classic Select your two currencies by clicking on a list, and wham – the exchange rate is provided.
Business-related websites	www.stern.nyu.edu/globalmacro Homepage of a professor of economics – Roubini – who has collated all the information on the Asian financial and economic crisis, and there's a lot.
General sites	www.nectec.or.th/ Homepage for Thailand in Bangkok, good links to other websites in the country.
	http://pears.lib.ohio-state.edu/AsianStudies/AsianStudies.html Huge range of links with information on topics from sports and travel to economics and engineering.
	http://coombs.anu.edu.au/WWWVL-AsianStudies.html Assortment of material from across Asian region.
	http://coombs.anu.edu.au/asia-www-monitor.html Produced by ANU's Research School of Pacific and Asian Studies, this site provides evaluations and summaries of Asian sites.
	http://www.nbr.org Centre for papers on Asia covering strategic, economic and political issues.
	www.library.wisc.edu/guides/SEAsia 'Gateway to Southeast Asia' from University of Wisconsin, numerous links.
History & culture	www.chula.ac.th Managed by Thailand's premier university, Chulalongkorn, and intended to introduce people to Thailand's history, culture, society, politics and economics.
	www.thaifolk.com Good site for Thai culture from folk songs and handicrafts through to festivals like Loi Kratong and Thai myths and legends. Information posted in both English and Thai – although the Thai version of the site is better.
	http://www.cs.ait.ac.th/~wutt/wutt.html More historical and cultural information at this site operated from the Asian Institute of Technology based just north of Bangkok.
	http://www2.hawaii.edu/~tsomo Resources on women and Buddhism.
	http://www.asiasociety.org Homepage of the Asia Society with papers, reports and speeches as well as nearly 1,000 links to what they consider to be the best educational, political and cultural sites on the web.

http://www.hmongnet.org Information on Hmong culture, history and language.

www.nautilus.org Homepage of the Nautilus Institute which focuses on issues **Environment**
connected with the environment and sustainability in the Asia-Pacific region.

http://www.geocities.com/~nesst/ The homepage of the Network for
Environmentally & Socially Sustainable Tourism (Thailand), with information on
tourism in Thailand, book reviews and a discussion page.

http://www.leidenuniv.nl/pun/ubhtm/mjk/intro.htm Library of 100 slides of Thailand **Picture libraries**
(Phimai, Chiang Mai, Lamphun) and other mainland Southeast Asian countries. **& books**

http://thailine.com/lotus Homepage of White Lotus, a Bangkok-based publishing house
specializing in English-language books (many reprints of old books) on the region.

Bangkok

3

Bangkok

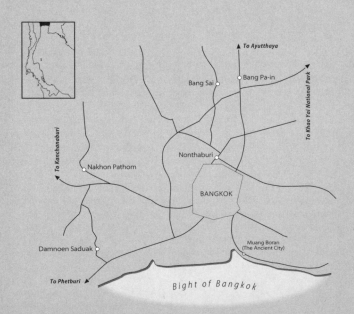

Bangkok is not a city to be trifled with: a population approaching 11 million struggle to make their living in a conurbation with perhaps the worst traffic in the world; a level of pollution which causes some children, so it is (rather improbably) said, to lose four intelligence points by the time they are seven; and a climate which can take one's breath away. (The Guinness Book of Records credits Bangkok as the world's hottest city because of the limited seasonal and day-night temperature variations.) As journalist Hugo Gurdon wrote at the end of 1992: "One would have to describe Bangkok as unliveable were it not for the fact that more and more people live here". But, Bangkok is not just a perfect case study for academics looking into the strains of rapid urban growth. There is charm and fun beneath the grime, and Bangkokians live life with a joie de vivre which belies the congestion. There are also numerous sights, including the spectacular Grand Palace, glittering wats (monasteries) and the breezy river, along with excellent food and shopping.

Background

The official name for Thailand's capital city begins Krungthep – phramaha – nakhonbawon – rathanakosin – mahinthara – yutthayaa – mahadilok – phiphobnobpharaat – raatchathaanii – buriiromudomsantisuk. It is not hard to see why Thais prefer the shortened version – Krungthep, or the 'City of Angels'. The name used by the rest of the world – Bangkok – is derived from 17th-century western maps, which referred to the city (or town as it then was) as Bancok, the 'village of the wild plum'. This name was only superseded by Krungthep in 1782, and so the western name has deeper historical roots.

Bangkok & vicinity

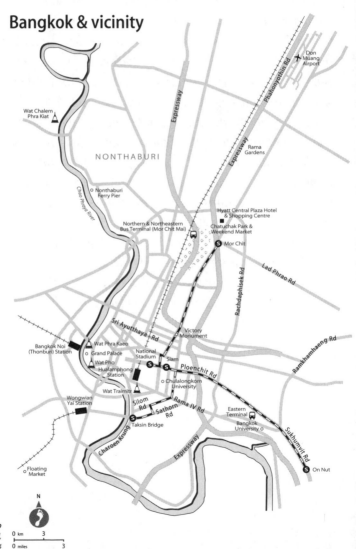

*Related map
Bangkok General,
page 74*

••
Bangkok: primate city of Thailand

	% of national total
Land area	0.3%
Population (end 1998)	9.2%
Gross regional product (1996)	39.1%
Commercial bank deposits (end 1998)	65.3%
Commercial bank loans (end 1998)	76.5%
Passenger car registrations (end 1997)	63.8%
Telephones (end 1998)	50.1%
Physicians (end 1995)	39.4%
Hospital beds (end 1995)	21.1%

••

In 1767, Ayutthaya, then the capital of Siam, fell to the marauding Burmese for the second time and it was imperative that the remnants of the court and army find a more defensible site for a new capital. Taksin, the Lord of Tak, chose Thonburi, on the western banks of the Chao Phraya River, far from the Burmese and from Phitsanulok, where a rival to the throne had become ensconced. In three years, Taksin had established a kingdom and crowned himself king. His reign was short lived, however; the pressure of thwarting the Burmese over three arduous years caused him to go mad and in 1782 he was forced to abdicate. General Phraya Chakri was recalled from Cambodia and invited to accept the throne. This marked the beginning of the present Chakri Dynasty.

In 1782, Chakri (now known as Rama I) moved his capital across the river to Bangkok (an even more defensible site) anticipating trouble from King Bodawpaya who had seized the throne of Burma. The river that flows between Thonburi and Bangkok and on which many of the luxury hotels – such as *The Oriental* – are now located, began life not as a river at all, but as a canal (or *khlong*). The canal was dug in the 16th century to reduce the distance between Ayutthaya and the sea by shortcutting a number of bends in the river. Since then, the canal has become the main channel of the Chao Phraya River. Its original course has shrunk in size, and is now represented by two khlongs, Bangkok Yai and Bangkok Noi.

Bangkok: the new capital

This new capital of Siam grew in size and influence. Symbolically, many of the new buildings were constructed using bricks from the palaces and temples of the ruined former capital of Ayutthaya. But population growth was hardly spectacular – it appears that outbreaks of cholera sometimes reduced the population by a fifth or more in a matter of a few weeks. An almanac from 1820 records that "on the seventh month of the waxing moon, a little past 2100 in the evening, a shining light was seen in the northwest and multitudes of people purged, vomited and died".

In 1900 Bangkok had a population of approximately 200,000. By 1950 it had surpassed one million, and by the end of 1998 it was, officially, 5,647,799 (don't you just love the spurious accuracy?). But the official figure considerably understates the true population of the city – 10-11 million would be more realistic. Many people who live in the capital continue to be registered as living up-country, and the physical extent of the capital has long overrun its administrative boundaries. By 2010, analysts believe Bangkok will have a population of 20 million. As the population of the city has expanded, so has the area that it encompasses: in 1900 it covered a mere 13.3 sq km; in 1958, 96.4 sq km; while today the Bangkok Metropolitan region extends over 1,600 sq km and the outskirts of the city sprawl into neighbouring provinces. Such is the physical size of the capital that analysts talk of Bangkok as an EMR or Extended Metropolitan Region.

Population

Bangkok

Bangkok general

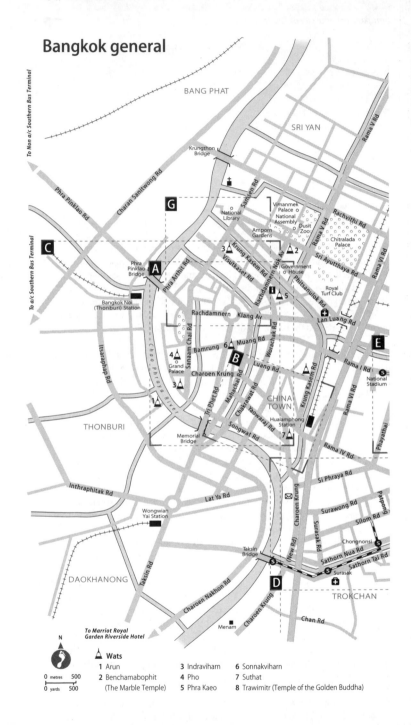

BANG PHAT

SRI YAN

To Non a/c Southern Bus Terminal

To a/c Southern Bus Terminal

Phra Pinklao Rd

Charan Sanitwong Rd

Krungthon Bridge

Samsen Rd

National Library

Vimanmek Palace
National Assembly

Dusit Zoo

Rachvithi Rd

Rama V Rd

Amporn Gardens

Chitralada Palace

Rama V Rd

Phra Pinklao Bridge

Phra Arthit Rd

Visuthkaset Rd

Krung Kasem Rd

Rachdamnern Nok Av

Government House

Sri Ayutthaya Rd

Rama VI Rd

Bangkok Noi (Thonburi) Station

Rachdamnern

Klang Av

Phitsanulok Rd

Royal Turf Club

Lan Luang Rd

Sanaam Chai Rd

Bamrung

Muang Rd

Worachak Rd

Rama I Rd

National Stadium

Phayathai

Grand Palace

Charoen Krung

Luang Rd

Krung Kasem Rd

Chao Phraya River

Tri Phet Rd

Maharathai Rd

Chakrawat Rd

Kaowraj Rd

CHINA TOWN

Rama VI Rd

THONBURI

Itsaraphap Rd

Hualamphong Station

Rama IV Rd

Memorial Bridge

Songwat Rd

Si Phraya Rd

Inthraphitak Rd

Lat Ya Rd

Charoen Krung

Surawong Rd

Silom Rd

Pattong

Wongwian Yai Station

Surasak Rd

(New Rd)

Chongnonsi

Taksin Rd

Taksin Bridge

Sathorn Nua Rd

Sathorn Tai Rd

Surasak

DAOKHANONG

Charoen Nakhon Rd

Charoen Krung

TROKCHAN

To Marriot Royal Garden Riverside Hotel

Menam

Chan Rd

N

0 metres 500
0 yards 500

Wats

1 Arun
2 Benchamabophit
   (The Marble Temple)

3 Indraviharn
4 Pho
5 Phra Kaeo

6 Sonnakviharn
7 Suthat
8 Trawimitr (Temple of the Golden Buddha)

Bangkok

To Northern & Northeastern
Bus Terminal (Mor Chit Mai)

Chatuchak
Weekend
Market

To Airport

Saphankhwai

Rama VI Rd

Second Stage Expressway

Phahonyothin Rd

SAPHANKHWAI

Aree

Sanampao

Expressway

HUAY
KHWANG

Expressway

Victory
Monument

Rachprarop Rd

DIN DAENG

Phayathai Rd

Siam City

Florida

Suan Pakkard Palace

Phya Thai

Ratchathewi

Pratunam Market

Phetburi Rd

Expressway

Siam

Ploenchit Rd

Chidlom

Ploenchit

New Phetburi Rd

Soi Nana Nua

Siam Society &
Kamthieng House

Chulalongkorn
University

Rachdamri Rd

Rachdamri

Nana

Soi Asoke

ASOKE

Rd

Henri Dunant Rd

Vietnam
Embassy

Asoke

Phrom Phong

Sukhumvit Rd

Rama IV Rd

Witthayu (Wireless) Rd

Lumpini
Park

F

Rachdaphisek Rd

Soi 26

Thonglor

Sala Daeng

Soi Sribamphen

Immigration
Department

Rama IV Rd

Soi Ngam Duphli

Nang Linchi Rd

THUNG
MAHAMEK

Eastern Terminal

Ekkamai

Related maps
A Bangkok – Old City,
page 82
B Chinatown,
page 94
C Bangkok's River &
Khlongs, page 97
D Silom & Surawong,
page 117
E Siam Square &
Ploenchit Road,
page 120
F Sukhimvit Road,
page 122

**Bangkok &
Thailand**

In terms of size, Bangkok is at least 23 times larger than the country's second city, Chiang Mai (40 times bigger, using the unofficial population estimates). It also dominates Thailand in cultural, political and economic terms. All Thai civil servants have the ambition of serving in Bangkok, while many regard a posting to the poor Northeast as (almost) the kiss of death. Most of the country's industry is located in and around the city, and Bangkok supports a far wider array of services than other towns in the country (see box). It is because of Bangkok's dominance that people often, and inaccurately, say 'Bangkok is Thailand'.

**Venice of
the East**

Bangkok began life as a city of floating houses; in 1864 the French explorer Henri Mouhot wrote that "Bangkok is the Venice of the East (in the process making Bangkok one of several Asian cities to be landed with this sobriquet) and whether bent on business or pleasure you must go by water". In 1861, foreign consuls in Bangkok petitioned Rama IV and complained of ill-health due to their inability to go out riding in carriages or on horseback. The king complied with their request for roads and the first road was constructed running south in the 1860s – Charoen Krung ('New Road'). This did not initially alter Bangkok's watery character, for bridges to span the many canals were in limited supply. In addition, Charoen Krung was frequently under water during the monsoons. It was not until the late 19th century that King Chulalongkorn (Rama V) began to invest large sums of money in bridge and road building; notably, Rachdamnern Avenue ('the royal way for walking') and the Makawan Rungsun Bridge, which both link the Grand Palace with the new palace area of Dusit. This avenue was used at the end of the century for cycling (a royal craze at the time) and later for automobile processions which were announced in the newspapers.

In the rush to modernize, Bangkok may have buried its roots and in so doing, lost its charm. But beneath the patina of modern city life, Bangkok remains very much a Thai city, and has preserved a surprising amount of its past. Most obviously, a profusion of monasteries (*wats*) and palaces remain. In addition, not all the *khlongs* have been filled in, and by taking a long-tailed boat through Thonburi (see page 98) it is possible to gain an idea of what life must have been like in the 'Venice of the East'.

Flooding

Bangkok is built on unstable land, much of it below sea-level, and floods used regularly to afflict the capital. The most serious were in 1983 when 450 sq km of the city was submerged. Each year the Bangkok Metropolitan Authority announced a new flood prevention plan, and each year the city flooded. The former populist Bangkok Governor, Chamlong Srimuang, was perhaps the first politician to address the problem of flooding seriously. His blindingly obvious approach was to clear the many culverts of refuse, and some people believe that at last serious flooding is a thing of the past. This may be over-optimistic: like Venice, Bangkok is sinking by over 10 cm a year in some areas and it may be that the authorities are only delaying the inevitable.

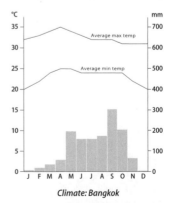

Climate: Bangkok

Bangkok

Bangkok's architectural nightmare

It doesn't, as they say, take a rocket scientist to realize that Bangkok is short of modern buildings with architectural merit. Indeed, there is a rather cruel joke doing the rounds: what is the difference between Bangkok and a toilet? At least you can flush a toilet. The reasons are manifold for this dearth of decent modern buildings. Of prime importance is the sheer speed of change in the capital. In the early 1970s there were less than 25 buildings over 6 storeys high; today there are well over 1,000. Most of the country's architects are young and inexperienced – and yet they are expected to be able to design high-rise buildings as they step out of college grasping their certificates. There are none of the critical apprenticeship years when architects hone their skills and eye on mundane garage blocks and single-storey old people's homes.

But it is not just that there is a dearth of experienced architects. Sumet Jumsai is possibly Thailand's most respected architect and he has little but derision for Bangkok's modern architecture. "Here – he suggested in a magazine article by John Hoskin – is money in its ugliest aspect, dictating building styles ... [producing] distorted Western neo-classical buildings and bad taste to satisfy the nouveau-riche's make-believe world".

Bangkok-based architect Robert Boughey also puts the blame on clients who want the largest building at the lowest cost – and young architects without the status or the desire to refuse, comply. As he put it, "Clients deserve the buildings they get". Sometimes, it can all go tragically wrong – as when the Royal Plaza Hotel in Korat collapsed killing 137. Some more cynical observers say that Bangkok's architectural poverty has a long-standing history. In his book Bali and Angkor published in 1936, Geoffrey Gorer wrote that Bangkok was "the most hokum place" he had ever seen, "a triumph of the imitation school". The tendency for buildings to combine Greek Classical with US Ranch style, Spanish Villa with Tudor Beamed seems to indicate that things really haven't progressed very far since the 1930s.

This is not to say that all Bangkok's contemporary architecture is so crass. There are the clean lines and elegance of the Regent Hotel on Rachdamri Road; and the appropriately stratospheric feel of the blue-glass walled HQ of Thai Airways on Phahonyothin Road on the way to the airport. There are also the older buildings which may have fulfilled Gorer's 'hokum' characterization in the 1930s, but which today seem positively refined.

First impressions

The immediate impression of the city to a first-time visitor is bedlam. The heat, noise, traffic, pollution – the general chaos – can be overwhelming. This was obviously the impression of Somerset Maugham, following his visit in 1930:

"I do not know why the insipid Eastern food sickened me. The heat of Bangkok was overwhelming. The wats oppressed me by their garish magnificence, making my head ache, and their fantastic ornaments filled me with malaise. All I saw looked too bright, the crowds in the street tired me, and the incessant din jangled my nerves. I felt very unwell."

Traffic & congestion – the perennial problem

Bangkok has become synonymous with traffic congestion. For many years it has been regarded as having some of the worst – perhaps *the* worst – traffic conditions of any capital city in the world. During peak periods the traffic congestion is such that 'gridlock' seems inevitable. The figures are sometimes hard to believe: US$500mn of petrol is consumed each year while cars wait at traffic lights; average traffic speeds can be less than 10 km per hour; one day in July 1992 it took 11 hours for some motorists to get home after a monsoon storm; in 1996, the Thai Farmers Bank's research centre estimated

● ●

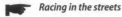

Racing in the streets

In Bangkok, bored young men gain short-lived fame and money by racing through the darkened streets of the capital on motorcycles late at night on weekends. Gang members put their reputations (and their lives) on the line, as they power down the wide and almost empty roads at over 160 km per hour. Large sums of money are gambled on the riders while 'rescue squads' wait to pick up the corpses that each night's racing produces. In Thai this dance with death is known as sing – from the English 'racing'. As journalist Gordon Fairclough explains: "Riders see themselves as members of an exclusive brotherhood, bound together by their willingness to risk death and dismemberment in the pursuit of thrills, notoriety and money". Although money is important, few of the riders are poor. Some even come from wealthy families. Critics of Thailand's climb into NIC-dom claim that the racing is a side-effect of the breakdown of traditional family life in the face of modernization. The racers themselves tend not to engage in amateur sociology. They explain "It's fun. It's a high. We like the speed, and its better than taking drugs".

● ●

that Bangkok's congestion costs the economy US$2.3bn in lost productivity, wasted energy, and health care costs; and the number of cars on the capital's streets was increasing by 800 each day prior to the economic crisis (the figure for the country is 1,300). In 1995 the singer Janet Jackson purposely avoided scheduling her concerts on Friday explaining, "with the traffic, who could make it on Friday?" It seemed that nothing could stop Bangkok simply grinding to a halt (see the box, The mother of all traffic jams). As one analyst observed: "Bangkok is only just beginning to happen". Even editorial writers at the *Bangkok Post* who, one might have imagined, would have become inured to the traffic found it a constant topic for comment throughout the 1980s and 1990s. At the end of 1993 the newspaper stated: "Bangkok's traffic congestion and pollution are just about the worst in the world – ever. Never in history have people had to live in the conditions we endure each day".

Ironically perhaps, the economic crisis that hit Thailand at the beginning of July 1997 gave the authorities a breathing space to try and sort out Bangkok's road nightmare. The bottom fell out of the new car market and many people took to alternative forms of transport to save money. This gave the capital's governor time to push through the necessary infrastructural projects designed, on the one hand, to improve the road system while also enticing people out of their cars and into a new and improved public transport network. At the beginning of 2000 Bangkok's first mass transit system opened – the BTS or Bangkok Transit System, popularly known as the Skytrain. This has made a real difference to travel in the areas that the network covers. The only trouble is that it is limited in coverage. In short, Bangkok has not become, overnight, another Singapore.

Solutions to Bangkok's traffic problem have been suggested, devised, contracts drawn up, shelved, cancelled and then revived since the early 1980s. The process of finding a solution became almost as slow as the traffic itself. In addition to the failure to approach transport planning in a co-ordinated way, Bangkok has a number of characteristics which make its problems particularly intractable. To begin with, Thailand was a city of canals; these have now been built over, but it means that the capital has a lower area of roads relative to its land area than any other capital – some 9% (some commentators put it as low as 5%) to New York's 24% and London's 22%. In addition, Bangkok is really Thailand's only city, making economic

The mother of all traffic jams

Bangkok's reputation for traffic congestion was already well-founded when, as the Bangkok Post put it, the Songkran exodus of 11-12 April 1995 created the 'mother of all traffic jams'. On Tuesday night, the capital saw the traditional mass movement of people to the provinces to celebrate Songkran. By late Wednesday afternoon, traffic on major routes was still heavily congested. One man telephoned a radio station to say that he had left his home in Bangkok at 2100 on Tuesday night and at 1100 on Wednesday had only made it to the Rangsit junction – barely out of the capital. One highway policeman remarked, perhaps with a touch of pride: "This is the first time in the 20-year history of the Vibhavadi Rangsit Highway that we have had traffic congestion for as long as 20 hours."

activity highly over-centralized. But there is more to it than just a series of historical accidents. Administration of roads is divided between numerous different agencies making co-ordination impossible. "It's like driving a bus with 16 hands on the wheel" one official was quoted as saying. The corruption that has accompanied many of the more grandiose projects, and the competition between various schemes – aerial railways, undergrounds, toll ways, computerized traffic control systems, freeways – has meant that none got off the ground until recently. Even when one project was finished – the 20 km-long, US$800 mn Bangkok Expressway which was completed in March 1993 – it didn't open to traffic until September that year. The government, under pressure from the public, tried to get the consortium to lower the agreed toll of ฿30. They refused, saying it would make the venture commercially unviable, so the city authorities gained a court order and opened the road themselves whereupon it promptly became snarled with traffic. Such actions on the part of the government threaten to scare away potential investors who require cast-iron agreements if they are to undertake such BOT (Build, Operate, Transfer) projects.

For wealthier commuters, the solution to the traffic problem is to transform their cars into mobile offices, to leave home at ungodly hours and, in some cases, to move elsewhere – like Chiang Mai (which, partly as a result, is experiencing its own traffic problems). Taxi drivers have taken to 'chicken footing' – skipping through hotel car parks to short-cut intersections. Government attempts to get people to leave their cars in the suburbs and bus in have failed because Bangkokians have an attachment to their cars which seems almost as devout as a Californian's. There was even talk of outfitting special buses with flashing lights declaring 'These passengers are car owners', so they could feel good about themselves!

A few years back, the motorcycle taxi hit the streets of Bangkok – a much faster alternative to sitting in a taxi in stationary traffic. Not that everyone is willing to endure weaving in and out of the traffic and sucking in great lung-fulls of the capital's noxious fumes just to get to their destination a little bit quicker. In June 2000 David Wilson, an executive with British-American Tobacco who was in Bangkok for the launch of the World Health Organisation's World No Smoking Day, likened smoking to taking a ride on one of these machines. "Every day people do things they choose to do that aren't terribly wise on reflection" he said, "like driving a motorbike taxi in Bangkok".

Bangkok

Pollution With the traffic comes pollution. Traffic police stationed at busy intersections have 'respite booths' with oxygen tanks, wear face masks to protect them from the fumes, and are entitled to regular health checks. Even so, directing traffic can, apparently, drive you mad. At the end of 1993, Lance Corporal Suradej Chumnet blew a fuse and switched all the traffic lights to green at one of Bangkok's busiest intersections. He then danced a jig amidst the chaos. Afterwards he claimed that he had seen King Rama V coming down the road towards him. A recent study found that 34% of police officers suffered from loss of hearing, and 23% had lung disease. Sitting in an open-sided tuk-tuk at traffic lights can seriously damage your health – or it seems as much with the fumes swirling around. It is for this reason that the tuk-tuk as a mode of transport in the capital is rapidly losing out to the air-conditioned taxi. Even so, one million of the capital's population are said to be suffering from respiratory ailments of one kind or another. It seems that even Silom Road's barn swallows, that have traditionally wintered on the road's telephone and electricity wires, have decided enough is enough. In 1984 there were an estimated 250,000 birds. In 1996-97 just 10-20,000 were prepared to carry on coughing their way through the winter months.

Bangkok has no sewerage system and most water gets pumped straight into the *khlongs* (canals) and waterways where it poses a health hazard before emptying into the Chao Phraya River which, in its lower stretches, is said to be biologically dead. The reputation of Bangkok's traffic keeps potential investors away, not to mention many tourists. And there are also around 1½ million people in the city living in squatter or slum conditions – a number which is growing due to the effects of the economic crisis. NGOs have identified a worrying increase in drug dealing and prostitution as people struggle to make a living – or struggle to forget their predicament – and there also seems to be a breakdown in some of the community social structures that formerly helped to maintain a semblance of stability.

But, despite the traffic conditions and pollution, Bangkok has a wealth of sights (even the traffic might be classified as a 'sight'): wats and palaces, markets and shopping, traditional dancing and Thai boxing, glorious food, tuk-tuks and water taxis. Ultimately, Bangkok and Bangkokians should win the affections of even the most demanding foreigner – although you may not be there long enough to get past the frustration phase. In Major Erik Seidenfaden's *Guide to Bangkok* published in 1928, the opening few sentences could be describing the city today:

"No other city in Southeastern Asia compares with Bangkok in the gripping and growing interest which leaves a permanent and fragrant impression on the mind of the visitor. It is difficult to set down in words, precisely whence comes the elusive fascination of Bangkok. With a wealth of imposing temples, beautiful palaces, other characteristic buildings and monuments, Bangkok offers a vista of fascinating views. In no other city is it possible to so often turn from the throng of the city street and find oneself, miraculously it would seem, in a little residential quarter. Even the most bitter misanthrope cannot but feel that in the very atmosphere of Bangkok, woven into all the stir and briskness of its daily life, is an impelling and pleasurable sense of more than mere contentment – of rare serenity and happiness everywhere."

Bangkok highlights

Temples *Bangkok's best known sight is the temple of Wat Phra Kaeo, situated within the grounds of the Grand Palace (page 84). Other notable temples include Wat Pho (page 83), Wat Arun (page 99), Wat Suthat (page 93) and Wat Traimitr (page 96).*

Museums *Bangkok's extensive National Museum houses the best collection in the country (page 90); other significant collections include those in Jim Thompson's House (page 104), the Suan Pakkard Palace (page 104) and Vimanmek Palace (page 102).*

Markets *The sprawling Chatuchak Weekend Market is the largest (page 107), but other markets include Nakhon Kasem or Thieves' Market (page 95), Pahurat Indian Market (page 94) and Chinatown's Sampeng Lane (page 95).*

Boat trips *On Bangkok's canals (page 96).*

Excursions *Day trips to the former capital and ruins of Ayutthaya (page 111), the Bridge over the River Kwai outside Kanchanaburi (page 113), the massive chedi at Nakhon Pathom (page 112), and the floating market at Damnoen Saduak (page 110).*

Bangkok

Sights

This section is divided into five main areas: the **Old City**, around the Grand Palace; the **Golden Mount**, to the east of the Old City; **Chinatown**, which lies to the south of the Golden Mount; the **Dusit** area, which is to the north and contains the present-day parliament buildings and the King's residence; and **Wat Arun and the khlongs**, which are to the west, on the other bank of the Chao Phraya River in Thonburi. Other miscellaneous sights, not in these areas, are at the end of the section, under **Other sights**.

Phone code: 02
Colour map 1, grid A2

Getting around the sights

Buses, both air conditioned and non-air conditioned, travel to all city sights (see Local transport, page 151). A taxi or tuk-tuk for a centre of town trip should cost ฿50-100. Now that taxis are almost all metered visitors may find it easier, and more comfortable (they have air-conditioning) – not to mention safer – than the venerable tuk-tuk, although a ride on one of these (fast disappearing) three-wheeled machines is a tourist experience in itself. If travelling by bus, a bus map of the city – and there are several, available from most bookshops and hotel gift shops – is an invaluable aid. The express river taxi is a far more pleasant way to get around and is also often quicker than going by road (see map, page 97 for piers, and box page 98).

The **Tourist Authority of Thailand** (TAT) has its main offices at 4 Rachdamnern Nok Avenue (at intersection with Chakrapatdipong Road), T2829775. ■ *Mon-Sun 0830-1630*. A second office is at Le Concord Building, 10th Floor, 202 Rachdaphisek Road (in the office block attached to the *Merchant Court Le Concorde Hotel* – north of town and rather inconvenient for most visitors), T6941222. ■ *Mon-Fri, 0830-1630*. In addition there is a counter at Don Muang airport (in the Arrivals Hall, T5238972) and the Chatuchak Weekend Market (Kamphaeng Phet 2 Road), T2724440. The two main offices are very helpful and provide a great deal of information for independent travellers – certainly worth a visit. A number of good, informative, English-language magazines provide listings of what to do and where to go in Bangkok.

Bangkok Metro, published monthly (฿100, www.bkkmetro.com) is well designed and produced and covers topics from music and nightlife, to sports and fitness, to business and children. A competitor to *Metro* is *Bangkok Timeout* which is much like its London namesake, but a tad less hip (฿80, published monthly, www.bkktimeout.com). Less independent, and with less quality information, is the oddly named *Guide of Bangkok* or GoB. Its advantage is that it is free.

The Old City

The Old City contains the largest concentration of sights in Bangkok, and for visitors with only one day in the capital, this is the area to concentrate on. It is possible to walk around all the sights mentioned below quite easily in a single day. For the energetic, it would also be possible to visit the sights in and around the Golden Mount. If intending to walk around all the sights in the old city start from Wat Pho; if you have less time or less energy, begin with the Grand Palace.

Old City

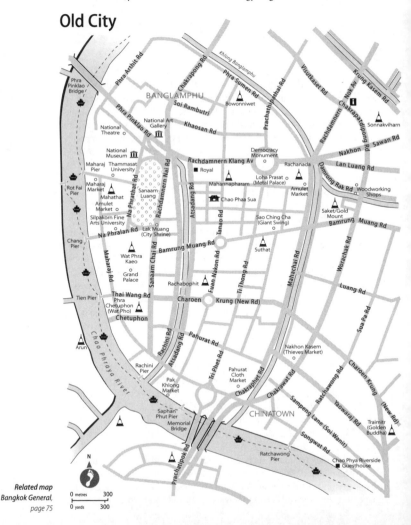

Related map
Bangkok General,
page 75

Bangkok

Wat Phra Chetuphon

The Temple of the Reclining Buddha, or **Wat Pho** as it is known to westerners (a contraction of its original name Wat Potaram), has its entrance on Chetuphon Road on the south side of the monastery complex. It is 200 years old and the largest wat in Bangkok. The wat is most famous for its 46-m long, 15-m high gold-plated reclining Buddha contained in a large viharn built during the reign of Rama III in 1832. The soles of the feet of the Buddha are inlaid with intricate mother-of-pearl decoration displaying the 108 auspicious signs of the Buddha.

The grounds of the wat contain more than 1,000 bronze images, rescued from the ruins of Ayutthaya and Sukhothai by Rama I's brother. The bot, or *ubosoth*, houses a bronze Ayutthayan Buddha in an attitude of meditation and the pedestal of this image contains the ashes of Rama I. Also notable is the 11-piece altar table set in front of the Buddha, and the magnificent mother-of-pearl inlaid doors which are possibly the best examples of this art from the Bangkok Period. They depict episodes from the Ramakien. The bot is enclosed by two galleries which house 394 seated bronze Buddha images. They were brought from the north during Rama I's reign and are of assorted periods and styles. Around the exterior base of the bot are marble reliefs telling the story of the Ramakien as adapted in the Thai poem the *Maxims of King Ruang* (formerly these reliefs were much copied by making rubbings onto rice paper). The 152 panels are the finest of their type in Bangkok. They recount only the second section of the Ramakien: the abduction and recovery of Ram's wife Seeda. The rather – to western eyes – unsatisfactory conclusion to the

Wat Phra Chetuphon (Wat Pho)

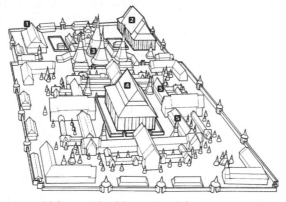

1 Sala kan parian or study hall
2 Viharn of the reclining Buddha
3 Enclosure of the royal chedis

4 Ubosoth (bot) or ordination hall
5 Cloister or phra rabieng

Source: adapted from a drawing by Kittisak Nualvilai based on aerial photographs and reproduced in Beek, Steve van and Tettoni, L. (1991) *The arts of Thailand*, Thames & Hudson: London

story as told here has led some art historians to argue they were originally taken from Ayutthaya. Thai scholars argue otherwise.

A particular feature of the wat are the 95 chedis of various sizes which are scattered across the 20-acre complex. To the left of the bot are four large chedis, memorials to the first four Bangkok kings. The library nearby is richly decorated with broken pieces of porcelain. The large top-hatted stone figures, the stone animals and the Chinese pagodas scattered throughout the compound came to Bangkok as ballast on the royal rice boats returning from China. Rama III, whose rice barges dominated the trade, is said to have had a particular penchant for these figures, as well as for other works of Chinese art. The Chinese merchants who served the King – and who are said to have called him *Chao Sua* or millionaire – loaded the empty barges with the carvings to please their lord. Rama III wanted Wat Pho to become known as a place of learning, a kind of exhibition of all the knowledge of the time and it is regarded as Thailand's first university.

For other centres of traditional Thai massage see page 143

Wat Pho is also probably Bangkok's most respected centre of traditional Thai massage (see page 143), and politicians, businessmen and military officers come here to seek relief from the tensions of modern life. Most medical texts were destroyed when the Burmese sacked the former capital, Ayutthaya, in 1776 and in 1832 Rama III had what was known about Thai massage inscribed on stone and then had these stones set into the walls of Wat Pho to guide and inform students of the art. ■ *Mon-Sun 0900-1700, ฿20. NB From Tha Tien pier at the end of Thai wang Rd, close to Wat Pho, it is possible to get boats to Wat Arun (see page 99). For westerners wishing to learn the art of traditional Thai massage, special 30-hr courses can be taken for ฿4,500, stretching over either 15 days (2 hrs per day) or 10 days (3 hrs per day). The centre is located at the back of the wat, on the opposite side from the entrance. A massage costs ฿100 for ½ hr, ฿180 for 1 hr with herbal treatment, the fee is ฿260 for 1½ hrs.*

Grand Palace &
Wat Phra Kaeo

About 10-15 minutes walk from Wat Pho northwards along Sanaam Chai Road is the entrance to the Grand Palace and Wat Phra Kaeo. (**NB** The main entrance is the Viseschaisri Gate on Na Phralan Road.) The Grand Palace is situated on the banks of the Chao Phraya River and is the most spectacular – some might say 'gaudy' – collection of buildings in Bangkok. The complex covers an area of over 1½ sq km and the architectural plan is almost identical to that of the Royal Palace in the former capital of Ayutthaya. It was started in 1782 and was subsequently added to. Initially the palace was the city, the seat of power, surrounded by high walls and built to be self-sufficient.

The buildings of greatest interest are clustered around **Wat Phra Kaeo**, or the 'Temple of the Emerald Buddha'. On entering the compound, the impression is one of glittering brilliance, as the outside is covered by a mosaic of coloured glass. The buildings were last restored for Bangkok's bicentenary in 1982 (the Wat Phra Kaeo Museum shows the methods used in the restoration process). Wat Phra Kaeo was built by Rama I in imitation of the royal chapel in Ayutthaya and was the first of the buildings within the Grand Palace complex to be constructed. While it was being erected the king lived in a small wooden building in one corner of the palace compound.

The **ubosoth** is raised on a marble platform with a frieze of gilded garudas holding nagas running round the base. Bronze *singhas* (lions) act as door guardians. The inlaid mother-of-pearl door panels date from Rama I's reign (late 18th century). Flanking the door posts are Chinese door guardians riding on lions. Inside the temple, the Emerald Buddha (see box page 86) sits high up, illuminated above a large golden altar. In addition, there are many other gilded Buddha images, mostly in the attitude of dispelling fear, and a series of mural paintings depicting the *jataka* stories. Those facing the Emerald Buddha show the enlightenment of the Buddha when he subdues the evil demon Mara. Mara is underneath, wringing out his hair, while on either side, the Buddha is surrounded by evil spirits. Those on one side have been subjugated; those on the other have not. The water from the wringing out of Mara's hair drowns the evil army, and the Buddha is shown 'touching ground' – calling the earth goddess Thoranee up to witness his enlightenment. (No photography is allowed inside the *ubosoth*.)

Around the walls of the shaded **cloister** that encompasses Wat Phra Kaeo, is a continuous mural depicting the Ramakien – the Thai version of the Indian Ramayana. There are 178 sections in all, which were first painted during the reign of King Rama I but have since been restored on a number of occasions.

To the north of the ubosoth on a raised platform, are the **Royal Pantheon**, the **Phra Mondop** (the library), two gilt stupas, a model of Angkor Wat and the **Golden Stupa**. At the entrance to the Royal Pantheon are gilded *kinarees*. The Royal Pantheon is only open to the public once a year on Chakri Day, 6 April (the anniversary of the founding of the present Royal Dynasty). On the same terrace there are two gilt stupas built by King Rama I in commemoration of his parents. The Mondop was also built by Rama I to house the first revised Buddhist scriptural canon. To the west of the mondop is the large Golden Stupa or chedi, with its circular base, in Ceylonese style. To the north of the mondop is a model of Angkor Wat constructed during the reign of King Mongkut (1851-1868) when Cambodia was under Thai suzerainty.

To the north again from the Royal Pantheon is the **Supplementary Library** and two viharns – **Viharn Yod** and **Phra Nak**. The former is encrusted with pieces of Chinese porcelain.

To the south of Wat Phra Kaeo are the buildings of the **Grand Palace**. These are interesting for the contrast that they make with those of Wat Phra Kaeo.

Wat Phra Kaeo & Grand Palace

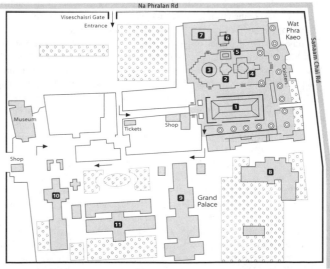

1 Temple of the Emerald Buddha (ubosoth)	4 Royal Pantheon	8 Boromabiman Hall
2 Phra Mondop (library)	5 Model of Angkor Wat	9 Amarinda Hall
3 Golden Stupa	6 Viharn Yod	10 Chakri Mahaprasart
	7 Viharn Phra Nak	11 Dusit Hall

● ●

 The Emerald Buddha

Bangkok

Wat Phra Kaeo was specifically built to house the Emerald Buddha, the most venerated Buddha image in Thailand, carved from green jade (the emerald in the name referring only to its colour), a mere 75 centimetres high, and seated in an attitude of meditation. It is believed to have been found in 1434 in Chiang Rai, and stylistically belongs to the Late Chiang Saen or Chiang Mai schools. Since then, it has been moved on a number of occasions – to Lampang, Chiang Mai and Laos (both Luang Prabang and Vientiane). It stayed in Vientiane for 214 years before being recaptured by the Thai army in 1778 and placed in Wat Phra Kaeo on 22 March, 1784. The image wears seasonal costumes of gold and jewellery; 1 each for the hot, cool and the rainy seasons. The changing ceremony occurs 3 times a year in the presence of the King.

Buddha images are often thought to have personalities. The Phra Kaeo is no exception. It is said, for example, that such is the antipathy between the Phra Bang image in Luang Prabang (Laos) and the Phra Kaeo that they can never reside in the same town.

● ●

Walk out through the cloisters. On your left can be seen **Boromabiman Hall**, which is French in style and was completed during the reign of Rama VI. His three successors lived here at one time or another. The **Amarinda Hall** has an impressive, airy interior, with chunky pillars and gilded thrones. The **Chakri Mahaprasart** (the Palace Reception Hall) stands in front of a carefully manicured garden with topiary. It was built and lived in by Rama V shortly after he had returned from a trip to Java and Singapore in 1876, and it shows: the building is a rather unhappy amalgam of colonial and traditional Thai styles of architecture. Initially the intention was to top the structure with a western dome, but the architects settled for a Thai-style roof. The building was completed in time for Bangkok's first centenary in 1882. King Chulalongkorn (Rama V) found the overcrowded Grand Palace oppressive and after a visit to Europe in 1897, built himself a new home at Vimanmek (see page 102) in the area to the north, known as Dusit. The present King Bhumibol lives in the Chitralada Palace, built by Rama VI, also in the Dusit area. The Grand Palace is now only used for state occasions. Next to the Chakri Mahaprasart is the raised **Dusit Hall**, a cool, airy building containing mother-of-pearl thrones. Near the Dusit Hall is a **museum**, which has information on the restoration of the Grand Palace, models of the Palace and many more Buddha images. There is a collection of old cannon, mainly supplied by London gun foundries. Close by is a small café selling refreshing coconut drinks. All labels in Thai, but there are free guided tours in English throughout the day. ■ *Mon-Sun 0900-1600. ฿50. Admission to the Grand Palace complex ฿200, ticket office open Mon-Sun 0830-1130, 1300-1530 except Buddhist holidays when Wat Phra Kaeo is free but the rest of the palace is closed. For further information T2220094 or www.palaces.thai.net The cost of the admission includes a free guidebook to the palace (with plan) as well as a ticket to the Coin Pavilion, with its collection of medals and 'honours' presented to members of the Royal Family and to the Vimanmek Palace in the Dusit area (see page 102). NB Decorum of dress is required (trousers can be hired for ฿10 near the entrance to the Grand Palace) which means no shorts, and no singlets or sleeveless shirts. It also means, slightly weirdly, no thongs. There are some rather nuanced drawings of accetable footwear at the entrance. If you are considered to have contravened this edict then there are tasteful plastic shoes for hire. For those who fear that they may leave Thailand with some incurable foot disease, socks are also helpfully made available for purchase. There are lots of touts offering to guide tourists around the Palace. It is also possible to hire a personal audio guide for ฿100 (2 hrs), available in English, French, German and some other languages.*

The Thai Ramayana: the Ramakien

The Ramakien – literally "The Story of Rama" – is an adaptation of the Indian Hindu classic, the Ramayana, which was written by the poet Valmiki about 2,000 years ago. This 48,000-line epic odyssey – often likened to the works of Homer – was introduced into mainland Southeast Asia in the early centuries of the first millennium. The heroes were simply transposed into a mythical, ancient, Southeast Asian landscape.

In Thailand, the Ramakien quickly became highly influential, and the name of the former capital of Siam, Ayutthaya, is taken from the legendary hero's city of Ayodhia in the epic. Unfortunately, these early Thai translations of the Ramayana were destroyed following the sacking of Ayutthaya by the Burmese in 1767. The earliest extant version was written by King Taksin in about 1775, although Rama I's rather later rendering is usually regarded as the classic interpretation.

In many respects, King Chakri's version closely follows that of the original Indian story. It tells of the life of Ram (Rama), the King of Ayodhia. In the first part of the story, Ram renounces his throne following a long and convoluted court intrigue, and flees into exile. With his wife Seeda (Sita) and trusted companion Hanuman (the monkey god), they undertake a long and arduous journey. In the second part, his wife Seeda is abducted by the evil king Ravana, forcing Ram to wage battle against the demons

of Langka Island (Sri Lanka). He defeats the demons with the help of Hanuman and his monkey army, and recovers his wife. In the third and final part of the story – and here it diverges sharply from the Indian original – Seeda and Ram are reunited and reconciled with the help of the gods (in the Indian version there is no such reconciliation). Another difference with the Indian version is the significant role played by the Thai Hanuman – here an amorous adventurer who dominates much of the third part of the epic.

There are also numerous sub-plots which are original to the Ramakien, many building upon events in Thai history and local myth and folklore. In tone and issues of morality, the Thai version is less puritanical than the Indian original. There are also, of course, differences in dress, ecology, location and custom.

Immediately opposite the entrance to the Grand Palace is **Silpakorn Fine Arts University**. It contains an exhibition hall. ■ *Mon-Sun 0900-1900 (see boards outside entrance for shows).* Turn left outside the Grand Palace and a five-minute walk leads to **Tha Chang pier and market**. The market sells fruit and food, cold drinks and the like. There is also a small amulet (lucky charm) and second-hand section. From Tha Chang pier it is possible to get a boat to Wat Arun for about ฿150 return, or a water taxi (see page 99). To the north of the Grand Palace, across Na Phralan Road, lies the large open space of the Pramane Ground (the Royal Cremation Ground), better known as **Sanaam Luang**. This area was originally used for the cremation of kings, queens and important princes. Later, foreigners began to use it as a race track and as a golf course. Today, Sanaam Luang is used for the annual **Royal Ploughing Ceremony**, held in May. This ancient Brahmanistic ritual, resurrected by Rama IV, signals the auspicious day on which farmers can begin to prepare their riceland, the

Other sights near the Grand Palace
Kite fighting can be seen at Sanaam Luang in the late afternoons between late-Feb & mid-Apr (the Kite Festival season). On Sun, salesmen & women sell kites for 15-20 baht

Bankok

● ●

☞ *Kite fighting*

Kite fighting is a sport which is taken very seriously – perhaps because they were used as weapons of war during the Sukhothai Period, as well as being used to ward off evil spirits during Brahmanic rites. King Rama V was an avid kite-flyer and allowed Sanaam Luang to be used for the sport from 1899. There are usually two teams, each with a different kind of kite: the 'chula' or male kite is the bigger of the two and sometimes requires a number of people to fly it. The

'pukpao' or female kite is smaller and more nimble and opposes the chula. The field is divided into two and the aim of the contest is to land the opposition in your half of the field. Attached to the chula kite are a number of hooks (champa) with which the kite-flyer grapples the pukpao and forces it to land in the opposite side of the field. The pukpao meanwhile has a loop with which the flyer lassoes the chula – which then crashes to the ground.

● ●

time and date of the ceremony being set by Royal Astrologers. Bulls decorated with flowers pull a red and gold plough, while the selection of different lengths of cloth by the Ploughing Lord predicts whether the rains will be good or bad. Sanaam Luang is also used by the Thai public simply to stroll around – a popular pastime, particularly at weekends.

In the southeast corner of Sanaam Luang opposite the Grand Palace is Bangkok's **Lak Muang**, housing the City Pillar and horoscope, originally placed there by Rama I in 1782 even before the Grand Palace was built. This original pillar is the taller of the two. However, the original shrine deteriorated due to lack of maintenance and Rama VI erected a second, squatter pillar, with the horoscope of the city inscribed in gold. The original pillar was removed and left to lie against the shrine walls until 1986, when it was reinstated. Rama IV needed to erect a new pillar, with a new horoscope, to legitimate his kingship and to protect the city from new threats – namely, the European colonial powers rather than the traditional Burmese. It is protected by an elaborate pavilion with intricate gold-inlay doors, and is set below ground level. According to Pornpun Kerdphol there is no evidence of this tradition of erecting city pillars prior to 1782. The shrine is believed to grant people's wishes, so it is a hive of activity all day. In a small pavilion to the left of the main entrance, Thai dancers are hired by supplicants to dance for the pleasure of the resident spirits – while providing a free spectacle for everyone else. ■ *Open 24 hrs Mon-Sun.* **NB** *There is no entrance charge to the Lak Muang compound; touts sometimes insist there is. Donations can be placed in the boxes within the shrine precincts.* At the northeast corner of Sanaam Luang, opposite the *Royal Hotel*, is a small statue of the **Goddess of the Earth** erected by King Chulalongkorn to provide drinking water for the public.

Wat Mahathat   North along Na Phrathat Road, on the river side of Sanaam Luang is **Wat Mahathat** (the Temple of the Great Relic), a temple famous as a meditation centre, which is tucked behind a façade of buildings and hard to find; walk under the archway marked 'Naradhip Centre for Research in Social Sciences' to reach the wat. For those interested in learning more about Buddhist meditation, contact monks in section five within the compound. The wat is a royal temple of the first grade and a number of Supreme Patriarchs of Bangkok have based themselves here.

The revision of the Tripitaka (the Buddhist Canon) took place at the temple in 1788, and an examination system was established for monks and novices after a meeting at the wat in 1803. In 1801 the viharn was burnt down during an over-enthusiastic fireworks display. In 1824 the future Rama IV began his 24

Magic designs and tokens: tattoos and amulets

Many, if not most, Thai men wear amulets or khruang. Some Thai women do so too. In the past tattooing was equally common, although today it is usually only in the countryside that males are extensively tattooed – sometimes from the ankle to the neck. In the case of both tattoos and amulets the purpose is to bestow power, good luck or protection on the wearer. (Members of secret societies and criminal gangs also use tattoos to indicate their allegiances.)

Amulets have histories: those believed to have great powers sell for tens of thousands, even millions, of baht and there are several magazines devoted to amulet buying and collecting (available from most magazine stalls). Vendors keep amulets with their takings to protect against robbery, and insert them into food at the beginning of the day to ensure good sales. An amulet is only to be handled by the wearer – otherwise its power is dissipated, and might even be used against the owner.

Amulets can be obtained from spirit doctors and monks and come in a variety of forms. Most common are amulets of a religious nature, known as Phra khruang. These are normally images of the Buddha or of a particularly revered monk. (The most valuable are those fashioned by the 19th-century monk Phra Somdet – which are worth far more than their weight in gold). Khruang rang are usually made from tiger's teeth, buffalo horn or elephant tusk and protect the wearer in very specific ways – for example from drowning. Khruang rang plu sek, meanwhile, are magic formulas which are written down on an amulet, usually in old Khmer script (khom), and then recited during an accident, attack or confrontation.

Tattooing is primarily talismanic: magic designs, images of powerful wild beasts, texts reproduced in ancient Khmer and religious motifs are believed to offer protection from harm and give strength.

(The word tattoo is derived from the Tahitian word tattau, meaning 'to mark'. It was introduced into the English language by Captain James Cook in 1769.) Tattoos are even believed to deflect bullets, should they be sufficiently potent. One popular design is the takraw ball, a woven rattan ball used in the sport of the same name. The ball is renowned for its strength and durability, and the tattoo is believed to have the same effect on the tattooed. The purpose of some tattoos is reflected in the use of 'invisible' ink made from sesame oil – the talismatic effects are independent of whether the tattoo can be seen. Most inks are commercial today (usually dark blue) although traditionally they were made from secret recipes incorporating such ingredients as the fat from the chin of a corpse (preferably 7 corpses, taken during a full moon).

The tattooist is not just an artist and technician. He, like the tattoos he creates, is a man of power. A master tattooist is highly respected and often given the title ajarn (teacher) or mor phi (spirit doctor). Monks can also become well-known for their tattoos. These are usually religious in tone, often incorporating sentences from religious texts. The tattoos are always beneficial or protective and always on the upper part of the body (the lower parts of the body are too lowly for a monk to tattoo).

Tattoos and amulets are not only used for protection, but also for attraction: men can have tattoos or amulets instilled with the power to attract women; women, alternatively, can buy amulets which protect them from the advances of men. Khruang phlad khik (or 'deputy penis') are phallic amulets carved from ivory, coral or rare woods, and worn around the wrist or the waist – not around the neck. Not surprisingly, they are believed to ensure sexual prowess, as well as protection from such things as snake bites.

Bangkok

years as a monk here, and it was again reconstructed between 1844 and 1851. Both viharn and bot, crammed in side-by-side, are undistinguished. Note that there are only four *bai sema* (boundary stones), and they are affixed to the walls of the building – presumably because there is so little room. The main Buddha images in the viharn and ordination hall are of brick and mortar. In the mondop are 28 bronze Buddha images, with another 108 in the gallery around the ordination hall. Most date from the Sukhothai Period. ■ *Mon-Sun 0900-1700*. At No 24 Maharaj Road a narrow soi (lane) leads down towards the river and a large amulet market.

Attached to the wat is a fascinating daily market selling exotic herbal cures, amulets, clothes and food. It is worth a wander as few tourists venture into either the market or the wat. At weekends, the market spills out onto the surrounding streets (particularly Phra Chan Road) and amulet sellers line the pavement, their magical and holy talismen carefully displayed.

Thammasat & the National Museum

Further north along Na Phrathat Road, is **Thammasat University**, the site of viciously suppressed student demonstrations in 1973. Sanaam Luang and Thammasat University remain a popular focus of discontent. Most recently, at the beginning of May 1992, mass demonstrations occurred here to demand the resignation of Prime Minister General Suchinda. The rally was led by former Bangkok Governor Chamlong Srimuang.

Next to Thammasat lies the National Museum, reputedly the largest museum in Southeast Asia. It is an excellent place to view the full range of Thai art before visiting the ancient Thai capitals, Ayutthaya and Sukhothai.

Gallery No 1, the gallery of Thai history, is interesting and informative, as well as being air-conditioned, so it is a good place to cool off. The gallery clearly shows kings Mongkut and Chulalongkorn's fascination with western technology. The other 22 galleries and 19 rooms contain a vast assortment of arts and artefacts divided according to period and style. If you are interested in Thai art, the museum alone might take a day to browse around. A shortcoming for those with no background knowledge is the lack of information in some of the galleries and it is recommended that interested visitors buy the *Guide to the National Museum, Bangkok* or join one of the tours. ■ *฿40, together with a skimpy leaflet outlining the galleries. Wed-Sun 0900-1600, tickets on sale until 1530. For English, French, German, Spanish and Portuguese-speaking tour information call T2241333. The tours are free and start at 0930, lasting 2 hrs (usually on Wed and Thu).*

The Buddhaisawan Chapel, to the right of the ticket office for the National Museum, contains some of the finest Bangkok period murals in Thailand. The chapel was built in 1795 to house the famous Phra Sihing Buddha. Folklore has it that this image originated in Ceylon and when the boat carrying it to Thailand sank, it floated off on a plank to be washed ashore in Southern Thailand, near the town of Nakhon Si Thammarat. This, believe it or not, is probably untrue: the image is early Sukhothai in style (1250), admittedly showing Ceylonese influences, and almost certainly Northern Thai in origin. There are two other images that claim to be the magical Phra Buddha Sihing, one in Nakhon Si Thammarat (see page 378) and another in Chiang Mai (Northern Thailand). The chapel's magnificent murals were painted between 1795 and 1797 and depict stories from the Buddha's life. They are classical in style, without any sense of perspective (as was usual), and the narrative of the Buddha's life begins to the right of the rear door behind the principal image, and progresses clockwise through 28 panels. ■ *German-speaking tours of the chapel are held at 0930 on the 3rd Tue of the month.*

Next to the National Museum is Thailand's **National Theatre**, a newish, large, Thai-style building on the corner of Na Phrathat and Phra Pinklao Bridge roads. Thai classical drama and music are staged here on the last Friday of each month at 1730 as well as periodically on other days. ■ *Current programmes can be checked by calling T2241342, 0830-1630 Mon-Fri.* Opposite the National Theatre is the **National Art Gallery** on Chao Fa Road. It exhibits traditional and contemporary work by Thai artists. ■ *Tue-Thu, Sat and Sun 0900-1600. ฿30.*

The Golden Mount, Giant Swing and surrounding wats

The Democracy Monument is a 10-15 minute walk from the north side of Sanaam Luang, in the middle of Rachdamnern Klang Avenue. This rather stolid structure was completed in 1940 to commemorate the establishment of Siam as a constitutional monarchy. Its dimensions signify, in various ways, the date of the 'revolution' – 24 June 1932. For example, the 75 buried cannon which surround the structure denote the Buddhist year (BE – or Buddhist Era) 2475 (1932 AD). In May 1992, the monument was the focus of the anti-Suchinda demonstrations, so brutally suppressed by the army. Scores of Thais died here, many others fleeing into the nearby *Royal Hotel.*

Democracy Monument

From the Democracy Monument, across Mahachai Road, at the point where Rachdamnern Klang Avenue crosses Khlong Banglamphu can be seen the Golden Mount (also known as the Royal Mount), an impressive artificial hill nearly 80 m high. The climb to the top is exhausting but worth it for the fabulous views of Bangkok. On the way up, the path passes holy trees, memorial plaques and Chinese shrines. The construction of the mount was begun during the reign of Rama III who intended to build the greatest chedi in his kingdom. The structure collapsed before completion, and Rama IV decided merely to pile up the rubble in a heap and place a far smaller golden *chedi* on its summit. The *chedi* contains a relic of the Buddha placed there by the present king after the structure had been most recently repaired in 1966. ■ *Mon-Sun 0800-1800. ฿5.*

Golden Mount

Wat Saket lies at the bottom of the mount, between it and Damrong Rak Road – the mount actually lies within the wat's compound. Saket means 'washing of hair' and Rama I is reputed to have stopped here and ceremoniously washed himself before being crowned King in Thonburi (see **Festivals**, November). The only building of real note is the library (*hor trai*) which is Ayutthayan in style. The door panels and lower windows are decorated with wood-carvings depicting everyday Ayutthayan life, while the window panels show Persian and French soldiers from Louis XIV's reign. ■ *Mon-Sun, 0800-1800 .*

Wat Saket

Also in the shadow of the Golden Mount but to the west and on the corner of Rachdamnern Klang Avenue and Mahachai Road lies Wat Rachanada and the Loha Prasat. Until 1989 these buildings were obscured by the Chalerm Thai movie theatre, a landmark which Bangkok's taxi and tuk-tuk drivers still refer to. In the place of the theatre there is now a neat garden, with an elaborate gilded sala, which is used to receive visiting dignitaries. Behind the garden the strange-looking Loha Prasat or Metal Palace, with its 37 spires, is easily recognizable. This palace was built by Rama III in 1846 as a memorial to his beloved niece Princess Soammanas Vadhanavadi, and is said to be modelled on the first Loha Prasat built in India 2,500 years ago. A second was constructed in Ceylon in 160 BC, although Bangkok's Loha Prasat is the only one still standing. The 37 spires represent the 37 Dharma of the Bodhipakya. In 1996 a major

Loha Prasat

Bangkok

Golden Mount place names

Amulet market	Wat Rachanada
ตลาดพระเครื่อง	วัดราชนัดดา
Golden Mount	Wat Saket
ภูเขาทอง	วัดสระเกศ
Wat Rachabophit	Wat Suthat
วัดราชบพิธ	วัดสุทัศน์เทพวราราม

renovation and expansion project was initiated on this wedding cake of a building. Rama III's original plans were never fully realised and so the Loha Prasat Restoration Committee has taken on the task. The pink cement is being peeled off and the chedis coated with bronze. The upper *chedi* was completed by 2000 but work on the smaller *chedis* will continue for another few years yet. The monks who look after the building have had problems with homeless men and woman who use the Prasat's many nooks and crannies as handy places to sleep: they are turfed out (in a suitable meritorious manner) by the monks before the place opens each morning. ■ *Daily 0830-1600.*

Wat Rachanada Next to the Loha Prasat is the much more traditional Wat Rachanada. Wat Rachanada was built by Rama III for his niece who later became Rama IV's queen. The principal Buddha image is made of copper mined in Nakhon Ratchasima province to the northeast of Bangkok, and the ordination hall also has some fine doors. ■ *Mon-Sun 0600-1800.* What makes the wat particularly worth visiting is the **Amulet Market** (see page 89) to be found close by, between the Golden Mount and the wat. The sign, in English, below the covered part of the market reads 'Buddha and Antiques Centre'. The market also contains Buddha images and other religious artefacts and is open every day.

The Giant Swing A five minute walk south of Wat Rachanada, on Bamrung Muang Road, is the
& Wat Suthat Sao Ching Cha or Giant Swing, consisting of two tall red pillars linked by an elaborate cross piece, set in the centre of a square. The Giant Swing was the original

Wat Suthat

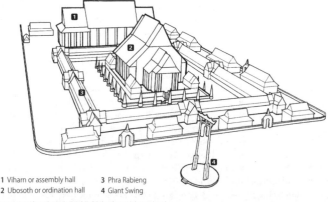

1 Viharn or assembly hall   3 Phra Rabieng
2 Ubosoth or ordination hall   4 Giant Swing

centre for a Brahmanic festival in honour of Siva. Young men, on a giant 'raft', would be swung high into the air to grab pouches of coins, hung from bamboo poles, between their teeth. Because the swinging was from east to west, it has been said that it symbolized the rising and setting of the sun. The festival was banned in the 1930s because of the injuries that occurred; prior to its banning, thousands would congregate around the Giant Swing for two days of dancing and music. The magnificent Wat Suthat faces the Giant Swing. The wat was begun by Rama I in 1807, and his intention was to build a temple that would equal the most glorious in Ayutthaya. The wat was not finished until the end of the reign of Rama III in 1851.

Engraving of the Sao Ching Cha from Henri Mouhot's Travels in the central parts of Indo-China *(1864)*

The viharn is in early-Bangkok style and is surrounded by Chinese pagodas. Its six pairs of doors, each made from a single piece of teak, are deeply carved with animals and celestial beings from the Himavanta forest. The central doors are said to have been carved by Rama II himself, and are considered some of the most important works of art of the period. Inside the viharn is the bronze Phra Sri Sakyamuni Buddha in an attitude of subduing Mara. This image was previously contained in Wat Mahathat in Sukhothai, established in 1362. Behind the Buddha is a very fine gilded stone carving from the Dvaravati Period (2nd-11th centuries AD), 2½ m in height and showing the miracle at Sravasti and the Buddha preaching in the Tavatimsa heaven.

The bot is the tallest in Bangkok and one of the largest in Thailand. The murals in the bot, painted during the reign of Rama III are traditional Thai in style, and largely unaffected by western artistic influences. They use flat colours and lack perspective. The *bot* also contains a particularly large cast Buddha image. ■ *0900-1700; viharn only opens on weekends and Buddhist holidays.*

Wat Rachabophit

The little visited Wat Rachabophit is close to the Ministry of the Interior on Rachabophit Road, a few minutes walk south of Wat Suthat down Ti Thong Road. It is recognizable by its distinctive doors carved in high relief with jaunty-looking soldiers wearing European-style uniforms. The temple was started in 1869, took 20 years to complete, and is a rich blend of western and Thai art forms (carried further in Wat Benchamabophit 40 years later, see page 103). Wat Rachabophit is peculiar in that it follows the ancient temple plan of placing the Phra Chedi in the centre of the complex, surrounded by the other buildings. It later became the fashion to place the ordination hall at the centre.

The 43 m-high gilded chedi's most striking feature are the five-coloured Chinese glass tiles which richly encrust the lower section. The ordination hall has 10 door panels and 28 window panels each decorated with gilded black lacquer on the inside and mother-of-pearl inlay on the outside showing the various royal insignia. They are felt to be among the masterpieces of the Rattanakosin Period (1782-present). The principal Buddha image in the ordination hall, in an attitude of meditation, sits on a base of Italian marble and is covered by the umbrella that protected the urn and ashes of Rama V. It also has a surprising interior – an Oriental version of Italian Gothic, more like Versailles than Bangkok. ■ *Mon-Sun 0800-1700.* ฿*10.*

Wat Mahannapharam North of Wat Rachabophit, on Tanao Road is Wat Mahannapharam, in a large, tree-filled compound. A peaceful place to retreat to, it contains some good examples of high-walled, Bangkok-Period architecture decorated with woodcarvings and mother-of-pearl inlay. Just south of here is the bustling **Chao Phaa Sua**, a Chinese temple with a fine tiled roof surmounted with mythological figures.

Markets near Wat Rachabophit From Wat Rachabophit, it is only a short distance to the **Pahurat Indian Market** on Pahurat Road, where Indian, Malaysian and Thai textiles are sold. To get there, walk south on Ti Thong Road which quickly becomes Tri Phet Road. After a few blocks, Pahurat Road crosses Tri Phet Road. **Pak Khlong Market** is to be found a little further south on Tri Phet Road at the foot of the Memorial Bridge. It is a huge wholesale market for fresh produce, and a photographer's paradise. It begins very early in the morning and has ended by 1000. The closest pier to the Pak Khlong Market is Tha Rachini, which is remembered for a particularly nasty episode in Thai history. It is said that in the 1840s a troublemaking up-country *chao* or lord was brought to Bangkok and sentenced to death. His eyes were burnt out with heated irons and then the unfortunate man was suspended above the river at Tha Rachini in a cage. The cage was so positioned that the *chao* could touch the water with his finger tips but could not cup water to drink. He died of thirst and sunstroke after three days and for years afterwards people would not live near the spot where he died.

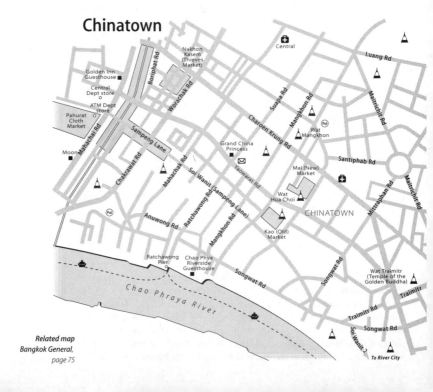

Chinatown

*Related map
Bangkok General,
page 75*

Chinatown and the Golden Buddha

Chinatown covers the area from Charoen Krung (or New Road) down to the river and leads on from Pahurat Road Market; cross over Chakraphet Road and immediately opposite is the entrance to Sampeng Lane. This part of Bangkok has a different atmosphere from elsewhere. Roads become narrower, buildings smaller, and there is a continuous bustle of activity. There remain some attractive, weathered examples of early 20th-century shophouses. The industrious Sino-Thais of the area make everything from offertory candles and gold jewellery to metalwork, gravestones and light machinery.

A trip through Chinatown can either begin with the Thieves' Market to the NW, or at Wat Traimitr, the Golden Buddha, to the SE. An easy stroll between the two should not take more than 2 hrs

Nakhon Kasem (strictly speaking Woeng Nakhon Kasem), or the Thieves' Market, lies between Charoen Krung and Yaowarat Road, to the east of the *khlong* that runs parallel to Mahachai Road. Its boundaries are marked by archways. As its name suggests, this market used to be the centre for the fencing of stolen goods. It is not quite so colourful today, but there remain a number of second-hand and antique shops which are worth a browse – such as the *Good Luck Antique Shop*. Amongst other things, musical instruments, brass ornaments, antique (and not so antique) coffee grinders are all on sale here.

Just to the southeast of the Thieves' Market are two interesting roads that run next to and parallel with one another: Yaowarat Road and Sampeng Lane. Yaowarat Road, a busy thoroughfare, is the centre of the country's gold trade. The trade is run by a cartel of seven shops, the Gold Traders Association, and the price is fixed by the government. Sino-Thais often convert their cash into gold jewellery, usually bracelets and necklaces. The jewellery is bought by its 'baht weight' which fluctuates daily with the price of gold (most shops post the price daily). Should the owner need to convert their necklace or bracelet back into cash it is again weighed to determine its value. During the economic crisis of 1997-98 the Gold Traders Association encouraged people to hand over gold in exchange for bonds to help support the slumping baht. They set a target of collecting 1 kg of gold per shop, or some 10,000 kg in total.

Yaowarat Road

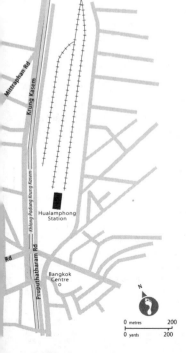

The narrower, almost pedestrian Sampeng Lane, also called **Soi Wanit**, is just to the south of Yaowaraj Road. This road's history is shrouded in murder and intrigue. It used to be populated by prostitutes and opium addicts and was fought over by Chinese gangs. Today, it remains a commercial centre, but rather less illicit. It is still interesting, and shaded with awnings, but there is not much to buy here – it is primarily a wholesale centre specializing in cloth and textiles although it is a good place to go for odd lengths of material, buttons of any shape and size, costume jewellery, and such like. It appears to have changed scarcely at

Sampeng Lane

Bangkok

all since James McCarthy wrote of it in his book *Surveying and exploring in Siam* published in 1900 (and since republished by the Bangkok-based publisher White Lotus): "The Chinaman is a born trader, and the country people prefer dealing with him. The consequence is the narrow streets of Sampeng, seen by few Europeans, are thronged with busy

Chinatown place names

Wat Traimitir

วัดไตรมิตรวิทยาราม

Woeng Nakhon Kasem

เวิ้งนครเกษม

crowds, and the little shop-front awnings, meeting in the middle of the street, make the heat more stifling to the half-naked, happy-go-lucky passers-by".

Wat Traimitr The most celebrated example of the goldsmiths' art in Thailand sits within Wat Traimitr, or the **Temple of the Golden Buddha**, which is located at the eastern edge of Chinatown, squashed between Charoen Krung, Yaowaraj Road and Traimitr Road (just to the south of Bangkok's Hualamphong railway station). The Golden Buddha is housed in a small, rather gaudy and unimpressive room. Although the leaflet offered to visitors says the 3 m-high, 700 year-old image is 'unrivalled in beauty', be prepared to be disappointed. It is in fact rather featureless, showing the Buddha in an attitude of subduing Mara. What makes it special, drawing large numbers of visitors each day, is that it is made of 5½ tonnes of solid gold. Apparently, when the East Asiatic Company was extending the port of Bangkok, they came across a huge stucco Buddha image which they obtained permission to move. However, whilst being moved by crane in 1957, it fell and the stucco cracked to reveal a solid gold image. During the Ayutthayan Period it was the custom to cover valuable Buddha images in plaster to protect them from the Burmese, and this particular example stayed that way for several centuries. In the grounds of the wat there is a school, crematorium, foodstalls and, inappropriately, a money changer. Gold beaters can still be seen at work behind Suksaphan store. ■ *Mon-Sun, 0900-1700. ฿20.*

Between the river and Soi Wanit 2 there is a warren of lanes, too small for traffic – this is the Chinatown of old. From here it is possible to thread your way through to the River City shopping complex which is air-conditioned and a good place to cool off.

Recommended reading Visitors wishing to explore the wonders of Chinatown more thoroughly, should buy Nancy Chandler's *Map of Bangkok*, a lively, detailed (but not altogether accurate) map of all the shops, restaurants and out of the way wats and shrines. ฿70 from most bookstores.

Thonburi, Wat Arun and the Khlongs

Thonburi Thonburi is Bangkok's little-known alter ego. Few people cross the Chao Phraya to see this side of the city, and if they do it is usually only to catch a glimpse from the seat of a speeding *hang yaaw* (long-tailed boat) and then climb the steps of Wat Arun. But Thonburi was, for a few brief years, the capital of Thailand (or Siam, as it was then) under King Taksin. It was only King Rama I's belief that Bangkok would be more easily defended from the Burmese that led him to switch sides in 1782. Perhaps because history gave Thonburi the cold shoulder, it retains a traditional character which, some people would say, has been lost to Bangkok.

One of the most enjoyable ways to see Bangkok is by boat – and particularly by the fast and noisy *hang yaaws*. You will know them when you see them; these powerful, lean machines roar around the river and the *khlongs* (canals) at break-neck speed. There are innumerable tours around the *khlongs* of Thonburi taking in a number of sights which include the floating market, snake farm and Wat Arun. Boats go from the various piers located along the east bank of the Chao Phraya River. The journey begins by travelling downstream along the Chao Phraya, before turning 'inland' after passing beneath Krungthep Bridge. The route skirts past laden rice-barges, squatter communities on public land and houses overhanging the canals. This is a very popular

Long-tailed boats & the Floating Market

Bangkok

Bangkok's river & khlongs

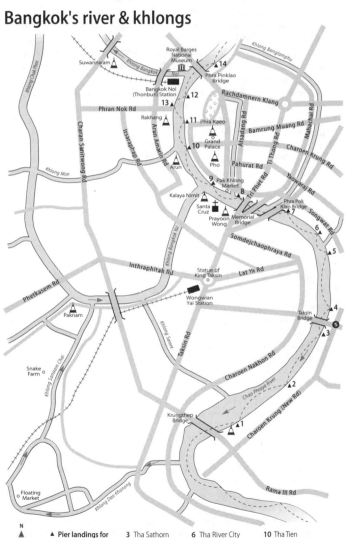

N

0 metres 400
0 yards 400

▲ **Pier landings for Chao Phraya Express River Taxi**
1 Tha Wat Rajsingkorn
2 Tha Vorachanyawat

3 Tha Sathorn
4 Tha Orienten *(Oriental Hotel)*
5 Tha Siphya *(Royal Orchid Hotel)*

6 Tha River City
7 Tha Ratchawong
8 Tha Saphan Phut *(Memorial Bridge)*
9 Tha Rachini

10 Tha Tien
11 Tha Chang
12 Tha Rot Fai
13 Tha Maharaj
14 Tha Saphan Phra Pinklao

Related map Bangkok General, page 74

Bangkok

The Chao Phraya River Express

One of the most relaxing – and one of the cheapest – ways to see Bangkok is by taking the Chao Phraya River Express. These boats (or rua duan) link almost 40 piers (or tha) along the Chao Phraya River from Tha Wat Rajsingkorn in the south to Tha Nonthaburi in the north. The entire route entails a journey of about 1¼-1½ hours, and fares are ฿4, ฿6 or ฿8. Adjacent to many of the piers are excellent riverside restaurants. At peak periods, boats leave every 10 minutes, off-peak about every 15-25 minutes. Note that boats flying red or green pennants do not stop at every pier; they also exact a ฿1 surcharge. Also, boats will only stop if passengers wish to board or alight, so make your destination known. NB The boats don't always stop at all the piers; it depends upon the water level.

Selected piers and places of interest, travelling upstream

Tha Orienten *by the* Oriental Hotel; *access to* Silom Road.

Tha River City *in the shadow of the* Royal Orchid Hotel, *on the south side and close to River City shopping centre.*

Tha Ratchawong Rabieng Ratchawong Restaurant; *access to* Chinatown *and* Sampeng Lane.

Tha Saphan Phut *Under the* Memorial Bridge *and close to* Pahurat Indian Market.

Tha Rachini Pak Khlong Market; *just upstream, the* Catholic seminary *surrounded by high walls.*

Tha Tien *Close to* Wat Pho; Wat Arun *on the opposite bank; and just downstream from* Wat Arun *the* Vichaiprasit Fort *(headquarters of the Thai navy), lurking behind crenellated ramparts.*

Tha Chang *Just downstream is the* Grand Palace *peeking out above white-washed walls;* Wat Rakhang *with its white corn-cob prang lies opposite.*

Tha Maharat Lan The Restaurant; *access to* Wat Mahathat *and* Sanaam Luang.

Tha Phra Arthit Yen Jai Restaurant; *access to* Khaosan Road.

Tha Visutkasat Yok Yor Restaurant; *just upstream the elegant central* Bank of Thailand.

Tha Thewes Son Ngen Restaurant; *just upstream are boatsheds with royal barges; close to the* National Library.

Tha Wat Chan *Just upstream is the* Singha Beer *Samoson brewery.*

Tha Wat Khema Wat Khema *in large, tree-filled compound.*

Tha Wat Khian Wat Kien, *semi-submerged.*

Tha Nonthaburi *Last stop on the express boat route (see map, page 97).*

route with tourists, and boats are intercepted by salesmen and women marketing everything from cold beer to straw hats. You may also get caught in a boat jam; traffic snarl-ups are not confined to the capital's roads. Nevertheless, the trip is a fascinating insight into what Bangkok must have been like when it was still the 'Venice of the East', and around every bend there seems to be yet another wat – some of them very beautiful. On private tours the first stop is usually the **Floating Market** (*Talaat Nam*). This is now an artificial, ersatz gathering which exists purely for the tourist industry. It is worth only a brief visit – unless the so-called 'post-tourist' is looking for just this sort of sight. The nearest functioning floating market is at Damnoen Saduak (see excursions from Bangkok, page 110).

Snake Farm   The Snake Farm is the next stop where man fights snake in an epic battle of wills. Visitors can even pose with a python. The poisonous snakes are incited to burst balloons with their fangs, 'proving' how dangerous they are. There is also a rather motley zoo with a collection of crocodiles and sad-looking animals in small cages. ■ ฿70, *shows every 20 mins. Refreshments available.* (The other snake farm in Central Bangkok (see page 107) is, appropriately, attached

Wat Arun place names

Royal Barges National Museum

พิพิธภัณฑสถานแห่งชาติ
เรือพระราชพิธี

Wat Arun

วัดอรุณราชวราราม

Wat Prayoon Wong

วัดประยูรวงศ์

Wat Rakhang

วัดระฆัง

Wat Suwannaram

วัดสุวรรณาราม

to the Thai Red Cross and is more professional and cheaper.) On leaving the snake farm, boats enter Khlong Bangkok Yai at the site of the large **Wat Paknam**. Just before re-entering the Chao Phraya itself, the route passes by the impressive **Wat Kalaya Nimit**.

To the south of Wat Kalaya Nimit, on the Thonburi side of the river, is **Wat Prayoon Wong**, virtually in the shadow of Saphan Phut (a bridge). The wat is famous for its *Khao Tao* or turtle mountain. This is a concrete fantasyland of grottoes and peaks, with miniature chedis and viharns, all set around a pond teeming with turtles. These are released to gain merit and the animals clearly thrive in the murky water. To coin a phrase, rather grotty, but unusual. Also unusual is the large white chedi with its circular cloister surmounted with smaller chedis, and the viharn with a mondop at each corner, each containing an image of the Buddha. The bot adjacent to the viharn is attractively decayed with gold inlay doors and window shutters, and *bai sema* protected by large mondops. This wat is rarely visited by tourists. ■ *Khao Tao open 0830-1730. Getting there: can be reached by taking a cross-river shuttle boat from Tha Saphan Phut (฿1).* The large white chedi of Wat Prayoon Wong is clearly visible from the Bangkok side of the river. A short walk (five minutes) upstream from here is **Santa Cruz Church**, facing the river. The church, washed in pastel yellow with a domed tower, was built to serve the Portuguese community who lived in this part of Thonburi. ■ *Getting there: cross-river shuttles also stop at Tha Santa Cruz, running between here and Tha Rachini, close to the massive Pak Khlong fresh produce market.*

Wat Arun Facing Wat Pho across the Chao Phraya River is the famous Wat Arun, or the Temple of the Dawn. Wat Arun stands 81 m high, making it the highest prang (tower) in Thailand. It was built in the early 19th century on the site of Wat Chaeng, the Royal Palace complex when Thonburi was briefly the capital of Thailand. The wat housed the Emerald Buddha before the image was transferred to Bangkok and it is said that King Taksin vowed to restore the wat after passing it one dawn. The prang is completely covered with fragments of Chinese porcelain and includes some delicate gold and black lacquered doors. The temple is really meant to be viewed from across the river; its scale and beauty can only be appreciated from a distance. Young, a European visitor to the capital, wrote in 1898: "Thousands upon thousands of pieces of cheap china must have been smashed to bits in order to furnish sufficient material to decorate this curious structure. Though the material is tawdry, the effect is indescribably wonderful".

Until recently, energetic visitors could climb up to the halfway point and view the city, however this is no longer permitted. ■ *Mon-Sun, 0830-1730 ฿20. The men at the pier may demand ฿20 to help 'in the maintenance of the pier'. NB It is possible to get to Wat Arun by water-taxi from Tha Tien Pier (at the end of Thai Wang Road near Wat Pho), or from Tha Chang (at the end of Na Phralan near Wat Phra Kaeo) (฿1). The best view of Wat Arun is in the evening from the Bangkok side of the river when the sun sets behind the prang.*

Royal Barges After visiting Wat Arun, some tours then go further upstream to the mouth of Khlong Bangkok Noi where the Royal Barges are housed in a hangar-like boathouse – the **Royal Barges National Museum**. These ornately carved boats, winched out of the water in cradles, were used by the king at *krathin* (see Ok Phansa festival, page 47) to present robes to the monks in Wat Arun at the end of the rainy season. The ceremony ceased in 1967 but the Royal Thai Navy restored the barges for the revival of the spectacle, as part of the Chakri Dynasty's bicentennial celebrations in 1982. The oldest and most beautiful barge is the Sri Supannahong, built during the reign of Rama I (1782-1809) and repaired during that of Rama VI (1910-1925). It measures 45 m long and 3 m wide, weighs 15 tonnes and was created from a single piece of teak. It required a crew of 50 oarsmen, and two coxwains, along with such assorted crew members as a flagman, a rhythm-keeper and singer. Its gilded prow was carved in the form of a *hamsa* (or goose) and its stern, in the shape of a *naga*. ■ *Mon-Sun 0830-1630 ฿30 (children free), extra for cameras and video cameras (see Festivals, September, page 144).*

Wat Rakhang Two rarely visited wats are Wat Suwannaram and Wat Rakhang. The royal Wat Rakhang is located just upstream from Wat Arun, almost opposite Tha Chang landing, and is identifiable from the river by the two plaster sailors standing to attention on either side of the jetty. The original wat on this site dates from the Ayutthaya Period: it has since been renovated on a number of occasions including during the reign of King Taksin and Rama I. The **Phra Prang** in the grounds of the wat is considered a fine, and particularly well proportioned example of early Bangkok architecture (late 18th century). The **ordination hall** (not always open – the abbot may oblige if he is available) was built during the reign of Rama III and contains a fine gilded Buddha image in an attitude of meditation, over which is the nine-tiered umbrella used to shelter the urn of Rama I during the Royal Cremation. Also here is a fine mural recording the 10 previous lives of the Buddha (note the trip to hell) painted by Phra Wannavadvichitre, an eminent monk-artist of the time. The bot was extensively renovated in 1995. The beautiful red-walled wooden **Tripitaka Hall** (originally a library built in the late 18th century) to the left of the viharn and bot when facing away from the river, was the residence of Rama I while he was a monk (before he became king) and Thonburi

was still the capital of Siam. Consisting of two rooms, it is decorated with faded but nonetheless highly regarded murals of the Ramakien (painted by a monk-artist), black and gold chests, a portrait of the king, and some odd bits of old carved door. It is one of the most charming buildings in Bangkok. The hall is towards the back of the complex, behind the large white *prang* and it is in excellent condition, having been recently restored. ■ *Mon-Sun 0500-2100 ฿2 (the river ferry stops at the wat).*

Wat Suwannaram is a short distance further on from the Royal Barges on Khlong Bangkok Noi, on the other side of the canal. The main buildings – which are particularly well proportioned – date from Rama I's reign (late 18th century), although the complex was later extensively renovated by Rama III. There was a wat on this site even prior to Rama I's reign, and the original name, Wat Thong (Golden Wat) remains in popular use. The *ubosoth* displays some fine wood-carving on the gable ends of the square pillared porches (Vishnu on his vehicle, Garuda), while the interior contains a series of murals, painted by two artists in professional competition with one another and commissioned by Rama III, and regarded by many as among the finest in Bangkok. The murals are in two 'registers'; the murals on the long walls between the windows show the Ten Lives of the Buddha. Entering the building through the right-hand door (with the river behind), on the right-hand wall, is a representation of a boat foundering with the crew being eaten by sharks and sea monsters as they thrash about in the waves. Closer inspection shows that these unfortunates are wearing white skull-caps – presumably they are Muslims returning from the haj to Mecca. The principal image in the bot is made of bronze and shows the Buddha calling the Earth Goddess to witness. Sukhothai in style, it was presumably brought down from the old capital, probably in the first reign, although no records exist of its prior history. Next to the bot is the viharn abutted, unusually, by two cross halls at the front and rear. It was built during the reign of Rama IV. Wat Suwannaram is elegant and rarely visited and is a peaceful place to escape after the bustle of Wat Arun and the Floating Market.

Wat Suwannaram
For plan see page 444

Almost opposite Wat Suwannaram on the opposite bank of the river is the home of an unusual occupational group – Chao Phraya's divers. The men use traditional diving gear – heavy bronze helmets, leaden shoes, air pumps and pipes – and search the bed of the murky river for lost precious objects, sunken boats, and the bodies of those who have drowned or been murdered. How they find anything is one of life's deeper mysteries.

Either book a tour at your hotel (see tours, page 113), or go to one of the piers and organize your own customized trip. The most frequented piers are located between the *Oriental Hotel* and the *Grand Palace* (see map, or ask at your hotel), or under Taksin Bridge (which marks the end of the Skytrain line – at Sapan Taksin). The pier just to the south of the Royal Orchid Sheraton Hotel is recommended. Organizing your own trip gives greater freedom to stop and start when the mood takes you. It is best to go in the morning (0700). For the trip given above (excluding Wat Rakhang and Wat Suwannaram), the cost for a *hang yaaw* which can sit 10 people should be about ฿600 for the boat for a half-day. If visiting Rakhang and Suwannaram as well as the other sights, expect to pay about another ฿200-300 for the hire of a boat. Be sure to settle the route and cost before setting out.

Arranging a boat tour

Bangkok

The Dusit Area

Dusit area place names

Dusit Zoo

สวนสัตว์ดุสิต

Vimanmek Palace

พระที่นั่งวิมานเมฆ

Wat Benchamabophit

วัดเบญจมบพิตร

Vimanmek Palace The Dusit area of Bangkok lies north of the Old City. The area is intersected by wide tree-lined avenues, and has an almost European flavour. The Vimanmek Palace lies off Rachvithi Road, just to the north of the National Assembly. Vimanmek is the largest golden teakwood mansion in the world. It was built by Rama V in 1901 and designed by one of his brothers. The palace makes an interesting contrast to Jim Thompson's House (see page 104) or Suan Pakkard (page 104). While Jim Thompson was enchanted by Thai arts, King Rama V was clearly taken with western arts. It seems like a large Victorian hunting lodge – but raised off the ground – and is filled with china, silver and paintings from all over the world (as well as some gruesome hunting trophies). The photographs are fascinating – one shows the last time elephants were used in warfare in Thailand. Behind the palace is the Audience Hall which houses a fine exhibition of crafts made by the Support Foundation, an organization set up and funded by Queen Sirikit. Support, rather clumsily perhaps, is the acronym for the Foundation for the Promotion of Supplementary Occupations and Related Techniques. Also worth seeing is the exhibition of the king's own photographs, and the clock museum. Dance shows are held twice a day at 1030 and 1400. Visitors are not free to wander, but must be shown around by one of the charming guides who demonstrate the continued deep reverence for King Rama V (tour approximately 1hr). ■ *Mon-Sun 0900-1600 (last tickets sold at 1500) ฿50, ฿20 for children. Note that tickets to the Grand Palace include entrance to Vimanmek Palace. For further information T2811569, www.palaces.thai.net Refreshments available.* **NB** *Visitors to the palace are required to wear long trousers or a skirt; sarongs available for hire (฿100, refundable). Buses do go past the palace, but from the centre of town it is easier to get a tuk-tuk or taxi (฿50-60).*

Amporn Gardens & Dusit Zoo From Vimanmek, it is a 10-15 minute walk to the Dusit Zoo, skirting around the **National Assembly** (which, before the 1932 coup was the Marble Throne Hall and is not open to visitors). The route is tree-lined, so it is possible to keep out of the sun or the rain. In the centre of the square in front of the National Assembly stands an equestrian statue of the venerated King Chulalongkorn. To the left lie the **Amporn Gardens**, the venue for royal social functions and fairs. Southwards from the square runs the impressive **Rachdamnern Nok Avenue**, a Siamese Champs Elysée. Enter the **Dusit Zoo** through Uthong Gate, just before the square. A pleasant walk through the zoo leads to the Chitralada Palace and Wat Benchamabophit. The zoo has a reasonable collection of animals from the region, some of which look rather the worse for wear. There is a children's playground, restaurants and pedal-boats can be hired on the lake. ■ *Mon-Sun 0800-1800. ฿30, ฿10 children.*

From the Dusit Zoo's Suanchit Gate, a right turn down the tree-lined Rama V Road leads to the present King Bhumibol's residence – **Chitralada Palace**. It was built by Rama VI and is not open to the public. Evidence of the King's forays into agricultural research may be visible. He has a great interest and concern for the development of the poorer, agricultural parts of his country, and invests large sums of his own money in royal projects. To the right of the intersection of Rama V and Sri Ayutthaya roads are the gold and ochre roofs of Wat Benchamabophit – about a 10 minute walk from the zoo.

The **Marble Temple**, or Wat Benchamabophit, is the most modern of the royal temples and was only finished in 1911. It is of unusual architectural design (the architect was the king's half brother, Prince Naris), with carrara marble pillars, a marble courtyard and two large *singhas* guarding the entrance to the bot. Rama V was so pleased with the marble-faced ordination hall that he wrote to his brother: 'I never flatter anyone but I cannot help saying that you have captured my heart in accomplishing such beauty as this'. The interior is magnificently decorated with crossbeams of lacquer and gold, and in shallow niches in the walls are paintings of important stupas from all over the kingdom. The door panels are faced with bronze sculptures and the windows are of stained-glass, painted with angels. The cloisters around the assembly hall house 52 figures (both original and imitation) – a display of the evolution of the Buddha image in India, China and Japan. The walking Buddha from the Sukhothai Period is particularly worth a look. The rear courtyard houses a large 80-year-old bodhi tree and a pond filled with turtles, released by people hoping to gain merit. ■ *Mon-Sun 0800-1700. ฿10.*

Wat Benchamabophit
The best time to visit this temple complex is early morning, when monks can be heard chanting inside the chapel

Bangkok

Government House is south of here on Nakhon Pathom Road. The building is a weird mixture of cathedral gothic and colonial Thai. It is only open on Wan Dek – a once yearly holiday for children held on the second Saturday in January. The little visited **Wat Sonnakviharn** is on Krung Kasem Road, located behind a car park and schoolyard. Enter by the doorway in the far right-hand corner of the schoolyard, or down Soi Sommanat. It is peaceful, unkempt, and rather beautiful, with fine gold lacquer doors, and a large gold tile-encrusted chedi. ■ *Mon-Sun.*

Government House

Wat Benchamabophit

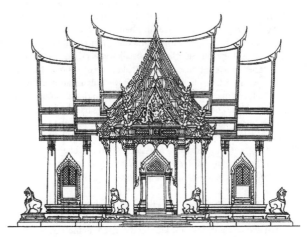

Adapted from Döhring, Kar (1920) *Buddhistische Tempelanlagen in Siam*, Asia Publishing House: Bangkok.

Bangkok

Other sights

Other area place names

Chatuchak Weekend Market

ตลาดนัดสวนจัตุจักร

Jim Thompson's House

บ้านจิม ทอมป์สัน

Siam Square

สยามสแควร์

Suan Pakkard Palace

วังสวนผักกาด

Suan Pakkard Palace
The grounds are very peaceful

In addition to the Vimanmek Palace, Bangkok has a number of other beautiful Thai-style houses that are open to the public. Suan Pakkard Palace or Lettuce Garden Palace is at 352-354 Sri Ayutthaya Road, south of the Victory Monument (see map page 75). The five raised traditional Thai houses (domestic rather than royal) were built by Princess Chumbhot, a great granddaughter of King Rama IV. They contain her fine collection of antiquities, both historic and prehistoric (the latter are particularly rare). Like the artefacts in the National Museum, those in Suan Pakkard are also poorly labelled. The rear pavilion is particularly lovely, decorated in black and gold lacquerwork panels. Prince Chumbhot discovered this temple near Ayutthaya and reassembled and restored it here for his wife's 50th birthday. ■ *Mon-Sun 0900-1600. ฿100 – including a fan to ward off the heat. All receipts go to a fund for artists.*

Jim Thompson's House

Jim Thompson's House is on the quiet Soi Kasemsan Song (2), opposite the National Stadium on Rama I Road. It is an assemblage of traditional teak Northern Thai houses, some more than 200 years old, transported here and re-assembled (these houses were designed to be transportable, consisting of five parts – the floor, posts, roof, walls and decorative elements constructed without the use of nails). Jim Thompson arrived in Bangkok as an intelligence officer attached to the United States' OSS (Office of Strategic Services) and then made his name by reinvigorating the Thai silk industry after the Second World War. He disappeared mysteriously in the Malaysian jungle on 27 March 1967, but his silk industry continues to thrive. (The *Jim Thompson Silk Emporium*, selling fine Thai silk, is at the northeast end of Surawong Road (see map page 117). This shop is a tourist attraction in itself. Shoppers can buy high-quality bolts of silk and silk clothing here – anything from a pocket handkerchief to a silk suit. Prices are top of the scale.) Jim Thompson chose this site for his house partly because a collection of silk weavers lived nearby on Khlong Saensaep. The house contains an eclectic collection of antiques from Thailand and China, with work displayed as though it was still his home. Shoes must be removed before entering; walking barefoot around the house adds to the appreciation of the cool teak floorboards. Bustling Bangkok only intrudes in the form of the stench from the khlong that runs behind the house. Compulsory guided tours around the house and no photography allowed. ■ *฿100, children ฿25 (profits to charity). Mon-Sat 0900-1630. There is a sophisticated little café attached to the museum as well as a shop selling Jim Thompson products. Getting there: bus along Rama I Rd, taxi or tuk-tuk.*

Siam Square

A 10 minute walk east along Rama I Road is the shopping area known as Siam Square (or *Siam Sa-quare*, see map page 120). This has the greatest concentration of fast-food restaurants, boutiques and cinemas in the city. Needless to say, it is patronized by young Thais sporting the latest fashions and doing the sorts of things their parents would never have dreamed of doing – girls smoking and couples holding hands, for instance. For Thais worried about the direction their country is taking, Siam Square encapsulates all their fears in just a few *rai*. This is crude materialism; this is Thais aping the west; this is the erosion of Thai values

Bangkok: animal supermarket of the world

Thailand has few laws restricting the import of endangered species of wildlife – either alive or dead – and the country acts as a collection point for animals from Burma, Cambodia and Laos, as well as further afield. Tiger skins and penises (the latter much prized by the Chinese), ivory, rhino horns and nails, cayman skins (from Latin America), live gibbons and tiger cubs, clouded leopard skins, hawksbill turtle shells, and rare palm cockatoos are all available in Bangkok, a city which has been called the 'wildlife supermarket of the world'. This is nothing particularly new: in 1833, government records show that 50-60 rhinoceros horns were exported, along with 26,000 pairs of deer's antlers and 100,000 deer hides.

But pressure on Thailand's natural environment means that the scale of the threat is different. In 1991 the World Wide Fund for Nature labelled Thailand as "probably the worst country in the world for the illegal trade in endangered species". Before the Olympic Games in Seoul, South Korea, in 1988 it is said that 200 Malayan sun bears were smuggled from Thailand to Korea so that local athletes could consume their energy-enhancing gall bladders and meat. Even Korean tourists are able to dine on bear meat in

restaurants in Bangkok – the animals are lowered alive in cages into vats of boiling water. The rear left paw is considered very lucky and cooked and cut off first. A plate of bear paw soup costs US$1,000. A whole bear, US$14,000.

Critics claim that the Thai government flagrantly violates the rules of the Convention on International Trade in Endangered Species (CITES) – which it has officially acceded to – and ignores blatant trading in both live and dead endangered species. At the end of 1994 a house was raided and discovered to contain piles of animal carcasses, frozen bears' paws, and live bears, monkeys and snakes – all destined for the cooking pot. In recent years there has been increasing pressure from conservationists and from other governments to try and force the Thai authorities to clean up their act. Perhaps as evidence of some success, in 1997 the Chatuchak Weekend Market – where hitherto it was possible openly to see and buy endangered species – fenced off the animal-selling sections in an effort to control the trade in protected fauna. They also erected signs and banners telling people to avoid buying protected animals, and set up a permanent information booth to inform the public.

and culture with scarcely a thought to the future. Because of the tourists and wealthy Thais who congregate around Siam Square it is also a popular patch for beggars. During the 'miracle' years of rapid economic growth the number of beggars actually increased. It may have been that this economic expansion didn't reached the poor in rural areas (Thailand has become a more unequal society over the last decade or so); or it may be that with greater wealth, begging had become a more attractive – in terms of economic return – occupation. A study by the Thai Farmers Bank in the mid-1990s found that beggars could earn more than the minimum wage. They also found that many of the beggars were not even Thai: many were Cambodians.

The land on which this chequerboard of shops at Siam Square are built is owned by Chulalongkorn University – Bangkok's, and Thailand's, most prestigious. While Thammasat University on Sanaam Luang is known for its radical politics, Chulalongkorn is conservative. Just south of Siam Square, on the campus itself (off Soi Chulalongkorn 12, behind the massive Mahboonkrong or MBK shopping centre; ask for *sa-sin*, the houses are nearby) is a collection of beautiful **traditional Thai houses**, erected to help preserve Thai culture. Also on campus is the **Museum of Imaging Technology** with a few hands-on

Chulalongkorn University

Bangkok

The Patpong Story

On 30 September 1996, Udom Patpongsiri died at the age of 79. In 1946 his family bought a small plot of land between Silom and Surawong roads for the princely sum of US$3,000 – presumably with some advice from the young Udom who had returned from an overseas education well informed about all the latest business and management trends. (He attended the London School of Economics and the University of Minnesota). At the time of his death half a century later the land was worth around US$100 mn and his name – or a part of it at least – had acquired an international profile: Patpong.

When they bought the land Patpong had no name; indeed there was not even a road on the plot of land to give a name. Udom's family built a track from Surawong to the canal which is now

Silom Road. Later when the canal was covered over, Udom began using his language skills and knowledge of American and British culture to entice foreigners to base their operations on his family's land. The fact that Udom joined the Free Thai Movement during the war and received training from the Offices of Strategic Services (OSS – the forerunner to the CIA) no doubt also introduced Udom to the predilections of US servicemen. When the war in Indochina saw a massive influx of American servicemen into Thailand, Udom saw a market niche crying out to be filled and with his encouragement and guidance Patpong Road and the parallel Patpong 2 Road quickly made the metamorphosis from quiet business streets to a booming red-light emporium.

photographic displays. Occasional photographic exhibitions are also held here. ■ *Mon-Fri 1000-1530 ฿100. To get to the museum, enter the campus by the main entrance on the east side of Phaya Thai Rd and walk along the south side of the playing field. Turn right after the Chemistry 2 building and then right again at the entrance to the Mathematics Faculty. It is at the end of this walkway in the Dept of Photographic Science and Printing Technology.*

Erawan Shrine East of Siam Square is the Erawan Shrine on the corner of Ploenchit and Rachdamri roads, at the Rachparasong intersection. This is Bangkok's most popular shrine, attracting not just Thais but also large numbers of other Asian visitors. The spirit of the shrine, the Hindu god Thao Maha Brahma, is reputed to grant people's wishes – it certainly has little artistic worth. In thanks, visitors offer garlands, wooden elephants and pay to have dances performed for them accompanied by the resident Thai orchestra. The popular *Thai Rath* newspaper reported in 1991 that some female devotees show their thanks by covorting naked at the shrine in the middle of the night. Others, rather more coy about exposing themselves in this way, have taken to giving the god pornographic videos instead. Although it is unlikely that visitors will be rewarded with the sight of naked bodies, the shrine is a hive of activity at most hours, incongruously set on a noisy, polluted intersection tucked into a corner, and in the shadow of the Sogo Department Store.

Siam Society One other traditional house worth visiting is the home of the Siam Society, off Sukhumvit Road, at 131 Soi Asoke (see map page 122). The Siam Society is a learned society established in 1904 and has benefited from almost continual royal patronage. The **Kamthieng House** is a 120-year-old Northern Thai house from Chiang Mai. It was donated to the society in 1963, transported to Bangkok and then reassembled a few years later. It now serves as an ethnological museum, devoted to preserving the traditional technologies and folk arts of Northern Thailand. It makes an interesting contrast to the fine arts displayed in Suan Pakkard Palace and Jim Thompson's House. The Siam Society houses a library, organizes lectures and tours and publishes books, magazines and pamphlets. ■ *Mon-Sat 0900-1700 ฿100, T6616470 for information on lectures or info@siam-society.org*

Wat Indraviharn is rather isolated from the other sights, lying just off Visutkaset Road. It contains a 32 m-high standing Buddha encrusted in gold tiles that can be seen from the entrance to the wat. The image is impressive only for its size. The topknot contains a relic of the Buddha brought from Ceylon. Few tourists. ■ *Mon-Sun.* **Wat Indraviharn**

For those with a penchant for snakes, the **Snake Farm** of the Thai Red Cross is very central and easy to reach from Silom or Surawong roads (see map page 117). It was established in 1923, and raises snakes for serum production, which is distributed worldwide. The farm also has a collection of non-venomous snakes. During showtime (which lasts half an hour) various snakes are exhibited, and venom extracted. Visitors can fondle a python. The farm is well maintained and professional. ■ *Mon-Fri 0830-1630 (shows at 1100 and 1430), Sat/Sun and holidays 0830-1200 (show at 1100) ฿70 . The farm is within the Science Division of the Thai Red Cross Society at the corner of Rama IV and Henri Dunant roads.*

Bangkok *(side tab)*

Chatuchak Weekend Market

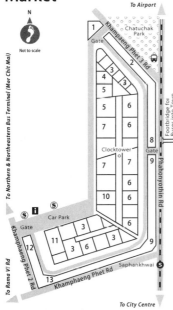

To Airport

N

Not to scale

To Northern & Northeastern Bus Terminal (Mor Chit Mai)

Khamphaeng Phet 3 Rd

Chatuchak Park

Gate

Footbridge for Buses into Town

Clocktower

Gate

Phahonyothin Rd

Car Park

Gate

Khamphaeng Phet 2 Rd

To Rama VI Rd

Khamphaeng Phet Rd

Saphankhwai

To City Centre

1 Decorative rocks & Bonsai	8 Plants & clothing
2 Agricultural products & clothing	9 Plants
3 Miscellaneous	10 Fresh & dried fruits & ceramic wares
4 Pets & handicrafts	11 Antiques
5 Pets	12 Buddha images, plants & books
6 Clothing	13 Paintings & plants
7 Fresh & dried fruits	

Slightly further out of the centre of Bangkok is the Chatuchak Weekend Market which is off Phahonyothin Road, opposite the Northern bus terminal (see map page 75). Until 1982 this market was held at Sanaam Luang, but was moved because it had outgrown its original home and also because the authorities wanted to clean up the area for the Bangkok bicentenary celebrations. It is a huge conglomeration of 8,672 stallholders spread over an area of 12 ha (28 acres), selling virtually everything under the sun, and an estimated 200,000 people visit the market over a weekend. It is probably the best place to buy handicrafts and all things Thai in the whole Kingdom. There are antique stalls, basket stalls, textile sellers, shirt vendors, carvers and painters along with the usual array of fish sellers, vegetable hawkers, butchers and candle-stick makers. In the last couple of years a number of bars and food stalls geared to tourists and Thai yuppies have also opened so it is possible to rest and recharge before foraging once more. In addition to the map here, Nancy Chandler's Map of Bangkok has an inset map of the market to help you get around. ■ *Believe it or not, the market is open on weekends, officially from*

Chatuchak Weekend Market
Definitely worth a visit – allocate ½ a day at least

0900-1800 (although in fact it begins earlier around 0700). It's best to go early in the day. Getting there: a/c buses 2 (from Silom Rd), 3, 10, 13 and 29 go past the market, and non-a/c buses 8, 24, 26, 27, 29, 34, 39, 44, 59, and 96. Or take a taxi or tuk-tuk. In 1994 plans were announced to transform the market by building a three-storey purpose-built structure with car parking and various other amenities. Such has been the outcry that the planners have retired to think again. But the fear is that this gem of shopping chaos will be reorganized, sanitized, bureaucratized and, in the process, ruined. **Beware pickpockets**. There is a tourist information centre at the entrance gate off Kamphaeng Phet 2 Road, and the clock tower serves as a good reference point should visitors become disoriented. Also here, in the north section of Chatuchak Park adjacent to Kamphaeng Phet Road is the **Railway Museum** with a small collection of steam locomotives as well as miniature and model trains. ■ *0500.*

The **Science Museum and Planetarium** is just past Sukhumvit Soi 40, next to the Eastern bus terminal (see map page 122). It contains a planetarium, aeroplanes and other exhibits but don't expect many of them to work. As one recent report put it, there are lots of interactive buttons, but nothing much happens when you press them. ■ *Tue-Sun 0900-1600. Closed public holidays. ฿40 adults, ฿20 children. Getting there: bus (a/c 1, 8, 11, 13, non-a/c 2, 25, 38, 40, 48, 71, 119), taxi or tuk-tuk.* (There is a newer and much better science museum, the National Science Museum, see page 111).

Excursions

Ancient City   The Ancient City or *Muang Boran* (T2241057) lies 25 km southeast of Bangkok in the province of Samut Prakarn and is billed as the world's largest outdoor museum. It houses scaled-down constructions of Thailand's most famous wats and palaces (some of which can no longer be visited in their original locations) along with a handful of originals relocated here. Artisans maintain the buildings while helping to keep alive traditional crafts. The 50-ha site corresponds in shape to the map of Thailand, with the wats and palaces appropriately sited. Allocate a full day for a trip out to the Ancient City. ■ *Mon-Sun 0800-1700. ฿50, ฿25 children. Getting there: there are 3 ways of getting to the Ancient City – either on the a/c city bus 8 or 11, or non-a/c 25 to Samut Prakarn and then a short songthaew ride; or by bus from the Eastern bus terminal to Samut Prakarn; or on one of the innumerable organized tours (see **Tours**, below).*

Crocodile   The Samut Prakarn Crocodile Farm and Zoo claims to be the world's oldest
Farm & Zoo   crocodile farm. Founded in 1950 by a certain Mr Utai Youngprapakorn, it contains over 50,000 crocs of 28 species. Thailand has become, in recent years, one of the world's largest exporters of farmed crocodile skins and meat. Newly rich Asians have a penchant for crocodile skin handbags, briefcases and shoes, and the Chinese are said to have developed a liking for crocodile steaks. Never slow in seeing a new market niche, Thai entrepreneurs have invested in the farming of the beasts – in some cases in association with chicken farms. (The old battery chickens are simply fed to the crocs – no waste, no trouble.) The irony is that the wild crocodile is now, to all intents and purposes, extinct in the country – there are said to be two left alive, and unfortunately living in different areas. The show includes the 'world famous' crocodile wrestling. The farm also has a small zoo, train and playground. ■ *Mon-Sun 0700-1800 (approximately), ฿300, ฿200 children, T7034891. Croc combat and elephant show-time is every hour between 0900 and 1600 Mon-Fri (no show at 1200), and every hour between 0900 and 1700 Sat/Sun and holidays. Getting there: a/c bus 8 or 11, or*

Other area place names

Ancient City
เมืองโบราณ

Ayutthaya
พระนครศรีอยุธยา

Bang Pa-In
บางปะอิน

Floating market at Damnoen Saduak
ตลาดน้ำดำเนินสะดวก

Hua Hin
หัวหิน

Khao Yai National Park
อุทยานแห่งชาติเขาใหญ่

Nakhon Pathom
นครปฐม

Nonthaburi
นนทบุรี

Phetburi
เพชรบุรี

Bangkok

*regular bus 25, 45, 102 or 119 along Sukhumvit Rd; or a bus from the Eastern bus terminal to Samut Prakarn and then take a minibus to the Crocodile Farm; or a tour (see **Tours**, below).*

Apart from the *khlong* trips outlined on page 96, there are other places to go on the river. The cheapest way to travel the river is by regular **water taxi**. There are three types (not including the *hang yaaws*): **Watery excursions**

First, the **Chao Phraya Express River Taxi** (*rua duan*) which runs on a regular route from Wat Rajsingkorn (near Krungthep Bridge, at the south end of Charoen Krung) northwards to Nonthaburi. Fares range from ฿4-16 and the service operates every 8 to 25 minutes depending on the time of day, 0600-1800 Monday-Sunday (see map page 97 for stops). The boats are long and fast. There are also **ferries** which ply back and forth across the river, between Bangkok and Thonburi. The fare for these slower, chunkier boats is ฿1. Lastly, there are a number of **other boat services** linking Bangkok with stops along the *khlongs* which run off the main Chao Phraya River and into Thonburi. These are a good, cheap way of getting a glimpse of waterside life. Services from Tha Tien pier (by Wat Pho) to Khlong Mon, 0630-1800 Monday-Sunday (every half an hour) ฿4; from Memorial Bridge pier to Khlong Bang Waek, 0600-2130 Monday-Sunday (every 15 minutes) ฿10; from Tha Chang pier (by the Grand Palace) to Khoo Wiang floating market (market operates 0400-0700) and Khlong Bang Yai, 0615-2000 Monday-Sunday (every 20 minutes) ฿10; and from Nonthaburi's Phibun Pier (north of the city) to Khlong Om, 0400-2100 Monday-Sunday (every 15 minutes).

An interesting day trip by long-tailed boat takes visitors to a **traditional Thai house** 30 km from Bangkok, in Nonthaburi (see next entry). A day trip, including lunch costs ฿500. It is possible to stay here as guests of the owner Mr Phaiboon (**A**, the rate includes breakfast, fan rooms, outside bathrooms and no hot water). Call *Asian Overland Adventure*, T2800740, F2800741.

Nonthaburi is both a province and a provincial capital immediately to the north of Bangkok (see map page 72). Accessible by express river taxi from the city, the town has a provincial air that contrasts sharply with the overpowering capital: there are saamlors in the streets (now banished from Bangkok) and the pace of life is tangibly less frenetic. About half an hour's walk away are rice **Nonthaburi**

🐽 My kingdom for a durian

To many Thais, durians are not just any old fruit. They are Beaujolais, grouse and dolcellata all rolled into one stinking, prickly ball. The best durian in Thailand – the cognoscenti would say the whole world – come from Nonthaburi, north of Bangkok. And the best varieties are those like the kan yao durian. The problem is that Nonthaburi has been taken over by factories and housing estates. Durian orchards are disappearing as development proceeds and many of the most famous orchards are now under concrete. In early 2000 it was said that there were just 3,000 rai of orchards left in the province (less than 500 ha). Such is the scarcity of these fruit that wealthy Thais reserve their fruit on the tree – each of which sells for ฿1,200-1,500. Nor is it just a case of land being redeveloped. Durian trees are said not to like thundering traffic and the fumes that go with Nonthaburi's gradual industrialization. The sensible things just refuse to fruit or produce second-class offerings.

fields and rural Thailand. A **street market** runs from the pier inland past the *sala klang* (provincial offices), selling clothes, sarong lengths, dried fish and unnecessary plastic objects. The buildings of the *sala klang* are early 19th century, wooden and decayed. Note the lamp posts with their durian accessories – Nonthaburi's durians are renowned across the Kingdom. Walk through the *sala klang* compound (downriver) to reach an excellent riverside restaurant. Across the river and upstream (five minutes by long-tailed boat) is **Wat Chalem Phra Kiat**, a refined wat built by Rama III as a tribute to his mother who is said to have lived in the vicinity. The gables of the bot are encrusted in ceramic tiles; the chedi behind the bot was built during the reign of King Mongkut or Rama IV (1851-1868). ■ *Getting there: by express river taxi (45 mins) to Tha Nonthaburi or by Bangkok city bus (Nos 32, 64, 97 and 203).*

Floating market at Damnoen Saduak

It is possible to combine this trip with a visit to the Rose Garden (see page 112)

Damnoen Saduak floating market, in Ratchaburi Province, 109 km west of Bangkok, is (almost) the real thing. Sadly, it is becoming increasingly like the Floating Market in Thonburi (see page 97), although it does still function as a legitimate market. ■ *Getting there: catch an early morning bus (No 78) from the Southern bus terminal in Thonburi – aim to get to Damnoen Saduak between 0800-1000, as the market winds down after 1000, leaving only trinket stalls. The trip takes about 1½ hrs. A/c and non-a/c buses leave every 40 mins from 0600 (฿30-49) (T4355031 for booking).* The bus travels via Nakhon Pathom (where it is possible to stop on the way back and see the Great Chedi – see Nakhon Pathom page 112). Ask the conductor to drop you at Thanarat Bridge in Damnoen Saduak. Then either walk down the lane (1½ km) that leads to the market and follows the canal, or take a river taxi for ฿10, or a mini-bus (฿2). There are a number of floating

Damnoen Saduak Floating Market

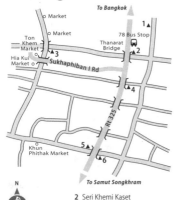

To Bangkok

Market
Market
Ton Khem Market
Hia Kui Market
Sukhaphiban I Rd
78 Bus Stop
Thanarat Bridge
Rt 325
Khun Phithak Market
To Samut Songkhram

N
Not to scale
▲ Piers
1 Soem Suk
2 Seri Khemi Kaset
3 Potchawan
4 Lek Silom
5 Mongkhon
6 Soem Suk

markets in the maze of *khlongs* – Ton Khem, Hia Kui and Khun Phithak – and it is best to hire a *hang yaaw* to explore the back-waters and roam around the markets, about ฿300 per hour (agree the price before setting out). Tour companies also visit the floating market.

Situated 31 km west of Bangkok on Pinklao-Nakhon Chaisri highway, the Thai Human Imagery Museum is the Madame Tussauds of Bangkok. 'Breath-taking' sculptures include famous monks, Thai kings, and scenes from Thai life; the museum is probably more interesting to Thais than foreigners. ■ *Mon-Fri, 0900-1730, Sat, Sun and holidays 0830-1800. ฿200. T034-332109. Getting there: by bus from the Southern bus terminals (either a/c or non-a/c) towards Nakhon Pathom; ask to be let off at the museum.* **Thai Human Imagery Museum**

The National Science Museum or NSM opened in Pathum Thani province in 2000, north of town, past the airport. The money for the project – a cool one billion baht – was allocated before the economic crisis. New buildings, air-conditioned, internet centre, and lots of hands-on exhibits to thrill children and the childlike is the result. The exhibits are labelled in English and Thai and the recorded information is also in both languages. It really is surprisingly good, well designed and with charming student helpers for that human touch. The cafeteria needs some more thought though. ■ *Tue-Sun, 0900-1700. ฿50, ฿20 children. T5774172, Pasopsuk@lox1.loxinfo.com Getting there: not that easy because it is some way north of the city centre. In Thai the Museum is known as Ongkaan Phiphitiphan Withayasaat Haeng Chaat (or Or Por Wor Chor). But even if you can manage that the chances are that the taxi driver will not know where you mean, so get someone from your hotel or guesthouse to make sure. Take the Chaeng Wattana-Bang Pa-in expressway north and exit at Chiang Rak (for Thammasat University's new out-of-town campus). Continue west on Khlong Luang Rd, over Phahonyothin Rd, and follow your nose over khlong 1 to khlong 5 (canals) until the road ends at a 'T' junction. Turn right and the NSM is 4 km or so down here on the left.* **National Science Museum**

Ayutthaya, 85 km north of Bangkok, was the capital of Thailand until 1767 when the Burmese razed the city. Despite the efforts of the Burmese – or perhaps because of them – it remains a splendid place with 84 palaces, shrines, monasteries and *chedis*. The city is situated on an island at the confluence of three rivers – the Chao Phraya, Pa Sak and Lopburi. The 'historical park' covers some 3 sq km and walking around in the evening, with the sun illuminating the deep red-brick ruins, it is possible to imagine the grandeur of this city which so amazed early European visitors. In December 1991 UNESCO added the Phra Nakhon Si Ayutthaya Historical Park to its list of World Heritage sites. Among the more notable monuments here are: Wat Ratchaburana, Wat Phra Mahathat, Wat Phra Ram, Wat Boromaphutharam, Wat Phra Sri Sanphet, Viharn Phra Mongkol Bopitr, Wat Lokaya Sutha, Wat Thamrikrat, Chao Sam Phraya Museum, Chandra Kasem Palace, Wat Chai Wattanaram, and the Elephant kraals. **Sleeping** There are ample places to stay, in all price brackets, in Ayutthaya. ■ *Getting there: it is an easy 1-hr journey from Bangkok's Northern bus terminal to Ayutthaya so it is easily accessible as a day tour. There are also regular train connections with Hualamphong station – and the station in Ayutthaya is centrally located. Another option is to arrive by boat, which takes a leisurely 3 hrs from Tha Tien pier in Bangkok (see page 114).* **Ayutthaya**

Bang Pa-In, just over 60 km north of Bangkok, became the summer residence of the Ayutthayan kings of the 17th century. King Prasat Thong (1630-56) started the trend of retiring here during the hot season, and he built both a **Bang Pa-in** palace and a temple – Wat Chumphon Nikayaram – on an island in the middle of the Chao Phraya River. The palace is in turn located in the middle of a lake that the king had created on the island. After the capital of Thailand was moved to Bangkok, Bang Pa-In was abandoned and left to degenerate. It was not until Rama IV stopped here on a journey to Ayutthaya that a restoration programme was begun and both he and his son, King Chulalongkorn (Rama V), visited Bang Pa-In regularly. The palace is now a museum and is easily accessible from Bangkok, by bus or train or on a tour. ■ *Bang Pa-In complex ฿50 (guidebook included). Mon-Sun 0830-1630. Getting there: regular bus connections from Bangkok's Northern terminal (1 hr) and 3 train connections each day from the capital's Hualamphong station.*

Bang Sai The **Royal Folk Arts and Crafts Centre** is based north of Bangkok at Amphoe (district) Bang Sai, around 24 km from Bang Pa-In, and covers an area of nearly 50 ha. Local farmers are trained in traditional arts and crafts such as basketry, weaving and wood carving. The project is funded by the Royal Family in an attempt to keep alive Thailand's traditions. Visitors are offered a glimpse of traditional life and technologies. All products – artificial flowers, dolls, silk and cotton cloth, wood carvings, baskets and so on – are on sale. Other attractions at Bang Sai include a freshwater aquarium and a bird park. ■ *Tue-Sun, 0830-1600. ฿50, ฿30 children. T366666, bangsai@wnet.net.th Getting there: by bus from the Northern bus terminal, or by boat up the Chao Phraya.*

Khao Yai National Park Khao Yai is Thailand's oldest national park and one of the most accessible, lying only 165 km northeast of Bangkok. ■*Getting there: 3 hrs by car. Regular connections by bus from the Northern bus terminal to Pak Chong. From here there are regular buses into the park.*

Rose Garden A Thai 'cultural village' spread over 15 ha of landscaped tropical grounds, 32 km west of Bangkok. Most people go for the cultural show – elephants at work, Thai classical dancing, Thai boxing, hilltribe dancing and a Buddhist ordination ceremony. The resort also has a hotel, restaurants, a swimming pool and tennis courts, as well as a golf course close by. ■ *Mon-Sun, 0800-1800. The cultural show is at 1445 Mon-Sun ฿300. (Bangkok office: 195/15 Soi Chokchai Chongchamron Rama III Rd, T2953261). Daily tour from Bangkok, half day (afternoons only).*

Nakhon Pathom The ancient city of Nakhon Pathom, less than 70 km from Bangkok, can be reached on a day trip from the capital, whether by train or road, and makes a nifty getaway from the madness of the city. While the Bangkok effect is noticeable even in Nakhon Pathom, the town does still have a provincial charm which makes it a refreshing counterpoint to the capital. Nakhon Pathom is one of the oldest cities in Thailand (though there is little left to show for it). Some scholars believe that the great Indian Emperor Asoka dispatched two missionaries here from India in the third century BC to expound the teachings of Buddhism. It later became the centre of the Dvaravati Kingdom (from the sixth to the 11th centuries). The impressive Phra Pathom Chedi is the largest in Thailand and dominates the heart of the town. The existing *chedi* was begun in 1853 at the instigation of King Mongkut (who visited its ruined predecessor while still a monk) and took 17 years to complete. **Sleeping** While there are no particularly attractive places to stay in Nakhon Pathom there are hotels from comfortable to budget. ■ *Getting there: the train station is to the north of the fruit market, an easy walk to/from the chedi. Regular connections with Bangkok's Hualamphong station, 1 hr. A/c buses also stop to the north of the fruit market, and there are regular connections (every 15 mins) with Bangkok's Southern bus terminal, 1-2 hrs.*

Kanchanaburi

Kanchanaburi, 122 km northwest of Bangkok, is famous for its proximity to the Bridge over the River Kwai – built at such human cost during the Second World War. This is also an area of great natural beauty and is a good jumping-off point for visits to national parks, trips on the River Kwai or excursions to one of a number of waterfalls and caves. Along with the bridge, a museum and two war cemeteries, there are cave monasteries outside town as well as the Muang Singh Historical Park, which preserves the ruins of a Khmer settlement that flourished during the 12th-13th centuries. **Sleeping** There is ample accommodation in Kanchanaburi, from simple riverside guest houses to lavish resort hotels. ■ *Getting there: the State Railways of Thailand offer a worthwhile all-day tour from Bangkok to Kanchanaburi on weekends and holidays. There are also regular buses from Bangkok's Southern bus terminal, 2-3 hrs.*

Phetburi

The ancient city of Phetburi lies 160 km southwest of Bangkok. It can just be visited in a day from the capital (see page 206). ■*Getting there: by bus from the Southern bus terminal (2 hrs) or by train from Hualamphong station, 2½ hrs.*

Hua Hin

Hua Hin, a beach resort, lies 230 km south of Bangkok. It is accessible as a day tour by either bus from the Southern terminal 3½ hours or by train from Hualamphong station 3½-4 hours (see page 214).

Safari World

Three-hundred-acre complex in Minburi, 9 km from the city centre, with animals and amusement park (T5181000, www.safariworld.com). Most of the animals are African – zebras, lions, giraffes – and visitors can either drive through in their own (closed) vehicles or take one of the park's air-conditioned coaches. There is also a marine park and a bird park. ■ *Mon-Sun 0900-1700. ฿600, ฿360 (children). Getting there: bus no 26 from the Victory Monument to Minburi where a minibus service runs to the park.*

Siam Water Park

Water World (with artificial surf, fountains, waterfalls and shutes), theme park, zoo, botanical gardens and fair all rolled into one, 101 Sukhapibarn 2 Rd, Bangkapi, T5170075. Half an hour east of town, or 1 hr by bus 26 or 27 from Victory Monument. ■ *Mon-Fri 1000-1800, Sat-Sun 0900-1900 ฿200. Getting there: bus nos 26 and 27 from the Victory Monument.*

Tours

Bangkok has innumerable tour companies that can take visitors virtually anywhere (see page 150 for a listing). If there is not a tour to fit your bill – most run the same range of tours – many companies will produce a customized one for you, for a price. Most top hotels have their own tour desk and it is probably easiest to book there (arrange to be picked up from your hotel as part of the deal). The tours given below are the most popular; prices per person are about ฿400-800 for a half day, ฿1,000-2,000 for a full day (including lunch).

Half-day tours

Grand Palace Tour; Temple Tour to Wat Traimitr, Wat Pho and Wat Benjamabophit; *Khlong Tour* around the *khlongs* (canals) of Bangkok and Thonburi, to Floating Market, Snake Farm and Wat Arun (mornings only); *Old City Tour; Crocodile Farm Tour; Rice Barge and Khlong Tour* (afternoons only); *Damnoen Saduak Floating Market Tour.*

Full-day tours

Damnoen Saduak and Rose Garden; Thai Dinner and Classical Dance, eat in traditional Thai surrounding and consume toned-down Thai food, ฿250-300,

1900-2200. *Pattaya*, the infamous beach resort; *River Kwai*, a chance to see the famous Bridge over the River Kwai and war cemeteries, as well as the great chedi at Nakhon Pathom; *Ayutthaya and Bang Pa-In*. There are also boat tours to Ayutthaya and Bang Pa-In (see below).

Alternative tours A number of so-styled 'alternative' tour companies are springing up in Bangkok. One of the best is run by the Thai Volunteer Services' (TVS) *Responsible Ecological and Social Tour (REST)* project. TVS is a non-governmental organization with links to other up-country NGOs. People visit and stay in rural villages, go trekking and camping, are shown round local development projects and are encouraged to participate in community activities. Costs are around ฿3,000-4,000 for a three- to four-day tour. Contact T6910437/ 6910438. Another similar, and also recommended firm is *Alternative Tour*, 14/1 Soi Rajatapan, Rajaprarop Road, T2452963, F2467020, which offers excellent 'alternative' tours, enabling visitors to see the 'real' Thailand, and not just tourist sights.

Boat tours There are more than 30 boats (in addition to the *hang yaaws* and regular ferries) offering cruises on the Chao Phraya. The *Oriental Queen* sails up the Chao Phraya River daily from the *Oriental Hotel* to the old capital, Ayutthaya, returning to Bangkok by air-conditioned bus, ฿1,550 (children 3-10 years old, ฿900), 0800-1700 with mediocre lunch (T2360400). The tour includes rather hurried visits to Bang Pa-In, Wat Phra Sri Sanphet and Wat Khun Inthapramun. The *Ayutthaya Princess* operates from the *Shangri-La Hotel* pier or the *Royal Sheraton* pier. The *Ayutthaya Princess* is a two-level vessel resembling a Royal Barge. Leaving at 0800 daily, there are cruises to Bang Pa-In, an air-conditioned bus tour around Ayutthaya, returning to Bangkok by coach at 1730. You can also do the reverse: coach to Ayutthaya and then a boat back to Bangkok, arriving at 1730, ฿1,100, including buffet lunch on board. (Kian Gwan Building, 140 Wireless Road, T2559200.)

Mekhala is operated by the *Siam Exclusive Tours* on the same route. The difference is that *Mekhala* leaves Bangkok in the late evening and puts ashore for one night in Ayutthaya, supplying a romantic dinner on deck. The *Mekhala* is a converted rice barge accommodating 12-16 passengers in six air-conditioned cabins with attached bathrooms. The barge arrives in Ayutthaya at Wat Kai Tia in the evening and departs the following morning for Bang Pa-In. To visit other sights, passengers are transferred to a long-tailed boat. An air-conditioned minibus transports passengers back to Bangkok. The reverse, proceeding by road up to Ayutthaya/Bang Pa-In and returning on the rice barge, is also available ฿5,290 (single), ฿4,200 (twin). Book through travel agents or *Siam Exclusive Tours*, Building One, seventh floor, 99 Witthayu Road, T2566153, F2566665. Cheaper are the day boat tours to Bang Pa-In via Queen Sirikit's handicraft centre at Bang Sai and the stork sanctuary at Wat Phai Lom operated by the *Chao Phraya Express Boat Company*. Tours leave on Saturday and Sunday only from the Maharaj and Phra Athit piers at 0800 and 0805 respectively, returning 1530, ฿180 or ฿240, T2225330.

Another company offering a professional cruise service is *Pearl of Siam* which operates three 'yachts'. Like other companies, they offer passengers either a bus trip up to Ayutthaya and a cruise down, or vice versa (฿1,600). In the evenings the company also offer dinner cruises for ฿1,100.

Dinner cruises *Chao Phraya*, T4335453; *Loy Nava*, T4374932, ฿700. *Wanfah Cruise*, T4335453, ฿650. *Ayutthaya Princess*, T2559200 organizes Sunday dinner cruise for ฿850.

The State Railway of Thailand organize day trips to Nakhon Pathom (see page 112) and the Bridge over the River Kwai and to Ayutthaya (see page 111). Both trips run on weekends and holidays. The latter tour leaves Bangkok at 0630 and returns from Ayutthaya by boat along the Chao Phraya River.

Train tours

For organizing visas to Vietnam, Laos, Cambodia and Myanmar (Burma), see page 150.

International tours

Essentials

Sleeping

Bangkok

Bangkok offers a wide range of accommodation at all levels of luxury. There are a number of hotel areas in the city, each with its own character and locational advantages (and disadvantages). Accommodation has been divided into five such areas with a sixth – 'other' – for the handful situated elsewhere. A new type of hotel which has emerged in Bangkok in recent years is the 'boutique' hotel. These are small, with immaculate service, and represent an attempt to emulate the philosophy of 'small is beautiful'.

For the last few years Bangkok has had a glut of hotel rooms – especially 5-star – as hotels planned during the heady days of the late 1980s and early 1990s have opened. Many hotels will offer considerable discounts off the rack rate.

NB For business women travelling alone, the *Oriental*, *Dusit Thani* and *Amari Airport* hotels allocate floors to women travellers, with all-female staff.

Many of the more expensive places to stay are on the **Chao Phraya River** with its views, good shopping and access to the old city. Running eastwards from the river are **Silom** and **Surawong** roads, in the heart of Bangkok's business district and close to many embassies. The bars of Patpong link the two roads. This is a good area to stay for shopping and bars, but transport to the tourist sights can be problematic. Not far to the north of Silom and Surawong roads, close to Hualamphong (the central railway station), is **Chinatown**. This, as one might expect, is a place of feverish commercial activity. There are a handful of hotels and guesthouses here – but it remains very much an alternative location to the better established accommodation centres. A more recently developed, but now well-established area is along **Sukhumvit Road** running east from Soi Nana Nua (Soi 3). The bulk of the accommodation here is in the **A-B** range, and within easy reach is a wide range of restaurants, bars, and reasonable shopping. The hotels are a long taxi or tuk-tuk ride from the sights of the old city, but the long-tailed boats which race along the *khlongs* (canals) provide access in under 20 mins to the historic centre. The journey is cheap and thrilling. There is a pier near the far end of Soi Nana Nua (Soi 3) (see map). In the vicinity of **Siam Square** are a handful of deluxe hotels and several 'budget' class establishments (especially along Rama 1 Soi Kasemsan Nung). Siam Square is central, a good shopping area, with easy bus and taxi access to Silom and Sukhumvit roads and the sights of the Old City. The main concentration of guesthouses is along and around **Khaosan Road** (an area known as Banglamphu, within walking distance of the Grand Palace). There is a second, smaller and quieter cluster of guesthouses just north of Khaosan Road, at the northwest end of **Sri Ayutthaya Road**. A third concentration of budget accommodation is on **Soi Ngam Duphli**, off Rama IV Road. These hotel areas encompass about 90% of Bangkok's accommodation, although there are other places to stay scattered across the city; these are listed under **Other**.

Silom, Surawong & the River In all Bangkok, this area most resembles a western city, with its international banks, skyscrapers, first-class hotels, shopping malls, pizza parlours and pubs. Development has not abated, with still more skyscrapers under construction. It is also home to one of the world's best-known red-light districts – Patpong. The opening of the Skytrain has made Silom more accessible to other parts of the city too: the line runs north through Siam Square to Mor Chit and the Weekend Market while another line runs east along Sukhumvit Road.

L *Dusit Thani*, 946 Rama IV Rd, T2360450, F2366400. A/c, restaurants, disappointing pool. When it was built, the *Dusit Thani* was the tallest building in Bangkok. Still excellent, it has been continually refurbished and upgraded. Recently played host to several celebrities, including boy band wonders *Ultra*. Excellent service and attention to detail. Recommended. **L** *Evergreen Laurel Hotel*, 88 Sathorn Nua, T2669988, F2667222. A/c, restaurants, pool, looks somewhat undersized compared to some of the newer high-rise blocks. Taiwanese-owned, all facilities and excellent service. **L** *Montien*, 54 Surawong Rd, T2348060, F2365219. A/c, restaurants, pool, one of the first high-rise hotels (opened 1967) with good location for business, shopping and bars, slick service, and continuing good reputation with loyal patrons. **L** *Oriental*, 48 Soi Oriental, Charoen Krung, T2360400, F2361939. A/c, restaurants, pool, one of the best hotels in the world, beautiful position overlooking the river, superb personal service despite its size (400 rooms). The hotel claims that Joseph Conrad, Somerset Maugham and Noel Coward all stayed here at one time or another, although the first

Silom & Surawong

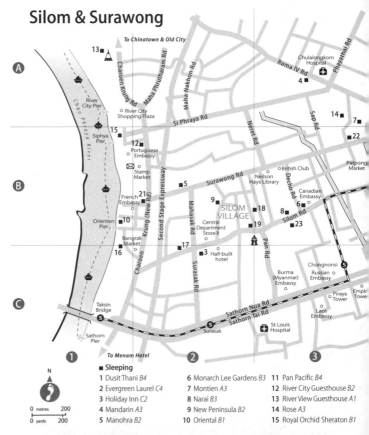

N

0 metres 200
0 yards 200

■ Sleeping

1 Dusit Thani *B4*	6 Monarch Lee Gardens *B3*
2 Evergreen Laurel *C4*	7 Montien *A3*
3 Holiday Inn *C2*	8 Narai *B3*
4 Mandarin *A3*	9 New Peninsula *B2*
5 Manohra *B2*	10 Oriental *B1*
	11 Pan Pacific *B4*
	12 River City Guesthouse *B2*
	13 River View Guesthouse *A1*
	14 Rose *A3*
	15 Royal Orchid Sheraton *B1*

of these probably did not – he lived aboard his ship or, perhaps, stayed in the now defunct *Universal Hotel*. Good shopping arcade, programme of 'cultural' events, 6 excellent restaurants, and a spa on the other side of the river opposite the hotel. Some of the equipment and bathrooms could be said to be a little old, however the hotel still comes highly recommended. **L** *Royal Orchid Sheraton*, 2 Captain Bush Lane, Si Phraya Rd, T2660123, F2372152. A/c, restaurants, pool. At times strong and rather unpleasant smell from nearby *khlong*, lovely views over the river, and close to River City shopping centre (good for antiques). Rooms are average at this price but service is very slick. **L** *Shangri-La*, 89 Soi Wat Suan Plu, Charoen Krung, T2367777, F2368579. A/c, restaurants, lovely pool, and great location overlooking the river. This hotel is preferred by some to the *Oriental* although others consider it dull and impersonal. Claims to be in the Top 10 World Hotels and is certainly an excellent hostelry. Recommended. **L** *The Westin Banyan Tree*, 21/100 Sathorn Tai Rd, T6791200, F6791199, www.westin-bangkok.com A/c, restaurant, pool and health spa. New hotel and the tallest in Bangkok – the spa on the 51st-54th floors has stunning views. It is targetting the business traveller, all rooms are suites with working area, in-room fax and copier, computer port and voice mail. Good location for central business district and set back from busy Sathorn Rd. The atmosphere is quiet sophistication. Recommended. **L-AL** *Holiday Inn Crowne Plaza*, 981 Silom Rd, T2384300, F2385289. A/c, restaurants, pool, vast, pristine marble-filled hotel, all amenities, immensely comfortable, minimum atmosphere and character. **L-AL** *Sukhothai*, 13/3 Sathorn Tai Rd, T2870222, F2874980. A/c, restaurants (especially good poolside Italian restaurant), pool, beautiful rooms and

Bangkok

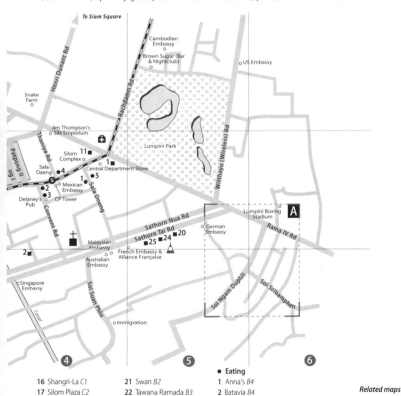

Related maps
A *Soi Ngam Duphli,*
page 119
Bangkok General,

excellent service. The design is clean and elegant, what might be termed Thai postmodern, and there are those who say it is even better than such established hotels as *The Regent* or even *The Oriental*. Since it opened a few years back it has become the favourite place to stay for regular visitors to Bangkok with deep pockets – the fact that their ads don't even bother with an address says it all. Recommended.

AL *Marriott Royal Garden Riverside Hotel*, 257/1-3 Charoen Nakorn Rd, T4760021, F4761120, www.marriot.com A/c, restaurant, excellent swimming pool, almost resort-like, very spacious surroundings with over 10 acres of grounds. On the other side of the river from the *Oriental Hotel*, near the Krung Thep Bridge, with free shuttle-boat service every half an hour between hotel and the *Oriental* and River City piers. Attractive low-rise design with some attempt to create Thai-style ambience. *Trader Vic's* is situated here. **AL** *Menam*, 2074 Charoen Krung, T2891148, F2911048. A/c, restaurant, pool, good value for river-view rooms but inconvenient location; shuttle-boat makes sightseeing easier. **AL** *Monarch Lee Gardens*, 188 Silom Rd, T2381991, F2381999. A/c, restaurants, pool, stark and gleaming high-tech high-rise, all facilities, still trying hard to attract custom, discounts available. **AL** *Pan Pacific Hotel*, 952 Rama IV Rd, T6329000, F6329011. A/c, restaurant, pool, 235 room hotel, good central position for business and shopping. **AL** *Sheraton Grande Sukhumvit*, Sukhumvit Rd, T6530333, F6530400, grande.sukhumvit @luxurycollection.com A bronzed, gilded affair offering the usual range of international hotel services, opposite the *Delta Grande*. **AL** *Tarntawan Place*, 119/5-10 Surawong Rd, T2382620, F2383228. A/c, restaurant, pool, good service and rooms. Recommended. **AL** *Tawana Ramada*, 80 Surawong Rd, T2360361, F2363738. A/c, restaurant, pool, average hotel given the stiff competition at this grade. **A** *Mandarin*, 662 Rama IV Rd, T2380230, F2371620. A/c, restaurant, small pool, friendly atmosphere, comfortable rooms, popular nightclub. **A** *Silom Plaza*, 320 Silom Rd, T2368441, F2367566. A/c, restaurant, small pool, caters mainly for East Asian tour groups, central but characterless, gently decaying. **A** *Silom Street Inn*, 284/11-13 Silom Rd, opposite the junction with Pan Rd (between Sois 22 and 24), T2384680, F2363619. A/c, restaurant, pool, small hotel, 30 well equipped but small rooms with CNN News, grubby and rather seedy lobby, set back from the road. **A** *Silom Village Inn*, 286 Silom Rd, T6356816, F6356817. Part of the Silom Village Shopping Complex, nothing to separate it from the masses, and not especially good value. **A** *Tower Inn*, 533 Silom Rd, T2344051, F2344051. A/c, restaurant, pool, simple but comfortable hotel, with large rooms and an excellent roof terrace, good value. **A** *Trinity Place*, 150 Silom Soi 5, T2380052, F2383984. A/c, restaurant, pool, attractive, small hotel. **A-B** *Narai*, 222 Silom Rd, T2370100, F2367161. A/c, restaurant, pool, rather non-descript, with cold, marble-clad lobby and small rooms.

B *Collins House (YMCA)*, 27 Sathorn Tai Rd, T2871900, F2871996. A/c, restaurant, large pool. Set back from Sathorn Tai Rd, clean, excellent value and friendly management. Not particularly central for sights and shopping but it is only a 10-15 min walk to the Sala Daeng Skytrain station. **B** *Manohra*, 412 Surawong Rd, T2345070, F2377662. A/c, coffee shop, small pool, unattractive rooms, mediocre service. **B** *New Peninsula*, 295/3 Surawong Rd, T2343910, F2365526. A/c, restaurant, small pool, small rooms. **B** *River City Guesthouse*, 11/4 Charoen Krung Soi Rong Nam Khang 1, T2351429, F2373127. A/c, not very welcoming but rooms are spacious and clean, good bathrooms, short walk to River City and the river. **B** *Rose*, 118 Surawong Rd, T2337695, F2346381. A/c, restaurant, pool, opposite Patpong, favourite among single male visitors, but getting seedier by the month. **B** *Swan*, 31 Charoen Krung Soi 36, T2348594. Some a/c, great position, clean but scruffy rooms.

A *Grand China Princess*, 215 Yaowarat Rd, T2249977, F2247999, pgb @dusit.com High-rise block mainly catering to the Asian market, with choice of Asian cuisine, business facilities, fitness centre (but no pool).

Chinatown
For a map of Chinatown, see page 94

Bangkok

C *Chao Phya Riverside Guesthouse*, 1128 Songward Rd (opposite the Chinese school), T2226344, F2231696. Some a/c, old-style house overlooking river, clean rooms, atmospheric, unusual location in commercial Chinatown where *sip lors* (ten-wheelers) loading rice, and metal workers fashioning steel. Seems to be a little more run-down than a few years back and characteristically brusque management but worth considering for its position and ambience. **C** *River View Guesthouse*, 768 Songwad Soi Panurangsri, T2345429, F2375771 (see map page 117). Some a/c, the restaurant/bar is on the top floor and overlooks the river, food is mediocre. Noisy and rather dirty, some rooms with balconies, some with hot water, overlooking (as the name suggests) the river. This hotel is worth considering for its location away from the bulk of hotels, close to the river. Reasonably good value too.

D *Moon Hotel*, Mahachai Rd, T2357195. A rabbit warren of cellular a/c rooms joined by damp corridors, excellent value however. **D-E** *Golden Inn Guesthouse*, Mahachai Rd, no telephone, excellent situation in the heart of Chinatown. Dark rooms and very noisy, but then this is Chinatown.

Soi Ngam Duphli is much the smaller of Bangkok's 2 main centres of guesthouse accommodation. Locationally, the area is good for the shopping and bars of Silom Rd but inconvenient for most of the main places of interest in the old city. Generally, the area is rather run-down these days and nowhere near as happening as Banglamphu. The only exception is *Charlie's*, which is good value. After *Charlie's*, the other places worth considering (at our last visit) are *Lee 3*, *Lee 4*, *Madam* and *Sala Thai*. See the Soi Ngam Duphli map for locations.

Soi Ngam Duphli

AL *Pinnacle Hotel*, 17 Soi Ngam Duphli, T2870111, F2873420. Clean and pleasant rooms with all mod cons, helpful staff, restaurant, night club. **B-C** *Malaysia*, 54 Rama IV Soi Ngam Duphli, T2867263, F2871457. A/c, restaurant, pool. Once a Bangkok favourite for travellers but now rather seedy and not great value.

C *Charlie's House*, Soi Saphan Khu, T6798330, F6797308. According to its own PR, this place is not a hotel, nor a guesthouse, but a home. It lives up to this description. The owners are helpful, the atmosphere is friendly, the rooms are carpeted and very clean. This is the probably the best place in Soi Ngam Duphli if you are willing to pay that little bit extra. There is a restaurant and coffee corner downstairs with good food at reasonable prices. Recommended. **D** *ETC*, northern end of Soi Ngam Duphli, T2869424. Big, clean rooms with nice sitting area on the 4th Floor, but the management are a little *laissez faire*. Price includes breakfast. **D** *Honey House*, 35/2-4 Soi Ngam Duphli, T2863460. An interesting

Soi Ngam Duphli

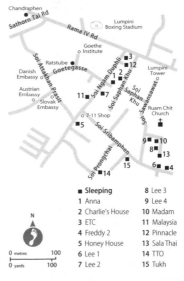

■ Sleeping	8 Lee 3
1 Anna	9 Lee 4
2 Charlie's House	10 Madam
3 ETC	11 Malaysia
4 Freddy 2	12 Pinnacle
5 Honey House	13 Sala Thai
6 Lee 1	14 TTO
7 Lee 2	15 Tukh

Related map
Bangkok General,
page 74

building architecturally. Big and clean rooms with attached bathrooms, some with small balconies, but sloppy management. **D** *Sala Thai Guesthouse*, Soi Saphan Khu, T2871436. At end of peaceful, almost leafy, soi, clean rooms, family run, good food, shared bathrooms. Recommended. **D** *TTO*, 2/48 Soi Sribamphen, T2866783, F2871571. Some a/c, well-run and popular. Homely atmosphere, with only 8 reasonably sized rooms all with attached bathrooms. Not particularly good value, however. **D-E** *Lee 3*, 13 Soi Saphan Khu, T2863042. Some a/c. Wooden house with character, down quiet soi, rooms are clean, shared bathrooms. Recommended. **D-E** *Madam*, 11 Soi Saphan Khu, T2869289. Wooden house, friendly atmosphere, attached bathrooms, no hot water, quiet. Recommended.

E *Lee 2*, 21/38-39 Soi Ngam Duphli, T2862069. Dirty and with sometimes hostile staff. **E** *Lee 4*, 9 Soi Saphan Khu, T2867874. Spotless rooms and bathrooms, some with balconies and views over the city. Recommended. **E-F** *Anna*, 21/30 Soi Ngam Duphli, clean rooms, some with bathrooms, travel desk downstairs. **E-F** *Lee 1*, Soi Sribamphen. OK for what you pay, quite clean, but nothing special. Asian toilets. **F** *Freddy 2*, Soi Sribamphen (next door to *Lee 1*), full on our last visit, so it must be popular. Similar to *Lee 1*.

Siam Square, Rama I, Ploenchit & Phetburi Rds
L *Grand Hyatt Erawan*, 494 Rachdamri Rd, T2541234, F2535856, guest @erawan.co.th, erawan@loxinfo.co.th, reservation@erawan.co.th The replacement hotel for the much-loved *Erawan Hotel*. A towering structure with grandiose entrance and a plastic tree-filled atrium plus sumptuous rooms and every facility. The hotel is hard to fault in its range of services but old hands maintain it has none of the atmosphere of the old *Erawan*. The *Spasso Restaurant/Club* here is very popular and very pricey. **L** *Novotel*, Siam Square Soi 6, T2556888, F2551824, novotel.com.th A/c, restaurant, pool, undistinguished but comfortable with a good location in the heart of

Siam Square & Ploenchit Road

To Florida & Siam City Hotels

	Sleeping	6	Grand Hyatt Erawan	12	Novotel
	1	A1 Inn	7	Hilton	13	Regent
	2	Amari Watergate	8	Imperial	14	Siam
	3	Arnoma	9	Kritthai Mansion		Intercontinental
	4	Asia	10	Le Meridien President	15	White Lodge
	5	B & B Guesthouse		& President Tower	16	White Orchid Guesthouse
		& Wendy House	11	Mercure		

Related map
Bangkok General,
page 74

Siam Square. **L** *Siam Intercontinental*, 967 Rama I Rd, T2530355, F2532275, bangkok@interconti.com A/c, restaurants, small pool, relatively low-rise hotel with a central position yet set in an amazing 11 ha (26 acres) of grounds. Good sports facilities and excellent service. A real haven in over-bearing Bangkok. **L-AL** *Hilton*, 2 Witthayu Rd, T2530123, F2536509, www.hilton.com A/c, restaurants, attractive pool. An excellent hotel set in lovely grounds with a remarkable garden feel for a hotel that is so central. Comparatively small for such a large plot first-class service, good restaurants, attractive rooms, a great hotel. In addition, US$1 is deducted for the WWF to salve environmental consciences and make you feel good about using all those towels. Recommended. **L-AL** *Imperial*, 6-10 Witthayu Rd (on the edge of Siam Square area), T2540023, F2533190. A/c, restaurants, pool, lovely grounds but hotel seems rather jaded next to Bangkok's newer upstarts. 370 rooms and numerous bars and restaurants where, apparently, it is possible to rub shoulders with the city's 'beautiful people'. Partition walls are thin for a hotel of this calibre and recent visitors have been disappointed at how it has declined in quality. **L-AL** *Regent Bangkok*, 155 Rachdamri Rd, T2516127, F2539195, www.regenthotels.com A/c, restaurants (see Thai Restaurants, page 139), pool (although rather noisy, set above a busy road), excellent reputation among frequent visitors who insist on staying here. Stylish and postmodern in atmosphere with arguably the best range of cuisine in Bangkok. It is also perhaps the most impressive piece of modern hotel architecture in Bangkok – which admittedly isn't saying much. Recommended.

AL *Amari Atrium Hotel*, 1880 New Phetburi Rd, T7182000, F7182002, www.amari.com (see map page 122). A/c, restaurants, pool, Clark Hatch fitness centre, opened early 1996, 600 rooms, all facilities, including babysitting. Reasonably accessible for the airport but not particularly well placed for the sights of the old city or for the central business district. **AL** *Arnoma*, 99 Rachdamri Rd, T2553411, F2553456. A/c, several restaurants, pool, health club, business centre. 403 well-equipped rooms, though much like any others in this price bracket, good location for shopping and restaurants. **AL** *Hotel Mercure*, 1091/336 Phetburi Rd, T2530510, F2530556. 650 rooms in this rather dated-looking hotel with pool, business centre and health centre. **AL** *Le Meridien President*, 135/26 Gaysorn Rd, T2530444, F2537565. Pool, health club, 400 rooms in this, one of the older but still excellent luxury hotels in Bangkok (it opened in 1966). Tranquil atmosphere, good service, excellent French food; a new sister hotel, *The President Tower*, was completed in 1996. It towers 36 storeys skywards. The original hotel is still recommended. **AL** *Radisson*, 92 Soi Saengcham, Rama 9 Rd, T6414777, F6414884. Overblown marble-clad lobby, sells itself as a business hotel, 431 ordinary rooms in this high-rise block, choice of cuisine, bakery, pub and cocktail lounge with good views of the city, fitness centre and pool. **AL** *Siam City*, 477 Sri Ayutthaya Rd, T2470120, F2470178. A/c, restaurants, pool, stylish hotel with attentive staff, large rooms, all facilities (gym, etc) and well managed. Good Mediterranean restaurant and bakery. Recommended. **A** *Amari Watergate*, 847 Phetburi Rd, T6539000, F6539045, www.amari.com A/c, restaurants (including the excellent Thai on 4 – see restaurant section), pool, Clark Hatch fitness centre, squash court, situated close to the Pratunam Market, great freeform pool (which makes swimming lengths a little tricky), but close to 600 rooms makes this a hotel on a grand scale. Lots of marble and plastic trees, uninspired block, good facilities and good value, great views from the upper floors on the south side of the building. **A** *Asia*, 296 Phayathai Rd, T2150808, F2154360. A/c, several restaurants from different continents (the *Rio Grill* – Brazilian food – has been recommended, with a good and reasonably priced buffet), pool. The jewellers within the hotel is one of the best in Bangkok. Entrance implies a certain degree of sophistication, but rooms are basic and the hotel is situated on a noisy thoroughfare. Overall, this old hotel is showing its age. Good deals available when booking in advance.

Bangkok

B *Kritthai Mansion*, 931/1 Rama I Rd, T2153042. A/c, restaurant, situated on a noisy thoroughfare. **B** *Florida*, 43 Phayathai Rd, T2470990. A/c, restaurant, pool, one of Thailand's first international hotels – and it shows – average even at this price. **B-C** *Chom's Boutique and Thai Kitchen*, 888/37-39 Ploenchit Rd, T2542070. A/c, central location, good rooms, small boutique hotel. The owner is a well-known chef. **C-D** *A1 Inn*, 25/13 Soi Kasemsan Nung (1), Rama I Rd, T2153029, aoneinn@thaimail.com A/c, well-run, intimate hotel. Recommended. **C-D** *Bed and Breakfast*, 36/42 Soi Kasemsan Nung (1), Rama 1 Rd, T2153004, F2152493. A/c, friendly and efficient staff, clean but small rooms, good security, bright 'lobby', price includes basic breakfast. Recommended. **C-D** *Wendy House*, 36/2 Soi Kasemsan Nung (1), Rama I Rd, T2162436, F2168053. A/c, spotless but small rooms, eating area downstairs, hot water. **C** *White Lodge*, 36/8 Soi Kasemsan Nung (1), Rama I Rd, T2168867, F2168228, pnktour @hotmail.com A/c, hot water, airy, light reasonably sized rooms. Recommended. **C** *White Orchid Guesthouse*, Soi 2 Siam Square, T2552186. 8 small rooms with pleasant atmosphere. **C-E** *Alternative Tour Guesthouse*, 14/1 Rachaprarop Soi Rachatapan, T2452963, F2467020. Friendly, excellent source of information, attached to *Alternative Tour Company*, promoting culturally and environmentally sensitive tourism, clean.

Sukhumvit Rd Sukhumvit is not one of Bangkok's traditional centres of tourist accommodation and really only emerged as such in the 1970s. Since then there has been almost continual

Sukhumvit Road

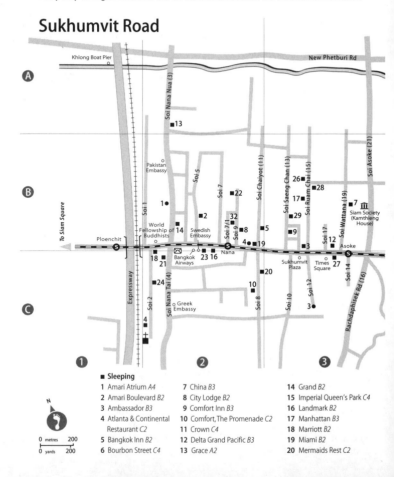

■ **Sleeping**
1 Amari Atrium *A4*
2 Amari Boulevard *B2*
3 Ambassador *B3*
4 Atlanta & Continental Restaurant *C2*
5 Bangkok Inn *B2*
6 Bourbon Street *C4*
7 China *B3*
8 City Lodge *B2*
9 Comfort Inn *B3*
10 Comfort, The Promenade *C2*
11 Crown *C4*
12 Delta Grand Pacific *B3*
13 Grace *A2*
14 Grand *B2*
15 Imperial Queen's Park *C4*
16 Landmark *B2*
17 Manhattan *B3*
18 Marriott *B2*
19 Miami *B2*
20 Mermaids Rest *C2*

expansion so that today almost all the facilities that a tourist might need – shops, tour and travel agencies, stalls, bars and restaurants – are to be found here. The main disadvantage of staying in this area is its distance from the main places of interest in the Old City like the Grand Palace, Wat Pho and the National Museum. However it is possible to take a long-tailed boat in under 20 mins from the pier near the far end of Soi Nana Nua (Soi 3) (see map). In addition, the opening of the Skytrain (which runs down Sukhumvit all the way to On Nut) has made the area much more convenient for travel to Siam Square and Silom.

L *Amari Boulevard*, 2 Sukhumvit Rd Soi 5, T2552930, F2552950, www.amari.com Great location in the heart of Sukhumvit, good rooms, adequate fitness centre, small pool with terraced Thai restaurant. Popular place with European visitors. **L** *Imperial Queen's Park*, Sukhumvit Soi 22, T2619000, F2619530. A massive hotel with a mind boggling 1,400 rooms. How service can, in any sense, be personal is hard to imagine, but it provides all possible facilities and an excellent French restaurant is also based here – Les Nymphéas. Its remoteness from most sights and the main business district means battling with traffic to do most things. **L** *Landmark*, 138 Sukhumvit Rd, T2540404, F2534259. One of the most glamorous hotels in the area. Excellent facilities, 12 restaurants, pool, health centre, smart shopping plaza and business facilities. Terrific views from the 31st floor. Recommended. **L** *Marriott*, 4 Sukhumvit Soi 2,

Bangkok

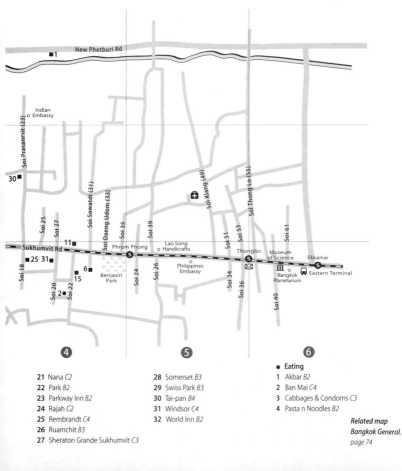

21 Nana *C2*	28 Somerset *B3*	• **Eating**
22 Park *B2*	29 Swiss Park *B3*	1 Akbar *B2*
23 Parkway Inn *B2*	30 Tai-pan *B4*	2 Ban Mai *C4*
24 Rajah *C2*	31 Windsor *C4*	3 Cabbages & Condoms *C3*
25 Rembrandt *C4*	32 World Inn *B2*	4 Pasta n Noodles *B2*
26 Ruamchit *B3*		
27 Sheraton Grande Sukhumvit *C3*		

Related map
Bangkok General,
page 74

T6567700, F6567711. Extremely elegant, with hints of art-deco design. 4 restaurants, pool, health club and spa, shops, bakery, the works. Recommended. **L** *Windsor Suites*, 8 Sukhumvit Soi 20, T2621234 F2621212, varaport@mozart.inet.co.th A/c, restaurants, pool, next door to the entrance hall has a Paddington-Station ambience, now under new ownership. **AL** *Delta Grand Pacific*, 259 Sukhumvit Rd, T2544330, F2544431, www.grandpacifichotel.com A/c, restaurants, pool, a very elegant hotel with a good pool and 4 restaurants. Even the standard rooms are expensive – but better value than the others, as ridiculous price increases are not reflected by a corresponding growth in amenities. **AL** *Rembrandt*, 15-15/1 Sukhumvit Soi 20, T2617040, F2617017. A/c, restaurants, pool, lots of marble but limited ambience. Pool, restaurant and usual facilities.

A *Ambassador*, 171 Sukhumvit Rd, T2540444, F2534123. A/c, restaurants, pool. Large, impersonal and rather characterless hotel but with great food hall (see places to eat). No email as yet **A** *Comfort, The Promenade*, 18 Sukhumvit Soi 8, T2534116, F2547707. A/c, restaurant, small pool, fitness centre, rather kitsch. **A** *Manhattan*, 13 Sukhumvit Soi 15, T2550166, F2553481. Smart hotel with 3 good, but expensive restaurants, pool. Lacks character but rooms are comfortable enough. Tours available and tri-weekly cabaret. **A** *Park*, 6 Sukhumvit Soi 7, T2554300, F2554309. A/c, restaurant. A peaceful oasis but showing signs of shabbiness and is overpriced given the competition in the area. **A** *Ruamchit*, 199 Sukhumvit Soi 15, T2540205, F2532406. A fairly well-furnished hotel with good views and excellent pool. The staff speak little English and it mainly serves Asian clientele. **A** *Swiss Park*, 23-24 Sukhumvit Soi 11, T2540228, F2540378. A/c, restaurant, excellent roof-top pool, business centre, another overbearing neo-classical hotel, but friendly service. **A** *Tai-pan*, 25 Sukhumvit Soi 23, T2609888, F2597908. A/c, tastefully decorated with restaurant and pool. **A-B** *Somerset*, 10 Sukhumvit Soi 15, T2548500, F2548534. A/c, restaurant, small but rather ostentatious hotel with shallow indoor pool. Rooms are non-descript but comfortable, bath-tubs are designed for people of small stature. Reception on the second floor.

B *Bourbon Street*, 29/4-6 Sukhumvit Soi 22 (behind Washington Theatre), T2590328, F2594318. A/c, a handful of rooms attached to a good Cajun restaurant. Recommended. **B** *Comfort Inn*, 153/11 Sukhumvit Soi 11, T2519250, F2543562. Small a/c hotel with rather dark, slightly musty rooms, coffee shop and friendly service. **B** *Grace*, 12 Sukhumvit Soi Nana Nua (Soi 3), T2530651, F2530680. A/c, restaurant, pool, bowling alley, disco. Once *the* sex hotel of Bangkok now trying to redeem itself but still overshadowed by its seedy reputation and rather gauche feel. **B** *Grand*, 2/7-8 Sukhumvit Soi Nana Nua (Soi 3), T2549021, F2549020. A/c, small hotel with rather dark rooms, café. **B** *Rajah*, 18 Sukhumvit Soi 2, T2550040. A rather dated hotel but with an attractive pool area, good-value restaurant, travel agents and craft shop. The atrium is reminiscent of the former eastern bloc. **B-C** *Atlanta*, 78 Sukhumvit Soi 2, T2521650. Basic a/c or fan-cooled rooms. A good large pool and a children's pool are a big plus. "Oiks, lager louts and sex tourists" are requested to go elsehere! "Those who cannot behave themselves abroad are advised to stay at home". Good restaurant (see **Eating**). Prides itself on its literary, peaceful atmosphere. Appears to be the cheapest and is certainly the most appealing hotel in the area at this price, particularly suited for families, writers and dreamers, 24-hr email available. Highly recommended. **B-C** *China*, 19/27-28 Sukhumvit Soi 19, T2557571, F2541333. A/c, restaurant, a small hotel masquerading as a large one, but rooms are up to the standard of more expensive places, so good value. Beware the karaoke lounge. **B-C** *City Lodge*, Sukhumvit Soi 9, citylodge9@amari.com A fairly smart, small hotel with bright rooms and a personal feel. Good room discounts at time of writing. The absence of a pool is counteracted by free access to the pool at the *Amari Boulevard*. Trendy pasta and noodle restaurant (see **Eating**). **B-C** *Parkway Inn*, 132 Sukhumvit Rd, T2553711, F2542180. Small establishment centred around the bar, which is a cross between an English pub lounge and Thai decor, basic rooms, book exchange. **B-C** *Nana*, 4 Sukhumvit Soi Nana Tai (Soi 4), T2520121, F2551769. A/c, coffee bar, cocktail bar, disco, shops, pool and travel agency. Frequented by dozens of unregistered female guests, like the *Grace* this hotel has a long-standing reputation for its links with the sex industry.

C *Bangkok Inn*, 12-13 Sukhumvit Soi 11/1, T2544884, F2543544. German management, clean, basic rooms, with a/c, TV and attached shower. **C** *Miami*, 2 Sukhumvit Soi 13, T2530369, F2531266. A/c, a distinctly run-down hotel, but quite good value considering its central Sukhumvit location. Reasonable pool. **C** *World Inn*, 131 Sukhumvit Soi 7/1, T2535391, F2637728. Basic rooms with the standard TV, minibar and en suite bathroom. Coffee shop with Thai and western food. **C-D** *Crown Hotel*, Sukhumvit Soi Lahet 29, friendly with transport-style café, a/c rooms, nothing special even by backpacker standards. **C-D** *Reno Hotel*, Rama 1 Soi Kasemsan 40, T2150026, F2153430, a/c, laundry, etc, grocery store on site.

Khaosan Road lies northeast of Sanaam Luang, just off Rachdamnern Klang Ave, close to the Democracy Monument. It is continually expanding into new roads and sois, in particular the area west of Chakrapong Rd. The *sois* off the main road are often quieter, such as Soi Chana Songkhran or Soi Rambutri. Note that rooms facing on to Khaosan Rd tend to be very noisy. Khaosan Rd is not just a place to spend the night. Also here are multitudes of restaurants, travel and tour agents, shops, stalls, tattoo artists, bars, bus companies – almost any and every service a traveller might need. (Note that toiletries and bottled water, etc are considerably cheaper in the Thai supermarkets, just outside the main tourist drag.) In general, the guesthouses of Khaosan Rd itself have been eclipsed in terms of quality and cleanliness by those to the north, closer to the river. The useful little post office that used to be at the top of Khaosan Rd and operated a Poste Restante service and a fax facility has recently closed; whether it will reopen is not certain.

Banglamphu (Khaosan Road) & surrounds

AL *Royal Princess*, 269 Lan Luang Rd, T2813088, F2801314. A/c, restaurants, pool, part of the Dusit chain of hotels, good facilities and good deals if booked through

Khaosan Road

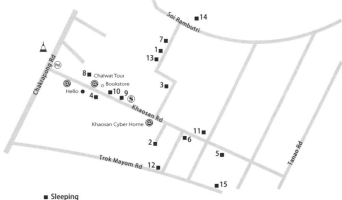

■ **Sleeping**
1 Arunothai (AT) Guesthouse	6 Dior Guesthouse	11 Nat Guesthouse
2 Bonny Guesthouse	7 Green House	12 Sawasdee Krungthep Inn
3 Buddy	8 Hello	13 Suneeporn Guesthouse
4 Chart Guesthouse	9 Lek Guesthouse	14 Viengtai Hotel
5 CH Guesthouse	10 Mam's Guesthouse	15 7 Holder Guesthouse

Related map
Bangkok General,
page 74
Banglamphu,
page 127

N
Not to scale

Khaosan Road: a world of its own

Banglamphu, as the place for backpackers to stay, dates from the mid-1970s. The Viengtai Hotel opened in 1962, and as it gained a reputation for budget accommodation, so some local families began to rent out rooms to tourists. Most of these places were concentrated along Khaosan Road, which as Marc Askew has written in his study The Banglamphu District: a portrait of change in inner Bangkok (TDRI, 1993), soon became known as Thanon Farang Khaosan. As he explains, and which is evident from first sight: "There is nothing Thai about the character of Khao San Road: everything is for the Farang, from the clothing, the jewellery, to the food. Most local residents in surrounding neighbourhoods tend to keep the road at an arms length and do not claim a close familiarity with it ..." Prior to this transformation Khaosan Road was an ordinary street of middle-class Thai educated families, with a commercial specialization of dress-making and tailoring. Today, the tourist focus has spilt over into surrounding streets, particularly to the north and east. The Tourist Authority of Thailand estimated at the beginning of the 1990s that there were 83 guesthouses in the area and that 238,000 tourists stayed in the district each year. The irony perhaps is that the group of tourists which is usually perceived to live closest to the Thai way of living – backpackers – have helped to create a world which is wholly their own.

Vieng Travel. **A** *Royal*, 2 Rachdamnern Klang Ave, T2229111, F2242083, www.rattanakosin-hotel.com (*Rattanakosin* is the name of the hotel in Thai). A/c, restaurant, pool. Another old (by Bangkok standards) hotel which acted as a refuge for demonstrators during the 1991 riots. Rooms are dated and featureless. This hotel is popular amongst Thais. **A** *Viengtai*, 42 Tanee Rd, Banglamphu, T2815788. A/c, restaurant, pool. Rooms here are good, if a little worn, clean and relatively spacious, with all the advantages of this area in terms of proximity to the Old City. Helpful management.

B *Pra Arthit Mansion*, 22 Phra Arthit Rd, T2800744, F2800742. Leafy though slightly dated hotel, popular with German tour operators. Rooms are good value with all the trimmings. Well-run with helpful management. **B** *Trang Hotel*, 99/1 Visutkaset Rd, T28221414, F2803610, www.trang-hotel.co.th A/c, restaurant, pool. Clean and friendly mid-range hotel which comes recommended by regular visitors to Bangkok. It opened way back in 1962 but is still a good establishment at this price. Discount vouchers available from *Vieng Travel* in the same building, with breakfast included.

C *New Siam*, Phra Arthit 21 Soi Chana Songkram, T2824554, F2817461. Some a/c, good restaurant, modern and clean, friendly and helpful staff, airy rooms, but featureless block with scarcely an ounce of atmosphere. Extensive services include tickets and tour information, fax facilities, email, lockers available. Quiet and a popular place – but it remains overpriced. **C-E** *Baan Sabai*, 12 Soi Rongmai, T6291599, F6291595, baansabai@hotmail.com A large, colonial style building with a green pillared entrance in front. Construction work being done on a new building at the back at the time of writing. Although it is not very expensive, it is not the typical backpacker's scene. Rooms are simple but large and airy. Storage is available at ฿10 per bag/suitcase. Occasionally local Thai bands are invited to play here. **C-E** *Chart Guesthouse*, 58 Khaosan Rd, T2803785. Restaurant, some a/c, majority of rooms are directly over a busy restaurant, so it can be noisy till early in the morning. Some rooms are small and a bit tatty, others are relatively spacious by Khaosan standards, while still others have no windows – so ask to see a range. **C-E** *New World Lodge Hotel and Guesthouse*, 2 Samsen Rd, T2815596 (hotel), T2812128 (guesthouse), F2825614, www.new-lodge.com Some hotel rooms have a/c whereas the guesthouse only offers fans, good location for the Old City yet away from the hurly-burly of Khaosan Rd. Not particularly inviting or characterful, rooms are large but barren and beginning to look worn. The Lodge has satellite TV for a higher price. Safety boxes are free for guests, as is the use of a small but worn-out gym. **C-E** *Sawasdee House*, 147 Chakrapong Soi Rambutri, T2818138, F6290994, sawasdee_house@hotmail.com Feels like a cross between a guesthouse and a hotel. Shared loos and showers are kept clean, and rooms, though box-like, are fine. Outside at the front is an atmospheric, wooden lounging area and beer 'garden'. Cocktails are slightly overpriced, but jazz and reggae music at night may make it worth the extra. This place has all the travellers' trimmings – email, travel service, TV, etc. **C-E** *Sawasdee Krungthep Inn*, 30 Praathi Rd, T6290072, F6290079. Recently opened, with a lively communal atmosphere. Clean and simple rooms, all with cable TV. Family rooms available with 2 double beds for ฿560.

D *My House*, 37 Phra Arthit Soi Chana Songkram, T2829263. Helpful and friendly management, rooms are very clean and the place maintains excellent standards of cleanliness. Popular, good travel service (minibus to airport every hour). **D** *7 Holder*, 216/2-3 Khaosan Rd, T2813682. Some a/c, some rooms a little grubby, but clean shared toilets. Friendly, located on the narrow soi behind Khaosan Rd, so quieter than those places situated right on the street. **D-E** *Arunthai (AT)*, 90/1, 5, 12 Khaosan Soi

Banglamphu & Ayutthaya Road

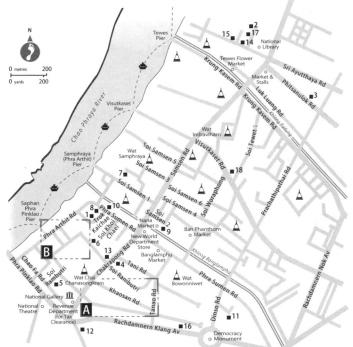

■ **Sleeping**

1 Apple II Guesthouse	7 Home & Garden & River Guesthouse
2 Backpacker's Lodge	8 KC Guesthouse
3 Bangkok Youth Hostel	9 New World Lodge
4 BK Guesthouse	10 PS Guesthouse
5 Chai's House	11 Pra Suri Guesthouse
6 Chusri Guesthouse	12 Royal

13 Sawasdee House	
14 Sawatdee Guesthouse	
15 Shanti Lodge	
16 Sweety Guesthouse	
17 Tavee Guesthouse	
18 Trang	

Related maps
Bangkok General,
page 74
Khaosan Road,
page 125
B Phra Arthit
Road,
page 128

Bangkok

Rambutri, T2826979. Situated in a quiet little courtyard with 4 or 5 other guesthouses. Rooms are adequate but staff are unfriendly. **D-E** *Buddy*, 137/1 Khaosan Rd, T2824351. Off main street, some a/c, rooms are small and dingy but it remains popular for some reason. Large open restaurant area bustles with people exchanging information. **D-E** *Chai's House*, 49/4-8 Chao Fa Soi Rongmai, last house down Soi Rambutri, so away from the competition, T2814901, F2818686. Some a/c, friendly atmosphere. Rooms are in traditional Thai style, with wood panelling. They vary in size but are clean and the a/c rooms are good value. Colourful with bougainvillea growing from the balconies and bamboos and orchids in the restaurant, making it a cool, quiet and relaxing place to eat. Recommended. **D-E** *CH Guesthouse*, 216/1 Khaosan Rd, T2822023. Some a/c, good reputation, and very popular – fully booked on our last visit, so unable to check the rooms. Probably the cheapest dorm rooms on Khaosan Rd. Left luggage (₿7 per day, ₿40 per week). **D-E** *Green House*, 88/1 Khaosan Soi Rambutri, T2819572. Some a/c. Rooms are spacious but variable, and some can be quite noisy. Helpful staff and a large and airy restaurant with a pleasant sitting area (a/c with TV and books). **D-E** *Hello*, 63-65 Khaosan Rd, T2818579. Some a/c, popular place, which means that we were unable to check rooms on our last visit. Internet café and popular restaurant with big screen downstairs (7 films shown daily). **D-E** *New Merry V*, 18-20 Phra Athit Rd, T2829267, merryv@loxinfo.co.th Adequately sized rooms but many are dark with windows facing onto an unlit shaft within the building (make sure the slats and curtains into the shaft are shut if you don't want to share everything with your neighbours). Excellent baguettes at cheap prices in the restaurant downstairs. **D-E** *Peachy Guesthouse*, 10 Phra Athit Rd, T2816659. Some a/c, the courtyard – which was its selling point – is starting to look neglected. Rooms are large but dark if you don't have a window, but clean. **D-E** *Pra Suri Guesthouse*, 85/1 Soi Pra Suri (off Dinso Rd), T2801428, F2801428. 5 mins east of Khaosan Rd not far from the Democracy Monument, fan, restaurant, own bathrooms (no hot water), clean, spacious and quiet, very friendly and helpful family-run travellers' guesthouse with all the services to match – videos, travel details, western food. Recommended. **D-E** *Privacy Tourist House*, 69 Tanow Rd, T2827028. Popular, quiet. Recommended. **D-E** *Sawasdee Smile Inn*, 35 Soi Rongmai, T6292340, F6292341. Large, spacious, sitting area in front under a gaudy looking green, Thai-style roof. Restaurant and 24 hr bar, so ask for a room at the back if you want an early night. Rooms are clean and simple, all with cable TV. Free safety boxes available.

E *Dior*, 146-158 Khaosan Rd, T2829142. Tiny, dirty rooms, unhelpful staff, avoid. **E** *KC Guesthouse*, 60-64 Phra Sumen Rd Soi Khai Chae, T2820618, kc_guesthouse @hotmail.com Small friendly place with a cosy and personal ambiance. Rooms and toilets are clean and well kept. Not far enough off the main road to be quiet. **E** *Lek*, 90/9 Khaosan Soi Rambutri, T2812775. Up a long flight of steps off the main road. Rooms are clean but boxy. Rooms at the front can suffer from the noise of Khaosan Rd. Helpful staff and friendly atmosphere, popular. **E** *Mam's*, 119 Khaosan Rd, double rooms only. Adequately clean, and friendly staff. Some

Phra Arthit Road

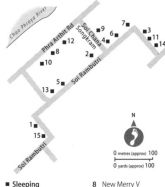

■ **Sleeping**	8 New Merry V
1 Baan Sabai	9 New Siam
2 Bella Bella	10 Peachy Guesthouse
3 Chusri Guesthouse	11 Popiang House
4 Green Guesthouse	12 Pra Arthit Mansion
5 Krungthop Inn	13 Rose Garden
6 Merry V	14 Sawasdee House
7 My House	15 Sawasdee Smile Inn

rooms are a little dark and noisy. **E** *Merry V*, 33-35 Phra Arthit Soi Chana Songkram, T2829267. Clean, tidy and cheap. Some rooms with good views out over the city from the upper floor balconies, although not from the rooms (some of which have no windows), which are small and dirty around the edges. Toilets kept clean. A well run place with good information. **E** *Nat*, 217 Khaosan Rd. Small, stuffy rooms which face onto a balcony overhanging the restaurant (thus noise disturbance into the early hours). **E** *PS Guesthouse*, 9 Phra Sumen Rd, T2823932. Kept clean and well-run, with good security. Rooms at the back have windows over the river (but it's not scenic). Some rooms have no windows. Aligns with main road, so noisy at the front. There is an airy, open restaurant in the front downstairs that does some of the best filtered coffee in the area (almost everywhere else serves instant sachets of Nescafé). It offers an international and reasonably priced menu, and guests may help out in the kitchen if they want to learn a bit of Thai cookery on the side. **E** *Suneeporn*, 90/10 Khaosan Soi Rambutri, T2826887. The entrance looks like a junk shop, with a ramshackle, characterful appearance. Run by a friendly old lady who keeps the rooms and toilets clean. Quiet location and recommended by guests. **E** *Sweety*, 49 Thani Rd, sandwiched between 2 roads, so noisy. Rooms are large and clean, with adequately clean shared toilets. **E-F** *Apple 2 Guesthouse*, 11 Phra Sumen Rd, T2811219. Quite hard to find: if you turn off Phra Arthit Rd, take the soi opposite Baan Chaophraya (with Compost 9 in front of it). If turning off the Phra Sumen Rd, take Trok Kaichee (soi). Not to be confused with *Apple*, which is grimy and unfriendly. Very friendly management (run by the same lady for 20 years, who exercises a tough love policy), this place, with its homely feel and quiet, clean rooms in an old wooden house, remains a firm favourite. Dorm beds available. **E-F** *Bonny*, 132 Khaosan Rd, T2819877. Situated down a narrow alley off Khaosan itself, a quiet location and family-run, but rooms are dirty. Cheap dorm beds available. **E-F** *Chusri Guesthouse*, 1-2 Soi Rambutri, T2829941, chusri_gh@hotmail.com Rooms are very simple, but not particularly clean. Cheap and open restaurant area in front. **E-F** *Green Guesthouse*, 27 Phra Arthit Soi Chana Songkram, T2828994. Not to be confused with the *Green House*, rooms are very small but are clean and cheap. **E-F** *Home and Garden*, 16 Samphraya Rd (Samsen 3), T2801475. Away from the main concentration of guesthouses, down a quiet soi, a small house in a delightful leafy compound and with a homely atmosphere. The rooms are a fair size with large windows, some face onto a balcony. Friendly owner and excellent value. Recommended. **E-F** *The River Guesthouse*, 18 Samphraya Rd (Samsen 3), T2800876. A small, family house with a homely and friendly atmosphere. Small but clean rooms. **F** *Clean and Calm Guesthouse*, 17 Samphraya Rd (Samsen 3), T2822093. It may be clean and calm, but this is probably due to the lack of visitors as there is no communal area.

Sri Ayutthaya Road

Sri Ayutthaya is emerging as an 'alternative' area for budget travellers. It is a central location with restaurants and foodstalls nearby, but does not suffer the over-crowding and sheer pandemonium of Khaosan Road and so is considerably quieter and more peaceful. It is also close to the Tewes Pier for the express river boats (see the Banglamphu map). The guesthouses are, overall, a little more expensive than those in Khaosan Road but the rooms are better and the places seem to be generally better managed. One family runs 4 of the guesthouses, and with a 5th one opening nearby in Nov 2000, this means that if one is full you will probably be moved on to another.

D-E *Shanti Lodge*, 37 Sri Ayutthaya Rd, T2812497. Reservation necessary during high season. Range of rooms from large a/c rooms to dorm beds for ฿80. Most rooms are housed in an old wooden house full of character. Rooms are clean and cosy and there is an attractive garden. Friendly management. Expensive but good restaurant with extensive menu (and a turtle). Very popular (particularly with long-term guests), good location for bus connections. Recommended. **D-F** *Bangkok Youth Hostel*, 25/2 Phitsanulok Rd (off Samsen Rd), T2820950. North of Khaosan Rd, away from the bustle, the dorm beds are great value (฿90) being newly furnished and with a/c. Other rooms are clean, small and basic and remain good value. If you don't have a valid YHA membership card, it will cost an extra ฿50 per night. **D-F** *Tavee*, 83 Sri Ayutthaya Rd, Soi 14, T2825983. Restaurant, a quiet, relaxed, and respectable place with a small garden and a number of fish tanks. Friendly management – a world away from the chaos of Khaosan Rd. The Tavee family keep the rooms and shared bathrooms immaculately clean and are a good source of information for travellers. Dorms are also available for ฿80 per night. This place has been operating since 1985 and has managed to maintain a very high standard. Highly recommended.

E *Backpackers Lodge*, 85 Sri Ayutthaya Rd, Soi 14, T2823231. Very similar to its neighbour, *Tavee* (whose owner is brother of the *Backpackers'* manager). The rooms are a little small but it has friendly service and there is an intimate feel to the place. Quiet and recommended. **E** *Sawatdee*, 71 Sri Ayutthaya Rd, T2825349. Western menu, pokey rooms, popular with German travellers, management brusque and off-hand.

Others   **NB** For hotels at, or close to, the airport, see page 23.

L *Central Plaza Hotel*, 1695 Phahonyothin Rd, T5411234, F5411087, centel @ksc5.th.com   Out of town, close to Chatuchak Market, huge 600-room block, pool, fitness centre, tennis, jogging track, 18-hole golf course, extensive business/conference facilities, good location for shopping either in Central Plaza or at the market. **L** *Merchant Court Hotel*, 202 Ratchadapisek Rd, Huay Kwang, T694222, F6942223, www.merchantcourthotels.com   Recently renovated hotel (which used to be *Le Concorde*), struggling with low occupancy rates, but banking on the opening of the underground by 2002 which will mean a station right outside the hotel and and an easy link to the skytrain and other areas of the city. Impeccably high standard, with friendly staff, faultless rooms and good facilities including pool and gym. A spa on the fourth floor will be completed by the time this book goes to press. Meeting rooms and conference amenities also extensive. *Doc Cheng's* restaurant (original one to be found in Raffles Hotel, Singapore) provides sumptuous fusion food (see entry in restaurant section). 24-hr coffee shop and Japanese restaurant. 50% off rack rate through 2001. **A-B** *Ramada Renaissance Bridge View*, 3999 Rama III Rd, T2923160, F2923164. A/c, numerous restaurants, pools, tennis, squash, new 476 room high-rise overlooking Chao Phraya River, all facilities, poor location for sights, shopping and business.

C-E *The Artists Club*, 61 Soi Tiem Boon Yang, T8620056. Some a/c, run by an artist, this is a guesthouse cum studio cum gallery in Thonburi (ie the other side of the river), clean rooms and a really alternative place to stay with concerts and drawing lessons, away from the centre of guesthouse activity.

Eating

Bangkok has the largest and widest selection of restaurants in Thailand – everyone eats out, so the number of places is vast. Food is generally very good and cheap – this applies not just to Thai restaurants but also to places serving other Asian cuisines, and western dishes. Roadside food is good value – many Thais eat on the street, businessmen and civil servants rubbing shoulders with factory workers and truck drivers.

Until a few years ago, with one or two notable exceptions, it was best to recommend that visitors stick to Thai restaurants if they are gastronomes who know their foie gras from their fettucini. This has changed. There is now a good range of excellent restaurants in the city and an increasing number of first-rate foreign chefs.

NB Many restaurants – especially Thai ones – close between 2200 and 2230. Many of the more expensive restaurants listed here take credit cards. Not that most bars also

Bangkok

● ●

Buffet meals in Bangkok

The following restaurants offer buffet 'eat all you like' meals. They are often very good value. Phone to check. The prices quoted are 2000 prices; children are usually charged half price or less and under 12s are sometimes allowed to gorge gratis. Daily newspapers also often provide information on new promotions as do listings magazines like Bangkok Timeout.

Sukhumvit Road

Ambassador Café, Ambassador Hotel, T2540444. Buffet Amercian breakfast (฿210), international lunch (฿260) and seafood dinner (฿300).
Grand Pacific Hotel, T6511000. Buffet Sunday brunch (฿480).
Tara Coffee Shop, Imperial Tara Hotel, T2592900. Porridge buffet Monday-Saturday, 1800-2400 (฿200).
Atrium, Landmark Hotel, T2540404. International lunch buffet (฿515).

Silom, Suriwong and Charoen Krung roads

The Pavilion, Dusit Thani Hotel, T2360450. Changing buffet themes, lunch and dinner (around ฿450-500)
Coffee Garden and Mae Nam Terrace,

Shangri-La Hotel, T2367777. Sunday brunch featuring Asian dishes as well as international cuisine (฿625).

Sathorn and Wittayu roads

Café Laurel, Evergreen Laurel Hotel, T2669988. International buffet, Monday-Friday (฿380)
Colonnade Restaurant, The Sukhothai, T2870222. Sunday brunch – one of the classiest (฿950).

Phetburi, Rama 1, Ploenchit and Rachdamri roads

The Garden Bar, Indra Regent Hotel, T2080022. International buffet, daily lunch and dinner.
Sivalai Restaurant, Siam Intercontinental Hotel, T2530355. Special children oriented Sunday brunch (฿450).
The Dining Room, Grand Hyatt Erawan Hotel, T2541234. Sunday brunch, live music (฿650).
The Expresso, Le Royal Meridien Hotel, T6560444. Sunday brunch with live music (฿690).

Sri Ayutthaya Road

Patummat Restaurant, Siam City Hotel, T2470123. Sunday brunch (฿580).

● ●

serve food. For those with either a large or an empty stomach who want a blow out, a number of restaurants, especially in hotels, offer (usually lunchtime) good-value buffet meals where you can eat till you drop or explode. See the box on page 131 for a listing. For a fuller listing of places to eat see *Bangkok Metro Magazine* or *Bangkok Timeout*, both published monthly. The former is better. Both magazines are also good for bars, music venues, shopping, etc.

For bars with live music also see *Music*, below, under **Entertainment**, page 141.

The greatest concentration of bars are in the 2 'red light' districts of Bangkok – Patpong (between Silom and Surawong roads) and Soi Cowboy (Sukhumvit). Patpong was transformed from a street of 'tea houses' (brothels serving local clients) into a high-tech lane of go-go bars in 1969 when an American made a major investment. In fact there are 2 streets, side-by-side, Patpong 1 and Patpong 2. Patpong 1 is the larger and more active, with a host of stalls down the middle at night (see page 145); Patpong 2 supports cocktail bars and, appropriately, pharmacies and clinics for STDs, as well as a few go-go bars. The *Derby King* is one of the most popular with expats and serves what are reputed to be the best club sandwiches in Asia, if not the world. Opposite Patpong, along Convent Rd is *Delaney's*, an Irish pub with draft Guinness from Malaysia (where it is brewed) and a limited menu, good atmosphere and well-patronized by Bangkok's expats – sofas for lounging and reading (upstairs). Limited and predictable menu – beef and guinness pie, etc. ■ *Daily 1100-0200*. *O'Reilly's* , corner of Silom and Thaniya is another themed Irish pub, run by a Thai

Silom, Surawong & the River
See map page 116

Bangkok

 Food Courts

If you want a cheap meal with lots of choice, then a food court is a good place to start. They are often found along with supermarkets and in shopping malls. Buy coupons and then use these to purchase your food from one of the many stalls – any unused coupons can be redeemed. A single-dish Thai meal like fried rice or noodles should cost around ฿25-30. The more sophisticated shopping malls will have stalls servings a wider geographical range of cuisines including, for example, Japanese and Korean. There are food courts in the following (and many more) places:	Mah Boon Krong (MBK), Phayathai Rd (just west of Siam Square, BTS Siam station) Panthip Plaza, Phetburi Road Ploenchit Centre, 2 Ploenchit Road (BTS Nana station) Robinson, 139 Ratchadapisek Road Siam Discovery Centre, Rama 1 Road (BTS Siam station) The Garden Terrace, The Emporium, 622 Sukhumvit Road (corner of Soi 24) United Centre Building, 323 Silom Road (near intersection with Convent Road, BTS Sala Daeng station) World Trade Centre, Ratchdamri Road (BTS Chitlom station).

(Chak) but with all the usual cultural accoutrements – Guinness and Kilkenney, rugby on the satellite, etc. ■ *0800-0200*.

Soi Cowboy is named after the first bar here, the ***Cowboy Bar***, established by a retired US Air Force officer. Although some of the bars also offer other forms of entertainment (something that quickly becomes blindingly obvious), there are, believe it or not, some excellent and very reasonably priced bars in these two areas. A small beer will cost ฿45-65, with good (if loud) music and perhaps videos thrown in for free. However, if opting for a bar with a 'show', be prepared to pay considerably more.

Warning Front men will assure customers that there is no entrance charge and a beer is only ฿60 (or whatever), but you can be certain that they will try to fleece you on the way out and can become aggressive if you refuse to pay. Even experienced Bangkok travellers find themselves in this predicament. Massages and more can also be obtained at many places in the Patpong and Soi Cowboy areas. **NB** AIDS is a significant and growing problem in Thailand so it is strongly recommended that customers practice safe sex (see page 54).

Expensive *Angelini*, *Shangri-La Hotel*, 89 Soi Wat Suan Plu, T2367777, open 1130 'till late', one of the most popular **Italian** restaurants in town – a lively place with open kitchens, pizza oven and the usual range of dishes. Menu could be more imaginative. ***Dusit Thani Thai Restaurant***, 946 Rama IV Rd. Beautiful surroundings – like an old Thai palace, exquisite **Thai** food, very expensive wines. ***Bussaracum***, 139 Pan Rd (off Silom Rd), T2666312. **Thai**, changing menu, popular, classy Thai restaurant with prices to match. Recommended. *La Normandie*, *Oriental Hotel*, 48 Oriental Avenue, T2360400. **French** food. Despite many competitors, *La Normandie* maintains extremely high standards of cuisine and service (with guest chefs from around the world), jacket and tie required in the evening but the service is still not overbearing. Very refined and while it is expensive for Thailand it is not pricey considering the quality of the food and service – set lunch and dinner menus are the best value. Open Mon-Sat for lunch and dinner and Sun for dinner. Recommended. ***Thaniya Garden Restaurant***, Thaniya Plaza, 3rd Floor, Room 333-335, 52 Silom Rd, T2312201. Open Mon-Sat 1100-2200, excellent **Thai** food and enormous portions. ***Trader Vic's***, *Marriott Riverside Hotel*, 257/1-3 Charoen Nakhon Rd, T4760021. Bangkok's only restaurant serving **Polynesian** food which is seafood based and takes inspiration from Chinese culinary traditions. Open for lunch and dinner (1200-1400, 1800-2230). *Le Bouchon*, 37/17 Patpong 2, T2349109, open daily

1100-0200, **French** country cuisine (Provence), family run, reasonable prices. *Once Upon a Time*, 32 Phetburi Soi 17 (opposite Pantip Plaza), T2528629. Up-market and inventive **Thai** cuisine including seafood soufflé in coconut and more traditional dishes like a delectable duck curry. Open for lunch and dinner, Tues-Sun. *The Barbican*, 9/4-5 Soi Thaniya, Thaniya Plaza, Silom Rd, T2343590. Chic café bistro with duck, steaks, sophisticated sandwiches, fish, open 1100-0200, DJ on Thu, Fri and Sat evenings. *Zanotti*, 21/2 Sala Daeng Colonnade, Silom Soi Sala Daeng, T6360002. Sophisticated **Italian** restaurant just off Silom Rd with wide-ranging menu including pizzas and pasta, risotto dishes, meat and poultry, all served in a clean modern atmosphere (no raffia chianti bottles here) with starched table clothes in a renovated early 20th-century building. Open daily for lunch and dinner. *Anna's*, 118 Silom Soi Sala Daeng, T6320619. Great **Thai-cum-fusion** restaurant in a vegetation-surrounded villa off Silom Rd named after Anna of *King & I* fame. Some classic Thai dishes like *laap*, *nua yaang* and *somtam* along with fusion dishes such as Alaska clams and western food including apple crumble and banoffee pie. Refined atmosphere and a good place to linger for coffee and conversation. Open daily 1100-2200. *Bua Restaurant*, Convent Rd (off Silom Rd). Classy post-modern **Thai** restaurant with starched white table linen and cool, minimalist lines, the food also reflects the decor (or the other way around?): refined and immaculately prepared. *T.G.I. Friday's*, Kamol Sukosol Building, 317 Silom Rd, T2667488. Large and popular American joint with burgers, Cajun food, pasta, steaks and salads. Frozen drinks too. Open 1100-0200.

Mid-range *Banana Leaf*, Silom complex (basement floor), Silom Rd, T3213124. Excellent and very popular **Thai** restaurant with some unusual dishes, including *kai manaaw* (chicken in lime sauce), *nam tok muu* (spicy pork salad, Isan style) and fresh spring rolls 'Banana Leaf', along with excellent and classic *laap kai* (minced chicken Isan style), booking recommended for lunch. There are several excellent **Thai** restaurants in *Silom Village*, a shopping mall, on Silom Rd (north side, opposite Pan Rd), excellent range of food from hundreds of stalls, all cooked in front of you, enjoyable village atmosphere. Recommended. *Ban Krua*, 29/1 Saladaeng Soi 1, Silom Rd. Simple decor, friendly atmosphere, a/c room, traditional **Thai** food, unfortunately the old garden sitting area has gone. *Le Basil*, Silom Complex, basement, Silom Rd, T2313114. **Vietnamese** food. Recommended. *Batavia*, 1/2 Convent Rd, T2667164. 'Imported' **Indonesian** chefs, good classic dishes like *saté*, *gado-gado* (vegetable with peanut sauce and rice) and *ayam goreng* (deep-fried chicken). *Bobby's Arms*, 2nd Floor, Car Park Building, Patpong 2 Rd, T2336828. **English pub** and grill, with jazz on Sun from 2000, open 1100-0100. Roast beef, fish and chips, pies and mixed grill – in other words English food which is increasingly difficult to get in the more chic restaurants in London. *Le Café de Paris*, Patpong 2 Rd, T2372776. Traditional **French** food from steaks to pâté. Open for lunch and dinner, daily. Recommended. *Himali Cha Cha*, 1229/11 Charoen Krung, T2351569. Good choice of **Indian** cuisine, mountainous meals for the very hungry, originally set up by Cha Cha and now run by his son – 'from generation to generation' as it is quaintly put. *MK*, Silom Complex, basement, Silom Rd. **Thai**. Very popular DIY restaurant. *Ristorante Sorrento*, 66 North Sathorn Rd (next to the Evergreen Laural Hotel), T2349841. Excellent **Italian** food along with imported steaks. *Shangarila*, 154/4-7 Silom Rd, T2340861. Bustling **Shanghai** restaurant with dim sum lunch. *Side Walk*, 855/2 Silom Rd (opposite *Central Dept Store*). **Thai**. Grilled specialities, also serves French. Recommended. *Sweet Basil* (branch at Sukhumvit also, see above) 1 Silom Soi Srivieng (opposite Bangkok Christian College), T2383088. **Vietnamese** food in an attractive 1930s era house with live music. Open daily for lunch and dinner. *Terrazzo*, *Sukhothai Hotel*, 13/3 South Sathorn Rd, T2870222. Stylish al fresco **Italian** restaurant overlooking the pool, wonderful Italian breads and good pasta dishes. Recommended.

Cheap *Banana House*, Silom Rd/Thaniya Rd (2nd floor). Very good and reasonably priced **Thai** food; few tourists here but lots of locals. *Isn't Classic*, 154 Silom Rd. Excellent BBQ, king prawns and **Isan** specialities like spicy papaya salad (*somtam*). *Nawab*, 64/39 Soi Wat Suan Plu, Charoen Krung. **North and South Indian** dishes. *Harmonique*, 22 Charoen Krung. Small elegant **coffee shop** with good music, fruit drinks and coffee. *Rung Pueng*, 37 Saladaeng, Soi 2, Silom Rd. Traditional **Thai** food at reasonable prices. *Tia Maria*, 14/18 Patpong Soi 1, T2588977. For the price, this is the best **Mexican** restaurant in Bangkok. Nachos, *enchiladas*, *fajitas* and more of the usual. Open daily for lunch and dinner 1100-2300. *Tamil Nadu*, 5/1 Silom Soi (Tambisa) 11, T2356336. Good, but limited **South Indian** menu, cheap and filling, *dosas* are recommended, there are 4 or 5 **Indian** restaurants in a row on Sukhumvit Soi 11.

Afternoon tea and morning coffee *The Authors' Lounge*, Oriental Hotel. Also for afternoon tea go to the *Dusit Thani Hotel* library, Rama IV Rd. *Starbucks*, six branches by 2000 and more opening as the drug spreads: Central Plaza, Phahonyothin Rd (Lad Phrao); Sivadol Building, Convent Rd (off Silom); 54 Surawong Rd (5 mins from Sala Daeng BTS station); Central Chitlom, Ploenchit Rd; Bumrungrad Hospital, Sukhumvit Soi 3 (Nana BTS station) Amarin Plaza, Ploenchit Rd – Californian coffee culture comes to Bangkok. **Bakeries** *Jimmy*, 1270-2, near Oriental Lane, Charoen Krung. A/c, **cakes** and **ice creams**, very little else around here, so it's a good stopping place.

Bars A particularly civilized place to have a beer and watch the sun go down is on the veranda of the *Oriental Hotel*, by the banks of the Chao Phraya River, expensive, but romantic (and strict dress code of no backpacks, no flip flops and no T-shirts). *Boh*, Tha Tien, Chao Phraya Express Boat Pier, Maharat Rd, open 1900-2400. A popular student hangout, with good sunset views over Wat Arun. *Hyper*, 114/14 Silom Soi 4, a very trendy joint, popular with celebrities. *King's Castle*, Patpong 1 Rd. Another long-standing **bar** with core of regulars. *Royal Salute*, Patpong 2 Rd. **Cocktail bar** where local *farangs* end their working days.

Soi Ngam Duphli
See map page 119

Expensive *Chandraphen*, Rama 1V Rd, popular, classy, catering for a superior clientele. Expensive but worth it. *Ratstube*, Goetegasse, German food, good quality but rather pricey. *Basement Pub* (and restaurant), 946 Rama IV Rd. A **bar** with live music, also serves international food, open 1800-2400.

Bakeries *Folies*, 309/3 Soi Nang Linchee (Yannawa) off southern end of Soi Ngam Duphli, T2869786. French expats and bake-o-philes maintain that this bakery makes the most authentic **pastries** and **breads** in town, coffee available, a great place to sit, eat and read.

Siam Square, Rama I, Ploenchit & Phetburi
See map page 120

Expensive *Spice Market*, Regent Hotel, 155 Rachdamri Rd, T2516127. **Westernized Thai**, typical hotel decoration, arguably the city's best Thai food – simply delectable. If the lists of dishes bamboozle, then choose the excellent set menu. Open daily for lunch and dinner. *Biscotti*, Regent Hotel, 155 Rachdamri Rd, T2555443. **Italian 'fusion'**, a second superb restaurant at this top-class hotel. Cuisine here is difficult to categorise. The chef is Italian and while there are pizzas and porcini mushrooms, there is also salmon and smoked duck. Excellent. *The Bay*, 2032 New Phetburi Rd, T7160802, **American** restaurant but serving more than just the usual burgers and fries – pork, duck, seafood, attached micro-brewery and live music in the evening from 2130. Good atmosphere, enjoyable decor. *Paesano*, 96/7 Soi Tonson (off Soi Langsuan), Ploenchit Rd, T2522834. **Italian** food in friendly atmosphere. This long-established restaurant has a loyal following and is very popular with *farangs* and westernized Thais. Our last visit was a mediocre culinary experience, but many disagree and come here time and again.   *Pho*, 2F Alma Link Building, 25 Soi Chidlom, T2518900.

Supporters claim this place (there are three other branches) serves the best **Vietnamese** in town even though the owner is not Vietnamese herself, but Thai. Modern trendy setting, non-smoking area. Open daily for lunch and dinner. *Wit's Oyster Bar*, 20/10 Ruamrudee Village, T2519455. Bangkok's first and only **Oyster Bar**, run by an eccentric Thai, one of the few places where you can eat late, good salmon fishcakes, international cuisine. *Ma Maison*, 2 Witthayu Rd, T2530123. Classic **French** cuisine from duck escoffier to wild mushroom soup and great soufflés. Restaurant is in a traditional Thai teak house which adds something to the ambience. Pricey. Open for lunch and dinner Mon-Sat and dinner only on Sun. *Thai on 4*, Amari Watergate Hotel, 847 Phetburi Rd, T6539000, classy, modernist restaurant on the 4th floor of this hotel. The food is excellent: some very traditional, some more like nouvelle cuisine, bordering on fusion. Pricey for Thai but good value for a hotel restaurant with high standards. The laid-back jazz music gives lie to the image the restaurant is trying to project.

Mid-range *Bali*, 20/11 Ruamrudee Village, Soi Ruamrudee, Ploenchit Rd, T2500711. Those who know say that this is the only authentic **Indonesian** food in Bangkok. Friendly proprietress and a charming old-style house with garden. Open for Mon-Sat for lunch and dinner and Sun for dinner only. *Ban Khun Phor*, 458/7-9 Siam Square Soi 8, T2501732. Good **Thai** food in stylish surroundings. *China*, 231/3 Rachdamri Soi Sarasin. Bangkok's oldest **Chinese** restaurant, serving full range of Chinese cuisine. *Hard Rock Café*, 424/3-6 Siam Square Soi 11, T2510792. Home-from-home for all burger-starved *farangs*, overpriced, videos, live music sometimes, and all the expected paraphernalia, a couple of **Thai** dishes have been included, large portions but it is appalling that a place serving burgers at ฿250 a shot (twice the daily salary of a farm worker) can't even offer water gratis. Moreover, the food is poor (over-cooked chicken, second-rate fries...); it's living off its name. *Kobune*, 3rd Floor, Mahboonkhrong (MBK) Centre, Rama 1 Rd. **Japanese**, Sushi Bar and tables, very good value. Recommended. *Mandalay*, 23/17 Ploenchit Soi Ruamrudee. Authentic **Burmese** food, most gastronomes of the country reckon their food is the best in the capital. Recommended. *Moon Shadow*, 145 Gaysorn Rd. **Thai food**, good seafood, choice of dining-rooms – a/c or open-air. *Otafuku*, 484 Siam Square Soi 6, Henri Dunant Rd. Sushi Bar or low tables, **Japanese**. *Peppers*, 99/14 Soi Langsuan, T2547355. Open during the day from 1000 to 1700, closed on Sun, small restaurant with just 20 seats run by Aussie-trained Sunissa Hancock, home-cooked Italian food and international dishes, friendly atmosphere, wholesome, tasty food. Great for a lunch stop. *Planet Hollywood*, Gaysorn Plaza, 1st Floor, Ploenchit Rd, T6561358, open 1130-0200. Live music nightly, typical American chow, salads, nachos, burgers, ribs and the decor you would expect from this show-biz-linked place. *Sarah Jane's*, 36/2 Soi Lang Suan, Ploenchit Rd, T2526572. Run by American woman, married to a Thai, best Thai salad in town and good duck, **Isan** food especially noteworthy, excellent value. Recommended. *Vito's Spaghetteria*, Basement, Gaysorn Plaza, Ploenchit Rd (next to *Le Meridien Hotel*). **Italian**. Bright and breezy pasta bar, make up your own dish by combining 10 types of pasta with 12 sauces and 29 fresh condiments, smallish servings but good for a hurried lunch. *Whole Earth*, 93/3 Soi Langsuan, Ploenchit Rd, T2525574. Thailand's best-known and arguably first **vegetarian** restaurant. This is the second and slightly less plush of the two branches (the other is on Sukhumvit Rd), but both have the same eclectic menu from Thai to Indian dishes, lassis and herbal teas and coffees. They have recently introduced some meat dishes. A trifle expensive, but good ambience. Open daily for lunch and dinner. *Wannalee Earth Kitchen*, 63/12 Langsuan, T6522939. 'Mother Earth' theme to this Thai restaurant, with background whale music and simple decor, there's a good choice of food from each region of the country. Open daily for lunch and dinner *Vegetarian House*, 4/1-4/2 6th Floor, Isetan World Trade Centre, Rachdamri Rd, T2559898. Wide-ranging menu from Asian to western. This bright and airy **vegetarian** restaurant is a place where vegetables are made to look like meat: beef stroganoff, shark's fin soup and the like all cunningly crafted from soybean.

Bangkok

Cheap *Caravan Coffee House*, Siam Square Soi 5. Large range of coffee or tea, food includes pizza, curry and some Thai dishes. *Princess Terrace*, Rama I Soi Kasemsan Nung (1). **Thai** and **French** food with BBQ specialities served in small restaurant with friendly service and open terrace down quiet lane. Recommended. *Round Midnight*, 106/12 Soi Langsuan. A **bar** with live blues and jazz, some excellent bands play here, packed at weekends, good atmosphere and worth the trip, also serves Thai and Italian food, open 1700-0400. *Seafood Market*, Sukhumvit Soi 24. A deservedly famous restaurant which serves a huge range of seafood "if it swims we have it", choose your seafood from the 'supermarket' and then have it cooked to your own specifications before consuming the creatures at the table, very popular. **Thai**.

Most **Thai** restaurants sell Chinese food, but there are also many dedicated Chinese establishments. **Siam Square** has a large number, particularly those specializing in shark's fin soup. Those who are horrified by the manner by which fins are removed and the way in which fishing boats are decimating the shark populations of the world should stay clear. But Siam Square also has two of the best noodle shops around, side-by-side on Siam Square Soi 10. *Hong Kong Noodles* is usually packed with university students and serves stupendously good *bamii muu deang kio kung sai naam* (noodle soup with red pork and stuffed pasta with shrimp) while *Kuaytiaw Rua Khuan Boke* is equally popular. More expensive than most noodle shops, but definitely worth the extra few baht.

Afternoon tea and morning coffee the *Bakery Shop*, Siam Intercontinental Hotel. *The Cup*, 2nd floor of Peninsula Plaza, Rachdamri Rd. *The Regent Hotel* lobby (music accompaniment), Rachdamri Rd. *Starbucks*, Central Chitlom, Ploenchit Rd and Amarin Plaza, Ploenchit Rd – the usual Starbuck's fare.

Bakeries *Basket of Plenty*, Peninsula Plaza, Rachdamri Rd (another branch at 66-67 Sukhumvit Soi 33). Bakery, deli and trendy restaurant, very good things baked and a classy (though expensive) place for lunch. *La Brioche*, ground floor of *Novotel Hotel*, Siam Square Soi 6. Good range of French patisseries. *Au Bon Pain*, Ground Floor Siam Discovery Centre, Rama 1 Rd. Excellent bakery and coffee shop with French pastries, croissants, muffins, cookies and great sandwiches as well as salads and some other dishes. *Sweet Corner*, *Siam Intercontinental Hotel*, Rama I Rd. One of the best bakeries in Bangkok. *Swedish Bake*, Siam Square Soi 2. Good Danish pastries.

Bars *Mingles*, *Amari Atrium Hotel*, New Phetburi Rd, open 1700-0100 calls itself a 'Rustic Thai Fun Pub', but the vodka bar suggests otherwise, theme nights throughout the week, some food available.

Sukhumvit
See map page 122

Expensive *Rossini*, *Sheraton Grande Sukhumvit*, Sukhumvit Rd, T6530333. This hotel-based Italian restaurant is open for lunch and dinner. A limited, but tantalizing array of dishes. Particularly good is the seafood. Italian chef. Vies for the 'best Italian in town' award. *Beccassine*, Sukhumvit, Soi Sawatdee. **English** and **French** home cooking. Recommended. *Cucina Bangkok Steak and Seafood*, 29/1 Sukhumvit Soi 49, T6626015. Run by a Thai who learnt about steaks in New York and returned to Thailand to spread the word. The name says it all, pricey but the quality of the ingredients is first rate and the service slick. *Hibiscus*, 31st Floor, *Landmark Hotel,* 138 Sukhumvit Rd, T2540404. **Italian** food which extends to more than pasta and pizza. Worth it for the views. Open for lunch and dinner. *La Grenouille*, 220/4 Sukhumvit Soi 1, T2539080. Traditional **French** cuisine, French chef and manager, small restaurant makes booking essential, French wines and French atmosphere. Recommended. *Le Banyan*, 59 Sukhumvit Soi 8, T2535556. Classic **French** food from foie gras to crêpes suzette, expensive with tougher dress code than most places. Open only for dinner, Mon-Sat. Highly regarded food, a shade stuffy. *L'Hexagone*, 4 Sukhumvit Soi 55 (Soi Thonglor), T3812187. **French** cuisine, in 'posh' surroundings. *L'Opera*, 55 Sukhumvit

Soi 39, T2585606. **Italian** restaurant with Italian manager, conservatory, good food (excellent salted baked fish), professional service, lively atmosphere, popular, booking essential. Recommended. *Les Nymphéas*, Imperial Queen's Park Hotel, Sukhumvit Soi 22, T2619000. An excellent restaurant (the interior theme is *Monet's Waterlillies* – hence the name) in an over-large and inconveniently located (unless you are staying here!) hotel – but don't be put off. The English chef creates probably the best 'modern' French cuisine in Bangkok. *Rang Mahal*, *Rembrandt Hotel*, Sukhumvit Soi 18, T2617107. Best **Indian** food in town, very popular with the Indian community and spectacular views from the roof-top position, sophisticated, elegant and expensive.

Mid-range *Art House*, 87 Sukhumvit Soi 55 (Soi Thonglor). **Chinese**. Country house with traditional Chinese furnishings, surrounded by gardens, particularly good seafood. *Akbar*, 1/4 Sukhumvit Soi 3, T2533479. **Indian, Pakistani** and Arabic. *Bane Lao*, Naphasup Ya-ak I, off Sukhumvit Soi 36. **Laotian** open-air restaurant (doubles as a travel agent for Laos), Laotian band, haphazard but friendly service. *Bei Otto*, 1 Sukhumvit Soi 20. Thailand's best-known German restaurant, sausages made on the premises, good provincial food, large helpings. *Black Scene*, 120/29-30 Sukhumvit Soi 23. A **bar** with live jazz, also serves Thai and French food, open 1700-0300. *Bourbon Street*, 29/4-6 Sukhumvit Soi 22 (behind Washington Theatre), T2594317. Cajun specialities including gumbo, jambalaya and red fish, along with steaks and Mexican dishes (Mexican buffet for ฿170 every Tue), served in a/c restaurant with central bar – good for breakfast, excellent pancakes. Open 0700-0100. *Crêpes and Co*, 18/1 Sukhumvit Soi 12, T6533990. The name says it all, specialises in crêpes but also serves good salads. Some local culinary touches – like the *crêpe musssaman* (a Thai curry). Open 0900-2400. *Larry's Dive*, 8/3 Sukhumvit Soi 22, T6634563. **American** bar which bills itself as the 'only private beach restaurant in Bangkok'. Burgers, nachos, ribs, chicken wings – what you would expect. Good value. *Le Dalat Indochine*, 47/1 Sukhumvit Soi 23, T6617967. Reputed to serve the best **Vietnamese** food in Bangkok, arrive early or management may hassle. Open daily for lunch and dinner. *Den Hvide Svane*, Sukhumvit Soi 8. **Scandinavian** and **Thai** dishes, former are good, efficient and friendly service. *Gino's*, 13 Sukhumvit Soi 15. **Italian** food in bright and airy surroundings, set lunch is good value. *Gourmet Gallery*, 6/1 Soi Promsri 1 (between Sukhumvit Soi 39 and 40). Interesting interior, with art work for sale, unusual menu of **European** and **American** food. *Haus Munchen*, 4 Sukhumvit Soi 15, T2525776. **German** food in quasi-Bavarian lodge, connoisseurs maintain cuisine is authentic enough. *Lemon Grass*, 5/1 Sukhumvit Soi 24, T2588637. **Thai** food and Thai-style house, rather dark interior but very stylish, one step up from *Cabbages and Condoms*. Open daily for lunch and dinner. Recommended. *Mrs Balbir's*, 155/18 Sukhumvit Soi 11, T2532281. **North Indian** food orchestrated by Mrs Balbir, an Indian originally from Malaysia, regular customers just keep going back, chicken dishes are succulent, Mrs Balbir also runs cookery classes. *Longhorn*, 120/9 Sukhumvit Soi 23. **Cajun** and **Creole** food. *Nasir al-Masri*, 4-6 Sukhumvit Soi Nana Nua, T2535582. Reputedly the best **Eastern (Egyptian)** food in Bangkok, *felafale, taboulie, humus*, frequented by large numbers of Arabs who come to Sayed Saad Qutub Nasir for a taste of home. *Señor Pico*, Rembrandt Hotel, 18 Sukhumvit Rd, T2617100. **Mexican**, pseudo-Mexican decor, staff dressed Mexican style, large, rather uncosy restaurant, average cuisine, live music, open only for dinner 1700-0100 daily. *Seven Seas*, Sukhumvit Soi 33, T2597662. Quirky 'nouvelle' **Thai** food, popular with young sophisticated and avant garde Thais. *Tum Nak Thai*, 131 Rachdapisek Rd, T2746420. **Thai** food, 'largest' restaurant in the world, 3,000 seats, rather out of the way (฿100 by taxi from city centre), classical dancing from 2000-2130. *Whole Earth*, 71 Sukhumvit Soi 26, T2584900. This is the slightly swisher of the two Whole Earth **vegetarian** restaurants (the other branch is on Soi Langsuan). Both offer the same eclectic menu from Thai to Indian dishes, live music, *lassis* and good range of coffee. Ask to sit at the back downstairs, or Thai-style upstairs on cushions. They have recently introduced some meat dishes. A trifle expensive, but good ambience. Open daily for lunch and dinner.

Cheap *Ambassador Food Centre*, *Ambassador Hotel*, Sukhumvit Rd. A vast self-service, up-market hawkers' centre with a large selection of **Asian** foods at reasonable prices: Thai, Chinese, Japanese, Vietnamese, etc. Recommended. *Ban Mai*, 121 Sukhumvit Soi 22, Sub-Soi 2. **Thai** food, in old Thai-style decorations in an attractive house with friendly atmosphere, good value. *Cabbages and Condoms*, Sukhumvit Soi 12 (around 400 m down the soi). **Thai**. Population and Community Development Association (PDA) restaurant so all proceeds go to this charity, eat rice in the Condom Room, drink in the Vasectomy Room, good *tom yam kung* and honey-roast chicken, curries all rather similar, good value. Recommended. *Continental*, *Atlanta Hotel*, 78 Sukhumvit Soi 2. **Thai**. Not clearly signed but worth seeking out at the end of Soi 2. The proprietor is a self-confessed foodie and his enthusiasm is reflected in the quality of the fare. A 1930s feel is created by the classical and jazz music played and art-deco fittings. Terrific menu, delicious food, excellent value. Highly recommended. *New Korea*, 41/1 Soi Chuam Rewang, Sukhumvit Sois 15-19. Excellent **Korean** food in small restaurant. Recommended. *Pasta n Noodles*, attached to *City Lodge*, Sukhumvit Soi 9. A trendy **Italian** and **Thai** restaurant, a/c, spotless open-plan kitchen. *September*, 120/1-2 Sukhumvit Soi 23. **Thai**. Art nouveau setting, also serves Chinese and European, good value for money. *Trumpet Pub* (and restaurant), 7 Sukhumvit Soi 24. A **bar** with live blues and jazz, also serves **Thai** food, open 1900-0200. *Veg House*, 2nd Floor, 1/6 Sukhumvit Soi 3 (Nana Nua). Friendly place with a menu of Thai and Indian **vegetarian** dishes. Good value and tasty. *Wannakarm*, 98 Sukhumvit Soi 23, T2596499. Well established, very **Thai** restaurant, grim decor, no English spoken, but rated food.

Seriously cheap *Suda*, 6-6/1 Sukhumvit Rd, Soi 14. Rather basic looking but popular with westerners. Wide menu. **Thai**. Recommended.

Bakeries Bangkok has a large selection of fine bakeries, many attached to hotels like the *Landmark*, *Dusit Thani* and *Oriental*. There are also the generic 'donut' fast-food places although few lovers of bread and pastries would want to lump the 2 together. *The Bakery Landmark Hotel*, 138 Sukhumvit Rd. Many cakes and pastry connoisseurs argue that this is the best of the hotel places, popular with expats, wide range of breads and cakes. *Bei Otto*, Sukhumvit Soi 20. A *German bakery* and *deli*, makes really very good pastries, breads and cakes. *Cheesecake House*, 69/2 Ekamai Soi 22. Rather out of town for most tourists but patronized enthusiastically by the city's large Sukhumvit-based expat population, as the name suggests **cheesecakes** of all descriptions are a speciality – and are excellent. *Gitanes*, 52 Soi Pasana 1, Sukhumvit Soi 63. A bar with live music, open 1800-0100. *Hemingway Bar and Grill*, 159/5-8 Sukhumvit Soi 55. A bar with live jazz and country music at the weekend, plus Thai and American food, open 1800-0100.

Bars There are plenty of bars in the Sukhumvit area, a couple of trendy nightspots are *Café 50*, Thonglor Rd (Sukhumvit Soi 50), *See, Too*, Ekamai Rd, T7116089, open until 0200, also serves reasonably priced Thai food. Undoubtedly the bar of the moment is the *Q Bar*, Sukhumvit Soi 11, T2523274 which opened in Dec 1999. Housed in a modern building, it is the reincarnation of photographer David Jacobson's bar of the same name in Ho Chi Minh City. Highly sophisticated, designed for conversation not for posing. Come here to drink, not to eat – the food is said to be poor and pricey. Live acid jazz on Sun.

Seriously cheap *May Kaidee*, 117/1 Tanao Rd, Banglamphu. This is a tiny, simple vegetarian restaurant tucked away down a soi at the eastern end of Khaosan Rd. Delicious, cheap Thai vegetarian dishes served at tables on the street.

Banglamphu
See maps page 125
& 127

Travellers' food available in the guesthouse/travellers' hotel areas (see above). Nearly all the restaurants in Khaosan Rd show videos all afternoon and evening. If on a tight budget it is much more sensible to eat in Thai restaurants and stalls where it should be possible to have a good meal for ฿15-30.

Bars *Buddy Beer*, 153 Khaosan Rd, a popular spot with Beer Garden, pool table and even a swimmng pool! *Dali*, 227 Soi Rambutri, open 1600-0200, huge choice of alcohol and vintage music too. *Blues Bar and Marjan Reech*, 4th and 5th Floor, Sukhumvit Plaza, 212/34 Sukhumvit Soi 12, open 1900-0200. A tiny Japanese bar selling whisky and sake. *Cheap Charlie's*, 1 Sukhumvit Soi 11, open 1500 until very late. As the title suggests; alcohol at very reasonable prices. *Jools Bar*, 21/3 Nana Tai, Sukhumvit Soi 4, a favourite watering hole for Brits. Open 0900-0100, also serves classic English food. *Tasman Pub*, 159/9 Sukhumvit Soi, 55, opposite Bangkok Bank. The only place in Thailand to serve Boag's Beer from Tasmania. Open 1700-2400. *The Londoner Brew Pub*, Basement, UBC II Building, Sukhumvit 33, open 1100-0200. A large pub, now brewing its English-style ales and also sells usual lagers.

Expensive *Kaloang*, 2 Sri Ayutthaya Rd, T2819228. 2 dining areas, one on a pier, the other on a boat on the Chao Phraya River, attractive atmosphere, delicious Thai food. Recommended.

Sri Ayutthaya

Very expensive *D'jit Pochana Oriental*, 1082 Phahonyothin Rd, T2795000. Thai, extensive range of dishes, large and rather industrial but the food is good. *Doc Cheng's*, 202 Ratchadapisek Rd (in the *Merchant Court Hotel*), Huay Kwang, T694222. A newly opened branch of the well-known Doc Cheng's in Singapore. Although the restaurant is none too happy with being described as concocting fusion cuisine (because the terms is viewed as hackneyed) that's exactly what it does. However the food and the restaurant are excellent. Imaginative creations, stylish presentation. Recommended.

Others

Expensive *Ban Chiang*, 14 Srivdieng Rd, T2367045. Thai food, quite hard to find – ask for directions, old style Thai house, large menu of traditionally prepared food. *Kanasa*, 34 Soi Phahonyothin 9, T6183414. This is not an easy place to get to for many casual visitors to Bangkok – it is in a residential area, north of town. Large garden as well as rooms in an European-style house. Serves what can best be described as nouvelle Thai – good, sometimes excellent but variable. Popular with Bangkok's intelligentsia.

Bangkok now has a large number of western fast-food outlets, such as *Pizza Hut*, *McDonalds*, *Kentucky Fried Chicken*, *Mister Donut*, *Dunkin' Donuts*, *Shakey's*, *Baskin Robbins* and *Burger King*. These are located in the main shopping and tourist areas – Siam Square, Silom/Patpong roads, and Ploenchit Rd, for example.

Fast Food

Scattered across the city for a rice or noodle dish, where a meal will cost ฿15-30 instead of a minimum of ฿50 in the restaurants. For example, on the roads between Silom and Surawong Rd, or down Soi Somkid, next to Ploenchit Rd, or opposite on Soi Tonson.

Foodstalls

Entertainment

Art galleries *The Artist's Gallery*, 60 Pan Rd, off Silom. Selection of international works of art. *The Neilson Hays Library*, 195 Surawong Rd. Has a changing programme of exhibitions. *The Sunday Gallery*, at Chatuchak Weekend Market exhibits up and coming Thai artists. The gallery is in Section 3, Soi 2, open 0930-1830 Sun, T5851556. The *British Council*, on Siam Square also hold exhibitions, T6116830.

Buddhism The headquarters of the World Fellowship of Buddhists is at 33 Sukhumvit Rd (between Soi 1 and Soi 3). Meditation classes are held in English on Wed at 1700-2000; lectures on Buddhism are held on the first Wed of each month at 1800-2000.

Classical music At the *Goethe Institute*, 18/1 Sathorn Tai Soi Atthakan Prasit; check newspapers for programme.

Cinemas Most cinemas have daily showings at 1200, 1400, 1700, 1915 and 2115, with a 1300 matinée on weekends and holidays. Cinemas with English soundtracks include *Central Theatre 2*, T5411065. *Lido*, T2526729. *Pantip*, T2512390. *Pata*, T4230568. *Mackenna*, T2517163. *UA Emporium. Washington 1*, T2582045. *Washington 2*, T2582008. *Scala*, T2512861. *Villa*, T2589291. *The Alliance Française*, 29 Sathorn Tai Rd, T2132122. Shows French films. Remember to stand for the National Anthem, which is played before every performance. Details of showings from English-language newspapers.

Discos *Dianas*, 3rd Floor, Oriental Plaza, Charoen Krung Soi 38. *Grand Palace*, 19th Floor, Rajapark Building, Sukhumvit Soi Asoke, 2100-0200. *Spasso's*, *Grand Hyatt Erawan Hotel*, 494 Rachdamri Rd, T2541234. This Italian restaurant turns into a dance floor as the evening progresses.

Dream World Mixed fairground-cum-fantasy land-cum-historical recreation located 10 mins drive from Don Muang Airport at Km 7 on the Rangsit-Ong Kharak Rd (T5331152). ■ *Mon-Fri 1000-1700, Sat and Sun 1000-1900. ฿450. Getting there: bus nos 39, 59 and 29 to Rangsit and then local bus.*

Fortune tellers There are up to ten soothsayers in the *Montien Hotel* lobby, Surawong Rd, on a regular basis.

Health club *Phillip Wain International*, 8th Floor, Pacific Place, 140 Sukhumvit Rd, T2542544. ■ *Mon-Sat 0700-2200.*

Magic Land 72 Phahonyothin Rd, T5131731. Amusement park with ferris wheel, roller coaster, etc. ■ *Mon-Fri 1000-1700, Sat and Sun 1000-1900. ฿100, plus additional charges for rides. Getting there: near Central Plaza Hotel – ask for 'Daen Neramit'.*

Meditation *Wat Mahathat*, facing Sanaam Luang, is Bangkok's most renowned meditation centre (see page 88). Anyone interested is welcome to attend the daily classes – the centre is located in Khana 5 of the monastery. Apart from Wat Mahathat, classes are held at *Wat Bowonniwet* in Banglamphu on Phra Sumen Rd (see the Bangkok – Old City map 82), and at the *Thai Meditation Centre* in the World Fellowship of Buddhists building on 33 Sukhumvit Rd, T2511188. *International Buddhist Meditation Centre*, Mahachulalongkorn Buddhist University, Wat Mahadhatu, Ta-Prachan, T2222835 Ext 130. For weekend retreats, talks, meditation sessions. *House of Dhamma*, 26/9 Soi Chompol Laadprao Lane 15 Chatuchak, T5113549.

Blues-Jazz, 25 Sukhumvit Soi 53. Open Mon-Sun 1900-0200, 3 house bands play really **Music** good blues and jazz, food available, drinks a little on the steep side. *Blue Moon*, 73 Sukhumvit 55 (Thonglor). Open Mon-Sun 1800-0300, for country, rhythm, jazz and blues – particularly Fri and Sun for jazz – some food available. *Brown Sugar*, 231/20 Sarasin Rd (opposite Lumpini Park). Open Mon-Fri 1100-0100, Sat and Sun 1700-0200, 5 regular bands play excellent jazz, a place for Bangkok's trendies to hang out and be cool (there are a couple of other popular bars close by too). *Cool Tango*, 23/51 Block F, Royal City Av (between Phetburi and Rama IX roads). Open Tue-Sat 1100-0200, Sun 1800-0200, excellent resident rock band, great atmosphere, happy hour 1800-2100. *Front Page*, 14/10 Soi Saladaeng 1. Open Mon-Fri 1000-0100, Sat and Sun 1800-0100, populated, as the name might suggest, by journos who like to hunt in packs more than most, music is country, folk and blues, food available. *Hard Rock Café*, 424/3-6 Siam Square Soi 11. Open Mon-Sun 1100-0200, speaks for itself, burgers, beer and rock covers played by reasonable house band, food is expensive for Bangkok though. *Magic Castle*, 212/33 Sukhumvit Plaza Soi 12. Open Mon-Thu 1800-0100, Fri and Sat 1800-0200, mostly blues, some rock, good place for a relaxed beer with skilfully performed covers. *Picasso Pub*, 1950-5 Ramkamhaeng Rd (close to Soi 8). Open Mon-Sun 1900-0300, house rock band, adept at playing covers. *Q Bar*, Sukhumvit Soi 11, T2523274, acid jazz on Sun (but phone to check) in one of Bangkok's hippest bars. *Round Midnight*, 106/12 Soi Langsuan. Open Mon-Thu 1900-0230, Fri and Sat 1900-0400, jazz, blues and rock bands.

Facilities for sports such as badminton, squash or tennis are either available at the 4 to **Sport** 5-star hotels or are listed in Bangkok's Yellow Pages and the monthly publications *Bangkok Metro Magazine* and *Bangkok Timeout*.

Bowling: *PS Bowl*, 1191 Ramkamhaeng Rd, Huamark. ■ *Mon-Thu 1000-0100, Fri-Sun 1000-0200*. *Sukhumvit Bowl*, 2 Sukhumvit Soi 63 (Ekamoi). ■ *Mon-Sun 1000-0100*.

Diving: *Dive Master*, 110/63 Ladprao Soi 18, T5121664, F5124889. Organize dive trips, NAVI and PADI courses and sell (or rent) diving equipment.

Golf: Most courses open at 0600 and play continues till dusk. Green fees vary from ฿400-2,000. Most also have clubs for hire. Telephone beforehand to check on availability. *Royal Thai Army*, 459 Ram Inthra Rd, Bangkhen, T5211530. 25 mins from city centre, weekday green fee ฿400, weekends and holidays ฿600, club hire ฿300, caddy fee ฿150, 36 holes. *Krungthep Sports Golf Club*, 516 Krungthep Kritha Rd, Huamark, Bangkapi, T3740491. Half an hour east from city centre. *Railway Training Centre Golf Club*, Vibhavadi Rangsit Rd, Bangkhen, T2710130. 15 mins from city centre. *Royal Thai Airforce Golf Club*, Vibhavadi Rangsit Rd, Bangkhen, T5236103. *UNICO Golf Course*, 47 Mu 7, Krungthep Kritha Rd, Phra Khanong, T3779038. 20 mins from city centre. Each has an 18-hole course and clubs can usually be hired for about ฿250. Green fees are usually double at weekends. Phone to check availability. *Rose Garden*, Mu 4, Tambon Tha Talaat, Nakhon Pathom, T034322771. Green fees weekdays ฿450, weekends and holidays ฿1,100, club hire ฿260, caddy fee ฿180, 18 holes. *Royal Dusit*, Phitsanulok Rd, T2814320. Green fees ฿320 weekdays, ฿530 weekends, club hire ฿200. *Muang-Ake*, 34 Mu 7, Phahonyothin Rd, Amphoe Muang, Pathum Thani, T5359335. 40 mins from city centre. Green fees ฿300 weekdays, ฿600 weekends, club hire ฿300. Phone to check regulations for temporary membership. There are also a number of golf **practice/driving ranges** off New Phetburi and Sukhumvit roads. Check the Yellow Pages, *Bangkok Metro Magazine* or *Bangkok Timeout*, for details.

Hash House Harriers: low-key runs with heavy bouts of drinking. There are mixed hashes on Mon, 1730. Call: Frank Allum, T9254344; men only hashes on Sat at 1700, call Randell Burke on T4068896.

Horse racing: at the *Royal Turf Club* and *Royal Sports Club* on alternate Sun from 1230 to 1800, each card usually consists of 10 races. Check newspapers for details.

Kite flying: kites are sold at Sanaam Luang for ฿15-20 on Sun and public holidays during the 'season' (see page 88).

Meditation and yoga: the *Dharma Study Foundation*, 128 Soi Thonglor 4, Sukhumvit Soi 55, T3916006 (■ *Mon-Fri 0900-1800*) and the *World Fellowship of Buddhists*, 33 Sukhumvit Rd (between sois 1 and 3), T2511188 (■ *Mon-Fri 0900-1630*). Both offer classes in meditation and some religious discussions. Yoga classes available at *Sunee Yoga Centre*, 2nd Floor, Pratunam Centre, 78/4 Rachprarop Rd, T2549768. ■ *Mon-Sat, 1000-1200 and 1700-1900*.

Spectator sports: Sanaam Luang, near the Grand Palace, is a good place to sample traditional Thai sports. From late Feb to the middle of Apr there is a traditional Thai Sports Fair held here. It is possible to watch **kite-fighting**, and **takraw** (the only Thai ball game – a *takraw* ball is made of rattan, 5 inches to 6 inches in diameter. Players hit the ball over a net to an opposing team, using their feet, head, knees and elbows – but not hands – and the ball should not be touched by the same team member twice in succession. Regions of Thailand tend to have their own variants of the sport; *sepak takraw* is the competition sport with a nationwide code of rules), **Thai chess**, **krabi** and **krabong** (a swordfighting contest). For Thai boxing, see below.

Swimming: *NTT Sports Club*, 612/26 Soi Lao Lada, Phra Pinklao Bridge Rd. Large pool open to public with sports centre, just north of Sanaam Luang, on the river (฿100). Another reasonably priced and central pool is at the *Department of Physical Education*, Rama I Rd (next to Mahboonkrong Shopping Centre). Open Tue-Sun 1500-1800. There are a number of other public pools as well as private pools which allow non-members/non-residents to swim for a small fee. For a full listing with addresses and rates, see the capital's two listing magazines, *Bangkok Metro Magazine* or *Bangkok Timeout*.

Tennis: courts in many hotels. Public courts available at: *Central Tennis Club*, Sathorn Tai Soi Attakarnprasit, T2867202. ■ *Mon-Fri 0700-2200, Sat and Sun 1100-2100, ฿80-150 per hour, 5 courts, showers, racket hire and food available*. *Volvo Sports Club*, Ramkhamhaeng Soi 13 (near mall 3), T3180322. ■ *Mon-Sun 0700-2200, ฿120 per hour, good facilities, 6 courts, racket hire, hot showers*.

Thai boxing: is both a sport and a means of self-defence and was first developed during the Ayutthaya Period, 1350-1767. It differs from western boxing in that contestants are allowed to use almost any part of their body. Traditional music is played during bouts. There are 2 main boxing stadiums in Bangkok – Lumpini (T2514303) on Rama IV Rd, near Lumpini Park, and Rachdamnern Stadium (T2814205) on Rachdamnern Nok Ave. At Lumpini, boxing nights are Tue and Fri (1800-2200) and Sat (1700), up to and over ฿1,000 for a ringside seat (depending on the card); cheaper seats cost from about ฿150. At Rachdamnern Stadium, 1 Rachdamnern Rd (near the TAT office), boxing nights are Mon and Wed (1800-2200), Thu (1700 and 2100), Sun (1600 and 2000), seats from ฿160-500. Bouts can also be seen occasionally at the National Stadium on Rama I Rd (Pathumwan) and at Hua Mark Stadium near Ramkhamhaeng University on Khlong Ton Rd. Or you can just turn on the television – bouts are often televised live. If you want to learn more about the sport contact the Muai Thai Institute, 336/932 Prachathiphat, Pathum Thani, www.muaythai.th.net

Thai Cookery Courses   The *Oriental Hotel* organizes an intensive 4-day course, with different areas of cuisine covered each day, 0900-1200. ฿2,500 per class or ฿11,500 for 5 classes. T4376211 or 4373080. The classes take place in an old teak house on the other bank of the Chao Phraya – student

● ●
Traditional Thai massage

While a little less arousing than the Patpong-style massage, the traditional Thai massage or nuat boraan *is probably more invigorating, using methods similar to those of Shiatsu, reflexology and osteopathic manipulation. It probably has its origins in India, and is a form of yoga. It aims to release blocked channels of energy and soothe tired muscles. A full massage should last 1-2 hours and cost around ฿150 per hour, although rates vary considerably.*

The thumbs are used to apply pressure on the 10 main 'lines' of muscles, so both relaxing and invigorating the muscles.

Headaches, ankle and knee pains, neck and back problems can all be alleviated through this ancient art (a European visitor to the Siamese court at Ayutthaya 400 years ago noted the practice of Thai massage). Centres of massage can be found in most Thai towns – wats and tourist offices are the best sources of information on where to go. In Bangkok, Wat Pho is the best-known centre and murals on the temple buildings' walls help to guide the student. For Thais, this form of massage is as much a spiritual experience as a physical one – hence its association with monasteries and the Buddha (see page 83).

● ●

gastronomes are ferried across from the hotel. For US$2,500 it is possible to combine the course with staying at the hotel, breakfast and a jet lag massage. *Wandee's Kitchen School*, 134/5-6 Silom Rd (on the 5th Floor, above the Dokya Book Shop), T2372051. Also offer a 5-day, 40-hr course from Mon-Fri but at the slightly cheaper rate of ฿5,200. Successful students emerge with a certificate and reeking faintly of chillies and *nam plaa*. Yet cheaper courses still are run by Mrs Balbir every Fri 0930-1130, in which she instructs small classes of 10 or so, ฿100, 155/18 Sukhumvit Soi 11, T2352281. At *UFM Baking and Cooking School*, 593/29-39 Sukhumvit Soi 33, T2590620, classes are held Mon-Fri 0900-1000, again in groups of about 10; and at the prosaically and politically incorrectly named *Modern House-wife Centre*, 45/6-7 Sethsiri Rd, T2792831, 2792834.

Classical dancing and music is often performed at restaurants after a 'traditional' Thai meal has been served. Many tour companies or travel agents organize these 'cultural evenings'. *National Theatre*, Na Phrathat Rd (T2214885 for programme). Thai classical dramas, dancing and music on the last Fri of each month at 1730 and periodically on other days. *Thailand Cultural Centre*, Rachdaphisek Rd, Huai Khwang, T2470028 for programme of events. *College of Dramatic Arts*, near National Theatre, T2241391. *Baan Thai Restaurant*, 7 Sukhumvit Soi 32, T2585403, 2100-2145. *Chao Phraya Restaurant*, Pinklao Bridge, Arun Amarin Rd, T4742389. *Maneeya's Lotus Room*, Ploenchit Rd, T2526312. 2015-2100. *Piman Restaurant*, 46 Sukhumvit Soi 49, T2587866, 2045-2130. *Ruen Thep*, Silom Village Trade Centre, T2339447, 2020-2120. *Suwannahong Restaurant*, Sri Ayutthaya Rd, T2454448, 2015-2115. *Tum-Nak-Thai Restaurant*, 131 Rachdaphisek Rd, T2773828 2030 2130.

Thai Performing Arts

See individual entries – *Magic Land, Siam Water Park, Dream World, Safari World*.

Theme parks

(See box page 143). Many hotels offer this service; guesthouses also, although most masseuses are not trained. The most famous centre is at Wat Pho (see page 84), a Mecca for the training of masseuses. Wat Pho specializes in the more muscular Southern style. The Northern-style is less exhausting, more soothing. Other centres offering quality massages by properly trained practitioners include: *Marble House*, 37/18-19 Soi Surawong Plaza (opposite Montien Hotel), T2353519. Open Mon-Sun 0100-2400, ฿300 for 2 hrs, ฿450 for 3 hrs and *Vejakorn*, 37/25 Surawong Plaza, Surawong Rd, T2375576. Open Mon-Sun 1000-2400, ฿260 for 2 hrs, ฿390 for 3 hrs.

Traditional Thai massage
Make sure you are getting 'raksaa tang nuat' (traditional Thai massage), otherwise you'll be in for the more pornographic variety

Bangkok

Bangkok

Festivals and major events

January *Red Cross Fair* (movable), held in Amporn Gardens next to the Parliament. Stalls, classical dancing, folk performances, etc.

January/ February *Chinese New Year* (movable), Chinatown closes down, but Chinese temples are packed. *Handicraft Fair* (mid-month), all the handicrafts are made by Thai prisoners.

March-April *Kite Flying* (movable, for 1 month), every afternoon/evening at Sanaam Luang there is kite fighting (see page 88). An *International Kite Festival* is held in late Mar at Sanaam Luang when kite fighting and demonstrations by kite-flyers from across the globe take place.

May *Royal Ploughing Ceremony* (movable), this celebrates the official start of the rice-planting season and is held at Sanaam Luang. It is an ancient Brahman ritual and is attended by the king (see page 87).

September *Swan-boat races* (movable), on the Chao Phraya River.

November *Golden Mount Fair* (movable), stalls and theatres set-up all around the Golden Mount and Wat Saket. Candles are carried in procession to the top of the mount. *Marathon* road race, fortunately at one of the coolest times of year.

December *Trooping of the Colour* (movable), the elite Royal Guards swear allegiance to the king and march past members of the Royal Family. It is held in the Royal Plaza near the equestrian statue of King Chulalongkorn.

Shopping

See also page 45. Most shops do not open until 1000-1100. Nancy Chandler's *Map of Bangkok* is the best shopping guide. Bangkok still stocks a wonderful range of goods, but do not expect to pick up a bargain – prices are high. Having said that, there are many items which find their way to smart London shops at double the price. Stallholders, entirely understandably, are out for all they can get – so bargain hard here. The traditional street market, although not dying out, is now supplemented by other types of shopping. Given the heat, the evolution of the a/c shopping arcade and a/c department store in Bangkok was just a matter of time. Some arcades target the wealthier shopper, and are dominated by brand-name goods and designer wear. Others are not much more than street side stalls transplanted to an arcade environment. Most department stores are now fixed price. For shoppers with limited time and little knowledge of Bangkok there is a new service available in the city. *ShopS I am Co Ltd* runs full-day or half-day shopping tours for private individuals or couples. Run by an Englishman, the company will provide a car, driver and personal shopping expert to take customers to the best places with the minimum of stress. The company charges a fee and takes no commission from shops. For more information and prices contact *ShopsS I am Co Ltd*, Bangkok, Thailand, T662-3821849, F662-3902750, www.shoppingsiam.com

Bangkok's main shopping areas are:

Sukhumvit Sukhumvit Rd, and the sois to the north are lined with shops and stalls, especially around the *Ambassador* and *Landmark* hotels. Many tailors and made-to-measure shoe shops are to be found in this area. Higher up on Sukhumvit Rd particularly around Soi 49 are various antique and furnishing shops. The big Emporium Department Store and Shopping Mall is to be found near Soi 24 (get off at the BTS Phrom

Buying gems and jewellery

More people lose their money through gem and jewellery scams in Thailand than in any other way (60% of complaints to the TAT involve gem scams). **DO NOT** *fall for any story about gem sales, special holidays, tax breaks – no matter how convincing.* **NEVER** *buy gems from people on the street (or beach) and try not to be taken to a shop by an intermediary. Any unsolicited approach is likely to be a scam. The problem is perceived to be so serious that in some countries Thai embassies are handing out warning leaflets with visas. For more background to Thailand and Burma's gems see page 189.*

Rules of thumb to avoid being cheated:

Choose a specialist store in a relatively prestigious part of town (the TAT will informally recommend stores).

Note that no stores are authorized by the TAT or by the Thai government; if they claim as much they are lying.

It is advisable to buy from shops which are members of the Thai Gem and Jewellery Traders Association.

Avoid touts.

Never be rushed into a purchase.

Do not believe stories about vast profits from re-selling gems at home.

Do not agree to have items mailed ("for safety").

If buying a valuable gem, a certificate of identification is a good insurance policy. The Department of Mineral Resources (Rama VI Rd, T2461694) and the Asian Institute of Gemological Sciences (484 Rachadapisek Rd, T5132112) will both examine stones and give such certificates.

Compare prices; competition is stiff among the reputable shops; be suspicious of 'bargain' prices.

Ask for a receipt detailing the stone and recording the price.

For more information (and background reading on Thailand) the Buyer's Guide to Thai Gems and Jewellery, *by John Hoskin can be bought at Asia Books.*

Bangkok

Phong station which has a direct escalator link), where the top brand names are to be found, along with some bargain designer items.

Central Two areas close to each other centred on Rama I and Ploenchit roads. At the intersection of Phayathai and Rama I roads there is Siam Square (for teenage trendy western clothing, bags, belts, jewellery, bookshops, some antique shops and American fast-food chains) and the massive – and highly popular – *Mah Boonkhrong Centre* (MBK), with countless small shops and stalls and the *Tokyu Department Store*. Siam Square used to be great for cheap clothes, leather goods, etc, but each year it inches further up-market. The arrival of the six-floored *Siam Tower* has made it even more chi-chi (all the top designers have a presence here). Peninsular Plaza, between the *Hyatt Erawan* and *Regent* hotels is considered one of the smarter shopping plazas in Bangkok. A short distance to the east, centred on Ploenchit/Rachprarop roads, are more shopping arcades and large department stores, including the *World Trade Centre*, *Thai Daimaru*, *Robinsons*, *Gaysorn Plaza*, *Naraiphan* shopping centre (more of a market-stall affair, geared to tourists, in the basement) and *Central Chidlom* (which burnt down in a catastrophic fire in 1995 but is now completely renovated. North along Rachprasong Rd, crossing over Khlong Saensap, at the intersection with Phetburi Rd is the *Pratunam Market*, good for fabrics and clothing.

Patpong/Silom Patpong is more of a night market (opening at 2100), the streets are packed with stalls selling the usual array of stall goods which seem to stay the same from year to year (fake designer clothing, watches, bags, etc), although some welcome additions include such items as binoculars, all-in-one pliers, etc (and other boys' toys). **NB** Bargain hard. The east end of Silom has a scattering of similar stalls open during the day time, and Robinsons Department Store. Surawong Rd (at the other end of Patpong) has Thai silk, antiques and a few handicraft shops.

Bangkok

West Silom/ Charoen Krung (New Road)	Antiques, jewellery, silk, stamps, coins and bronzeware. Stalls set up here at 2100. A 15 min walk north along Charoen Krung (close to the *Orchid Sheraton Hotel*) is the *River City Shopping Plaza*, specializing in art and antiques.
Banglamphu/ Khaosan Road	Vast variety of low-priced goods, such as ready-made clothes, shoes, bags, jewellery and cassette tapes.
Lardphrao- Phahonyothin	Some distance north of town, not far from the Weekend Market (see page 107) is the huge *Central Plaza* shopping complex. It houses a branch of the *Central Department Store* and has many boutiques and gift shops.
Antiques	Chinese porcelain, old Thai paintings, Burmese tapestries, wooden figures, hilltribe art, Thai ceramics and Buddhist art. Be careful of fakes – go to the well-known shops only. Even they, however, have been known to sell fake Khmer sculpture which even the experts find difficult to tell apart from the real thing. Permission to take antiques out of the country must be obtained from the *Fine Arts Department* on Na Phrathat Rd, T2214817. Shops will often arrange export licences for their customers. Buddha images may not be taken out of the country – although many are. A large number of the more expensive antique shops are concentrated in *River City*, a shopping complex next to the *Royal Orchid Sheraton Hotel* and an excellent place to start. Reputable shops here include *Verandah* on the top floor, *The Tomlinson Collection Room* 427-428 and *Acala Room* 312 for Tibetan and Nepalese art. More antique shops can be found in *Gaysorn Plaza* on Ploenchit Rd and at the *Jewellery Trade Centre* 919/1 Silom Rd in the shopping mall on the ground floor called *The Galleria Plaza* or *Silom Galleria*. At the time of writing the management of this building has been taken over by the Central Group and it has been successful in attracting some of the more up-market antique shops of River City ilk. *NeOld*, 149 Surawong Rd has a good selection of new and old objects, but it's pricey. *Peng Seng*, 942/1-3 Rama IV Rd, on the corner of Surawong Rd, has an excellent selection of antiques. *Thai House Antiques*, 720/6 Sukhumvit (near Soi 28). *L'Arcadia*, 12/2 Sukhumvit Soi 23, Burmese antiques, beds, ceramics, carvings, doors, good quality and prices are fair. The affable owner Khun Tum is helpful and informative. Another quality shop off Sukhumvit is *Paul's Antiques*, 41 Sukhumvit Soi 19 (behind the *Grand Pacific Hotel*), mostly furniture from Thailand and Burma. *Jim Thompson's*, Surawong Rd, for a range of antiques, wooden artefacts, furnishings and carpets. For the serious, see Brown, Robin (1989) *Guide to buying antiques and arts and crafts in Thailand*, Times Books: Singapore.
Books	*Kinokuniya Books*, on the 3rd floor of the Emporium Shopping Centre on Sukhumvit Soi 24 (BTS Phrom Phong Station) has the best selection of English-language books in town (there is another branch on the 6th floor of the Isetan Department Store, World Trade Centre, Rachdamri Rd). On the 3rd floor of the Emporium there is also a branch of the longer established *Asia Books*, which is excellent for books on Asia but less comprehensive than Kinokuniya. Asia books have other branches at at 221 Sukhumvit Rd, between Sois 15 and 17; 2nd Floor Peninsula Plaza, Rachdamri Rd; Thaniya Plaza (3rd Floor), Silom Rd; 2nd Floor, Times Square, Sukhumvit Rd; and World Trade Centre (3rd Floor), Rachdamri Rd. Patpong has 2 book stores – *The Bookseller* (81, Patpong I) and *Bangkok Christian Bookstore*. *Chulalongkorn University Book Centre*, in University compound (ask for '*suun nang suu Chula*') for academic, business and travel books. *DK (Duang Kamol) Books* in Siam Square, on the 3rd floor of the Mahboonkhrong Centre, at 180/1 Sukhumvit (between Sois 8 and 10), and 90/21-25 Rachprarop Rd is the best source of locally published books in English. They also have branches on the 3rd floor of the Mahboonkrong Centre (MBK) at the corner of Phayathai and Rama I roads, and at 180/1 Sukhumvit (between Sois 8 and 10). *Elite Used Books*, 593/5 Sukhumvit Rd, near Villa Supermarket (and with a branch at 1/2 Sukhumvit Soi Nana Nua [Soi 3]),

offers a good range of second-hand books in several languages. *White Lotus*, 26 Soi Attakarnprasit, Sathorn Tai Rd, for collectors' books on Southeast Asia and reprints of historical volumes under their own imprint (also available from many other bookshops). *Dokya*, 258/8-10 Soi Siam Square 3. Books are also sold in the various branches of *Central Department Stores*, 1027 Ploenchit Rd, 1691 Pahonyothin Rd, and 306 Silom Rd. Second-hand books are also available at the *Chatuchak Weekend Market* (see page 107) in sections 22 and 25. For **Maps**, see below.

Bronzeware

Thai or the less elaborate western designs are available in Bangkok. There are a number of shops along Charoen Krung, north from Silom Rd, eg *Siam Bronze Factory* at No 1250 also at 714/6-7 Sukhumvit Road between Sois 26 and 28. The cutlery has become particularly popular and is now even available at the big department stores.

Celadon

Distinctive ceramic ware, originally produced during the Sukhothai Period (from the late 13th century), and recently revived. *Thai Celadon House*, 8/8 Rachdapisek Rd, Sukhumvit Rd (Soi 16), also sells seconds, or from *Narayana Phand*, 127 Rachdamri Rd.

Clothes

Cheap designer wear with meaningless slogans and a surfeit of labels (on the outside) available just about everywhere and anywhere, and especially in tourist areas like Patpong and Sukhumvit. Imitation *Lacoste* and other garments are less obviously on display now that the US is pressurizing Thailand to respect intellectual copyright laws but they are available. Note that the less you pay, generally, the more likely that the dyes will run, shirts will spontaneously down-size, and buttons will eject themselves at will. For unique funky designer clothes of Indian inspiration visit *Vipavee* on the first floor of *The Emporium* at Sukhumvit Soi 24 (there are lots of other places here as well). *Kai Boutique* on the 4th floor of Times Square Building is worth visiting for those interested in what the best designers in Thailand are doing. Many of Bangkok's smartest ladies patronise this establishment.

Department stores

Central is the largest chain of department stores in Bangkok, with a range of Thai and imported goods at fixed prices; credit cards are accepted. Main shops on Silom Rd, Ploenchit Rd, and in the Central Plaza, just north of the Northern bus terminal. Other department stores include *Thai Daimaru* on Rachdamri and Sukhumvit (opposite Soi 71). *Robinson's* on corner of Silom and Rama IV roads, Sukhumvit (near Soi 19) and Rachdamri roads. *Tokyu* in MBK Tower on Rama I Rd. *Sogo* in the Amarin Plaza on Ploenchit Rd, and *Zen*, World Trade Centre, corner of Rama I and Rajdamri roads, soon to have an ice rink.

Designer ware

Clothing, watches, leather goods, etc, all convincing imitations, can be bought for very reasonable prices from the many roadside stalls along Sukhumvit and Silom roads, Siam Square and in other tourist areas. Times Square, on Sukhumvit 14, has several 'designer clothing' shops.

Dolls

There is a Thai doll factory on Soi Ratchataphan (Soi Mo Leng) off Rachprarop Rd in Pratunam. The factory sells dolls to visitors and also has a display. ■ *Mon-Sat 0800-1700, T2453008.*

Furniture

Between Soi 43 and Soi 45, Sukhumvit Rd, is an area where rattan furniture is sold. *Rattan House*, 795-797 Sukhumvit Rd (between Soi 43 and 45). *Corner 43*, 487/1-2 Sukhumvit Rd (between Soi 25-27). For stylish modern furniture visit the shopping mall attached to the Hilton Hotel on Witthayu Rd or *Home Place*, a shopping mall on Sukhumvit Soi 55 (Thonglor) at sub-soi No.13

Bangkok

Gold This is considerably cheaper than in USA or Europe; there is a concentration of shops along Yaowaraj Rd (Chinatown), mostly selling the yellow 'Asian' gold. Price is determined by weight (its so-called 'baht weight').

Handicrafts The *State Handicraft Centre* (*Narayana Phand*), 127 Rachdamri Rd, just north of Gaysorn, is a good place to view the range of goods made around the country. *House of Handicrafts*. *Regent Hotel*, 155 Rajdamri Rd. *House of Handicrafts*, 3rd Floor, Amarin Plaza, 496-502 Ploenchit Rd. On the opposite side of the road on the corner is *Gaysorn Plaza*. On the top two floors of the building is a collection of stalls called *The Thai Craft Museum* shop. This has a bit more style than Narayana Phand and feels less like a tour bus shopping stop. Also here on the 3rd floor is a relatively new and very "in" shop called *Cocoon*. Here traditional Thai objects have been transformed by altering the design slightly and using bright colours. Great for unusual and fun gifts.

Interior Design Siam Discovery Centre, otherwise known as Siam Tower, has some great Interior Design shops, including *Habitat*, and *Anyroom*, on the fourth floor.

Jewellery Thailand has become the world's largest gem cutting centre and it is an excellent place to buy both gems and jewellery. The best buy of the native precious stones is the sapphire. Modern jewellery is well designed and of a high quality. Always insist on a certificate of authenticity and a receipt (see box page 145 for gem-buying checklist). *Ban Mo*, on Pahurat Rd, north of Memorial Bridge is the centre of the gem business although there are shops in all the tourist areas particularly on Silom Rd near the intersection with Surasak Rd, eg *Rama Gems*, 987 Silom Rd. *Uthai Gems*, 28/7 Soi Ruam Rudi, off Ploenchit Rd, just east of Witthayu Rd are recommended, as is *P. Jewellery* (Chantaburi), 9/292 Ramindra Rd, Anusawaree Bangkhan, T5221857. For western designs, *Living Extra* and *Yves Joaillier* are to be found on the 3rd floor of the Charn Issara Tower, 942 Rama IV Rd. *Jewellery Trade Centre* (aka Galleria Plaza), next door to the *Holiday Inn Crowne Plaza* on the corner of Silom Rd and Surasak Rd contains a number of gem dealers and jewellery shops on the ground floor. *Tabtim Dreams* at Unit 109 is a good place to buy loose gems.

Maps *Asia Books* sell a very accurate map of Bangkok called *Bangkok, Central Thailand Travel Map*, published by Periplus Editions, ฿85. *Nelles* also publish a good Bangkok map with an excellent detailed map of the city centre.

Markets The markets in Bangkok are an excellent place to browse, take photographs and pick up bargains. They are part of the life blood of the city, and the encroachment of more organized shops and the effects of the re-developer's demolition ball are inimical to one of Bangkok's finest traditions. Nancy Chandler's map of Bangkok, available from most bookshops, is the most useful guide to the markets of the capital. The largest is the *Weekend Market* at Chatuchak Park (see page 107). The *Tewes Market*, near the National Library, is a photographer's dream; a daily market, selling flowers and plants. *Pratunam Market* is spread over a large area around Rachprarop and Phetburi roads, and is famous for clothing and fabric. Half of it was recently bulldozed for redevelopment, but there is still a multitude of stalls here. The *Bai Yoke Market* is next door and sells mostly fashion garments for teenagers – lots of lycra. A short distance south of here on Rachprarop Rd is the *Naraiphan Shopping Centre* and *Narayana Bazaar* an indoor stall/shopping centre affair (concentrated in the basement) geared to tourists and *farang* residents. *Nakhon Kasem* known as the *Thieves' Market*, in the heart of Chinatown, houses a number of 'antique' shops selling brassware, old electric fans and woodcarvings (tough bargaining recommended, and don't expect everything to be genuine – see page 95). Close by are the stalls of *Sampeng Lane* (see page 95), specializing in toys, stationery, clothes and household goods, and the

Pahurat Cloth Market (see page 94) – a small slice of India in Thailand, with mounds of sarongs, batiks, buttons and bows. *Bangrak Market*, south of the General Post Office, near the river and the *Shangri-La Hotel*, sells exotic fruit, clothing, seafood and flowers. *Pak Khlong Market* is a wholesale market selling fresh produce, orchids and cut flowers and is situated near the Memorial Bridge. An exciting place to visit at night when the place is a hive of activity, (see page 94). *Phahonyothin Market* is Bangkok's newest, opposite the Northern bus terminal, and sells potted plants and orchids. *Banglamphu Market* is close to Khaosan Rd, the backpackers' haven, on Chakrapong and Phra Sumen roads. Stalls here sell clothing, shoes, food and household goods. The nearby *Khaosan Rd Market* (if it can be called such) is much more geared to the needs and desires of the foreign tourist: CDs and cassettes, batik shirts, leather goods and so on. *Patpong Market*, arranged down the middle of Patpong Rd, linking Silom and Surawong roads, opens up about 1700 and is geared to tourists, selling handicrafts, T-shirts, leather goods, fake watches, cassettes and videos. *Penang Market*, Khlong Toey, situated under the expressway close to the railway line specializes in electronic equipment from hi-fis to computers, with a spattering of other goods as well. Watch out for pick-pockets in this market! A specialist market is the *Stamp Market* next to the GPO (see map page 116) on Charoen Krung which operates on Sun only. Collectors come here to buy or exchange stamps.

Tapes and CDs can be bought from many stalls in tourist areas, although the choice is limited to better-known artists. Cheap copies are harder to come by these days although as the genuine article is just ฿100 for a cassette or ฿500 for a CD it makes sense to buy the real McCoy. For a wider range of choice visit *Tower Records* on the top floor of *Siam Centre*, Rama 1 Rd or on the 3rd floor of *The Emporium* at Sukhumvit Soi 24. **Music**

There are several pottery 'factories' on the left-hand side of the road on the way to the Rose Garden, near Samut Sakhon (see page 112). **Pottery**

The *Siam Bootery* is a chain of shops for handmade footwear. **Shoes**

Beware of 'bargains', as the silk may have been interwoven with rayon. It is best to stick to the well-known shops unless you know what you are doing. Silk varies greatly in quality. Generally, the heavier the weight the more expensive the fabric. One-ply is the lightest and cheapest (about ฿200 per metre), four-ply the heaviest and most expensive (about ฿300-400 per metre). Silk also comes in 3 grades: Grade 1 is the finest and smoothest and comes from the inner part of the cocoon. Finally, there is also 'hard' and 'soft' silk, soft being rather more expensive. Handmade patterned silk, especially *matmii* from the northeast region, can be much more expensive than simple, single-coloured industrial silk – well over ฿10,000 per piece. There are a number of specialist silk shops at the top of Surawong Rd (near Rama IV), including the famous *Jim Thompson's* (which is expensive, but has the best selection). ■ *Mon-Sun 0900-2100*. There are also a number of shops along the bottom half of Silom Rd (towards Charoen Krung) and in the Siam Centre on Rama I Rd. *Anita Thai Silk*, 294/4-5 Silom Rd, slightly more expensive than some, but the extensive range makes it worth a visit. *Home Made (HM) Thai Silk*, 45 Sukhumvit Soi 35 (silk made on premises), good quality *matmii* silk. *Jagtar* at 37 Sukhumvit Soi 11 has some lovely silk curtain fabrics as well as cushion covers in unusual shades and other accessories made from silk. Originality means prices are high. Village-made silks also available from *Cabbages and Condoms* (also a restaurant) on Sukhumvit Soi 12 and Raja Siam, Sukhumvit Soi 23. *Khompastr*, 52/10 Surawong Rd, near *Montien Hotel*, distinctive screen-printed fabric from Hua Hin. Factory (industrial) silk available from *Shinawatra* on Sukhumvit Soi 31. Numerous stalls at the *Chatuchak Weekend Market* also sell lengths from Laos and northeast Thailand (see page 107). **Silk**

Bangkok

Spectacles Glasses and contact lenses are a good buy in Bangkok and can be made up in 24 hrs. Opticians are to be found throughout the city.

Shopping Malls No longer do visitors to Bangkok need to suffer the heat of the market stall, Bangkok is fast becoming another Singapore or Hong Kong, with shopping malls springing up all over the place. Some, like the long established *MBK* on the corner of Phayathai and Rama 1, are down-market and packed full of bargains, whilst others, like the *Siam Discovery Centre* (or Siam Tower), across the road from Siam Square, are more sophisticated and you are unlikely to pick up many cut-price goods. *The Emporium*, on Sukhumvit Soi 24 (directly accessible from BTS Phrom Phong Station) is an enormous place, dominated by the *Emporium Department Store* but with many other clothes outlets as well as record and book shops, designer shops and more. The ground and first floors are monopolised by the big names in fashion – *Kenzo*, *Chanel*, *Versace* are all there along with some expensive looking watch and jewellery shops. For the less extravagant there are a number of trendy clothes shops on the 2nd floor namely, *Phalene* and *Soda* (the names of two different shops as opposed to a new drink). The 3rd floor has the more prosaic offerings in the way of shops – *Boots the Chemists* have recently opened a store here. *Exotique Thai* occupies the space between the escalators on the 4th Floor. Here you can find a nice selection of decorative items for the home while the 5th Floor is dedicated to household goods along with a large food hall.

Supermarkets *Central Department Store* (see Department stores listing). *Robinsons* – open until midnight (see Department stores listing). *Villa Supermarket*, between Sois 33 and 35, Sukhumvit Rd (and branches elsewhere in town) – for everything you are unable to find anywhere else. The *Villa* supermarkets are the best place to go for the more exotic imported foods and the branch on Sukhumvit road is open 24 hrs a day. *Isetan* (World Trade Centre), Rachdamri Rd.

Tailoring services Bangkok's tailors are skilled at copying anything; either from fashion magazines or from a piece of your own clothing. Always request a fitting, ask to see a finished garment, ask for a price in writing and pay as small a deposit as possible. Tailors are concentrated along Silom, Sukhumvit and Ploenchit roads and Gaysorn Square. Indian tailors appear to offer the quickest service. *N and Y Boutique*, 11 Chartered Bank Lane (Oriental Avenue), near the *Oriental Hotel* (for ladies' tailored clothes), *New Devis Custom Tailors*, 179/2 Sukhumvit Rd, Soi 13 and *Rajawongse*, 130 Sukhumvit Rd (near Sukhumvit Soi 4) have both been recommended. There are many other places, though.

Textiles *Prayer Textile Gallery*, 197 Phayathai Rd, good range and excellent quality traditional and Laotian textiles.

Woodworking Lots of woodworking shops along Worachak Rd at the point where it crosses Khlong (canal) Banglamphu. *Bua Thong* is recommended, although the sign is only in Thai. Good places to buy bracelets, curtain rings and other knobs and trinkets fashioned from tropical hardwoods.

Tour operators

Travel agents abound in the tourist and hotel areas of the city – Khaosan Rd/Banglamphu, Sukhumvit, Soi Ngam Duphli, and Silom (several down Pan Rd, a soi opposite Silom Village). All major hotels will have their own in-house agent. Most will book airline, bus and train tickets, arrange tours, and book hotel rooms. Because there are so many to choose from, it is worth shopping around for the best deal. For those wishing to travel to Vietnam, Laos, Cambodia and Burma, specialist agents are recommended as they are usually able to arrange visas – for a fee. *Asian Holiday Tour*, 294/8 Phayathai Rd, T2155749.

Asian Lines Travel, 755 Silom Rd, T2331510, F2334885. *Banglamphu Tour Service*, 17 Khaosan Rd, T2813122, F2803642. *Dee Jai Tours*, 2nd Flr, 491/29 Silom Plaza Building, Silom Rd, T2341685, F2374231. *Diethelm Travel*, Kian Gwan Building II, 140/1, Witthayu Rd, T2559150, F2560248. *Dior Tours*, 146-158 Khaosan Rd, T2829142. *East-West*, 46/1 Sukhumvit Soi Nana Nua, T2530681. *Exotissimo*, 21/17 Sukhumvit Soi 4, T2535240, F2547683 and 755 Silom Rd, T2359196, F2834885. *Fortune Tours*, 9 Captain Bush Lane, Charoen Krung 30, T2371050. *GM Tour & Travel*, 273 Khaosan Rd, T2823979, F2810642. One of the more efficient operations, with impartial flight information. *Guest House and Tour*, 46/1 Khaosan Rd, T2823849, F2812348. *MK Ways*, 57/11 Witthayu Rd, T2555590, F2545583. *Patco Chiang Mai*, Hualamphong Railway Station tourist office, organizes treks in the north, it comes recommended. *Pawana Tour and Travel*, 72/2 Khaosan Rd, T2678018, F2800370. *Roong Ruang Tour Travel Centre Co*, 183-185 Samsen Rd, T2801460. *Siam Wings*, 173/1-3 Surawong Rd, T2534757, F2366808. *Skyline Travel Service*, 491/39-40 Silom Plaza (2nd Flr), Silom Rd, T2331864, F2366585. *St Louis Travel*, 18/7 Soi St Louis 3, Sathorn Tai Rd, T2121583, F2121583. *Thai Travel Service*, 119/4 Surawong Rd, T2349360. *Top Thailand Tour*, 61 Khaosan Rd, T2802251, F2823337. *Tour East*, Rajapark Building (10th Flr), 163 Asoke Rd, T2593160, F2583236. *Transindo*, Thasos Building (9th Flr), 1675 Chan Rd, T2873241, F2873246. *Vieng Travel*, branch on the ground floor of the Trang Hotel, 99/8 Wisutkaset Rd, T2803537. *Vista Travel*, 244/4 Khaosan Rd, T2800348. *Western Union*, branch in the foyer of *Atlanta Hotel*, 78 Sukhumvit Soi 2, T2552151. Good all-round service.

Transport

Bus This is the cheapest way to get around town. A bus map marking the routes is indispensable. The *Bangkok Thailand* map and *Latest tours guide to Bangkok and Thailand* are available from most bookshops as well as many hotel and travel agents/ tour companies. Major bus stops also have maps of routes and instructions in English displayed. There is quite a range of buses, including a/c and non-a/c, micro, express and new improved, generally colour coded. Standard non-a/c buses (with blue stripe) cost ฿3.50. Beware of pickpockets on these often-crowded buses. Red-striped express buses are slightly more expensive, slightly less crowded, and do not stop at all bus stops. A/c buses cost ฿6-18 depending on distance and are coloured solid blue. Travelling all the way from Silom Rd to the airport by a/c bus, for example, costs ฿14; most inner city journeys cost ฿6. There are also smaller a/c 'micro buses' (a bit of a misnomer as they are not micro at all, not even 'mini'), which follow the same routes but are generally faster and less crowded because officially they are only meant to let passengers aboard if a seat is vacant. They charge a flat fare of ฿20. New arrivals on Bangkok's complicated bus system are white a/c buses which charge a flat fare of ฿10 and orange a/c buses which cost ฿12.

Local
More people have their belongings stolen on Bangkok's city buses than almost anywhere else

Car hire Approximate cost, ฿1,000-1,200 per day, ฿6,000-8,000 per week; Hertz and Avis charge more than the local firms, but have better insurance cover. See page 34 for general advice on driving in Thailand. **Avis**, 2/12 Witthayu Rd, T2555300. **Central Car Rent**, 115/5 Soi Ton-Son, Ploenchit Rd, T2512778. **Dollar Car Rent**, 272 Si Phraya Rd, T2330848. **Grand Car Rent**, 233-5 Asoke-Din Daeng Rd, T2482991. **Hertz**, 420 Sukhumvit Soi 71, T3900341. **Highway Car Rent**, 1018/5 Rama IV Rd, T2357746. **Inter Car Rent**, 45 Sukhumvit Rd, T2529223. **Silver International**, 102 Esso Gas Station, 22 Sukhumvit Rd, T2596867. **SMT Rent-a-Car**, 931/11 Rama I Rd, T2168020, F2168039.

Skytrain (BTS) At last Bangkok has a mass transit system! It may have taken years to make an appearance, and it may not cover even most of the city, but at least it's here. It runs on an elevated track several stories up in the sky – hence its popular name, Skytrain. But it is officially know as BTS or the Bangkok Transit System, which are the letters emblazoned at the stations. There are two lines which cross at Siam Station (Siam

Bangkok

Bangkok's public transport numbers

taxis	145,000
tuk tuks	127,405
motorcycle taxis	120,000
illegal taxis	126,000

Square): one runs from Mor Chit on Phahonyothin Road (close to the Chatuchak Weekend Market, to the north of the city centre) to Phrakanong on Sukhumvit Rd. The second lines runs from the National Stadium on Rama I Rd to Taksin Bridge (Saphan Taksin) at the end of Silom Rd in the heart of the business district. While the Skytrain doesn't cover anywhere close to all of the city, it does include a large chunk of the tourist, business and shopping areas so is very useful. It is also quick and cool – although the tramp up to the stations can be a fag (10 stations were having escalators installed in mid-2000) and the stations themselves are not air-conditioned. Trains run from 0600-2400, every 3-5 mins during peak periods and every 10-15 mins out of the rush hour. Fares are steep by Thai standards but worth it for most overseas visitors: ฿10 for one stop, ฿40 for the whole route. See the map on page 74 for its planned route. The skytrain may be the first mass transit system in the capital, but there are others being mooted and one already under construction: an underground which is scheduled for completion in 2002. For up-to-date information T6177300 or www.bts.co.th

Express boats Travel between Nonthaburi in the north and Wat Rajsingkorn (near Krungthep bridge) in the south. Fares are calculated by zone and range from ฿10 upwards. At peak hours boats leave every 10 mins, off-peak about 15-25 mins (see map, page 97 for piers, and page 96). The journey from one end of the route to the other takes 75 mins. Note that boats flying red or green pennants do not stop at all piers (they also exact a ฿2 express surcharge). Also, boats will only stop if passengers wish to board or alight, so make your destination known.

Ferries Small ferries take passengers across the Chao Phraya River, ฿1 (see map on page 97 for piers).

Khlong or long-tailed boats can be rented for ฿200 per hour, or more (see page 101).

Motorcycle taxi A relative newcomer to Bangkok (and now present in other towns in Thailand) they are the fastest, and most terrifying, way to get from A to B. Riders wear numbered vests and tend to congregate in particular areas; agree a fare, hop on the back, and hope for the best. Their 'devil may care' attitude has made them bitter enemies of many other road users. Expect to pay ฿10-20.

Check that the meter is 'zeroed' before setting off

Taxi Taxis are usually metered (they must have a/c to register) – look for the 'Taxi Meter' illuminated sign on the roof. There are a number of unmarked, unofficial taxis which are to be found around the tourist sites. Flag fall is ฿35 for the first 3 km, and ฿5 per kilometre thereafter. Most trips in the city should cost ฿40-100. If the travel speed is less than 6 km per hour – always a distinct possibility in the traffice choked capital – a surcharge of ฿1 per minute is automatically added. Passengers also pay the tolls for using the expressway. Taxi drivers sometimes refuse to use the meter despite the fact that they are required to do so by law. We have had numerous complaints about Bangkok's taxi drivers who view foreign visitors to the city as ripe for ripping-off. If they refuse to use the meter simply get out and hail another – there are usually scores around. Another popular ruse is for drivers to deny they have any change. It's best to make sure you have sufficient 20s and 100s to pay but if not just get out and get change from a nearby shop. They'll wait! Taxis should not be tipped, although it is usual to round fares up to the nearest ฿5. For most tourists the arrival of the metered taxi has lowered prices as it has eliminated the need to bargain (assuming, of course, that the meter is being used). To call a taxi T1545 or T1661, they charge ฿20 plus the fare on the meter. Note that taxi drivers are not renowned for their knowledge of Bangkok. Many are up-country boys and with *farang* visitors massacring their language it is handy to have a rough idea of where you want to go, and a map (preferably with Thai lettering too).

Tuk-tuk The formerly ubiquitous motorized saamlor is rapidly becoming a piece of history in Bangkok, although they can still always be found near tourist sites. Best for short journeys: they are uncomfortable and, being open to the elements, you are likely to be asphyxiated by car fumes. Bargaining is essential and the fare must be negotiated before boarding, most journeys cost at least ฿40. Both tuk-tuk and taxi drivers may try to take you to restaurants or shops – do not be persuaded; they are often mediocre places charging high prices.

Long distance

Bangkok lies at the heart of Thailand's transport network. Virtually all trains and buses end up here and it is possible to reach anywhere in the country from the capital. Bangkok is also a regional transport hub, and there are flights to most international destinations. For international transportation, see page 17.

Air

Don Muang Airport is 25 km north of the city. Regular connections on **THAI** to many of the provincial capitals. For airport details see page 23. There are a number of **THAI** offices in Bangkok, Head Office for domestic flights is 89 Vibhavadi Rangsit Rd, T5130121, but this is inconveniently located north of town. 2 more central offices are at 6 Lan Luang Rd (T2800070) and 485 Silom Rd. Tickets can also be bought at most travel agents. **Bangkok Airways** flies to Koh Samui, Hua Hin, Phuket, Sukhothai, Chiang Mai, Ranong, Hat Yai, U-Tapao (Pattaya) and Mae Hong Son. They have an office in the domestic terminal at Don Muang, and 2 offices in town. Note that Bangkok Airways have their own check-in area and departure lounge on the ground floor of the domestic terminal (not on the first floor).

Train

Bangkok has 2 main railway stations. The primary station, catering for most destinations, is Hualamphong, Rama IV Rd, T2237010/2237020; condensed railway timetables in English can be picked up from the information counter in the main concourse. Trains to Nakhon Pathom and Kanchanaburi leave from the Bangkok Noi or Thonburi station on the other side of the Chao Phraya River. See page 18 for more information on Thailand's railways.

Road

Bus There are 3 main bus stations in Bangkok serving the north and northeast, the east, and the south and west. Destinations in the Central Plains are also served from these terminals – places north of Bangkok from the northern and northeastern bus terminal, southwest of Bangkok from the southern terminal, and southeast from the eastern bus terminal. The new **Northern bus terminal** or *Mor Chit Mai* (new Mor Chit), aka Mor Chit 2, is at the western side of Chatuchak Park on Kamphaeng Phet 2 Rd. It serves all destinations in the north and northeast as well as towns in the Central Plains that lie north of Bangkok like Ayutthaya and Lopburi. Non-a/c buses 77, 134, 136 and 145 and a/c buses 3, 8, 12, 134, 136 and 145 all pass the terminal. Note that the original Mor Chit bus terminal, on Phahonyothin Rd, closed in 1998. The non-a/c **Southern bus terminal** is on Phra Pinklao Road (T4110061) near the intersection with Route 338. Buses for the west (places like Nakhon Pathom and Kanchanaburi) and the south leave from here. A/c town bus No 7 travels to the terminal. A/c buses to the south and west leave from the terminal on Charan Santiwong Rd, near Bangkok Noi Train Station in Thonburi, T4351199. The **Eastern bus terminal**, Sukhumvit Rd (Soi Ekamai), between Soi 40 and Soi 42, T3912504 serves Pattaya and other destinations in the eastern region.

Buses leave for most major destinations throughout the day, and often well into the night. There are overnight buses on the longer routes – Chiang Mai, Hat Yai,

Bangkok

Chiang Rai, Phuket, Ubon Ratchathani. Even the smallest provincial towns such as Mahasarakham have deluxe a/c buses connecting them with Bangkok. Note that in addition to the government-operated buses there are many private companies which run 'tour' buses to most of the major tourist destinations. Tickets bought through travel agents will normally be for these private tour buses which leave from offices all over the city as well as from the public bus terminals listed above. Shop around as prices may vary. Note that although passengers may be picked up from their hotel/guesthouse therefore saving on the ride (and inconvenience) of getting out to the bus terminal, the private buses are generally less reliable and less safe. Many pick up passengers at Khaosan Rd, for example.

Directory

Airline offices For airport enquiries call, T2860190. *Aeroflot*, Regent House, 183 Rachdamri Rd, T2510617. *Air China*, 2nd Flr, CP Building, 313 Silom Rd, T6310731. *Air France*, Vorawat Building, 20th Flr, 849 Silom Rd, T6351199. *Air India*, SS Building, 10/12-13 Convent Rd, Silom, T2350557. *Air Lanka*, Ground Flr, Charn Issara Tower, 942 Rama IV Rd, T2369292. *Alitalia*, SSP Tower 3, 15th Flr, Unit 15A, 88 Silom Rd, T6341800. *American Airlines*, 518/5 Ploenchit Rd, T2511393. *Asiana Airlines*, 18th Flr, Ploenchit Center, 2 Sukhumvit 2 Rd, T6568610. *Bangkok Airways*, Queen Sirikit National Convention Centre, New Rajdapisek Rd, Klongtoey, T2293456/2293454, and 140 Pacific Place Building, Sukhumvit Rd, T2293434. *Bangladesh Biman*, Ground Flr, Chongkolnee Building, 56 Surawong Rd, T2357643. *British Airways*, 14th Flr, Abdulrahim Place, 990 Rama 1V Rd, T6361747. *Canadian Airlines*, 6th Flr, Maneeya Building, 518/5 Ploenchit Rd, T2514521. *Cathay Pacific*, 11th Flr, Ploenchit Tower, 898 Ploenchit Rd, T2630606. *China Airlines*, 4th Flr, Peninsula Plaza, 153 Rachdamri Rd, T2534242. *Continental Airlines*, CP Tower, 313 Silom Rd, T2310113. *Delta Airlines*, 7th Flr, Patpong Building, Surawong Rd, T2376838. *Eva Airways*, Green Tower, 2nd Flr, 425 Rama IV Rd, opposite Esso Head Office. *Egyptair*, 3rd Flr, CP Tower, 313 Silom Rd, T2310504. *Finnair* 6th Flr, Vorawat Bldg, 849 Silom Rd, T6351234. *Garuda*, 27th Flr, Lumpini Tower, 1168 Rama' IV Rd, T2856470. *Gulf Air*, 12th Flr, Maneeya Building, 518 Ploenchit Rd, T2547931. *Japan Airlines*, 254/1 Ratchadapisek Rd, T6925151. *KLM* 19th Flr, Thai Wah Tower 11, 21/133-134 South Sathorn Rd, T6791100. *Korean Air*, Ground Flr, Kong Bunma Building (opposite *Narai Hotel*), 699 Silom Rd, T6350465. *Kuwait Airways*, 12th Flr, RS Tower, 121/50-51 Ratchadapisek Rd, T6412864. *Lao Aviation*, 491 17 Ground Flr, Silom Plaza, Silom Rd, T2369822. *Lufthansa*, 18th Flr, Q-House (Asoke), Sukhumvit Rd Soi 21, T2642400. *MAS (Malaysian Airlines)*, 20th Flr, Ploenchit Tower, 898 Ploenchit Rd, T2630565. *Myanmar Airways*, 23rd Flr, Jewellery Trade Centre, Silom Rd, T6300334. *Orient Express*, 17th Flr, 138/70 Jewellery Centre, Naret Rd, T2673210. *Pakistan International*, Chongkolnee Building, 56 Surawong Rd, T2342961. *Qantas*, 14th Flr, Abdulrahim Place, 990 Rama IV Rd, T6361747. *Royal Brunei*, 4th Flr, Charn Issara Tower, 942 Rama IV Rd, T2330056. *Royal Air Cambodge*, 17th Flr, 2 Pacific Place, 142 Sukhumvit Rd, T6532261. *Royal Nepal Airlines*,9th Flr, Phyathai Plaza Building, 128/108 Rajthevee Rd, T2165691. *Sabena*, 12th Flr, Charn Issara Tower, Rama 1V Rd, T2672100. *SAS*, 8th Flr, Glas Haus I, Sukhumvit Rd Soi 25, T2600444. *Saudi*, 19th Flr, United Centre Building, Silom Rd, T2667393. *Singapore Airlines*, 12th Flr, Silom Centre, 2 Silom Rd, T2365295/6. *Swissair*, 21st Flr Abdulrahim Place, 990 Rama 1V Rd, T6362160. *THAI*, 485 Silom Rd, T2343100. 89 Vibhavadi-Rangsit Rd, T5130121. *Vietnam Airlines*, 7th Flr, Ploenchit Centre, 2 Sukhumvit 2 Rd, T6569056.

Banks There are countless exchange booths in all the tourist areas open 7 days a week, mostly 0800-1530, some from 0800-2100. Rates vary only marginally between banks, although if changing a large sum, it is worth shopping around.

Church services *Evangelical Church*, Sukhumvit Soi 10 (0930 Sun service). The *International Church* (interdenominational), 67 Sukhumvit Soi 19 (0800 Sun service). *Baptist Church*, 2172/146 Phahonyothin Soi 36 (1800 Sun service). *Holy Redeemer*, 123/19 Wittayu Soi Ruam Rudee (Catholic, 5 services on Sun). *Christ Church*, 11 Convent Rd (Anglican – Episcopalian – Ecumenical, 3 Sun services at 0730, 1000 and 1800).

Communications Internet cafés abound, especially in the backpackers' centres. Eg *Khaosan Cyber Home*, Khaosan Rd. Open 0900-2200. *Bangkok Internet Café*, Khaosan Rd.

Chaiwat Tour, Khaosan Rd. *Byte in @ cup*, Rm 401, 4th Flr, Siam Discovery Centre, 989 Rama I Rd, open 1000-1900, www.byte-in-a-cup.com 4 laptops available for ฿150 per 2 hrs (free if you bring your own laptop). Coffee, cakes and sandwiches as well as maps and books available. *The Café*, Surawong Rd, Corner of Soi Thaniya (ryoidii@rms.ksc.co.th). Open 1100-2200. 4 terminals and modern plugs for bringing your own laptops. *Cyberia*, 654/8 Sukhumvit Rd, corner of Soi 24. Open Sun-Wed 1030-2300. Thu-Sat 1030-2400. 18 terminals, ฿250 per hour, classy joint, food and live music towards the end of the week. *Explorer Internet Café*, Patpong Soi 1, a new place with plans to expand; they hope to be open 24 hrs a day, at present they are open 1700-0100. **Central GPO** (*Praysani Klang* for taxi drivers): 1160 Charoen Krung, opposite the *Ramada Hotel*. Open 0800-2000 Mon-Fri and 0800-1300 weekend and holidays. The money and postal order service is open 0800-1700, Mon-Fri, 0800-1200 Sat. Closed on Sun and holidays. 24-hr telegram and telephone service (phone rates are reduced 2100-0700) and a packing service.

Cultural centres *British Council*, 254 Chulalongkorn Soi 64 (Siam Square), T6116830, F2535311. For films, books and other Anglocentric entertainment; check in 'What's On' section of *Sunday Bangkok Post's* magazine for programme of events. *Alliance Française*, 29 Sathorn Tai Rd. *Goethe Institute*, 18/1 Sathorn Tai Soi Atthakan Prasit. *Siam Society*, 131 Soi 21 (Asoke) Sukhumvit, T2583494. Promotes Thai culture and organizes trips within (and beyond) Thailand. Open Tue-Sat.

Embassies & consulates *Australia*, 37 Sathorn Tai Rd, T2872680. *Brunei*, 154 Ekamai Soi 14, Sukhumvit 63, T3815914, F3815921. *Cambodia*, 185 Rachdamri Rd, T2546630. *Canada*, 15th Flr Abdulrahim Place, 990 Rama 1V Rd, T6360541. *Denmark*, 10 Sathorn Tai Soi Attakarnprasit, T2132021. *Finland*, 16th Flr, 500 Amarin Tower, Ploenchit Rd, T2569306. *France*, 35 Customs House Lane, Charoen Krung, T2668250. (There is also a French consulate at 29 Sathorn Tai Rd, T2856104.) *Germany*, 9 Sathorn Tai Rd, T2132331. *Greece*, 79 Sukhumvit Soi 4, T2542936, F2542937. *India*, Sukhumvit Rd Soi 23, T2580300. *Indonesia*, 600-602 Phetburi Rd, T2523135. *Israel*, 25th Flr, Ocean Tower II, 75 Soi Wattana, Sukhumvit 19, T2604854. *Italy*, 399 Nang Linchi Rd, T2854090. *Japan*, 1674 New Phetburi Rd, T2526151. *Laos*, 502/1-3 Soi Ramkhamhaeng 39, T5396667. *Malaysia*, 33-35 Sathorn Tai Rd, T6792190. *Myanmar* (Burma), 132 Sathorn Nua Rd, T2332237. *Nepal*, 189 Sukhumvit Soi 71, T3917240. *Netherlands*, 106 Witthayu Rd, T2547701. *New Zealand*, 93 Witthayu Rd, T2542530. *Norway*, UBC 11 Building, 18th Flr, 591 Sukhumvit 33 Rd, T2611213. *People's Republic of China*, 57 Ratchadapisek Rd, Dindaeng, T2457032. *Philippines*, 760 Sukhumvit Rd, T2590139. *Singapore*, 129 Sathorn Tai Rd, T2862111. *South Africa*, 6th Flr, Park Place, 231 Soi Sarasin, Rachdamri Rd, T2538473. *Spain*, 7th Flr, Diethelm Building, 93 Witthayu Rd, T2526112. *Sweden*, 20th Flr, Pacific Place, 140 Sukhumvit Rd, T2544954. *UK*, 1031 Witthayu Rd, T2530191/9. *USA*, 95 Witthayu Rd, T2054000. *Vietnam*, 83/1 Witthayu Rd, T2517202, F2517201.

Language schools Bangkok has scores. The best known is the *AUA school* at 179 Rachdamri, T2528170.

Libraries *British Council Library*, 254 Chulalongkorn Soi 64 (Siam Square). Open Tue-Sat 1000-1930, membership library with good selection of English-language books. *National Library*, Samsen Rd, close to Sri Ayutthaya Rd. Open Mon-Sun 0930-1930. *Neilson Hays Library*, 195 Surawong Rd, T2331731. Next door to British Club. Open 0930-1600 Mon-Sat, 0930-1230 Sun. A small library of English-language books housed in an elegant building dating from 1922. It is a private membership library, but welcomes visitors who might want to see the building and browse; occasional exhibitions are held here. Open Mon-Sat 0930-1600, Sun 0930-1230. *Siam Society Library*, 131 Sukhumvit Soi 21 (Asoke). Membership library with excellent collection of Thai and foreign language books and periodicals (especially English) on Thailand and mainland south east Asia. Open Tue-Sat 0900-1700.

Medical services *Bangkok Adventist Hospital*, 430 Phitsanulok Rd, Dusit, T2811422/2821100. Efficient vaccination service and 24-hr emergency unit. *Bangkok General Hospital*, New Phetburi Soi 47, T3180066. *Bangkok Nursing Home*, 9 Convent Rd, T2332610. *St Louis Hospital*, 215 Sathorn Tai Rd, T2120033. **Health clinics:** *Dental Polyclinic*, New Phetburi Rd, T3145070. *Dental Hospital*, 88/88 Sukhumvit 49, T2605000, F2605026. Good, but expensive. *Clinic Banglamphu*, 187 Chakrapong Rd, T2827479.

Useful addresses *Tourist Police*, Unico House, Ploenchit Soi Lang Suan, T1699 or 6521721. There are also dedicated tourist police offices in the main tourist areas. **Immigration**: Sathorn Tai Soi Suanphlu, T2873101.

The Eastern Seaboard

4

The Eastern Seaboard

The Eastern region is sandwiched between the Gulf of Thailand to the south and the Damrek range of mountains to the north. It covers 37,507 sq km and stretches 400 km from Bangkok, southeast to Trat on the Cambodian border. It is similar to the Western region, in that it is small in area, without any focal city, and lacking a characteristic regional culture. It is also akin to the West in that, at least until not very long ago, the East was a relatively quiet and traditional area of fruit trees, gem mining and forests. It also had a flourishing fishing industry exploiting the waters of the Gulf of Thailand and serving the Bangkok market.

Although these activities have been overshadowed by recent developments, there are still orchards between Rayong and Chantaburi, a multitude of fishing communities along the Gulf coast, and a major centre for gem mining at Chantaburi, where many of Thailand's finest sapphires are sourced.

Development and tourism in the East

The east has been transformed since the 1960s. Illegal loggers have largely cleared the area of trees, and landless families from other parts of the kingdom – with the encouragement and support of Chinese middlemen – have moved in to plant the land to upland crops such as cassava and maize. As the forests were being replaced by crops, the beaches of the eastern Gulf were witnessing an extraordinary growth in tourism. This was focused on the famous (to some infamous) beach resort of Pattaya, about 150 km from Bangkok. Beginning as a resort for small numbers of Thais and *farangs* who wished to escape from the capital for weekend breaks, Pattaya developed into one of the key destinations for American GIs on leave during the Vietnam War. With the end of that war, Pattaya adroitly switched its attention to the international tourist market, attracting increasing numbers of men (and a few women). A Tourist Authority of Thailand survey revealed that over one-fifth of all tourists to Thailand visited the area of Pattaya and Chonburi. Assuming the survey is accurate (never a sensible assumption to make in Thailand), this would mean that well over a million international tourists visit this resort each year. When you add in domestic tourists, the numbers reach three million.

Although tourism is important to the economy of the east – and there is still room for further expansion – in recent years this has been superceded by its role as an overspill area for Bangkok. As Bangkok's infrastructure came under ever greater pressure, the government began looking for ways to ease the strain on the capital. In the early 1980s, it came up with the much vaunted Eastern Seaboard Development Project, a massive scheme which brought roads, ports, rail links, pipelines and gas separation plants to eastern Thailand – mostly concentrated along a corridor between the towns of Chonburi and Rayong.

Chonburi to Pattaya

Route 3 from Bangkok follows Thailand's eastern seaboard to the Cambodian border. The first 130 km (on the newish Highway 34) is a ribbon of development – effectively Bangkok's industrial overspill. Companies have moved here to escape the high land prices and congestion of the capital. As a result former sleepy towns like Chonburi and Si Racha have been engulfed. 147 km from Bangkok is the renowned beach resort of Pattaya, brash and brazen. Past Pattaya, Route 3 swings eastwards and passes through the town of Rayong (70 km from Pattaya), and then Ban Phe, where boats leave for the island of Koh Samet. Continuing on Route 3, Chantaburi is 109 km from Rayong, and Trat another 70 km on from here. Both towns are highly regarded for their fruit and gems. From the port of Laem Ngop, 17 km from Trat, boats leave for Koh Chang.

Chonburi

Phone code: 038
Colour map 1, grid A2

Chonburi is the first significant town travelling southeast from Bangkok along Route 3. It is an important commercial centre with oyster farms and fruit processing and canning plants serving the sugarcane, cassava and coconut farms and plantations of the area. It also has a reputation as a battlefield for the Chinese mafia. There is not much of interest for the tourist in this dusty town. The oldest and most important wat in the province is **Wat Intharam**, which is near the old market. The wat, dating from the Ayutthaya Period, is unusual in that it has not been extensively restored. The bot contains an excellent series of formally structured murals with no sense of perspective dating from the late 18th century. Near the centre of town is **Wat Dhamma Nimitr**, which contains a 37-m high image of the Buddha in a boat and covered in gold mosaic. Not only is this Buddha image the largest in the region, it is also one of the few in the country with a maritime theme.

There is a lot of accommodation in Chonburi, but it is rarely used by visitors to Thailand. This is an area of condominiums and time-share apartments for Bangkok's wealthy, get-aways for locals rather a holiday destination for foreigners. **B-C** *Sukjai Bungalow*, 17/32 Phayasatya Rd, T282255. Some a/c. **C** *Likhit*, 781 Chetchamnong Rd, T273810, F273811. Some a/c, restaurant.

Sleeping

Oct *Buffalo Races* (movable). Races and contests between buffalo and man.

Festivals

Road Bus: regular connections with Bangkok's Eastern bus terminal, Pattaya (67 km) and other eastern destinations.

Transport
80 km from Bangkok

The Eastern Seaboard

Bang Saen

Bang Saen is a beach resort popular with middle-class Thais. It is crowded at the weekends but practically deserted during the week and has good seafood. The town is clearly attempting to become another Pattaya, although it is difficult to see how it will succeed. That said, it does have a Hotels and Tourism Training Institute, so it should provide skilled services – and the town is surprisingly clean. On Monkey Hill there is the **shrine of Chao Mae Khao Sammuk**, a Chinese girl who drowned herself in the 18th century after her parents refused to allow her to marry the man she loved. Now a Goddess, many Sino-Thais visit the shrine to improve their luck. The oyster beds for which the town is known can be seen from the hill. There is usually a welcome onshore breeze on the sandy palm-fringed beach. The **Ocean World Amusement Park** is on the Beach Road, T383096. ■ *Mon-Sun ฿150 adults, ฿100 children.*
There is a **Marine Science Museum** in Srinakarinwirot University.

Phone code: 039
Colour map 1, grid A2

Like Chonburi, Bang Saen is mainly used by Bangkokians looking for a weekend away from the grime within easy reach of the capital. Overseas visitors rarely come here. **A-C** *Bang Saen Beach Resort*, 55-150 Beach Rd, T381675, B2536385. A/c, restaurant, pool, close to the action. **A-C** *Bang Saen Villa*, T282088, F311726. A/c, restaurant, pool, good views, well run and recommended attached restaurant. **C-D** *Saen Sabai Bungalow*, 153 Beach Rd, T381063, a/c, restaurant.

Sleeping

Road Bus: regular connections with Bangkok's Eastern Bus terminal (1½ hrs) and with Chonburi (18 km south) and Pattaya.

Transport
98 km from Bangkok

Banks *Siam Commercial*, 53/1 Bang Saen Rd.

Directory

Si Racha

Si Racha, some 100 km from Bangkok, is the home of a locally famous hot chilli sauce (*nam prik Si Racha*), usually eaten with seafood, for which the town also has a reputation. The town has a profusion of seafood restaurants, the most enjoyable of which are built on jetties which protrude out to sea. Westerners usually visit Si Racha in order to reach the island of Koh Si Chang (see page 163), but the town does have character and is worth more than a cursory wander.

Sights A short distance to the north of town is a small, gaudy but nevertheless enjoyable **Sino-Thai wat** built on a rocky islet – **Koh Loi** – connected to the mainland by a long causeway. The monastery commemorates a monk who spent many years on the rock and it boasts a footprint of the Buddha as well as an image of the Chinese Goddess of Mercy, Kuan Yin. On Choemchomphon Road, the waterfront road, and almost opposite Soi 16, is the **Jaw Phor Samut Dam Chinese temple** said to be 100 years old. Up the road towards the clock-tower at the southern end is a large covered **market**. However, perhaps the most enjoyable feature of Si Racha (and of Koh Si Chang) are the overpowered, chariot-like **motorized saamlors**. Purring along, with deep bucket seats and massive engines, the machines seem like outrageous modernized rickshaws. They cannot be a terribly efficient form of transport and it probably will not be long before they are elbowed out by the ubiquitous tuk-tuk – unless their macho appeal helps them to survive.

Si Racha place names

Jaw Phor Samut Dam Chinese temple

วัดเจ้าพ่อสมุทรดำ

Laem Chabang

แหลมฉบัง

The Eastern Seaboard, and in particular the length of coast between Chonburi and Rayong, was selected in the 1980s as the overspill area for Bangkok's industry and as a result there has been an upsurge in activity around Si Racha. **Laem Chabang**, just the other side of Khao Nam Sap, a modest hill 10 km to the south of town, has been developed into a major deep-water port and can be seen from the road to Pattaya. Even closer to Si Racha, just a few kilometres south, is the Thai Oil refinery. So far, and surprisingly, Si Racha has maintained its poise amidst all this activity.

Excursions Si Racha Tiger Farm is a little less than 10 km east of town, off route 3241. This really has a remarkable collection of tigers – well over 100 Bengal tigers at the last count – which appear to breed like rabbits. In addition to the tigers there is a scorpion zone and a crocodile farm as well as assorted camels, elephants and deer. ■ *Mon-Sun, 0800-1800, ฿250, ฿150 (children). Getting there: take a tuk-tuk from town.*

Sleeping Like its restaurants, all the hotels mentioned below except the *Laemthong* are built over the sea – which makes a pleasant change from the usual featureless budget accommodation available in Thai towns. Many of these hotels are well run, clean and atmospheric affairs, most with great restaurants attached.

B-C *Grand Bungalow*, 9 Choemchomphon Soi 18, T312537. South end of town, range of bungalows built off a jetty. Better for larger groups or families rather than couples. **B-C** *Laemthong Residence Hotel*, Sukhumvit Rd, T322888, F312651. A/c, restaurant, pool, tennis. Modern hotel lacking the character of the others listed here, but the closest thing to a starred establishment. Central location. **C-D** *Srivichai*, Choemchomphon Rd, Soi 8, T311212. Wooden hotel, much like the *Sri Wattana*, just a shade pricier, friendly, good attached restaurant, clean and classy. Recommended. **D-E** *Bungalow Sri Wattana*, Choemchomphon Rd, Soi 8, T311037. Wooden hotel constructed on a jetty, friendly and clean with great atmosphere and enthusiastic service. Good restaurant attached. Recommended. **D-E** *Samchai*, Choemchomphon Rd, Soi 10, T311134. Some a/c, wooden hotel, clean rooms, good atmosphere, great food. Recommended.

Eating Si Racha is known for its seafood, which is generally excellent. Many restaurants are Chinese rather than Thai, or at least Sino-Thai. Mussels and oysters are particularly good, and many of the dishes come with Si Racha's famed chilli sauce. Price depends to a great extent on what type of seafood takes your fancy: grilled lobster is several times more expensive than a simple *pla kapong* dish. However all of the following are good. **Seafood**: *Si Racha Seafood*, Choemchomphon Rd (near the bus stop). *Cherinot*, Choemchomphon Rd, Soi 14 (pier). *Jaw Sii*, 98 Choemchomphon Rd. *Hua Huat*, 102 Choemchomphon Rd. *Chua Li*, Choemchomphon Soi 10, most pricey of the seafood restaurants in town with an established, and well-deserved reputation for quality victuals.

Road Bus: Connections every 30 mins or so with Bangkok's Eastern bus terminal as well as with Pattaya (29 km north) and Chonburi (24 km south). Songthaews for Naklua in Pattaya leave from close to the clock tower at regular intervals.

Transport
105 km from Bangkok

Train: While just about everyone arrives here by bus, there are a handful of trains each day from Hualamphong station in Bangkok. Cheap, slow but considerably more attractive than the bus journey.

Boat: Ferries for Si Racha depart from the pier at the end Jermjomphon Rd, Soi 14 (see Si Racha entry for details).

Banks *Bangkok Bank of Commerce*, Surasak Rd.

Directory

Koh Si Chang

Koh Si Chang is a small island about 45 minutes ferry ride from Si Racha with a resident population of fewer than 5,000 people. Although it is quite feasible to visit the island as a day trip, there are hotels and camping facilities for those who might wish to stay longer.

Phone code: 038
Colour map 1, grid B2

Koh Si Chang used to be the trans-shipment point for both cargo and passenger vessels before the Chao Phraya River was dredged sufficiently to allow ships to reach Bangkok. Even though many vessels now bypass Si Racha, the surrounding water is still chock-a-block with ships at anchor (normally about 50, but sometimes as many as 100 ships), their cargoes being unloaded into smaller lighters and barges. The island's main trade is now as a service base for the freighter crews. Their visas often do not allow them to disembark, so all R & R is taken to them by the varied residents of Koh Si Chang. In the bay just out from the town can be seen a white ship – the *Phnom Phenh* – previously a floating hotel but severely damaged by fire two years ago. Ever since then, the ship's crew have been confined, so it is said, to ship. The island also has a reputation as a sanctuary for criminals. The drugs trade is reportedly rife and corruption within the police force endemic. Reports of individual travellers being asked for customary gifts of whisky and the like have been known. This is reportedly more of a problem in isolated spots like Tham Phang.

At the northern edge of the town, set high up on a hill (a tiring walk to the top), there is a **Chinese temple – Chaw Por Khaw Yai**. With an assortment of variously decorated shrines and caves, and with views of the island and town, it makes a good first stop after docking at the jetty beneath the temple. A particular favourite with the Chinese at Chinese New Year, it is said that during the festivities, over 5,000 people visit the shrine each evening, more than doubling the island's population.

On the west side of the island is **Khaw Khad**, a popular weekend fishing spot for Bangkokians. Not far away to the south, and overlooking the town, is a **Buddhist retreat** set among limestone caves (unlit). A large, yellow, seated

Sights
Don't come to Koh Si Chang expecting a tropical idyll.

The Eastern Seaboard

Buddha image looks out over the bay. On the east coast, south of the retreat, are the **ruins of a palace** built by Rama V. It was abandoned in 1893 when the French took control of the island during their confrontation with the Thais regarding each country's respective rights of suzerainty over Laos. Not much remains – in fact, most of the structure was dismantled and rebuilt in Bangkok. Rather eerie stairways, balustrades and an empty reservoir remain scattered across the rocky, frangipani-covered hillside – as if the palace had been vaporized. There has been some, limited re-building work but even so the only building of any size remaining is **Wat Atsadangnimit**. This monastery is still revered and attracts a surprising number of pilgrims largely because King Chulalongkorn used to meditate here. The Buddha image within the sanctuary is unusual in style if not remarkable in artistic accomplishment. ■ *0800-1800.*

The island also has a number of **beaches** and reasonable swimming and snorkelling. The quietest beach with the best coral and swimming is **Tham Phang** on the western side of the island (฿10 by tuk-tuk); easier to reach are **Tha Wang** (next to the palace) – a rocky beach and not suitable for swimming – and **Hat Sai Khao** (over the hill from the palace). At weekends the island becomes crowded with Thai day-trippers; it is more relaxed during the week. While it is possible to swim here, note that the waters are really pretty turbid and at certain times of year the currents can wash all sorts of trash onto the beach.

Sleeping **A-B** *Si Chang Palace*, Atsadang Rd, T216276. A/c, restaurant, pool. The top of the pile on the island, this hideous building seems very out of place and is overpriced. Its redeeming feature is that is has great views (and a pool).

B-D *Si Phitsanu Bungalows*, Hat Tham, T216024. Some a/c, a range of rooms and bungalows available here with views over the sea, out of town not far from Hat Tham. **B-D** *Tew Phai*, T216084. Some a/c, restaurant (pricey), welcoming management and usually busy with activity, the best of the cheaper places to stay, but not as good as the hoardings suggest. A tout will meet you at the pier as you alight from your boat which goes a long way to explaining why it is so popular.

C-D *Benz*, T216091. Some a/c, unusual stone bungalows, clean and well kept, close to the sea. **D** *Green House*, T216024. Simple green rooms at the edge of the town, in a style reminiscent of 1960s Skegness. A good view, if it wasn't for the uncontrolled undergrowth.

Camping This is possible, but bring your own equipment; at weekends Thais from the mainland camp in large numbers.

Eating *Si Chang Palace Coffee Shop*, an a/c refuge offering a range of coffee and cakes.

Transport **Local** There are a number of the massive motorized **saamlors** that are also found in Si Racha and Chonburi. Given that the roads (in reality, paths) only allow the drivers to attain a speed of about 30 km per hour, they must be among the most overpowered taxis in the world. A tour of all the sights should not be more than ฿150 – and in chariot-like splendour (the owner of No 38, Nerng, speaks reasonable English and distributes maps free of charge).

Boat Regular daytime ferry service from Jermjomphon Rd, Soi 14 in Si Racha, 0900-1700 outward, 0630-1630 return, 40 mins, but frequently more, because of drop-offs to the many ships moored in the harbour (฿30). The more expensive hotels can be booked from the pier in Si Racha.

Directory **Banks** *Thai Farmers*, 9-9/1-2 Coast Rd.

Pattaya

Pattaya or 'Southwest wind' is argued by some to be Thailand's premier beach resort, yet only 25 years ago it was a little-known coastal village frequented by fishermen, farmers and a handful of Thai and farang weekenders.

Ins and outs

Pattaya is well connected with Bangkok. Most people arrive here by bus from the capital's Eastern bus terminal, and there are dozens of departures daily from VIP to economy. The road from Bangkok is good and fast and the journey takes about 2 hrs. There are even direct connections from Bangkok's Don Muang Airport. U-Tapao is the nearest airport to Pattaya but the only scheduled service is **Bangkok Airways**' daily connection with Koh Samui. There is also a train station, although the service with Bangkok is limited.

Getting there
Phone code: 038
Colour map 1, grid B2

The town itself is simple to get around. It consists of one long straight seafront road running the length of the beach (Pattaya Beach Road), together with another parallel road just inland (Pattaya 2 Road). Linking the two there are innumerable sois (lanes) packed with bars, restaurants and hotels. The greatest concentration of restaurants and bars is at the south end of town. Local transport is abundant. Songthaews run regularly between all the tourist centres and there are also scores of people hiring out bikes, motorbikes and jeeps. The **tourist office**, *TAT*, 382/1 Beach Rd, T428750, F429113, has helpful staff and lots of information. Areas of responsibility are Pattaya and Samut Prakan. There are several free tourist magazines and maps available. Unlike some other areas of Thailand, obtaining information is easy.

Getting around

The Eastern Seaboard

The resort

Pattaya began to metamorphose when the US navy set up shop at the nearby port of Sattahip (40 km further down the coast) and American sailors began to demand something more than just sand and sea. As the war in Vietnam escalated, so the influx of GIs on 'rest and recreation' also grew and Pattaya responded enthusiastically. (Not by chance, Pattaya was selected as an R & R destination for the UN peacekeeping forces in Cambodia in 1992-93 bringing the town the title 'city of peace'.) Today, it provides around 36,000 hotel rooms and supplies everything you could ever need from a beach holiday – except, arguably, peace and quiet. Given its origins in the Vietnam War, it is hardly surprising that Pattaya's stock in trade is entertainment for unaccompanied men who arrive in droves, many of them on package tours. At any one time, about 4,000 girls are touting for work around the many bars and restaurants of Pattaya. In the past, most of Pattayas tourists came from the US, Australasia and Western Europe. However over the last few years these traditional sources have been in decline while visitors from Eastern Europe and Russia have escalated. There are now even tourist magazines in Russian and most of the bars stock a good range of vodkas and the bar girls have a smattering of Russian.

Around 3 mn people are said to visit Pattaya each year

  While Pattaya's official population is a comparatively paltry 60,000, most people believe that at any one time there are between 200,000 and 300,000 staying in town, whether international tourists or migrant workers. This has inevitably led to environmental problems. Lack of treatment of polluted water has meant that the beaches are not as clean as they once were – and the waters offshore can have a coliform count that should make most people stick to their hotel swimming pools or baths. This applies particularly to South Pattaya

Pattaya

To Ocean Marina Yacht Club, Siriporn Orchid Garden, Sattahip & Nong Nooch Village (Rt 3)

Related maps
A Pattaya Beach,
page 171

■ **Sleeping**

1	Asia Pattaya	11	Silver Sand Villa
2	Central Wong Amat	12	Sugar Hut
3	Gardenia		
4	Garden Lodge		🚌 **Buses**
5	Island View	1	BKS non a/c to Bangkok
6	Mermaid's Beach Resort	2	A/c bus to North & Northeast
7	Pattaya Park Beach	3	A/c bus terminal
8	Royal Cliff Beach	4	Bus to Sattahip
9	Sawasdee Palace	5	Sri Mongkhon Tour - buses to northeast
10	Sea Breeze	6	407 Pattana Tour - buses to Nong Khai

Beach where swimming, as yet, is not recommended. However, in 1992, the government allocated US$42mn in an effort to clean up Pattaya's act and Pattaya is already Thailand's first provincial city to have a water treatment plant. South Pattaya Beach, according to the authorities, should (should being the operative word) be clean enough to swim off, now that new waste water works have been completed.

Indeed, Pattaya – according to official statements at least – is going out of its way to play down its go-go bar image and promote a 'family' resort profile. This is deemed to be good for business, and perhaps the only way that occupancy rates can be maintained when the sex industry in Thailand is coming under such scrutiny, both for health and social reasons. (In 1996 average occupancy rates barely touched 50%.) This emphasis on good ol' wholesome family fun is hard to reconcile with the reality. But still the effort continues. It was no coincidence that an international conference on 'sustainable tourism' was held in Jomtien, outside Pattaya, a few years ago. The conference produced the so-called Pattaya Protocol, a series of guidelines on how to promote culturally and environmentally sensitive tourism. As well as trying to entice families to come here, local planners are also trying to re-cast Pattaya as a conference and incentive break venue. But just when things look like they are improving, something comes along to makes a mess of all the efforts. In 1997 there was an algae bloom that made the water even less appealing than it usually is, and in July 1997 there was a blaze at the 16-storey *Royal Jomtien Resort*, with the death of 80 people. Most recently of all, in 2000 a British tourist was gored by an enraged elephant at the Nong Nooch Tropical Garden. She died in hospital shortly afterwards.

The busiest and noisiest area is at the southern end of town (South Pattaya or 'The Village'); from about Soi 11 to Soi Post Office (with Pattayaland 1, 2 and 3 being the gay areas of town), there must be one of the highest concentration of bars, discos, massage parlours, prostitutes and transvestites of any place in the world. Many people find this aspect of Pattaya repugnant. However, there is no pretence here – either on the part of the hosts or their guests. This is a beach resort of the most lurid kind. **Warning** It is worth bearing in mind that whatever people might tell you, Thailand *does* have an **AIDS** problem, the most serious in Asia (see page 54).

Pattaya may be infamous in the west as a city of sin, but there is more to the resort than this popular perception might indicate. It is also a haven for watersports lovers: there is sailing, para-sailing, windsurfing, ski-boating, snorkelling, deep-sea fishing and scuba diving. And for the non-beach lover, there are trips to sapphire mines, orchid farms and elephant kraals as well as tennis, golf (the Siam Country Club has the best course in Thailand), bowling and a multitude of other sports. Pattaya is also remarkably good value. It is probably this, coupled with the range of activities and services on offer (and Pattaya's accessibility) which explains why – despite the bad press – the resort has so many repeat guests (25-50%). Indeed, Pattaya's negative press has been overdone; it is not the tourist hell-hole one might expect from some of the reports. It may be raucous and somewhat tarnished – but it is also a bargain.

Pattaya place names

Bang Saray

บางเสร่

Elephant Village

หมู่บ้านช้าง

Khao Khieo 'Open Zoo'

สวนสัตว์เปิดเขาเขียว

Mini Siam

เมืองจำลอง

Nong Nooch Orchid Wonderland

สวนนงนุช

The Eastern Seaboard

Sights

Big Buddha   There are few sights, as such, in Pattaya to compare with many other places in the Kingdom. However, many visitors do make their way to the **Big Buddha** on the hill at the southern end of the beach (see map page 166). There are good views over the resort from the vantage point and the monks based here are usually willing to talk to interested visitors. The main Buddha image is surrounded by smaller images representing each day of the week. In the evenings **South Pattaya Road** is entertaining to explore because it is closed off to traffic. It's the best time to check out the bars, shops and so on.

Jomtien Beach   South of Pattaya Bay, past the Big Buddha on the hill, is the quieter **Jomtien Beach**, which is becoming more popular by the month. Here there are more hotels, restaurants and sports facilities as well as a slightly cleaner beach. One of the highlights of our most recent visit to Pattaya was a trip up the **Pattaya Park Tower**. Situated on the headland at Jomtien, this 240-m pinnacle provides spectacular views of the surrounding area, and for some extra excitement, it is possible to travel down the zip-wire from 170 m to ground level (see sports below). For ฿200, visitors travel to the top of the tower and get one ride down the zip wire. For another ฿300, a buffet meal is provided in the *Pinnacle Revolving Restaurant*. T251201 for more information.

Other things to do – and bear in mind that these are modest attractions to say the very most – include a visit to the verbosely named **Million Years Stone Park and Pattaya Crocodile Farm** at 22/2 Moo 1, Tambon Nong Pla Lai, Banglamong, T249347, where there are granite rock gardens, with fossils, bonsai trees and various rare animals. ■ *0900-1800*. Alternatively, you could try the **Siriporn Orchid Farm** at 235/14 Moo 5, Tambon Nong Prue, T429013, where there is an array of orchids on show (and for sale). ■ *Mon-Sun, 0800-1700 ฿10*. The **Bottle Museum** at 79/15 Moo 10, Sukhumvit Road, T422957, displays over 300 pieces of artwork, the result of 15 years hard labour by the Dutch sculptor Leter Bedelais. Finally, the **Ripleys Believe it or not Museum**, T710294, is on the third floor of the *Royal Garden Plaza*, easily identified by the red biplane stuck on the side of the building. It consists of a collection of curiosities, both originals and replica. All a bit tacky. ■ *Mon-Sun, 1000-2400 ฿150*.

Excursions

Mini Siam   Mini Siam is a cultural and historical park where 80 of Thailand's most famous 'sights' – including, for example, Wat Phra Kaeo and the Bridge over the River Kwai – are recreated at a scale of 1:25. There are also replicas of some other sights including the Eiffel Tower and the Statue of Liberty. ■ *T421628 for details. 0700-2200. Getting there: by tour or by songthaew; the park lies 3 km north of Pattaya Beach, on the Sukhumvit highway (Route 3) running to Bangkok, at the Km 143 marker.*

Khao Khieo 'Open Zoo'   Khao Khieo 'Open Zoo' is a 500 ha forested area supporting 130 species of bird and 38 mammal (including a few leopards); there is also a wildlife education centre with museum, and the requisite waterfall (*Chanta Then*). There is no overnight accommodation. ■ *Daily 0800-1800. ฿20, ฿5 children, ฿20 for a car, T311561. Getting there: 30 km north on Route 3, turn inland near Bang Saen on Route 3144. The park lies close to Bang Phra Golf Course.*

Elephant Village   The Elephant Village is near the Siam Country Club. ■ *฿300, show at 1430.* There is also elephant trekking available which lasts two hours and takes the intrepid pachyderm jockey into the surrounding bush (฿700). Contact *Tropicana Hotel* for booking, T428645-8, Ext Elephant Village Counter or T249174 after 1800.

The Nong Nooch Tropical Garden is a 200-ha park containing immaculate gardens with lakes (and boating), an orchid farm, family zoo, Thai handicraft demonstrations and a thrice-daily (1015, 1500 and 1545) 'cultural spectacular' with Thai dancing, Thai boxing and an elephant show, T429321 for details. In 2000 a British tourist was gored here by an enraged elephant and later died. It is similar to the 'Rose Garden' complex outside Bangkok and is rather artificial, though it serves a purpose for tourists visiting nowhere but Pattaya and is popular with children. **Sleeping** Available in traditional Thai cottages and there are a number of restaurants. But much better is Sunset Village, about 2 km fron Nong Nooch. Very quiet, with a small beach, good bungalows, pool and excellent seafood. Good for lunch or to stay the night. ■ *Mon-Sun 0900-1800. ฿20, ฿200 for the cultural show, or take a tour from Pattaya for ฿250, T238063. Getting there: most people arrive on a tour; the garden is 15 mins from Pattaya town 3 km off the main road at the Km 163 marker.*

Nong Nooch Tropical Garden

Bang Saray is a fishing village 20 km south of Pattaya on Route 3, with seafood restaurants (notably the *Ruan Talay*) and a good base for game-fishing trips, which can be arranged at the Fisherman's Inn, Fisherman's Lodge, or the Sea Sand Club; a chartered boat costs about ฿2,500. **Sleeping B** Fisherman's Lodge, T436757. A/c, restaurant. **B** Fisherman's Inn, T436095. A/c, restaurant, pool, spacious grounds. **C** Bang Saray Villa, T436070. A/c, restaurant, pool. **C** The Sea Sand Club, T435163, F435166. A/c and facilities for windsurfing. Good seafood restaurants here. ■ *Getting there: by bus from Pattaya.*

Bang Saray

When Pattaya gets too much, many people retire to one of the offshore islands for rest and recreation of a different kind. The largest island (and the only one with accommodation) is **Koh Larn**, with good snorkelling and scuba diving waters surrounding it. Glass-bottomed boats are available for touring the reef, as is the full array of watersports. The island even has an 18-hole golf course. **Sleeping** *Koh Larn Resort*, its office is at 183 Soi Post Office, T428422. **B** for bungalows, which include the boat fare and transfer to the bungalows. ■ *Getting there: the Resort office will organize boats, or tickets can be purchased from the booth next to the Sailing Club. Boats depart at 0930 and 1130, returning at 1600, 45 mins (฿250).* Boats can be chartered for ฿1,500 per day. A shared sailing junk ฿250 (inclusive of lunch and coral reef viewing), or a chartered sailing junk costs ฿3,000 per day. 'Tours' to Koh Larn, have watersports organized by the travel agent.

Further afield are the islands of **Koh Lin**, **Koh Sak** and **Koh Phai**, where there is better coral but fewer facilities. Only charter-boats visit these islands, for double the price of Koh Larn.

Offshore Islands

There are countless tours organized by the many travel agents in town: the standard long-distance trips are to Koh Samet, the sapphire mines near Chantaburi, Ayutthaya and Bang Pa-In, Bangkok, the floating market, Kanchanaburi and the River Kwai Bridge (two days). There are also local tours to Nong Nooch village, the Elephant Village and Khao Khieo Open Zoo, among others. Prices for day tours (meal included) range from ฿600-1,200.

Tours

The Eastern Seaboard

Essentials

Sleeping Pattaya has the biggest selection of hotels in Thailand outside Bangkok (36,000 rooms at the last count), although there is little left here for the budget traveller, with rooms from ฿350 upwards. However, for those who are looking for places one notch up from budget places then there is lots to choose from and most are very good value. There are three distinct areas of accommodation. At the northern end of the beach is the area of **Naklua**. This is the quieter end of town, although it still has its fair share of clubs and bars with little attempt to disguise their raison d'être. **Pattaya beach** is busier and gets noisier and more active from north to south. On round the headland is **Jomtien**, with a better beach but less nightlife. All accommodation in our '**A**' range has a/c, restaurant, pool, and prices are exclusive of tax. A continuing room glut means reduced rates (up to 50%) should be offered except at weekends and high season. The high season is Nov-Mar.

Naklua AL *Central Wong Amat*, 277-8 Moo 5, Naklua, T426990, F428599, www.centralgroup.com Set in 25 acres, choice of 100 or so deluxe rooms or 65 chalet and bungalow rooms, business facilities, 2 pools (1 good sized laps pool), watersports facilities, good position away from the main drag. **A** *Woodlands Resort*, 164/1 Pattaya-Naklua Rd, T421707, F425663. On the edge of Pattaya and Naklua. This hotel has tried to recreate a colonial lodge-type atmosphere – only partially successfully – but it is quiet, leafy and airy with attractive rooms and pool and landscaped gardens.

B *Garden Lodge*, Naklua Rd, T429109, F421221. A/c, pool, bungalow rooms looking onto mature gardens, quiet and excellent value. Recommended. **B** *Gardenia*, near North Pattaya Rd, T426356, F426358. A/c, pool. **B** *Loma*, Soi Naklua 18, T426027, F421501. A/c, restaurant, pool. **B** *Sea View Resort*, Soi Naklua 18, T424825. A/c, restaurant, pool. **C** *Sawasdee Palace*, Naklua Rd (near Soi 16), T225651, F225616. A/c, pool. Recommended. **C** *Sea Lodge*, Naklua Rd, T425128, F425129. A/c, pool.

Pattaya Beach   L-AL *Royal Cliff Beach*, 353 Moo 12 Cliff Rd, South Pattaya, T250421, F250511, www.royalcliffco.th A/c, restaurants, pool, every imaginable facility in this almost 1,000-room hotel, a great favourite with conference and incentive groups, but so large that it is hard not to be just one of the crowd. Set high up on the promontory at the south end of the beach, it is also rather gross with 9 restaurants, 5 pools, fitness centre, tennis courts, 3-hole practice golf course and more. **L-A** *Royal Garden Resort*, 218 Moo 10, Pattaya 2 Rd, T428126, F429926. A/c, restaurants, pool, tennis, 4-storey shopping mall with boutiques, handicrafts and fast-food outlets. Similar to McDonald's downstairs – tasteless, the same wherever you go and nothing like the adverts.

L-AL *Dusit Resort*, 240 Beach Rd (north end), T425611, F428239. Health club, tennis, squash courts, children's pools, table tennis and a games room, watersports, clean, private beach, shopping arcade, disco, excellent hotel with 474 room, good service and all facilities. **AL** *Montien*, Beach Rd, T428155, F423155, B2337060. Central location, extensive mature gardens, still excellent hotel, despite its age and size. **AL-A** *Nova Lodge*, Beach Rd (northern end), T420016, F429959. Large pool and gardens, tennis, simple (given the rates) rooms with balconies, central position. **AL-A** *Siam Bayshore*, Pattaya Beach Rd, T427272, F428730. A/c, restaurant, pool, 270-room hotel, made up of rather sombre interlinking blocks, on large 20-acre plot of land at the southern end of Pattaya Beach, set back from the beach, great swimming pools, tennis, separate Garden Wing for families, with a playground and children's pool. **AL-A** *Siam Bayview*, 310/2 Moo 10 Pattaya 2 Rd, T423871, F423879. Rather ugly 270-room block, only some rooms with ocean views and balconies, small free-form pools, rather cramped site. **A** *Amari Orchid Resort*, Beach Rd, North Pattaya,

Pattaya Beach

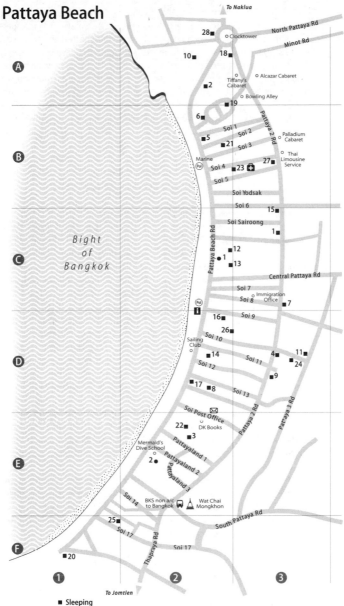

The Eastern Seaboard

- **Sleeping**
- 1 AA Pattaya *C3*
- 2 Amari Orchid Resort *A2*
- 3 ANZAC *E2*
- 4 Bay Breeze *D3*
- 5 Beach View *B2*
- 6 BJ's Guesthouse *B2*
- 7 Chris' Guesthouse *C3*
- 8 Caesar Palace *D2*
- 9 Diana Inn *D3*
- 10 Dusit Resort *A2*
- 11 Honey Inn *D3*

- 12 Merlin *C2*
- 13 Montien *C2*
- 14 Nautical Inn *D2*
- 15 Novotel Tropicana *C3*
- 16 Ocean View *D2*
- 17 Palm Garden *D2*
- 18 Palm Lodge *A2*
- 19 Regent Marina *A2*
- 20 Right Spot Inn *F1*
- 21 Royal Cruise *B2*
- 22 Royal Garden *E2*

- 23 Royal Night *B3*
- 24 Sawasdee Mansion
  & Guesthouse *D3*
- 25 Siam Bayshore *F1*
- 26 Siam Bayview *D2*
- 27 Thai Palace *B3*
- 28 Woodlands Resort *A2*

- ● **Eating**
- 1 Orient Express *C2*
- 2 Oslo *E2*

Related maps
Pattaya, page 166

T428161, F428165, www.amari.com A/c, restaurants, Olympic-sized pool, tennis, mini-golf, watersports. 230 room hotel on a tranquil 10 acre plot of lush landscaped gardens at the northern end of the beach, away from most of the bars and discos. **A** *Merlin Pattaya*, Pattaya Beach Rd (near Central Pattaya Rd), T428755, F421673, B2557611. One of Pattaya's original high-rise hotels with 360 rooms in 3 wings, a large compound, equally large pool, but rather impersonal. **A** *Novotel Tropicana*, 98 Pattaya 2 Rd, T428645, F423031, B2162278. Almost 200 rooms in this low-rise hotel which occupies a large plot in the centre of town, rooms are unimaginative and the hotel rather impersonal, competitive rates. **A** *Regent Marina*, 463/31 North Pattaya Beach Rd, T429977, F423296, B3902511. Situated in quiet northern end of town, well designed with excellent music bar – the *Laser Pub*. **A** *Royal Cruise*, 499 Beach Rd, near Soi 2, T/F424242. Novel design – the hotel looks like a cruise liner (the 'first cruise on land', as they bill it) – rooms (or 'cabins') are average however, though rates are good and it offers a wide range of facilities including sauna, gym and jacuzzi.

B *AA Pattaya*, 182-182/2 Beach Rd, Soi 13, T428656, F429057. In the midst of bar-land, attractive fourth-floor pool, well-equipped rooms. Recommended. **B** *Bay Breeze*, 503/2 Pattaya 2 Rd (near Soi 10), T428384, F429137. A/c, restaurant, pool, in the centre of town, away from beach but rooms are large and well equipped, rather featureless but good value. **B** *Beach View*, 389 Beach Rd, near Soi 2, T422660, F422664. A/c, restaurant, pool, one of Pattaya's older hotels, rooms are dated and the pool is small, but room rates are keenly priced. **B** *Grand*, 103 Mu 10, Soi 14, T428249. A/c, friendly, good service. **B** *Ma Maison*, Soi 13 Beach Rd, T429318. A/c, pool. As the name suggests, it's French run. Rooms are arranged around a pool, restaurant serves excellent food. **B** *Nautical Inn*, Soi 11 Beach Rd, T429890, F428116. A/c, restaurant, pool, older and now rather dated, low-rise hotel on large plot of land in the centre of town, large rooms are a little run-down, but has more character than most, with distinct seaside atmosphere. **B** *Ocean View*, Pattaya Beach Rd (near Soi 9), T428084, F424123. A/c, restaurant, pool, built over 20 years ago, which means rooms are a good size – if a touch dated and seedy – and the hotel benefits from a big compound in a prime position, good value. **B** *Palm Garden*, Pattaya 2 Rd (north end), T429386, F429188. A/c, restaurant, pool, rooms and corridors are rather dingy, but large compound, clean and well maintained, good pool and excellent value. **B-C** *Palm Lodge*, North Pattaya Beach Rd (near Soi 6), T428779. Small hotel catering mainly for single male visitors, small pool, central, good room rates.

The bulk of the cheaper accommodation is at the southern end of the beach and is in our '**C**' range; non a/c rooms are cheaper. **C** *BJ's Guesthouse*, 405 Beach Rd (northern end), T421148. A/c, good-value rooms in a small guesthouse above a restaurant. Unpredictable airconditioning. **C** *Caesar Palace*, Pattaya 2 Rd opposite Soi 8, T428607. A/c, restaurant, pool. **C** *Chris's Guesthouse*, Soi 12, Beach Rd, T429586, F422140. A/c, near centre of town down quiet soi in secluded courtyard, large, clean rooms, English management, friendly, the most welcoming place for backpackers. Recommended. **C** *Diana Inn*, 216/6-9 Pattaya 2 Rd, between Sois 11 and 12, T429675, F424566. A/c, restaurant, pool, on busy road but rooms have good facilities for price, modern, well-run, friendly and popular. Recommended. **C** *Honey Inn*, 529/2 Pattaya 2 Rd, Soi 10, T428117. A/c, restaurant, pool, large, clean rooms, small pool, frequented largely by single men – not a family hotel, but good value nonetheless, down quiet soi, away from beach. **C** *Right Spot Inn*, situated in south Pattaya. Clean and quiet with an excellent restaurant, there is no swimming pool but residents, provided they buy a drink, can use the pool at *Windy Inn* next door, central position and comes highly recommended by one multiple return visitor. **C** *Thai Palace*, 212 Pattaya 2 Rd, T423062, F427698. A/c, restaurant, small pool, central, rooms arranged around a courtyard, clean and competitively priced. **C-D** *Royal Night Hotel-bungalow*, 362/9 Pattaya Beach, Soi 5, T428038. Quiet hotel halfway down Soi 5, small shaded pool, good rooms, hot water, popular.

D *ANZAC*, 325 Pattayaland 1, T427822, F427823. A/c, restaurant, homely atmosphere with only 22 rooms, well run. **D** *Sawasdee Mansion and Guesthouse*, 502/1 Pattaya 2 Rd, Soi 10, T425360. Some a/c, one of the cheapest places in town, but don't expect a quaint bungalow on a palm lined beach ... this is a high-rise block down a built-up soi, but the rooms are clean, cool, serviceable and good.

Jomtien L *Ocean Marina Yacht Club*, 274/1-9 Moo 4, Sukhumvit Highway, T237310, F237325. Massive high-rise which is hard to miss, ostentatious hotel linked to the marina with choice of restaurants, a games deck with pool, tennis and squash courts, fitness centre, there is also a 25-m pool. Extensive business facilities. **L-A** *Asia*, 325 Cliff Rd, T250602, F250496, B2150808. Health club, tennis, golf, all facilities.

AL *Sugar Hut*, 391/18 Thaphraya Rd, on the way to Jomtien Beach, T251686, F251689. A/c, restaurant, 2 pools, overgrown gardens with rabbits and peacocks. Thai-style bungalows ('single' is adequate for 2 people), not on the beach, but very attractive grounds. Recommended. **A** *Ambassador City*, 21/10 Sukhumvit Rd, Km 55, Jomtien Beach, T255501, F255731, B2550444. Enormous. **A** *Pattaya Park*, 345 Jomtien Beach Rd (north end), T251201, F251209, B5110717. Watersports facilities (but you pay for them), ugly coffee bar, panoramic restaurant and bar charges ฿280 just to step inside. **A-B** *Silver Sand Villa*, 97 Moo 12, Jomtien Beach Rd, T231288, F231030. A/c, restaurant, pool, plain but reasonably sized rooms, large pool, on the beach.

B *Island View*, Cliff Rd, T250813, F250818, B2498941. A/c, restaurant, pool. **B** *Mermaid's Beach Resort*, 75/102 Moo 12 Nong Prue, Jomtien Beach Rd, T428755, F421673. A/c, restaurant, pool. **B** *Sea Breeze*, Jomtien Beach, T231057, F231059. A/c, restaurant, pool, good value.

Pattaya has the greatest choice of international cuisine outside Bangkok. This ranges from excellent 5-star restaurants, to European fast-food chains, to foodstalls on the beach or down the sois. Because so many of the guests are tourists, prices tend to be high by Thai standards – there aren't the locals to complain that a plate of fried rice shouldn't cost a king's ransom. **Eating**

Thai Expensive: *PIC Kitchen*, Soi 5. 4 traditional Thai pavilions, Thai classical dancing in garden compound, good food. Recommended. *Somsak*, 436/24 Soi 1, North Pattaya. Recommended. *Ruen Thai*, Pattaya 2 Rd, opposite Soi Post Office. Very good Thai food and not excessively overpriced. Recommended. *Benjarong*, Royal Wing, *Royal Cliff Beach Hotel*. *Deeprom*, 503 Moo 9 Central Pattaya Rd. Recommended. *Kruatalay*, Pattaya Park, Jomtien beach, plus seafood. **Mid-range**: *Kiss*, Pattaya 2 Rd, between sois 11 and 12 next to *Diana Inn*. Good range of Western and Thai food at low prices. An excellent place to watch the world go by.

Other Asian cuisine Expensive: *Akamon*, 468/19 Pattaya 2 Rd. Best-known Japanese restaurant in town. *Alibaba*, 1/15-16 Central Pattaya Rd. Indian. *Arirang*, Soi 5 Beach Rd. Korean. *Empress*, *Dusit Resort*, large Chinese restaurant overlooking Pattaya Bay. Good dim sum lunches. *Koreano*, Soi 1 Beach Rd. Korean. *Narissa*, *Siam Bayview*, North Pattaya. Chinese, speciality Peking Duck. *White Orchid*, 110/3 South Pattaya Rd. Good Chinese food. *Yamato*, Pattaya Beach Soi 13. Sushi bar (฿100) and sukiyaki, sashimi and tempura, all excellent. **Mid-range**: *Café India*, 183/9 Soi Post Office. *Mai Kai Supper Club*, Beach Rd. Polynesian, Haitian band. *Thang Long*, Soi 3 Beach Rd. Vietnamese.

International Expensive: *Alt Heidelberg*, 273 Beach Rd. Roadside bistro, open 0900-0200, German cook and owner, German sausages, draught beer. *Buccaneer*, Beach Rd. Seafood and steaks in rooftop restaurant above the *Nipa Lodge*. *Dolf Riks*,

Regent Marina Complex. Speciality Indonesian, some international, one of the original Pattaya restaurants. *El Toro Steakhouse*, 215 Pattaya 2 Rd. Top-quality steaks. *Green Bottle*, Pattaya 2 Rd (between Sois 10 and 11). Ersatz English pub with exposed 'beams', grills, seafood. *La Gritta*, Beach Rd (northern end past Soi 1). Some people maintain this restaurant serves the best Italian in town, pizzas, pasta dishes and seafood specialities. *Noble House*, Pattaya Beach Rd (near Soi 10). Italian, seafood and German dishes, good German breakfasts with fresh coffee. *Orient Express*, Beach Rd (just north of Central Pattaya Rd). 2 'Orient Express' coaches converted into dining cars serving average European food in novel surroundings. *Papa's*, 219 Soi Yamato. Range of international food including fondue, steaks and seafood. *Peppermill*, 16 Beach Rd, near Soi Post Office. First class French food. *Savai Swiss*, Pattaya 2 Rd, Soi 6. Swiss style, with international food. **Mid-range**: *Blue Parrot*, Pattayaland 2 Rd. Mexican. *Dream Bakery*, 485/3 Pattaya 2 Rd. English breakfasts, Thai. *Italiano Espresso*, 325/1 Beach Rd, South Pattaya. Traditional Italian food, and some Thai dishes. *Oslo*, 325/14 Pattayaland Soi 2, South Pattaya. Scandinavian style restaurant, with Scandinavian buffet and individual dishes. *Zum Wiener Schnitzel*, 98/7 Beach Rd. Traditional German and some Thai food, large helpings. **Cheap**: *Amsterdam*, Regent Marina Complex. Thai/German/English/breakfast. *Ice Café Berlin*, Pattaya 2 Rd. German. *Aussie Ken's Toast Shop*, 205/31 Pattaya 2 Rd. Fish and chips, sandwiches, cheap beer. *Bella Napoli*, Naklua Rd. Italian. *Pattaya Princess*, floating restaurant, pier at south end of Beach Rd.

Seafood The best seafood is on Jomtien beach or at the southern end of Pattaya beach. **Expensive**: *Lobster Pot*, 228 Beach Rd, South Pattaya. On a pier over the water, known for very fresh seafood. **Mid-range**: *Nang Nual*, 214/10 Beach Rd, South Pattaya, on the waterfront. Recommended (there is another *Nang Nual* restaurant in Jomtien). *Seafood Palace*, on the pier, southern end of Beach Rd.

Bars The majority of Pattaya's bars are concentrated at the south end of the beach, between Beach Rd and Pattaya 2 Rd and there are hundreds to choose from. They are mostly open-air, lined with stools. The men-only bars are around Pattayaland Soi 3, and the Karaoke bars are along Pattaya 2 Rd.

Entertainment Pattaya comes to life as dusk approaches – it is a beach version of Bangkok's Patpong. Music blares out from the many bars, discos and massage parlours which are mainly concentrated in South Pattaya, referred to as 'The Strip'.

Cabaret shows *Alcazar* and *Tiffany's*, both on Pattaya 2 Rd are the 2 biggest establishments in town. Shows at *Tiffany's* are daily at 1900, 2030 and 2200, T429642 for reservations. Although it might seem slightly odd visiting a cabaret show in Thailand, the acts are very professional and good value – nor are they anything like the acts in Patpong. This is family entertainment! There is also *Simon's*, on Pattayaland Soi 2 and the *Malibu Show* at the top end of Soi Post Office (all transvestite shows).

Disco Average admission ฿250, a selection are – *Marina Disco*, *Regent Marina Hotel*. *Captain's Club*, *Dusit Resort*. **Palladium**, 2nd Pattaya Beach Rd. **Spark**, southern end of Pattaya Beach. *Hollywood*, southern end of Pattaya Beach.

Sports **Badminton**: Soi 17. Open 1400-2400, 4 courts, ฿60 per hour, racquet hire ฿20, shuttlecock ฿25. **Bowling**: there are 3 bowling alleys in Pattaya. *Pattaya Bowl* (recommended), Pattaya 2 Rd. A/c, 20 lanes, open 1000-0200 Mon-Sun. *OD Bowl,* South Pattaya, *Royal Jomtien Hotel*, 8 lanes. **Bungee jumping**: near Jomtien Beach, *Kiwi Thai Bungee Jump* is said to be the highest in the world, T427555, open 1400-2100, Mon-Sun. **Diving**: there are more than 10 dive shops in Pattaya, offering a range of services – dives from the offshore islands, instruction and equipment hire. A recommended and established centre is *Seafari*, Soi 5, T429253, run by an American couple. Cost for a day's diving to the nearby islands is ฿800 (group rate), to the outer islands and a wreck dive, ฿1,150. A day's introductory instruction costs ฿2,300, and a 4 day course, about ฿10,300. Dive shops include *Mermaid's Dive School* on Soi Mermaid, Jomtien Beach, T232219 and *Dave's Divers Den*, Pattaya-Naklua Rd, T420411 (NAUI). *Aquanauts*, 437/17 Soi Yodsak, *Seafari Sports Centre*, 359/2 Soi 5 Beach Rd. **Fishing**: at Panarak Park, en route to the Siam Country Club, freshwater lake. **Fitness**: *Pattaya Fitness Centre* is near the *Regent Marina Complex*, North Pattaya. With weight-lifting facilities, gym and sauna, open 0800-2000 Mon-Sun. There is a *fitness park* on the road over the hill to Jomtien. **Game-fishing**: there are 4 or 5 game fishing operators in Pattaya. Fish commonly caught in local waters include shark, king mackerel, garoupa and marlin. Martin Henniker, at *Jenny's Hotel*, Soi Pattayaland 1, is recommended. *The Fisherman's Club*, Soi Yodsak (Soi 6) takes groups of 4-10 anglers and offer 3 different packages (including an overnight trip). The *Dusit Resort* organize angling contests. Angling equipment is available from Alan Ross at the *Pattaya Sports Supply* shop, opposite the *Regent Marina Hotel* (North Pattaya). For larger boat expeditions (30 or so anglers), expect to pay about ฿1,000, organized by Dieter at *Deutsches Haus*, Soi 4.

Golf: there are now 9 courses within 50 km of Pattaya. Green fees range between ฿250 and ฿1,000 during the week and ฿500 and ฿1,500 at the weekend. *Asia*, *Asia Hotel,* Jomtien. 9-hole course. Recommended. *Siam Country Club* is the closest to town, 20 mins from Pattaya, T428002. Restaurant and swimming pool available. Green fees ฿1,000, ฿150 caddy fee. *Royal Thai Navy Course*, near Sattahip, 35 mins from town, T428422. Slow and uneven greens but characterful. Green fees ฿250, ฿140 caddy fee. 2 other courses are the *Bangpra International* (one of the oldest courses in Thailand, accommodation and restaurant available, green fees ฿500, ฿150 caddy fee) and the *Panya Resort* (45 mins from town, large clubhouse with restaurant, green fees ฿800, ฿150 caddy fee), both near Chonburi. *Phoenix*, Sukhumvit Rd (15 km south of Pattaya). New course, 27 holes. Outings organized by *Cherry Tree Golf Tours* from the Red Lion Pub, South Pattaya, T422385 or by Mike Smith at *Caesars Bar*, Beach Rd – he's chairman of *Pattaya Sports Club*. 9-hole course behind the *Asia Pattaya Hotel*. Mini golf course, Naklua Rd, 500 m north of *Dusit Resort*. Rather further afield are: *Rayong Green Valley Country Club*, Ya Ra Rd, T603000-5, F614916. Green fees ฿700 weekdays, ฿1,200 weekends; and the *Eastern Star Country Club*, Pala Rd, T602500, F602754. Green fees ฿250 weekdays, ฿400 weekends. *Green Way Driving Range*, Sukhumvit Highway, 2 km south of South Pattaya. *Aussie Ken's*, Pattaya 2 Rd. Computer golf simulator for up to 4 players.

Go-Kart: *KR Go-Kart Pattaya*, 62/125 Moo 12 Thepprasit Rd, T3003479. Open 1000-1930, a 1.1 km circuit. **Helicopter Rides**: T535506. US$50 per person round trip to Koh Larn and Koh Sak, including the promise of 2 hrs funny time on Koh Sak. To charter for the hour, it will set you back US$1,500. **Jetskis**: for hire, about ฿350 per 15 mins. **Motor racing**: at *Bira International Circuit*, Km 14, Route 36. Races of Formula 3 cars, pick-ups and bikes held at weekends. **Paintball:** next to Go-Kart track on Thepprasit Rd, T300608. ฿300 for a 2 hr game. Games begin at 1000 daily. **Parasailing**: near *Montien, Royal Cliff, Asia Pattaya* and *Wong Amat* hotels. **Riding**: *Pattaya Riding Club*, Highway 36 Km 11. Imported horses will canter until you are content in jungle and mountain surroundings. T3020814 for free transport. **Running**: *Hash House Harriers* meet every Mon at 1600 at the *Hare House*, Soi Post Office. **Sailing**: Lasers, Hobie Cats and Prindles are available. *Royal Varuna Yacht Club*, T428959. *Sundowner Sailing Services*, Ocean Marina, T423686. **Shooting** *Tiffany's*, Pattaya 2 Rd, open 0900-2100 Mon-Sun, T429642. ฿120 range fee, range of rifles and handguns, rates charged per bullet. **Snooker**: fees vary from ฿60 to ฿100 per hour. *Pattaya Bowl*, Pattaya 2 Rd, North Pattaya, open 1000-0200 Mon-Sun. T429466. Above *Mike's Department Store*, Beach Rd, is a small club with 5 tables. *JB Snooker Club*, Jomtien Bayview Hotel, open Mon-Sun 24 hrs, T425889. **Snorkelling**: day trips to the offshore islands can be organized through the dive shops. **Speedboats**: for rent, about ฿600 per hour. **Squash**: *Cherry Tree*, on the *Siam Country Club* Rd, T423686,

English run. **Swimming**: there are now designated swimming 'zones' on Pattaya and Jomtien beaches. With the new waste-water treatment, it is hoped that the entire length of Pattaya Beach is now fit for swimming. **Tennis**: many hotels have courts. Instruction is often available, ฿100- ฿150 per hour. **Water scooters**: on the beach. **Water skiing**: the water off Pattaya Beach is not particularly good for this, as it is rarely calm. However, an artificial freshwater lake has been created for waterskiers at Lake Land, T232690, south of Pattaya on Sukhumvit Road, restaurant by the lake. They specialize in cable skiing. **Water World** at *Pattaya Park Beach Resort*, between Pattaya and Jomtien beach. Admission ฿50 for adults, ฿30 for children. **Windsurfing**: many different schools – more than 20 in all. Best time to windsurf is from Oct to Jun. **Zip Wire**: Pattaya Tower, Jomtien Beach. A 170-m ride down a wire from the top of the tower to the ground. ฿200 for the experience, T251201.

Traditional Thai dance: *PIC Kitchen*, Soi 5. Wed 1930, ฿100. *Ruen Thai*, Pattaya 2 Rd, opposite Soi PO. Recommended. ฿120.

Festivals **Jan** *Pattaya Carnival* is a purely commercial affair with floats, competitions and the like. **Mar** *Thai Music Festival*, the name of this festival really says it all, and it's not just Thai classical music but includes Thai country music, rock and roll, etc. **Apr** *Annual Pattaya Festival* celebrates nothing in particular but is a good excuse for a jamboree. **Jul** *Pattaya International Marathon*. This has expanded into a significant national sporting event and there are numerous other associated (and unassociated) attractions.

Shopping There are hundreds of market stalls and small shops on Pattaya 2 Road selling jewellery, fashion ware, handicrafts, leather goods, silk, fake watches and a good selection of shopping plazas where most western goods can be purchased.

Books *DK Books*, Pattaya Beach Rd, Soi Post Office. Best selection of books in Pattaya. *Asia Books*, Royal Garden Shopping Complex.

Department stores *Mike's*, Beach Rd. *Booneua Shopping Plaza*, South Pattaya Rd.

Gemstones/jewellery *World Gems*, Beach Rd. *Best Gems*, South Pattaya Rd. *Pattaya Lapidary*, Beach Rd.

Handicrafts *Northern Thai Handicrafts*, 215 Pattaya 2 Rd. *Shinawatra*, Pattaya 2 Rd.

Silk *Dada Thai Silk* (plus tailoring), 345 Beach Rd (southern end). *Shinawatra Thai Silk*, 78/13 Pattaya 2 Rd. *Fantasia* (hand-wrapped silk flowers). *Booneua Shopping Plaza*, South Pattaya Rd.

Supermarkets Plenty to choose from for Western food and pharmaceuticals (including *Boots The Chemist*).

Tailors *Royal Garden Boutique*, *Royal Garden Hotel*, Pattaya Beach Rd. *Princess Fashion*, *Complex Hotel*, 235/5 Beach Rd, South Pattaya. *Marco Custom Tailors*, opposite *Montien Pattaya*, 75/5-6 Pattaya 2 Rd.

Tour operators For cheap airfares and tours to Indo-China, the best informed travel agent is *Exotissimo*, 183/19 Soi Post Office, T422788. Other travel agents include: *Lee Tours*, 183 Soi Post Office, T429738. *Malibu Travel*, 183 Soi Post Office, T423180. *Tour East*, 437/111 Soi Yodsak, T429708. *RTD Travel*, 370/11-12 Moo 9 Pattaya 2 Rd, T427539.

Transport **Local Songthaews**: are in abundance along Beach Road (for travelling south) and on
147 km S of Bangkok Pattaya 2 Road (for travelling north), ฿5 for short trips around Pattaya Bay (although it is

not uncommon for visitors to be charged ฿10), ฿10 between Naklua and Pattaya beach, ฿20 to Jomtien. To avoid being charged more than the standard fare, present the driver with the correct money and walk away (of course, prices may go up). Similarly, when boarding, just get in – even if it is empty – and do not attempt to negotiate the price, as the driver will expect you to hire the vehicle as a taxi. **Bicycle/motorbike/ jeep/ car hire**: along Beach Road (bargaining required), bicycles ฿100 per day or ฿20 per hour, jeeps ฿500-700 per day, motorbikes ฿150 per day for a small bike upto ฿600 for a larger machine. **Avis** at *Dusit Resort* (T425611) and the *Royal Cliff Beach Resort* (T250421). **NB** Jeeps are rarely insured. **Boat charter**: from along Beach Road. ฿700-1500 per day (seats 12 people).

Air There is an airport at U-Tapao, not far from Pattaya. This is gradually expanding and in 1997 it received its first international scheduled arrival for some years. There are daily connections on **Bangkok Airways** with Koh Samui, but none with Bangkok.

Train The station is off the Sukhumvit Highway, 200 m north of the intersection with Central Pattaya Rd. There is a limited train service between Pattaya and Bangkok; running on weekends and holidays. The Bangkok-Pattaya train leaves at 0700, and the Pattaya-Bangkok at 1330, 3½ hrs.

Road Bus: A/c buses stop at the a/c bus terminal on North Pattaya Rd, near to the intersection with the Sukhumvit Highway. Songthaews take passengers to South Pattaya, past most of the Pattaya beach hotels (฿10) and to Jomtien beach (฿20) (as mentioned above, do not ask for price or this will be taken as an attempt to hire the taxi for yourself). Regular connections with Bangkok's Eastern bus terminal on Sukhumvit Soi Ekamai (Soi 63) 1¾-2½ hrs, ฿66 (0530-2100) or less frequent connections from the Northern bus terminal in Bangkok (*Mor Chit*), ฿67. There are also bus connection direct with Don Muang Airport. *THAI* run a service from the airport to the *Royal Cliff Beach Resort*, ฿250 (pre-flight check-in available at *Royal Cliff*) and there is also a public bus leaving every 2 hrs, 0700-1700. Hotels and travel agencies in Bangkok run tour bus services to Pattaya. Non-a/c buses to Bangkok leave from the BKS stop in front of Wat Chai Mongkhon, near the intersection of Pattaya 2 and South Pattaya roads. The main BKS terminal (non-a/c) for buses to other Eastern region destinations (for example Rayong, Sattahip, Si Racha) and beyond, is in Jomtien, near the intersection of Beach Rd and Chaiyapruk Rd. If staying in Pattaya City, it is possible to stand on the Sukhumvit Highway and wave down the appropriate bus. Tour buses to the north (Chiang Mai, Mae Hong Son, Mae Sai, Phitsanulok, etc) leave from the station on the Sukhumvit Highway, near the intersection with Central Pattaya Rd. Nearby, buses also leave for Ubon (*Sri Mongkhon Tour*) and Nong Khai (*407 Pattana Tour*), both in the northeast. **Limousine service**: *THAI* operates a service from Don Muang airport, Bangkok to Pattaya. T423140 for bookings from Pattaya. A chauffeur-driven car from travel agencies in Bangkok should cost about ฿1,600.

Airline offices *Bangkok Airways* office is on the 2nd floor, *Royal Garden Plaza*, 218 Beach Rd, **Directory** T411965, F411965. *Thai*, T602192. *Kuwait Airways*, 218 Beach Rd, T410493. **Banks** There are countless exchange facilities both on the beach road and on the many sois running east-west, many stay open until 2200. **Communications** Internet café: *Royal Garden Shopping Complex*, top floor. ฿5 per minute (minimum ฿40). **Post Office**: Soi Post Office. **Safety deposit**: overseas service on Soi Post Office, ฿200 per month. **Telephone exchange service**: South Pattaya Rd, open 24 hrs. **Embassies & consulates** *Sweden*, 75/128-29, Moo 12, Jomtien Beach, T231630. **Medical services** Hospitals: *Pattaya International Clinic*, Soi 4, Beach Rd, T428374. *Pattaya Memorial Hospital*, 328/1 Central Pattaya Rd, T429422, 24-hr service. Dr Olivier Clinic, 20/23 Moo 10, South Pattaya Rd (opposite the Day-Night Hotel), T723521, F723522. Operated by an English-French-German speaking doctor, Dr Meyer. **Chemists**: *Nong Nooch Village Pharmacists*, plenty of drug stores on South Pattaya Rd. **Useful numbers** Tourist Police: T429371 or T1699 for 24-hr service and **Sea Rescue**: T433752 are to be found on Beach Rd, next to the TAT office.

Pattaya to Koh Samet

Coastal towns south of Pattaya

The beaches of Rayong All along the coast from U-Tapao Airport southeast past Ban Phe to Laem Mae Phim are resort-style hotels. The beaches here are scarcely memorable and there is very little accommodation of the budget variety. It is mostly Thais who come to stay here and because they tend to drive themselves it is hard to get about on public transport.

Sattahip Sattahip is 20 km south of Pattaya and, like Pattaya, was also frequented by the US military. Now the port of Sattahip is the headquarters of the Thai navy which itself uses it as a vacation spot; many of the beautiful beaches are reserved for the military. It has recently been developed into an important commercial deep-sea port to take some of the pressure off Bangkok's stretched port facilities. The town has little to offer tourists: a modern and rather garish wat, a bustling market, and a few restaurants.

Samaesan Samaesan is a small, quiet and unspoilt fishing village, 52 km south of Pattaya. Offshore there are a number of beautiful islands: **Koh Ai Raet**, **Koh Samaesan**, **Koh Kham**, **Koh Chuang** and **Koh Chan**. It is possible to hire boats to visit the islands – enquiries can be made at the *Lam Samaesan Seafood Restaurant* (about ฿300). There is basic accommodation available in Samaesan. Boats to the islands also run from Ban Phe (see below), mostly at the weekend.

Rayong

Phone code: 038
Colour map 1, grid B2

The area around Rayong has many orchards and is famed for its fruit, as well as its sea cucumbers

Rayong is famous, at least in the Thai context, for its *nam pla* (fish sauce) – made from a decomposed silver fish. This is usually mixed with chillies to produce the fiery *nam pla prik*. For most Thais: no *nam pla*, no eat, and in Thai elections it used to be common to find voters being 'bought' with free bottles of the watery sauce. (In recent elections cash has changed hands – the electorate have outgrown gifts of *nam pla*.) Rayong town does not have much to offer, except a few beaches, a 12 m-long reclining Buddha at **Wat Pa Pradu** which, unusually, reclines to its left and dates from the Ayutthaya Period. Also worth visiting is **Wat Khot Thimtharaam** on Thimtharaam Road. The monastery was built in 1464 and features some interesting murals. There is also a statue of Thailand's most famous poet – Sunthorn Phu (see page 180). However, few people stay long in Rayong; they just pass through on their way to the island of Koh Samet.

Sleeping **AL** *Novotel Rim Pae Resort*, 4/5 Moo 3, Pae Klaeng Kram Rd, Chark Pong (roughly equidistant from Rayong and Ban Phe), T2371305/648008, F2364353/648002. A/c, restaurants, 4 pools, fitness centre, resort-style hotel with almost 200 rooms, very comfortable but not much to distinguish from all the other hotels of similar ilk. **A** *Palmeraie Princess*, Ban Phe-Mae Pim Rd, T638071, F638073. A/c, restaurant, pool, affiliated with the *Dusit Group* of hotels. **A** *Sinsiam Resort*, 235 Laem Mae-Pim, T2117026, B4373648. A/c, restaurant, pool. **B-E** *Otani*, 69 Sukhumvit Rd, T611112. Some a/c, large rooms but dirty. **C** *Rayong*, 65/1-3 Sukhumvit Rd, T611073. A/c, an ugly hotel with friendly staff, not much atmosphere but rooms are well priced. Good location for restaurants. **E** *Rayong International Youth Hostel*, 89/4 Moo 1, Mae Ramphung Beach Rd, T653374, B025137093. 100 m from the beach, nestled among a forest of high-rise hotels. 6 rooms with a total of 30 beds. Food available, but remote from other restaurants. Appears to be undergoing extensive expansion. They are not used to *farangs*, but recommended if you arrive in Rayong too late to cross to Koh Samet.

May *Fruit Fair* (movable) local fruits, handicrafts on sale.

Festivals

Local Car hire: *Rayong Mahanakorn Co*, 74/3 Ratbamrang Rd, opposite Manora Massage Parlour. **Road Bus**: regular connections with Bangkok's Eastern bus terminal, Pattaya and other east-coast towns.

Transport
221 km from Bangkok
70 km from Pattaya

Banks *Thai Farmers*, Sukhumvit Rd. **Tourist offices** *TAT*, 153/4 Sukhumvit Rd, T655420. Covers Chantaburi too.

Directory

Ban Phe

Once a small fishing village with a national reputation for its fish sauce, Ban Phe has become a way station for visitors heading for Koh Samet. It has many food and handicraft stalls, but few foreign tourists bother to stay any longer than it takes to catch the boat. In the vicinity of the village are a number of mediocre beaches lined with bungalows and resorts – **Hat Ban Phe**, **Hat Mae Ram Phung** (to the west), **Laem Mae Phim**, **Suan Son** and **Wang Kaew** (all to the east) which are largely frequented by Thai tourists.

Phone code: 038
Colour map 1, grid B3

The Eastern Seaboard

Resort and bungalow developments line the 25 km of coast east and west of Ban Phe. Few foreign visitors stay either in the village or in the hotels around abouts – this is a resort geared to and patronized by Thais.

Sleeping

In Ban Phe D *Nual Napu*, east of the market, close to the pier for Koh Samet, T651668. Some a/c.

Outside Ban Phe AL *Rayong Resort*, 186 Moo 1, Ban Phe, T651000, F651007, www.rayongresort.com A/c, restaurant, pool, 167 room resort, on a cape with private beach, average rooms for the price. **B** *Diamond Phe*, 286/12 Ban Phe Rd, T615826. A/c, east of Ban Phe near the pier for Koh Samet, plain and rather kitsch but comfortable and convenient. **D-E** *TN Place*, close to the pier. Some a/c, reasonable for a stopover.

Road Bus: regular connections direct from Bangkok's Eastern bus terminal and from Pattaya, 1 hr. Or via Rayong (20 km to the southeast), and then a songthaew to Ban Phe (฿10).

Transport
223 km from Bangkok

Banks *Krung Thai*, a short distance west of the pier (if going to Samet it is a good idea to change money here as the rates are better than on the island). **Communications** Lenso Cardphone available here for international calls.

Directory

Koh Samet

Phone code: 038
Many of the hotels only
have mobile numbers
(prefixed with 01)
Colour map 1, grid B3

Koh Samet is a 6-km-long, lozenge-shaped island which used to be known as Koh Kaeo Pisadan. Until the early 1980s it was home to a small community of fishermen and was visited by a few intrepid travellers. The famous 19th-century Thai romantic poet Sunthorn Phu retired to this beautiful island and, inspired, proceeded to write his finest work, the epic Phra Aphaimani. The poem recounts the story of a prince, banished by his father to live with a sea-dwelling, broken-hearted giantess. Escaping to Koh Samet with the help of a mermaid, the prince kills the pursuing giant with his magic flute and marries the mermaid.

Ins and outs

Getting there   Koh Samet is, as the crow flies, the nearest to Bangkok of Thailand's many resort islands. But unlike Koh Samui and Phuket there is no airport so it is necessary to bus to Ban Phe, about 3½ hrs from Bangkok, and then take one of the regular boats out to the island, another 40 mins or so.

Getting around   Koh Samet is only 6 km long so it is possible to explore the island on foot. Songthaews travel between the main beaches and there are also tracks negotiable by motorbike – which can be rented from a handful of places.

All visitors pay an entrance fee to visit Koh Samet, (฿50 for adults, ฿25 for children). The best time to visit is between October and May; heavy rains can be a problem between July and September. However, during the rainy season rates are cut and the island is less crowded. It is best to visit during the week; at weekends it is very popular with Thais and this is particularly true during public holidays when it can be chocka with visitors camped out on just about every sq ft of floor. Avoid these periods if humanly possible.

The island

It is unlikely Sunthorn Phu would find the necessary quiet today: over the past decade, Koh Samet has become increasingly popular with young Thai holiday makers and with foreign visitors. Because of its relative proximity to Bangkok (Ban Phe is only 223 km from the capital), it is particularly popular with Thais at the weekend and during public holidays, when the island is best avoided.

In 1981 Samet became part of the Khao Laem Ya National Park which also includes the neighbouring Kuti and Thalu islands as well as 100 sq km of surrounding sea (hence the admission fee). Authorities have ostensibly insisted that all accommodation remains limited to bungalows set back behind the tree line of the beach. This is difficult to reconcile with the scale and pattern of development that has occurred. The park authorities have periodically threatened to shut the island down on the basis that every bungalow owner is breaking the law. Indeed, they have actually closed the island to tourists on a couple of occasions, only to reopen it after protests from bungalow owners, many of whom were making a living on the island prior to 1981 when it was declared a national park. As the owner of the Wong Duan Resort said during one of the shut downs: "It is unfair. We fight, work hard, pay taxes and invest a lot of money ... the Forestry Department never invested anything. Now they are the owners and we are the encroachers." In March 2000 it was announced that after years and years of wrangling, the Royal Forestry Department and the bungalow operators were close to a deal. Apparently the operators are to sign over ownership of the land to the RFD and then the RFD has agreed to rent the land back to the operators on 10-, 20- or 30-year leases at a rental rate of ฿10-20 per rai (about ฿60-120 per hectare).

Like Phi Phi, the rubbish created by tourism is becoming an environmental threat on the island. It seems that however hard the park authorities, the TAT and the environmentalist pressure groups may try to protect Samet, they are fighting a losing battle; people continue to stay on the island in their thousands and yet more bungalows are being built.

Koh Samet place names

Ao Phrao

อ่าวพร้าว

Hat Sai Kaew

หาดทรายแก้ว

Na Dan

หน้าด่าน

Samet is a comparatively dry island (1,350 mm per year – Chantaburi 50 km away has rainfall of 3,164 mm per year) and therefore a good place to visit during the rainy season. However, between May and October there can be strong winds, and the seas are sometimes rough. The island's limited supply of fresh water was a constraint to tourist expansion for a number of years, now it is shipped in and most of the bungalows have a reasonable supply. In addition, malaria was quite prevalent but there is little or none left these days. Prophylactics are no longer recommended for the island but precautions – such as wearing long-sleeved shirts and trousers after sunset are nonetheless advisable.

Many visitors land at the main **Na Dan Pier** in the northeast of the island (but note that it is becoming more and more common for bungalow operators to run boats directly to their beaches from one or other of the piers in Ban Phe – see Road and Sea section below). There has been a settlement here for many years – while it is now a fishing settlement-come-tourist service centre, junks from China used to anchor here to be checked before the authorities would allow them to sail over the sandbar at the mouth of the Chao Phraya River and north to Bangkok. Along the beach here there is a collection of featureless bungalows. Unless you want to watch the boats come in (there is little else to do), head for one of the other bays.

Hat Sai Khao (Diamond Sand Beach) is a 10-minute walk from Na Dan Pier, and remains the most popular place to stay, perhaps because all other beaches must be reached by foot or boat. This was once a beautiful spot, but it has been disfigured by uncontrolled development. Shophouses, discos, bars and travel agents line the path from Na Dan to Hat Sai Khao and the beach itself. In front of the bungalow operations and resorts at the southern end of the beach are long lines of plastic tables sheltered from the sun and rain by vulgar, brightly coloured plastic roofing. In front of these lie deckchairs – five rows thick. In addition, jet-skis are a popular form of watersport. The northern end of the beach is very slightly less crowded and touristy. Despite the crowded, bustling atmosphere, the beach remains clean and it has a sandy bottom which makes it an excellent place to swim (especially for children). Just south along the coast from Hat Sai Khao is Ao Hin Khok where Koh Samet's one and only sight is to be found: a rather tatty statue depicting the tale of *Phra Aphaimani* (see above). A short distance further south still, just 1 km southwest from Hat Sai Khao, is **Ao Phai**, which is less developed and more peaceful. The bungalows here cater for *farang* rather than for Thai visitors. Two and a half kilometres from Ao Phai, past the smaller **Ao Tubtim**, **Ao Nuan** and **Ao Cho**, is **Ao Wong Duan**. This crescent-shaped bay has a number of more up-market resort developments. Consequently there is also a wider range of facilities: water-skiing, diving, boat trips, and windsurfing. Continuing south from Ao Wong Duan is **Ao Thian**, **Ao Wai** and **Ao Kiu Na Nok**. These are the most peaceful locations on Koh Samet, and the island's finest coral is also found off the southern tip of the island.

The Eastern Seaboard

Koh Samet

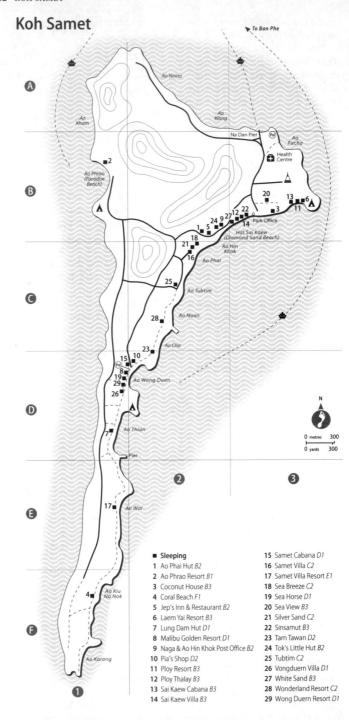

The Eastern Seaboard

■ **Sleeping**
1 Ao Phai Hut *B2*
2 Ao Phrao Resort *B1*
3 Coconut House *B3*
4 Coral Beach *F1*
5 Jep's Inn & Restaurant *B2*
6 Laem Yai Resort *B3*
7 Lung Dam Hut *D1*
8 Malibu Golden Resort *D1*
9 Naga & Ao Hin Khok Post Office *B2*
10 Pia's Shop *D2*
11 Ploy Resort *B3*
12 Ploy Thalay *B3*
13 Sai Kaew Cabana *B3*
14 Sai Kaew Villa *B3*

15 Samet Cabana *D1*
16 Samet Villa *C2*
17 Samet Villa Resort *E1*
18 Sea Breeze *C2*
19 Sea Horse *D1*
20 Sea View *B3*
21 Silver Sand *C2*
22 Sinsamut *B3*
23 Tarn Tawan *D2*
24 Tok's Little Hut *B2*
25 Tubtim *C2*
26 Vongduern Villa *D1*
27 White Sand *B3*
28 Wonderland Resort *C2*
29 Wong Duern Resort *D1*

Ao Phrao, or Paradise Beach (2 km from Sai Kaew), is the only beach to have been developed (so far) on the west side of the island.

Excursions

Hire a fishing boat (or go on a tour), take a picnic, and explore the **Kuti** and **Thalu islands.**

Tours

Small operators on many of the beaches organize boat trips to outlying islands such as Koh Kuti and Koh Thalu for fishing, diving and snorkelling. For example *Samet Villa* at Ao Phai run an adventure tour to Koh Mun Nok, Koh Mun Klang and Koh Mun Nai for ฿500 per person, trips to Thalu and Kuti for ฿300, and trips around the island for ฿200 per person.

Essentials

Sleeping

Koh Samet mostly offers bungalow accommodation, although there are an increasing number of more sophisticated 'resorts' (at Wong Duan, Hat Sai Khao and Ao Phrao). Due to the cost for the bungalow operators of shipping in water and the proximity of the island to Bangkok, the cost of equivalent accommodation is higher than in other Thai beach resorts. This is particularly so in the high season when a very basic bungalow with attached bathroom may cost ฿450, or on public holidays when you may pay that much to rent a tent for the night. At low season, particularly Aug-Sep, prices can be bargained down. Only a selection of the bungalows is given below (at last count there were something like 50 developments – a lot for an island this size). The best source of information on whether standards are being maintained is recent visitors – ask those leaving the island.

There is no mains electricity on the island so all the bungalow operations and resorts generate their own and electricity is only available at certain times of day (usually 1800 to 1000). Check before you book a room what hours electricity is available – some of them switch off at midnight – it can be very uncomfortable sleeping without a fan.

Hat Sai Khao (Diamond Sand Beach). Because there are so many shops, pubs and discos aligning the beach here, many of the bungalows look out onto the rear concrete walls of these establishments, so it's not the place to look for accommodation if you appreciate a seaview from your balcony. However, if you like to be where the action is, then this is the place to head for. Most of the bungalows are solid and uninspiring – take your pick from a number of different operators covering a wide range of budgets. All bungalows have attached restaurants. **AL** *Sai Kaew Villa*, T01-2186696. **A-D** *Coconut House*, T01-651661. **B-D** *Diamond Hut* T01-3210814. **B-C** *Diamond Beach and Sea View*, T01-2390208. **D** *White Sand*, T01-321734. **C-D** *Ploy Thalay*, T01-2186109. **D-E** *Sinsamut*.

Prices here vary enormously between high & low season

Ao Hin Khok **D** *Jep's Inn and Restaurant*, the restaurant here has a large range of dishes and is reputed to be very good. **E** *Tok's Little Hut*, T01-3230264. Used to be a favourite among the low budget travellers but following a change of ownership it is rumoured that standards of cleanliness have no longer been maintained. **E-F** *Naga*, T01-3532575, F01-3210732. English-run and friendly, offers home-baked cakes, bread and pastries. The only post office on Koh Samet is located here (Post Restante and satellite phone to Europe – expensive). Basic huts, some with fans, cheaper without, all have shared, if rather smelly, bathrooms.

Ao Phai **C-E** *Ao Phai Hut*, T01-3532644. Some a/c, friendly, clean operation, wooden huts higher up behind the tree line, mosquitoes prevalent. This place has a library and organizes minibuses to Pattaya. International phone available. **D** *Samet Villa*, T01-4948090. This clean and friendly Swiss-run establishment offers the best value

The Eastern Seaboard

accommodation on Samet, all rooms have fans and attached bathrooms and electricity is on round the clock (rare for Koh Samet). They organize a number of trips and excursions to neighbouring islands. Recommended. **D-E** *Silver Sand*, good value bungalows, popular restaurant offering wide range of dishes, large selection of recent videos, discos at the weekends. **E-F** *Sea Breeze*, T01-3211397. Bungalows are fairly cheap but are located facing the back wall of the restaurant and are fairly grotty inside and out, restaurant also poorly located set back from the sea beside the path. On the plus side, the seafood here is good and the staff friendly and helpful.

Ao Tubtim/Ao Phutsa **D** *Pudsa Bungalow*. **D** *Tubtim* more expensive huts have their own showers.

Ao Nuan **D-E** *Nuan Kitchen*, wooden huts with thatched roofs entered by crawling through a low door, no electricity (lamps are provided), all rooms have shared bathroom, there are lots of mosquitoes since the huts are higher up behind the treeline, but nets are provided, the food is reputed to be very good. This place certainly has more character than many of the concrete bungalows to be found on the island.

Ao Cho This bay, immediately north of Wong Duan features a couple of rather characterless operations with rather grotty concrete bungalows: **D** *Tarn Tawan*, has slightly better bungalows than *Wonderland* in a similar price bracket. **E** *Wonderland Resort*, T438409. Grotty bungalows and ugly glass-fronted building ruins any character this might ever have had – they do, however, organize trips around the island for ฿100 per person.

Ao Wong Duan This beach is becoming a close second to Hat Sai Khao in terms of shops, pubs, bars and nightlife, but the accommodation is not so cramped and it's not quite so crowded. Several of the guesthouses run boats to Ban Phe. **B-C** *Malibu Garden Resort*, T2185345. Offers a range of fairly solid and characterless bungalows situated (at time of writing) around a smelly, boggy patch. **B-C** *Wong Duern Resort*, T651777, F651819. Offers slightly nicer bungalows in the same price range in an attractive setting behind the tree line, restaurant offers a vast range of Thai and western dishes to suit all budgets. **A-C** *Vongduern Villa*, T651292. One of the most expensive resorts on the island with 2 VIP bungalows at the top end of their range even having hot water (very rare on Koh Samet), there are pool tables and the restaurant has its tables on rocks just beside the sea (or even in the sea at very high tides). **C-E** *Seahorse*, T01-3230049. Some a/c, friendly and popular with 2 restaurants and a travel agency but cheaper rooms in a longhouse aren't up to much. **E** *Samet Cabana*, basic dark wooden huts with shared bathroom. **E-F** *Pia's Shop*, behind the shop up the hill at the north end of the beach. Three bamboo huts with no electricity and shared bathroom, a good location for the low-budget traveller who would like a peaceful spot but doesn't want to be too far from the action.

Ao Thian – (Candlelight Beach) **E-F** *Lung Dam Hut*, T651810. Basic wooden and bamboo huts with grass roofs or you could try their treehouse just a few feet from the sea, only some of the huts have fans, some have own bath.

Ao Wai **B-C** *Samet Villa Resort*, bookable through the boat Phra Aphai at Ban Phe, T01-3211284. The only accommodation on this beach – good bungalows but quite expensive, very peaceful and attractive location, but lacks places to sit with views of the sea.

Ao Kiu Na Nok **B-D** *Coral Beach*, T652561. A range of rather grotty, overpriced huts and fan-cooled bungalows, the electricity goes off at midnight; food isn't up to much either.

Ao Phrao An altogether more peaceful experience on this side of the island, with the added bonus of sunsets. **A-B** *Ao Phrao Resort*, T651814. Once the most luxurious accommodation on the island, but unfortunately the management have got greedy and have crammed too many bungalows onto the plot, filling every available space. The only dive school on the island is located here. Regular boat service to Seree Ban Phe Pier in Ban Phe.

Camping Because the island is a national park, it is permissable to camp on any of the beaches. The best area is on the west coast, which means a walk on one of the many trails of not more than 3 km.

Just about all the resorts and guesthouses on Koh Samet provide a selection of the usual Thai dishes and travellers' food, including fresh seafood. There are also one or two dedicated restaurants. The following places have a particular reputation for their food, but note that chefs move at the drop of a saucepan and one season's Michelin-starred guesthouse becomes the following season's greasy spoon. *Jep's Inn and restaurant*; *Naga* (home-baked cakes, bread and pastries); *Sea Breeze* (good seafood); *Nuan Kitchen* (very good food); *Wong Duern Resort* (vast range of Thai and western dishes); and the *Bamboo Restaurant* on Ao Cho – open through the day, reasonable food and one of the island's few restaurants). **Eating**

The major beaches offer sailing, windsurfing (฿150 per hour), scuba-diving, snorkelling, and water-skiing (฿500 per 15 mins) and jet-skiing (฿1,000 per hour). However, many of the bungalows display notices requesting visitors not to hire jet-skis because they are dangerous to swimmers (there have been 2 deaths already), damage the coral, and disrupt the peace. It is also not unheard of for those renting them to lose their deposits or have difficulty getting their passports back because the renter claims they have damaged the machine in some way. Ao Wong Duan has the best selection of watersports. The best snorkelling is to be found at Ao Wai, Ao Kiu Na Nok and Ao Phrao. **Sports**

Citizen Travel, Hat Sai Khao. *Citizen Travel 2*, Ao Phai. *CP Travel Service*, Hat Sai Khao. *Sea Horse Tours*, Wong Duan Beach, T01-2132849. **Tour operators**

Local Koh Samet is a small island and it is possible to walk just about everywhere. There are rough tracks, some suitable for songthaews, rather more negotiable by motorbike. There are also rocky paths that wind over the headlands that divide each beach and which can only be negotiated on foot. **Songthaews**: are the main form of public transport, bouncing along the tracks that criss-cross the island. Rates are fairly expensive – from Na Dan it costs ฿15 per person to Hat Sai Khao, ฿20 to Ao Phai, ฿30 to Wong Duan or Ao Phrao, ฿40 to Ao Thian, and ฿50 to Ao Kiu Na Kok. It is also possible to charter songthaews; in fact, if a songthaew is not full the driver may insist that the passengers make up the fares to a full load. **Motorbike hire**: motorbikes can be hired from *Aladin* in Na Dan but this is expensive (฿100 per hour or ฿800 per day) and they disturb the peace (or what is left of it). The rental companies explain that because the roads are so bad their machines have a very short life expectancy. As Koh Samet is only 6 km long and 3 km wide, walking is always a possibility. **Transport**

Road and sea Regular connections from Bangkok's Eastern bus terminal to Ban Phe, the departure point for the boat to Koh Samet. It is also possible to catch a bus to Rayong or Pattaya and then a connecting songthaew to Ban Phe. But if arriving in the late afternoon in Rayong it can be difficult to find a regular public songthaew making its way out to Ban Phe. Other than staying in Rayong for the night (see above for accommodation in Rayong) and catching a ฿15 songthaew the following morning, the only alternative is to charter a vehicle for the trip (฿150 upwards for the 22 km journey). A private car from Bangkok to Ban Phe should cost around ฿1,600 and take 3 hrs. There are regular boats to Na Dan from Ban Phe Pier throughout the day departing when full, 30-40 mins (฿40), with the last boat leaving at 1700. There are also many boats to various beaches from Nuanthip Pier and Seree Ban Phe Pier which lie just to the west of the main pier. Most of these boats are run by bungalow operators and they tend to cost ฿40- ฿50. You may also be charged ฿10 for a boat taxi to the beach at the island end. It is usually well worth catching one of these boats if you can find one going to your chosen destination because you then avoid paying for the *songthaew* from Na Dan and also the park entry fee. Most boats dock at Na Dan or Ao Wong Duan. Some will also drop passengers off at Ao Phrao. Boats visit the southern beaches of Ao Thian, Ao Wai and Ao Kiu Na Nok less frequently – enquire before departure. Note that it may be difficult to find out which boat is going where; boat operators try hard to get visitors to stay at certain bungalows with which they are linked. It is best not to agree to stay anywhere until arrival on the island whereupon claims of cleanliness and luxury can be checked out. Travel agents on Khaosan Rd, Bangkok, also arrange transport to Samet, easier but slightly more expensive (and less fun?) than DIY.

Directory **Banks** The island has no banks, so for the best rates, change money on the mainland. Many of the bungalows and travel agents do offer a money changing service but take a 5% fee. The one exception is *Samet Villa* at Ao Phai which uses the mainland rates as published daily in the paper. **Communications** Post Office: situated inside *Naga Bungalows* at Hin Khok between Hat Sai Khao and Ao Phai (Poste Restante). Open 0830-1500 Mon-Fri, 0830-1200 Sat. **Telephone office:** between Hat Sai Khao and Na Dan (for overseas calls). It is also possible to make calls (including overseas calls) from many of the bungalows but rates may be more expensive. **Useful addresses** Police: Hat Sai Khao. **Health centre:** Koh Samet Health Centre, a small, public health unit, is situated on the road south from Na Dan to Hat Sai Khao [MARK ON MAP].

Chantaburi

Phone code: 039
Colour map 1, grid B5

Chantaburi, or the 'city of the moon', has played a central role on several occasions as Thailand has faced external threats. With the fall of Ayutthaya to the marauding Burmese in 1767, King Taksin retreated here to regroup and rearm before venturing back to the Central Plains to confront the Burmese and establish a new capital. A century and a quarter later, Chantaburi was occupied by the French for over 10 years between 1893 and 1904, a period during which the future of Siam as an independent kingdom was seriously at threat.

Ins and outs

Getting there Chantaburi is a small provincial capital 330 km from Bangkok. There is no airport here, and the eastern train line doesn't reach this far, so the only public transport links are by bus. There are regular connections with Bangkok's Eastern bus terminal and also services to other eastern towns like Rayong and Pattaya and destinations in the Northeast such as Korat.

Getting around Songthaews and local buses link Chantaburi with places nearby. Saamlors and tuk-tuks provide transport within the town.

Sights

Chantaburi has built its wealth on rubies and sapphires – and especially the famous 'red' sapphire or Thapthim Siam (see box page 189). Many of the gem mines were developed during the 19th century by Shan people from Burma, who are regarded as being among the best miners in the world.

● ●

Chantaburi place names

Bo Rai	Nam Tok Krating
บ่อไร่	น้ำตกกระทิง
Catholic Cathedral	Nam Tok Pliu
วิหารคาธอลิก	น้ำตกพลิ้ว
Khai Nern Wong	Oasis Sea World
ค่ายเนินวง	โอเอซีส ซีเวิลด์
Khao Ploi Waen	
เขาพลอยแหวน	

● ●

Muang Chan – as it is locally known – has a large Chinese and Vietnamese population, which is reflected in the general atmosphere of the town: narrower streets, shuttered wooden shophouses, Chinese temples and an air of industriousness. This atmosphere is most palpable along Rim Nam or Sukhaphiban Road which, as the name suggests, follows the right bank of the Chantaburi River. Old **shophouses**, some dating from the 19th century, house Chinese funeral supply and medicine shops. The active French-style **Catholic Cathedral** of the Immaculate Conception was built in 1880 and is the largest church in Thailand. Architecturally uninspiring (coloured beige and grey), it is significant merely for its presence. The interior though, is rather more interesting, Moorish pillars washed in cool colours, seashell chandeliers, and European stained glass. The Cathedral was built to serve the large number of Vietnamese Catholics who fled their homeland and settled here. On weekdays at 1600, children disgorge from the school near the Cathedral and an array of foodstalls miraculously appears in the compound, selling mouthwatering-looking snacks. The footbridge near the compound leads into the old part of town; the most interesting street architecture in the town is to be found in the road parallel to the river, westwards towards the main bridge. The Vietnamese part of town lies to the north of the cathedral, on the opposite side of the river.

It is Chantaburi's gems which attract most people's attention, but in addition, the province is highly regarded as a source of some of the best durians in Thailand, which flourish in the lush climate. The finest can cost several hundred baht (over a week's wages for an agricultural labourer), a fact which can seem astonishing to visitors who regard the fruit as repulsive - 'carrion in custard', as one Englishman is said to have remarked (see page 44).

Excursions

Khai Nern Wong – a ruined fort – lies 4½ km southeast of town off Tha Chalaep Road. Take the turning towards Tha Mai, and walk or drive for another 200 m. The fort is not as well preserved as the official tourist literature suggests. King Taksin retreated here after Ayutthaya fell to the Burmese in 1767. With his army consisting mainly of Chinese, it is thought Taksin decided to flee to the region of his kingdom with the largest number of Chinese settlers. Consequently, he proceeded from Chonburi to Rayong and finally to Chantaburi. Even so, he had to wage a battle against the ruler of Chantaburi in June 1767 to secure his position. Within the precincts of the fort an **Underwater Archaeological Museum** has opened. This does not mean that visitors have to don scuba gear, but rather that the objects displayed have been recovered from wrecks lying in this part of the Gulf. Most of the pieces are earthenware pots and Sawankhalok china.

Khai Nern Wong

Khao Ploi Waen Khao Ploi Waen is a small hill 4 km past the fort. There is an active wat at the bottom of the hill and a Ceylonese-style chedi on the top, built during the reign of King Rama IV. It is a steep climb up steps to the top of the hill, where there are good views of the surrounding countryside with its orchards. The hill is pockmarked with gem mines, although they are all now abandoned and the vegetation has made a good job of covering up the evidence.

Khao Sa Bap National Park **Nam Tok Phui** is a waterfall located within the 16,800-ha **Khao Sa Bap National Park**, gazetted in 1975. It is to be found off Route 3, south towards Trat. After about 14 km, at Ban Plui, a left turn is signposted to the waterfall (there is a large, rather grand, Chinese temple close to the turn-off). Facing the waterfall are two chedis, the Alongkon Chedi and one commissioned by Rama V as a memorial to Princess Sunantha Kumareeratana in 1876. Park bungalow accommodation available, T5790529. ■ *Getting there: by minibus from the municipal market.*

Chantaburi

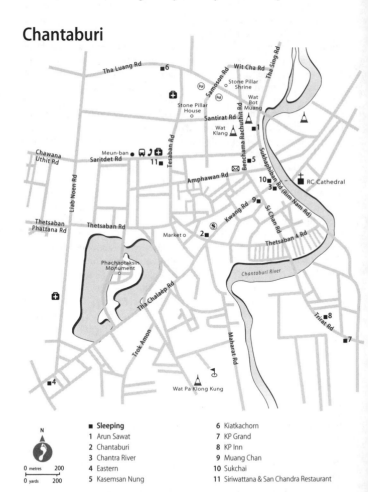

■ **Sleeping**
1 Arun Sawat
2 Chantaburi
3 Chantra River
4 Eastern
5 Kasemsan Nung
6 Kiatkachorn
7 KP Grand
8 KP Inn
9 Muang Chan
10 Sukchai
11 Siriwattana & San Chandra Restaurant

The tears of the gods: rubies and sapphires

Major deposits of two of the world's most precious stones are found distributed right across mainland Southeast Asia: rubies and sapphires are mined in Thailand, Burma, Vietnam, Cambodia and Laos. The finest of all come from Burma, and especially from the renowned Mogok Stone Tract, which supports a town of 100,000 almost entirely upon the proceeds of the gem industry. Here peerless examples are unearthed, including the rare 'pigeon's blood' ruby. One Thai trader was reported saying that "Asking to see the pigeon's blood is like asking to see the face of God".

Although the Burmese government tries to keep a tight grip on the industry, many of the gems pass into the hands of Thai gem dealers, often with the connivance of the Thai army. Corruption, violence, murder, arson and blackmail are all part and parcel of the trade. Through fair means and foul, Bangkok has become the centre of the world's gem business and Thailand is the largest exporter of cut stones – indeed, it has a virtual monopoly of the sapphire trade. Thai buyers conclude deals with mines in Australia, Kenya, Sri Lanka, the USA – across the globe – and have a stranglehold on the business. Those who try to buck the system and bypass Bangkok risk having a contract taken out on their lives.

Rubies and sapphires are different colours of corundum, the crystalline form of aluminium oxide. Small quantities of various trace elements give the gems their colour; in the case of rubies, chromium and for blue sapphires, titanium. Sapphires are also found in a spectrum of other colours including green and yellow. Rubies are among the rarest of gems, and command prices four times higher than equivalent sized diamonds. The Burmese call the ruby ma naw ma ya or 'desire-fulfilling stones'.

The colour of sapphires can be changed through heat treatment (the most advanced form is called diffusion treatment) to 1,500-1,600°C (sapphires melt at 2,050°C). For example, relatively valueless colourless geuda sapphires from Sri Lanka, turn a brilliant blue or yellow after heating. The technique is an ancient one: Pliny the Elder described the heating of agate by Romans nearly 2,000 years ago, while the Arabs had developed heat treatment into almost a science by the 13th century. Today, almost all sapphires and rubies are heat treated. The most valued colour for sapphires is cornflower blue – dark, almost black, sapphires command a lower price. The value of a stone is based on the four 'C's: Colour, Clarity, Cut and Carat (1 carat = 200 milligrammes). Note that almost all stones are heat treated to improve their colour. For information on buying gems in Thailand, see page 145.

Oasis Sea World is 25 km south of town off Route 3 near the small town of **Oasis Sea World** Laem Sing. The station covers 11 ha and was established to breed two species of dolphin – the humpbacked and Irrawaddy. Dolphin shows are performed at regular intervals through the day. *Mon-Sun 0900-1800, ฿120 (adults), ฿60 (children). For information T399015.*

Nam Tok Krating, another waterfall, can be found within the **Kitchakut** **Kitchakut** **National Park** (along with a few bat-filled caves), and is about 30 km north- **National Park** west of town. The water is believed to have healing powers. The park is one of the smallest in the country, covering under 60 sq km, and was established in 1977. The falls are within hiking distance of the park headquarters. It is also possible to walk to the summit of the Phrabat Mountain, so-called because there is an impression of a footprint of the Buddha. Allow four hours to reach the top. There is accommodation available in the park near park HQ (B T5790529/5794842). ■ *Getting there: regular public songthaews run past the entrance to the park on Route 3249; from here it is a 15 min walk to the park HQ.*

Bo Rai Bo Rai is a gem mining area near the Cambodian border, with a gem market (see page 192).

Wat Khao Sukim Wat Khao Sukim, situated at Ban Khao Sukim 35 km northwest of Chantaburi is a famous wat – visited daily by hundreds who come to see Luang Pho Somchai, an elderly monk with mysterious powers and a nationwide reputation as a meditation teacher. The monastery is sited on the side of Sukim mountain and a cable car runs up the side of the hill. Because so many gifts have been bestowed on the monastery by wealthy Thais there is now a **small museum** displaying the hoard. ■ *Getting there: take the 316 north out of Chantaburi, go west along Route 3, then north up the 3322.*

Essentials

Sleeping **A** *Caribou*, 14 Chawana Uthit Rd, T323431. Recently built luxury hotel, pool, business facilities, 3 restaurants, Thai restaurant has live traditional Thai music most nights. **B** *Chantaburi Riverside*, 63 Moo 9, Chanthanimit 5 Rd, on the east bank of the Chantaburi River, north of town, T311726, F311726. A/c, restaurant, pool recently constructed, with Thai-style bungalows set in a tatty garden, all looking rather scruffy. Staff, however, are said to be friendly and helpful. **B** *KP Grand*, 35/200-201 Trirat Rd, T323201, F323214. 18 floors, so easy to spot, a/c, restaurant, newish hotel with all mod cons.

B-C *Eastern*, 899 Tha Chalaep Rd, T312218, F311985. Pool, all rooms have a/c, TV and bath tub – larger rooms also have fridges and are almost twice the price, smaller rooms are good value. **C** *KP Inn*, Trirat Rd, T311756. Very friendly but rather boring – all rooms have hot water and a/c, located directly opposite *KP Grand*. **C-D** *Mark's Travelodge*, 14 Raksakchamun Rd, T311531. A/c, own bathroom, spacious but quite far out. **D-E** *Kiatkachorn*, Tha Luang Rd, north side of town, T311212. Some a/c, boring bland exterior, not much better inside, noisy. **D** *Chantaburi*, 42/6 Tha Chalaep Rd, T311300. Some a/c, extremely grotty and very noisy, just about the only thing going for it is that it is central. **D-E** *Kasemsan Nung* , 98/1 Benchama Rachuthit Rd, T312340. Some a/c, large, clean rooms in big hotel, well run, but some rooms can be noisy. **D** *Siriwattana*, 51/3-4 Saritdet Rd, T328073. 5 clean rooms all with a/c, some with small balcony but room at back has no window, bright, friendly management, probably best value accommodation in town, located directly above *San Chandra Rice and Noodle House*. **D-E** *Muang Chan*, 257-259 Si Chan Rd, T312909. Noisy and characterless.

E *Arun Sawat*, 239 Sukha Phibal Rd, T311082. Situated in the most attractive part of town, small but clean rooms with homely atmosphere. **E** *Sukchai*, 28 Tha Chalaep Rd, T311292. Basic but relatively clean, central. **F** *Chantra River Hotel*, 248 Sukha Phibal Rd, T312310. Clean and friendly, shared bathroom, some rooms overlook river (located directly opposite *Arun Sawat*).

Eating Most restaurants are on Tha Chalaep Rd. Where the road runs along the eastern side of King Taksin Lake, there is a profusion of pubs, bars and ice cream parlours – this is where Chantaburi's yuppies hang-out.

Cheap: *The Meun-ban* or 'Homely' restaurant is located directly next to the bus terminal and is probably the best low-budget restaurant in town. It offers a multitude of Thai dishes (including a huge vegetarian selection – something which it is not always easy to find in Thailand) and ice creams, at very low prices. The owners speak good English and are a helpful source of local information, it is also in an ideal location if you arrive tired and hungry after a long bus journey and need some refreshment. Recommended. *San Chandra (Chantaburi Rice and Noodle House)*, on Saritdet Rd, is another sparklingly clean and friendly restaurant offering delicious Thai food and ice creams, at the time of writing the menu is in Thai only but they are working on a translation – you can always point. Recommended.

Beware of **Chanthon Phochana** 98/1 Benchama Rachuthit Rd, the restaurant below the *Kasemsan I Hotel* – it serves unpleasant food at extortionate prices (there are no prices on the menu and *farangs* probably get charged more).

May or Jun *Fruit fair* (movable), celebrating local fruits such as durian, jackfruit, pomelo and rambutan; cultural shows, handicraft exhibitions.   **Festivals**

Gems and jewellery Si Chan Rd, or 'Gem Street' has the best selection of jewellery shops and gem stores. However you are unlikely to pick up a bargain. On Fri, Sat and Sun a gem street market operates along Krachang Lane.   **Shopping**

Rattan and basketwork Chantaburi is regarded as one of the centres of fine rattan work in Thailand. Available from numerous shops in town.

If coming from the northeast, it is possible to avoid the capital by taking routes 304, 33 and 317 south from Korat. The road descends from the Khorat plateau and follows the Thai/Cambodian border, through frequent checkpoints, south to Chantaburi.   **Transport**
330 km from Bangkok

Road Bus: regular connections with Bangkok's Eastern bus terminal. Also buses from Pattaya, Rayong, Ban Phe and other eastern seaboard towns. If coming from Koh Samet, get a boat to Ban Phe, songthaew to Rayong (฿20) and then a bus to Chantaburi – buses leave every hour, the journey takes 2 hrs and costs ฿30. There are less regular bus connections with destinations in the Northeast including Korat.

Banks *Thai Farmers*, 103 Sirong Muang Rd. *Bangkok*, 50 Tha Chalaep Rd. **Directory**
Communications Post Office: at the intersection of Amphawan and Si Chan roads.

Chantaburi to Koh Chang

Trat

Trat is the provincial capital and the closest Thai town of any size to Cambodia. Like Chantaburi, it is a gem centre (see box, page 145). As the prospects of lasting peace in Cambodia get ever-so-slowly brighter, and as the government in Cambodia opts for Gorbachev-style policies of *perestroika*, so Chinese businessmen in Trat are getting increasingly excited about business prospects across the border. For a while, between 1894 and 1906, Trat was part of French Indo-China. But the French agreed to repatriate the town in exchange for the Thais giving up their traditional claims to western Cambodia.   *Phone code: 039*
Colour map 1, grid C6

Most people visit Trat en route to beautiful Koh Chang, and the emergence of Koh Chang as the latest in a long string of tropical Thai islands to entice the *farang* visitor has brought considerable business to the place. But truthfully, there is little to keep visitors in the town any longer than they need to catch a bus or boat onwards.

However, if your boat/bus connection means that you are stranded here, then there is a bustling **covered market** (attractively known in official literature as the 'Municipal Shopping Mall') in the centre of town on Sukhumvit Road. It offers a good selection of food and drink stalls. On the same road, north of the shopping mall, there is also an active **night market**. **Wat**

Buppharam, also known as **Wat Plai Klong** dates from the late Ayutthaya Period. It is notable for its wooden viharn and monk's *kutis*, and is 2 km west of town, down the road opposite the shopping mall.

Excursions **Bo Rai** on the Cambodian border, used to be a really thriving gem market, cashing in on the supply of rubies from Cambodia as well as from local mines. However there are fewer and fewer high-quality gems being mined these days and so Bo Rai's significance has declined (it may also be that many of the gems are sold in Bangkok rather than through intermediaries in Bo Rai). While in the early 1990s there were several gem markets here, now there is just one – the **Khlong Yor Market** which operates during the morning. One unusual feature of the market is that it is the gem buyers who remain seated while the sellers walk around showing their wares. ■ *Getting there: songthaews leave from outside the market.*

An even better source of gems is over the border, in Cambodia. From 1991 for several years, thousands of Thais, after being taxed US$60 each by the Khmer Rouge, were penetrating the Cambodian jungles in search of their fortunes. One was quoted as saying, 'Over that mountain, a few days' walk away, you just stick your hands in the ground and the dirt is filled with precious stones'. Under pressure from the UN and the international community, the Thai government tried – or at least gave the impression of trying – to stop the flow of gems, so that the flow of funds to the Khmer Rouge would also stop. In this they were only partially successful. While Cambodia remains a tempting source of gems, the Khmer Rouge – thank goodness – are dead and buried.

Trat

Khlong Yai is the southernmost town on this eastern arm of Thailand and an important fishing port. The journey there is worthwhile for the dramatic scenery with the mountains of Cambodia rising to the east and the sea to the west. Khlong Yai is also a pretty and bustling little port, well worth the trip. There are several Cambodian markets and the seafood is excellent. **Sleeping** There is one hotel in Khlong Yai which, we understand, is serviceable. *Getting there: by songthaew from the back of the municipal market (฿25) or shared taxi from the front of the market (฿35 each).*

Sleeping **C-D** *OK Bungalow*, down a narrow tree-lined road (no sign in English) on the left-hand side as you head east along the Wiwattana Rd, opposite the *Nam Chok* restaurant, T512657-8. This is a second branch

9 Residang Guesthouse
10 Thai Rungrot
11 Trat Guesthouse
12 Trat Inn & Family Café
13 Windy Guesthouse

■ **Sleeping**
1 Coco's Guesthouse & Café
2 Foremost Guesthouse
3 Friendly Guesthouse
4 Garden Home Guesthouse
5 Jame's Guesthouse
6 Muang Trat
7 NP Guesthouse
8 OK Bungalow

● **Eating**
1 Jean Café
2 Max & Tick
3 Sang Fah

🚌 **Transport**
1 A/c buses to Bangkok
2 Non a/c Bus Station
3 Minibus & taxis to Laem Ngop
4 Buses to Chantaburi

Trat place names

Khlong Yai

คลองใหญ่

Laem Ngop

แหลมงอบ

of the *Muang Trat* and is the most up-market place to stay, it consists of a concrete line of bungalows, each separated from the next at ground level by a parking bay, the more expensive bungalows have hot water and a bath tub, most have a/c. **D-E** *Thai Rungrot*, 296 Sukhumvit Rd, T511141. Some a/c, north of town, to the right of Sukhumvit Rd, rather decrepit with boring rooms.

D *Muang Trat*, 4 Sukhumvit Rd, T511091. Some a/c, clean rooms, very centrally located on the south side of the lane which runs between the 2 markets – a fact which has put their restaurant out of business.

D-E *Trat Inn*, 66-71 Sukhumvit Rd, T511028. **E-F** *NP Guesthouse*, 1-3 Soi Luang Aet, Lak Muang Rd, T512564. Clean, friendly, well-run converted shophouse, with a bright little restaurant, shared bathroom, dorm beds. Recommended.

F *Foremost Guesthouse*, 49 Thoncharoen Rd, by the canal, last turn on the left off Sukhumvit Rd, towards Laem Ngop, T511923. First floor rooms, shared bathrooms, hot water, clean and friendly with lots of local information. Recommended. **F** *Windy Guesthouse*, Thoncharoen Rd. Across the road from *Foremost*, owned by same family, slightly cheaper rooms, dorm beds available.

Eating The municipal market has a good range of stalls to choose from – good value and delicious. Other markets which sell food include the night market next to the a/c bus station. **Expensive**: *Suan Phu*, Ban Laem Hin, 10 km southeast of town. One of the best places to sample seafood in the region, with crab being the speciality (it is attached to a crab farm). Attractive seating area on piers out over the water. **Mid-range**: *Max and Tick*, Soi Luang Aet, opposite the *NP Guesthouse*. A good place for breakfast, friendly owners who are a mine of local information. *Nam Chok*, corner of Soi Butnoi and Wiwatthana roads (off Thatmai Rd). Good local food served outdoors. *Sang Fah*, 156 Sukhumvit Rd. Thai food, extensive menu, especially seafood, a/c restaurant, quite good.

Festivals **Jun** *Rakham Fruit Fair* celebrates Trat's reputation as a fruit-growing centre.

Transport *400 km from Bangkok* **Local** **Motorbike hire**: from Soi Sukhumvit, just south of the municipal market and from *Windy Guesthouse* (they also have bicycles and may have canoes for exploring the canal).

Road **Bus**: a/c station is on Sukhumvit Rd, just north of the night market. Non-a/c buses leave from Wiwattana Rd, north, off Sukhumvit Rd. Regular connections with Bangkok's Eastern bus terminal 5½ hrs, Pattaya 3½ hrs, and with Chantaburi 1 hr 40 mins. **Songthaew**: to Laem Ngop from outside the municipal market on Sukhumvit Rd (฿15). **Shared taxi**: to Chantaburi 50 mins (฿30 each).

Boat From near the *Foremost Guesthouse*, boats leave very irregularly to Koh Kut and Koh Mak.

Directory **Banks** *Siam Commercial*, Sukhumvit Rd. *Thai Farmers*, 63 Sukhumvit Rd. *Thai Military*, Sukhumvit Rd. **Communications** **Post Office:** Tha Reua Jang Rd on northeast side of town. **Tourist offices** Found on Soi Sukhumvit, not far from the market; helpful and informative.

Laem Ngop

Phone code: 039
Colour map 1, grid C5

This sleepy fishing village – in fact the district capital – has a long pier lined with boats, along with good seafood and a relaxed atmosphere. But this is unlikely to last: Laem Ngop is poised to explode into life as Koh Chang – an offshore island – becomes Thailand's next island beach resort to hit the big time (see below). At the time of writing, the town had a handful of guesthouses and some restaurants by the main pier in town. Two new piers, one rather prosaically called Koh Chang Centre Point, have been completed some distance outside town, to the northwest. There is a small tourist information centre in the Amphoe (district) Office, offering information on bungalows on Koh Chang and the other islands in the Marine National Park. The headquarters for the park are at Laem Ngop. Few people stay in Laem Ngop and almost everyone arrives here merely to catch the boat to Koh Chang.

Sleeping There are a number of guesthouses on the main road into the village. **D-E** *Laem Ngop Inn*, T597044. Some a/c. **D-E** *Paradise Inn*, T512831. Some a/c. **E** *PI*, large clean rooms, open high season only. **F** *Chut Kaew*, good source of information and comes recommended.

Tour operators *AD Tour*, by the pier, T2128014.

Transport *17 km from Trat* **Road** **Songthaew**: from the stand outside the shopping mall, Sukhumvit Rd, in Trat (30 mins). Regular departures during daylight hours. After dark, songthaews must be chartered. **Boat**: regular boat departures for Koh Chang from the main pier in town; rather more intermittant from Koh Chang Centre Point outside town. For details, see Koh Chang entry, below.

Directory **Banks** Mobile exchange service at the pier. 0900-1600. **NB** exchange rates on Koh Chang are poor. **Medical services** *Malaria Centre* on main road, opposite *Laem Ngop Inn*. They give the latest information on malaria and can help with treatment. **Tourist offices** *TAT*, 100 Mu 1 Trat, Laem Ngop Rd, T597255. Areas of responsibility are Trat and the islands, including Koh Chang.

Koh Chang

Phone code: 039
Colour map 1, grid C5

This – as yet – unspoilt island is Thailand's second largest (40 km long and 16 km wide) and is part of a Marine National Park which also includes another 50-odd islands and islets covering just over 650 sq km. Despite the 'protection' that its national park status should offer, Koh Chang is developing rapidly, with resorts and bungalows springing up virtually overnight along its shores.

Ins and outs

Getting there *To reach Koh Chang in a day from Bangkok means a very early bus – before 0800*

Getting to Koh Chang is not easy – which probably explains why it has been slow to develop as a resort island. First of all it is necessary to get to Laem Ngop (see the previous entry), the departure point for boats to the island. From Bangkok catch a bus from the Eastern bus terminal to Trat (see page 193); from there, there are regular songthaews the 17 km to Laem Ngop. During the high season (Nov-May) boats leave every hour or so from Laem Ngop for Koh Chang. But during the low season departures are much more intermittent.

Getting around Koh Chang's best beaches are on the western side of the island – **Hat Sai Khao** (white sand), **Hat Khlong Phrao** and, on the southern coast, **Hat Bang Bao**. These can be reached either by jeep taxi from Ao Sapparot (price ranging from ฿20- ฿40, depending upon destination, if you manage to fill up the taxi) or by boat from Laem Ngop. There is a dirt road up the east coast and down the west coast as far south as Ao Kai Bae. For destinations further south such as Hat Bang Bao you must either walk or get a boat – although If planned improvements to the track have progressed according to schedule then this section may also be open to road vehicles. The steep mountainous stretch between Ao Khlong Son and Hat Sai Khao is now paved and work is on-going so it may well be that more of the island's dirt roads are now surfaced. The intention is to create a paved ring road encircling the whole island, which should be completed by 2001, or thereabouts. In addition to songthaews there are also motorbikes (around ฿400 per day) and mountain bikes for hire. For walkers, there is a path crossing the middle of the island from Ban Khlong Phrao to Than Ma Yom but it is a strenuous day-long hike and locals recommend taking a guide.

For snorkelling and diving the best time to visit is between November and May, when visibility is at its best. This is also the best time to visit from the weather point of view. Koh Chang is a wet island with an annual rainfall of over 3,000 mm (the wettest month is August).

Koh Chang

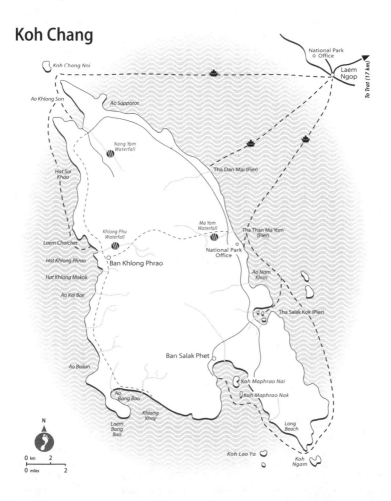

The area

Khlong Son, near Koh Chang's northern tip, is the largest settlement on the island. Even so, there's not much here: a health clinic, a few small noodle shops, a monastery, post office and school. Many of the other islands within the national park have villages, and a fair amount of land, particularly around the coast, has been cleared for agriculture – mostly coconut plantations. The park was only gazetted in 1982 and most of the

Koh Chang place names

Hat Bang Bao
หาดบางเบ้า
Hat Khlong Phrao
หาดคลองพร้าว
Hat Sai Khao
หาดทรายขาว
Than Ma Yom Waterfall
น้ำตกธารมะยม

people living within the parks boundaries were here many years beforehand. Even so, Koh Chang remains mainly undeveloped. But it is a matter of conjecture as to how long the island will remain uspoilt. Given the changes that have occurred elsewhere – Phuket, Samui and Samet – it is easy to be pessimistic about the environmental future of Koh Chang. Indeed, we are already receiving letters from people complaining of the rubbish. With no waste management system it doesn't take many visitors or guesthouses to create a serious refuse problem – and that is what appears to be emerging on Koh Chang's more popular beaches.

Sights

Than Ma Yom Waterfall Koh Chang is famed for its wild boar and the **Than Ma Yom Waterfall** – which is on the east side of the island. King Chulalongkorn (Rama V) visited this waterfall on no less than six occasions at the end of the 19th century, so even given the Thai predilection for waterfalls of any size, it counts as an impressive one (in fact there are three falls). To prove the point, the king carved his initials (or had them carved), on a stone to mark one of his visits. Rama VI and VII also visited the falls, although it seems that they didn't get quite so far – they left their initials inscribed on stones at the nearest of the falls. The falls are accessible from either Ban Dan Mai or Thaan Ma Yom, both on the east coast and getting to the first of the cascades involves a walk of around one hour. It is around 4 km to the furthest of the three falls.

Khlong Phu Falls More accessible from the west coast (which is where most people stay), and perhaps even more beautiful, are the **Khlong Phu Falls** at Ao Khlong Phrao. This waterfall can be reached by taxi or motorbike in 10 minutes from Hat Sai Khao. You can also travel to it from the road by elephant for ฿200 or for free by walking just 3 km. There is a good pool here for swimming as well as a restaurant and some bungalows. Because this is a national park it is also possible to camp.

The forest Koh Chang is also likely to prove rewarding for naturalists. The **forest** here is some of the most species-rich in the country and while the island's coast may be undergoing development the rugged, mountainous interior is still largely inaccessible and covered with virgin rainforest (around 70% is said to be forested). There is a good population of birds, including parrots, sunbirds, hornbills and trogons, as well as Koh Chang's well-known population of wild boar. While the waters around Koh Chang are clear there have been some reports of a deterioration in water quality connected with coastal gem mining on the mainland. Nonetheless, hard and especially soft corals are abundant.

Fish are less numerous and varied than on the other side of the Gulf of Thailand or in the Andaman Sea.

NB Mosquitoes (carrying malaria) and sandflies are a problem on Koh Chang and surrounding islands, so insect repellent and anti-malarials are essential. Take a net if camping.

Other nearby islands

There are many other smaller islands near Koh Chang, which are also part of the Koh Chang National Park and which are likewise gradually being developed. These are mostly off the south coast, and are the best areas for snorkelling and diving.

The next largest island after Koh Chang itself is **Koh Kut**. This island has lovely beaches, especially on the west side, and a number of small fishing villages linked by dirt roads. There is an impressive waterfall and the coral is also said to be good. However, mosquitoes are a problem. Koh Kut is not part of the national park and so there are almost no controls on development; the forest is being encroached upon by agriculture and developers are claiming the best pieces of shoreline. There are two resorts – the exclusive **AL** *Koh Kut Island Resort*, T039-511824 and **E-F** *Klong Chao Laguna*, basic huts near the waterfall. ■ *Getting there: two, sometimes more, boats per week leave from the pier on the Trat River in Trat (not Laem Ngop) for Koh Kut. During the high season (Nov-May) are on Mon at 1100 and Fri at 1400; day visitors from Koh Mak (see below) can make the trip on regular boats linking the two islands.*

Koh Kut

Koh Mak is the third largest island in the archipelago after Koh Chang and Koh Kut. It has been privately owned by a few wealthy local families and a little over half of the island has been cleared for coconut plantations. But there is still a reasonable area of forest and the coral is also good. The best beach is on the northwest shore. It is said that many of the prime pieces of shorefront have been sold to Bangkok-based developers, so it remains to be seen what happens to Koh Mak. Perhaps the economic downturn and the collapse of the property market will slow the pace of change. **Sleeping A-B** *Ban Laem Chan*, T01-9142593, F02-3982844. Seven wooden cottages with seaview, attached bathrooms and 'club house'. **A-B** *Koh Maak Resort*, reservations from Bangkok on T3196714 or from Trat on T3270220. **D** *Alternative House*, good bungalows in a pleasant location. **E-F** *Lazy Days*, basic huts. ■ *Getting there: boats leave daily for Laem Ngop for Koh Mak during the high season (Nov-May). Departures may be suspended during the low season.*

Koh Mak

The tiny island of Koh Kham has two bungalows (**F**), tents and the **E** *Koh Kham Resort*. Boats leave from Laem Ngop, 3½ hours (฿150). Koh Kham is well known for its swallows, nests and turtle eggs, as well as good coral and rock formations for divers.

Koh Kham

Other islands with bungalows are **Koh Phrao**, **Koh Ngam**, **Koh Whai**, which has two bungalow operations **D-F** *Pakalang Resort*, **E-F** *Koh Whai Paradise*, T579131, **Koh Lao Ya** (with accommodation at the **A** *Lao Ya Resort*, T512552. A/c, hot water, half board compulsory, excellent restaurant; the ultimate place for 'getting away from it all'). **Koh Sai Khao** (**A** *Hat Sai Khao Resort*, T511429), and **Koh Khlum**.

Many of the more sophisticated bungalow operations on Koh Chang organize day trips to the islands during the high season (when the seas are calmer,

The Eastern Seaboard

the visibility greater and there is generally more demand). In the low season few boats go between these islands and either Koh Chang or the mainland and most of the accommodation closes down.

Essentials

Sleeping

Caution: there are many thefts on Koh Chang. If you're staying in a basic bamboo hut be sure not to leave valuables in it when you are not there, or near open windows when you are asleep

- -
Koh Kut place names

Koh Khlum
เกาะคลุ้ม

Koh Kut
เกาะกูด

Koh Rang
เกาะรัง

- -

Rapid development means that the accommodation list below may date quickly. The best source of information is travellers returning from the island. Check the guest book at the *Foremost Guesthouse* in Trat. Almost all the accommodation is simple A-frames, with wood-slat walls, thatched roofs, communal showers and no protection against mosquitoes – although some establishments will provide netting. Longer-stay visitors should ask for a discount. During the high season (Nov-May) you can usually ask your boat driver to drop you at the beach of your choice. In the low season most boats land only at Ao Sapparot (or at Ban Dan Hao) – in which case the boat ticket will also include the songthaew journey from Ao Sapparot down the west coast to your destination if the seas are too rough for the boat to make it round there. Much of the accommodation closes during the low season so if you do find a boat willing to go to the west or south coasts check before you go that accommodation is open there – otherwise you may be faced with a night on the beach followed by a long walk the next day.

NB With the development of the tourist industry on Koh Chang prices are also increasing and particularly during the very busy months (Dec and Jan) prices may be much higher than you might expect for accommodation in that category (you may well pay ฿1,000 for a fairly smart bungalow with fan but no a/c and no hot water for example). Although there are now electric cables around the island, most places cannot afford the enormous connection fee and still generate their own electricity which means that electricity is restricted in many places and only available from 1800 to midnight or 0600, so if it is important to you to have a fan all night then check what time it goes off.

Ao Khlong Son Few people choose to stay here anymore but head instead for the beaches on the west or south coasts. There are only two operations still going here: **F** *Mannee*, rather run down but friendly and enthusiastic management. **D-E** *Premvadee*, some single rooms, and some larger bungalows with attached bathrooms.

Hat Sai Khao About 15 establishments here, all with similar facilities and prices – many provide mosquito nets. The water is very shallow. **B-C** *Phaloma Resort*, T01-3230164. German-Swiss-run operation on the southern tip of the bay, some bungalows with a view over the sea, again there is no beach here, the restaurant is very good if a little more expensive than average, small library, in the high season boat trips to Koh Yai, Rang and Khlum can be arranged, motorcycles can also be hired here. **C-D** *Mac Bungalow*, own bathrooms, quite nice bungalows. **D-E** *Ban Dung Rong Resort* T597184. **D-E** *Cookie*, south of Patthai, Hat Sai Khao. Efficiently run bungalows all with shower/WC in 3 rows at varying price, popular and cheap but closed in low season, long-stay discount. **D-E** *White Sand Beach Resort*, out of the way up at the northern end of the beach and rather run-down, some rooms with own bathroom. **E** *Apple Bungalow*, slightly smarter huts than other places in this price category. **E** *Hat Sai Khao Bungalow*, featuring some of the smartest and most expensive bungalows on the beach, in addition to some basic bamboo huts, good associated restaurant. **E** *Sunsai Bungalow*, clean and good value, some with attached bathroom, but no beach here. **E-F** *Ya Kah Bungalow*, basic but characterful little huts, friendly management. **F** *KC Bungalow*, clean huts arranged along the sea front in a very good location, quiet but not too secluded. **F** *Rock Sand Bungalow*, a few basic huts situated higher up above the beach.

Hat Khlong Phrao This is the next beach, 5 km south of Hat Sai Khao, and 2 km long, spread out each side of the mouth of the Khlong Phrao canal – a beautiful beach but the water tends to be very shallow. **AL** *Koh Chang Resort*, T538054-9. A/c, expensive bungalows, probably overpriced. **B** *Khlong Prao Resort*, T597216. Rather tatty and overpriced bungalows set around a lagoon, plus a 2-storey block, beautiful beach, good for swimming. **C-E** *Chaiyachet Bungalow*, T21930458. Bungalows set in an attractive garden at the top end of the bay, 1½ km walk to the beach. **C-E** *Coconut Beach Bungalow*, T01-21930432. Wooden huts with shared bath, well built, mosquito nets provided, set above the beach, rather unfriendly management. **E** *Hobby Hut*, quite far back from the beach, attractive wooden bungalows and restaurant in pleasant setting in wood on bank of canal. **E-F** *PSS*, lovely, clean bamboo huts on beach, good food. Recommended. **E-F** *NP*, next operation south of *PSS* and the last on the beach, overpriced run-down huts.

Ao Khlong Makok There is almost no beach here at high tide and there are just a couple of bungalow operations which are virtually deserted in the low season. **D-F** *Chok Dee* and **D-F** *Mejic* both offer huts with attached and shared bathrooms and have restaurants attractively located on stilts above the sea.

Ao Kai Bae This is the southernmost beach on the west coast. The beach is beautiful but swimming is not so good as the bottom is very shallow and covered with rocks with dead coral in places. **A-E** *Sea View Resort*, T597143. Very comfortable bungalows set on a steep hill in a landscaped garden, very good value (particularly in the low season when prices tend to halve), they also have a number of cheap basic huts right on the beach. **B-E** *Siam Bay Bungalow*, south end of the beach. Bungalows on the hill with sea views. **C-E** *Kai Bae Hut Resort*, T21930452. Some a/c, good bungalows, restaurant, good food, small shop. Recommended. **C-F** *Kai Bae Beach*, rather tatty huts with grass roofs, not very friendly management. **D-F** *Coral Bungalow*, offers mountain bikes for hire for ฿30 per hour, telephone service, flight reconfirmation and has a TV and video selection. **E-F** *Kai Bae Garden*, located 500 m up from the beach and hence cheaper huts, there is also a shop here. **E-F** *Nang Nuan Bung*, located at the north end of the bay (no beach here). Small, wooden huts, rather close together, no mosquito nets, but the management are very friendly and the restaurant offers a good range of meat and seafood dishes. **E-F** *Poon*, huts on the beach, basic and rather run-down, but cheap.

There are lovely views out to the small islands dotted along the coast here

Ao Bang Bao This is a lovely beach on the south coast of the island. The bay dries out at low tide and it is virtually inaccessible in the low season when the accommodation tends to shut down. There are no regular boats here – you can either charter a fishing boat or walk from Hat Kai Bae (about 5 km). **C-D** *Nice Beach Bang Bao*, situated directly on the beach, concrete bungalows with attached bathroom placed quite far apart, attractive restaurant. **D-F** *Bang Bao Blue Wave*, 15 wooden bungalows situated in a small shady wood (with and without bathroom), friendly atmosphere. **D** *Bang Bao Beach*, 10 mins from the beach and village. **D-F** *Bang Bao Laguna*, located at the eastern end of the bay, wooden huts, friendly management. **E-F** *Tantawan Bungalow*, only 7 huts here.

Although there is a scattering of bungalow operations on the **East coast** very few people choose to stay here even in the high season. The only beach is at Sai Thong but the bungalow operation here had closed down at last check.

The Eastern Seaboard

Tha Than Ma Yom D-E *Tha Than Ma Yom Bungalow*, overpriced, grotty huts on the opposite side of the road above the beach. **D-F** *Tha Than Ma Yom*, bungalows set above the sea in the woods.

Eating   Guesthouses tend to serve an unchanging array of Thai and travellers' fare; restaurants and bars are appearing gradually and the gastronomy should improve. Grilled seafood is the best bet. *JJ Sabai Land* is on Khlong Phrao beach, Thai and Western food available. *Bubby Bong's*, south end of Ao Sai Khao, recently opened by 2 Californians, seafood, Thai food and burgers, an open-sided torch-lit hut – will inevitably become popular. *Patthai Bungalows*, run by *farang* lady, midway along Hat Sai Khao, serves home-made bread and excellent Lao filter coffee.

Cookie, south of *Patthai*, Hat Sai Khao, good selection of Thai and travellers' food, popular and cheap. *The Fisherman's*, between *Patthai* and *Cookie* on Hat Sai Khao, good fresh fish. *Thor's Palace*, on Hat Sai Khao, excellent restaurant of the variety where you sit on the floor at low, lamp-lit tables, very friendly management, popular, library.

Sport   **Diving**: there is a Swiss-run diving school, Koh Chang Divers, on Hat Sai Khao which offers PADI and snorkelling; no credit cards accepted. There is a second outfit on Ao Kai Bae, the Seahorse Dive Centre.

Transport   To get to Koh Chang, take a bus to Trat (see Trat section), a songthaew to Laem Ngop and then a boat to the island. When leaving the island it is advisable to get immediately into a songthaew to Trat (if that is where you want to go) rather than hanging around because if you miss the one which meets the boat you may have to wait hours for the next one or have to charter one. Details on getting to the smaller islands of Koh Mak and Koh Kut are given above.

Local   No cars, but there are motorbike and jeep **taxis**. These are pretty expensive (about ฿20- ฿40 per 5 km) The usual rule of not getting into an empty one without checking the price first in case you charter it applies of course. The high prices date back to the days when the roads were poor and the machines had a very short lifespan but there is really no excuse for it now that the roads have been improved. **Motorbike hire**: from many of the guesthouses but, again, rates are high – ฿60 per hour, ฿400 per day. **Mountain bike hire**: some of the guesthouses now have mountain bikes for hire (around ฿100 per day).

Boat   Boats leave daily for the various beaches from one of the three piers in Laem Ngop (฿50 and up). The main pier is right at the end of the road from Trat, before you fall into the sea. The other two piers are several kilometres west of Laem Ngop and service the more expensive resorts. Boats to Khlong Son Beach take 1 hr, to Than Ma Yom Pier 50 mins, to Dan Mai Pier 35 mins. During peak season (Nov-May) there are almost hourly departures, some to Than Ma Yom Pier (east coast), others to the west coast. From the island, there are boats from 0730 from Than Ma Yom Pier (pick-ups leave from Hat Sai Khao). Between Jun and Oct – the low season – boats are more irregular and some routes do not operate at all because of rough seas combined with limited demand. **NB** It is only possible to reach Koh Chang in a day from Bangkok by taking an early morning bus (first a/c bus 0700, non-a/c 0420). Beware of *Sea Horse*, who reputedly run minibuses to Laem Ngop and drive deliberately slowly to miss the last ferry, so that they get to choose where you stay (and take a commission).

Car ferry   Car ferries leave from Koh Chang Centrepoint Pier, northwest of Laem Ngop, four times daily. Another vehicular ferry leaves from Laem Ngop's third pier, at Ao Thammachat on Route 3156 – five departures daily.

Banks There are no banks on Koh Chang, and rates are poor at the guesthouses that change money. **Communications** There is a telephone (overseas calls possible but at exorbitant rates), money exchange, stamps and letterbox and general grocery store at the southern end of Sai Khao beach. **Medical services** Doctors: in Ao Khlong Son and in Ao Khlong Phrao near *Hobby Hut*. For more serious injuries patients are transferred to Laem Ngop. **Tourist offices** There is an information centre on Sai Khao beach where boat trips, fishing and snorkelling can all be arranged. **Useful addresses** Police: there are 6 policemen permanently at the station in Khlong Son. Thefts should be reported immediately so that if there are suspects the next boat to the mainland can be intercepted by the mainland police.

Directory

The Eastern Seaboard

The Isthmus

5

The Isthmus

The Isthmus provinces of Thailand include Phetburi, Prachuap Khiri Khan, Chumphon, Ranong and Phangnga. It is in Prachuap that Thailand is at its narrowest - stretching just a few tens of kilometres from the Gulf of Thailand to the hills and forests of the Burmese border. Phetburi is, some art historians maintain, Thailand's best-preserved Ayutthaya-period town. Most others in the Central Plains were sacked by invading Burmese while Phetburi was bypassed and its fine monasteries protected from thieving hands.

Hua Hin, further south, was developed as Thailand's first beach resort from the late 19th century and, though much changed, maintains a quaintness which is absent from gauche places like Pattaya and areas of Phuket. Cha-am is another beach resort on the Gulf of Thailand, much favoured by Bangkok's middle classes. One of Thailand's smaller but more interesting national parks is also to be found in this area: the Khao Sam Roi Yod National Park, best known for its water fowl, although there are also good caves in the limestone hills and a well-designed network of walks.

Travelling further south, and on the Andaman Sea coast of Phangnga, a string a beach resorts has been established between Takua Pa and Khao Lak. These are generally low key and low rise, appealing to those looking for a more relaxed approach to getting a tan. Also here is one of southern Thailand's largest protected areas - the Khao Sok National Park which has a reasonable tourist infrastructure and impressive limestone karst landscapes. It is also rich in wildlife and there are camping, canoeing and walking tours.

Southern Peninsula: Phetburi to Chumphon

At its narrowest, this part of Thailand is only 20 km wide and only one road, the busy Route 4, links Bangkok with the South. The historic town of Phetburi, with perhaps the best-preserved Ayutthayan wats in Thailand, is 160 km south of Bangkok and can be visited as a day trip from the capital. Another 70 km south is Hua Hin, Thailand's original and premier beach resort, until it was eclipsed by Phuket and Pattaya. The route south is environmentally depressing: the forest has been almost totally extirpated, leaving only scrubland or degraded secondary forest.

Phetburi

Phone code: 032
Colour map 2, grid B3

Phetburi (or Phetchaburi) is an historic provincial capital on the banks of the Phetburi River. The town is one of the oldest in Thailand and because it was never sacked by the Burmese is unusually intact.

Ins and outs

Getting there Phetburi is just 160 km from Bangkok, so it is possible to visit the town on a day trip from the capital. Trains take 2½ hrs and the station is about 1½ km northwest of the town centre. The main bus terminal is about the same distance west of town, at the foot of Khao Wang, but the a/c bus terminal is more central, 500 m or so north of the centre. Buses take about 2 hrs from Bangkok. There are connections south to Cha-am, Hua Hin and onward.

Getting around Phetburi – or at least its centre – is small enough to explore on foot. *Saamlors* are the main form of local transport.

History

Initially, its wealth and influence was based upon the working of the coastal salt pans found in the vicinity of the town, and which Thai chronicles record as being exploited as early as the 12th century. By the 16th century, Phetburi was supplying salt to most of Siam and the Malay Peninsula. It became particularly important during the Ayutthaya Period (14th century) and because the town was not sacked by the Burmese (as Ayutthaya was in 1767) its fine examples of Ayutthayan art and architecture are in good condition. Later, during the 19th century, Phetburi became a popular retreat for the Thai royal family, and they built a palace here. Because of its royal connections, Phetburi was *the* town to visit and to be seen in. Today, Phetburi is famous for its paid assassins who usually carry out their work from the backs of motorcycles with large-calibre pistols. Each time there is a national election, 15-20 politicians and their canvassers (so-called *hua khanen*) are killed. As in Chonburi, Thailand's other capital of crime, the police seem strangely unable to charge anyone.

Sights

Phetburi is littered with wats – below is a selection of some of the more interesting examples. Although it is possible to walk around these monasteries in
half a day, travelling by saamlor is much less exhausting. Note that often the
ordination halls (or *bots*) are locked; occasionally, if the abbot can be found, he
may be persuaded to open them up.

Situated in the heart of the town on Damnoenkasem Road, Wat Phra Sri **Wat Phra Sri**
Ratana Mahathat can be seen from a distance. It is dominated by five, much **Ratana**
restored, Khmer-style white prangs, probably dating from the Ayutthaya **Mahathat**
Period (14th century). The largest is 42 m high. Inside the bot, richly decorated
with murals, are three highly regarded Buddha images, ranged one in front of
the other: **Luangpor Mahathat**, **Luangpor Ban Laem** and **Luangpor Lhao
Takrao**. The principal image depicts the crowned Buddha. The complex
makes an attractive cluster of buildings. Musicians and dancers are paid by
those who want to give thanks for wishes granted.

Across Chomrut Bridge and east along Pongsuriya Road is **Wat Yai** **Wat Yai**
Suwannaram, on the right-hand side, within a spacious compound and a large **Suwannaram**
pond. The wat was built during the Ayutthaya Period and then extensively
restored in the reign of Rama V. The bot contains some particularly fine
Ayutthayan murals showing celestial beings and, facing the principal Buddha
image, Mara tempting the Buddha. Note the six-toed bronze Buddha image on
the rear wall which is thought to be pre-Ayutthayan in date. Behind the bot is a

The Isthmus

Phetburi

N

0 metres   300
0 yards   300

● **Eating**
1 Hand Made Public
  House
2 Millenium Pub

🚌 **Transport**
1 A/C bus terminal
2 Buses to Bangkok
3 Buses to Cha-am & Hua Hin

*Related map
Phetburi Centre
Detail,
page 209*

The Isthmus

Phetburi place names

Khao Luang Cave	Wat Phra Sri Ratana Mahathat
ถ้ำเขาหลวง	วัดพระศรีรัตนมหาธาตุ
Phra Nakhon Khiri	Wat Sra-bua
พระนครคีรี	วัดสระบัว
Wat Boromvihan	Wat Trailok
วัดบรมวิหาร	วัดไตรโลก
Wat Bun Thawi	Wat Yai Suwannaram
วัดบุญทวี	วัดใหญ่สุวรรณาราม
Wat Kamphaeng Laeng	
วัดกำแพงแลง	

large teak pavilion *(sala kan parian)* with three doorways at the front and two at the back. The front door panels have fine coloured-glass insets, while the (sword?) mark on the right-hand panel is said to have been made by a Burmese warrior en route to attack Ayutthaya. The wat also houses an elegant old wooden library. **Wat Boromvihan** and **Wat Trailok** are next to one another on the opposite side of the road, and a short distance to the east of Suwannaram. They are distinctive only for their wooden dormitories (or *kuti*), on stilts.

Wat Kamphaeng Laeng
South down Phokarong Road, and west a short distance along Phrasong Road, is **Wat Kamphaeng Laeng**. The five Khmer laterite prangs (one in very poor condition) – reminiscent of those in the northeast – have been dated to the 12th century. Little of the original stucco work remains, but they are nonetheless rather pleasing. Surrounded by thick laterite walls, the wat may have originally been a Hindu temple – a statue of a Hindu goddess was found here in 1956.

Other wats
West back towards the centre of town, and south down Matayawong Road are, in turn, **Wat Phra Song**, **Wat Laat** and **Wat Chi Phra Keut**, all on the left-hand side of the road. Just before reaching a bridge over Wat Ko Canal, is **Wat Ko Kaeo Sutharam**. The bot contains early 18th-century murals showing scenes from the Buddha's life and from Buddhist cosmology. The fact that the mural of the Buddha subduing Mara is on the rear wall, behind the principal Buddha image, has led to speculation that the entrance to the building was relocated at some time, possibly to gain access to a newly constructed road. The wat also houses interesting quarters for monks – long wooden buildings on stilts, similar to those at Wat Boromvihan.

Phra Nakhon Khiri
At the west edge of the city is **Phra Nakhon Khiri**, popularly known as Khao Wang ('Palace on the Mountain'), and built in 1858 during the reign of Rama IV. Perched on the top of a 95-m-high hill, the palace represents an amalgam of Thai, Western and Chinese artistic styles. The hill complex is dotted with frangipani trees with three areas of architectural interest on the three peaks. On the west rise is the **royal palace** itself. This has recently been restored and is now a well-maintained museum, containing an eclectic mixture of artefacts collected by Ramas IV and V who regularly stayed here. The airy building, with good views over the surrounding plain, has a Mediterranean feel to it. ■ *Mon-Sun 0900-1600. ฿40.*

Also on this peak is the **Hor Chatchavan Viangchai**, an observatory tower which Rama IV used to further his astronomical studies. On the central rise of the hill is the **Phra That Chomphet**, a white stupa erected by Rama IV. On the east rise sits **Wat Maha Samanaram** (aka Wat Phra Kaeo). Within the bot there are mural paintings by Khrua In Khong, quite a well-known Thai painter. The wat dates from the Ayutthayan Period. (Watch out for the monkeys here. They seem innocent and friendly enough until you buy a bag of bananas or corn on the cob for ฿5. Sprawls between monkeys are quick to break out and, more often than not, the whole bag will be ripped from your hand. Just remember that they are wild animals!) A **cable car** (more a cable-tram than car) takes visitors up the west side of Khao Wang for ฿45 one way, ฿40 both ways. ■ *0800-1600.*

Wat Sra-bua at the foot of Khao Wang is late Ayutthayan in style. The *bot* exhibits some fine gables, pedestal and stucco work. Also at the foot of the hill, slightly south from Wat Sra-bua is the poorly maintained **Wat Phra Phuttha Saiyat**. Within the corrugated iron-roofed viharn is a notable 43 m-long brick and plaster reclining Buddha dating from the mid-18th century. The image is unusual both in the moulding of the pillow, and in the manner in which the arm protrudes into the body of the building.

Foot of Khao Wang

Excursions

Tham Khao Luang is on Route 3173, 3 km north from Phetburi. It offers stalactites, stupas and multitudes of second-rate Buddha images in various poses. This cave was frequently visited by Europeans who came to Phetburi in the 19th century. Mary Lovina Court (1886), an early example of the inquisitive but destructive Western tourist wrote: "At the mouth of the cave we found some curious rocks, and succeeded in breaking off several good specimens". She was also enchanted by the caves themselves in which, she records, there "are the greatest wonders". Mary Court ended her sojourn telling some Buddhist visitors about "the better God than the idols by which they had knelt". On the right hand side, at the entrance to the cave, is a monastery called **Wat Bun Thawi**, with attractive carved-wooden door panels. ■ *Getting there: by saamlor.*

Khao Luang Cave

See page 216 for more details on Kaeng Krachan National Park which lies around 50 km southwest of town. ■ *Getting there: buses from Phetburi run past the turn-off for Kaeng Krachan Dam (Route 3175). From here, there are occasional minibuses which take visitors to the dam and the park headquarters (another 8 km), or hitch a lift.*

Kaeng Krachan National Park

Phetburi centre detail

As Phetburi is only 160 km south of Bangkok (two hours by bus), it can be seen in a day from the capital. It has poor accommodation at the upper end – although there are one or two good budget places to stay – so for those wishing to spend more time viewing the town's wats, it is probably best to stay at Hua Hin, Cha-am, Nakhon Pathom or at the *Rose Garden Hotel* (see page 355).

The Isthmus

Essentials

Sleeping   **A-C** *Royal Diamond Hotel*, 555 Phetkasem Rd, T411061, F424310. Luxurious hotel compared to any others available in Phetburi, with a/c. The restaurant does a range of international food. Beer garden and pleasant, peaceful atmosphere.

C-D *Khao Wang*, 174/1-3 Ratwithi Rd, T425167, F410750. Some a/c, characterless overpriced rooms have attached bathrooms (with western toilet) and Thai TV but are rather tatty. The management are cold and generally unwelcoming and although there is a small restaurant at the edge of a snooker room it is very dark and unappealing. **D-E** *Phetkasem*, 86/1 Phetkasem Rd, T410973, F425581. Some a/c, clean rooms and friendly management, some rooms have hot water, there is no restaurant but it is located very close to some of the best eats in Phetburi (see **Eating** below). Best value place to stay in this category. **D-E** *Phet Chalet*, 7 km out of town on the Phetkasem Rd, T412748. Some a/c, noisy and isolated, no restaurant, attached bathrooms but no showers. **D-E** *Rabieng Guesthouse*, Damnoenkasem Rd, T425878, F410695. Well-decorated wood-panelled rooms with tiled floors. Great open-air seating area and clean communal facilities. Appealing restaurant overlooking the river (see **Eating**). Motorbikes can be rented here at ฿250 per day. Laundry service. Trekking and rafting tours in the National Parks are available. Recommended. **E** *Chom Klao*, on east bank of the river, T425398. Offers clean, quiet, and fair-sized rooms, though they are bare and unattractive. The rooms with views over the river are by far the best and have balcony areas. More expensive rooms have shower-rooms attached, ones without have basins. Friendly, helpful and informative management.

Eating   Phetburi is well known for its desserts, including *khanom mo kaeng* (a hard custard made of mung bean, egg, coconut and sugar, baked over an open fire), *khao kriap* (a pastry with sesame, coconut and sugar) and excellent *kluai khai* (sweet bananas). There are several good restaurants along Phetkasem Rd, selling Phetburi desserts including: **Cheap**: *Ban Khanom Thai* (literally, the 'Thai Sweet House', at No 130) and *Rotthip* (No 45/22). *Rabieng Restaurant Guesthouse*, Damnoenkasem Rd, attractively furnished riverside restaurant, serving a good range of Thai and Western food. Recommended. *Hand Made Public House*, Chisa-In Rd, is nicely decorated and serves a range of Thai and western food.

There is a small but excellent **night market** at the southern end of Surinreuchai Rd underneath the clock tower – you can get a range of delicious snacks here and may want to try the local '*patai*' (omelette/pancake fried with mussels and served with bamboo shoots).

Entertainment   *The Millennium Pub*, Ratwithi Rd (near the bridge). A wooden saloon with a western/Native American-Indian theme to it. Harley-Davidson posters alongside Manchester United and Liverpool banners; anything western goes. Every night a local Thai band plays live (so I was told). Does all the usual imported and local beers and whiskys. Accepts Visa and Mastercard. Open 5pm-1am every night.

Festivals   Feb *Phra Nakhon Khiri Fair* (movable) *son et lumière* show.

Transport   **Local Saamlors**: can be hired for about ฿100 per hour. **Motorbikes**: can be
160 km S of Bangkok   rented from *Rabieng Guesthouse* at ฿250 per day, and motorbike taxis cost about ฿20-30 per kilometre.

Train The station is 1,500 m northwest of town. Regular connections with Bangkok's Hualamphong station 2½ hrs, via Nakhon Pathom. Trains to Bangkok mostly leave Phetburi in the morning. Trains to Hua Hin, Surat Thani and southern destinations.

Road **Bus**: regular a/c connections with Bangkok's Southern bus terminal near the Thonburi train station, 2 hrs; non-a/c buses from the new terminal on Phra Pinklao Road, 2 hrs. These buses arrive and leave from the new bus station behind Khao Wang near the 'cable car'. Songthaews meet the buses and take passengers into the town centre for ฿5. Also connections with Cha-am, Hua Hin and other southern destinations, between 6am and 6pm. These buses leave from the centre of town (see map).

Banks *Siam Commercial Bank* on Damnoenkasem Rd changes cash and TCs, and has an ATM. **Directory**
Communications Overseas calls can be made from the Post Office (on Ratwithi Rd).

Cha-am

Cha-am is reputed to have been a stopping place for King Naresuan's troops when they were travelling south. The name 'Cha-am' may have derived from the Thai word *cha-an*, meaning to clean the saddle. Cha-am is a beach resort with no town to speak of, some excellent hotels and a sizeable building programme of new hotels and condominiums for wealthy Bangkokians. A number of new hotels have opened on the seafront, offering more bungalows and simple rooms in the **B-C** price range, with a few in the **D** range. Unless you speak Thai, it will be difficult to make a phone booking, but it is highly likely that you'll find free rooms if you just show up. The town also has a good reputation for the quality of its seafood.

Phone code: 032
Colour map 2, grid B3

The Isthmus

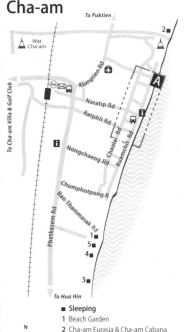

Cha-am

■ Sleeping
1 Beach Garden
2 Cha-am Eurasia & Cha-am Cabana
3 Dusit Resort & Polo Club
4 Golden Sand
5 Regent Cha-am

N
Not to scale

Cha-am does not have the charm of Hua Hin nor the facilities of Pattaya or Phuket, but it is easily accessible from Bangkok. It has become a popular weekend spot, so sizeable discounts are available during the week when most hotels are close to empty. At the weekend something of a transformation comes over this Jekyll & Hyde resort and it buzzes with life for 48 hours or so, before returning to its comatose state. You will need your Thai phrasebook or dictionary with you, as hand gestures and smiles alone will do little more than find you a room for the night in this town. There are a few locals who speak a little English. The **tourist office**, at 500/5 Phetkasem Road, T471005, is responsible for the areas of Cha-am and Prachuap Khiri Khan. There is a tourist information booth on the beach.

Maruekkhathayawan Palace, designed by an Italian and built by Rama VI in 1924 (the king is reputed to have also had a major hand in the design of the palace). The palace is made of teak and the name means 'Place of love and

Excursions

hope', which is rather charming. It is currently being renovated (and has been for the last 20 years) but consists of 16 pavilions in a very peaceful setting. ■ *Mon-Sun 0800-1600. Admission is free although you are expected to leave a small gratuity for the shoe custodian. Getting there: by saamlor, or catch a bus heading for Hua Hin and walk 2 km from the turn-off.*

Sleeping **L-AL** *Dusit Resort and Polo Club*, 1349 Phetkasem Rd, T520009, F520296, BT2360450. A/c, restaurant, pool, large, stylish hotel block (300 rms), with horse-riding and polo 'motifs' throughout. Superb facilities including range of watersports, fitness centre, tennis courts, horse-riding and an enormous swimming pool, Thai arts and crafts demonstrations. **L-AL** *Golden Sand*, 853 Phetkasem Rd, T451200, F451209, BT2598977. A/c, restaurant, pool, high-rise block with views onto the sea. Facilities including tennis, squash, watersports, fitness centre. **L-AL** *Regent*, 849/21 Phetkasem Rd, T451240, F471491, www.regent-chaam.com A/c, restaurants, pools, hotel and cottage accommodation on a 300-acre site, and every conceivable facility (squash, tennis, fitness centre, etc). **L-A** *Beach Garden*, 249/21 Phetkasem Rd, T508234, F508241, BT2372615. A/c, restaurant, pool, right on the beach, 3-storey block and some cottage accommodation, facilities including watersports, tennis, fishing and a mini-golf course. **L-A** *Mark-land Plaza Hotel*, T433833, F433834. Luxury high-rise hotel with the works (pool, gym, etc). **L-A** *Methavalai*, 220 Ruamchit Rd, T471028, F471590, BT6210600, BF2243960. A/c, good seafood and Thai restaurant, pool, some bungalows with several bedrooms – ideal for families – and a small area of private beach. **AL-A** *Cha-am Eurasia*, Klongtien Rd, T471327, F430397, BT2586589. A/c, restaurant, pool. **AL-C** *Cha-am Holiday Lodge*, T471595. Rather grotty rooms, management speaks no English.

A *Cha-am Phaisiri*, T471047, 3-roomed bungalows, very average for this price range. **A-B** *Santisuk*, 263/3 Ruamchit Rd, T471212, BT2511847. Range of accommodation, some a/c, 2 styles of accommodation – wooden cottages or a hotel block, both are good. **A-D** *Cha-am Villa*, 24/1 Ruamchit Rd, T471241, F471086. Nice rooms, friendly management, some a/c, good discounts during the week. Recommended. **B** *Thipdharee*, 274/34-35 Ruamchit Rd, T471879. Reasonable a/c rooms but rather boring. **B-C** *Kaenchan*, 241/3 Ruamchit Rd, T471314, F471531. Some a/c, small pool on the rooftop, range of accommodation. **B-D** *NP Place*, T471826, accommodation ranging from apartments with hot water and bath tub and a/c to bungalows with fan.

Cha-am detail

Snooker o Massage

Mini Mart

Naratip Rd

Buses to Bangkok

Ratphli Rd

Chaolai Rd

Ruamchit Rd

Not to scale

■ **Sleeping**
1 Anatachai	10 Rua Makam
2 Cha-am Guesthouse	11 Sam Resort
3 Cha-am Holiday Lodge	12 Santisuk
4 Cha-am Phaisiri	13 Savitree
5 Cha-am Villa	14 Som's Guesthouse
6 Kaenchan	15 Thipdharee
7 Mark-land Plaza	16 Thunya's Guesthouse
8 Methavalai	17 Viwathana
9 Nirandorn	18 White

The Isthmus

C *Anatachai*, T471980. Nice rooms with attached bathroom, TV and a/c, well run and competitively priced, ocean views. C *Golden Villa*, 248/13 Ruamchit Rd, T471881. A/c. C *Nirandorn*, T471893. Some a/c, wooden cottages. C *Pratarnchoke House*, 240/3 Ruamchit Rd, T471215. Range of rooms available here from simple fan-cooled through to more luxurious a/c rooms with attached bathrooms. C *Rua Makam*, T471073. Bland, boring, ugly, overpriced bungalows. C *Rung Aran Bungalow*, 236/26 Ruamchit Rd, T471226. A/c. C *Sam Resort*, 246/9 Ruamchit Rd, T471197. Reasonable rooms. C *Savitree*, 263/1 Ruamchit Rd, T434088. Rooms have TV and fridge but no hot water, perhaps rather overpriced. C *Viwathana*, 263/21 Ruamchit Rd, T471289. This hotel is one of the longer established with some simpler, fan-cooled wooden bungalows as well as a new brick-built block. All are set in a garden of sorts giving the place more character than most. The more expensive bungalows have 2 or 3 rooms and/or a/c – no restaurant or hot water – but good value for families. **C-D** *Cha-am Guest House*, T433400. Attached bathroom, some a/c, small balcony overlooking sea, no hot water, no restaurant. **C-D** *Jitravee*, 240/20 Ruamchit Rd, T471382. Clean rooms, friendly management, more expensive rooms have a/c, TV, fridge, room service, attached bathroom, cheaper rooms have clean, shared bathroom, some English spoken here.**C-D** *Thunya's Guesthouse*, T433504. Very nice rooms with attached bathrooms (western toilet and shower), TV, a/c, balcony, some have OK views over wooded area (rather than cement walls and roofs like much of the accommodation here). **D-E** *Som's Guesthouse*, 234/30 Ruamchit Rd, T433753. Nice clean rooms and one of the cheapest places to stay in Cha-am.

Eating Between the *Beach Garden* and the *Regent* there are several restaurants, notably *Family Shop* (**cheap**), on the beach, good barbecued fish. Plenty of seafood restaurants along Ruamchit Rd, mostly serving the same range of dishes, including such things as chilli crab and barbecued snapper with garlic.

Transport
25 km N of Hua Hin
Road Bus: regular connections with Bangkok's Southern bus terminal 2½ hrs, Phetburi, Hua Hin and south destinations. Buses from Bangkok drop you right on the beach but buses from Phetburi or Hua Hin stop on the Phetkasem Highway. Motorbike taxis from here to the beach cost ฿20 but they also try to take a ฿50 commission on your accommodation – so avoid being dropped at a hotel; ask to be dropped off on the beach. To get to other southern destinations catch a bus to Hua Hin and change there.

Directory **Banks** *Bangkok Bank*, 241/41 Ruamchit Rd. **Communications** The main Post Office is on the Narathip Rd 400 m north of the Phetkasem Highway. Overseas calls can be made from here. There is also a small Post Office on Ruamchit Rd.

Hua Hin

Thailand's first beach resort, Hua Hin has had an almost continuous royal connection since the late 19th century. In 1868, King Mongkut journeyed to Hua Hin to observe a total eclipse of the sun. In 1910, Prince Chakrabongse, brother of Rama VI, visited Hua Hin on a hunting trip and was so enchanted by the area that he built himself a villa. Sadly, today, Hua Hin has become a rather tawdry beach resort and the beach itself is an object lesson in what happens when people don't care.

Phone code: 032
Colour map 2, grid B3

Ins and outs

Getting there There are daily flights on Bangkok Airways to Bangkok and also connections with Koh Samui. The train station is on the western edge of town, within walking distance of the centre. The journey from Bangkok takes 4 hrs and there are connections ownards to all points south. The bus terminal is also reasonably central; regular connections with Bangkok and many southern towns.

• •
Hua Hin place names

Kaeng Krachan National Park

อุทยานแห่งชาติแก่งกระจาน

Khao Sam Roi Yod National Park

อุทยานแห่งชาติเขาสามร้อยยอด

Khao Takiab

เขาตะเกียบ

Getting around Hua Hin is an increasingly compact beach resort and many of the hotels, restaurants and places of interest (such as they are) are within walking distance of

• •

one another. But there is also a good supply of public transport. Songthaews run along fixed routes; there are taxis and saamlors; and bicycles, motorbikes and cars are all available for hire. The local **tourist office** is at 114 Phetkasem Rd, T512120. ■ *Mon-Sun 0830-1630.*

History

The first of the royal palaces was built by Prince Naris, son of Rama V – Saen Samran House. In the early 1920's, King Vajiravudh (Rama VI) – no doubt influenced by his brother Chakrabongse – began work on a teakwood palace, 'Deer Park'. The final stamp of royal approval came in the late 1920s, when King Phrajadipok (Rama VII) built another palace, which he named **Klai Kangwon**, literally 'Far From Worries' (not open to the public except when a permit has been obtained from the Royal Household in advance – a good hotel should be able to arrange this). It was designed by one of Prince Naris' sons. The name could not have been more inappropriate: the king was staying at Klai Kangwon in 1932 when he was dislodged from the throne by a *coup d'état*.

Early guidebooks, reminiscent of English seaside towns, named the resort Hua Hin-on-Sea. *Hua* (head) *Hin* (rock) refers to a stone outcrop at the end of the fine white-sand beach. The resort used to promote itself as the 'Queen of Tranquility'. Until the 1980s, it was a forgotten backwater of an earlier, and less frenetic, tourist era. However, in the last few years the constant influx of tourists have livened up the atmosphere considerably. With massage parlours, tourist shops selling the usual paraphernalia, and numerous western restaurants and bars lining the streets, it's hard to get a moment's peace in this town. And just when you think that the town is as chock-a-block as possible, the sound of drills and construction work reminds you that economic expansion has come to take precedence over all else in this seaside town. Even more condominiums are springing up along the coast to cater for wealthy holiday-makers from Bangkok, high-rise buildings scar the horizon, and vehicles clog the streets. New golf courses are being constructed to serve Thailand's growing army of golfers – as well as avid Japanese players – and the old-world charm that was once Hua Hin's great selling point has been lost.

Sights The famous **Railway Hotel** was built in 1923 by a Thai prince, Purachatra, who headed the State Railways of Thailand. It became Thailand's premier seaside hotel, but by the 1960s had fallen into rather glorious disrepair. It experienced a short burst of stardom when the building played the role of the Phnom Penh Hotel in the film the *Killing Fields*, but it still seemed destined to rot into oblivion. Saved by privatization, it was renovated and substantially expanded in 1986 and is now an excellent five-star hotel. Unfortunately, it has been renamed, and goes under the unromantic name of the *Sofitel Central*. At the other end of Damnoenkasem Road from the Railway Hotel, on the opposite

The Isthmus

side of the main highway, is the **Railway Station** itself. The station has a rather quaint Royal Waiting Room on the platform.

Khao Takiab (or Chopstick Hill), south of town, is a dirty, unremarkable hill with a large standing Buddha facing the sea. As Hua Hin expands, so this area is also developing. At present, it resembles a building site. Nearby is **Khao Krilat**, a rock covered in assorted shrines, stupas, ponds, salas and Buddha images. To get there, take a local bus from Dechanuchit Road.

Hua Hin

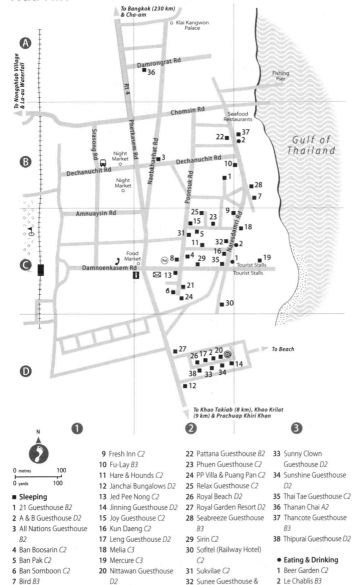

Sleeping

1 21 Guesthouse *B2*
2 A & B Guesthouse *D2*
3 All Nations Guesthouse *B2*
4 Ban Boosarin *C2*
5 Ban Pak *C2*
6 Ban Somboon *C2*
7 Bird *B3*
8 City Beach *C2*
9 Fresh Inn *C2*
10 Fu-Lay *B3*
11 Hare & Hounds *C2*
12 Janchai Bungalows *D2*
13 Jed Pee Nong *C2*
14 Jinning Guesthouse *D2*
15 Joy Guesthouse *C2*
16 Kun Daeng *C2*
17 Leng Guesthouse *D2*
18 Melia *C3*
19 Mercure *C3*
20 Nittawan Guesthouse *D2*
21 Patchara House *C2*
22 Pattana Guesthouse *B2*
23 Phuen Guesthouse *C2*
24 PP Villa & Puang Pan *C2*
25 Relax Guesthouse *C2*
26 Royal Beach *D2*
27 Royal Garden Resort *D2*
28 Seabreeze Guesthouse *B3*
29 Sirin *C2*
30 Sofitel (Railway Hotel) *C2*
31 Sukvilae *C2*
32 Sunee Guesthouse & Europa *C2*
33 Sunny Clown Guesthouse *D2*
34 Sunshine Guesthouse *D2*
35 Thai Tae Guesthouse *C2*
36 Thanan Chai *A2*
37 Thancote Guesthouse *B3*
38 Thipurai Guesthouse *D2*

● Eating & Drinking

1 Beer Garden *C2*
2 Le Chablis *B3*

As Hua Hin is billed as a beach resort, people come here expecting – this is Thailand after all – a beautiful tropical beach. Don't be fooled. It's filthy. The obvious side of this is the rubbish: plastic bottles, paper and tins litter the beach. But there's more. Uncontrolled discharges into the sea from the resort's hotels, guesthouses and restaurants means there is a nutrient overload too. The fact that Hua Hin is heading the way of Pattaya was recognized several years back, but nothing was done about it. Now, almost too late, there seems to be some action. The *Melia Hua Hin Hotel* has initiated a 'Save the Hua Hin Beach Environment' campaign because it discovered in customer feedback surveys that while they loved the hotel, they hated the beach and sea. As the manager of the hotel remarked to the *Bangkok Post*, it is a little tricky running a beach resort hotel successfully if people don't like the beach. Will the local authorities also see the urgency of the matter? Unlikely.

Excursions **Kaeng Krachan National Park**, 63 km northwest of Hua Hin, is Thailand's largest protected area covering 2,915 sq km. It was gazetted in 1981. It is said to support significant populations of large mammal species – elephant, tiger, leopard, gibbon, the Malayan pangolin – and birds, in particular, hornbills, minivets, pheasants and bee-eaters. Endangered species include the wooly-necked stork and the plain-pouched hornbill. (Few visitors see many, if any, of these animals, though.) Extensive trails lead through undisturbed forest and past a succession of waterfalls (the best being Pa La-U), to hot springs and a Karen village. Guides are advisable and cost ฿500 per day, though many of them don't speak English, so make sure you meet the guide who will be taking you before paying your money. The Tenasserim Mountain range cuts through the park, the highest peak stands at 1,207 m. Phanoen Thung Mountain offers superb views of the surrounding countryside (warm clothes are needed for the chilly mornings). It is a six-hour hike to the summit. En route to Pa La-U, 27 km from Hua Hin and close to Nongphlab village, are three caves: **Dao**, **Lablae** and **Kailon**, which contain the usual array of stalactites and stalagmites. Guides with lanterns will take visitors through the caves for ฿30. Boat trips can be made on the reservoir. Until recently, entrance to the park was only ฿20, but was suddenly increased to ฿200 with another charge of ฿200 for the Pa La-U waterfalls. Due to this dramatic increase, a number of tour operators have decided to boycott the park, in the hope they'll drop the price. **Sleeping** Bungalows are available at headquarters (฿750-1,000 per bungalow, which sleeps 5-6 people), but you must bring all necessities with you (eg blankets, food and water) as nothing is provided any longer. ■ *Getting there: take a minibus from the station on Srasong Road to the village of Fa Prathan, 53 km (฿15). For the caves, take the same bus but get off at Nongphlab village (฿10) and ask at the police station for directions – the caves are a 45 mins to 1 hr walk away. Tours are also available (see below).*

Khao Sam Roi Yod National Park, about 45 km south of Hua Hin, is one of the best-managed protected areas in the country (see page 221).

Tours Companies run day tours to the Sam Roi Yod (around ฿850-900) and Kaeng Krachan National Parks (around ฿1,000), and to the Pa La-U waterfall, with lunch (see above). A number of other tours are available, including the usual 'adventure' tours (rafting, trekking, elephant rides), day trips to Burma ($5 immigration fee, and a chance to extend your visa for another 30 days) and the Tennaserrim mountain range, as well as diving, snorkelling, and fishing excursions. Many tour companies in Hua Hin offer such tours at competitive prices (see **Directory** below).

L *Chiva Som International Health Resort*, 73/4 Phetkasem Rd, T536536, F511154, chivasom@ksc9.th.com A/c, restaurant, pool, this is a luxury health resort (*Chiva-Som* means 'Haven of Life'), set in 3 ha of land, with a large spa building housing a spacious gym, Roman bath, enormous jacuzzi, circular steam room and dance studio. There is also an outdoor freshwater pool. With health consultants, hydrotherapy and lots of herbal tea and healthy food, this is the place to come to lose weight or firm up those buttocks without feeling that life is too miserable. All for a considerable price, but at least one leaves feeling good about oneself, a truly pampering kind of hotel. **L-AL** *Melia Hua Hin*, 33 Naresdamri Rd, T511612, F511135, BT2713435, BF2713689, www.solmelia.com A/c, restaurants, pool with water slide and jacuzzi, ugly high-rise hotel with all facilities, all rooms have sea views. **L-AL** *Royal Garden Resort*, 107/1 Phetkasem Rd, T511881, F512422, BT4760021, BF4601805, www.royal-garden.com A/c, restaurant, pool, to complement the even larger L-shaped block, good sports facilities including tennis, fitness centre, watersports. There's also a mini-zoo and shopping arcade. Recommended. **L-AL** *Sofitel Central* (previously, the *Railway Hotel*), 1 Damnoenkasem Rd, T512021, F511014, BT5411463, BF5411464, www.sofitel.com A/c, restaurant, pool, Hua Hin's original premier hotel. Both maintain excellent levels of service and enjoy an excellent position on the beach, and while the new rooms are small they are well appointed. In addition the seafood restaurant here – with a French chef – is truly worth seeking out. Recommended. **L-A** *Hua-Hin Grand Hotel and Plaza*, 222/2 Petchakasem Rd, T511391, F511765, BT2547675, BF2547675, www.huahingrand.co.th Large swimming pool, all mod cons, spacious rooms, fully equipped meeting rooms, shopping plaza, restaurants and bars, 24-hr coffeeshop.

Sleeping

AL *Royal Garden Tower*, 43/1 Phetkasem Rd, T512412, F512417, BT2558822. A/c, suites only. **AL** *Royal Garden Village*, 45 Phetkasem Rd, T512412, F520259, BT2518659. A/c, restaurant, pool, teak pavilions set around a pool, good sports facilities but no beach to speak of. **AL-A** *City Beach Resort*, 16 Damnoenkasem Rd, T512870, F512488, www.citybeach.co.th A/c, restaurant, pool, pub with live music and karaoke, conference halls available for booking, central, unattractive interior. **AL-A** *Sailom*, 29 Phetkasem Rd, south of the centre, T511890, F512047, BT3922109, BF3902799. A/c, restaurant, pool. **A** *Mercure Hotel*, 1 Damnoenkasem Rd, T512036, F511014. A/c, restaurant, pool, 41 villas in garden compound. This hotel benefits from access to the good facilities at the *Sofitel Central* next door. **A** *Sport Villa*, 10/95 Phetkasem Rd, 3 km south of town, T511453. A/c, restaurant, large pool, sauna. **A-B** *Hua Hin Highland Resort*, 4/15 Ban Samophrong, north of town, T2112579, BT2800750. A/c, popular with golfers. **A-B** *Sirin*, Damnoenkasem Rd, T511150, F513571. A/c, quiet despite being central, standard, over-priced. **A-C** *Chanchai*, 117/1-18 Phetkasem Rd, T511461, F532376, banchanchay@hotmailcom Bungalows on the beach, a/c, satellite TV, telephones in rooms, slightly outside the ruckus of central Hua Hin, quieter beach.

B *Ban Boosarin*, 8/8 Poonsuk Rd, T512076, F512089. A/c, comfortable rooms and reliable and friendly management. Recommended. **B** *Fu Lay*, 110/1 Naresdamri Rd, T513670, F530320, www.huahinguide.com/guesthouses/fulay (an enquiry form can be filled out from here). A/c, small hotel, clean and friendly, sea view. They also have a cheaper guesthouse across the road (T513145, F530320). Recommended. **B** *PP Villa*, T533785, F511216. A/c, restaurant, pool, recently upgraded with the addition of a pool and the construction of an adjacent hotel under the same management, the *Puang Pen Hotel* (also in our **B** category). *Fresh Inn*, 132 Naresdamri Rd, T511389. A/c, restaurant, the *Melia* blots out any sea view it may once have had but the rooms are good and it is well priced. **B-C** *Jed Pee Nong*, 17 Damnoenkasem Rd, T512381, F532063. Uninviting pool surrounded by uprising buildings, some a/c, breakfast included, clean, boring and popular. Rooms in the older block are run down and over-priced for what they offer. The newer blocks are better. **B-D** *Thanan Chai*, 11 Damrongrat Rd, T511755. Some a/c, north of centre, but quite good value. **C** *Hua Hin*, 5/1 Soi Binthabat, Poonsuk Rd, T511653. A/c, restaurant. **C** *Patchara House*, Naresdamri Rd, T511787. Some a/c, clean, friendly, room service, hot water, TV, pleasant restaurant. Recommended.

Guesthouses A new area of slightly more expensive guesthouses has sprung up just south of the town. The area is called Soi Thipurai after the first guesthouse that opened up there, and all *tuk-tuk* drivers know it as such. It's very much its own little community, with internet facilities (though slightly expensive), restaurants in all the guesthouses, motorbike and bicycle rental, tours available, and even a fashion house for tailor-made clothes. Everyone speaks very good English and the people are very hospitable and friendly. The beach here is much quieter and cleaner than the noisy and harassing atmosphere at the main beach in Hua Hin. There are still the same watersports available, jetskis, windsurfs, etc, but at least you're not hassled so much. A highly recommended area for a quiet retreat.

All the following guesthouses have similar spacious rooms with a/c, hot water, satellite TV, and access to a swimming pool (though the beach might be a better option). Prices may enter the **A** price range during high season.

B-C *A&B*, T532340, F512711, www.travel.to/A&B Friendly Swedish management, minibar. **B-C** *Jinning Beach*, T513950, F532597, www.jinningbeachguesthouse.com Minibar and video channel available. **B-C** *Leng*, T513546, F532095, leng @workmail.com Minibar and fridges in rooms. **B-C** *Nilawan*, T512751, F533630, www.travel.to/nilawanhouse Internet service and coffeeshop. **B-C** *Royal Beach*, T532210, royalbeach@hotmail.com Minibar and video channel available. **B-C** *Sunny Clown*, T512936, F533368, sunnyclown@mail.tele.dk Restaurant area. **B-C** *Sunshine*, T515309, Cell661-8662352, sunshineguesthouse@yahoo.com Slightly cheaper than the others, and fridges in some rooms. **B-C** *Thipurai*, T532096, F512210, thipurai @prachuab.a-net.net.th Restaurant and bar.

The following are concentrated around Naresdamri Rd, one road in from the beach; some residents rent out rooms in their homes.

D *Ban Pak*, T511653. Fair rooms with wooden ceilings and comfortable chairs, some a/c, no balcony but clean. **D** *Ban Somboon*, T501338. Rooms OK but slightly on the small side, all have attached shower rooms with hot water and TVs, attractive restaurant and sitting area. **D** *Bird*, T511630. Rooms on wooden platform on stilts above the beach, no restaurant but you can get breakfast here, sitting area with views over the sea, more ambience and character than most. **D** *Kanokporn*, Damnoenkasem Rd. Recommended. **D** *Pala-U*, Naresdamri Rd. A/c, clean rooms with attached bathrooms, laundry service, well run by a German and his Thai wife. Recommended. **D** *Seabreeze*, next door to *Bird Guesthouse* with a similar set up – again no restaurant but drinks and snacks available. Rooms are OK, those with sea view are slightly more expensive – which might not be worth it as at low tide the beach is less than appealing. **D** *Thai Tae*, 8 bungalows on wooden stilts – fair size, some a/c. **D** *Thancote*, T513677. Some a/c, seafood restaurant, friendly owners. There is no reception area, but the owners can be found in the restaurant. **D-E** *21 Guest House*, T533619. Rather overpriced, grotty and dark, own bathroom, squat toilet. **D-E** *Joy*, T512967. Fair rooms if a little bit boring, some have own bathroom, nice communal sitting area and balcony upstairs, lively bar and restaurant downstairs with pool table and darts, friendly management. **D-E** *Sukvilae*, T513523. Range of rooms, some cement, some wood, some own bath, some a/c and hot water, OK rooms, communal balcony, but very noisy at night with beer garden below.

E *Pattana Guesthouse*, 52 Naretdamri Rd, T513393, F530081, huahinpattana @hotmail.com Attractive location down a small alley, making it a quiet spot. 13 twin-bedded rooms with fans in 2 original Thai teakwood buildings set around a flower-filled compound, some rooms with own bathrooms. 50 m from the beach, breakfast and dinner available, email and internet service. **E** *All Nations*, Dechanuchit Rd, T512747, F530474, gary@infonews.co.th Email facilities, shared bathrooms, own balcony, clean and friendly. One of the cheapest in Hua Hin. **E** *Europa*, 158 Naresdamri Rd, T513235. Restaurant (international food), own bathroom. **E** *Forum*, Soi off Naresdamri Rd. Some private bathrooms. **E** *Hare & Hounds*, 8/5-7 Soi Kanjanomai, T533757, mags118@hotmail.com Small, simple, clean rooms, communal showers. **E** *Kun Daeng*, cheap rooms, shared bathroom. **E** *Phuen*, Soi off Naresdamri Rd, T512344. Old wooden house, quiet, but rather small rooms all with own bathroom, fax and phone services, 24-hr coffee house. **E** *Relax*, located down a small quiet alley, nice rooms all with own bathroom, smaller rooms are cheaper, communal balcony at front. **E** *Sunee*, all rooms have shared bath (downstairs), a bit noisy.

Try the central market for breakfast. Good seafood is widely available particularly at the northern end of Naresdamri Rd. Most of the fish comes straight from the boats which land their catch at the pier at the northern end of the bay. There is also a concentration of restaurants and bars geared to *farang* visitors along Naresdamri surrounding lanes.

Eating

The Isthmus

Seafood Very expensive: *Sofitel Hotel Seafood Restaurant*, 1 Damnoenkasem Rd, the seafood restaurant in this refurbished hotel is probably the best in Hua Hin. Don't expect the usual range of Thai dishes; the chef is French. **Expensive**: *Meekaruna*, 26/1 Naresdamri Rd. Small pavilion. Recommended. *Seangthai*, Naresdamri Rd. Also serves Thai, large open-air restaurant on the seafront and long established by Hua Hin standards. Regular visitors maintain that it remains one of the better seafood restaurants. *Tappikaew House*, 7 Naebkaehat Rd. Attractive Thai restaurant, indoor and outdoor eating by the sea. *Charlie's Seafood*, Naresdamri Rd. Also serves Thai. *Charoen Pochana*, Naresdamri Rd. Also serves Thai. *Europa*, Naresdamri Rd. Also serves International and Thai. *Supharos*, 69/2-3 Phetkasem Rd. Also serves Chinese. *Tharachan*, Phetkasem Rd. Also serves Thai.

Chinese Chinese restaurants are to be found around the junction of Phetkasem and Naebkhaehat roads.

Indian *Moti Mahal*, Naresdamri Rd. Reasonable Indian restaurant serving the usual dishes.

International Expensive: *Le Chablis*, 33 Naresdamri Road. Highly recommended French (and Thai) cuisine, the restaurant was run by a Thai-French couple but since the death of the husband in 1998 the wife has successfully continued the enterprise. First-class and very reasonable food (and wine). Recommended. **Mid-range**: *Lo Stivale*, 132 Naresdamri Rd. The best Italian restaurant in town. Recommended. *Beer Garden*, Naresdamri Rd. Mostly serves western dishes from steaks to grilled chicken with a sprinkling of Thai dishes – a popular watering spot. *La Villa*, Poonsuk Rd, pizzas, pasta and other Italian dishes, nothing remarkable but pleasant surroundings.

Foodstalls There is an excellent new *Food Market* opposite the Town Hall on Damnoenkasem Rd. The night market just off Phetkasem Rd does the usual selection of cheap Thai food as well as seafood that is so fresh that they have to tie the crabs' and lobsters' pincers shut.

Shopping The most distinctive buy is a locally produced printed cotton called *pha khommaphat*. The usual tourist shops can be found lining most streets in the town. There are also a number of tailors shops that have opened recently, guaranteeing any style you want, made-to-fit within 3-4 days.

Night market Dechanuchit Rd, close to the bus station. Open dusk-2200; it sells a range of goods including Tibetan jewellery, paper dragons, T-shirts, cassettes, watches and silk scarves. **Seashell souvenirs** To be avoided. **Shopping centre** 1/9 Srasong Rd.

Sport **Golf**: *Royal Hua Hin Golf Course*, designed in 1926 by a Scottish engineer working on the Royal Siamese Railway, is the oldest in Thailand and recently upgraded. Open to the public Mon-Sun 0600-1800. Green fees ฿250 at the weekend and ฿150 during the week (per 9 holes). Caddies available ฿100. **Minigolf**: Phetkasem Road, T511585 (south of town), open Mon-Sun 0900-2300 ฿60-100 per person. 3 more golf courses are under construction. **Snooker**: parlours in town. **Watersports and horse riding**: along the beach.

Tour operators Concentrated on Damnoenkasem and Phetkasem roads. *Ken Diamond Company Ltd*, 162/6 Naresdarmi Rd, T513863, F513863. *Thip's Top Tours*, 162/4 Naresdarmi Rd, T532488, F532488, thiptop@loxinfo.co.th *Western Tours Hua Hin*, 11 Damnoenkasem Rd, T512560. *Pran Tour*, 1st flr, *Siriphetkasem Hotel*, Srasong Rd, T511654. *Hua Hin Travel*, *The Royal Garden Resort*.

Transport It is presently a 3-hr drive from Bangkok, along a hazardous 2-lane highway (particu-
230 km S of Bangkok larly bad over the last 80 km from Phetburi), jammed with *siplors* (10-wheel trucks).

Local **Bicycle hire**: ฿100 per day (on Damnoenkasem and Phetkasem roads). **Bus**: station on Dechanuchit Rd. Buses to Khao Krilas or Khao Takiab every 20 mins, ฿10. **Car hire**: jeeps ฿800-1,000 per day (on Damnoenkasem and Phetkasem roads). **Motorbike hire**: ฿200 per day upwards (on Damnoenkasem and Phetkasem roads). **Saamlor**: ฿20-40 around town, ฿150 for a sightseeing tour. **Songthaew**: run set routes around town and out to Khao Takiab, ฿10. **Taxis**: run prescribed routes for set fares, taxi stand on Phetkasem Rd, opposite *Chatchai Hotel*. Taxis can be hired for the day for ฿400 plus petrol. Motorcycle taxis (identified by 'taxi' sign) will take you wherever you want to go.

Air Bangkok Airways, T5352498, run daily connections with Bangkok at 1900, 35 mins.

Train The station is on Damnoenkasem Rd, T511073. Regular connections with Bangkok's Hualamphong station (same train as to Phetburi) 3½-4 hrs. Day excursions run on weekends, leaving Hualamphong at 0615, arriving Hua Hin at 1130, departing from Hua Hin at 1630, arriving Bangkok 2030. Regular connections with Phetburi 1 hr.

Road **Bus**: station is on Srasong Rd, next to the Chatchai market, T511654. Regular a/c connections with Bangkok's Southern bus terminal near the Thonburi train station 3½ hrs; non-a/c buses leave from the new terminal on Phra Pinklao Rd 3½ hrs. Also connections with Phetburi, Cha-am and other southern destinations. Overnight VIP buses to Phuket available (11 hrs). **Taxi**: 3 hrs from Bangkok (about ฿1,600-1,800).

Directory **Airline offices** *Bangkok Airways*, 114/17 Phetkasem Rd, T532113, F532115. **Banks** There are a number of currency exchange booths along Phetkasem Rd. **Communications Internet**: The post office provides email service and a number of small internet cafés have opened up around town. **Overseas telephone office**: Damnoenkasem Rd. **Post Office**: 21 Damnoenkasem Rd. **Medical services** 511-743 Phetkasem Rd, T511743 (4 km downtown). **Useful addresses Police station**: Damnoenkasem Rd, T511027.

Khao Sam Roi Yod National Park

Khao Sam Roi Yod National Park (Mountain of Three Hundred Peaks), lies about 45 km south of Hua Hin, east off Route 4. It was declared Thailand's third national park and first marine park in 1966. The park occupies an area of limestone hills surrounded by salt-water flats, and borders the Gulf of Thailand. Its freshwater marshes provide 11 different categories of wetland habitat (as much as the Red River Delta in Vietnam which covers an area nearly 200 times greater). A haven for water birds, the area has been extensively developed (and exploited) as a centre of prawn and fish farming limiting the marshland available to the waterbirds who breed here. The park has the advantage of being relatively small – it covers just 98 sq km – with readily accessible sights: wildlife (including the rare and shy serow), forest walks, caves (**Phraya Nakhon**, close to Ban Bang Pu beach, with two large sinkholes where the roof collapsed a century ago, and a pavilion which was built in 1896 for the visit of King Rama V and Sai Cave, which contains impressive stalactites and stalagmites and 'petrified waterfall', created from dripping water) and quiet beaches. At least 237 species of land and waterbirds have been recorded – including painted storks, herons, egrets and many different waders. Boats can be hired from local fishermen, organized at Park headquarters, to visit caves

Colour map 2, grid C2

The plains of Sam Roi Yod were also used as the location for Pol Pot's Killing Fields in the film of the same name

The Isthmus

Khao Sam Roi Yod National Park

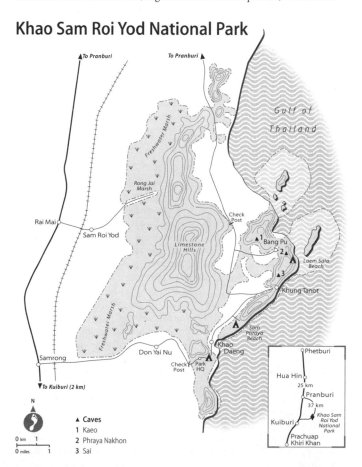

To Pranburi

To Pranburi

Gulf of Thailand

Freshwater Marsh

Rong Jai Marsh

Rai Mai

Sam Roi Yod

Check Post

Limestone Hills

1 Bang Pu
2
Laem Sala Beach
3
Khung Tanot

Freshwater Marsh

Sam Phraya Beach

Samrong

Don Yai Nu

Khao Daeng

Check Post   Park HQ

To Kuiburi (2 km)

Phetburi

Hua Hin
25 km
Pranburi
37 km
Khao Sam Roi Yod National Park
Kuiburi
Prachuap Khiri Khan

N

0 km   1
0 miles   1

▲ Caves
1 Kaeo
2 Phraya Nakhon
3 Sai

and beaches (β200-700). Boat trips usually sight schools of dolphin. The biggest challenge facing the park – which supports a remarkable range of habitats for such a small area – is encroachment by private shrimp ponds; more than a third of the park area was cleared for fish and shrimp farming in 1992. Ironically, most of the prawn farms are now deserted, due to prawn disease. The soil was highly acidic which caused bacteria to flourish and oxygen to reduce in the ponds. Money is now needed to restore the farms back to parkland –

Prachuap Khiri Khan names

Ao Manao

อ่าวมะนาว

Bang Saphan

บางสะพาน

Huai Yang waterfall

น้ำตกห้วยยาง

Khao Chong Krachok

เขาช่องกระจก

this may be received if the park becomes a world conservation site. The park now distributes a very useful guide with comprehensive details on fauna and flora and other natural sights in the park. Available at the park HQ. ■ *Getting there: by bus from Hua Hin to Pranburi (there are also trains to Pranburi, as well as trains and buses from Bangkok). From Pranburi it is necessary to charter a songthaew (β250) or take a motorcycle taxi (β150) to the park HQ. NB Be sure you are taken to Khao Sam Roi Yod National Park, and not Khao Sam Roi Yod village. For Laem Sala Beach (located within the park), there are regular songthaews from Pranburi market to Bang Pu village between 0600 and 1600, β20.*

Sleeping **B-D** Bungalows (for reservations, telephone BT5614292 ext 747), either for hire in their entirety or per couple (β100 per person per night) and a camping ground, although the tents for hire are now very worn and not really suitable for use. You can also pitch your own tent here for around β20. Bungalows are available at both the park HQ and at Laem Sala Beach. **NB** Take mosquito repellent.

Prachuap Khiri Khan

Phone code: 032
Colour map 2, grid C2

Prachuap Khiri Khan is a small and peaceful resort with a long crescent-shaped beach. The town is more popular with Thais than with *farangs* and it has a reputation for good seafood. An exhausting climb up **Khao Chong Krachok**, the 'Mountain with the Mirror' (past armies of preening monkeys), is rewarded with fine views of the surrounding countryside and bay. At the summit there is an unremarkable shrine containing yet another footprint of the Buddha. There is a good **night market** at the corner of Phitakchat and Kong-Kiat roads. The **tourist office** is on Sarathip Road.

Excursions **Ao Manao** is an attractive bay 5 km south of town with a rather disappointing beach and lots of day trippers. However there is one place to stay here which makes it is an alternative to sleeping in Prachuap. **Sleeping** *Sawadii Khan Wing*, BT611017. Small cottages, well maintained, sea views, attached bathrooms, some large bungalows available for families. The management here is poor and lacking in initiative but the rooms are OK. ■ *Getting there: easiest by motorbike taxi (β20-30). Alternatively, take the tourist road train (which looks like something from Disneyland). This goes regularly between Ao Manao and town and can be flagged down on the beach β15.*

Huai Yang Waterfall is 28 km south of Prachuap, and 7 km off the main road (turning west at Ban Huai Yaang). Not worth visiting in the dry season, it merely illustrates the Thai penchant for waterfalls (and caves) of all sorts.

Bang Saphan Several beaches along this strip are beginning to develop (see page 225). ■ *Getting there: by bus from Prachuap, or a slow train.*

Informal tours can be organized with *Mr Pinit*, who can often be found on the beach, or can be contacted on T550059. He has motorbikes and will take you to wats, caves, waterfalls, or nearby islands. If you need any information on the local surroundings, for example times and prices for the National Parks, he's recommended as the guru of all in the area, and speaks very good English.   **Tours**

Prachuap Khiri Khan

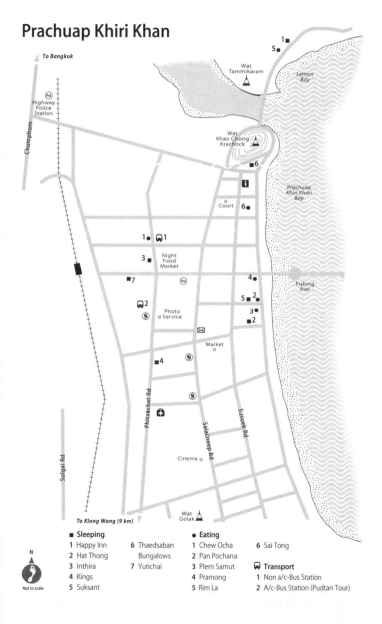

N Not to scale

■ **Sleeping**
1 Happy Inn
2 Hat Thong
3 Inthira
4 Kings
5 Suksant
6 Thaedsaban Bungalows
7 Yutichai

● **Eating**
1 Chew Ocha
2 Pan Pochana
3 Plern Samut
4 Pramong
5 Rim La
6 Sai Tong

🚍 **Transport**
1 Non a/c-Bus Station
2 A/c-Bus Station (Pudtan Tour)

Sleeping At weekends, accommodation is hard to find, with the influx of Thais. During the week, room rates can be negotiated down.

Watch out for wild monkeys who live on Khao Chong Krachok, as they sometimes try to raid the bungalows

AL-B *Hat Thong*, 7 Susuk Rd, T601050, F601057. A/c, restaurant (good Thai buffet lunch Mon-Fri), comfortable, overlooking the sea, good value, best in town. **A-D** *Thaedsaban Bungalows*, T611204. Solid concrete bungalows on stilts across the road from the beach, own bathroom, squat toilet, no TV, no hot water, some a/c. **C-D** *Golden Beach*, located 200 m south of *Happy Inn*, T601626. Similar prices and set-up but rooms are smaller, some a/c. **C-D** *Happy Inn*, located 500 m north of Khao Chong Krachok, T602082. Quite nice bungalows with TV and bathroom with squat toilet attached, some a/c. Just across the road from the beach, beside the river. **C-D** *Suksant*, T611145. Average rooms with TV, some with a/c but no hot water, rather seedy in the evenings. **D** *Kings*, 800/3 Phithakchat Rd, T611170. Fan rooms only. **D-E** *Prachuap Suk Hotel*, T611019, F601711. Simple but clean rooms with some fan, some a/c. **E** *Inthira*, T611013, Kong-Kiat Rd, T611013. Noisy and not very nice. **E** *Yutichai*, 35 Kong-Kiat Rd, T611055. OK rooms with own bathroom and fans.

Eating Prachuap is famous for its seafood and there are a number of excellent restaurants (as well as some more average ones) in the centre of town and along the seafront.

Expensive-mid-range: *Laplong Seafood*, also north of the river, south of *Prenkoon*. Offers an extensive range of seafood, probably the best selection in town (with a few meat dishes too), reasonably priced and friendly service. *Shiew Ocha I*, located near the non-a/c bus station. Offers a good range of Thai and Chinese dishes (including a fair amount of seafood). *Shiew Ocha II*, on the seafront towards the north of the town. Good range of seafood and meat dishes. **Mid-range**: *Plern Samut*, on the seafront near the *Had Thong Hotel*, large range of seafood and other meat dishes. **Mid-range-cheap**: *Mong Lai*, 2½ km north of Laplong on the north end of the bay below the mountain. Country-style restaurant, well known for its spicy dishes. *Pan Pochana*, in the centre of town. Only offers a small selection. *Pheuenkoon*, located north of the river on the seafront. Offers a good selection of seafood and other dishes. *Pramong*, is on the seafront beside the pier but only offers a small selection of prawn, chicken and pork dishes and is reputed more for the heavy drinkers that frequent it than the quality of the food.

Night markets Centre of town, near the police station. There is another night market in front of the Bangkok Bank on Salacheep Rd.

Shopping Prachuap is best known for its printed cotton, known as *pha khommaphat*, although it's better to buy this in Hua Hin.

Transport

323 km from Bangkok 93 km S of Hua Hin

Local Motorized saamlor: Prachuap has its own distinctive form of *tuk-tuk* – motorcycles with sidecars and benchseats.

Train The station is on the west side of town, regular connections with Bangkok's Hualamphong station 5 hrs, Hua Hin and destinations south.

Road Bus: the station is on Phithakchat Rd, regular a/c connections with Bangkok's Southern bus terminal near the Thonburi train station, 5 hrs; non-a/c buses leave from in front of the *Inthira Hotel*, but thse go to Chumphon, not to Bangkok. They leave every hour between 0600 and midday, but in low season there may be fewer.

Directory **Banks** The Government Savings Bank just off Salacheep Rd on the way to the pier cashes TCs and has an ATM. **Communications** Post Office: around the corner from *Hat Thong Hotel*.

Bang Saphan

There are several beaches along this strip of coast at Bang Saphan, 60 km south of Prachuap, and they are beginning to develop into small beach resort areas, geared as much to Thais as to foreigners. Hat Somboon is the nearest beach to Bang Saphan, just 1 km away. The position is attractive enough although the sand very soon degenerates into mud below the low water mark. Continuing south along Route 3374 from Bang Saphan are a series of other small groups of resorts and guesthouses – all still very low key. Tonthonglang Beach comes recommended by one recent visitor; there are a small number of cheaper places to stay here. Around 5 km further south is a ferry link to the off-shore island of Koh Talu where there is one bungalow resort.

Phone code: 032
Colour map 3, grid A2

Sleeping Hat Somboon: C *Nipa Beach Bungalows*, a/c, hot water, telephone and TV. Good value and comfortable.

Eating *Slab*, Hat Somboon, next door to the *Nipa Beach Bungalows*. Recommended.

Chumphon

Considered the 'gateway to the south', this is where the southern highway divides, one route running west and then south on Route 4 to Ranong, Phuket and the Andaman Sea side of the Peninsula; the other, south on Route 41 to Surat Thani, Koh Samui, Nakhon Si Thammarat and the waters of the Gulf of Thailand. In his book *Surveying and exploring in Siam*, published in 1900, James McCarthy writes of 'Champawn' marking the beginning of the Malay Peninsula. Though a group of French engineers had already visited the area with a view to digging a canal through the Kra Isthmus, it was clearly a little place: the "harbour was full of rocks covered with oysters. The usual cocoa-nut palms and grass shanties marked the position of the village".

Phone code: 077
Colour map 3, grid B2

At the end of 1988, Typhoon Gay tore its way through Chumphon province, causing extensive flooding and the death of more than 300 villagers. The positive side of the disaster was that it led to a ban on all logging in Thailand; deforestation was perceived to be to blame for the severe flooding.

Chumphon is 8 km off Route 4/41. There is not much to see, but there are some good beaches nearby and it can be used as an access point for Koh Tao (see the end of **Transport**, below). The **tourist information centre**, in front of the railway station, is not very informative.

Pak Nam Chumphon lies 11 km southeast of Chumphon (on Route 4901), on the coast, at the mouth of the Chumphon River. This is a big fishing village with boats for hire to the nearby islands where swiftlets build their nests for the Chinese speciality, bird's nest soup – *yanwo*, in Chinese (see page 304). Many concessionaires are accompanied by bodyguards; visitors should seek permission before venturing to the nest sites. Islands include Koh Phrao, Koh Lanka Chiu and Koh Rang Nok. ■ *Getting there: songthaews from opposite the morning market on the southern side of town.*

Excursions

Diving, jungle treks, boat trips to caves can all be organized through a guest-house or travel agent here. *Infinity* can help with boats to Koh Tao from Paknam and will arrange day tours. For example they organize one-day trips to Yai Ai Beach (a 3-km-long beach 45 km north of Chumphon) and the nearby Koh Khai, both of which are very good for snorkelling, for ฿600. Two-day trips cost ฿1,000 (including camping on the beach). At the time of

Tours

The Isthmus

writing there is no accommodation on the beach but there are plans to build a hotel here as soon as the Chumphon airport has been opened. *Infinity* also organize a one-day tour to **Rubror Cave**, on the hill near Wat Thep Charoen a kilometre from Chumphon, containing stalactites and stalagmites, **Phitsadarn Cave** and **Thung Wua Laen Beach** for ฿400. The *Chumphon Guesthouse* organizes one-day tours to Hat Sai Ri, Thung Wua Laen Beach, and both caves for ฿450 including lunch (leave 0900, arrive back 1800). *Mayazees Resthouse* rents out motorcycles for ฿150 per day if you would prefer to go out and explore the area on your own.

Sleeping **B** *Janson Chumphon*, off 188-65 Saladaeng Rd, T502520, F503403. A/c, restaurant, pool, newest in town. Fairly clean, well-equipped a/c rooms. Restaurant serves a wide range of Thai food. Discotheque attached. **C** *Pharadorn Inn*, 180/12 Pharadorn Rd, T511598. A/c, restaurant, pool, A/c rooms furnished with attractive bamboo furniture. The restaurant offers a wide range of reasonably priced food. **C** *Tha Taphao*, 66/1 Tha Taphao Rd, T511479, F502479. Large a/c rooms with cable TV; some also have a fridge. Attractive restaurant.

D *Sri Chumphon*, Saladaeng Rd. Hotel is not a very beautiful building, but it is comfortable to stay. These words are emblazoned on a window outside the hotel and sum the place up nicely. Clean rooms, some have a/c and TV, coffee shop. **D** *Suriwong*, 125/27-29 Saladaeng Rd, T511203. Somewhat dingy rooms, some a/c, TV but Thai

Chumphon

■ **Sleeping**
1 Chumphon Guesthouse
2 Infinity
3 Janson Chumphon
4 Mayazee's Resthouse
5 Nam Tai
6 Pharadorn Inn
7 Sooksamer
8 Sri Chumphon
9 Sri Taifa
10 Suriwong
11 Suriya
12 Tha Taphao
13 Thai Prasert

● **Eating**
1 Lin Garden
2 Para Seafood

🚌 **Transport**
1 A/c Bus Station
2 Bus Station
3 Local Buses
4 Minibus to Surat Thani
5 Songthaews to Tayang Pier
6 Songthaews to Thung Wua

N

0 metres 200
0 yards 200

channels only. **D** *Mayazee's Resthouse*, 111/35-36 Soi Bangkok Bank, Saladen Rd, Tha Taphao, T504452. Bright, clean, comfortable and welcoming guesthouse. Rooms are brightly decorated and spotlessly clean. Some have a/c, some have a small balcony. Spacious sitting area upstairs and down. Free drinking water, tea and coffee provided. Every effort is made to make the guest feel at home. Highly recommended. **D-E** *Sri Taifa*, 73-75 Saladaeng Rd, T511063. The a/c rooms are much nicer that the fan rooms which are quite dirty and unappealing. The entrance is through a bustling restaurant.

E *Ekawin Guesthouse*, 5/3 Krom Luang Chumphon Rd, T501821. The most expensive room has a private shower-room, but it is dark as it has, as yet, no window. The other rooms have basins and they are all very clean. The service is friendly and some food is served. Good tour information provided. Recommended. **E** *Chumphon Guesthouse* (otherwise known as *Maio Guesthouse*) located on 2 different sites on and close to the Krong Luam Chumphon Rd, T501242. Bright, clean, cosy rooms with wood-panelled floors, homely atmosphere, friendly and helpful management who speak good English. If you book the boat trip to Koh Tao from here they only charge ฿30 rather than ฿50 for the taxi to the ferry. **E** *Suriya*, 25/24-5 Saladaeng Rd, T511144. Rooms are a little tatty, but clean enough. Squat loos. Recommended. **E-F** *Infinity*, 68/2 Tha Taphao Rd, T501937. Only 3 rooms, one larger with balcony, 2 smaller with no windows – all have fans, very basic but clean, shared bathrooms. Very friendly and helpful management, but it closes at 2230 and you cannot get in (or out) between then and 0730. Good travel service offered here, some food served. **E-F** *Nam Tai*, 130/5 Saladaeng Rd, T511412. Fan-cooled rooms. **E-F** *Sooksamer* (or *Pat's Place*), 118/4 Suksamer Rd. Thai and European food, friendly, clean rooms, English-speaking owner, good source of information. Recommended. **E-F** *Thai Prasert*, OK rooms with fan, some have own bathroom, but not as nice as *Chumphon* and *Mayazees* guesthouses.

Eating There are 2 **night markets** on Krom Luang Chumphon Rd and on Tha Taphao Rd. There are also several restaurants on Tha Taphao and Saladaeng roads and on the Krom Luang Chumphon Rd. *Lin Garden* and *Para Seafood* have been recommended.

Tour operators *Infinity*, 68/2 Tha Taphao Rd.

Transport
500 km S of Bangkok
171 km N of Rayong

Air A new airport has recently opened in Chumphon and start-up domestic airline **PB Air** operate a service to Bangkok. **Train** Station at west end of Kram Luang Chumphon Rd. Regular connections with Bangkok's Hualamphong station, 7½-9 hrs and all stops south.

Road **Bus**: terminal on Tha Taphao Rd, not far from the night market. Regular a/c connections with Bangkok's Southern bus terminal near the Thonburi train station, 7 hrs; non-a/c buses leave from the new terminal on Phra Pinklao Rd, 7 hrs. Also connections with all south destinations.

Getting to Koh Tao This island (see page 368) can be reached by boat from the pier 10 km southeast of the town. There is a slow midnight boat which takes 6 hrs and costs ฿200 (taxi to the pier from town usually costs ฿50 but if you book through *Chumphon GuestHouse* they only charge ฿30 for the taxi). There is a speedboat at 0800 which arrives at 0940 and costs ฿400 (plus taxi). There is also a slower, larger speedboat at 0730 for ฿400 which takes 2½ hrs. Tickets for these boats can be bought at all the travel agents in town.

Directory **Banks** *Thai Farmers' Bank*, Saladaeng Rd. **Communications** Post Office: this has recently moved to new premises on the Paramin Manda Rd about 1 km out of town on the left-hand side. Telephone Office: for overseas calls slightly further on the right.

The Isthmus

Around Chumphon

Beaches

There are a number of good beaches around Chumphon, most of them with accommodation

Pharadon Phap Beach, 1 km south of Pak Nam on the Chumphon estuary: **A-B** *Porn Sawan Hotel Resort*, has 60 bungalows, a/c, restaurant, pool, tennis.

Hat Thung Wua Lean, 18 km north of Chumphon, is beautiful, probably the best beach in the area. **Sleeping** There are a number of hotels and bungalow operations here: **B-C** *Chumphon Cabana Resort*, T501990, has some nicely decorated a/c bungalows set in attractive gardens and two hotel blocks all with a/c and hot water. The newer buildings have all been designed on energy-saving principles in keeping with the owner's environmental concerns. The resort has all the usual facilities including a pool, a very peaceful location and a great view of the beach from the restaurant and some of the bungalows. Down sides are that the food served at the restaurant is very bland, and sometimes there is an unpleasant smell from the drains in some of the rooms in the hotel blocks. **B-C** *Chuan Phun*, has 40 rooms in an apartment block, all with a/c, hot water and TV, rooms at the back with no sea view are slightly cheaper. **B-C** *Kray Rim Lae*, has nice a/c bungalows of varying sizes. **B-D** *View Sea Food*, has nice bungalows. **C-D** *Clean Wave*, has some a/c and some cheaper fan-cooled bungalows. **C-E** *Sea Beach*, only has fan-cooled bungalows at varying prices depending upon the size. ■ *Getting there: catch a bus from the market in Chumphon for ฿30.*

Hat Sai Ri is 3 km south of Hat Pharadon and close to Koh Thong Luang – there is good snorkelling in the area. There is also a shrine to His Royal Highness Prince Chumphon, the so-styled father of the Royal Thai Navy. **Sleeping** The **D** *Tung Makham* offers good bungalows with fan and attached bathroom, and organizes snorkelling trips (15 minutes by speedboat) to Thong Luang. To get to this beach get a songthaew (฿20) from opposite *Infinity Travel* or from the post office.

Amphoe Thung Tako (Sunny Beach) is located 50 km south of Chumphon. **Sleeping B-C** *Chumphon Sunny Beach Resort*, T2811234. Has fan-cooled and a/c bungalows. ■ *Getting there: get a bus from the bus station in Chumphon.*

Amphoe Lang Suan is 62 km south of Chumphon. There are reports of two beautiful caves in the area – Tham Khao Ngoen and Tham Khao Kriep – although we have not been able to confirm this. The district is also locally renowned for the quality of its fruit. **Sleeping C-E** *Tawat Hotel*, T541341. A hotel with 100 rooms, some with fan and some a/c. **D-E** *Chumphon 99 Bay Resort*, T541481. Bungalows. **D-E** *Jane Resort*, T541330. A smaller hotel than *Tawat* and with slightly cheaper rooms (fan-cooled only). ■ *Getting there: get a bus from the bus station in Chumphon.*

The West Coast: Chumphon to Phuket

Just to the west of Chumphon the highway divides. Route 4 runs down the east coast of the peninsula, usually out of sight of the Andaman Sea. Ranong is about 130 km southwest of Chumphon and is famous for its hot springs. At this point the Kra Isthmus is at its narrowest.

From Prathong Island near Takua Pa (south of Ranong), right down to Phuket, virtually the entire western coast of Phangnga comprises great long sandy bays with the occasional small or larger peninsular or rocky headland. With the exception of the Thai Muang National Park, much of this coastline is currently being developed for tourism. The main centre is the Khao Lak area, but development is also beginning in the Bang Sak (see pages 233-242). With the Thai Muang National Park to the south, the Khao Lak Lam Ru National Park bordering the Khao Lak area, and the Khao Sok National Park inland to the north, tourism operators along the coast of Phangnga are targetting those interested in "getaway" and nature tourism. In addition, to the inland national parks, the western coast resorts in Phangnga are also the closest departure points for the Similan Islands (see page 276). Most resorts to date are low rise and fairly low key, and resort operators along the Khao Lak beach in particular have expressed their intent to prevent the bar scene in Phuket from migrating up to Phangnga.

Eighty-kilometres south of Khao Lak and you reach Phuket Island and province; the largest beach resort in the south. After Phuket, Route 4 skirts northeastwards to Phangnga (100 km from Phuket) and then south to Krabi (another 85 km). Krabi is the main departure point for the islands of Koh Lanta and Koh Phi Phi, and also has a number of good beaches close by. From Krabi, Route 4037 links up with Surat Thani and the east coast, while Route 4 continues southwards to Trang, 317 km from Phuket. Boats for islands in the Andaman Sea leave from Pakmeng, Trang's port.

Ranong

Ranong province is the first southern province bordering the Indian Ocean and Thailand's rainiest (often in excess of 5,000 mm per year), narrowest and least populated. Kra Buri, 58 km north of Ranong, is the point where the Kra Isthmus is also at its narrowest, and there has been debate for centuries about the benefits of digging a canal across the Isthmus, so linking the Gulf of Thailand with the Andaman Sea and short-cutting the long hike down the peninsula to Singapore and then north again through the Melaka Strait. The project is currently out of favour.

Phone code: 077
Colour map 3, grid B1

The Isthmus

The name Ranong is derived from *rae* (tin) *nong* (rich), and the town was established in the late 18th century by a family from Hokkien, China. Large numbers of Chinese labourers came to the town to work in the tin mines on which its prosperity was based and even today Ranong has a predominantly Sino-Thai population. In town there are a number of attractive 19th-century Chinese-style houses. There is a small **tourist office** on Kamlungsab Road.

Ranong

The Isthmus

Sights   Surrounded by forested mountains, Ranong is a scenic place to stay for a day or two. However, there is little to keep the demanding visitor here for much longer than this. It is a small and unpretentious provincial capital, an important administrative centre but hardly a place endowed with natural beauty or historical or artistic significance. Ranong's proximity to **Myanmar** is a plus (it is possible to visit Kawthoung on a day trip), there are the hot springs (see below), some islands off-shore which are accessible in the dry season, and a handful of houses built by the town's Hokkien Chinese immigrants. There are also some waterfalls, one of which, Punyaban, can be seen from the road as you approach the town.

Geo-thermal mineral water springs
The water is not too hot to touch, but hot enough to cook an egg in

The town contains **geo-thermal mineral water springs** (65°C) at **Wat Tapotharam**, 2 km east of the town and behind the *Jansom Thara Hotel*. The hot water bubbles up into concrete tubs named *bor mae, bor por* and *bor luuk saaw* – mother, father and daughter pools respectively. The springs provide the *Jansom Thara Hotel* with thermal water for hot baths and a giant jacuzzi. There is a small park with a cable bridge over the river, a number of bathing pools (sometimes empty of water), and a second-rate animal garden. The wat is rather dull, containing a footprint of the Buddha. ■ *Getting there: by songthaew along Route 2; ask for 'bor naam rawn' (hot water well).*

Continuing along Route 2 for another 6 km or so, the road reaches the old tin-mining village of **Hat Som Paen**. The tin that brought wealth to the area was worked out long ago, but **Wat Som Paen** is worth a visit to see the giant carp which reside here, protected because of their supposed magical qualities: catch and eat them – and regret it.

Excursions   **Port of Ranong** lies 3 km from town. Each morning the dock seethes with activity as Thai and Burmese fishing boats unload their catches. Boats can be hired at a pontoon next to the dock, to tour the bustling harbour and look across the Kra River estuary to the Burmese border (approximately ฿300). For those who wish to actually step ashore in Burma, then it is possible to visit Kawthoung (see below). **NB** Border officials can be touchy, carry your passport with you. Ranong is an important point of contact between Burma and Thailand. Not only is there considerable trade, but many Burmese, in search of higher wages, cross the estuary to work.

Kawthoung and **Thahtaykyun (Myanmar)**: recently it has become possible to visit Myanmar (Burma) from Ranong. A regular ferry plies between the port and the Burmese town of Kawthoung, and officials in Myanmar are currently providing visitors with day visas (sometimes longer). For those who do not wish to visit Kawthoung independently, the *Jansom Thara Hotel* also organizes tours – ฿600 (minimum eight people). For more details, see under Kawthoung on page 232. It is also possible to visit the luxury **L-A** *Andaman Club* on nearby Thahtaykyun Island in Burmese waters which is very popular among the Ranong Thais for its 24-hour casino. The boat costs ฿250 return and leaves regularly from the pontoon next to the dock. It is worth bearing in mind, however, that profits from the three-hour trip and from the casino go to the Burmese government and help support the régime there.

Surin and **Similan Islands**: boats sail from Ranong Port, see page 276.

There are a number of notable **beaches** and **islands** in the neighbourhood of Ranong, many within the limits of the **Laem Son National Park**, such as Hat Bang Baen, Koh Payam, Koh Nam Noi, Koh Kam Yai, Koh Chang and Koh Kam Tok. The islands are only easily accessible in the high season, between November and April. The park was gazetted in 1983 and covers a little over 300 sq km. The water here is not terribly clear – the park and the islands effectively lie at the outer limits of the Kra River estuary – so don't expect coral and excellent visibility. Mangroves fringe many of the islands and because of the high rainfall in the area the natural vegetation is tropical rainforest. While the islands may not have great water, or great beaches for that matter, they do have good birdlife (there are around 47 bird species in the park) and because there is no electricity it is peaceful and relaxed (some of the bungalows have generators). The only time to visit is between November and April; outside this period the guesthouses shut and the long-tailed boats stop operating. ■ *Getting there: long-tail boats run from Ranong Port out to Koh Chang around 3 or 4 times a day, in the morning. There is no fixed fare – it depends how many people are travelling. Return boats tend to leave Koh Chang in the afternoon.*

Sleeping on the islands There are around 10 bungalow operations on **Koh Chang**. Some can be booked through *Ranong Travel* in town. **E** *Koh Chang Resort* offers wooden huts, some with attached bathroom and has a restaurant. Snorkelling and fishing can be organized from here. **E** *Rasta Baby*, T833077. Small group of bungalows on north side of island, laid-back atmosphere in line with its name. **E** *Sunset*, this small operation offers clean bungalows and a friendly atmosphere. **E** *Chang Thong* and *Phung Thong* are next door to each other, just 5 mins walk from the pier. **F** *Sabai Jai*, probably the best value and one of the best-run places on the island. Clean and with good, home-cooked food, dorm beds available as well as range of bungalows. **B** *Andaman Peace Bungalows* on **Hat Bang Baen** is in an idyllic spot although the bungalows need some attention. They come with fan and fridge.

A-B *Jansom Thara*, 2/10 Phetkasem Rd, Bang Rin, F821821, BT4242050. A/c, restaurant, pool, international-style hotel, the bath-water comes straight from the thermal springs. Check in before 1600 to enjoy the thermal baths in the hotel. Lovely views from most of the rooms (many of which have balconies). **A-B** *Jansom Thara Resort* (out of town), Paknam Ranong, T821611, BT4242050. A/c, restaurant, pool, overlooks Kra River estuary.

Sleeping

B *Eiffel Inn*, 6 km out of town, T823271-2. Comfortable bungalows (and some rooms in apartment block), coffee shop, room service, rooms have a/c, hot water, TV, fridge, friendly but rather spoilt by a hideous misrepresentation of the Eiffel Tower sitting in the car park. Room maintenance sometimes leaves a little to be desired, so it's worth checking out your room first. **B-C** *Spa Inn*, 25/1 Phetkasem Rd, T811715. All rooms have hot water, bath tub, a/c and are comfortable with wall-to-wall carpeting. Slightly more expensive ones come with TV and fridge.

C-D *Ranong Inn*, 29/9 Petchkasem Rd, T822777. Most rooms have balconies overflowing with flowers, OK rooms, carpeted, some have a/c, swimming pool.

D *Ranong Guesthouse*, T833369. Some a/c, all have TV and attached bathrooms (Asian toilet) but no hot water. Spacious, clean and light rooms. Good value but rather stern management. **D-E** *Asia*, 39/9 Ruangrat Rd, T811113. Some a/c, clean rooms, well located hotel but can be noisy. Rooms are adequate and staff seem reasonably tuned in. **D-E** *Sin Ranong*, 26/23-4 Ruangrat Rd, T811454. Adequate.

E *Rattanasin*, corner of Ruangrat and Luwang roads, T811242. Large rooms with attached bathrooms (Asian toilet), some a/c, central location but noisy and watch out for the cockroaches.

In the centre of town on Ruangrat Rd the excellent **Cheap** *J&T Food and Ice*, serves a range of delicious but very reasonably priced Thai food and ice-creams, very popular place with locals and *farangs* alike, friendly owners. Recommended. *Somboon Restaurant*, opposite the *Jansom Thara Hotel*, serves delicious Thai and Chinese seafood much of which is displayed in tanks in front so it should be pretty fresh.

Eating

The Isthmus

Shopping *Batik Shop* on Thawi Sinkha Rd.

Tour operators *Ranong Travel*, 37 Ruangrat Rd is probably a better source of information than the tourist information office. They can book bungalows on Koh Chang (see **Excursions**), arrange fishing trips, and advise on visiting Burma.

Transport
600 km from Bangkok
Air The airport is 20 km south of town. **Bangkok Airways** fly once a day to and from Bangkok, leaving Ranong at 0900. **Road Bus**: The road journey from the north is arduous – 8 hrs – the last half of which is through mountains; not good for travel sickness sufferers. Consider taking the train from Bangkok to Chumphon and the bus from there (which takes the same amount of time). The bus terminal is on the edge of town, near the *Jansom Thara Hotel*. Regular a/c and non-a/c connections with Bangkok's Southern bus terminal near the Thonburi railway station. Also connections with Chumphon, Surat Thani and Phuket (304 km south). For private coach companies T2816939 or 2817011.

Directory **Airline offices** *Bangkok Airways*, 50/18 Mool, Phetkasem Highway, T835096, F835097. **Banks** On Tha Muang Rd there are branches of the *Bank of Ayudya*, *Thai Military Bank*, *Thai Farmers Bank* and *Siam Commercial Bank*, all with ATMs and/or exchange facilities. **Communications** Post Office: Chon Rao Rd, near the junction with Dap Khadi Rd. There is also a Poste Restante service. The **telephone office** is on Ruangrat Rd. **Medical services** Hospital: situated at the junction of Permphon and Kamlungsab roads (currently being extended).

Kawthoung (Myanmar)

Colour map 3, grid B1 Kawthoung, at the southern tip of Myanmar (formerly Burma), is just a few kilometres from the fishing port of Ranong. In Ranong, Burmese trawlers fishing the Andaman Sea dock to unload their catches and regular ferries ply the waters between Ranong and Kawthoung. As at some other crossings between Thailand and Myanmar, it is possible to secure a day visa, or an even longer visa, at the immigration office at Kawthoung Pier in Myanmar. However, the visa only permits travel in the immediate area. (This may soon change. In January 1999 the Thai and Burmese authorities were discussing the possibility of allowing tourists to cross into Burma via Ranong (Kawthoung) and continue into the Burmese heartland.) The road north is off-limits to foreigners – and in any case it is little more than a track – and, though there are flights to Yangon (Rangoon – the capital of Myanmar), it is not clear whether people arriving in Myanmar from Ranong would be permitted to board.

Because of Kawthoung's close economic links with Thailand, the town feels comparatively wealthy by Burmese standards. Many people work in Ranong, while others travel all the way to Bangkok to secure employment. Growing numbers of girls in Bangkok's brothels come from Myanmar and many of these are said to enter the country via Ranong. Whatever work these international labour migrants secure, some benefits filter back to Kawthoung in the form of cash and consumer goods. (Researchers have also pointed out that these migrants bring much more than money and gifts back to their families: AIDS is also being spread into Myanmar in this way.)

The limestone islands of the Myeik Archipelago have long been famous for the nests of the swiftlets which have been collected from the caves here for centuries. The Thai name for the bird – 'wind-eating bird' – apparently refers to the belief that these creatures took their sustenance from the air, and never alighted to feed. Although the King of Siam claimed the right to harvest the nests, such was their value that poaching quickly took hold. Norman Lewis recounts in his book *Golden Earth* (1952) how he stayed in the Mergui (Myeik) lodging house of Yok Seng, a Chinese gentleman who by chance happened to be in the nest-exporting business. He records that an early Chinese scientific expedition analysed the constituents of the life-giving nests and concluded that they were composed of 'solidified sea foam', which is rather more appetizing than the more scientific saliva explanation. Yok Seng also told the inquisitive travel writer that unscrupulous individuals had taken to selling fake nests composed of jelly made from seaweed. "Be sure", Yok Seng warned, "that when you order bird's nest soup in a restaurant, it will be a fake you will be served".

For those who do not wish to visit Kawthoung independently, the *Jansom Thara Hotel* in Ranong organizes tours – ฿600 (minimum eight people). **Tours**

C *Kawthoung Motel*, slightly better than most hotels in out-of-the-way spots like this in Myanmar, with attached facilities and a reasonable level of service, still pretty spartan though, considering the rates that are charged. **Sleeping**

There is also the plusher 250-room Andaman Club Resort Hotel on Thahtaykyun Island which opened in 1993 and a 2nd resort-style hotel is planned for Yadanakyun Island. It is scheduled to open in 2001.

Air Myanmar Airways flies to Kawthoung from Yangon. There are also connections with Dawei and Myeik. **Transport**

Road **Bus**: the road north is a track and not only are foreigners not permitted to travel along it but there is no regular bus service in any case.

Sea **Boat**: Myanmar Five Star Lines operate ships between Yangon and Kawthoung, calling at ports en route.

International connections with Thailand There are regular ferry connections between Kawthoung and the Thai port of Ranong from early morning to mid-afternoon. On arrival in Kawthoung visitors should report to the immigration office at the jetty where they will be issued with a day visa.

Takua Pa to Khao Lak

The western coastline is lined with beaches, but many are quite hard to get to. The **Bang Sak Beach** area lies just south of Takua Pa off the main road to Phuket. Although at least one resort has been operating for about ten years, this area has only just begun to draw the attention of tourism operations targetting non-Thai tourists. The beaches in the area are mostly gently sloping with pale yellow-to-white sands lined with casuarinas and backed with beach forest and some swamp forest. Unlike the Khao Lak area further south there are no hills as a backdrop to the resorts, but the isolation of many of these beaches, miles from anywhere, is an attraction in itself for those who want to escape completely. Bang Sak beach itself is a Thai tourism spot popular with local picnickers and well served with small seafood restaurants. It is too out of the way to be tacky, however, but it does look as though this will be the next area to take off in terms of tourism development.

**Takua Pa &
Bang Sak**
Phone code: 076
Colour map 4, grid A1

Takua Pa, no more than an hour's drive from Bang Niang, and considerably less than from Bang Sak, was once the centre of Phangnga province. Once a nationally important centre of tin mining, Takua Pa has lost much of its financial power since the collapse of the tin market in 1983, but it is a friendly place to wander, and the main shopping and administrative centre for this part of

Phangnga province. The town has a charming, rambling layout and some lovely old streets with Sino-Portugese buildings.

There are several islands off the Phangnga coast near Takua Pa

Prathong Island has one resort well known for its environmental focus: the Golden Buddha Beach Resort. The Chelon Institute carries out research on sea turtles at Prathong Island with the assistance of this resort, and also accepts volunteers. See details on the resort in the accommodation section below. **Khor Khao Island** further south has one newly opened resort. This island lies in a beautiful bay with views to the hills of Ranong and nearby islands to the north and west.

Excursions There is a stretch of **coral reef** lying off shore between *Sun Splendour Lodge* and *Bang Sak Beach Resort*, about 1 km north of *Bang Sak Beach Resort* which is revealed at low tide. The nearby village is a Moken community (also known as the Chao Le) who have settled in this area but continue to practice fishing with traditional fishing gear.

Several **national parks**, are within easy reach of this area including the Similan and Surin Marine National Parks, Khao Lak-Lam Ru National Park, Khao Sok (see page 242), and Sri Phang Nga National Parks.

Tours Information on tours can be found at almost every resort.

Sleeping **L-A** *Bang Sak Beach Resort*, about 15 mins drive from Takua Pa bus terminal, or 1-2 hrs from Phuket International Airport, T446520, F446520, annemathuros@hotmail.com Just opened, this is a delightful resort right on the beach with comfortable cottages built in local style from natural materials, and equipped with all the facilities (hot and cold shower, mini bar, a/c, telephone, but no television). A wooden walkway leads through some natural forest which has been left intact in various places in the grounds. Some of the cottages are tucked away in these forest patches. Two restaurants serve seafood dishes in Thai and international style. The presentation and flavour of the food is excellent although prices are rather high. Facilities also include a mineral spa (water is to be brought in from the Thai Muang area), massage, aromatherapy, body and beauty treatments, and a Thai cooking class. Nice pool with a deck, mini golf, petanque and a children's playground are all available and there will be a souvenir shop. Limousine services to and from the airport are available. Recommended.

AL-B *Similana Resort*, off the main Takua Pa – Phuket road, just a bit further south of the Bang Sak area, signposted down a dirt road. T420166-8, www.losthorizonsasia.com/simitxthtm Perched on a rocky hillside overlooking a private bay, the resort is beautifully – and thoughtfully – laid out. All the rooms are well decorated with Thai-style furnishings. The bungalows and tree houses are particularly attractive with high ceilings, wood furnishings and window seats. The hotel block has forest views and large balconies (and baths). Tree houses, in fact they are bungalows on high stilts, are at beach level. Bungalows and tree houses have both ceiling fans and a/c and are well screened against mosquitoes. Two

Takua Pa & Bang Sak

Not to scale

■ **Sleeping**
1 Bangsak Inn
2 Bangsak Beach Resort
3 Bangsak Resort
4 Diamond Beach Resort
5 Koh Khor Khao Resort
6 Similana Resort
7 Sun Splendor Lodge
8 Theptharo Lagoon Beach Resort

The Isthmus

restaurants serving Thai, Italian and northern European food. **NB** breakfast is included in the room price. Facilities include pool and recreation room, massage services, reflexology, gift shop, jeep rental and tours to the Similans and other national parks in the area. Very friendly and helpful staff. Limousine services from Phuket International Airport are available. Recommended, but the number of steps and narrow paths might make it difficult for those unsteady on their feet. **A-B** *Theptharo Lagoon Beach Resort*, Off the main Takua Pa-Phuket road follow the signs to the resort from Ban Khuk Khak village. T420151-5, www.khao-lak.com/theptharo Large, smart concrete bungalows with traditional shingle roofs, Thai-style furnishings (the doubles are quite romantic with four-poster beds), balconies and sunken baths (some with a view!). All a/c. Set in landcaped gardens overlooking the sea. All facilities including a pool. The setting is attractive but the resort is new and the garden looks rather sparse. **A-C** *Sun Splendor Lodge*, in Thai this is called the 'Tap Tawan Resort'. Down the same road as the *Bangsak Beach Resort* on the road leading to Tap Tim Beach off the main Takua Pa-Phuket road, this resort has been operating for about ten years and is located on a small sandy headland with very shallow waters on the beaches. Chalet-style accommodation (all with a/c) in open grounds, with a small pool. Some chalets have direct access to the beach. Larger chalets sleep four in two double beds (in the same large room). Rooms are simply furnished. The restaurant serves Thai food only – mostly seafood. Friendly staff. There are fan rooms above the reception and restaurant building. These are better value than the a/c rooms. **B** *Golden Buddha Beach Resort*, www.losthorizons.com/asia A full-board rate of an additional ฿550 is also available. Located on Prathong Island off the Phangnga coast, the *Golden Buddha Beach Resort* supports a turtle conservation project run by the Chelon Institute on the same beach as the resort. Volunteers for the project are accommodated at the resort. Biologists can get reduced rates if they want to work on the project (see the website for more details). Reports from those who have visited the resort describe it as 'idyllic' and 'paradise'. Accommodation is in one-bedroom bungalows. 5-day, 4-night tours of the area with accommodation at the resort can be pre-booked from overseas.

C-D *Bangsak Resort*, about 1 km on from the *Bangsak Inn* down the winding beach road and within sight of the *Bangsak Beach Resort*. A mixture of old and new fan bungalows in gardens. The new bungalows are quite nice, in a coconut plantation, the old bungalows are rather run-down and in regimental gardens with little charm. Nice beach and walking distance to several local seafood restaurants. Not bad value (for the new bungalows) if you don't mind being miles from anywhere. **D** *Diamond Beach Resort*, about 5 km out of Takua Pa down the road leading to the Khor Khao Pier, and Nam Khem fishing village, there is a turn-off to the left and a dirt road leads to the Diamond Beach Resort. T01-9584916. Very basic concrete bungalows in an open setting with some Casuarina trees. Closed during the low season. Looks very run-down. About 500 m from the nearest beach. The beach is quite pleasant, but nothing special for the area and there are no facilities, e.g. restaurants or other refreshments, nearby. **D** *Koh Khor Khao Resort*, past the turn-off to *Diamond Beach Resort*, the road winds through a fishing village to the pier to Koh Khor Khao. Boats can be taken to the resort for ฿10 per person each way, and ฿400 return for a vehicle. The resort is closed from May to Oct. T01-2292303, 593176. The resort can be contacted at the office at the entrance to the road to Nam Khem Fishing Village on the main Takua Pa-Phuket road. Fan rooms only. **D-E** *Bangsak Inn*, Take the road down to Bang Sak Beach off the main Takua Pa-Phuket road, there is a T-junction at the beach and *Bangsak Inn* is about 100 m down the road to the right just across the road from the beach. T422476 after 1700. Dingy, dirty rooms with ceiling fan on very low ceilings. Not recommended.

There is also a new luxury development under construction at Laem Pakarang (Coral Cape) and set to open at the end of 2000.

The Isthmus

Transport

Takua Pa is 134 km N of Phuket & 54 km N of Khao Lak

Road Bus: some a/c and non-a/c connections between the Southern terminal in Bangkok and Takua Pa (12 hrs). From Krabi and Phangnga, take a bus towards Phuket and change at Kochloi to a bus running north to Takua Pa. From Phuket take a local bus to Takua Pa. Local buses and songthaews provide transport between smaller communities.

Khao Lak

Phone code: 076
Colour map 4, grid B1

The Khao Lak area is a relatively recent discovery for visitors to Thailand, popular with Germans (which may account for the generally high standard of cleanliness at virtually all the resorts!). It stretches from just south of the Khao Lak-Lam Ru National Park, north to the Bang Niang beach. There is a string of resorts along a series of shallow, secluded beaches, roughly midway between Takua Pa (30 km north) and Thai Muang (30 km south), 80 km north of Phuket on the Andaman Sea coast. From north to south the beaches are: Chong Fah, Bang Niang, Nang Thong and Khao Lak. There is a small **tourist information** stand on the beach, between *Nang Thong Bay Resort* and *Garden Beach Resort*, staffed by people with an extensive knowledge of the area. They will organize tours to any of the places mentioned in **Excursions** below. ■ *0900-1100, 1600-1800.*

Khao Lak Beach itself is actually quite small, separated from the longer Nang Thong Beach by a small rocky headland where some more resort development is currently taking place. South of Khao Lak lies the National Park headquarters on another forested rocky headland. There are small beaches here which you can get to from the National Park headquarters and *Khao Lak Nature Resort*. South of the National Park is the *Poseidon Bungalow Resort* which also has its own beach. To date, Khao Lak beach is targetting the upper end of the Khao Lak market, particularly people looking for peace and quiet. The beach is very clean and bungalow-resorts are generally equipped with all the facilities.

Nang Thong Beach has a wider range of accommodation and facilities, although it is still fairly pricey. Budget accommodation is usually set back a little way from the beach. There are several beach restaurants and bars at the northern end. The main strip of small bars and restaurants that used to run through the middle of the beach is being evicted from what is government land, ostensibly so that the local government can create a park in this area.

After another small headland, there is **Bang Niang Beach** which runs into Chong Fah Beach. Bang Niang Beach has a mixture of accommodation (from budget to tourist class), some small shops and two dive shops (*Sea Dragon* and *High Class Adventure* both have booking offices here). There isn't a real sense of identity to Bang Niang yet, and it is uncertain which way tourism is likely to develop along here, but apparently a

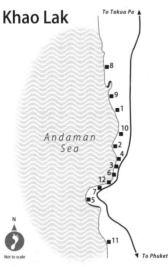

Khao Lak

To Takua Pa

Andaman Sea

N

Not to scale

To Phuket

■ **Sleeping**
1 Chong Fah Beach Resort
2 Khao Lak Andaman Beach Resort
3 Khao Lak Bay Front Resort
4 Khao Lak Laguna Resort
5 Khao Lak Nature Resort
6 Khao Lak Palm Beach
7 Khao Lak Resort
8 Khao Lak Tropicana Resort
9 Mai's Quiet Zone
10 Palm Andaman Beach Resort
11 Poseidon Bungalows
12 Sunset Resort

Khao Lak place names

Chongfa

ช่องฟ้า

Lumpee

ลำพี

Turtle Beach

หาดเต่า

huge 600-room hotel is planned for the area in the next year, and this could change the beach considerably.

Chong Fah Beach has a stronger backpacker/budget feel with fairly long-stay visitors in several bungalow outfits. There are the tourist-class resorts too, but these do not really affect the overall character of the beach. Somewhat incongruous mixed clientele: many come for the quiet but there are also some who are attracted by the raucous Full Moon Parties (complete with booming bass which can be heard for a couple of kilometres) which are held at the far northern end of the beach.

Waterfalls, there are several along the coast, two of them are **Chong Fah** (5 km north) and **Lumpee** (20 km south). ■ *Getting there: the easiest way is by hired motorbike, ฿200 per day (see Local transport).*

Coral reef, an interesting half-day trip is to a local reef, 45 minutes by long-tail boat. Charges are about ฿300 for snorkelling equipment and ฿1,000 for diving, which includes equipment and two dives.

Excursions

Turtle Beach, at the Khao Lumpee-Had Thai Muang National Park, is a 20 km-long stretch of beach where turtles, including the giant leatherback, come ashore at night to nest from November to February (entrance fee ฿20). Young turtles can be seen hatching from March to July. Hawksbill and Olive Ridley turtles are currently being raised in ponds near the park headquarters.

Turtle releases are held every Mar as the highlight of an annual district festival

Khao Sok National Park is within fairly easy reach of Khao Lak – and many tour companies offer trips to the park (see page 242).

Khao Lak-Lam Ru National Park stretches from a small bay just south of the main Khao Lak tourism area, inland up into the hills. There is a tiered waterfall with walks from the main path at the top of the hill, and forest rangers can take trekkers through the hills. However, the level of English spoken leaves rather a lot to be desired and trails are not regularly maintained so it can be fairly heavy-going.

Khao Lampee-Had Thai Muang National Park is a relatively small national park, covering an area of 72 square km, and comprising two distinct geographical areas: the Thai Muang Beach area and the Khao Lampee area. The western portion, Thai Muang Beach, has 14 km of undisturbed beach lined with casuarina trees. The park continues inland for about 1 km and includes mangrove forest along the edge of the sea inlet, some swamp forest (*pa samet*) and freshwater lagoons from the old mine works from which Thai Muang derives its name (Muang in this case means mine). The eastern portion, inland, covers several waterfalls and surrounding forested hills. There is an office in the Khao Lampee area, but the park headquarters are based in the Thai Muang area near the entrance. Accommodation is available in four fan-cooled bungalows in the Thai Muang part of the park. Prices range from ฿800 for a bungalow which can accommodate 6 people, to ฿1,000 for a bungalow which can accommodate 10 people. Bookings can be made at the central Forestry Department office in Bangkok (Reservations office, Marine National Parks Division, Royal Forest Department, Chatuchak, Bangkok, 10900 – T02-5797047-8) or at the park headquarters in Thai Muang. The bungalows

The Isthmus

may not be available while they are being improved, however, so it is best to have a back-up alternative if you do wish to stay here. Camping is allowed and food and drinks can be purchased at the canteen.

Dusit Hot Spring Beach lies south of the Thai Muang National Park and can be reached from the main Phuket-Takua Pa road (Petchkasem Road) by following the signs to Na Tai Beach and then taking the turn off to the Dusit Hot Spring Beach. The hot springs are being developed into a spa-type resort, with separate hot mineral spas for men and women set in gardens. Bungalow-type accommodation is under construction. For details contact T581360. If you just want to use the spa pools, entrance is ฿20 per person for non-Thais and ฿10 per person for Thais. The extensive grounds are being landscaped with access to the beach via footbridges over some freshwater lagoons.

Tours   Information on tours can be found at almost every resort. Tours to the **Similan Islands** (see page 276) are organized by *Poseidon Bungalows* and by *Khao Lak Bungalows*. A three-day trip costs around ฿3,500, including transport, accommodation and all food. They will also organize diving and snorkelling trips. *Poseidon Bungalows* will shortly be organizing five-day trips to the **Surin Islands** (see page 277). The *Thai Dive Company*, T571434, have an office in Thai Muang and will organize transport from Phuket. This is a British-managed company, with a friendly and professional manner. They are well equipped and supply excellent food. A three-day dive tour costs ฿9,200, two days, ฿6,900. There is a 25% discount for non-divers. Diving companies can be found at the *Khao Lak Laguna Resort* (*Sea Dragon* and *Phuket*) and *Khao Lak Bayfront* (*Kon Tiki*), and at offices in Nang Thong and Chong Fah for the other two dive companies. They are well signposted at all resorts. *Garden Beach Resort* organize snorkelling and fishing trips (฿300 per day including meals) and trips to waterfalls (฿250-450 per day). Peter and Mani, of the *Khao Lak Restaurant* organize walking jungle trips (฿450 per day, including food), boat tours around Phangnga Bay, diving to Similan and Surin.

Sleeping   **Chong Fah Beach** is reached by taking the signposted road off the main Phuket-Takua Pa Highway (Route 4 to Ranong). Once you get to the beach, the resorts are off to the right down a dirt track. **B-D** *Barn Soraya Bungalows, Restaurant and Pub*, 55 Moo 5, Petchkasem Rd, Khukkhak, T420192-4, baansoraya@yahoo.com Just past the *Chong Fah Beach Resort*, this is a small concrete block next to, but not facing the sea, with 6 well-appointed fan and a/c bungalows (the a/c bungalows are more expensive). Clean and comfortable with a small balcony by the door. Koen (the owner) and his wife and mother-in-law are all very friendly and happy to help guests. They will also discount for long stays. Fishing tours can be arranged from a small stall at the front. Koen plans to open a restaurant and pub which will play jazz-type music and serve a mixture of western and Thai food. At the far northern end of the beach right next to the mouth of a small river, a new bungalow outfit, the *Wunder Resort*, is under construction. Adjacent to *Wunder* is **C-D** *Mai's Quiet Zone Bungalows*, 53 Moo 5 Banbangniang, T420196 F420197. Bungalows vary in size and charm – it's worth having a look at a few before you decide where you want to stay. One room comes complete with kitchen for a longer stay. All fan, all equipped with mosquito nets. Doug and Mai are the friendly owners and relatively long-term residents at Chong Fah. They will rent motorbikes, jeep and bicycles and arrange elephant trekking, airport taxi, and boats to go fishing or snorkelling. Apparently the Full Moon Parties up the beach can be pretty noisy on the one night in the month they occur (cheaper in the low season or for long lets).

A-C *Bang Niang Beach Resort*, T420171-5, F420176, bangniangresort @png.a-net.net.th Set about 500 m back from the sea behind the *Chong Fah Beach*

Resort, this is a small hotel-style resort with fan and a/c concrete bungalows arranged in a round with a swimming pool in the middle and a small garden. Rooms are spacious and clean. A/c rooms are all to be equipped with TV, fridge and minibar. Restaurant serves Thai, Chinese and Western food. Discounts available for low season. *Pascha Resort*, just along from the *Bang Niang Beach Resort* are a series of sea-facing wood and brick bungalows belonging to the *Pascha Resort*. The bungalows look well constructed and the garden is pleasant. About a 2 min walk to the sea. The view could be blocked by future development. **A-D** *Chong Fah Beach Resort*, 6 Moo 5 Kukkak, Petchkasem Rd, Takua Pa, T420056-9, F420055. Simple but very clean rooms with fan and bathroom, excellent Thai and international food, friendly staff. More expensive, spacious, and well-equipped a/c bungalows with large balcony, fridge, TV and hot water also available – rather characterless and in a very sparse garden of sorts. The fan rooms have nicer views. Can arrange fishing tours and diving. **C-E** *Coconut*, T420256 T01-9264567, which is just before *Pascha*, is something a bit different from the usual resort; staying at *Coconut* is more like staying in a home-stay. Acharn Pat Junkaew, the owner and retired teacher of the Phuket Teachers' College, wants to introduce visitors to the traditional lifestyles of Thailand's past. Three of the five rooms are in his house. Two "rooms" are reconstructions of traditional Thai houses from the Yaw Island in the Songkhla Lagoon (Songkhla Province). One is wood and the other bamboo. These houses are the best value, set in what feels like their own kitchen gardens. The accommodation is very simple with mosquito nets and basic bathrooms, but this is in keeping with its style. Acharn Pat is starting a small herb garden near these two rooms. He and his wife are both charming and will go out of their way to introduce guests to southern Thailand. *Coconut* comes complete with dogs, cats and chickens! No luxury, but lots of atmosphere. Recommended. **D-C** *Gerd & Noi's Sabai Bungalows*, T(01)2292197 the first bungalow outfit on your left as you come into the main area of Chong Fah Beach. A row of simple bamboo bungalows facing the sea but set back about 200 m. You can book dive trips through *High Class Adventure Diving* from their office at this bungalow outfit.

Bang Niang Beach can be reached by taking the road to Chong Fah Beach (Had Chong Fah) and then taking the dirt road off to the left, about 500 m off the main Phuket-Takua Pa Highway. The first resort you come to on the right hand side is **B-C** *The Beach Resort*, 48 Moo 5 Kukkak, Takuapa, Phangnga 82190 T420103-6 F420107. Raised concrete bungalows in a garden plot about 2 mins walk from the beach. Fan and a/c accommodation, with the higher prices for a/c rooms. All rooms have hot water showers. Swimming pool due to open in late 2000. New, clean, spacious. Friendly management. Restaurant serving Thai and western food with a good selection for breakfast. Hotel-style facilities including laundry service, gift shop, room service, airport pick-up (฿800 one way). Good value especially in low season. Motorbikes are available for rental for ฿250 a day. Next door in a small row of shops is an office for *High Class Adventure Diving*. **A-B** *Palm Andaman Beach Resort*, 59 Moo 5, Tambol Kukkak, Takuapa, Phangnga 82190, T420185-8, F420189 Large a/c bamboo cottages with airy bathrooms and an interior garden. For some reason the bamboo has been painted grey on the outside which makes the cottages look as though they are built from unpainted concrete. Generous sea-facing hardwood balconies on all bungalows. A pleasant quiet setting with a good restaurant, beach bar and soon-to-be completed pool. **C-D** *Paradise Bungalow and Restaurant*, T420184, 420254, 01-2709849, just across from the *Palm Andaman Beach Resort*, several bamboo bungalows on the beach. Larger bungalows at the front are more expensive. Very simply decorated, bathrooms are very basic. Not particularly good value. Friendly staff. Run trekking and canoeing tours to Khao Sok National Park and take bookings for *Sea Dragon Diving*. Restaurant serves the usual Western dishes (spaghetti, sandwiches, etc) and Thai food. Prices are negotiable for long-lets and during low season.

The Isthmus

Nang Thong Beach is reached by taking the road signposted Nang Thong Beach just after the Khao Lak area. The *Khao Lak Laguna Resort* and *Barn Khao Lak Resort* can be reached directly from the main road, and the road marking Nang Thong Beach is just after these resorts. This area is rapidly developing so it is worthwhile taking a look around to see if there are any new resorts. These will often give good discounts as they may not yet have a regular clientele or tour bookings. Along Highway 4 just near the turn-off to Nang Thong Beach you will also find the greatest accumulation of shops, internet facilities, and some new restaurant developments in the Khao Lak area. **A-B** *Khao Lak Tropicana Beach Resort*, T420231-40, F420240, www.khaolak-tropicana.com About 2 km along from *Nang Thong Beach* signs for the *Khao Lak Tropicana Beach Resort* direct you down a short surfaced road to the sprawling, 82-bungalow resort. Set back from the sea (the land beside the sea is owned by the government) the resort is not very imaginatively laid out and rather over-priced for average rooms. Small pool, restaurant. Can arrange tours. **A-C** *Barn Khao Lak Resort* is along from Khao Lak Laguna Resort and next to Nang Thong Bay Resort. Access is from the main road down a short dirt road. T420199, F420198, www.baankhaolak.com 28 modern, 'mimimalist'-style rooms in architect-designed bungalows. Rooms are quite sparse in decoration but pleasant and airy as are the bathrooms. A/c prices are higher than fan rooms but all rooms come with both options. If you want to pay fan rates tell the desk and they will lock the air-conditioning off. Good mosquito screens and plenty of natural light. Restaurant, pool. Can arrange tours. Good value for the area. **B** *Khao Lak Laguna Resort*, 1 km south of town at the far southern end of Nang Thong Beach accessible from the main road, T420200, F431297. A real resort with shops, barbers, etc. Very nice and spotlessly clean rooms. **B-C** *Khao Lak Andaman Beach Resort*, the northernmost resort on Nang Thong Beach, next to *Khao Lak Bungalows*, T420134-5. A huge resort with a rather boring regimented layout: rows on rows of bungalows all of the same design and facing the same way. Inside the bungalows are clean and spacious if rather boring, and a/c, hot showers etc, are all of a high standard. More expensive bungalows are near the sea. A/c and fan are available. Restaurant is on the beach, about 100 m from the main resort, in an area where some expansion is due to take place. **B-C** *Khao Lak Bungalows*, next door to the *Garden Beach Resort* at the northern end of Nang Thong Beach. Take the road signposted Nang Thong Beach and turn right at the T-junction, *Khao Lak Bungalows* is about 500 m down the road. T420145. Small beachfront restaurant, traditional Thai-style bungalows, set in jungly garden, some luxury bungalows, and family apartments. Older bungalows are a bit faded but better designed than the newer bungalows. Both fan and a/c available. The owners, Gerd and Noi, organize exotic trips (quite expensive), such as a cave tour and snorkelling/diving trips to the Similan Islands. **B-C** *Nang Thong Bay Resort I*, Km 60 Hat Nang Thong, T420088-9, F420090. Large, 2-storey restaurant with extensive menu serving European and Thai food (recommended), good-value breakfasts. 60 rooms all with bathrooms, some a/c, some fans, the manageress Yoy speaks excellent English and is very helpful. Onward bus tickets can be booked from here. **B-C** *Nang Thong Bay Resort II*, T420078-9, F420080. Take the Hat Nang Thong (Nang Thong Beach) exit off the main Phuket-Takua Pa road and turn left at the T-junction. An excellently run, if unimaginatively titled, resort. A lovely place to stay with large and immaculately kept rooms. Extensive menu in the restaurant and the beach is a stone's skim away. Quieter than *Nang Thong Bay Resort I* (the elder sister resort). **B-D** *Khao Lak Green Beach Resort* Take the road signposted Nang Thong Beach and turn right at the T-junction, this is the first resort on the left-hand side. T420043-7, F420047. Three styles of bungalows in well-shaded gardens (with fan or with a/c). The rooms are comfortable and clean and the staff friendly and helpful. Good restaurant serving mainly Thai dishes with some European favourites at the beach, and lots of picnic tables. Discounts area available for longlets. Tours can be arranged to Khao Sok National Park, and the Similan and Surin Islands. **C-D** *Garden Beach Resort*, a few minutes walk north of *Nang Thong Bay Resort I*, T7231179. Extensive menu at beachfront

£4000 worth of holiday vouchers to be won!

... that can be claimed against any exodus, Peregrine or Gecko's holiday, a choice of around 570 holidays that set industry standards for responsible tourism in 90 countries across seven continents.

exodus

The UK's leading adventurous travel company, with over 25 years' experience in running the most exciting holidays in 80 different countries. We have an unrivalled choice of trips, from a week exploring the hidden corners of Tuscany to a high altitude trek to Everest Base Camp or 3 months travelling across South America. If you want to do something a little different, chances are you'll find it in one of our brochures.

Peregrine

Australia's leading quality adventure travel company, Peregrine aims to explore some of the world's most interesting and inaccessible places. Providing exciting and enjoyable holidays that focus in some depth on the lifestyle, culture, history, wildlife, wilderness and landscapes of areas that are usually quite different to our own. There is an emphasis on the outdoors, using a variety of transport and staying in a range of accommodation, from comfortable hotels to tribal huts.

Gecko's

Gecko's holidays will get you to the best places with the minimum of hassle. They are designed for younger people who like independent travel but don't have the time to organise everything themselves. Be prepared to take the rough with the smooth, these holidays are for active people with a flexible approach to travel.

To enter the competition, simply tear out the postcard and return it to Exodus Travels, 9 Weir Road, London SW12 0LT. Or go to the competition page on www.exodus.co.uk and register online. Two draws will be made, Easter 2001 and Easter 2002, and the winner of each draw will receive £2000 in travel vouchers. The closing date for entry will be 1st March 2002. If you do not wish to receive further information about these holidays, please tick here. ☐ No purchase necessary. Plain paper entries should be sent to the above address. The prize value is non-transferable and there is no cash alternative. Winners must be over 18 years of age and must sign and adhere to operators' standard booking conditions. A list of prizewinners will be available for a period of one month from the draw by writing to the above address. For a full list of terms and conditions please write to the above address or visit our website.

To receive a brochure, please tick the relevant boxes below (maximum number of brochures 2) or telephone (44) 20 8772 3822.

exodus	Peregrine	Gecko's
☐ Walking & Trekking	☐ Himalaya	☐ Egypt, Jordan & Israel
☐ Discovery & Adventure	☐ China	☐ South America
☐ European Destinations	☐ South East Asia	☐ Africa
☐ Overland Journeys	☐ Antarctica	☐ South East Asia
☐ Biking Adventures	☐ Africa	☐ India
☐ Multi Activity	☐ Arctic	

Please give us your details:

Name: --

Address: --

Postcode: --

e-mail: --

Which footprint guide did you take this from?

----

getaway tonight on **www.exodus.co.uk**

The Different Holiday

The Different Holiday

getaway tonight on

www.exodus.co.uk

The Different Holiday

exodus

9 Weir Road
LONDON
SW12 0BR

BUSINESS REPLY SERVICE
Licence No SW4909

restaurant, mainly Thai food, but a few European favourites, all rooms have fans and attached bathroom. The bungalows closest to the beach, where guests are lulled to sleep by the sound of the waves, are more expensive. Onward bus and air tickets bookable here (see **Tours**). Rather too many bungalows, not particularly attractive design. **NB** may close from May to Oct. **C-D** *Krathom Khaolak Resort and Restaurant*, on the main Takua Pa-Phuket Rd just beyond the turn-off to Nang Thong Beach as you travel north. T420149, phutesuan@hotmail.com A nice bamboo, wood and brick restaurant and 9 clean, cosy bungalows tastefully decorated with local materials. The bungalows are set in a coconut plantation. The beach can be reached by walking through the plantation. Managed by a doctor and his son, the doctor also runs a small clinic (Dr Seree's clinic) for tourists. Friendly, helpful owners. Recommended.

Khao Lak Beach **L-A** *Khao Lak Palm Beach Resort*, 26/10 Moo 7, T. Khuk Khak, adjacent to the *Khaolak Sunset Resort* on the main road from Phuket to Takua Pa, T420099-102, F420095, www.khaolakpalmbeach.com Large, comfortable bungalows in gardens with all facilities, the attached bathrooms have step-down tiled baths and showers. Pool and restaurant overlooking the beach. The resort faces due west and is in a lovely quiet location to sit and watch the sun set. Standard rooms are probably better value than the suites, the living room of which is rather sparsely furnished. Friendly and helpful staff. **AL-A** *Khao Lak Bay Front Resort* next to the *Khao Lak Palm Beach Resort*, T420111-17, F420118, khaolak@cscoms.com Thai-style furnishings and bungalows, well equipped, all with a/c. More expensive rooms have a sea view. Beachside pool and bar. Restaurant serves Thai, Chinese, Vietnamese and European dishes. Can arrange tours in the area. *Kon Tiki Diving* has an office in a shop on the premises. Facing due West on a quiet beach. The resort looks into some splendid forest on its northern side, but it's anybody's guess how long this will last now that it has been cleared on all sides and if there is more resort development. **A-C** *Khao Lak Sunset Resort*, 26/7 Moo 7, T. Khuk Khak, A. Takuapa, at the southern end of the the Khao Lak Beach area, T420075-77, F420147, khaolaksunset @hotmail.com The more expensive rooms have beautiful views over the sea, but the management is a little haphazard for the price. Fan rooms are set back in a separate building near the road. Beachfront restaurant.

B-C *Khao Lak Nature Resort*, past *Poseidon Bungalows*, and just before the entrance to the National Park Headquarters as you travel north from Phuket. The reception is in the main restaurant (Thai and Chinese) building. T420179-81, F420182, nature_resort@hotmail.com Very new and sensitively laid out. This resort is right next to the boundary with the Khao Lak-Lam Ru National Park. 40 bungalows have been arranged so as to avoid felling any trees and are spread out up into the forest on the hill. There is a bar with a view over the bay to the west, and a steep walk down some steps to a private beach. A swimming pool and deck have been built at the top of the hill with mosquito screening for the pool! A/c rooms are available but are less appealing than the fan rooms as they can become a bit musty in the damp of the forest. All rooms have excellent mosquito screening and nice bathrooms (hot water only with the a/c rooms). Very friendly and helpful owner with an interest in the environment. Transport from Phuket airport and other transport centres can be arranged. The resort has a small open-air meeting room for the use of groups. Recommended. **C-D** *Poseidon Bungalows*, 1/6 Tambon Lam Kaen, Mu 2, Amphoe Thai Muang, T443258. 5 km south of main Khao Lak area, range of rooms, some with bathrooms and beachfronts. Restaurant built out over the sea on stilts, Thai and European food. The bungalows are situated in a sheltered bay with a secluded beach, surrounded by jungle and rubber plantations. The owners are very friendly and are a mine of local information, they can organize day and longer trips to local places of interest, boat trips and snorkelling, including a live-aboard to the Similans dedicated to snorkellers. Closes from May to Oct. Recommended.

The Isthmus

D *Phu Khao Lak*, T420140 situated on the opposite side of the road to the beach. As a result this resort is cheaper. Closed in the wet season. **D-E** *Khao Lak Resort*, Km 58 Si Takua Pa Rd, T721061. Coming from the south, through Khao Lak National Park, this is the first set of bungalows, some rooms have attached bathrooms, others are very basic. Unattractive resort, fallen into disrepair, only open in high season.

Eating   Several good restaurants attached to the bungalows, see above. A row of **foodstalls** can be found next to the Information Stand, on the beach. **Cheap** *Khao Lak Restaurant*, on the main road, Thai, International and American breakfast (see **Tours**). Restaurants in the Ruen Mai complex on the main road to Takua Pa in the Nang Thong area. Tiny bar/snack shop on the beach run by Thai fishermen – no English spoken.

Bars   There are bars at most of the larger bungalow establishments and at Ruen Mai on the main road to Takua Pa in the Nang Thong area. Beach bars can be found next to *Khao Lak Green Beach Resort*, and on the beach at Bang Niang and the northern end of Chong Fah. A 'sunset' bar on the promotory overlooking the whole Khao Lak area is to be found at the *Khao Lak Nature Resort*.

Sport   **Diving**: the *Sea Dragon*, *Phuket Dive* and *Kon Tiki* all offer diving to the Similan and Surin Islands. They have offices near and in various resorts along the coast from Khao Lak to Chong Fah. The Swiss-run *Kon Tiki*, Laguna Centre is a well organised dive shop and comes recommended.

Transport   **Local Jeeps**: for hire from *Nang Thong Resort* and from *Garden Beach Resort*, ฿800
80 km N of Phuket   per day. **Motorbikes**: for hire from *Nang Thong Resort* and from *Garden Beach Resort* and from *Khao Lak Restaurant*, ฿200 per day.

Road Bus: some a/c and non-a/c connections with the Southern terminal in Bangkok. Departs 1900, about 13 hrs. From Krabi and Phangnga, take a bus towards Phuket and change at Kochloi to a bus running north towards Takua Pa and Ranong. From Phuket take a local bus to Takua Pa or an a/c bus towards Ranong. Be careful – it is easy to miss this place, there is no actual sign on the roadside, but there are signs for the guesthouses. It is a 5 min walk from the road through a rubber plantation to the beach. Many buses now travel on a new road which bypasses Khao Lak and goes straight to Phangnga town, and then on to Phuket. Check that your bus passes through Khao Lak/Takua Pa/Ranong. Different bus companies have different routes.

Directory   **Banks**   At *Nang Thong Resort*. **Communications**   Internet: services can be found in the Nang Thong area and at certain resorts (eg *Khao Lak Sunset*). **Post Office**: the nearest Post Office is at Lam Kaen, a small village 5 km south of Khao Lak. Banks, shops and post offices can also be found in Takua Pa and Thai Muang, both 30 km north and south of Khao Lak respectively.

Khao Sok National Park

Colour map 4, grid A2   Khao Sok National Park is bordered by the Sri Phangnga National Park to the
Phone code: 076   west, the Khao Phanom National Park to the south, and the Khlong Saen and Khlong Nakkha Wildlife Sanctuaries to the north. It is part of the largest protected area in Southern Thailand. The total area protected is 4,400 sq km making this a core conservation area for Southeast Asia. The National Park spreads across Surat Thani and Phangnga provinces. The closest town is Takua Pa but many companies from Phuket, Phangnga, Krabi and Surat operate day and overnight tours. (Try to take an overnight tour, as otherwise it's a long drive with little time to explore the national park and not really worth the money.)

With its dramatic limestone karst mountains (the tallest reaches over 900 m), low mountains covered with evergreen forest, streams and waterfalls, and a large reservoir and dam, Khao Sok has it all. The impressive scenery alone would be a good enough reason to visit, but Khao Sok also has a high degree of endemism (ie many species found in Khao Sok can be found here alone), and an exceptionally large number of mammals, birds, reptiles and other fauna. The list of 48 confirmed species of mammals include: wild elephants, tigers, barking deer, langur, macaques, civets, bears, gibbons and clouded leopards. Of the 184 confirmed bird species, perhaps the most dramatic include: the rhinoceros hornbill, the great hornbill, the Malayan peacock pheasant and the crested serpent-eagle. The plants to be found there are also of considerable interest. If you visit between December and February, the Rafflesia Kerri Meijer (found only in Khao Sok) is in flower. This parasitic flower (it depends on low-lying lianas) has an 80-cm bloom which smells of rotting flesh! There are also at least two palms endemic to the Khao Sok area.

In the centre of the park is the Rachabrapah Reservoir. Near the dam there is a longhouse of sorts, and several houseboats. Tours can be taken to the dam area for day trips or for overnight stays. Visitors to Khao Sok should, of course, be aware that one has to be extremely lucky or very experienced to see wild animals, particularly in evergreen forest such as is found in the south of Thailand. However, for Khao Sok, the best location for animal spotting is near the reservoir where grassland at the edge of the reservoir attract animals. If you really want to get into the forest, it is probably a good idea to take an overnight tour into the park with an experienced guide. Tours are available from virtually all the various bungalows near the park. Park rangers will also act as guides. Have a chat with your intended guide before you make up your mind to go so you can be sure you feel comfortable about the level of English (or other languages) they speak, familiarity with the park, and general knowledge of the environment and wildlife. Expect to pay from ฿300 per person for a guide to take you on a day trek, and around ฿2,000 per person for an overnight trip to the reservoir (this includes accommodation and all meals. **NB** prices will vary depending on how many people are in the group). In addition to camping, canoeing and walking tours, you can take elephant treks at Khao Sok. The routes taken must be outside the park, however, as elephant trekking is not permitted within the confines of the national park.

To get more enjoyment out of the park we recommend the excellent book written by Thom Henley: *Waterfalls and gibbon calls: exploring Khao Sok National Park*. This is available in various outlets in Southern Thailand, from the visitors centre at Khao Sok National Park, and from many of the bungalow operators at Khao Sok. It is well worth the ฿470 it costs, containing a background to the park, local histories, descriptions and lists of the fauna and flora found there, maps, guides to interpretive trails and some notes on accommodation.

Sleeping There is a well-developed tourism business centred on Khao Sok, and visitors have a considerable degree of choice in how they travel to the park and where they stay. There are several bungalow operations near the park headquarters and new operations seem to be sprouting up every year in the general area. Prices range from around ฿200 to about ฿800. Particularly noteworthy are *Art's Riverview Lodge, Khao Sok Rainforest Resort*, and *Our Jungle House. Art's Riverview Lodge* F421614, or write to Art's Riverview Jungle Lodge PO Box 28, Takuapa, Phangnga 82110 Thailand) has a range of rooms some built like Thai houses with several rooms together, all have simple bathrooms, mosquito nets, etc. The only lighting provided is in the form of candles. The reception area and restaurant is right beside the river near a swimming hole. *Our Jungle House*, T01-8939583, F421706, our_jungle_house@hotmail.com is also right on a river bend with several styles of accommodation. The Thai managers are very friendly and helpful and the setting is peaceful and inviting with the central Thai-style house and restaurant set in a large park-like garden. The *Khao Sok Rainforest Resort*, the first resort on the left as you go down the entrance to the park, is located right next to the forest (most other bungalows are off to the right as you go towards the entrance and are near orchards and fields). This provides excellent opportunities to see birds and other wildlife from your room!

Further afield, the **B-C** *Khao Sok Riverside Cottages*, Km 106.5 (Highway 401), T01-2293750, F075-612544, is a simple but stylish alternative. About 2.5 km down a dirt road off the main Takua Pa-Phun Phin road, east of the National Park Headquarters, there are several wooden and bamboo cottages dispersed through an area of forest on a small hill beside a bend in the river. The restaurant, right beside the river, serves very good, simple Thai food. Cottages with twin beds are slightly larger and more expensive than doubles (prices include breakfast). The cottages are delightful, built using traditional materials, with lots of windows, spacious balconies and clean bright bathrooms. The manager and designer of the resort, Khun Daycho, is the president of the local conservation group. *Khao Sok Riverside Cottages* run walking tours and elephant trekking to forest adjacent to the resort (not actually in the National Park) and also do overnight camping and day visits to the lake.

Transport Tours are run from most tourism centres from Phangnga, Phuket, Krabi and Surat Thani. Alternatively, take a local bus from Takua Pa to Phun Phin near Surat Thani town, or vice versa, and ask the driver to stop at the Khao Sok National Park (*oo-tayaan-haeng-chart-khao-sok*). When you arrive at the stop there will frequently be a number of bungalow operators waiting to whisk you off to their establishment, or you can walk, take transport into the park. If you decide to walk take a small pack as it's quite a hike to some bungalows! Incidentally the drive from Takua Pa to Panom (about halfway between Takua Pa and Surat) is very scenic with views of dramatic limestone karst, forested mountains and valleys.

The Andaman Sea Coast

6

The Andaman Sea Coast

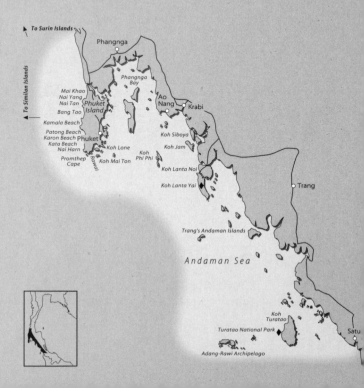

From a tourism perspective, Phuket dominates this portion of southern Thailand. Originally an island which built its wealth on tin and rubber, Phuket metamorphosed into a beach resort during the 1970s. From modest backpacker beginnings, it exploded into a centre attracting international visitors from the very deep-pocketed to those of more modest means. Over time, budget accommodation has been squeezed out and budget travellers have now moved on to quieter and cheaper corners of the South. It is still, though, a beautiful island which has the bonus of fine hotels and a great range of amenities.

But there is more to the area than just Phuket and the coast here is probably more suited to visitors with a yen for tropical seaside idylls than anywhere else in Thailand. Phangnga Bay has spectacular limestone scenery and the area around Krabi has developed to exploit these natural advantages. The island of Phi Phi and more recently Lanta have expanded their tourist infrastructure – sometimes excessively so – and enterprising tour companies provide varied activities from sea canoe safaris to rock climbing, scuba diving and deep-sea fishing. Small, family-run bungalows and cafés offer a refreshing counterpoint to the more commercialized atmosphere of Phuket.

Travelling further south along Thailand's Andaman Sea coast to the town of Trang and yet more islands and beach destinations open up. Trang's offshore islands and the islands of the Turatao National Park provide alternative, and more pristine, destinations – although the seasons here limit travel to the months between November and April.

Phuket Island

Phone code: 076
Colour map 4, grid B1

Phuket, Thailand's premier resort island, lies on the west coast of the Kra Isthmus in the warm Andaman Sea and is connected to the mainland by the 700 m-long Sarasin causeway. The name Phuket is derived from the Malay word bukit, *meaning hill, and it is Thailand's only island to have provincial status. Known as the 'Pearl of Thailand' because of its shape, it measures 21 km at its widest point, and is 48 km long. With a land area of 550 sq km, it is about the same size as Singapore – making it Thailand's largest island.*

Ins and outs

Getting there   Phuket is nearly 900 km south of Bangkok. Even so, it is well connected and getting to the island is easy – especially if you are willing to pay for the air fare. Phuket International Airport is in the north of the island, about 30 km from Phuket Town, but rather closer to many of the main beaches and hotels. There are international connections with Hong Kong, Kuala Lumpur, Singapore, Penang, Taipei and Tokyo, as well as Munich and Dusseldorf. There are multiple daily connections on THAI with Bangkok as well as connections with Koh Samui (on Bangkok Airways), Chiang Mai and Hat Yai. The southern railway line doesn't come to the island. However it is possible to take a train to Phun Phin near Surat Thani and then catch a connecting bus. The main bus terminal is in Phuket Town and there are regular connections with Bangkok (a long 14 hrs) as well as destinations in the South.

Getting around   Buses run from Phuket Town to all the beaches at regular intervals from 0600 to 1800. There are also numerous places to hire cars and motorbikes as well as mini vans that can be used as meterless taxis.

History

Phuket was first 'discovered' by Arab and Indian navigators around the end of the ninth century, although it is said to have been marked on charts as far back as the first century. The first Europeans (Dutch pearl traders), arrived in the 16th century. **Phuket Town**, the island's capital in the southeast, was built in the middle of the last century to replace Thalang, which had been destroyed by the Burmese in 1800.

Historically, the province derived much of its wealth from tin production. Phuket was first mentioned as a major source of tin in the mid-16th century (when it was known as Junkceylon). Modern tin-mining methods were introduced by the Englishman Captain Edward Miles in 1907, with elephants living on the island transporting the ore from the mines to the smelting works. Such was the wealth generated that Phuket Town was probably the first place in all Thailand to have paved roads and cars, around 1910. Today, Phuket remains the centre of tin production in Thailand although tourism has far-and-away exceeded tin in its contribution to the province's gross regional product. Rubber (which

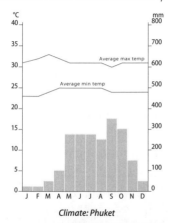

Climate: Phuket

A Thai curse on Malaysia

There have always been close trading relations between the former Malay sultanates and the south of Thailand. It was only during the colonial period that Siam lost suzerainty over the northern Malaysian states. But in 2000, the Malaysian authorities in Langkawi invited the seventh generation descendant of a Thai woman who lived – and died – in Langkawi over 200 years ago to visit the island. It was hoped this might bring to an end a curse that had been hanging over the island.

Around two centuries ago a Thai couple from Phuket settled on Langkawi. The woman, Mahsuri, was particularly gorgeous and the dowdy female population of Langkawi grew jealous. When her husband left the island on a war campaign the wife of a village leader unjustly accused Mahsuri of adultery and she was sentenced to death. Stabbed with a ceremonial kris, her blood flowed white – proving her innocence – and as she died she cursed Langkawi to seven generations of barrenness. Shortly after Mahsuri's execution, a Siamese force attacked Langkawi and killed most of the inhabitants. Mahsuri's family left and returned to Phuket.

And that is where 14 year-old Aishah Mawawi, the daughter of a tuk-tuk driver, comes into the picture. She is the seventh generation descendant of Mahsuri (who had given birth to one son before she was so foully accused and executed). Aishah was invited to Langkawi to put to rest the curse of her ancestors. Aishah may not be Malaysian, she may not even speak Malay, but she is Muslim. Crowds greeted Aisah's arrival in Langkawi where she was said – spookily – to look like her ancestor. (Long memories in Langkawi.) She had audiences with Prime Minister Mahathir and the Sultan of Kedah, and has been interviewed on television. She has also been offered Malaysian citizenship, a free house and a job.

accounts for 29% of the land area), coconut, and fisheries also all contribute to the island's wealth. Indeed, the inhabitants of Phuket are among the wealthiest in Thailand, a fact reflected in the richly endowed temples. This does not mean, though, that there are not poor people on Phuket. Indeed, in 1995, strike action by employees at one of the island's hotels was agreed – the first time, apparently, in Phuket's history – because wages were felt to be too low to sustain a reasonable standard of living. The population of the province has risen from 6,000 in the early 1900s, to 140,000, with five times that number of visitors every year.

Phuket offers little in the way of sights of historical interest, but much of natural beauty, although the wild elephants, rhinos and tigers which once roamed the island have long since been killed. There are national parks, long sandy beaches (particularly on the west coast), good snorkelling and diving, peaceful coconut groves and rubber plantations, and some traditional (well, -ish) villages. Phuket seems big enough to absorb large numbers of tourists and still maintain a semblance of 'tradition' in some areas – although Thai and *farang* tourism activists would dispute this vehemently.

Sights

There are a handful of historical and cultural sights around the island. South of Phuket Town, down Sakdidej Road which becomes Route 4023, in the grounds of the *Cape Panwa Sheraton Hotel*, is **Panwa House**, a fine example of Sino-Portuguese architecture. At the tip of Panwa Cape is the **Marine Biological Research Centre and Aquarium**. The air-conditioned aquarium is well laid out, with a moderate collection of salt and fresh water fish, lobsters, molluscs and turtles. ■ *Mon-Sun 0830-1600, ฿20, T391128.* Getting there: there are regular public *songthaews* every hour (฿10) from the market area on

South of Phuket Town

The Andaman Sea Coast

● ●

Phuket Island place names

Bang Pae Waterfall
น้ำตกบางแพ

Khao Phra Thaeo Wildlife Park
อุทยานสัตว์ป่าเขาพระแทว

Thalang National Museum
พิพิธภัณฑสถานแห่งชาติถลาง

Tha Rua
ท่าเรือ

Wat Chalong
วัดบุญทวี

Wat Phranang Sang
วัดพระนางสร้าง

Wat Phra Thong
วัดพระทอง

● ●

Ranong Rd to the Aquarium. It is possible to charter **long-tailed boats** from here to **Koh Hii** (฿600) and **Koh Mai Ton** (฿1200) or to go fishing (฿1200).

Six kilometres south of Phuket Town, just north of Chalong Junction, is the ostentatious **Wat Chalong**, best known for its gold-leaf encrusted statues of the previous abbots, Luang Pho Chaem and Luang Pho Chuang. The former was highly respected for his medical skills, which proved to be particularly valuable when Phuket's Chinese miners revolted in 1876. The halving of the international price of tin coupled with Bangkok's attempt to extract excessive taxes from the province raised the ire of the Chinese. Some 2,000 gathered around the governor's house, and when they failed to take the building turned their attention to the less well-defended villages. The spree of killing and looting was only finally brought to an end at Wat Chalong.

North of Phuket Town Twelve kilometres north from Phuket Town on Route 402, towards the airport, is the village of **Tha Rua**. At the crossroads there is a statue of two female warriors: **Muk** and **Chan**. These sisters helped to repel an army of Burmese invaders in 1785 by dressing up all the women of the town as men, so fooling the Burmese. Rama I awarded them titles for their deeds, and they are celebrated in bronze, swords drawn. The statue was erected in 1966 and Thais rub gold-leaf on its base as a sign of respect and to gain merit. The **Thalang National Museum** is just east of this crossroads on Route 4027. It has a well-presented collection, displaying various facets of Phuket's history and culture. ■ *Wed-Sat 0900-1600, ฿30.* Also in Thalang is the extraordinary **Wat Phranang Sang**. Designed as if the architect did not know what he was building, this monastery is surrounded by a modern crenellated castle wall. Inside the wall, a statue of the Chinese goddess Kuan Yin, encircled by a dragon, stands in front of a particularly gaudy bot (ordination hall). This place is worth visiting – if in Thalang anyway – for its highly syncretic interpretation of Theravada Buddhism.

Continuing north on Route 402, just beyond the district town of Thalang, is **Wat Phra Thong**, surrounded by life-sized concrete animals. The wat contains a buried Buddha image, with just its head protruding from the ground, covered in gold-leaf. Legend has it that shortly after a boy had tethered his buffalo to a post, they both fell mysteriously ill. On excavating the post, villagers discovered this golden Buddha. It is believed that anyone trying to disinter the image will meet with a disaster – Burmese invaders attempted to do so in 1785 and they were attacked by a swarm of hornets. There is also a museum here with a bizarre and motley collection: Chinese porcelain, an old typewriter, sea shells, mouldering books, faded photographs, animal heads and, in the centre of the room, an old gramophone with a 78 of Victor Sylvester singing *Why did she fall for the leader of the band?* on the turntable.

The Andaman Sea Coast

Sea, water and weather conditions on Phuket

November-April *Fair seas with morning breezes of 15-20 knots, lessening as the day wears on. Winds increasing during March and April. Water conditions and visibility best during these months.* **May-October** *Moderate winds and seas.*

Squalls becoming more common from June. Seas can be rough and water conditions and visibility suffer accordingly. Stiff currents and rip tides on the West Coast – observe warning flags and ask about conditions daily.

Khao Phra Thaeo Wildlife Park lies 20 km from Phuket Town. Turn east off the main road in Thalang and follow signs for Ton Sai Waterfall. This beautiful, peaceful road winds through stands of rubber trees and degraded forest. The park supports wild boar and monkeys and represents the last remnant of the island's natural forest ecosystem. The **Ton Sai Waterfall** is located within the park, but is really only worth a visit during the rainy season; even then the falls are a bit of a disappointment. There are bungalows and a lakeside restaurant here, and a number of hiking routes. Visitors can paddle in the upper pool. ■ *0600-1800.*

Khao Phra Thaeo Wildlife Park

The road east from the waterfall becomes rough and can only be negotiated on foot or by motorbike. This track leads to **Bang Pae Waterfall**. Alternatively, the falls can be approached from the other direction, by turning off Route 4027 and driving 1 km along a dirt track. There is a beautiful lake, refreshment stands, forest trails, and bathing pools. ■ *0600-1800.* Just south of the waterfall is a **Gibbon Centre**; a rehabilitation centre for these endangered animals funded from the US and apparently the only such initiative in Southeast Asia. Follow signs off Route 4027. Also off Route 4027, at **Ao Poh**, there is a long wooden jetty where boat tours leave for Naka Noi Island and Pearl Farm – Thailand's largest (see below).

Most people do not go to Phuket for history or culture. They go for **beaches**, and in this respect the island is hard to beat. Its size, and the length of its beaches means that it is still possible to find a peaceful spot to sunbathe. The best beaches are on the west coast, although the resort of Patong is far from peaceful. The east coast is rocky and fringed with mangroves and the beaches are poor for swimming. There are now some excellent luxury hotels on Phuket; the island is no longer a haven for backpackers – most have moved on to cheaper locations such as Phi Phi, Samui and Lanta. That said, it is still possible (just) to stay relatively cheaply on Phuket.

Beaches *Details of the various beaches are given after the section on Phuket Town*

In order to explore some of the sights mentioned above, it is best to hire a motorbike or jeep for the day. A suggested route might run north from Phuket Town or east from Patong to Tha Rua, the Heroines' Monument and the National Museum at Thalang. Take a side trip to Ton Sai Waterfall and the National Park, then continue north on Route 402, before turning left for Nai Yang Beach and National Park. Crossing Route 402, drive east through rubber plantations, taking in Bang Pae Waterfall, before returning to the main road at the Heroines' Monument. A half to one day trip.

Tour by motorbike or jeep

Koh Yao Noi and **Koh Yao Yai** are two largish islands to the east of Phuket Island. They remain untouched by the tourist industry and hold a scattering of fishing villages. There is good diving off the islands and many dive shops run expeditions out here. ■ *Getting there: boats leave from the village of Ban Rong.*

Excursions

Full-day tours to **Phi Phi** (see page 301) are organized by *Aloha Tour, Cruise Centre, Pee Pee Hydrocraft* (฿750), *Silver Queen*, and *Songserm Travel* (who

Tours

The Andaman Sea Coast

Phuket Island

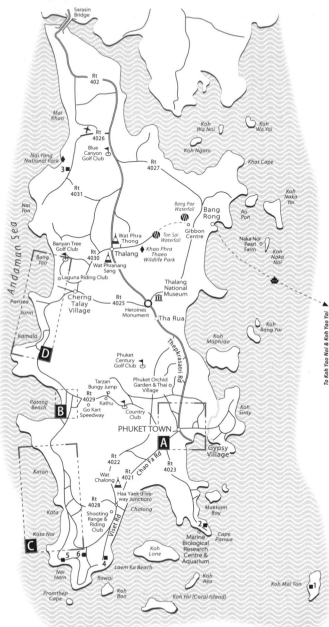

Rt 402

Sarasin Bridge

Mai Khao

Rt 4026

Blue Canyon Golf Club

Nai Yang National Park

3

Rt 4031

Rt 4027

Koh Wa Noi

Koh Wa Yai

Koh Ngam

Khat Cape

Nai Ton

Andaman Sea

Koh Nai Yai

Ao Poh

Bang Pae Waterfall

Bang Rong

Banyan Tree Golf Club

Rt 4030

Wat Phra Thong

Ton Sai Waterfall

Gibbon Centre

Naka Noi Pearl Farm

Thalang

Khao Phra Thaeo Wildlife Park

Koh Naka Noi

Bang Tao

Wat Phranang Sang

Laguna Riding Club

Pansea

Cherng Talay Village

Rt 4025

Thalang National Museum

Koh Rang Yai

Surin

Heroines Monument

Tha Rua

Koh Maphrao

Kamala

D

Phuket Century Golf Club

Thepkasatri Rd

Phuket Orchid Garden & Thai Village

Tarzan Bungy Jump

Patong Beach

Rt 4029

Kathu

Go Kart Speedway

Country Club

Koh Siray

B

PHUKET TOWN

A

Gypsy Village

Karon

Rt 4022

Chao Fa Rd

Rt 4023

Wat Chalong

Rt 4021

Haa Yaek (Five-way Junction)

Rt 4028

Chalong

Makham Bay

Kata

Shooting Range & Riding Club

Viset Rd

2

Marine Biological Research Centre & Aquarium

Cape Panwa

Kata Noi

C

5 6

4

Koh Lone

Nai Harn

Rawai

Laem Ka Beach

Koh Aeo

Koh Mai Ton

1

Promthep Cape

Koh Bon

Koh Hii (Coral Island)

To Koh Yao Noi & Koh Yao Yai

The Andaman Sea Coast

N

0 km 2
0 miles 2

■ **Sleeping**

1 Mai Ton Resort
2 Panwa House & Cape Panwa Sheraton Hotel
3 Pearl Village

4 Phuket Island Resort
5 Phuket Yacht Club
6 Rawai Garden Resort

operate a large catamaran called the *King Cruiser*). Day trips to Phi Phi are also available on the *Andaman Queen*, T215261, leaving at 0830 (฿750-950).

Similan Islands (see page 276). Full-day tours leave from Chalong or Patong beaches. *Phuket Travel and Tour Co* and *Songserm Travel* (T222570), organize tours for about ฿1,500, which includes a tour of the reef in a glass bottomed boat, lunch, and dinner on the boat back to Phuket. Many other tour companies in Phuket Town and on Patong Beach organize similar tours.

Phangnga Bay (see page 280). A day trip costs about ฿650.

Coral Island (Koh Hii) Full-day tours include swimming, snorkelling and fishing. Regular boats leave from Chalong Bay, 0930, ฿50 per person one way. Chartered boats leave from Chalong, Rawai and Laem Ka, ฿600 per person including hotel transfer, lunch, snorkelling equipment, etc, T218060, F381957.

Naka Noi Island and the Pearl Farm Boats leave from Ao Poh, in the northeast of the island, for the 15-minute-trip at 1030 daily. Tours, including admission to the Pearl Farm and a 'demonstration,' cost ฿500, T219870 for information. ■ *Pearl Farm open Mon-Sun 0900-1530.* Accommodation available at bungalow resort. **NB** Ensure your visit is to Naka Noi, rather than Naka Yai, where the 'Pearl Farm' seems to be a fake.

Tour by glass-bottomed boat Two-hour cruises in the Andaman Sea, ฿300 (or on a chartered basis for ฿5,000 per two hours).

Yacht charter from November-May, boats can be chartered to sail around Phuket. *Thai Yachting Co*, B1-2 Patong View Plaza, 94 Patong Beach (Thaweewong) Rd, T341253, depending on the number of people in the party, a week's trip costs about US$2,000, including meals, professional crew, transfers, fishing and snorkelling equipment. *South East Asia Yacht Charter*, 89 Patong Beach (Thaweewong) Rd, T340460, four- to seven-day diving tours to Similan and Surin Islands, PADI diving courses also available.

Nature tours There is not much 'nature' left on Phuket but nonetheless *Phuket Nature Tours*, 5/15 Chao Fah Road, T225522, F215126, have managed to climb on board the eco-tourism bandwagon and offer tours to forests, rice fields, villages, plantations, secluded beaches and so on. *Siam Safari* offer *Eco Nature Tours*, T213881, F210972; a similar set up to the above. *Etc Asia*, www.ultimate -asia.com also offer nature and other tours.

Diving The warm, clear water off Phuket is rich in marine life, and affords excellent diving opportunities. Dive centres – over 25 of them – will normally offer introductory courses for those who have never dived before, leading to one of the internationally recognized certificates (such as PADI and NAUI). For an open water course

The Andaman Sea Coast

Phuket's Romeo and Juliet

At the end of the 1970s a tragic love story unfolded in Phuket. A poor school bus driver with few prospects and a school girl from a middle-class family fell in love. Realizing that society would never let them stay together, the two lovers tied themselves together and threw themselves off the Sarasin Bridge into the strong currents that flow through the narrow waters that separate Phuket from the mainland. Since then numerous Thai singers and film makers, attracted by the tragedy of a love affair that never stood a chance, have mined the story for artistic material. But the tragedy did not end with the lovers' deaths. The girl's parents suffered not just the grief of their young daughter's suicide, but also the accusation of neighbours that they had brought about the suicide pact by forbidding the relationship.

the cost is about ฿8,000-10,000. The course stretches over four days, beginning in a hotel pool and ending on a reef. A simple introductory dive, fully supervised, will cost ฿1,500-2,000 (one dive) to ฿2,000-2,500 (two dives). For those with diving experience there are a range of tours from single day, two-dive outings to dive spots like Koh Phi Phi, Koh Raja Yai and Koh Raja Noi (both due south of Phuket), and Shark Point (off to the east of Phuket); to one-week expeditions to offshore islands such as the Similan and Surin Islands. Prices vary, but a day-trip to Phi Phi with two dives should cost about ฿2,500-3,000 per person, and to the Similans about ฿3,000-3,500 per person. Four days and three nights, around ฿11,000-12,000 (eight dives) and five days and four nights about ฿14,000 (10 dives). Snorkelling is good on the outer islands; the waters around Phuket Island itself are mediocre. It is best to catch one of the boat tours to Phi Phi Island for the day and snorkel on either side of the land bridge that separates the two halves of Phi Phi Don (see page 303). But even here, development has reduced the clarity of the waters. For the best snorkelling and diving it is necessary to go to the Similan Islands.

Best time to visit The driest months are November-April, which also have the most sunshine. May to October are wetter with more chance of overcast conditions, although daily sunshine still averages five to eight hours.

Essentials

Sleeping Phuket has literally hundreds of places to stay, largely at the upper price end. See individual areas for listings. **NB** During the low season (Jun-Oct) room rates may be as little as half the high season price. All rates quoted are high season. It is recommended that visitors book hotel rooms during high season (particularly at Christmas and New Year).

Entertainment **Thai cookery courses** At the *Boathouse Inn Cookery School*, Kata Beach, T2514707 (see Kata Beach accommodation for full address).

Festivals March *Thao Thep Kasattri and Thao Sisunthon Fair* (13th). An annual fair held to celebrate the the 2 female warriors, better known as Muk and Chan, who helped repel an army of Burmese invaders in 1785 (see page 250).
April *Fish Releasing Festival* timed to coincide with Songkran or Thai new year (see page 276). Baby turtles are released at several of Phuket's beaches.
May *Seafood Festival* not much of a festival; more of a tourism PR junket which is meant to celebrate Phuket's wealth of seafood. Lots of carved ice-sculptures, piles of lobsters and mussels, and so on.
July *Marathon* (2nd week).

Diving in Phuket

Diving in Phuket is regarded as top quality because of the combination of number of dive shops (over 25), the professionalism of the instructors, the range of dive sites, and the variety of other entertainment and facilities from excellent hotels to superb food.

Dive sites within easy reach of Phuket Shark point and **Koh Dok Mai** are 1 hour and 1½ hours east of Phuket Island. As the name of the former indicates, this site is known for its sharks and has been declared a marine sanctuary. Koh Dok Mai offers a good wall dive. Depth: 10-27 metres; visibility: fair to excellent. The twin Rajah islands (Rajah Yai and Rajah Noi – Big and Little Rajah) lie due south of Phuket, about 1½-2 hours by boat. Raja Noi

attracts large schools of skipjack tuna and barracuda and Rajah Yai is known for the clarity of its water. There are hard and soft corals and steep drop-offs. Depth: 10-35 metres; visibility: good to excellent. Less good, but better for non-divers and snorkelling is **Coral Island**, 40 minutes by boat south of Phuket. The **Phi Phi Islands** are another popular dive site. See page 301 for further details.

Dive sites further afield Perhaps the finest diving, however, is to be found off the **Surin and Similan Islands** in the Andaman Sea, to the west of Phuket. Diving here requires an overnight stay, but many dive shops organize trips. See page 276 for further details on the two groups of islands.

See page 301 for further details.

See page 276 for further details on the two groups of islands.

October *Chinese Vegetarian Festival* or *Ngan Kin Jeh* (movable), lasts 9 days and marks the beginning of Taoist lent. No meat is eaten, alcohol consumed nor sex indulged in (in order to cleanse the soul) and men pierce their cheeks or tongues with long spears and other sharp objects and walk over hot coals and (supposedly) feel no pain. The festival is celebrated elsewhere, but most enthusiastically in Phuket, and especially at Wat Jui Tui on Ranong Rd in Phuket Town (see box). This must be one of the star attractions of a visit to Phuket. Visitors are made to feel welcome and to take part in the event.

November *Phuket Travel Fair* (1st). Another ersatz PR event designed to raise Phuket's tourism profile. More activity than during May's Seafood festival though.

December *King's Cup Regatta* (5th). Yachting competition in the Andaman Sea, timed to coincide with the King's birthday (the King is a yachtsman of international repute). The event attracts competitors from across the world.

Diving centres The greatest concentration of diving companies is to be found along Patong Beach Rd, on Kata and Karon beaches, at Ao Chalong and in Phuket Town. **Phuket Town**: *Phuket Aquatic Safaris*, 62/9 Rasada Centre, Rasada Rd, T216562. *Andaman Sea Diving*, 3rd Flr, Tian Sin Bldg, 54 Phuket Rd, T215766. **Patong**, all on the Beach Rd: *Ocean Divers*, Patong Beach Hotel, T321166, or T341273, F340625. *Scuba Cats*, Beach Rd, T293120. *Pioneer Diving Asia*, Patong Beach, T342508. *Santana*, Sawatdirak Rd, T294220. *Andaman Divers*, T321155. *Fantasea Divers*, T340088, F340309 (instructors for English, French, German and Japanese); *South East Asia*, T340406 (instructors for English, French, Swedish, Italian and German). **Kata/Karon**: *Siam Diving Centre*, Kata-Karon Beach, T330936 (instructors for English and Swedish); *Kon Tiki*, T396312. *Marina Cottage*, Kata Beach, T381625. *Phuket International Diving Centre (PIDC)*, Le Meridien, Karon Noi Beach, T321480. **Chalong**: *Sea Bees Diving*, T381765

Canoeing: *Sea Canoe* (who also operate from Krabi and Phi Phi), and *Andaman Sea Kayak*, hire out specially designed 2-man canoes to explore the grottoes, capes and bays that line Phuket's coast but which are often not accessible by road. Day trips cost about ฿2,500-3,000; 6-day expeditions, all inclusive, ฿24,000. For *Sea Canoe* T/F212172.

Sport

The Andaman Sea Coast

Phuket's festival of mortification

The Chinese Vegetarian Festival or Ngan Kin Jeh *is said to have its origins about 150 years ago when a Chinese opera troupe's visit to the island coincided with a terrible plague. The artistes decided it was in some way connected with their pre-performance rituals and they sent one of the cast back to China to light and bring to Phuket a vast jos stick. In this way, the Nine Emperor Gods of China might be invited to Phuket in order to cure the population of the plague. They succeeded, so it is said, and today's festival commemorates the event.*

To open the proceedings, participants light candles and lanterns to invite the Nine Emperor Gods to return to Phuket. The first four days of the festival are comparatively peaceful and ordinary – as festivals go. It is during the last five days that events, for most foreigners, turn really weird. Each of the five Chinese temples or pagodas of Phuket Town in turn arranges a procession. Devotees show their commitment and the power of the Nine Emperor Gods by piercing their cheeks, tongues and various other parts of their anatomy. The processions end in a large field where razor ladders, caldrons of boiling oil, and pits of red-hot embers await the supplicants. Most appear to get off relatively lightly, although in some years tourists – possibly excessively carried away with the festivities – also try their hand (or their feet, or their cheeks) at such mortifications, and end up severely injured.

On the ninth day, a crowd of thousands converge on Saphan Hin to the south of Phuket Town (see page 258), and offerings are cast into the sea, thereby allowing the Nine Emperor Gods to return to their heavenly abode, and many of the participants to return home and eat a meal of meat.

Andaman Sea Kayak, T235353, F235353. **Santana Canoeing**, 92/18 Sawatdirak Rd, Patong, T340360. River canoeing through the jungle as well as sea canoeing. **Fishing**: *Big Game Fishing*, Phuket Sport Fishing Centre, Patong Beach, T214713, F330680. *Ao Chalong Game Fishing*, Chalong Beach, T280996. **Golf**: *Blue Canyon*, to the north of the island, near the airport, T327440, F327449. The most expensive, but also the best course on the island. *Phuket Country Club*, Route 4029 to Patong, T321025, F321721. *Phuket Century*, in the middle of the island, T321929, F321928. *Banyan Tree*, part of the Laguna Phuket Complex, a new course, so it needs time to 'mature', T324350, F324351. *Thai Muang Beach*, north of Phuket on the coast, T571533, F571214. Part of a new complex with hotel, sports facilities, etc. **Paintball**: *Asia 'Top Gun'*, Ao Chalong Shooting Range, Kata Rd, T381667. Open Mon-Sun 0900-1800, ฿275 for 25 round game. **Riding**: *Laguna Riding Club*, Bang Tao Bay, just before Phuket Laguna complex, T324009. Open Mon-Sun. *Phuket Riding Club*, south of Chalong Circle on Viset Road, T288213. Open Mon-Sun 0700-1100 and 1400-1830. *Crazy Horse Club*, look out for signs near Nai Harn Bay from Rawai, open 0800-1700, ride through jungle or on the beach. **Swimming**: swimming and snorkelling are safe from Nov to Apr when the sea is calm. But during the monsoon between May and Oct, there can be strong surf and undertows – especially after storms. Swimmers should check the beaches for red flags, which indicate whether conditions are dangerous. **Sailing**: Phuket is an important sailing centre and many boats pick up and drop off crew here. The *Kanda Bakery*, 31-33 Rasada Road, in Phuket Town have a notice board advertising crewing opportunities.

Transport
890 km S of Bangkok

Local Bus: for Patong, Kamala, Surin, Makham Bay, Nai Yang, Kata, Karon, Nai Harn, Rawai, Thalang and Chalong buses leave every 30 mins between 0600 and 1800 from the market on Ranong Rd in Phuket Town. Fares range from ฿20 to whatever the ticket collector thinks he can get away with. **Car hire**: jeeps can be hired from small outfits along most beaches, expect to pay ฿600-1,200 per day, depending on age of car, etc. **Avis** has an office opposite Phuket airport, T311358 and desks at various hotels including *Le Meridien*, the *Holiday Inn*, the *Phuket Cabana* (all on Patong Beach), the *Dusit Laguna* (on Bang Tao Beach) and the *Metropole* (in Phuket Town) (฿1,200 per day, ฿7,200 per week). **Hertz** has a desk at the airport, T311162, and at the *Patong Merlin* and *Tara Patong*; prices are similar to Avis. There are other local companies down Rasada Rd in Phuket Town (see Phuket Town). **Long-tailed boat**: these can be hired to visit reefs and the more isolated coves, ฿600-1200 per day. **Motorbike hire**: as above, ฿150-350 per day. There are also several places on Rasada Rd in Phuket Town. Note that not all places insist on taking your passport as a deposit/collateral and it is best not to let it out of your hands. **Motorbike taxi**: men (and a few women) with red vests will whisk passengers almost anywhere for a minimum of ฿10. They congregate at intersections. **Small minibuses**: can be chartered for journeys around the island. Karon to town – ฿130, town to airport – ฿250, Patong to town – ฿130.

Air The airport is to the north of the island, 30 km from Phuket Town. For flight reservations, T211195 (domestic) and T212855 (international) on Phuket, and T2800070 in Bangkok. Regular domestic connections on THAI with Bangkok, 1 hr 15 mins, Chiang Mai 2 hrs, Hat Yai 55 mins, Nakhon Si Thammarat 1 hr 40 mins, Surat Thani 35 mins and Trang 40 mins. **Bangkok Airways** also run daily connections with Koh Samui 50 mins. **International connections** with Hong Kong, Penang and KL (Malaysia), Singapore, Taipei, Tokyo and Munich and Dusseldorf. Airlines include ANA, Bangkok Airways, Dragonair, MAS, Qantas, THAI and Tradewinds. **Airport facilities**: café, left luggage (open 0700-2030, ฿25 per day), THAI reconfirmation desk, **Hertz** car rental, tourist information counter, currency exchange, and hotel information. **Transport to town**: Thai Airways appear to have a virtual monopoly on transport from the airport and prices are not cheap (unless being picked up by your hotel). There are 2 ways to avoid the ฿70 fare into Phuket Town. One is to walk the 3 km to the main north-south road, Route 402, and pick up a public bus or songthaew there. Alternatively, walk out of the airport gate and wait for a motorcycle taxi dropping someone off (฿30). (They cannot pick up fares at the airport itself). Motorcycle taxis wait at the intersection with Route 402 to ferry people to the terminal (฿30); it's getting from the airport to Route 402 which is more difficult. THAI run a minibus service into Phuket Town for ฿70 (from Phuket Town to the airport, the minibus leaves from the THAI office, 78 Ranong Rd), they also have a taxi and limousine service to town. Buses take passengers to Patong, Kata and Karon beaches for ฿100, or by private taxi for ฿400.

Train There is no rail service to Phuket. However, some visitors take the train to Phun Phin, outside Surat Thani (usually the overnight train), where buses wait to take passengers on to Phuket 6 hrs (see page 335).

Road **Bus**: station (*bor ko sor* – BKS) is on Phangnga Rd in Phuket town, T211480. Tickets bought here are cheaper than through travel agents. The information desk here usually stocks a timetable and fare list produced by the TAT detailing all departures as well as local transport. Regular a/c and non-a/c connections with Bangkok's Southern bus terminal 14 hrs. A/c tour buses also ply this route. In Bangkok many depart from Khaosan Rd where substantial numbers of guesthouses are concentrated. Regular morning connections with Hat Yai 8 hrs, Trang 6 hrs, Surat Thani 6 hrs and Satun 7 hrs. Regular connections with Phangnga 2 hrs, Takua Pa 3 hrs, Ranong 6 hrs and Krabi 4 hrs. Note that buses leave for the beaches from the market area from around 0600 – although the taxi drivers may try to convince you otherwise! **Taxi**: taxis will leave when they are full (usually with 5 passengers). For Surat Thani, they leave from the coffee shop opposite the Pearl Cinema on Phangnga Rd (฿150 per person).

Phuket Town

Sights
Phone code: 076
directory assistance
& overseas phone
service: 100
Colour map 4, grid B2

Phuket Town is interesting for its **Sino-Portuguese architecture** (similar to that of Penang and Macao), dating back 100-130 years. Wealthy Chinese tin barons built spacious colonial-style residences set in large grounds to celebrate their success. The best examples are along Thalang, Yaowarat, Ranong and Damrong roads and include the Chartered Bank (the first foreign bank to establish offices in Thailand), the Thai Airways office on Ranong Road opposite the market, and the Sala Phuket on Damrong Road. Less grand, but nonetheless elegant, are the turn-of-the-century shophouses on, for example, Thalang Road. There is some talk of renovation, in an attempt to preserve these deteriorating buildings but an appreciation of the architectural wealth that still exists in Phuket Town appears to be only slowly developing. There are **night markets** on Ong Sim Phai and Tilok Uthit 1 roads.

Khao Rang, a hill overlooking Phuket Town, can either be reached by foot (a longish climb), or by songthaew or tuk-tuk. It is a public park, with fitness track, and affords a good view of the island and countryside to the southwest. Other views of the island are obscured by trees (chartered tuk-tuk ฿50 round trip).

Koh Sire/Siray – or Sire Island – is connected to Phuket by a short bridge. There is not much to see here; fishing boats unload their catches (turn right immediately after crossing the bridge) and there is a village of sea gypsies (or *chao talay*) and fishermen who embrace animist beliefs. They are thought to be descended from Andaman/Nicobar islanders to the west of Phuket (chartered tuk-tuk ฿60 round-trip).

Saphan Hin, a small promontory to the south of town, is a place where Thais congregate in the evening. With the on-shore breeze, array of street sellers, and a wonderful spirit house, it is worth the trip. It is just a shame the beach is like a rubbish tip.

The **Crocodile Farm and Elephant Land** is on Chana Charoen Road. It is run down and poorly managed and would offend the sensibilities of those with any love for crocodilians. . ■ *Mon-Sun 0900-1800. Daily shows at 1230 and 1530. ฿200.* The **Snake Farm** is on Thepkrasatri Road, just north of the turn-off to Patong. Snake-leather goods for sale. ■ *Snake shows from 1100-2400.* Another very touristy affair is the **Phuket Orchid Garden and Thai Village** with the usual assortment of cultural shows with dancing, Thai boxing and handicraft displays, elephant rides and an orchid garden. Pretty forgettable, overall. ■ *Show times at 1100 and 1730, ฿230. Getting there: the centre is off Thepkrasatri Rd, just north of town, T214860 for further details.*

The **tourist office**, *TAT*, 73-75 Phuket Rd, T212213, F213582, is good for specific local questions and problems relating to Phuket and Phangnga. They provide useful town maps and transport details. A free monthly magazine is also produced for visitors, *Travel and Style Phuket*. It is financed by advertising, so don't expect too much critical comment. Nonetheless it does contain some useful background information. More critical in its comment is the *Phuket Gazette*, a monthly tabloid newspaper (English language), produced for, and by, *farang* residents and visitors (฿20). There is also a good, free colour map of Phuket and the beaches with most hotels and other places of interest marked, distributed by *Thaiways Magazine*.

Tours   Travel agents in town will organize full or half-day tours to Phangnga Bay, Phi Phi Island, Coral Island, the pearl farm, or scuba-diving around Phuket Town.

Hotels in town are rather uninspired; most people avoid staying here and head straight for the beaches, although those on business or needing to catch an early morning bus connection might need to spend a night here. **Sleeping**

AL *Metropole*, 1 Montri Rd, T215050, F215990. A/c, restaurant, pool, ostentatious hotel with pretensions of grandeur. Massive and impersonal with rather heavy, over-elaborate decor. **AL** *Novotel Royal Phuket City*, T233333, F233335 opposite the main bus station in town. Swimming pool, business centre, gym but no beach and no holiday atmosphere. Expensive but up to 50% discount in the wet season, this place is

Phuket Town

■ **Sleeping**
1 City
2 Daeng Plaza
3 Downtown Inn
4 Imperial
5 Laemthong
6 Metropole
7 Nara Mansion
8 Novotel Royal
    Phuket City
9 On On
10 Pearl
11 Pengman
12 Phuket Garden
13 Phuket Inn
14 Phuket Island Pavilion
15 Phuket Merlin
16 Siam
17 Silver
18 Sinthavi
19 Siri
20 Talang Guesthouse
21 Thavorn Grand Plaza
22 Thavorn Hotel
23 Wasana Guesthouse

● **Eating**
1 Bondeli Café
2 Kanda Bakery
3 Koh Lao Luat Mu
4 Lai-An Lao
5 Mae Porn
6 Thiptawan House
7 Vegetarian
8 Venus

🚍 **Transport**
1 Long distance bus
    terminal to
    destinations beyond
    Phuket (Bor Kor Sor)
2 Local buses to
    beaches, Thalong,
    Sarasin Bridge &
    turn off for
    airport

▲ **Other**
1 Ocean Shopping Mall
2 Rasada Shopping
    Centre
3 Suriyadet Circle

Related maps
Phuket Island,
page 252
Patong Beach,
page 264
Karon & Kata
Beaches, page 269
Bang Tao,
Pansea & Kamala
Beaches, page 274

surprisingly tacky for such a large establishment. **AL-A** *Thavorn Grand Plaza*, 40/5 Chana Charoen Rd, T222240, F222284. A/c, restaurants, 2 pools, 125 rooms, large high-rise hotel geared to businessmen not to holiday-makers, located away from town centre. **AL-B** *City*, Thepkrasatri Rd, T216910, F213554, B2535768. A/c, restaurant, pool, ugly high-rise block near centre of town. **AL-B** *Pearl*, 42 Montri Rd, T211044, F212911, B2601022. A/c, Chinese rooftop restaurant, pool, small attractive garden, clean rooms. **AL-B** *Phuket Merlin*, 158/1 Yaowarat Rd, T212866, F216429. A/c, restaurant, pool, clean, comfortable high-rise block, free shuttle bus to Patong Beach throughout the day. 35% discount available in the wet season. Overstaffed. **A** *Phuket Garden*, 40/12 Bangkok Rd, T216900, F216909. A/c, restaurant, helpful staff, the suite rooms are good value. **A** *Phuket Island Pavilion*, 133 Satool Rd, T210444, F210458. Very nice rooms with a different layout to most places. Superior rooms are sumptuous. Swimming pool and all facilities. Outdoor reception at the bottom of this circular sky-rise.

B-C *Sinthavi*, 89 Phangnga Rd, T211186, F211400. Clean, fair rooms, but typically slow staff. Restaurant and bakery attached. **C** *Daeng Plaza*, 57 Phuket Rd, T216428. A/c, restaurant, a multi-storeyed hotel in the centre of town with 75 rooms and helpful staff, despite their lack of English. Not much to recommend this place unless somewhere to rest one's head is all that is required. **C-D** *Thavorn*, 74 Rasada Rd, T211333, F215559, A/c, restaurant, pool, central and dull but good-value rooms. Cheesy historical feel, the staff are about as active as some of the exhibits in the attached museum. Some attempts to develop a sense of style, for example the attached *Collector Pub and Restaurant* is really rather stylish and tasteful, but it sits incongruously next to the gloomy lobby where Thai female coffee shop crooners in tight sequined dresses congregate at night, overall this is probably the best hotel in this price bracket. **C- D** *Imperial*, 51 Phuket Rd, T212894, F213155. Co-operative staff, good clean rooms at realistic rates. **C-D** *Downtown Inn*, 56/16-19 Ranong Rd, T216884. A/c. Probably a brothel but clean and reasonable rooms.

D *Nara Mansion*, 15/1 Soi Mongkon, Yaowarat Rd, T259238. Cheap and reasonable rooms, but the management didn't even seem to realize they were running a hotel. Some a/c. **D** *Talang Guesthouse*, Krabi Rd, T215892. Welcoming rooms, helpful owner, good rates. **D-E** *On On*, 19 Phangnga Rd, T211154. Attractive hotel dating from 1929 situated in the heart of town. Clean and comfortable a/c rooms with attached cold-water showers can sometimes be rather gloomy, fan rooms a bargain. This place has real character, attached a/c coffee shop and good restaurant plus tour desk. Recommended. **D-E** *Wasana Guesthouse*, 159 Ranong Rd, T211754. Central location just by the fresh market, bargain basement a/c rooms with attached shower rooms, cavernous lobby looking a little like an extremely grubby operating theatre, rooms are clean enough though, and friendly at our last visit. **E** *Siam*, 13-15 Phuket Rd, T212328. Noisy location but clean rooms. **E** *Pengman*, Phang-nga Rd, near the *On-On Hotel*. Noisy small rooms but OK for the money and its location is convenient. **F** *Laemthong*, 24-26 Soi Romanee, Thalang Rd, T212310. Very basic rooms in attractive old street.

Eating **Thai Expensive**: *Ka Jok See*, 26 Takua Pa Rd, T217903. Excellent Thai restaurant, booking is essential. The success of the restaurant is leading to some pretty sharp pricing policies, but nonetheless we have had comments from customers who believe the atmosphere, character, style, and first-rate cuisine make it worth paying the extra few hundred baht. *Krua-Thai*, 62/7 Rasada Centre. Clean restaurant with well-presented food. Recommended. *Lucky Seafood*, 66/1 Phuket Rd. Saphan Hin, seafood, large restaurant with Chinese/Thai food, not central. *Phuket Seafood*, 66/2 Phuket Rd. Saphan Hin, seafood, large, Chinese/Thai restaurant, not central. *Tunk-Kao*, Khao Rang. Seafood, good views over town from here, food is reasonable. **Expensive-mid-range**: *Thiptawan House*, Takua Pa Rd. Good, well-priced Thai food in a/c restaurant. Recommended. **Mid-range**: *Phuket View*, Khao Rang. Seafood, good position on Rang Hill with views overlooking Phuket Town, average food. *Sip Gaeng*, Yaowarat Rd. Translates as '10 curries'. **Cheap**: *Mae Porn*, 50-52 Phangnga Rd. Excellent food available from this unprepossessing corner restaurant, including ice creams, shakes, Thai dishes and seafood specialities, a/c room available. Recommended.

Other Asian cuisines Expensive: *Lai-An Lao*, 58 Rasada Rd. Chinese restaurant with seafood specialities. Recommended. *Venus Chinese Restaurant*, next to *Mae Porn Restaurant*, classy establishment serving a variety of Chinese and Thai dishes. **Mid-range**: *Vegetarian Restaurant*, Ranong Rd. Respectable place with a good choice of veggie dishes. *Kaw Yam and Bakery*, 11/1 Thung Kha Rd. *Erawan*, 41/34 Montri Rd. Seafood, Chinese. *Omar E Khyam*, 54/1 Montri Rd. Indian.

International Expensive: *Bondeli Café*, Rasada Rd (corner of Phuket Rd). A/c café and boulangerie with good pastries and savouries including pizzas and quiche, sophisticated place for a coffee (excellent – probably the best in town) and cool off. **Mid-range-Cheap** *Kanda Bakery*, 31-33 Rasada Rd. Spotlessly clean a/c restaurant with art deco undertones, serves breakfast, Thai and international dishes and good cakes like cinnamon rolls, croissant and chocolate brownies. Recommended. **Mid-range** *Le Café*, Rasada Centre. Elegant café serving burgers, steaks, sandwiches, cappuccino and milkshakes. *Le Glacier*, 43/3 Rasada Centre. Ice creams, coffee and drinks. *Suthep Roast Chicken*, 480 Phuket Rd.

Fast food In the *Ocean Shopping Mall* – which has been closed for renovation since 1998 but presumably will re-open at some point – there was (and should be again) *McDonalds, Burger King, Pizza Hut, KFC, Svensons, Mister Donut*, enough for even the most dedicated fast foodie.

Foodstalls The best place to browse on the street is around the market on Ranong Rd. Here, roadside stalls serve such delicacies as deep fried chicken feet, *khao niaw mamuang* (sticky rice and mango – when in season), grilled bananas, squid and *kanom* (Thai sweets). A very good and cheap restaurant close by is *Koh Lao Luat Mu* (name only in Thai), on the circle linking Ranong and Rasada roads, which serves tasty noodle and rice dishes. Alternatively, *Khai Muk*, Rasada Rd (opposite the *Thavorn Hotel*) serves superb *kuaytiaw* (noodle soup).

Cinema 4 cinemas renting headphones with English dialogue. *The Pearl* is on corner of Montri and Phangnga roads, 3 shows daily at 1230, 1900 and 2130. Some shows with the English soundtrack (ask at ticket office). **Entertainment**

Cultural shows *Orchid Garden and Thai Village*, 2 km off Thepkrasatri Rd, T214860. Sword fighting, Thai boxing, Thai Classical dancing, folk dances, almost 1 ha of orchid gardens, handicraft centre and elephants. Open 1000-2200. Daily cultural shows 1100-1200 and 1730-1830.

Discos Most discos run from 2100-0200. *Marina Club* at the *Phuket Merlin*, 158/1 Yaowarat Rd. *The Wave* at the *Pearl Hotel*, Montri Rd. *Diamond Club* at the *Thavorn Hotel*, Rasada Rd (cover charge ฿50 for women, ฿70 for men).

Most souvenirs found here can be bought more cheaply elsewhere in Thailand, and if travelling back to Bangkok, it is best to wait. Best buys are pearls and gold jewellery. **Shopping**

Antiques *Ban Boran Antiques*, 39 Yaowarat Rd (near the circle), recently moved from old shop on Rasada Rd, this is arguably the best antique shop on Phuket; interesting pieces from Thailand and Burma especially, well-priced, charming service. *Antiques*

House, Rasada Centre, central location, limited stock of Thai and other Asian antiques. *Puk Antiques*, Phangnga Rd (close to *On On Hotel*); *Chan's Antiques*, Thepkrasatri Rd, just south of the Heroines Monument, not many 'antiques', but a selection of Thai artefacts.

Books *Seng Ho Phuket Co*, 2/14-16 Montri Rd. *The Books*, Phuket Rd, a few English language and German books and magazines, coffee bar.

Department stores *Rasada Centre*, Rasada Rd, or *Ocean Shopping Mall*, opposite the *Metropole Hotel* facing the clocktower has been closed since 1998 for renovation but should re-open. Further down the road is the *Ocean Plaza* shopping centre which is very good.

Handicrafts *Cheewa Thai Crafts Centre*, 250/1 Thepkrasatri Rd. *Dam Dam*, Rasada Rd (near the fountain circle), interesting selection. From numerous stalls at the *Rasada Centre*, Rasada Rd.

Jewellery There are a number of shops on Montri and Rasada roads, designs tend to be 'Asian'.

Pewterware *Phuket Pewter Centre*, 52 Phuket Rd.

Silk *Silk Master*, Thepkrasatri Rd, just north of turn-off to Patong Beach. Hand-weaving demonstrations, huge range of silk products, tailor-made clothes, leather goods, 'antiques', pots.

Tailors There are a number of tailors and fabric shops on Yaowarat Rd, near the circle. Clothes can be copied and made up in as little as a day.

Textiles *Ban Boran Textiles*, 51 Yaowarat Rd. Modern Thai and hilltribe textiles and some other handicrafts.

Sport Bowling: *Pearl*, behind Pearl theatre, Phangnga Rd. **Diving**: see page 255. **Game fishing**: *Phuket Tourist Centre*, 125/7 Phangnga Rd, T211849. *Andaman Queen Tour*, 44 Phuket Rd, T211276, F215261. **Golf**: see page 267. **Jogging**: Fitness Park on Khao Rang. **Shooting range**: indoor and outdoor, snooker club and restaurant, at 82/2 Patak Rd (west of Chalong 5-way intersection). ■ *Open Mon-Sun 0900-1800.* **Snooker**: *Nimit Snooker Club*, 53/57 Nimit 1 Rd, T213202. ■ *Open 0900-late, VIP table ฿120 per hour, standard ฿50 per hour.* **Thai boxing**: every Fri at 2000 (tickets available from 1600), unfriendly place. The stadium is on South Phuket Rd (Saphan Hin). ฿350 (overpriced).

Tour operators There are several around Rasada Rd and the Rasada centre, and along Phuket Rd. See the introduction to Phuket (page 251), for a full background on the tours available. Among the companies in Phuket Town are: *Dits Travel*, 11 Sakdidej Rd, T212848, F213934. *Songserm Travel*, 51-53 Satool Rd, Phuket Town, T222570. *Silver Queen*, 1/10 Thung Kha Rd, T214056, they also have a desk at the *Patong Merlin Hotel*. *Aloha Tour*, Chalong Bay, T216726. *Cruise Centre*, Rawai Beach, T381793.

Transport Local **Car hire**: Pure Car Rent, 75 Rasada Rd, T211002 ฿900 per day. **Phuket Horizon Car Rent**, 235/4 Yaowarat Rd, T215200. **Avis**, *Metropole Hotel*, 1 Montri Road, T215050, ฿950 per day. **Motorbike hire**: from the same places and many others from ฿150 per day. **Tuk-Tuk**: ฿7 within town, ฿10 from town to suburbs.

Long distance See page 256 for information on transport beyond Phuket. The bus terminal is just off Phangnga Rd.

Directory

Airline offices *Bangkok Airways*, 158/2-3 Yaowarat Rd, T212341. *Dragonair*, 37/52 Montri Rd (from Hong Kong). *Malaysia Airlines*, Merlin Hotel, T216675. *SilkAir*, 183/103 Phangnga Rd, T213891, F213887. *Thai*, 41/33 Montri Rd, T212400. *Thai* (domestic), 78 Ranong Rd, T211195. *Tradewinds*, 95/20 Phuket Rd, T213891 (from Singapore). **Banks** Along Rasada, Phuket, Phangnga and Thepkrasatri roads there are branches of all the major banks, all with ATMs and currency exchange. **Communications** Post Office: Montri Rd (at the corner of Thalang Rd). **Telephone centre:** 122/2 Phangnga Rd, open 24 hrs. Overseas telephone and fax also available from the post office in town. **Medical services** *Mission*, Thepkrasatri Rd, T212386. *Wachira*, Yaowarat Rd, T211114. *Bangkok Phuket Hospital*, Yangyok Uthit Rd, T254421. **Places of worship** Christian Church: Chao Fa Rd, Sun service at 1030. **Useful addresses** American Express agent: *Sea Tour*, 95/4 Phuket Rd, T216979. Immigration office: South Phuket Rd (close to Saphan Hin). Ask for the boxing stadium; the office is next door. T212108. **24 hrs petrol station:** Esso, Thepkasatri Rd. **Tourist Police** Emergency call, T219878 (till 1630), then Police on T212115. Police station on corner of Phuket and Phangnga roads.

Phuket's beaches

The beach areas listed below begin with the principal resort of Patong, followed by the beaches south of Patong from Karon and anti-clockwise to Chalong. Finally, there is a section on the less-visited beaches of the west coast, north of Patong.

Patong Beach

The most developed beach on Phuket is the 3 km-long **Patong**, 15 km due west of Phuket Town. It began to metamorphose from a hippy paradise into a commercial centre during the 1970s. It is the Pattaya of the south, with a mass of neon signs advertising the many hotels, massage parlours, restaurants, straight bars, gay bars, nightclubs, clothes stalls and discos. The cheap accommodation has now been almost entirely displaced to remoter parts of the island although cheaper places do exist, especially on Rat Uthit Road. Sadly, there is little indication that any thought has been given to the overall planning of the area: individual hotels and restaurants can be excellent, but the whole ensemble is a shambles; enormous, impersonal skyscraper hotels tower over rather more attractive two-storey guesthouses. Developers bypass planning restrictions by offering 'gifts' to the appropriate officials. In an article published in the London *Sunday Times* in 1996, Mark Ottaway lamented that "Many commentators, myself included, spent much of the last decade agonizing as to whether it was 'going the way of Pattaya'", adding that "the omens get worse with every visit". One thing cannot be denied though: Patong generates a great deal of foreign exchange.

Having said all this, Patong seems popular with families these days and is less frenetic than Pattaya, with the sex tourism scene not really in evidence. It also offers the widest selection of watersports on Phuket and in spite of the hotel development, it is still possible to snorkel on the reef at the southern end of the bay. Patong could not, in any sense, be described as peaceful, but it is the best place to stay if you are looking for a nightlife. The beach is also safe for children, as the seabed shelves gently and the water is generally calm. The beach at the northern end of the bay is quiet but rocky; at the southern end also quiet but sandy and better for swimming.

Express boats leave Patong for day trips to the Similan Islands (see page 276), or to Phi Phi (see page 303). *Thai Tour Patong Beach*, T213275, organize two-hour tours in a glass-bottomed boat to view the coral reef. Daily departures from Patong Beach at 1000, 1200, 1400 and 1600 (฿300).

Phone code: 076
Looking down the main drag, Patong could be anywhere: south of France, the west coast of the US ... there is little sense of 'Thai-ness' here

The Andaman Sea Coast

Tours

Sleeping There are dozens of hotels on Patong and new ones still under construction; the following is only a small selection. Most hotels are situated on Patong Beach Rd (also known as Thaweewong Rd), but there are also quite a few on Rat Uthit Rd. Most hotels are situated south of Sawatdirak Rd.

AL *Amari Coral Beach*, 104 Trai Trang Rd, T340106, F340115, coralbea@ loxinfo.co.th On secluded promontory at southern end of beach, 200 a/c rooms, all with balconies, restaurants, pools, fitness centre, tennis courts, private beach – one of the more peaceful places here. **AL** *Club Andaman*, 77/1 Patong Beach Rd, T340530, F340527, B2701627. A/c, restaurant, pool, large new block and some older thatched cottages, set in large spacious grounds. Fitness centre, tennis courts, watersports, children's games room. **AL** *Merlin*, 99/2 Song Roi Pee Rd, T340037, F340394, B2532536. A/c, restaurant, 3 sculptured pools and a children's pool, large 4-storey hotel, quite attractively laid out with well-designed, spacious rooms. Nice garden, watersports, fitness club. Rather out on a limb, away from the activity of Patong. **AL** *Seapearl Beach*, 101 Beach Rd, T341901, F341122, seapearl@ phuket.ksc.co.th, at the southern end of the beach. Pool, mini shopping centre. A relative newcomer, 60 rooms with rather ostentatious decor, pleasantly low-rise, right on the beach and most rooms have a seaview. **AL** *Sea View*, 102 Thaweewong Rd, T341300, F340103.

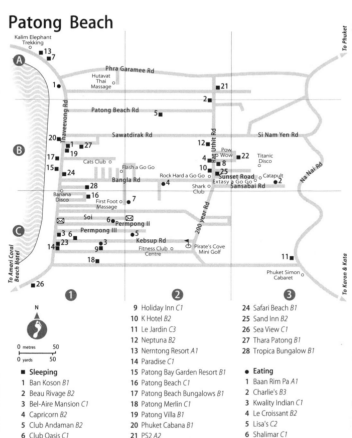

Patong Beach

Sleeping	
1 Ban Koson *B1*	
2 Beau Rivage *B2*	
3 Bel-Aire Mansion *C1*	
4 Capricorn *B2*	
5 Club Andaman *B2*	
6 Club Oasis *C1*	
7 Diamond Cliff *A1*	
8 Golden Field *B2*	
9 Holiday Inn *C1*	
10 K Hotel *B2*	
11 Le Jardin *C3*	
12 Neptuna *B2*	
13 Nerntong Resort *A1*	
14 Paradise *C1*	
15 Patong Bay Garden Resort *B1*	
16 Patong Beach *C1*	
17 Patong Beach Bungalows *B1*	
18 Patong Merlin *C1*	
19 Patong Villa *B1*	
20 Phuket Cabana *B1*	
21 PS2 *A2*	
22 Royal Paradise Hotel *B3*	
23 Royal Palm Resotel *C1*	
24 Safari Beach *B1*	
25 Sand Inn *B2*	
26 Sea View *C1*	
27 Thara Patong *B1*	
28 Tropica Bungalow *B1*	

● Eating	
1 Baan Rim Pa *A1*	
2 Charlie's *B3*	
3 Kwality Indian *C1*	
4 Le Croissant *B2*	
5 Lisa's *C2*	
6 Shalimar *C1*	
7 Waikiki Dive Café *C2*	

Related maps
Phuket Island,
page 252
Phuket Town, page 259
Karon & Kata Beaches,
page 269
Bang Tao,
Pansea & Kamala
Beaches, page 274

The Andaman Sea Coast

A/c, restaurant, pool, attractive hotel at southern end of the bay, facing onto a section of beach which is less cluttered and busy than elsewhere on Patong. This, by Patong standards, is a classy hotel, well designed, good pool, attentive service. Recommended. **AL-A** *Diamond Cliff Resort*, 61/9 Kalim Beach, T340510, F340507, B2455815. A/c, restaurant, pool, northern end of Patong, large impressive resort on side of hill but not much beach immediately in front of hotel, tennis courts, mini-golf, health club. **AL-A** *Holiday Inn*,52 Patong Beach Rd, T340608, F340435, B2554260. A/c, restaurants, pool very close to the main road, making it rather public to passers by. Ugly concrete hotel block on the beach, popular with tour groups. Tennis, watersports, gym, golf driving range, diving centre. **AL** *Patong Beach Hotel*, 124 Patong Beach Rd, T340301, F340541, B2612986, patong@sun.phuket.ksc.co.th A fairly ugly 11-storey block situated in the middle of Patong beach, several restaurants to choose from, free form pool, jacuzzi, fitness centre, health club, bars and disco – a happening place. **A** *Patong Bay Garden Resort*, 61/13 Patong Beach Rd, T340297. A/c, restaurant, small pool, 2-storey Spanish-style hotel, 60 rather small rooms but intimate atmosphere and it has the advantage of being on the beach. **A** *Patong Beach Bungalows*, 96/1 Patong Beach Rd, T340117, F340213. A/c, restaurant, small pool, a 35 room strip of rather small and damp bungalows, not particularly attractive, but it's right on the beach which explains why the rooms here go for a premium. There are better and cheaper places to stay – but they don't have a beach front position. **A** *Phuket Cabana*, 41 Patong Beach Rd, T340138, F340178, B2782239. A/c, open-air café, small pool for size of hotel (about 140 rooms), wooden cabins quite well laid out in leafy winding paths, rather close together, but hotel is in a good location by the beach and has a longer pedigree than most and something approaching an intimate atmosphere. **A-B** *Le Jardin*, Na Nai Rd, T340391, F344182. Pool, restaurant, obviously aimed at the French tourists but not noticeably hostile to other nationalities. **A-B** *Neptuna*, 82/49-50 Rat Uthit Rd, T340824, F340627. A/c, restaurant, tiny pool, 2-storey small hotel, a bit cramped. **C** *Sand Inn*, 93/35 Rat Uthit Rd, T340275, F340273. Very pleasant rooms, well run, good restaurant downstairs.

B *Bel-Aire Mansion*, 76 Beach Rd, T340280. Superb rooms, great location but perhaps a little noisy. Located 20 m from the beach and for this price, a bargain. Recommended. **B** *K Hotel*, 82/4/ Rat Uthit Rd, T340832, F340124. Some a/c, restaurant, decent-sized pool for a low-key hotel, well-maintained compound, quiet 2-storey hotel with 40 rooms, largely German clientele, quite expensive. Recommended. **B** *Patong Villa*, 85/3 Patong Beach Rd, T340132, F340133. Centre of beach, restaurant, pool. **B** *Safari Beach*, 83/12 Patong Beach Rd, T340230, F340231. A/c, restaurant attached, small pool, small 2 and 3-storey hotel set around pool in leafy compound just north of Soi Bangla, peaceful, considering how central it is. **B** *Thara Patong*, 81 Patong Beach Rd, T340135, F340446, B3214989. A/c, restaurant, attractive pool, 3-storey hotel with 130 rooms, good value. **B** *Tropica Bungalow Hotel*, 94/4 Patong Beach Rd, T341463, F340206. A/c, *Malee's Seafood Restaurant* in front of hotel, small pool, very leafy compound set back from road, quite dark rooms, but it's central, quiet and good value for the middle of town.

C *Capricorn*, 82/29 Rat Uthit Rd, T340390, F295468. Private bathroom. **C** *Nerntong Resort*, Kalim Beach, T340572, F340571. A/c, restaurant, pool, north of Patong and away from the beach, attractive for its seclusion. **C** *Paradise*, 93 Patong Beach Rd, T340172. Southern end, a/c. **C** *PS 2 Bungalow*, Rat Uthit Rd, T342207, F290034. (Good) restaurant, some a/c, 60 rooms, newer (and more expensive, with hot water) ones in a block, older in individual bungalows, this hotel is looking a little jaded now although the newer rooms are in reasonable condition, the guesthouse is located about 10 mins walk from the beach on a large garden plot so rooms are quiet, remains popular, motorcycles for hire. **C-D** *Beau Rivage*, 77/15-17 Rat Uthit Rd, T340725. Some a/c, large rooms – some suites – with clean bathrooms, spacious and good value although like the other hotels on Rat Uthit Rd it is some way from the beach. **D** *Ban Koson*, 81/3 Patong Beach Rd, T340135. Near Soi Post Office. **D** *Club Oasis*, 86/4 Patong Beach Rd, T293076. Near Soi Post Office. **D** *Golden Field*, Patong Beach Rd, T340375. **D** *Jeep I*, 81/7 Bangla Rd, T340264. Huts in a grassy compound. **D** *Jeep II*, 38/8 Rat Uthit Rd, T340100. Centre of beach. **D** *Royal Palm Resotel*, 86/4 Patong Beach, T340141. Near Soi Post Office. **D** *White*, 81/4 Rat Uthit Rd. Quiet guesthouse down a narrow lane running off Rat Uthit Rd, attractive garden, clean rooms. Recommended.

Eating As with accommodation, there is a huge selection of restaurants selling all types of food; seafood is recommended. Though it may sound less than Holmsian, the best way to find somewhere to suit your palate and wallet is to wander around until you strike lucky. Places are easy to find at night when the neon lights spring to life. Most restaurants have their menus displayed outside.

Thai Very expensive: *Baan Rim Pa*, 100/7 Kalim Beach Rd, T340789. Open terrace, on cliff overlooking bay, great position but expensive. *Krua Thai*, 99/61 Rat Uthit Rd (south end); **Expensive**: *Malee's Seafood*, 94/4 Patong Beach Rd. Also serves Chinese and International dishes. *No 4 Seafood*, Bangla Rd. Seafood. *Patong Seafood*, 98/2 Patong Beach Rd. Seafood, basic but good. **Expensive-mid-range**: *Hungry Tiger*, intersection of Bangla and Second roads, Thai as well as western dishes, one recent visitor reported with relish that "they have the guts to serve [the food] unmoderated ... hot really means hot!". *Sabai Sabai*, Soi Post Office, it may not be a terribly original name, but this small restaurant serves good and well-priced Thai food.

Indian Expensive: *Shalimar*, 89/59 Soi Post Office. Seafood specialities. *Kashmir*, 83-50 Patong Beach Rd. **Mid-range**: *Kwality Indian Cuisine*, Soi Kepsab. This is a good place if you need a curry fast, good choice.

International Many of the sois off Patong Beach Rd sell a good range of international food. **Expensive**: *Buffalo Steak House*, 94/25-26 Soi Patong Resort, off Bangla Rd, T340855. Scandinavian fare with lots of beef. *Da Maurizio*, on Kalim Beach, north of Patong, opposite *Diamond Cliff Hotel*, T344079. Italian food in attractive setting. *La Mousson*, Sawatdirak Rd. Quite sophisticated French cuisine. *Patong Beer Garden*, by *K Hotel*, 82/47 Rat Uthit Rd. Attractive garden setting, Viennese food cooked by Austrian chef. **Mid-range**: *Rock Hard Café*, 82/51 Bangla Rd. Garden, steaks, pizzas. *Lai Mai*, 86/15 Patong Beach Rd. Great Western breakfasts. *Babylon*, 93/12 Bangla Rd. Italian. *Mon Bijou*, 72/5 Rat Uthit Rd. German. *Vecchio Venezia*, Bangla Rd. Pizza. *Blackbeard's*, behind *Holiday Inn*, on site of Pirates Cove Minigolf. Great burgers, good for families, reasonable prices. *Waikiki Dive Café*, Soi Patong Resort. Food and pool and internet. A cool place to chill out, open until 0200, more a bar than a restaurant. *Le Croissant*, Soi Bangla. Thai/European restaurant/bakery. Good selection. *Lisa's Scandinavian Restaurant*, Soi Permpong. Easy to find, plenty of choice and good value. *Charlie's Restaurant*, Soi Sansabai. Thai and Tex-Mex. Barbecue every Fri from 2100. Good bar.

Fast food Lots of choice along the Beach Rd.

Fruit stalls At northern end of Rat Uthit Rd.

Bars Bars in Patong are concentrated along Rat Uthit Rd and Bangla Rd. The latter is throbbing with activity in the evening with dozens of bars catering for all nationalities and persuasions. *Black and White*, 70/123 Paradise Complex. *Bounty Bar*, Bangla Road. *Captain Hook's*, 70/142 Paradise Complex. *Maxim's*, Rat Uthit Road. *Oasis*, off Bangla Road. *Stardust a go-go*, *Extasy*, *Titanic*, *Fawlty Towers*, all on Soi Sunset, Rat Uthit Road.

Cabaret *Phuket Simon Cabaret*, Patong Rd, T342114, 1930-2130.   **Entertainment**

Cultural shows A Thai-style house on the hill before Patong Beach provides Thai boxing, classical dance, sword fighting. 2 shows a night, with Thai dinner, T7230841.

Discos *Banana* at *Patong Beach Hotel*, **Deep Sea Video Theque** at *Phuket Arcadia Hotel* and at *Le Crocodile*. *Tin Mine 21* in *Royal Paradise Hotel*, Rat Uthit Road. *Shark Club and disco*, Soi Bangla, popular, brand new place with state-of-the-art audio visuals.

Horror on Patong Beach T293123. Asia's biggest Horror House. ■ *Daily 1700-0100.*

Music *Le Crocodile*, just off Bangla Rd, and at many of the bars. Also the usual assortment of massage parlours, straight and gay bars, and revues.

Traditional Thai massage From countless (usually untrained) women on the beach or from *Hide Away*, 47/4 Na Nai Rd, Patong Beach, T340591, or *Hutavat Thai Massage*, 45/11-12 Phra Baramee Rd, Patong Beach, T342427. **First Foot Massage**, Soi Bangla, T340027.

All the usual tourist goods available here: T-shirts, sandals, mediocre handicrafts,   **Shopping** sea-shells (unfortunately). Stalls line Patong Beach Rd and several sois off here. *Centre Point* is a covered market area on Rat Uthit Rd. There are several **jewellery** shops in the centre of Patong Beach Rd.

Bungy jumping: *Jungle Bungee Jump*, on Route 4029 into Patong. ■ *Mon-Sun*   **Sport** *0900-1800, T321351*. **Catapult**, Soi Sunset, run by the same group. ■ *2000-2400*. **Diving**: centres are concentrated along Patong Beach Rd. Trips range from 1-day tours to Phi Phi Island, to week-long expeditions to the Similan Islands National Park and the Surin Islands. See general diving section on page 255 for listings. **Fitness**: the *Fitness Club Centre* T340608, with aerobics, sauna and body building is in the *Holiday Inn* on Patong Beach. ■ *Mon-Sat 0900-2100, Sun 1200 2100. Daily, weekly and monthly membership is available*. **Game fishing**: quite a few operators along Patong Beach Rd. Expect to pay about ฿1,500-2,000 per day. **Go-Kart racing**: track on left, at the bottom of the hill leading to Patong (Route 4029), T321949. ■ *Mon-Sun 1000-2200*. **Golf**: *Phuket Country Club*, on main road between Phuket Town and Patong, T213383, 18-hole, ฿150. ■ *0800-1800*. Caddy ฿100. **Crazy golf**: *Pirate's Cove*, behind *Holiday Inn*, two 18-hole courses ฿150, good restaurant attached (*Blackbeards* – see above). **Elephant trekking**: *Kalim Elephant Trekking*, Kalim Beach, T290056. ■ *0800-1000*.

A wide range of **watersports**: windsurfing, waterskiing, sailing, diving, snorkelling, deep-sea fishing. Ask at your hotel or at one of the sports shops along Patong Beach Rd.

Magnum Travel, Patong Beach Rd, T381840. *Travel Company*, 89/71 Patong Beach   **Tour operators** Rd, T321292.

Local Jeep and motorbike hire: from outlets along Patong Beach Rd. Motorbikes   **Transport** on Rat Uthit Rd. **Avis** has desks at the *Holiday Inn* (T340608) and *Phuket Cabana Hotel*   *15 km W of town* (T340138), **Hertz** is at the *Merlin* (T340037).

Road Chartered tuk-tuk: ฿130 one way, from Patong to town or vice versa. **Songthaews/minibuses**: regular departures from Ranong Rd, by the market in Phuket Town (฿10).

The Andaman Sea Coast

Directory **Banks** Banks and currency exchange booths are concentrated on Patong Beach Rd (Thaweewong Rd). **Communications** **Post Office:** Patong Beach Rd (the beachfront road), near Soi Permpong Pattana (aka Soi Post Office). International telephone service next door to the Post Office on Patong Beach Rd. Open 0800-2300. **Medical services** *Kathu Hospital* on Rat Uthit Rd. **Useful addresses** Tourist Police: on Patong Beach Rd.

Karon and Kata Beaches

Phone code: 076   The horseshoe-shaped Karon and Kata Beaches south of Patong are divided by a narrow rocky outcrop. Karon started tourist life as a haven for backpackers; it is now well developed, with a range of hotels and bungalows and a wide selection of restaurants. But the density of building is much less than at Patong. Hotels are more widely spread, the atmosphere is more relaxed, less frenetic. Karon's major drawback, perhaps, is the beach which is exposed, offering almost no shade from trees. At crab-eye level it must seem an inhospitable expanse of baking sand. Most hotels are also set some distance away from the beach, so that reaching the sea requires a walk across scrubland and a road. Nonetheless, there are good mid-range places to stay on Karon, and the slower moving pace of life here will appeal to many.

Kata consists of two beaches: **Kata Yai** (Big Kata) and **Kata Noi** (Little Kata), divided by a cliff. Kata Noi is dominated by the *Amari Kata Thani Hotel*, although there are a few bungalows here. The snorkelling is good around Koh Pu, the island in the middle of the bay, and at the south end of Kata Noi. Kata Yai is a sprawling mass of development: hotels, souvenir shops and roadside restaurants abound. It has no real charm – although it does provide excellent facilities for the holidaymaker.

Sleeping   **In Karon** **AL** *Arcadia*, T396038, F396136, Bangkok T2640291. Centre of beach, a/c, restaurant, pool, modern, overbearing high-rise with countless rooms, all overlooking the sea, health club, tennis, watersports, set back, away from the beach. **AL** *Le Meridien* , T340480, F340479, Bangkok T6532201. A/c, restaurants, pools, nightclub, plenty of entertainment including fitness centre, tennis, squash, mini-golf, watersports, very private and secluded with large landscaped pool to complement this massive 470-room L-shaped block. **AL** *Thavorn Palm Beach*, 128/10 Moo 3, T396090, F396555, Bangkok T2475150. A/c, 5 restaurants, 5 pools, squash, tennis, snooker, a large hotel facing the beach with all facilities but not much style, it has outgrown itself. **AL-A** *Islandia Park Resort*, T396200, F396491, B5136756. A/c, restaurant, pool, high-rise block, all rooms facing sea, new and plush (for how long?). **A** *Felix Karon View Point* (*Swissôtel*), 4/8 Patak Rd, T396666, F396853. A/c, restaurant, pool smallish, low-rise hotel with 125 rooms at the northern end of Karon Beach, the style of the place is more Spanish than Thai, but nonetheless it is more attractive than most, small pool, away from the beach, inland from the road. **A** *Karon Beach Resort*, 5/2 Moo 3 Patak Rd, T330006, F330529, katagrp@loxinfo.co.th A/c, restaurant, simple laps pool, right on the beach at the Southern end of the bay, slightly frayed interior, all rooms with balconies overlooking beach, owned by the Kata Group, the managing director is an English woman. **A** *Karon Villa Royal Wing*, T396139, F396122, B2516615. Centre of beach, a/c, restaurant, pool. **A** *Marina Cottage*, PO Box 143, southern end of beach, T381625/330493, F381516. A/c, 2 good restaurants, beautiful secluded pool, individual cottages in lush grounds, no private beach, *Marina Divers* here, tours and boat trips organized. Recommended. **A** *Phuket Island View*, T396452, F396632. Southern end of beach, a/c, restaurant, pool. **A** *Sand Resort*, T212901. A/c, restaurant, simple bungalows, clean, small rooms. **A** *South Sea Resort*, 36/12 Moo 1, Patak Rd, T396611, F396618. A/c, restaurant, pool, nearly 100 rooms in this hotel which is almost Wild West in design, attractive central pool, good range of facilities, location in a relatively quiet spot at the north end of the bay, set away from the beach, rooms are unremarkable with little local feel, good balconies. **A-B** *Kharon Inn*, T330530, F330128. A/c, restaurant, pool, some 60 bungalows and 40 more modern rooms in a low-rise block on large plot, small pool, overall feels rather dated but not unattractively so.

B-C *Shady Bungalow*, T330677. Well located on the beach but slightly cramped with so many other places in operation in this small space at the southern end of Kata. **B-C** *Phuket Ocean Resort*, 9/1 Moo 1, Karon Beach, T396176, F396470, B7320608. A/c, restaurant, pool, a rather ramshackle affair with older bungalows and newer rooms in tiered blocks on the hillside, position is at the quieter, northern end of the bay, away from the beach, good mid-range place to stay, no pretensions, comfortable.

C *Karon Guesthouse*, T396860, F396117. A decent, very average mid-range place. **C-D** *Lumi and Yai Bungalow*, northern end of beach, T396096. 15 reasonable rooms, well located for access to both Karon/Kata and Patong. **C-D** *Kata Noi Club Bungalow*, T330194. Isolated position on this lovely beach and at a reasonable price, well managed. **C-D** *Kata Noi Riviera Bungalow*, T330726. Similar rates to *Kata Noi Club* and likewise benefitting from being relatively alone on the beach. **C-E** *My Friend*, northern end of beach, T396344. Simple huts within easy reach of the beach. **D** *Happy Hut*, 121/2 Kata-Karon Beach, T330230. Small, clean and green. **D** *Karon Sea View* (next to *Sand Resort*), T396798. Good value chalets. **E** *Bell Guesthouse*, T330111. One of the cheapest places to stay in Karon/Kata, but away from the beach.

In Kata (All with restaurant, pool and a/c.) **L-AL** *Boathouse Inn*, T330015, F330561. Southern end of beach, a/c, several restaurants (good seafood), pool, attractive high-end choice, big hotel, but retains the feel of a small hotel. Very well run, large central jacuzzi, one of the best and most refined places to stay on Phuket, small touches delight even the most world-weary expense account traveller, there is also the added excitement of a Thai cookery school here for those who wish to leave knowing how to handle a chilli.

Karon & Kata Beaches

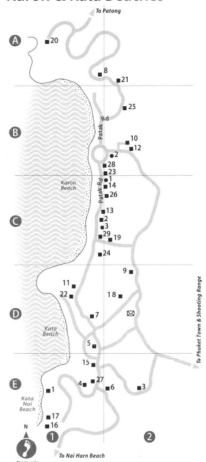

To Patong

The Andaman Sea Coast

Ta Phuket Town & Shooting Range

To Nai Harn Beach

Not to scale

■ Sleeping

1 Amari Kata Thani *E1*
2 Arcadia *C1*
3 Bell Guesthouse *E2*
4 Boathouse Inn *E1*
5 Club Med *D1*
6 Cool Breeze *E2*
7 Fantasy Hill *D1*
8 Felix Karon View Point *A1*
9 Happy Hut *D2*
10 Islandia Park Resort *B2*
11 Karon Beach Resort *D1*
12 Karon Guesthouse *B2*
13 Karon Sea View *C1*
14 Karon Villa & Karon Villa Royal Wing *C2*
15 Kata Beach Resort *E1*
16 Kata Noi Club *E1*
17 Kata Noi Riviera *E1*

18 Kata Tropicana *D2*
19 Kharon Inn *C2*
20 Le Meridien *A1*
21 Lumi & Yai Bungalow *A2*
22 Marina Cottage *D1*
23 My Friend *B2*
24 Phuket Island View *C1*
25 Phuket Ocean Resort *B2*
26 Sand Resort *C2*
27 Shady Bungalow *E1*
28 South Sea Resort *B2*
29 Thavorn Palm Beach *C1*

● Eating

1 Al Dente *C2*
2 Little Mermaid *B2*
3 Old Siam *C1*

AL *Club Med*, T285225, F330461, B2540742. Centre of beach, looking rather threadbare, superb sports activities, large piece of private beach, excellent for children. **AL** *Kata Beach Resort*, 5/2 Mue 2 Patak Rd, T330530, F330128, B9394062, katagrp@loxinfo.co.th Southern end, 262 rooms in L-shaped block set around a freeform pool, run by an English lady married to a Thai, this is an efficiently run hotel, paired with *Karon Beach Resort* and *Kharon Inn*. **A** *Amari Kata Thani*, Kata Noi Beach, T330127, B2675213. A/c, restaurants, unexciting pools, large average hotel, popular with package holidays, but lovely beach. **A** *Mansion*, T381565. A/c, restaurant, quiet area of beach. **D** *Kata Tropicana*, T330141. Simple chalets, friendly and clean. Recommended. **D-E** *Fantasy Hill*, between Karon and Kata, T330106. Rather noisy. **E** *Cool Breeze*, Kata Noi, T330484. Very good value, with excellent restaurant (which is in the guesthouse but doesn't belong to it).

Eating   **Thai** *Ruan Thep*, southern end of beach. *Old Siam*, T396090. Traditional Thai food in traditional Thai atmosphere. Great position on the beach with indoor and terrace dining. Expensive, and while *farangs* may not realise that it is overpriced, most Thais do.

International Very expensive-expensive: *Maxim*, seafood, southern end of Karon. **Expensive**: *Hayashi*, T381710. Japanese. *Co Co Cabana*, pizza, northern end of Karon. *Gustos* and *No 2* near *Kata Thani Hotel*. **Mid-range**: *Swiss Bakery*, *Western Inn*, Recommended. *Little Mermaid*, T396628. Good value, extensive menu. *Al Dente*, T396569, Italian fare.

Shopping   **Books** *Good Earth*, second-hand book shop next to the Rose Inn.

Sport   **Diving**: *Siam Diving Centre*, 121/9 Patak Rd, southern end of Karon Beach, T330936. – Organize diving expeditions to the Similan Islands. *Marina Divers*, southern end of Karon Beach, T330272, F330516. PADI certified courses, very professional set-up. Recommended; and *PIDC Divers* at *Le Meridien Hotel*, T321479. **Horse riding**: next to shooting range, T381667. ฿600 per hour. ■ *0700-1200, 1300-1830*. **Shooting range**: Phuket Shooting Range, 82/2 Patak Road, T381667. Off Route 4028 between Kata and Chalong. ■ *Mon-Sun 1000-1800.*

Transport   **Local Car hire**: **Avis** has a desk at the Phuket *Arcadia* (T381038), *Le Meridien* (T340480)
20 km from   and *Kata Beach Resort* (T381530). **Hertz** has a desk at the *Thavorn Palm Beach* (T381034).
Phuket Town

Road Minibus: chartered minibus to/from town, ฿130; **Songthaews**: to both Karon and Kata leave regularly from the Ranong Rd Market, Phuket Town (฿15).

Nai Harn and Promthep Cape

Phone code: 076   Nai Harn, 18 km southwest of Phuket Town, is one of the island's most beautiful locations, with spectacular sunsets. It is now possible to stay here in luxury at the *Phuket Yacht Club* (built, illegally, on protected land). During the monsoon season between May and October, the surf and currents can be particularly vicious and care should be taken when swimming. From Nai Harn it is possible to walk to **Promthep Cape**, the best place to view the sunset. Walk out to the cape itself or simply look down on the surrounding sea and coastline from the road, for a spectacular view. Near the highest point there is a shrine covered in gold leaf and surrounded by wooden elephants.

Sleeping   **L** *Le Royal Meridien Phuket Yacht Club*, T381156, F381164, BT2545435, info @phuket-yachtclub.com A/c, restaurants, pool, lovely position on hill, overlooking Nai Harn and Promthep Cape, well run with109 luxurious rooms, secluded. Spacious and recently refurbished rooms have large secluded balconies with sea views, massive bathrooms. Excellent food, fitness club, tennis courts, lovely beach, the hotel was built contravening environmental laws but as money can move mountains in Thailand, little could or can be done. **AL** *Nai Harn Villa*, 14/29 Wiset Rd, T381595, F381961. Overpriced but well run. There are better-value places elsewhere. **AL-C** *Jungle Beach*, T381108. Some a/c, pool, remote, attractive position, has a long and pretty good track record – a lot of local *farangs* swear by it – although there are reports that it is on a slow slide. **C** *Nai Harn Beach Resort*, 14/29 Moo 21 Wiset Rd, T381810. Some a/c, good rooms for the price. Clean and well kept. **D** *Ao Saen*, T288306. On the beach. **E** *New Sunset Bungalow*, 93/1 Moo 6, clean bungalows in nice setting.

Riding: *Crazy Horse Club*, rides on the beach or along mountain trails (฿300 per hour). Other 'sports' available here include: Waterskiing, windsurfing, mini-golf, herbal sauna.

Entertainment

Rawai

To the north of Promthep Cape, up the eastern side of the island the first beach is Rawai, 14 km from Phuket Town. This crescent-shaped beach is now relatively developed although not to the same degree, nor in the same style, as Patong or Karon. It is patronized by Thai tourists rather than foreigners and as a result has a quite different atmosphere. There is a small market selling assorted handicrafts and various snacks. The bay is sheltered from the monsoon and it is safe to swim throughout the year. But the beach is rather dirty and it is rocky. At Rawai there is a 'sea gypsy' tribal village, **Chao Le**.

Phone code: 076

Koh Kaew Pisadarn can be seen from Promthep Cape and is a short 15-minute ride by boat from Rawai Beach. The island is the site of not one, not two, but an amazing three footprints of the Buddha. Two of the footprints are located among the boulders and stone on the upper shore; the third is situated just below the low watermark. For many years important Buddhist festivals were celebrated here because of the island's supposed spiritual power and significance; then, about 40 years ago, these religious pilgrimages stopped. Sam Fang, who researched a story on the island for the *Bangkok Post*, discovered a tragedy had occurred about this time. A storm had sunk some rowing boats making the trip out to the island, and locals assumed that a resident sea serpent, angered by the visits, was involved. When a series of attempts were made to construct images of the Buddha on the island between 1952 and 1967, these were continually thwarted by bad weather and high seas. In this way there developed a belief that the island was in some way cursed. Only in 1994 were attempts at erecting a Buddha image renewed. The 1½ m-high standing image cast in concrete is on the northeastern side of the island, overlooking Promthep Cape, and about a 10-minute walk along a laid path from the boat landing. The image is surrounded by two protective nagas that slither over the top of the encircling balustrade. The footprints themselves are located on the shore beneath the Buddha; steps lead down to them. In 1995 the celebration of Loi Krathong at Koh Kaew Pisadarn was reintroduced. ■ *Getting there: by long-tailed boat from Rawai Beach. Negotiate with one of the boat-owners, take a picnic, and arrange to be picked up at a convenient time.*

Excursions

AL-A *Phuket Island Resort*, T381010, F381018, BT2525320. A/c, restaurant, pool, luxurious hotel with almost every conceivable facility. Well run by helpful staff. **C** *Salaloi Resort*, 52/2 Wiset Rd, T381370. Some a/c, well established, good restaurant, cheaper rooms are good value. **C** *Rawai Resort*, T381298. A/c, restaurant. **D** *Rawai Garden Resort*, T381292. Restaurant, small affair but pleasant. **D** *Pornmae*, T381300.

Sleeping & eating

The Andaman Sea Coast

Sport   **Diving**: equipment can be hired from the *Phuket Island Resort*. **Paintball**: *Top Gun*, 82/2 Patak Rd, T381667.

Laem Ka and Chalong beaches

The next beaches up the east coast are **Laem Ka Beach** and **Chalong**. Ao Chalong is 1 km off the main road. There is not much here for the sun and sea-worshipper and the beach is rather dirty. Offshore tin-dredging is said to have ruined the beach. Boats can be caught to the offshore islands for game fishing, snorkelling and scuba diving from Chalong's long pier, and there is a small collection of good seafood restaurants. The rest of the east coast has not been developed for tourists as the coast is rocky.

Sleeping   **B-C** *Laem Ka Beach Inn*, T381305. Restaurant. **B-C** *Phuket Fishing Lodge*, T281003,
■ on maps   F281007. Easier to reach than some of the other places to stay. Fair rooms but not
Price codes: see   overly receptive reception. **B-C** *Wichit Bungalow*, 16/1 Wiset Rd, T381342. To the
inside front cover   south of Chalong bay. Nice area, but a bit out of the way. **B-D** *Atlas Resort*, 14 Wiset Rd, T381279, F381279. Isolated from the other establishments and in the middle of the long beach. Reasonable rooms, fair prices. **C** *Boomerang Bungalow*, T281068, F381690. Not on the beach but the price doesn't reflect its inferior position. Not bad, nonetheless. **E-F** *Ao Chalong Bungalow*, T282175. Restaurant.

Eating   **Expensive**: *Kan Eang Seafood*, on the beach, excellent selection of seafood. Recommended. *Ruan Thai Seafood*.

Sport   **Golf**: 18-hole mini-golf course (open 1000-2300 Mon-Sun) left of the narrow road to Ao Chalong from the main road. Herbal sauna, sailing centre and dive shop (see dive section, page 255).

Tour operators   *Aloha Tours* (T381220) and the *Chalong Bay Boat Centre* (T381852) are both on Wisit Rd. *Ao Chalong* arrange trips to Phi Phi, Coral, and Raja Islands as well as fishing and diving expeditions.

Cape Panwa

The Marine Research Centre and aquarium are to be found on this remote point (see page 249), as well as Panwa House, in the grounds of the only significant hotel here – the *Cape Panwa Sheraton*. Boat trips to nearby islands leave from the cape.

Sleeping   **AL-A** *Cape Panwa Sheraton*, T391123, F391117, B2339560. Beautifully secluded, some bungalows for families, tennis courts, fitness centre, electric train down to the private beach, coral reef 40 m off-shore. This hotel plays on the fact that Leo of *The Beach* fame stayed here but we have had reports from disgruntled guests who have complained of cockroaches and half-baked service.

Koh Tapao Yai, a small island off the cape is home to a couple of hotels, the **A** *Tapao Yai Island Resort*, T391217, all facilities and **B** *Phuket Paradise Resort*, T391217, F214917, B3941949.

Eating   *Yaun Yen* (200 m from the aquarium), reasonable food, seafood is best.

Koh Lone and Koh Mai Ton

Phone code: 076

There are places to stay on several of the islands off the east and southeast coasts of Phuket. All the resorts here play on the desert island getaway theme. These places may be hard to reach in the monsoon season. Koh Mai Ton, for instance, is a private island 9 km southeast of Phuket with very little on it except the *Mai Ton Resort*. This fits the bill for those truly 'deserted tropical island' holidays, except the Resort seems rather out of place with mock-classical pillars by the pool and rooms that could be on any tropical island. All a bit pretentious.

Koh Lone B *Lone Pavilion*, T381374. A/c, restaurant. **C** *Lone Island Resort*, T211253. **Koh Mai Ton L** *Mai Ton Resort*, T214954, F214959, maiton@ksc.th.com A/c, restaurants, pools, 75 individual Thai pavilions with wooden floors and separate sitting-room, good sports facilities and beautiful white-sand beaches.

Sleeping

Other islands: Koh Hii AL-A *Coral Island Resort*, T281060, F381957. **Koh Raya Yai** *Raya Andaman Resort*, T381710, F381713. **Koh Sire D** *Sire Resort*, T221894. **Koh Taphao Yai B** *Phuket Paradise Resort*, T391217, F214917.

North from Patong

Travelling north from Patong, there remain some beautiful unspoilt beaches. This part of Phuket's shoreline has virtually no cheap accommodation but a number of exclusive hotels.

A *Thavorn Beach Village*, 6/2 Moo 6, Nakalay-Patong Beach (between Kamala and Patong beaches, on the Kao Phanthurat Pass, 5 km from Patong), T340436, F340384. Attractively designed Thai-style villas, with 4 rooms each (2 ground floor, two first) many with poolside verandas, large lagoon-like pool. A secluded spot on an almost private beach (rocky at low tide).

Sleeping

Kamala Beach

Kamala Beach is 10 km north of Patong and the road to this still quiet bay has recently been surfaced and upgraded – although sections may remain rough. The beach is rather bare, with little shade, but the (Muslim) village has a nice atmosphere, with its own post office, telephone service, police station, health centre, dive centres (*Seahawk Divers* and *Thai Dive*), tour operator and travel agent and vehicle rental outfits. Indeed, visitors wishing a quiet and relaxing holiday need never leave Kamala – except to get home again. How long Kamala will remain a quiet corner of Phuket is a moot point. Land speculators have made their mark and development is underway.

Phone code: 076 As many of the local people here are Muslim, topless bathing is regarded as beyond the pale & will offend

AL *Kamala Bay Terrace Resort*, 16/12 Moo 6, Tambon Kamala, T270801, F270818, B6426107, kamala@samart.co.th A/c, restaurants, disappointingly small pool, tennis, built on hillside overlooking the sea, quieter location than most with virtually its own private beach, but rooms unremarkable for the price and a bit of an eyesore to boot. **AL** *Kamala Beach Estate*, T324111, F324115. **A** *Phuket Kamala Resort*, T324396. Right on the beach, a big complex but this doesn't seem to spoil the relaxed ambience. **C** *Bird Beach Bungalow*, quiet and relatively cheap but not very exciting. **C-D** *Maya's House* and *Yada's Cottage* are 2 small bungalow operations on Kamala Beach, little to choose between them, although the garden at *Yada's* is more mature and luxuriant, these are clean, simple bungalows on a quiet beach.

Sleeping

Eating There are a number of reasonable restaurants on Kamala. Along with the usual seafood places. **Expensive-mid-range**: *White Orchid* serves French cuisine and *Paul's Place* (at the southern end and overlooking the bay), T324111. An excellent restaurant serving good Thai food (with a marine flavour – try the fried pomfret with garlic).

Entertainment *Phuket Fantasea*, a ฿3.3 billion entertainment complex, is currently being built near Kamala Beach, to be completed by 1999. It will inevitably lure tourists to this as yet relatively undeveloped area.

Surin Beach

Phone code: 076

Lined with casuarina trees and open-air restaurants, patronized mostly by Thais. The seabed shelves away steeply from the shoreline and swimming can be dangerous. Small golfcourse and no hotels on the beach. Surin Beach is particularly dirty.

Bang Tao, Pansea & Kamala Beaches

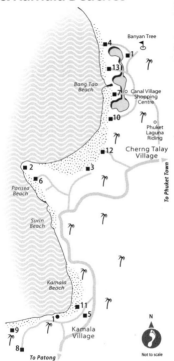

Sleeping
■ on maps
Price codes: see
inside front cover

Pansea Beach is a tiny beach just north of Surin with two exclusive hotels on it: **L** *Amanpuri Resort*, 118/1 Pansea Beach, T324333, F324100, BT2870026, a/c, restaurant, pool, more expensive rooms are beautifully designed Thai pavilions, with attention to every detail. Superb facilities include private yacht, watersports, tennis and squash courts, fitness centre, private beach, library, undoubtedly the best on Phuket but not recommended for small children, because of many steps around the resort. For a place of such style the food is mediocre – the surroundings, style and service incomparable. **L-AL** *Chedi Phuket* (formerly the *Pansea Resort*), T324017, F324252, BT2374792, south of *Amanpuri*, a/c, restaurant, pool, exclusive resort with range of traditional Thai cottages to sleep from 2-10 people, superb facilities, including all watersports, cinema, library, games room, secluded beach. *Hertz* have a desk here. High season surcharge that itself is more than the price of many rooms on the island.

Related maps
Phuket Island,
page 252
Phuket Town, page 259
Patong Beach,
page 264
Karon & Kata Beaches,
page 269

Eating The Thai restaurant (**Very expensive**) at the *Amanpuri* is considered one of the best on the island (and the setting is sensational), at least 48 hrs advanced booking needed during peak season (T324394).

■ Sleeping

1 Allamanda	9 Kamala Beach Estate
2 Amanpuri Resort	10 Laguna Beach Club
3 Bangtao Lagoon	11 Phuket Kamala Resort
Bungalows	12 Royal Park Resort &
4 Banyan Tree	Lanna Resort
5 Bird Beach Bungalow	13 Sheraton Grande
6 Chedi Phuket (Pansea	Laguna
Resort)	
7 Dusit Laguna	● **Eating**
8 Kamala Bay Terrace	1 Paul's Place

The Andaman Sea Coast (vertical text, left margin)

Bang Tao (Laguna)

Development on Bang Tao Bay is in two distinct areas. To the north is the *Laguna Phuket*, a complex consisting of four **L-AL** hotels built around a lagoon. Free tuk-tuks and boats link the hotels and guests are able to use all the facilities. Excellent range of watersports and good provision for children – all facilities free. The recently opened Canal Village offers 40 or so shops and a lagoon-side café, serving satay. The adjoining bakery serves good pastries and cakes. To the south of the *Laguna Phuket* (and quite a long way round by road) there is a smattering of other places to stay.

Phone code: 076

L *Banyan Tree*, T324374, F324375, banyan@samart.co.th, banyantree.com A/c, restaurant, pool, excellent, elegant hotel with all facilities and superb service. *The Allamanda*, T324359, F324360, www.lagunaphuket.com/allamanda The most recent addition to the Laguna Phuket, situated behind the *Sheraton Grande*, half the rooms look east over the *Banyan Tree Golf Club*, pools, restaurants, a large scale resort. **L-AL** *Dusit Laguna*, T324320, F324174, BT2384790. A/c, restaurants, attractive pool, the quietest and most refined of the *Laguna Phuket* complex. Excellent service, immaculate gardens, beautifully laid out unimposing hotel, tennis courts, watersports and a Children's Corner. **Avis** have a desk here. **L-AL** *Laguna Beach Club*, Bang Tao Beach, T324352, F324353. A/c, restaurants, pool, 250 rooms in low-rise blocks on an 8-ha (20-acre) site. This hotel has a sports emphasis: the pools are simply spectacular: a sort of marine Angkor – Raiders of the Lost Ark affair with spouting statues, caves and slides, there is also tennis, diving, squash, golf driving, etc, good for children and those with a penchant for activity/sports-filled holidays. **L-AL** *Sheraton Grande Laguna*, T324101, F324108, BT2366543. A/c, 5 restaurants (with a good choice of cuisine), interesting design in the 'Chess Bar', large pool with interlinked sections, including a sandy 'beach' and a sunken bar, rather impersonal accommodation some of which is out on stilts on the lagoon, tennis courts, health centre, massage, children's corner.

Sleeping

A *Lanna Resort*, T212553, F222502. 4 bungalows sleeping 2 to 6 people each, Thai style, 10 mins from beach, no a/c, but secluded with space, rather overpriced. **A** *Royal Park Travelodge Resort*, Southern end of the beach, T324021, F324243, BT5411524. A/c, several restaurants, pool, large 3-storey hotel, with watersports, tennis, fitness room, gift shops.

B-D *Bangtao Lagoon Bungalow*, 72/3 Moo 3, Tambon Cherng Talay, T324260, F324168. Some a/c, small pool, a rather haphazard bungalow development in a comparatively isolated position. Range of chalets from simple (and rather worn) fan bungalows to 'deluxe' a/c affairs, the latter are small and featureless, but very clean, family cottages also available, all set within a large coconut and casuarina grove 100 m from a rubbish-strewn beach. This resort doesn't really feel as though it is on Bang Tao, as access is much further south.

Canal Village, shops including *Jim Thompson's*, several gem stores, clothing and handicrafts. All quite pricey and exclusive. Another 'arcade' of shops is opening up just after the turn-off from Cherng Talay to the Laguna Complex.

Shopping

Golf: the 18-hole *Banyan Tree Golf Club* is situated here, with driving range attached, on Wed nights, a 9-hole tournament takes place, T324350, F324351.

Sport

Nai Ton

Phone code: 076   Between Bang Tao and Nai Yang is the isolated beach of Nai Ton which consists of little more than a handful of drinks stalls, where deck-chairs and umbrellas can be hired. However, the track leading to the beach is in the process of being improved and the rate of development may soon accelerate. So the drinks stalls may soon be joined by other more grandiose developments. South of Nai Ton is an exquisite cove, most easily accessible by boat.

Sleeping   **B-C** *Nai Thon Beach Resort*, only place to stay here and apparently only open in the high season, T213928, F222361.

Nai Yang

Phone code: 076   Nai Yang is the northernmost beach and part of the **Nai Yang National Park**. It is close to the airport and 37 km from Phuket Town (entrance ฿5 for car). The park encompasses Nai Yang and Mai Khao beaches, which together measure 9 km, making it the longest stretch of beach on the island. The area was declared a national park in 1981 to protect the turtles which lay their eggs here from November to March. Eggs are collected by the Fisheries Department and young turtles are released around about the second week of April each year (check on the date as it changes from year to year), on 'Turtle Release Festival Day'. Not as exciting as it may sound. The north end of the beach (where there is good snorkelling on the reef) is peaceful and secluded, with the only accommodation being in the National Park bungalows. ■ *The Visitors Centre is open Mon-Sat 0830-1630. Further south, there is more activity, with a range of luxury hotels and bungalows.*

Sleeping   **AL** *Crown Nai Yang Suite Hotel*, T327420, F327323. A/c, restaurant, pool. **AL** *Pearl Village*, T327006, F327338, BT2601022. A/c, restaurant, attractive pool, well run, friendly management, beautiful gardens, facilities including tennis courts, horse riding, elephant riding, good for families. Recommended. **B-D** *National Park bungalows*, T327047. **C-E** *Garden Cottage*, T327293, F327292. 2 mins from the airport, cottage-style guesthouse, friendly owner who is willing to show you the island. **Camping**: available in the National Park (฿60).

Eating   Several seafood places, for example *Nai Yang Seafood*.

Transport   **Road Bus**: from the market on Ranong Rd in Phuket Town.
30 km from Phuket Town

Directory   **Banks** Mobile exchange van.

Koh Similan

Colour map 4, grid A1   The **Similan Islands National Park** consists of nine islands. They lie 80 km northwest of Phuket and are some of the most beautiful, unspoilt tropical idylls to be found in Southeast Asia. The water surrounding the archipelago supports a wealth of marine life and is considered one the best diving locations in the world as well as a good place for anglers. A particular feature of the islands is the huge granite boulders. These same boulders litter the sea-bed and make for interesting peaks and caves for scuba divers. On the west side of the islands the currents have kept the boulders 'clean', whilst on the east, they have been buried by sand.

Avoid taking too much luggage, as visitors must transfer from ferry to precarious long-tailed boat mid-ocean

Koh Miang houses the park office and some dormitory and camping accommodation. Koh Hu Yong, the southernmost island is the most popular diving location. From some 16,000 tourists in 1994, the numbers visiting the Similan Islands has risen to over 25,000. Anchor damage and the dumping of rubbish is a big problem here, although buoys have now been moored and some people say that the rubbish situation is slowly improving.

The best time to visit is December to April. The west monsoon makes the islands virtually inaccessible during the rest of the year; be warned that boats have been known to capsize at this time. Also, be warned that transport away from the islands is unpredictable and you might find yourself stranded here, rapidly running out of money. At the end of March/beginning of April, underwater visibility is not good, but this is the best time to see manta rays and whale sharks.

Tours See page 253. Most dive companies in Phuket offer tours to the Similan Islands (see page 255). Hotels in Khao Lak (see page 290), organize boat and dive trips to Similan.

Sleeping Bungalows are available on Koh Ba Ngu (**E-F**). There are also some bungalows and a restaurant on Koh Pa Yang. Reservations can be made at the Similan National Park Office, Thai Muang, or at Tap Lamu Pier (T411914). There are several (overpriced) huts on Koh Miang, but no fans, no mosquito nets and uncooperative kitchen staff, very limited menu and poor overpriced food.

Camping On Koh Ba Ngu, Koh Similan and Koh Miang. Bring your own tent, although there are some battered tents available on Koh Miang. ฿20.

Similan Islands

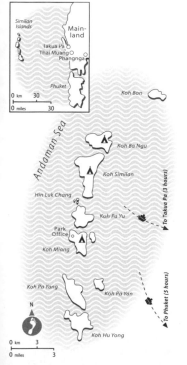

Transport
40 km off shore

Boat Boats leave from Ao Chalong and Patong Beach (T222570, *Songserm Travel*) every Sat, Thu, and Tue from Dec-Apr, Phuket 6-10 hrs. Vessels also depart from Thap Lamu pier, 20 km north of Thai Muang, 3 5 hrs. Finally, boats leave from Ranong, a busy deep-sea fishing port. Although it is possible to visit the Similan Islands independently, it can be an expensive and/or time-consuming business; it is far easier to book onto a tour (see above).

Directory **Useful addresses** For information on weather conditions T2580437.

Koh Surin

Five islands make up this Marine National Park, just south of the Burmese border, and 53 km off the mainland. The two main islands are **Koh Surin Tai** and **Koh Surin Nua** (South and North Surin respectively), separated by a narrow strait which can be waded at low tide. Both islands are hilly, with few inhabitants; a small community of Chao Le fishermen live on Koh Surin Tai. The diving and snorkelling is good here and the coral reefs are said to

The Andaman Sea Coast (vertical sidebar text)

be the most diverse in Thailand. Dr Thon Thamrongnawasawat, a marine biologist, has established an underwater nature trail with markers and underwater information pamphlets sealed in plastic. However, overfishing has led some people to maintain that diving is now better around the Similan Islands. Novices will still find the experience both exhilarating and enchanting. The National Park office is at Ao Mae Yai, on the southwest side of Koh Surin Nua.

Best time to visit December to March. **NB** Koh Surin Tai may close to visitors during the full moon each March, when the Chao Le hold an important festival.

Sleeping At **Ao Mai Yai**, southwest side of Koh Surin Nua, 3 dormitories, ฿1,500 (for whole dormitory), T411545 for details. There is also a bungalow that sleeps 6, ฿600.

Camping On south side of island, there is a campground, ฿80 for a tent for 2 people.

Eating Food is supplied at the bungalow, ฿250 per day for 3 set meals.

Transport **Local Long-tailed boats** can be hired, ฿400 for 4 hrs.

Boats Leave from Patong or Rawai on Phuket (10 hrs), from Ranong (through the *Jansom Thara Hotel*) or from the pier at Ban Hin Lat, 1 km west of Khuraburi 4-5 hrs (฿500).

Directory **Useful addresses** For information on weather conditions T2580437.

Phuket to Satun

The drive to Phangnga from Phuket passes through impressive limestone scenery. En route, it is possible to watch rubber being processed by smallholders. Not long ago, over-mature rubber trees (those more than 25 years old) were cut down and processed into charcoal. Today, due to the efforts of an enterprising Taiwanese businessman, a rubber-wood furniture industry has developed. As the road nears Phangnga, there are a number of roads down to the coast, from where tours to Phangnga Bay depart. At these junctions, men frantically beckon potential customers.

Phangnga

Sights
Phone code: 076
Colour map 4, grid B2

Phangnga itself is a bit of a one-horse town – or at least a one-road town – though spectacularly located in the midst of limestone crags. Due to the limestone geology, there are a number of caves in the vicinity. Just at the outskirts of town on Route 4 towards Phuket, on the left-hand side, are the **Sinakharin Gardens**, visible from the road. Within the gardens is **Tham Luu Sii**, a watery, sun-filled cave which would be beautiful if it were not for the concrete pathways. At the entrance to the cave sits Luu Sii, the cave guardian, under an umbrella. **Tham Phung Chang** is a little closer into town on the other side of the road, within the precincts of **Wat Phraphat Phrachim Khet**. There is a spring and Buddha images in this unremarkable cave, and a small pool where local boys swim. The wat itself is probably more interesting, with its fine position against the limestone cliff and set within a large compound. To get to the wat and cave, take a songthaew from town. About 300 m past the traffic lights (themselves past the *Lak Muang 2 Hotel*) is the arched entrance to the wat.

In the centre of town, behind the *Ratanaphong Hotel* is the fresh produce **market** while along the main street near the *Thaweesuk Hotel* are some remaining examples of the **Chinese shophouses** that used to line the street.

Phangnga Bay is best known as the location for the James Bond movie *The Man with the Golden Gun*. Limestone rocks tower out of the sea (some as high as 100 m) and boats can be hired to tour the area from Tha Don, the Phangnga customs pier (see Tours, below). ■ *Getting there: take a songthaew to the pier* (฿10) from Phangnga town. 7 km along Route 4 there is a turning to the left (Route 4144 – signposted Phangnga Bay and the Ao Phangnga National Park Headquarters), and the pier is another 3 km down this road. Best time to visit: Nov-Apr. Park entrance fee: ฿5. **Long-tailed boats** can be chartered from the pier for a trip around the sights of Phangnga Bay for about ฿350-450 although it is cheaper to take a tour (see Tours, below). **Sleeping** Bungalows are available at the headquarters of the National Park (which incorporates the Bay).

Tham Suwan Kuha is 12 km from Phangnga on Route 4 to Phuket. A turning to the right leads to this airy cave temple. It is popular with Thais and is full of Buddha images, the largest of which is a poorly proportioned reclining Buddha. Stairs lead up to a series of tunnels, containing some impressive natural rock formations. King Chulalongkorn visited the cave in 1890 and his initials are carved into the rock. The cave is associated with a wat, Wat Suwan Kuha or Wat Tham. ■ *฿10. Getting there: take a bus travelling southwest along Route 4 towards Phuket.*

Wat Tham Khao Thao is 12 km from Phangnga on Route 4152 to Krabi, on the left-hand side of the road, under a cliff wall. There are views of the surrounding plain which can be seen from a stairway being built up the cliff-face. The road here passes through nipa palm which then becomes an area of mangrove. Aquaculture is an important sideline industry, and tiger prawns are raised in the brackish waters of the mangroves and in purpose-built ponds.

Excursions

The Andaman Sea Coast

Phangnga Bay

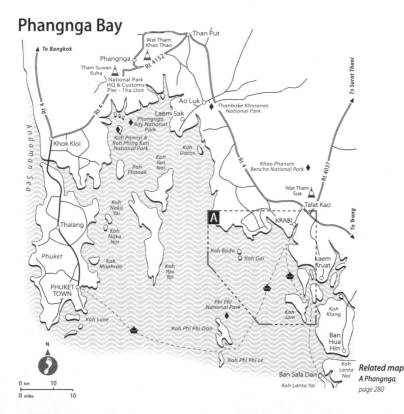

Related map
A Phangnga,
page 280

■ *Getting there: take a bus along Route 4152 towards Krabi.*

Tours The standard tour of **Phangnga Bay** winds through mangrove swamps and nipa palm, past striking limestone cliffs, before arriving at **Tham Lod** – not really a cave at all, but a tunnel cut into the limestone, through which boats can pass. From Tham Lod, the route skirts past the Muslim fishing village of **Koh Pannyi** with its turquoise green mosque (and seafood restaurants), and then reaches the 'highlight' of the trip: **James Bond Island**, or **Koh Phing Kan** or, sometimes, **Koh Tapoo**. Greatly overrated, the 'famous' overhanging rock, like a chisel, seems much smaller than it should be, and the beach and cave are littered with trinket-stalls and other tourists. Close to Koh Pannyi are some **ancient cave paintings** of dolphins and other creatures (rather disappointing). There are two main tour companies in town, *Sayan* and *Kean*. Both advertise widely: at the bus terminal, in the *Thaweesuk* and *Ratanaphong* hotels. Both companies run very similar tours and charge the same – ฿300 for half day, ฿600 for full day. The tours are worthwhile and good value – and for an extra ฿250 *Sayan Tour* will put you up in a Muslim village for the night and provide a seafood dinner.

Canoeing and jungle tours are organized by the environmental tour company *Green Spirit*, T411521.

Sleeping **A** *Phangnga Bay Resort*, 20 Thadon Rd (out of town, near the customs pier), T412067, F412057, B2162882. A/c, restaurant, pool, mostly tour groups, modern, overpriced but excellent views. **B** *Phangnga Valley Resort*, 5/5 Phetkasem Rd, T412201, F411201. Restaurant, just before the turn-off for Phangnga from Route 4, about 6 km or so from the town centre, lovely setting, 15 bungalows. **C-D** *Lak Muang 2*, 540 Phetkasem Rd, T412218, F411500. Some a/c, restaurant, pool, good value rooms with hot water tubs, carpets and TVs, but featureless and located 2 km or so from the bus station and the centre of town, note that rooms facing onto the road are very noisy. **D-E** *Ratanaphong*, 111 Phetkasem Rd, T411247. Some a/c, in town centre, friendly with clean, though unremarkable and noisy, rooms, good and popular restaurant. **E** *Lak Muang 1*, 1/2 Phetkasem Rd, T412486, F411512. Some a/c, restaurant. **E** *Thaweesuk*, 79 Phetkasem Rd, T411686. Clean rooms of variable size, strange, rather elusive management, good information but not unlike sleeping in a prison. **E** *Rak Phangnga*, on the main street in town, cheap but rather drab interior and noisy due to its location.

Phangnga place names

Phangnga Bay
อ่าวพังงา

Tham Suwan Kuha
ถ้ำสุวรรณคูหา

Wat Tham Khao Thao
วัดถ้ำเขาเต่า

Phangnga

■ Sleeping
1 Lak Muang 1
2 Lak Muang 2
3 Phangnga Valley Resort
4 Phang Nga Bay Resort
5 Rak Phang-nga
6 Ratanaphong
7 Thaweesuk

Cafés on Phetkasem Rd, near the market, sell the usual array of Thai dishes; including **Eating**
excellent *khaaw man kai* (chicken and rice) and *khaaw mu daeng* (red pork and rice).
Try the rather dark but very popular *Kha Muu Restaurant* opposite the *Thaweesuk
Hotel*. There are several coffee houses across from the *Thaweesuk*.

Mid-range: *Duang Seafood*, 122 Phetkasem Rd (opposite Bank of Ayudhya). Excellent seafood restaurant, Chinese specialities. **Cheap**: *Khru Thai* (Thai Teacher),
Phetkasem Rd (opposite the Post Office). Clean and cheap place, local civil servants
eat here and the dishes are openly displayed making selection easy.

Local Ancient, cramped **songthaews** constantly ply the main road – rather slowly **Transport**
(฿5). **Motorbike hire**: from the *Thaweesuk Hotel*. **Road Bus**: the bus station is on *100 km from Phuket*
Phetkasem Rd, near the centre of town and a short walk from the *Thaweesuk* and *Lak* *93 km from Krabi*
Muang 1 hotels. Motorcycle taxis wait to take passengers further afield and regular *879 km from Bangkok*
songthaews run up and down the main road (฿5). Buses from Bangkok's Southern bus
terminal, 15 hrs; T434119 for a/c bus information and T4345557 for non-a/c bus information. 3 VIP buses leave in the evenings for Bangkok. Regular connections with
Phuket's bus terminal on Phangnga Rd, 2 hrs and with Krabi, 2 hrs. Also buses to
Ranong, Takua Pa, Hat Yai and Trang.

Banks Mostly on the main street, Phetkasem Rd. **Communications** **Post Office:** on Phetkasem **Directory**
Rd, 2 km from centre on main road entering town from Phuket. Overseas telephone service.

Krabi

From Phangnga to Krabi, the road passes mangrove swamps and nipa palm, **Sights**
more dramatic karst formations and impressive stands of tropical forest. *Phone code: 075*
Krabi is a small provincial capital, situated on the banks of the Krabi River, *Colour map 4, grid B3*
close to where it discharges into the Andaman Sea. Formerly Krabi's economy
was based squarely on agriculture and fishing; but since the mid to late-1980s
tourism has grown by leaps and bounds so that today it probably contributes
more to the town's – and possibly the province's – economy than any other
single activity. This transformation is all too evident.

The town is visited by tourists largely because it is a jumping-off point for
Phi Phi Island (see page 301), **Koh Lanta** (see page 307), **Ao Nang** and **Rai
Leh** (see page 290). Many people find they need to spend a night here, and the
guesthouses and hotels, not to mention the multitude of tour agents and restaurants, have sprouted to serve this community. While Krabi town itself does
not contain much to keep a visitor here, the rising cost of accommodation in
beach-side areas and on nearby islands is leading increasing numbers of visitors to choose to stay in Krabi and day-trip to the many attractions the province as a whole has to offer. There is a **general market** on Srisawat and Sukhon
roads, and a **night market** close to the Chao Fah Pier. The Promenade, on the
river front is a pleasant place to walk in the evenings.

There is a small *TAT* **tourist office** on Uttarakit Road and a newer office near
Chao Fah Pier on Khong Kha Road. Both are helpful. ■ *Mon-Sun 0830-1630.*
Many other places also advertise themselves as offering 'tourist information'; be
aware that this is not done for altruistic reasons but in order to sell tours, tickets
and rooms. A very useful locally produced guidebook is the *Krabi Holiday Guide*
by Ken Scott (฿40). It provides far more information on Krabi, Ao Nang, Phra
Nang, Raileh, Phi Phi and Koh Lanta and the smaller neighbouring islands than
we can offer here. Good maps of Krabi and the surrounding area can be obtained
from numerous shops and tour agents around town.

The Andaman Sea Coast

Excursions   **Wat Tham Sua** or the Tiger Cave Temple (see map page 279), is 3 km northeast of town just past Talat Kao down a track on the left and has dozens of *kutis* (monastic cells) set into the limestone cliff. Walk behind the ridge where the bot is situated to find a network of limestone caves, which eventually lead back to the entrance. There is also a steep staircase on the left; 1270 steps leading to the top of a karst hill with fantastic views of the area and some meditation areas for the monks. An exhausting climb, this is best reserved for cool weather and cooler times of day. ■ *Getting there: Wat Tham Sua is east along Route 4. Take a red songthaew from Phattana Rd, in town to Route 4. From here either walk along Route 4 to the Cave Temple or take a motorcycle taxi (about ฿10). Walk to the cave from the main road.*

The caves of **Tham Phi Hua To** and **Tham Lod** can be reached by boat from a pier just down the road from Hat Nopparat Thara (take the first left as you exit towards Khlong Muang), or you can take one of many tours by boat or canoe to the same caves. Phi Hua To cave is so named because of the large prehistoric human skulls found there. *Phi* means ghost or spirit, *Hua* means head, and *To* means large. Tham Lod is in fact a tunnel through the limestone karst through which you can travel by boat. The boat ride to these caves passes mangroves and limestone karst outcrops – a good day or half-day trip.

Butterfly World just established as a butterfly zoo, this small locally operated natural history centre is in landscaped gardens on the road leading to Ao Nang from Krabi approximately 3 km out of the municipality. Also a souvenir shop. ■ *Getting there: white songthaews from Krabi municipality from Phattana or Maharat Rd. (฿10).*

Susaan Hoi literally 'shell cemetery', lies 20 km southwest of Krabi, near the village of Laem Pho (not far from Ao Nang Beach). See page 290 for location and more information. ■ *Getting there: white songthaews from Krabi from the corner of Phattana and Maharat Rd, or from the pier every hour (฿20).*

Mangroves line the river opposite the municipality. This is a protected area, although heavy logging in the past has left most of the forest quite immature. Long-tail boats can be hired for a trip into the mangroves at the Chao Fa pier (rates are negotiable and depend on the time of year, length of time and number of people in the boat). Worth visiting for the birds and other wildlife, including several families of macaques, but ask the boatman to go slowly when in the mangroves so as not to startle the animals and birds. It may also be possible to get a *rua jaew* for this trip – this is the traditional boat used in the Krabi area (including Koh Lanta). Paddles are used instead of a motor (though most now use both), with the boatman standing on the bows to paddle.

Thanboke Khoranee National Park is a beautiful, cool and peaceful forest grove with emerald rock pools, streams and walkways. Swimming is permitted in the upper pool. Near the pool there is a small nature trail leading up into the limestone cliffs (sturdy shoes are advised). ■ *Getting there: take Route 4 back towards Phangnga; turn left down Route 4039 for Ao Luk, after 45 km. Two kilometres down this road there is a sign for the gardens, to the left. By public transport, take a songthaew from Krabi Town to Ao Luk, and then walk or catch a local songthaew.*

Laem Sak juts out from the mainland just North of Ao Luk and makes a good trip before or after a visit to the Thanboke Khoranee National Park. Turn left as you come out of the park and continue on Route 4039 into the town of Ao Luk and beyond down a small road to the end of the peninsular. There is a good seafood restaurant to the left, down a steep slope, near the fishing pier. Views back towards the mainland are impressive with a wall of limestone karst in the distance fringed by mangroves. Out to sea and to the west are a group of rocky islands. The fishing pier is a hive of activity and the restaurant serves excellent seafood and is a good place to watch the fishing boats pass by. ■ *Getting there:*

take Route 4 back towards Phangnga; turn left down Route 4039 and continue on through the town and along the winding road along the peninsular.

Garos Island lies off the coast of mainland Krabi near Ban Thung (before Ao Luk). A local tour leaves from a pier down a rough dirt track which can be reached from Ban Thung. (Turn left at Barn Tung, drive about 500 m and take a right turn down the dirt track. There are signs to the pier after about 5 km, and the pier is about 12 km in total from the main road). A day trip in a small

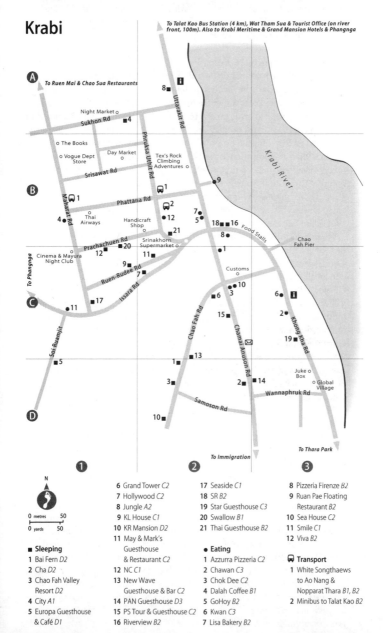

Krabi

To Talat Kao Bus Station (4 km), Wat Tham Sua & Tourist Office (on river front, 100m). Also to Krabi Meritime & Grand Mansion Hotels & Phangnga

The Andaman Sea Coast

6 Grand Tower *C2*	17 Seaside *C1*	8 Pizzeria Firenze *B2*
7 Hollywood *C2*	18 SR *B2*	9 Ruan Pae Floating
8 Jungle *A2*	19 Star Guesthouse *C3*	Restaurant *B2*
9 KL House *C1*	20 Swallow *B1*	10 Sea House *C2*
10 KR Mansion *D2*	21 Thai Guesthouse *B2*	11 Smile *C1*
11 May & Mark's		12 Viva *B2*
Guesthouse	● **Eating**	
& Restaurant *C2*	1 Azzurra Pizzeria *C2*	🚐 **Transport**
12 NC *C1*	2 Chawan *C3*	1 White Songthaews
13 New Wave	3 Chok Dee *C2*	to Ao Nang &
Guesthouse & Bar *C2*	4 Dalah Coffee *B1*	Nopparat Thara *B1, B2*
14 PAN Guesthouse *D3*	5 GoHoy *B2*	2 Minibus to Talat Kao *B2*
15 PS Tour & Guesthouse *C2*	6 Kwan *C3*	
16 Riverview *B2*	7 Lisa Bakery *B2*	

N

0 metres 50
0 yards 50

■ **Sleeping**
1 Bai Fern *D2*
2 Cha *D2*
3 Chao Fah Valley Resort *D2*
4 City *A1*
5 Europa Guesthouse & Café *D1*

long-tail fishing boat will take you past mangroves and limestone karst islands to Garos Island, where you can see some prehistoric wall paintings, and several caves used as traditional burial grounds for "sea gypsies" (Chao Le). Good for birdwatching, and for seeing the traditional lifestyles of local fishing communities. The tour provides a fantastic lunch cooked on a small island beach where you can also enjoy a swim. Operated by members of the local community. Recommended. ■ *Pre-arrange tour by calling T649149. Mr Mos speaks reasonably good English. His partner (Mr Mudura) can also take the tour but speaks much less English, although he knows more about the general area having lived there for most of his 60 years!*

It is easy to get stranded if you have not made arrangements to get back because not very many people visit the park

Khao Phanom Bencha National Park provides a magnificent backdrop to the town, with the peak rising more than 600 m above the surrounding land. Near the national park entrance is the lovely **Huai To Waterfall**. The drive to the waterfall is very pleasant with a distinctly rural feel, and the area around the park entrance has some lovely trees and open grassland which makes for a good picnic spot. Park rangers can take people on treks up to the peak and across down to a waterfall on the other side. To date, however, tourists seem to miss Khao Phanom Bencha park so the level of English spoken by park rangers can vary – check that you feel comfortable with any potential guide before setting out. The trek takes more than one day as the climb is quite steep. ■ *Getting there: motorcycle or other transport out on the main road going towards Trang (past Talat Kao). The turn-off comes before the exit for Wat Tham Sua.*

Khao Nor Chu Chi lowland forest, the **Crystal Pool and Hot Springs** are all located in Khlong Thom district to the south of Krabi province. Khao Nor Chu Chi has a forest trail and bungalow-style accommodation that was initiated as part of an ecotourism project aimed at conserving the seriously endangered Gurney's Pitta, a bird believed to be extinct but found recently by the well-known ornithologists Philip Round and Uthai Treesucon. Sadly, local influence has led to so much encroachment and plans for infrastructure development for tourism in this area that the project to support conservation of the Gurney's Pitta is generally considered to have been a failure. It is uncertain what the future of this forest and its animal inhabitants will be with the Tourism Authority of Thailand and various provincial figures all encouraging road development so that tourists can reach the crystal pool and other attractions. Once again tourists and tourism have a lot to answer for.

The Crystal Pool is so called because of the exceptional clarity of the water and its emerald colour. In fact the colour derives from mineral deposits which can be seen through the water. The pool is quite shallow and the water very bouyant. However while the pool may look attractive enough, the deposits feel rather crunchy and not particularly pleasant under foot and the slopes leading into the pool are very slippery. Fun to swim in if you have no nerves about the water, but probably not recommended for nervous swimmers as it can be quite a struggle to get out of the pool once in!

A visit to **hot springs** on a hot day may seem rather odd, but the temperature of the water is quite comfortable and it's a relaxing place to spend some time in amidst the trees. ■ *Getting to Khao Nor Chu Chi lowland forest, the Crystal Pool and the Hot Springs: tours can be arranged from most tour offices in town. For self-drive, the turn-off to Khao Nor Chu Chi is just after the major intersection in Khlong Thom town. It is marked. That said, once you get on to the road to the crystal pool and hot springs, signposting tends to deteriorate and it can be quite an adventure getting to the final destination (be it hot springs, lowland forest or crystal pool).*

Ao Nang and **Nopparat Thara Beaches** See page 291 for details. ■ *Getting there: white songthaews leave regularly from 0600 to 1800 from Maharat and Phattana roads stopping at both Nopparat Thara and Ao Nang (β30).*

Most tour companies operate daily and overnight tours around Phangnga Bay (see page 280), often incorporating a visit to Wat Tham Suwan Kuha and other local sights. Also available are river trips, birdwatching, tours to national parks and reserves (including Khao Nor Chu Chi lowland forest and crystal pool, Khao Phanom Bencha and Khao Sok), motorcycle treks and sea canoeing. **Tours**

In Krabi, the word guesthouse often means neither a warm, family welcome nor a homely atmosphere – with a few exceptions, hotels and guesthouses are very ordinary. Few people want to stay in town more than the single night it may take to catch a ferry to one of the outlying islands, or a bus back to Bangkok or south to Malaysia and Singapore. As a result, perhaps, most rooms are very plain and functional. Some newer guesthouses do have a bit more style, and it appears there is a shift in markets now with more backpackers spending time in Krabi town to avoid the high cost of accommodation on the beaches. The guesthouses on Ruen-Ruedee Rd are generally cramped and stuffy; those up the hill and elsewhere in the town are a little more spacious. Note that prices during the high season can be double the rates for the low season. **Sleeping**

A *Krabi Meritime Hotel* [sic], T620028-46, F620047 Krabi town's first luxury hotel, it is located about 2 km from town, off the road towards the bus station. Built overlooking the mangroves and limestone karst, they run a ferry service to a private beach and club. Expensive, and there have been complaints about poor service. They have another, newer, better-run hotel at Ao Nang, the *Ao Nang Pakasai Resort*. **B-C** *Boon Siam Hotel*, 27 Chao Khun Rd, T632511-5 F632510. One of the newest hotels in the town, the rooms are all a/c (with hot water) spacious and comfortable. A bit far out of the town, but still within walking distance of the centre (it's not a large town). Good value – the best in this price range. **B-C** *Grand Mansion*, 289/1 Uttarakit Rd, T611371. Some a/c, clean with good-sized rooms and spotless bathrooms. The main drawback is that this 4-storey hotel is 2 km or so from the centre of town, on the road towards the bus station. **C** *Thai*, 7 Issara Rd, T6111474, F620564. Some a/c, large hotel with 150 rooms, grotty corridors but the rooms are fine, large and clean with reasonable bathrooms, an acceptable mid-range place in need of a character transplant. Rooms vary quite a bit according to rate with the most expensive rooms having much better furnishing and facilities than the cheaper rooms. Discounts available in the low season. **C-D** *Chao Fah Valley Resort*, 50 Chao Fah Rd, T612499. Some a/c, this used to have attractive, clean and well-maintained wood and rattan bungalows but a recent visitor reports that it is sinking into decreptitude. The bathrooms are none too clean and food is best avoided. **C-D** *City Hotel*, 15/2-3 Sukhon Rd, T621280, F621301. Some a/c, 3-storey hotel for which we have received good reports, rooms are clean with attached bathrooms and friendly service, faces onto one of the quieter streets in town. Better value than the *Thai*.

D *Europa Café and Guesthouse*, 1/9 Soi Ruamjit Rd, T620407. Under Thai and Danish management, the *Europa Café* has five rooms above the restaurant. All rooms are nicely decorated, and clean, but the smallest rooms are rather dark as they don't have a window. Shared bathroom with hot water. The restaurant, which is decorated a bit like a pub (and features many photographs including one of Leonardo di Caprio during his stay in Krabi), serves good-quality northern European food (imported meats and cheeses). Henrich and Tip are good sources of local information – both speak excellent English and German, and Danish of course. The guesthouse closes up at 2300 so guests have to be back by that time. **D** *Hollywood*, 26 Issara Road, T620508.

Large-ish restaurant and bar serving western and Thai food in a shop house dressed up to look like a log cabin. Friendly staff but service can be a bit slow. Upstairs there are 10 rooms, all with shared bathrooms (separate male and female). Rooms are large, well-furnished, cool and very clean with ceiling fans, some rooms have a nice view. The water colours for sale on the walls of the restaurant are by a local artist – Boonkasem Soykaew. **D** *KR Mansion*, 52/1 Chao Fah Rd, T612761, F612545. Some a/c, well-priced restaurant, clean, bright and airy rooms, friendly staff, roof-top balcony for an evening beer and good views, videos shown nightly. This place is at the quieter top end of town, a 10 min walk from most of the bars and restaurants, one criticism we have received is that they can be rather pushy with their overpriced tours and tickets. Apparently, however, security at this guesthouse leaves a lot to be desired. There have been complaints of thefts from the rooms. **D** *Rai Leh Hotel* 28 Maharaj Road Soi 5, T613031-2 F613046. Very new. Simple rooms in a rabbit warren of a building. Not all rooms have windows. Very friendly service and not a bad place for the price, but located in a street with a lot of bars and karaoke places; this may not be the most comfortable place for a single woman to stay. **D** *Star Guest House* Chao Fah Rd, (opposite the market), T611721. A charming wooden guesthouse over the top of a small convenience store and tour office, the rooms (7) are tiny, leaving little space for more than a bed, but there is a pleasant balcony with tables and chairs overlooking the night market and the river. The whole house has been painted white and is bright and cheery. Separate bathrooms are downstairs near a small bar area in a garden at the back. Recommended. **D-E** *Bai Fern Guesthouse*, 24/1 Chao Fah Rd, T611254. Attached shower, clean fan rooms all with balcony. **D-E** *PAN Guesthouse*, 182 Uttarakit Road, near the Post Office, T612555/612041. More expensive rooms have own bathroom. Set in garden on hill with a restaurant, tour office and car rental at the front. Rooms are very simple and the garden is not very well maintained, but it's not a bad choice for Krabi town. **D-F** *Grand Tower*, 73/1 Uttarakit Rd, T611741. Good restaurant, a large guesthouse which, though not exactly towering, does have 5 floors, rooms are bare but clean, some with attached showers, videos are shown nightly in the ground-floor restaurant-cum-meeting area, and there is also a roof-top balcony to sit out in the evenings. Good travel agency attached. As with *KR Mansion*, there have been some complaints of poor security.

E *Ano Guest House* Just off *Maharaj Rd*, mostly caters to a Thai clientele. Quite old and a bit jaded, but the rooms are clean and well-kept, and adequate with bathrooms en suite (but partition walls only). **E** *KL House*, 24-32 Ruen-Ruedee Rd, T612511. Warren of a place above a tour office, small rather stuffy rooms with shared bathrooms, their claim of 'spacious and luxurious' rooms should be viewed as taking poetic license to extremes. **E** *NC Guesthouse* Prachachuen Rd. Large, smart rooms, restaurant downstairs. Central location and amenable staff. **E** *Siboya*, T611258, F630039. Wooden building brightly painted with a small café downstairs, souvenir shop and agent for the *Siboya Island Bungalow Resort* on Siboya Island. Rooms are priced depending on whether or not they have a window. Share bathroom. Clean, simple. **E** *SR Guesthouse*, Khong Kha Rd (next door to *River View Guest House*). Big, clean rooms with shared bathroom, hospitable owners, great value. Downstairs there is a large second-hand bookstore. **E** *Thai Guesthouse*, on the corner of Issara and Phruksa-Uthit Road above a clothes shop. Very simple rooms, no natural light but well lit. Not very well maintained. **E-F** *New Wave Bar and Guest House*, 25-1/2 Chao Fah Rd. Simple accommodation in 3 rooms of a wooden house with a common area and a west-facing balcony overlooking one of the greener parts of town. The New Wave Bar is in the garden adjacent to the Guest House (advertisements for full moon parties suggest the guest house may be rather noisy when the season is in full swing). Run by an English woman, Emma, and her Thai boyfriend, both very friendly. **E-F** *PS Guest House*, 71/1 Uttarakit Rd T620480. Small guesthouse with just 4 rooms. Clean with shared bathroom. Quite dark and very simple, but friendly and helpful owners. Room rates depend on the size. **E-F** *River View Guesthouse* Khong Kha Rd. Only 4 rooms with views of the river, above the Thammachart Tour Company and Restaurant, but clean, decent and good value – and with a friendly owner (Acharn Lek), who speaks excellent English and will (for a fee) act as translator should anyone need assistance in legal affairs. The *Thammachart Restaurant* specializes in vegetarian food, although they also serve non-vegetarian dishes. **E-F** *Swallow Guesthouse* Prachachuen Rd. Very friendly and well run. Plain but clean rooms, shared bathrooms. **F** *Cha*, Chao Fah Rd, T611141. Restaurant, basic huts set in garden compound on the main road but set back. Dirty but friendly, motorbike and jeep hire. **F** *Jungle Tours & Guesthouse*, Uttarakit Rd. Restaurant serving basic meals, shared bathroom facilities, tiny, dark rooms but comfy beds and very friendly family owners, tickets and tours sold.

Thai Expensive: *Ruan Pae*, Uttarakit Rd (floating restaurant). Attractive location but overpriced and very mediocre food.   **Eating**

Expensive-mid-range: *Ruen Mai*, on Maharaj Rd well beyond the *Vogue Department Store* up the hill on the left-hand side as you leave the town. Excellent Thai food in a quiet garden setting. Popular with locals, with good English-language menu and help-ful staff. Has a number of southern specialities. Fish dishes are particularly good, as are the salads (yam). *Chao Sua*, on Maharaj Rd, along the road from the *Ruen Mai* (the sign, with a leopard on it, is in Thai). Another restaurant that attracts large numbers of locals. The restaurant itself has a rambling slightly chaotic feel and service can be highly vari-able. Serves excellent Thai food. Barbecued seafood and virtually anything that is fried are especially good. A very original menu with lots of house specialities, for example, the Chao Sua eggs are delicious. They also have an English-language menu.

Mid-range: *May and Mark's Restaurant*, Ruen-Ruedee Rd. Good information, friendly atmosphere and good food, home-made bread, Mexican and Italian dishes, Thai food, excellent fresh coffee, breakfasts and all the usual from banana porridge to pizza. *Go Hoy*, Uttarakit Rd at the junction with Issara Rd. One of the oldest restaurants in the town, they have been operating for over 50 years, the restaurant has changed along with the rest of Krabi. The building used to be built entirely from wood standing above water. Behind the restaurant along what is now Maharaj Rd was forest. Go Hoy serves *jok* (rice porridge) in the morning and Hainanese chicken, red pork and other basics for the rest of the day. Closed for the evening. Friendly, very informal, service and a good range of food on an English-language menu. They do vegetarian dishes too. **Mid-range-cheap** *Kwan Coffee Corner*, 75 Uttarakit Rd. Fresh coffee, sandwiches, milk shakes, ice creams, cheap and tasty Thai food, good breakfasts of fruit and muesli, almost everything even if, as they put it, "coffee is not your cup of tea". Recommended. There are several other places on Khong Kha Rd by the pier. **Mid-range-cheap** *Chawan*, serves Thai food and the usual western dishes (sandwiches, spaghetti, etc). The Thai food comes in generous portions for a reasonable price – caters to a western palate.

Cheap: *Smile*, opposite Soi Ruanjit on Issara Rd. Shiny new place with outdoor seat-ing, serving fast food (as well as non-fast), ice cream and coffee. **Expen-sive-mid-range**: *Pizzeria Firenze*, Khong Kha Rd. Usual mix of Thai and Italian dishes, nothing culinarily notable. **Cheap**: *Sea House*, Chao Fah Rd. Reasonable prices, menu includes freshly ground coffee. **Mid-range-cheap**: *Chok Dee*, Chao Fah Rd. Reason-able prices, some dishes are really delicious, and very good value prices for the quality and quantity of food. The owner has two televisions with cable and video – good selection of movies. It can get a bit loud, but the owner is responsive if you can't hear a movie or you want the sound turned down. Friendly management and staff.

Expensive-mid-range: *Azzurra*, Uttarakit Rd just passed the police box. Pretty good pizza and pasta. Nice fresh coffee. There is a branch in Ao Nang. *Europa Café*, 1/9 Soi Ruamjit Rd, T620407 Serves tasty Northern European food with imported ingredients. A favourite with locals and local expats. *Viva*, Phruksa-Uthit Rd between Pattana and Issara roads. Serves a range of European, Italian and Thai food and good fresh coffee (Lavazza). Looks set to become quite a hang-out for travellers, but the music can be very loud and the food is nothing special. **Cheap**: *Dalah Coffee* Maharaj Rd, on the other side of the road to *Vogue*, next to the access to the forest temple and across from a doctor's clinic. Serves fresh coffee, tea and ice cream in a pleasant, clean coffee shop with a small 'garden' down the side of the shop. Popular with locals, the owner and his wife both speak reasonable English.

Bakeries *Lisa Bakery*, 120-123 Uttarakit Road. For rather synthetic cakes and reasonable croissants. *May & Mark's Restaurant*, Ruen Rudee Rd. Home made bread: sourdough, rye and whole wheat. Fresh bread is also available from the *Pizza Firenze* and *Chawan* near the pier.

Foodstalls A **night market** sets up in the early evening on Khlong Kha Road, along the Krabi River, good seafood dishes. Tasty ice cream from the ice cream stall, and good Thai desserts from the dessert stall furthermost up the hill. Stall food is also available from the **fresh market** between Srisawat and Sukhon roads, and from scattered places along Uttarakit Rd, facing onto the Krabi River. The *Vogue Department Store* on Maharat Rd also has an a/c 'food court' on the 3rd floor with dishes only marginally more expensive than out on the street.

Bars *Toyaiman*, 228 Uttarakit Rd (on the hill). *Juke Box Pub* and *Global Village* both on Khong Kha Rd. The latter is probably the better of the 2.

Festivals *Boat races* on the river, very noisy. *Berg Fa Andaman Festival* in the gardens beyond the pier in Nov (coinciding with *Loy Krathong*) – a showcase for traditional dancing and singing from around Thailand, sadly there is little information in English available at the festival. Also features local handicrafts from the Andaman region.

Shopping **Books** *The Books*, 78-80 Maharat Rd (next to *Vogue Department Store*). Many of the guesthouses and tour companies also run book exchanges. **Department stores** *Vogue Department Store*, Maharat Rd. **Supermarkets** *Sri Nakhorn*, opposite the *Thai Hotel*. **Clothes and tailoring** There is a tailor on the corner of Issara and Khong Kha roads. Lots of clothes stores on Phattana, Prachachuen and Uttarakit roads mostly selling beach wear. **Souvenirs** *Khun B Souvenir*, and other souvenir shops on Khong Kha and Uttarakit Rd sell a range of souvenirs from all around Thailand and Southeast Asia; *Hot & Spicy* on Prachachuen Rd, sells handicrafts mostly from the Northern region, and *Thai Silver* opposite *Thai Hotel* sells silverware mostly from Nakhon Sri Thammarat.

Sport **Game fishing**: *Phi Phi Marine Travel Co* can arrange expeditions to catch marlin, sailfish, barracuda and tuna.

Tour operators Concentrated on Uttarakit and Ruen-Ruedee roads and close to the Chao Fah Pier. Guesthouses often double up as tour companies and travel agents. There are so many tour and travel companies/agents, and information is so freely and widely available, that it is not necessary to list outfits here. Prices and schedules are all openly posted and a 30-min walk around town will reveal all. We have, though, received negative reports regarding the professionalism of *Pee Pee Sea Tour*, 35 Issara Rd. **Rock climbing** *Tex's Rock Climbing Adventure* has an office and shop in Krabi town, on Uttarakit Rd, at the back of *Jam Travel*, as well as at Rai Leh East.

Local Motorbike hire: many of the guesthouses and tour companies hire out scooters and motorbikes, ฿150 – 200 per day. **Songthaews**: drive through town, stopping at various places such as Phattana Rd, in front of *Travel & Tour*, for Ao Phra Nang and in front of the foodstalls on Uttarakit Rd for Noppharat Thara Beach. They also run regularly to the bus station at Talaat Kao, 5 km from town.

Transport
93 km from Phangnga
180 km from Phuket
867 km from Bangkok

Air Krabi airport is located about 8 km out of town on the road towards Trang. THAI and PB Air operate daily flights (for about ฿4,200 return). It is usually possible to get hotels/resorts to arrange a pick-up. Alternatively, PB Air will arrange a pick-up (from their flights) if you call their office in town (T622048-9). There is usually a songthaew waiting for incoming flights. Alternatively, regular connections with Phuket, and from there take a bus to Krabi.

Train Some people take the train (usually the overnight sleeper) to Phun Phin (Surat Thani) where the train is met by buses for the 3-hr journey to Krabi. Buses drop travellers at the tourist office in Krabi, where bookings for the islands can be made. Alternatively travel to Trang or Nakhon Si Thammarat.

Road Bus: station is 5 km out of town, in Talat Kao (Old Market), close to the intersection of Uttarakit Rd and Route 4. Red songthaews regularly run between the bus station and town (฿5). Motorcycle taxis also wait to ferry bus passengers into town. Numerous evening a/c, VIP and non-a/c connections with Bangkok's Southern bus terminal, 16 hrs. Regular a/c and non-a/c connections with Phuket via Phangnga, 3 hrs and 1½ hrs respectively. Morning buses to Koh Samui, via Surat Thani with ferry connection, 6 or 7 hrs by *Songserm Travel's* express boat. Regular connections with Surat Thani (3 hrs) and Trang, a/c minibuses to Hat Yai. Tickets and information about bus connection (both public buses and private tour buses) available from countless travel agents. **Taxi**: to Trang 2 hrs (฿150). For Ao Nang and Nopparat Thara take a white songthaew from Phattana Rd (฿15).

International connections with Malaysia and Singapore: by a/c minibus to Singapore, Kuala Lumpur and Penang (departs 0700 and 1200, 7-11 hrs, ฿300). Buses stop in Hat Yai, for passports to be checked. Some travel agents charge ฿10 'border service' – avoid paying if possible.

Train and road Combination tickets from Bangkok via Surat Thani. Travel agents will book tickets.

Boat All boats leave from Chao Fah Pier. Daily boats to Phi Phi 0930 and 1430, returning 0900 and 1300, 1½ hrs (฿150). Express boats to Phi Phi 1030 and 1430, (may be more frequent in the high season) returning 0900 and 1300, 1 hr. Daily boat to Koh Lanta at 1330, returning 0800, 2½ hrs (฿150). Also boats to Phra Nang. Every Tue and Thu at 0830 express boats from Makham Bay, Phuket 3½ hrs, stopping at Phi Phi, 1½ hrs en route. To Phuket, the boat leaves at 1300 on Tue and Thu.

Banks Branches of all major banks with ATMs. **Communications** Internet: lots of services available around the town, especially on Uttarakit Rd, Chao Fah Rd (towards the pier) and around *Hollywood*. Prices per minute vary. Connections are still quite slow in Krabi. **Post Office**: Uttarakit Rd (half way up the hill, not far from the Customs Pier). It has a Poste Restante counter. **International telephone**: quite a way out of the town on the way to the Krabi Meritime Hotel. Alternatively, look for services in some tour offices on Uttarakit Rd. **Useful addresses** Immigration office: Uttarakit Rd, a little way up from the post office on the same side of the road. The office will extend visas for an extra 30 days (฿500) and provide 14-day visas (free) for people arriving by sail boat. They can also provide re-entry permits for those travelling on longer-stay visas. Open 0830-1200, 1300-1630, Mon-Fri. **NB** Photocopies can be made at a couple of shops just across the road from the Immigration office in the row of wooden shophouses.

Directory

The Andaman Sea Coast

Ao Nang and Nopparat Thara

Phone code: 075   The beaches at Ao Nang and Nopparat Thara lie 18 km and 22 km respectively to the west of Krabi town. Many of the local people in the area are not Buddhist but Muslim Thais and it is noticeable, for example, that pork is rarely on the menu of restaurants hereabouts. (It should also be noted that as for most places in Thailand, but especially with respect to Muslim communities, topless

Around Krabi

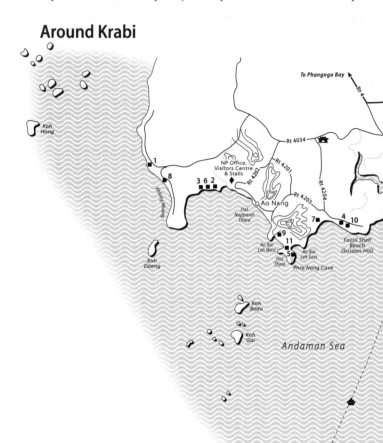

Related maps
Ao Nang,
page 294
Krabi, page 283

N

0 km 2
0 miles 2

■ **Sleeping**
1 Andaman Holiday Resort
2 Andaman Inn
3 Bamboo
4 Dawn of Happiness
5 Dusit
6 Emerald
7 Holyland Bungalows
8 Pine Bungalow
9 Rai Leh Village
10 Sea & Sand Bungalows
11 Sunrise Bungalows

sunbathing is very definitely frowned upon in the area). The road to the coast winds for 15 km past spectacular limestone cliffs, a large reclining Buddha, rubber stands and verdant forest. Arriving at the coast in the evening, with the setting sun turning the limestone cliffs of Ao Nang a rich orange, and the sea interspersed with precipitous limestone crags, is a wonderful sight.

Ao Nang provides a range of accommodation and facilities including diving, windsurfing, fishing and tours to the surrounding islands. It is still quite relaxed, with a relatively peaceful atmosphere, although sometimes the noise of the long-tail boats plying back and forth to Rai Leh and nearby islands can be disturbing. The sandy, gently shelving beach is being eroded at one end by run-off from the beach road, but the beach is good for swimming out of the monsoon season with calm waters, and beautiful limestone scenery. The surrounding beaches, coves, caves and grottoes provide good trekking and boat trip destinations. Note that between June and October the monsoon makes swimming risky and many bungalows shut down for the season. Excellent seafood available here.

Three kilometres northwest of Ao Nang, **Nopparat Thara Beach** is a long sandy beach, popular with Thai picnickers and part of the **Had Nopparat Thara – Phi Phi Islands National Marine Park**, although you'd never guess that looking at the Ao Nang end of the beach where accommodation, bars and stalls are rapidly moving in. There is a visitors' centre here with a small exhibition and a multitude of foodstalls. ■ *0830-1630*. At low tide it is possible to walk out to some of the islands in the bay. In the opposite direction, beyond the limestone crags, is **Phra Nang** and the beaches (and accommodation) of **Rai Leh** – accessible only by long-tailed boat (see below).

The Andaman Sea Coast

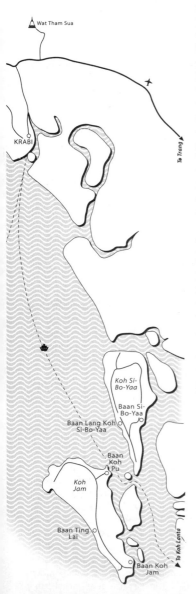

Excursions

Time your visit to coincide with low tide when more of the pavement is exposed

Fossil Shell Beach or *Susaan Hoi* lies 5 km east of Ao Nang. Great slabs of what looks like concrete are littered along the shoreline but on closer inspection turn out to be countless fossilized freshwater shells, laid-down 75 million years ago. It is one of only three such cemeteries in the world; the others are in the USA and Japan. **Sleeping C** *Dawn of Happiness Resort*, PO Box 35, Krabi 81000, T612730. This is a guesthouse with a difference, good traditional bungalows, environmentally and culturally sensitive, library, hammocks, trips to local monasteries, the owners try to educate their guests but not in an overbearing way, isolated position in Ao Nam Mao, close to Susaan Hoi. *Sea and Sand Bungalows*, up the road from the *Dawn of Happiness Resort* down a small dirt road. Set back from the beach which is about a two-minute walk past a shrimp nursery and through another resort. Simple bungalows, but furnished with a bit of care, some a/c, cheaper with fan. Not a great walk to the beach and only half the bungalows have sea views. The owners are in a partnership to build a three-storey resort with bungalows in the land between this bungalow resort and the sea. *Holyland Bungalows*, between Ao Nang and the Fossil Shell Beach down a dirt road through rubber plantations in a stunning location at the far end of Ao Nam Mao next to the limestone crags that fringe Rai Leh. The layout of the bungalows, sadly, makes little use of its wonderful location. There are some bamboo bungalows with better views and location overlooking the bay, but most are concrete and set back in sparse gardens. A couple of motorbikes can be rented at ฿200 per day.

Khlong Muang and around Krabi the *Green Earth Botanical Garden Co Ltd* operated by Mr Gift (of Gift's Bungalows that used to be on the beach at Ao Nang) operates tours between Hat Nopparat Thara via boat and land ending up with a tour of the botanical gardens and including lunch. He also operates small group mountain bike tours of the province and walking tours up the highest peak in Krabi province. Equipment is well maintained, and staff are friendly and helpful. Prices range from ฿900-฿1,200 per person, usually including a meal. Contact: T637190 or T637190.

Koh Boda (see map page 279) is 30 minutes by boat from Ao Phra Nang. It is a haven for snorkellers, with wonderfully clear water. Round-trip excursions last five hours. There are bungalows available on the island for ฿350, book through the *Krabi Resort* (T611389 or B2518094). The bungalows are a good size, restaurant, 'Western' loos, not particularly friendly staff. Camping is possible on the island (฿50). The nearby **Koh Gai** is also a 30 minutes boat trip from Ao Phra Nang.

Koh Phi Phi is accessible as a day trip from Ao Nang (see page 301). Arrange a ticket for the boat trip through your guesthouse. The boat departs from Ao Nang at 0900 returning at 1630.

Phra Nang and **Rai Leh** are also easily accessible. Long-tailed boats leave regularly from the beach opposite *Sea Canoe*, 15 minutes (฿50).

Sleeping

High-season (Nov-May) room rates may be as much as double (or more) the low-season (Jun-Oct) rates

Accommodation in Ao Nang is currently in a state of flux. Guesthouses and bungalows are appearing further and further inland, while more expensive hotels are being developed nearer the beach. Some of the old favourites in the centre of the beach area have had to move on as the owners of the land have terminated contracts and this central area is now becoming dominated by shops, restaurants and bars. Behind these developments there are some rooms available, but it's rather over-crowded. Some new hotels have been developed up in the hills overlooking Hat Nopparat Thara – most are fairly pricey, and this is the location of Ao Nang's two luxury resorts (the *Ao Nang Pakasai Resort* and the *Thai Village Resort*. A new hotel by the Pavillion Group is under construction in this area. It's difficult to see where development of this area is going. The Hat Nopparat Thara beach area is changing rapidly from a quiet, undeveloped and beautiful beach to, frankly, a rather tacky beach front. Sadly, the forested hills have also been targeted by large-scale developers, even though apparently these were once designated as reserve forest (in this case it's tempting to say, 'what's new?').

Ao Nang **L-AL** *Ao Nang Pakasai Resort*, 88 Moo 3, Ao Nang, T637777, F637637, yoonpk@loxinfo.co.th A new plush resort, owned and managed by the same company that owns and operates the *Krabi Meritime* in the town, up a small road off the main road running between Hat Nopparat Thara and Ao Nang. Complete with vanishing-edge pool with a great sea view. Not all rooms have sea views. Rooms are spacious and offer pretty much everything you'd expect for the price, although only the deluxe rooms have baths as well as showers. Huge range of rooms with some incredibly expensive suites. One restaurant and a pool bar. Well managed, professional service. Also offer cookery classes and bicycle rental. The resort advertises itself as 'nature-loving', but this would appear to be based more on the fact that its location is up in amongst the trees with a view of the sea than a reflection of any pro-environmental policies (part of the mountain had to be 'landscaped' to build the resort, and the resort is located in amongst some prime forest, some of which had to be cleared for building). **L-AL (promotional rate)** *Thai Village Resort*. A huge hotel up in the forest with views over Nopparat Thara beach and bay. Although a new resort (being developed by the Pavillion Group) is being constructed opposite, this does not obscure views of the bay from the rooms at the Thai Village. Built in central Thai style but without any special charm and with rather large paved areas throughout the resort. There are three large swimming pools including a pool bar, and also a children's pool. Expensive, luxury resort with all the extras – beauty salon, fitness room, several restaurants, bakery and coffee shop, gift shop. Belongs to the same group as the *Siam Beverley*. Rooms are well equipped as one would expect for this price bracket, and have large balconies. Still, expensive at the upper bracket price given that this is not a beach-front property.

AL (high)-A (low) *Lai Thai Resort*, 25/1 Moo 2, Ao-Nang T637281 F637282, info@laithai-resort.com, http://laithai-resort.com/ About 1 km from the beach, but with a shuttle service for free. Family-run resort with great views of the mountains at the back of Ao Nang. The swimming pool (black-tiled) is one of the best in Ao Nang. Friendly owners (Robert and his Thai wife). Rooms are spacious, well decorated and very comfortable. Restaurant and bar have good ambiance and a range of food including Mexican. **A** *Krabi Resort* (office in Krabi at 53-57 Phattana Rd, T611389, BT2089165). At northwest end of the beach, a/c, restaurant overlooking the sea, nice pool, some bungalows, rooms are some of the best available on Ao Nang, large and airy, with satellite TV and baths. In need of refurbishment but a good location and friendly staff. Apparently the bungalows are better than the hotel rooms. **A-B** *Ao Nang Villa*, 133 Ao Nang Rd, southeast end of the beach, T/F637270. A/c, restaurant, pool, a range of rooms here, the most expensive are in a 3-storey block built around a swimming pool (small for the size of hotel), there are also bungalows with attached bathrooms, both a/c and fan. Excellent views from upper-floor rooms in new block. Could do with better maintenance and cleaning. **A (high)-B (low)** *AP Resort*, T637342. Very pleasant proprietor, simple, decent rooms, but rather overpriced, also have a travel desk and email facilities. **A (high)-B (low)** *Arcadian Villa*, 264/1 Moo 2, Ao Nang, T637837. Five concrete bungalows by the side of the road near the Ao Nang School, quite a distance (over 2 km) from the sea. Sensibly they are facing in towards the coconut plantation behind. Twin beds in all rooms, very new, very clean and well-equipped with satellite TV, a/c, fridge. Pleasant location, but a bit pricey for somewhere this far from the beach. **A (high)-B (low)** *Ao Nang Beach Resort*, T637766-9, F637812. Hotel style accommodation in a block along the seafront. The entrance is set back from the front but the hotel lives up to its claim that many of the rooms have excellent sea views. Clean, standard type of rooms, central location. **A-B** *Beach Terrace*, 154 Moo 2, Ao Nang, TB7220060, FB7220061. A/c, there are really 2 hotels here: one is a 6-storey block rather incongruously sited on a beach where most places are just a single storey tall; the second 'hotel' is a series of large, solidly made concrete bungalows. At these prices you don't really get very much: comfortable enough rooms with superb views from the upper floors of the block, but a down-at-heel coffee shop that would look average in a hotel charging half these rates, and not even a swimming pool. **A (high)-B (low)** *Frito Misto Villa*, T637692, F637691,

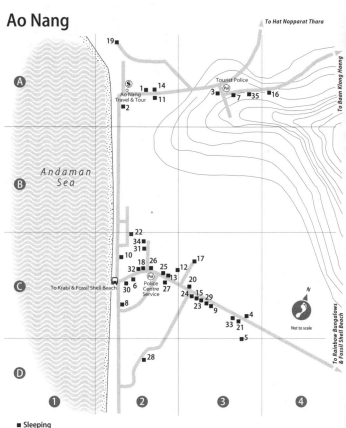

Ao Nang

To Hat Nopparat Thara

To Baan Klong Haeng

Andaman Sea

To Krabi & Fossil Shell Beach

To Rainbow Bungalows & Fossil Shell Beach

Not to scale

The Andaman Sea Coast

frittomisto1@hotmail.com Italian-owned time-share property that rents out apartments and rooms to guests when the owners are not in residence. Up on the hill away from the beach in a quiet location, with pool and good facilities (excellent bathrooms with bidets no less!). Variable decorations. A bit far from everything, but represent pretty good value for the facilities. **A (high)-B (low)** *Krabi Nopparat Resort*, 83 Moo 3, Ao Nang T637632-3 F637634 Small two-storey blocks facing towards the sea. Upper rooms have balcony and are separate. Lower rooms have balcony and are connecting. Simply furnished, a/c, hot water, satellite TV, telephone. There are two rows of rooms close together. The front row has views of the sea. The back row has views of the front row! Behind the resort there is a small lawn overlooking the *khlong* and the mangroves. **A (high)-B (low)** *Ocean Garden View Resort*, T637527-31, F637211. Large new development with several two-storey blocks of rooms on the hillside back from the main road. Located next to the Ocean Mart, just up from the *Phranang Inn*. Rooms are well equipped and comfortable with balconies. All rooms have views of the sea, rooms at the back, higher up the hill have the best views. Pool under construction. Not a bad choice for the price, but the steps are quite steep up the hill. **A (high)-C (low)** *BB Bungalows*, T637542-3, F637304. Both fan and a/c available. Older cottages here are now showing their age and the attached bathrooms with Asian toilets are rather grotty, newer bungalows much better – large and solidly built, but constructed too close together and overpriced for what they offer. **A (high)-D (low)** *Ao Nang Paradise Resort*, T637650-1, F637652, aonangparadise @hotmail.com, continuing down the road from the *Lai Thai Resort* and near the older boxing stadium, this is a new bungalow resort with a very welcoming reception area and good lighting throughout. Good views of the mountains with coconut palms in the foreground. Bungalows are well designed with lots of natural light and some nice decorative features. The owners/managers/designers live on-site and obviously care about the quality of experience they offer (including maintenance of the bungalows). They plan to offer fans and a/c for every bungalow and to provide mosquito nets for those who prefer fans. Can book tours at the front desk. Recommended.

B *Ban Ao Nang Resort*, 31/3 Moo 2, Ao Nang, T7220258, F612914, TB7220258. A/c, 3-storey modern block with balconies overlooking the sea. Rooms have satellite TV and fridge, solid wooden floors, large bathrooms with hot-water showers. This place is competitively priced and the rooms are better than those at most of the more expensive resorts. **B** *Phra Nang Inn*, PO Box 25, T637130, F637134. A/c, restaurant, small pool, older wing of hotel is on one side of the road, a new 3-storey concrete structure faced in wood to try and make it more 'natural' on the other. Rooms are mediocre at this price, although the views in the evening from the top floor of the new wing are spectacular. **B-C** *Ao Nang Thara Lodge*, T7230517, F3916245. Between Ao Nang and Nopparat Thara, good restaurant, own bathroom, but generally looking pretty jaded. Views are obscured by the trees in front of the bungalows, water garden, friendly management. **B (high)-C (low)** *BB Inn Hotel*, T627148, F637147. A new hotel block owned and operated by the same owner as the *BB Bungalows*, and adjacent to them. Rooms are spacious and clean with tiled floors but tacky decor. Well equipped with baths, small TV, fridge. **B-C** *Hill Side Village*, 168/10 Moo 2 Ao Nang, T637604, Leem@loxinfo.co.th Opposite the *Lai Thai Resort*. Recently converted concrete row of rooms. Rooms come in sets of two (double at back, twin at front) and would make good family rooms. Rooms to the back are smaller and cheaper, with shower only and no hot water. Rooms at the front are twin beds with a bath and hot water. All rooms come with a/c, TV (satellite), and a fridge. Friendly staff also provide information on tours at the front desk, and will take guests to and from the beach. Restaurant serves the usual international favourites. **B-D** *Krabi Seaview Resort* (Krabi office at 171-173 Uttarakit Rd, T611648). Some a/c, solidly built brick A-frame bungalows with zinc roofs, looking almost alpine, set around a rather unattractive pond. Attached bathrooms, there are also some much cheaper cottages set back further away from the road, with good views over the treetops and out to sea. **B-D** *Peace Laguna Resort*, 193 Moo 2, T611972, BT7231005. Some a/c, this is one of the more attractive and better designed of the mid-range places, virtually in the shadow of the limestone crag that dominates the southeastern end of Ao Nang. Solid brick and tile-roofed bungalows built around a large pond and off the road so much quieter than many other places, all bungalows with hot-water in bathrooms, cheaper cottages with fan, a path leads down to Ao Nang Beach allowing guests to avoid the road. **B (high)-D (low)** *Sea of Love*, T637204. Trendy bar and restaurant with accommodation in 4 rooms in rustic style behind. If you can get over the embarrassment of staying somewhere called the 'Sea of Love', this is a good choice – rooms are all different, nicely designed with a bit of style, and though the back area is quite closely packed the feel is villagey rather than over-crowded.

C *Ao Nang Palm Hill Valley* , up and across the road from the *Lai Thai Resort* there are several concrete bungalows in mature gardens. Variable state of repair. Tours are offered at the front desk. **C** *Ao Nang Royal Resort*, T7231071. Group of 15-odd a/c bungalows built in a circle around a concrete pond. Rooms are functional, they have no view (the hotel is set back from the beach), but are some of the best-value, a/c rooms available here (especially good rates in the low season), bathrooms with hot-water showers, a good place to stay if intending to remain out during the day and just want somewhere cool to sleep at night. **C** *Dutch Mansion*, 249/2 Moo 2, Ao Nang, T01-3968152. Newly renovated and decorated rooms in a shophouse. Rooms are huge, all with a/c, warm water, TV and fridge. Very clean. Simply furnished. Rooms vary so ask to see a few if you can. Some rooms at the back have little natural light, but these are probably quieter as they are away from the road. Good value. **C** *Lavinia House*, good clean rooms in the centre of the beach at the back, behind the shops. **C-D** *Ao Nang Blue Bayou Bungalow*, T637558. About a third of the way along the road between Ao Nang and the National Parks offices, the *Blue Bayou Bungalows* used to be the only accommodation (even development) on Hat Nopparat Thara beach. Now obscured behind the *Rim Leh Seafood Restaurant*, these basic fan or a/c bungalows, no hot water, are looking very run-down. Friendly staff. Tours available from the front desk. They have their own restaurant. **C (high)-D (low)** *Ao Nang Mountain Paradise*, 26/11 Moo 2, Ao Nang, T637659, 9 rooms in bungalow-style accommodation (identical to *Ao Nang Garden Home Resort* in style). Ceiling fan with some a/c, hot water. Simply furnished but clean, in a quiet location down a dirt road near the *Lai Thai Resort* with good views of the limestone mountains. Friendly management. Well-priced basic breakfasts are available at the tiny restaurant/office at the front. **C-D** *Leela Valley*, 262/1 Ao Nang T635673. Some simple bamboo bungalows on the ground and some smarter fan and a/c houses on tall stilts with balconies, set in spacious grounds rather lacking in shade. Good views of the mountains. Rooms are clean. Discounts are given for long lets. Quite a distance from the sea, but excellent value. **C-D** *Seagull Huts*, next to *Lai Thai Resort*. Brick and wood bungalows with the limestone karst mountains in the background. About 50 m off the main road. Fan rooms. Basic.

D *Ao Nang Ban Lae*, T7220243. Reasonable and adequate. **D** *Ao Nang Garden Home Resort* , T637586 Bungalow style is almost identical to the *Ao Nang Mountain Paradise* which is just down the road, but these are raised above the ground and have nice wooden bannisters to the balconies. No hot water. Serves only coffee for breakfast. **D** *Rainbow Restaurant and Bungalows*, 248 Moo 2, Ao Nang, T/F637336 About 1.5 km away from the beach, after the turn-off from the Fossil Shell Beach. Bungalows are up on the hill. Very simple with shared bathrooms (clean). Quiet location. The owners have found a sensible solution to the problem of the distance to the beach by providing residents with the free use of a bicycle each. Bicycles can also be hired for ฿100 per day. **D** *Phra Nang Place*, Laem Nang, T512172, F612251. On private plantation, catch a boat from Ao Nang or Krabi, restaurant, quiet location and well designed. **D-E** *Ao Nang Beach Bungalows*, near the centre of the beach, thatched bamboo bungalows spaced widely enough apart so as not to be oppressive, attractive garden setting. **D-E** *Ao Nang Village*, simple tidy rooms and only 5 mins from the beach despite being the last on the row. **D-E** *Jungle Hut Bungalows*, simple, rustic, split bamboo huts up the road, away from the beach, these are among the cheapest bungalows on Ao Nang.

E *Green Park*, 13/1 Mu 2. Some of the cheapest bungalows available here, but showing their age, they are also some of the quietest, set back from the road and virtually in the middle of a forest, there are no views and although the basic cottages have good verandas the trees shade out most of the sun, more expensive cottages have simple attached shower rooms.

Guesthouses There is a line of older guesthouses (*Orchid, Dream Garden House, Mountain View, Nong Eed House* and *Penny's*) on one side of the road to the Fossil Shell Beach; they all offer traditional second- and third-storey rooms in our **E** category. *Nong Eed House* has a block of new rooms at the back, but at our last visit the staff were anything but friendly. Penny's has also made some changes and upgraded accommodation (http://phket.loxinfo.co.th/~johneyre, Pennys@loxinfo.co.th, T637295). There is also a group of places on the opposite side of the road, all exactly the same. The rooms are clean and quite large, usually with shared bathrooms. In the low season rates are in our **F** category, rising to **E** in the high season. The line of guesthouses, fronted by a row of restaurants, include *Sea World, PK Mansion* (set off the road), *Sea Beer, Jinda, One* and *Lottas* (on the road).

Nopparat Thara B-C The headquarters of the *Nopparat Thara and Phi Phi Islands National Park* has some bungalows and camping facilities, T5790529. **D** *Emerald Bungalow*, Don Son Beach, T611944. Catch a boat from Nopparat Thara pier across the estuary, westwards, this place is very peaceful with large, fan bungalows, to get here follow instructions as per *Bamboo*. **D** *Sara Cove*, 10 rooms in an isolated position but otherwise much the same as other places. **D-E** *Andaman Inn*, T612728. 35 rooms and some basic huts. **E-F** *Bamboo*, on round the coast from Noppharat Thara over the river, restaurant (good food), shared facilities, very basic, friendly staff. Recommended. **E-F** *Nature Restaurant and Bungalow*, very basic place run by friendly young Thais, the most remote place on the beach. To get there, take a bus from Krabi to the National Park office; the staff from *Bamboo* will pick you up from here (5 mins boat trip over river).

Khlong Muang L-AL *Andaman Holiday Resort*, T7220207, BT7111942. Large resort which extends right down to the beach in a peaceful and isolated spot. Pool is a bit under-sized for the number of rooms. Rooms vary, with the more expensive villas representing better value. Over-priced for what it is. Service at the restaurant is lacking professionalism given the price of the rooms and the food. **C** *Green Earth Botanical Garden Co, Ltd.* Two rooms in the main building. Rooms are nicely, if simply furnished with twin beds and a fan, and the setting is delightful in nearly an acre of tropical gardens. This is operated by Mr Gift of *Gift's Restaurant and Bakery*. Also operates various tours (see **Tours**), teaches Thai cookery, and runs this nursery/botanical garden. Mr Gift ascribes to strong environmental principles, and keeps things very low impact and peaceful. Recommended. Both *Klai Wang* and Mr Gift's place are for those looking for something very peaceful and off-the-beaten track. **D** *Klai Wang* Thai house with two simply-decorated rooms and a bathroom set in a lovely garden near a waterfall and a couple of fish ponds. A couple of kilometres from the sea, the house is right by the stream running down from the waterfall. Friendly owner who will take visitors on a trek up past fields and mountain forest to a cave (for a fair price). Vegetables served at the restaurant are organic, grown in a small plot opposite the accommodation. He rents the whole house for ฿500 a night. Recommended. **E** *Pine Bungalow* (Krabi T612192). Basic grass huts with mosquito nets, friendly staff, Asian toilets, cold water, boat trips to nearby islands arranged, dirt road all the way there. Recommended.

Eating As one would expect, the best food available at Ao Nang is seafood. Almost all the restaurants along the beach front road, and then lining the path northwest towards the *Krabi Resort*, serve BBQ fish, chilli crab, steamed crab, prawns and so on. There is little to choose between these restaurants – they tend to serve the same dishes in the same way. Most lay their catches out on ice for customers to peruse – snapper, shark, pomfret, tiger prawns and glistening crabs. Evening is certainly the best time to eat, drink and relax, with the sun illuminating the cliffs and a breeze taking the heat off the day.

There are also some places serving more specialist dishes. For example, **Wanna's Place**, Beach Front Rd. Produces Swiss cuisine – veal escalopes, rösti and chicken and also serves wine; there are three good Italian restaurants: **Azzurra**, which has a branch in Krabi town, **La Luna** and **Fantasia Mediterranea**. All three are on the beach-front road. The 'Italian' restaurant on the corner near *Krabi Resort* is using an old sign and menu from a previous establishment and should not even pretend to be capable of cooking Italian food, even if pizza is on the menu! Their Thai food isn't bad. There is also a German garden restaurant next door to the *Baan Lae* guesthouse. **The Roof Restaurant** attractive building and setting although not on the beach. Good extensive menu. Note: All the land on the beachfront road at Ao Nang is rented, not owned, by the shops and restaurants. Apparently, the owner of some of the land here is planning on terminating the contracts with most of the current restaurant and shop proprietors and redeveloping the land as newer, smaller units. It will be interesting to see which old faces remain and which new ones come in.

Bars Plenty to choose from but they tend to open and close with great frequency. Try the *Full Moon House* on the beach front, and *Hotaru* next to *Ao Nang Thara Lodge*. The *Luna Beach Bar* on Hat Nopparat Thara has a good location but a scary reputation with reports of regular fights.

Shopping Shops open on the beach front during the evening selling garments, leather goods and other products made specifically for the tourist market. There's little unusual on sale – except for batik 'paintings', usually illustrating marine scenes, which are produced from small workshops here.

Sport **Canoe trips**: *Sea Canoe*, T212252, F212172, anurak@hotmail.com, or Anurak @seacanoe.com), run out of an office next to the *Phra Nang Inn*, provide small-scale sea canoeing trips (self-paddle), exploring the overhanging cliffs and caves, and the rocky coastline of Phra Nang, Rai Leh and nearby islands (see www.seacanoe.com). Also see **Sea World Kayaking** (T637334, F637334) and **Sea Kayak Krabi** (T630270), both on the front. It seems fairly difficult to choose between these companies. *Sea Canoe* has some strong environmental policies, including restrictions on the number of people per trip, and no foam or plastic-packaged lunches. The best thing is probably to spend some time chatting to your prospective guide to see if you like the way they operate and whether you are happy with the level of English they speak. **Diving**: **Seafan Divers** (NAUI and PADI certification) by the *Phra Nang Inn*. **Calypso** (PADI certification), also near the *Phra Nang Inn*. **Phra Nang Divers** near the new guesthouses. **Aqua Vision Diving** next to *Beach Bungalows*. **Ao Nang Divers** (PADI Certification) at

Krabi Seaview Resort. **Rock-climbing**: *King Climbers* has an office down towards *Phra Nang Inn*. **Muay Thai** there is a new and well-supported stadium for Thai boxing in the Ao Nang area. The old one, just recently closed, was next to *Ao Nang Paradise*. The new and much larger stadium which attracts national standard boxers is set back from Hat Nopparat Thara beach by about 300 m.

Ao Nang Ban Lae Travel (close to *Krabi Resort*). *AP Travel* very helpful and friendly. **Tour operators**

Local Jeep hire (฿800-1,200 per day) and **motorbike hire** (฿250 per day) from travel agents and guesthouses.

Transport
20 km from Krabi

Road Songthaew: regular white *songthaew* connections with Krabi town 30 mins (฿20). From Krabi town, *songthaews* leave from Phattana Rd, opposite the *New Hotel* and travel to Ao Nang via Nopparat Thara Beach. For the return trip, songthaews leave from the eastern end of the Beach road, opposite *Sea Canoe*. The service runs regularly 0600-1800.

Boat Regular long-tailed boats to Rai Leh during the high season (Oct-May), 15 mins (฿50). The *Ao Nang Princess* links Ao Nang with Rai Leh and Koh Phi Phi daily during the high season, 2 hrs (฿150). Tour agents and some guesthouses (for example *Gift's)* advertise crewing jobs on sail boats to Malaysia and Singapore.

Banks Mobile exchange booths along Ao Nang beachfront and a more permanent place next to the *Phra Nang Inn*, run by the Siam City Bank. Thai Military Bank booth next to *AP Resort*, open daily 1000-1730. During low season (Jun-Oct) exchange booths may not open. **Communications** Fax and overseas telephone facilities available from numerous tour and travel agents along the beachfront road. **Useful addresses** Police station: half way along the beach road – really just a police booth. **Tourist Police** near the *Ao Nang Pakasai Resort* and another general police box near the *Phra Nang Inn*.

Directory

Rai Leh and Phra Nang

Phra Nang is the peninsular to the south of Ao Nang. There are no roads on Phra Nang, which makes it a beautifully secluded place to stay. The point consists of **Rai Leh West** and **Hat Tham** on the west side and **Rai Leh East** on the east. The best beach is on the west side – a truly picture postcard affair. The beach on the east coast is poor. There is good snorkelling and swimming in archetypal crystal-clear water. The limestone rock formations are spectacular, and there are interesting caves with stalagmites and stalactites to explore. At the southern extremity of the bay is a mountain cave dedicated to the goddess of the area – Phra Nang. There's a walkway from Rai Leh east through to Hat Tham (there are no accommodation or restaurants on Hat Tham). On the walkway, there is a sign to an inland lagoon, a tough 15-minute climb (good views from the top). There are several climbing schools (see **Sport**, below, for details) and the tower karst formations offer some truly outstanding climbing opportunities – as well as spectacular views.

Phone code: 075

Over the last few years Rai Leh has become something of a Mecca for rock climbers.

Like Phi Phi (see page 301), a very similar place in a variety of ways, Rai Leh is suffering from being too popular. The area available for development is small, sandwiched between limestone cliffs and crags, and already the bungalows are cheek-by-jowl in some places. Development will need to be carefully controlled if tourists and tourism are not to over-run this scenically glorious site.

There is not much to distinguish between the various lower-end bungalow operations at Rai Leh. Most offer a range of bungalows from older, smaller, more run-down

Sleeping

and cheaper cottages to larger and more sophisticated places. Unfortunately, some owners have crammed too many structures onto too small an area, and others have grown too large (with 40 or more cottages) and service has consequently suffered. All places to stay have their own restaurants, bars and often minimarts, tour desks and international phone facilities. Many also have an exchange service.

Rai Leh West   A beautiful beach, but huts have been built too closely together, making for overcrowded conditions and very basic (but not cheap) accommodation. To get there, take a boat from Ao Nang. Boats to Phi Phi stop at Rai Leh West. **AL-B** *Lanka Daeng*, T01-4644338, rbclub@phuket.ksc.co.th   Off on its own section of beach (at the opposite end to the *Premier Rayavadee*) this has to be one of the most stylish places to stay at Rai Leh. Traditional Thai-style houses have been built and sold on as holiday homes. Their owners now let them out whenever they are not in residence. Fully equipped with kitchens and bathrooms but no a/c. Electricity goes off after midnight. Prices vary depending on the size. Houses are available for 2 people or more. **A-B** *Railey Village Bungalows*, T2284366. Large outfit with a range of bungalows with attached bathrooms arranged in a strip running inland, pleasant rooms in attractive grounds. A/c is more expensive. Book exchange, masks and fins for hire, traditional Thai massage, western-style toilets. **A** *Sand Sea Bungalows*, T611944. 60-odd a/c bungalows, has grown too large to offer much in the way of personal service, reasonable range of facilities. **A-C** *Rai Leh Bay Bungalows*, T611789. Restaurant, the cheaper rooms are hot and somewhat dingy, but a/c ones are better.

Rai Leh East   **B-C** *Diamond Cave*, only a few rooms on a hill next to a huge limestone outcrop. Solidly built and clean bungalows. **C** *Sunrise*, standard bungalows, restaurant serves mediocre food. Movies played at the restaurant every night. **C** *Viewpoint*, T2304619. Friendly, well run, clean and well-maintained rooms. Good restaurant. The least accessible of all the places to stay at the far end of Rai Leh East, but some of the best bungalows available, especially given the rates. **D-E** *Coco Bungalows*, T612915. Very basic and natural bungalows made of split bamboo and roofed with thatch, small operation so has the personal touch that other larger places now lack. Excellent food. **D-E** *Yaya*, T611585. 6 rooms set in 2-storey (some higher) groups. Wooden constructions, different and aesthetically pleasing! Friendly place to stay, but if you're the shy retiring type this may not be for you as it is quite loud. Reasonable rooms and well priced. Also offers camping but at ฿200 a night per person this is fairly pricey. One of the few places that offer fresh coffee in the morning. Bit of a hang-out for rock climbers (and coffee addicts).

Phra Nang headland   **L** *Premier Rayavadee*, 67 Moo 5 Susaan Hoi Rd, T620740, F620630. A/c, restaurant, pool, luxurious isolated get-away with 75 villas and suites set in 10 ha (26 acres) of gardens, beautiful pool and romantic sitting rooms with grand bathrooms, access is by boat, the *Premier's* attempt to 'protect the environment' means that no motorized watersports are allowed. No longer a part of the Dusit group, but still very expensive. The quality of the food has been criticised (given the price) and there is a long-standing campaign by one outspoken activist concerning the location (she asserts the hotel has been built within the limits of the national park).

Ton Sai Bay   has a few bungalow operations accessible after a walk across to the beach. **C** *Dream Valley*, T01-4646479. Simple bamboo bungalows with fans and en suite bathrooms. **C** *Andaman Nature*, simple bamboo bungalows. **D** *Ton Sai Hut*, T075-637092, simple bungalows with shared bathrooms. Most of these close during the low season. This beach is a favourite spot for the rock climbers, and is also reasonably quiet compared with Rai Leh West.

Canoeing: kayaks available to explore the limestone grottoes off the Phra Nang headland. **Diving and snorkelling**: most guesthouses hire out masks and flippers and many
places now have their own dive operations. *Baby Shark Divers*, based at *Sunrise Bay
Bungalows* (NAUI certification). *Phra Nang Divers* has an office in Ao Nang (in the row of
shophouses near the *Phra Nang Inn*). They offer introductory courses as well as more
advanced dives at sites like Koh Boda. **Rock climbing**: rock climbing is now one of the
best-known and most popular attractions to the Rai Leh area. Professional *farang* and
Thai climbers will instruct novices on Phra Nang's limestone cliff faces and their equipment and safety record are both said to be excellent. Most operations are based on Rai
Leh East. These include *Tex Rock Climbing* (www.thaibiz.com/texsrockclimbing/), *Phra
Nang Rock Climbers*, and *King Climbers*. There are several other places operating out of
resorts. See www.simonfoley.com/climbing/krabi.htm for a personal take on climbing
in Rai Leh and lots of travel information. Half-day introductory climbing courses should
costs ฿500, ฿1,000 for a full-day course and ฿3,000 for a three-day course. All prices are
per person.

Boat Regular long-tailed boats from Ao Nang Beach, southeastern end, throughout
the day during the high season from Nov to May, 15 mins (฿20). From Krabi town
long-tailed boats leave through the day from the pier, 45 mins (฿50 (if there are
enough passengers at any one time, otherwise you can wait for more passengers or
take the whole boat for an agreed sum). The *Ao Nang Princess* links Phi Phi, Ao Nang
and Rai Leh during the high season, 2 hrs (฿150). Note that the sea can be rough
between Jun and Oct which is one reason why there are no boats between Ao Nang
and Rai Leh at this time.

Banks It is possible to change money at Rai Leh but rates are poor. Better to change money
before arriving in Krabi.

Koh Phi Phi

Koh Phi Phi consists of two beautiful islands – Phi Phi Le and Phi Phi Don. All   Phone code: 075
accommodation is on the larger Phi Phi Don. Shaped like an anvil and fringed by   Colour map 4, grid C2
*sheer limestone cliffs and golden beaches, it offers good swimming, snorkelling
and diving.*

Ins and outs

The only way to get to Phi Phi is by boat. There are daily connections with Krabi, 1 hr **Getting there**
on an express boat and 1½ hrs on the normal service. Boats also run from the beaches
of Ao Nang and Rai Leh close to Krabi, 2 hrs. There are boats from Koh Lanta (1 hr) and
Koh Tarutao and finally from various spots on Phuket (1-1½ hrs). The quickest way of
getting to Phi Phi from Bangkok is to fly to Phuket and catch a boat from there.

There are no roads on Phi Phi Don, so the only way to get around the island – which is a **Getting around**
National Park – is on foot. However long-tailed boats can be hired from the village to
explore the nearby sister island of Phi Phi Le and the coastal waters around Phi Phi Don.

The island

The western arm has no tourist accommodation on it. Boats dock at the 'neck'
– **Ton Sai Bay** – near the village of the same name. Formerly, a quiet Muslim
fishing community, it is now almost entirely geared to the demands of tourists,
with restaurants, dive schools, tour companies, currency exchanges, laundry

The Andaman Sea Coast

Koh Phi Phi

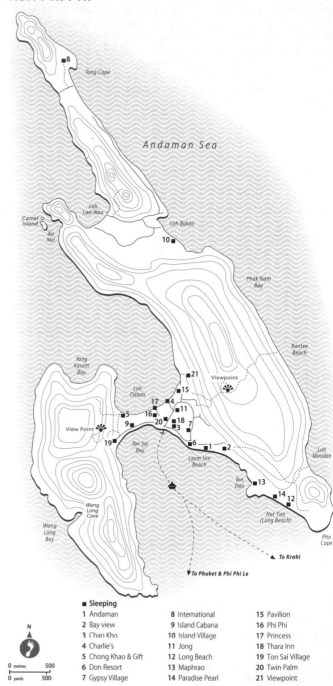

Andaman Sea

Tong Cape

Loh Laa-Naa

Camel Island

Ao Nui

Loh Bakao

Phak Nam Bay

Yong Kasem Bay

Loh Dalam

Viewpoint

Rantee Beach

View Point

Ton Sai Bay

Laem Hin Beach

Loh Moodee

Wang Long Cave

Ton Dao

Hat Yao (Long Beach)

Wang Long Bay

Pho Cape

To Krabi

To Phuket & Phi Phi Le

N

0 metres 500
0 yards 500

■ Sleeping
1 Andaman
2 Bay view
3 Chao Kho
4 Charlie's
5 Chong Khao & Gift
6 Don Resort
7 Gypsy Village
8 International
9 Island Cabana
10 Island Village
11 Jong
12 Long Beach
13 Maphrao
14 Paradise Pearl
15 Pavilion
16 Phi Phi
17 Princess
18 Thara Inn
19 Ton Sai Village
20 Twin Palm
21 Viewpoint

The Andaman Sea Coast

services and souvenir shops. Unfortunately, the island is too small to absorb the number of visitors that flock here; evident in the piles of rubbish and the worrying statistic that 80% of the fresh water wells are contaminated with faeces. Some attempts are now being taken to combat this deterioration of the environment. Funds have been allotted to improve rubbish disposal and water supply, and to reduce noise pollution by encouraging long-tailed boat operators to fit mufflers to their exhausts. On our last visit we got a sense that development had peaked – only one resort was expanding – and that the guesthouses and resorts had begun to clean up their acts. The rubbish situation, for example, appears to have improved.

The best snorkelling on the island is at **Hat Yao** (Long Beach). **NB** It is possible to travel to Koh Phi Phi all year round but during the rainy season (October-May), the boat trip can be very rough and not for the faint-hearted.

Phi Phi Le is a National Park, entirely girdled by sheer cliffs, where swiftlets nest (see box). It is not possible to stay on Phi Phi Le but it can be visited by boat. Most boat excursions include a visit to the **Viking Cave**, which contains prehistoric paintings of what look like Viking longboats, and the cliffs where birds' nests are harvested for bird's nest soup (see box, page 304).

Hire a **long-tailed boat** from the village, or from your resort to take a **trip around the island**. Boats seat eight people, half-day trip, ฿500 per boat.

Excursions

It is possible to climb to one of the **viewpoints** on the island by walking east from the village. The ascent takes about 30 minutes. A walk to Long Beach along the beach, or on the track, takes about 20 minutes.

A day trip snorkelling around the island is well worthwhile (฿300 per person, including lunch, snorkels and fins).

Tours

Phi Phi Le There are regular trips to see the cliff formations, the Viking Cave, Lo Samah Bay and Maya Bay (about ฿140 per person). Maya Bay was used in the filming of *The Beach* starring Leonardo DiCaprio (see box, page 306).

Hotels and bungalows are poor value for money in comparison to other beach resorts in Thailand. Most accommodation is clustered on the central 'neck' of the anvil, close to Ton Sai village, on both the north and south shores. Rooms get very booked up during peak season at Christmas and New Year and people have had to sleep on the beach or restaurant floors. Prices fluctuate enormously, depending on the season, prices quoted are high-season prices.

Sleeping
■ *on maps*
Price codes: see inside front cover

Ton Sai Bay **A** *Ton Sai Village*, contact *Phi Phi Marine Travel*, 201 Uttarakit Rd, Krabi, T/F612132, BT2557600. A/c, pool, best hotel on this side of the island, it consists of nearly 250 a/c rooms with hot-water bathrooms, satellite TV, overpriced. **A** *Phi Phi*, T611233, F2303138. A/c, hot water, restaurant, big hotel right in the middle of things, but considering the price facilities are limited. **A-B** *Island Cabana*, T620634, F612132. The old *Cabana* remains with reasonable rooms at the lower rate, and the new extension is immaculate. Good staff and excellent rooms, pool and other facilities. Recommended. **C-E** *Phi Phi Don Resort*, T2284252. Stone bungalows on the beach, newer ones built behind, limited electricity supply, some rooms have mosquito nets. **D-E** *Chao Kho*, T611313. Slow staff but a nice stretch of beach, small bungalows.

Loh Dalam Facing north, this beach is clean and relatively quiet and is gently shelving, so is suitable for children. **A** *Phi Phi Princess*, T612188, F620615. A/c, restaurant, satellite TV, individual bungalows, rather close together. **A-B** *Phi Phi Pavilion*, next to *Charlie's*, T/F620633. Friendly management, well-maintained bungalows right on the beach, up to 50% discount in low season. Breakfast included. **C-D** *Charlie's*,

Bird's nest soup

The tiny nests of the brown-rumped swift (Collocalia esculenta), *also known as the edible-nest swiftlet or sea swallow, are collected for bird's nest soup, a Chinese delicacy, throughout Southeast Asia. The semi-oval nests are made of silk-like strands of saliva secreted by the birds which, when cooked in broth, softens and becomes a little like noodles. Like so many Chinese delicacies, the nests are believed to have aphrodisiac qualities, and the soup has even been suggested as a cure for AIDS. The red nests are the most highly valued, and the Vietnamese Emperor Minh Mang (1820-40) is said to* have owed his extraordinary vitality to his inordinate consumption of bird's nest soup. This may explain why restaurants serving it in Southern Thailand are usually also associated with massage parlours. Collecting the nests is a precarious business and is only officially allowed twice a year – between February and April and in September. The collectors climb flimsy bamboo poles into total darkness, with candles strapped to their heads. In Hong Kong a kilo of nests may sell for US$2,000 and nest-concessions in Thailand are vigorously protected.*

T7230495. Close to the beach, clean, reasonable rooms, OK restaurant, good value. **C-E** *Thara Inn*, built on the back of the hill, the more expensive rooms are your best bet, cheaper rooms are grotty. **D** *Jong*, restaurant, only 6 rooms, all with double bed and fan, friendly management, open high season only. **D-E** *Chong Khao*, noisy location next to the generator. **D-E** *Gift*, noisy location next to the generator. **E** *Phi Phi Viewpoint*, T722011 or in Krabi T611318, F611541. Built on the side of the hill, wooden bungalows with good views, indifferent management. **E** *Twin Palm Guesthouse*, spacious rooms, reasonable value.

East from Ton Sai Bay Laem Hin: beautiful fine sand and tree-lined beach: **B-C** *Bay View Resort*, T7231144. Restaurant, private bathroom. **C-E** *Phi Phi Andaman*, T7231073. Large number of small huts in uniform rows, 3 standards of room, all have mosquito nets, some have fans and own bathrooms. **D** *Gypsy Village* (behind *Phi Phi Don Resort*), big stone bungalows, quieter and cleaner than most here. Recommended. **Ton Dao Beach**: **D-E** *Maphrao*, restaurant, quiet, private beach, bungalows set on a shaded hill, 3 grades of accommodation, the most expensive have own bathrooms, 24-hr electricity and fans, all rooms have mosquito nets. **Long Beach (Hat Yao)**: a long-tailed boat ride from Ton Sai (฿20-30 per person, one way, ฿50-100 at night time). Good-value accommodation on a lovely beach, away from all the bustle of Ton Sai. Good snorkelling off shore here. **C-F** *Paradise*, T7230484. Big restaurant, quiet, 80 bungalows with a range of rooms all with own bathrooms, the cheaper ones have limited electricity and no fan, the more expensive ones are spacious, tours organized to Phi Phi Le, etc, snorkels and fins for hire, videos, boats to Ton Sai. Recommended. **D-E** *Phi Phi Long Beach*, good food, some private bathrooms, salt water showers in dry season, simple but OK, unfriendly staff.

On the East coast Loh Bakao: **A** *Phi Phi Island Village*, T2111907 or BT2770704. Set alone to the north of the island, some a/c overpriced. **Laem Tong**: **AL-B** *Phi Phi International* T7231250, BT9828080. To the north of the island, good diving and snorkelling.

Eating
● *on maps*
Price codes: see inside front cover

There are about 5 good seafood restaurants in the village, all with similar menus. All display (and barbecue) their catch on the street. **Mid-range**: *Captain's*, good Thai food and Western breakfasts. *Malinda* for steaks. *Mama*, French, friendly, popular and excellent food. Recommended. *Patcharee Seafood*. Recommended. *Pizza House*,

Sharks' fin

Throughout Asia, wherever there are large populations of Chinese, sharks' fin soup is on the menu of the more expensive or traditional restaurants. For those tempted to partake, be aware however, that the shark is a little understood animal with important and complex interactions with key marine systems such as coral reefs. Sharks are critical to maintaining a natural balance in reef systems. Take away the sharks, and parrot fish and other fish which graze on coral increase, leading to excessive grazing and later destruction of the reef system.

Shark fisheries have been increasing dramatically as demand not only for shark fins, but also for other shark products, rises year by year. In 1994, 182,000 million tonnes of sharks were brought to shore by the fisheries sector. This does not include the millions of sharks thrown away into the sea after being caught accidentally during fishing for more lucrative commercial species such as blue tuna. The real total catch is estimated to be as much as twice as great as the statistics show.

Nowadays, sharks are usually stripped of their fins before being discarded in the oceans, and there is a growing fisheries sector focusing on sharks. The biology of the shark, unlike other fish, does not lend itself to large-range exploitation. Sharks are at the very top of the food chain. They live for a long time and produce few young, most of which will survive to adulthood. This is vastly different from most commercial fisheries where the catch species produce many young, most of which die, and live for only a few years. Furthermore, little is known about many shark species which are highly migratory. We do not, therefore, know the impact of this increase in fishing of sharks for products, such as the fins. We cannot even say whether any species of shark is currently threatened by this fishing activity, but past experience in shark fisheries does not bode well. To date every fishery directed at sharks has quickly collapsed as the shark populations have been decimated.

Until we know more about shark fisheries and understand the impacts of our desires for shark products, please take the precautionary approach and stay clear of sharks' fin soup. In June 2000, responding to passenger concern, Thai Airways took sharks' fin soup off its in-flight menu.

(Statistics taken from the 1997 TRAFFIC South East Asia report on species in danger: Managing Shark Fisheries: Opportunities for International Conservation, by Michael L Weber and Sonja V Fordham)

The Andaman Sea Coast

Italian, French bakery sells delicious croissants. *Top Ten* for burgers. **Cheap**: *PP Bakery* good selection of pastries and sweet things with restaurant area as well.

A number of bars are to be found on the track from Ton Sai to the northern shore. Many show latest video releases. *Crazy Bar* is the loudest. *Lazy Bar* is the most laid back. **Disco** *Casa Blanca*. **Bars & nightclubs**

Thai massage ฿100 per hour (many masseurs are untrained). **Videos** At bungalows. **Entertainment**

Second-hand books for sale or to rent on track from Ton Sai to the northern shore. **Shopping**

Boxing: 'stadium' occasionally holds fights on national holidays. **Diving**: there have been worries expressed that Phi Phi's frantic development has degraded the marine environment. A 1995 report by one diver maintained that this was not so. Pollution is minimal, and animal life flourishing. There are about 12 dive schools on the island and rates are very competitive. *SSI (Scuba School International)*, which offers a 5-day **Sport**

Life's a Beach

During 1998 and early 1999 Phi Phi attracted more column inches of media attention than you would expect for a tiny island. The reason: Leonardo DiCaprio came head-to-head with environmental correctness.

Towards the end of the year, 20th Century Fox began filming The Beach, based on Alex Garland's novel, having selected DiCaprio as the bankable heart-throb and Phi Phi as a suitably sun-drenched island. (In fact Phi Phi Le, just to the south of the main island, Phi Phi Don.) But there were three problems – not enough atmospheric palm trees, too much scrubby grass, and lumpy sand dunes. Easy: ship in 92 trees, turf out the grass and bulldoze the dunes. But Phi Phi is also part of a National Park, so when Thailand's environmental movement got wind of what was going on they realised they were onto an environmental winner. Environmental lawyers, local people and activists joined forces to bring the devastation to the wider world. "In a society which shuns confrontation except in the

heat of the moment," opponents said as they took the film company to court to prevent filming, "this is an unprecedented step taken in desperation".

In response to an increasingly hysterical and effective anti-Leo campaign, producer Andrew McDonald said that he had sought and received permission from the National Parks' office and had made a payment of US$100,000. He also made a commitment to return everything to its natural state on completion of filming. "We are being picked on," he complained to The Nation, "because we are a big studio name and because Leonardo DiCaprio is involved". He said that before filming could begin the crew had to remove six tons of rubbish from Maya Beach. He also asked why similar attention has not been brought to bear on the conflagration of restaurants and bungalow operations, the piles of rubbish, the constant coming-and-going of boats, the pillaging of the reefs... He has a point. Phi Phi – still a beautiful island – is a mess; over-crowded and over-developed.

certificate course, has been recommended. Alternatively, book up with one of the many dive centres on Phuket. Areas of interest for divers include the Bida Islands, south of Phi Phi Le, where the variety of coral is impressive. There is a 50 m underwater tunnel here for more experienced divers. Wrecks can be found behind Mosquito Island. The best visibility is from Dec-Apr (25-40 m). **Game fishing**: can be organized in the village. Prices are normally ฿1,600 per day for a long-tailed boat and 2 lines. Lunch included. **Kayaking**: *Phi Phi Viewpoint Resort* rents out kayaks for ฿400 for 8 hrs or ฿100 per hour. A good way to visit deserted bays. **Paddle boats**: for rent for ฿100 per hour from the northern shore. **Paragliding**: ฿500 a time. **Rock climbing**: the limestone cliffs here are known internationally. Sometimes there are climbers available to give tuition on the Ton Sai cliffs. **Snorkelling**: Snorkels and fins can be hired from most bungalows or in the village (฿50 per day). **Walking**: to the viewpoint (drinks available here) or around the island. See map for marked paths. **Waterskiing**: off the north shore. **Yacht charter**: *Top Ten Burger Bar* for information. Yachts sail to Phangnga Bay, Similan Islands and Andaman Islands in high season.

Tour operators There are several agents in Ton Sai, all charging similar prices and able to organize all sorts of tickets.

Transport Phi Phi lies between Krabi and Phuket and can be reached from both.

Boat Connections from the Chao Fah Pier in Krabi at 0930 and 1430, 1½ hrs, or 1 hr for the express boats which leave at 1030 and 1430. Return boats from Phi Phi to Krabi depart at 0900 and 1300 for both the normal and express services. Daily connections with Ao Nang and Rai Leh on the *Ao Nang Princess*, 2 hrs. There are also boat connections with Koh Lanta 1 hr and Koh Tarutao. Connections with Phuket from Patong, Siray and Chalong (*Aloha Tours*, T381215) 2 hrs. The '*King Cruiser*', run by *Ferryline* and *Songserm* (51-53 Satool Rd, Phuket Town, T222570) makes 2 trips a day from Makham Bay 1½ hrs. There is also an express boat from Tien Sin on Phuket (on the *Andaman Queen*, T215261) at about 0830, 1 hr 20 mins.

Banks there is a small branch of Krung Thai Bank with exchange facilities open daily 0830-1530 in between Ton Sai and Loh Dalam. **Communications** Stamps can be bought, and letters can be posted in the postboxes in the village. **Medical services** Rescue unit and first aid: next to *Phi Phi Andaman*. **Directory**

Koh Lanta

Koh Lanta is actually a group of islands, the three largest of which are Koh Lanta Yai (which is the one with the resorts), Koh Lanta Noi and Koh Klang. It is one of the more recent beach developments in Southern Thailand, but, like so many other islands and beaches in Thailand has had to contend with a very rapid expansion in business. Land speculation is rife, with one *rai* (0.15 ha, 0.4 acre) of prime land with resort potential worth about ฿1-2 mn. Locals are being encouraged not to sell out to speculators and efforts are being made to prevent the island from becoming another Phi Phi, where rapid and uncontrolled growth has led to problems. Even with this laudable attempt to control and manage development, it is all too clear that bungalow owners are free to build whatever they like, just about anywhere they like.

Phone code: 075
Colour map 4, grid C3
This is somewhere where you can truly 'get away from it all'

Various developments are underway: electrification is being extended, phone links are being improved and rubbish collection is being stepped up. In addition, there are plans to surface more of the island's tracks to improve accessibility. Koh Lanta is recognized by the Thai government as a 'site of natural beauty' and a portion of the south of the island has recently been gazetted and designated as a National Park. This should keep this part of the island, at least, relatively untouched.

The beaches on the west, particularly to the north, are sandy and safe for swimming. There are boat trips to neighbouring islands for snorkelling and there are attractive forest and cliff-top trails, but little else. There is also a sizeable sea gypsy village to the southeast of the island, where the inhabitants continue with a lifestyle they have maintained for generations. It is said that they have no wish to become yet another 'tourist attraction' – the appalling experiences of the sea gypsies of Phuket may be at the forefront of their minds in apparently rejecting the tourist dollar.

Tham Khao Mai Kaeo is a series of caves, situated in the middle of the island; follow the signs to the supernatural caves. The best way to visit them is by hired motorbike, but they are not that easy to find so ask for directions at your hotel or guesthouse. The old administrative centre and port on Koh Lanta, now known as 'Ban Koh Lanta' is slowly developing its own tourism niche. With stunning views across to the islands and mainland to the east of the island, and most of its original old wooden shophouse/fishing houses still standing, the small town has a certain charm. Local entrepeneurs are beginning to open galleries and souvenir shops, and there are plans in the offing to start offering accommodation and cultural activities. This is also where many of the islands internet services can be found.

All bungalows offer day trips to Trang's Andaman Islands (see page 317), ฿350 per person or ฿600 per boat including lunch and snorkelling gear. (Note that it **Tours**

The Andaman Sea Coast

Koh Lanta

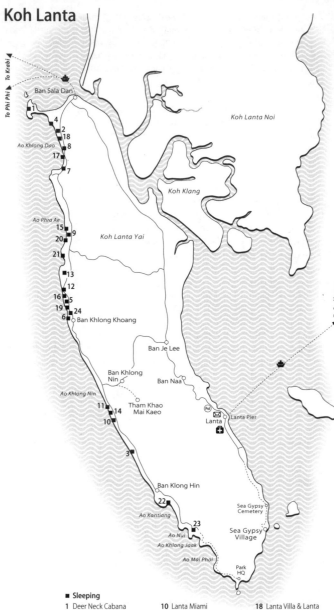

■ Sleeping

1 Deer Neck Cabana
  & Kaw Kwang Beach
2 Diamond Sand Inn
3 Dream Team
4 Golden Bay Cottages
5 Lanta Emerald Bungalow
6 Lanta Coral Beach
7 Lanta Garden Home
8 Lanta Island Resort
9 Lanta Long Beach

10 Lanta Miami
11 Lanta Nature Beach
   Resort
12 Lanta New Beach
13 Lanta New Beach
   Bungalows
14 Lanta Paradise
15 Lanta Palm Beach
16 Lanta Riviera
17 Lanta Sea House

18 Lanta Villa & Lanta
   Royal Resort
19 Lanta's Lodge Bungalows
20 Rapala Long Beach
   Resort
21 Relax Bay Tropicana
22 Seasun
23 Waterfall Bay Resort
24 Where Else

is a long trip – three hours each way – and some people find the noise unbearable for just an hour or two's snorkelling.) A ferry leaves Sala Dan at 0830 for the day-trip to Phi Phi, ฿240 per person. Fishing trips are organized by *La Creperie*, ฿450 per day, ฿1,200 for two days (which includes camping on a deserted island with food provided). Encourage your boatman to anchor at a buoy, not using an anchor – as this damages the coral.

Most bungalow operations are scattered down the west coast of Koh Lanta Yai and usually offer free pick-up from the pier at Sala Dan. Travel agents and tour companies in Krabi and Ao Nang advertise accommodation on Koh Lanta so it is possible to get a pretty good idea of the various places before arriving. With very few exceptions the bungalow operations are much of a muchness. The choice is basically between simple concrete bungalows (some with a/c) and bamboo or wood bungalows (usually fan). Some resorts have been nicknamed 'army camps' or 'chicken farms' for the unimaginative and over-crowded layout. This is particularly true of resorts at Ao Khlong Dao. However, this is the main area where bungalows are open year round. In most other places, bungalows close during the wet season. Further up the coast, there are some new and more interesting resorts, and the whole area is much less crowded and has a gentle peaceful atmosphere (although there are regular parties during the high season). Note that like other beaches and islands hereabouts there is considerable variation between high-season (roughly, Nov-May) and low-season (Jun-Oct) rates. Expect to pay half the high-season rate during low season. The attraction of visiting in the low season is that the island is virtually deserted and room rates are very competitive. Agents in Krabi and Ao Nang will provide information of which places are open.

Sleeping

■ *on maps*
*Price codes: see
inside front cover*

Ao Khlong Dao **A (high)-C (low)** *Lanta Andaman Resort*, towards the south is the first real hotel on Koh Lanta. The 2-storey building is not very pretty, and although there is a pool, the very ordinary rooms are over-priced for what they are. Note also that prices rise by a third during the high season and during peak months another ฿600 is added to the bill. Games room, snooker, restaurant. **B-C** *Sayang Beach*, T01-4766357, situated just south of the *Lanta Villa*. This operation is run by a local lady called Tukta and they have taken care to protect the environment while constructing their bungalows (unlike many). Excellent food with fresh fish nightly. Large bugalows; no a/c. **C-E** *Diamond Sand Inn*, T2284473. Some a/c. Spotless big rooms and huge attached bathrooms. Limited electricity supply, but this is the only negative thing to say about this place. The restaurant is good, with nice views and the proprietors are extremely welcoming and amiable. Very competitive rates in the low season, reflected in the price range quoted here. Recommended. **C-E** *Lanta Sea House*, T2284160. Well kept plot, with casuarina trees and tidy garden, 2 grades of room, both are clean and well supplied, the more expensive have spacious balconies and their own bathroom. Very good value in the low season (reflected in the price grading here). Recommended. **C-E** *Lanta Villa*, T/F611944. Another place which has declined in quality over the last couple of years. Range of rooms from simple A-frame bungalows with attached shower rooms to larger and more sophisticated Thai-style, red-roofed cottages with wood floors, and large tiled bathrooms. However the bungalows are too close together and during the high season it is crowded and noisy. Credit cards accepted. **C-F** *Kaw Kwang Beach Bungalow*, restaurant, lovely beach with safe swimming, double rooms with fans, some very cheap and basic wooden huts available. Closed in low season. **D** *Lanta Royal*, impersonally large restaurant, large, rather bare rooms with unattractive cement floors. This is one of the larger places on the island with over 50 cottages, as a result, perhaps, it lacks the family atmosphere of the smaller outfits but does have a range of facilities. **D-E** *Deer Neck Cabana*, T7230623. Northern end of Koh Lanta, on the promontory, the beach here is rather muddy, but the sea bed shelves very gently making it a good place

The Andaman Sea Coast

for children to play and paddle but hopeless for proper swimming and snorkelling. A better beach lies a short walk across the neck of the promontory. The bungalows are good for the price and the management are very friendly and helpful, excellent restaurant with Thai and western food, good value. Recommended. **D-E** *Golden Bay*, clean, own bathroom, electricity, some simple wood and bamboo huts, some concrete. Very good value (especially in the low season when it is down to **F** for a good room). Friendly, helpful owners and an easy place to get to. **D-E** *Lanta Garden Home*, a small number of A-frame basic huts and some wooden bungalows on stilts, shady plot. New resorts in this area include the *Lanta Island Cabana* which has a curious restaurant designed to look like a large boat and a row of simple, solidly built wooden bungalows, the *Lanta Island Resort* which definitely falls into the army camp category, and the fairly ordinary *Merry Beach Bungalows* and *Cha Ba*. All are fairly close together just up from the *Lanta Villa*.

Ao Phra-Ae (a lovely beach) **AL (high)-B (low)** *Lanta Resotel*, Bungalow development that definitely falls into the 'army camp' or 'chicken farm' (for 'hatching tourist eggs') categories. Large solidly built wooden bungalows with a/c and all hotel amenities. It advertises itself as a home rather than a hotel, but the regimented layout of row on row of bungalows with no gardens to speak of, and plans to add another 50 bungalows belies the publicity material. **A-D** *Wang Thong Resort*, lies about 250 m from the beach and is set in amongst trees and along the banks of a canal. The thatched bamboo and wood bungalows on high stilts that are on the left-hand side (looking towards the beach) are lovely. Nicely spaced out and with a secluded natural feeling to the layout, there are lots of walkways between the bungalows and small wooden bridges over the water. These are all fan only. On the right-hand side are newer houses currently under construction. Also set in amongst the trees, the 2-bedroom affairs are ideal for families, with a cooking space under the house and a spacious deck beside the bedrooms. These are also fan only. The only blots on the landscape are the blocks of a/c rooms at the front on the right-hand side. These are totally out of character with the rest of the resort, being made of concrete and hideous red-tiled walls. One can only hope the owner sees sense and redesigns them, soon! **C** *Rapala Long Beach*, small swimming pool, rather out of place, pretentious, new resort, hexagonal bungalows with small triangular shower rooms and a rocky beach. Closed in the low season. **C-E** *Relax Bay Tropicana*, 1 Moo 2, BT7220089, T/F620618. Restaurant, 48 large wooden bungalows raised high off the ground and scattered through beachside grove of trees, every effort has been taken to keep this development *au naturel* and the beach and location are very quiet, all rooms have glass and/or mosquito panels in the windows, fans and shower rooms in the open-air adjoining. **D** *Last Horizon Resort*, 175 Moo 2, Baan Phu Klom Beach, T01-2283625, last_horizon@hotmail.com Opened in late 1999, 25 stone bungalows in a coconut grove with attached showers, 24-hr electricity, restaurant and beach bar. Friendly management, motorbikes for hire, tours arranged. The only downside is that the beach here is only suitable for swimming at high tide. Recommended. **E** *Lanta Long Beach*, bamboo huts with mosquito nets provided. Also a number of smaller huts. **E-F** *Lanta Palm Beach*, T7230528. Adequate restaurant, small rather shabby huts rather close together, some electricity, all with bathrooms, tents ฿30, free taxi service to Sala Dan.

From *Lanta Palm Beach* onwards to Hat Khlong Khuang there are several new bungalow operations. With the exception of *Wang Thong* which has a lot of charm, and *Lanta Resotel* which has none, these are all very similar. Either they are concrete bungalows (usually over-crowded) or bamboo bungalows (often with a bit more space). In most cases, they are set back a little from the beach in coconut plantations or in gardens just off the road. Any of these would probably be a pleasant enough place to stay, but none have any special qualities to distinguish from the rest. All fall under our **C-D** price range and all close during the low season. The list includes: *Tamrin Resort*, *Lanta*

Emerald Bungalow, *Lanta Riviera*, *Lanta New Beach Bungalows*, *Baan Gayee*, and the *Good Day Resort*, but no doubt there will soon be more names to add!

Hat Khlong Khoang C (high)- E (low) *Lanta Coconut Green Field*, pleasant bamboo bungalows in a coconut plantation by a rocky shore. Friendly staff and peaceful setting. Restaurant with movie showings. **D (high)-E (low)** *Bee Bee*, a 'village'-like set-up of unusual-looking bamboo bungalows set just back from the beach in a coconut plantation. Some with two levels and all with bamboo bathrooms! Charming and different from its neighbours. Closed during the low season. **D-F** *Lantas Lodge Bungalows*, restaurant, lovely beach, 'A' frames, some wooden huts and tents, very attractive plot amongst coconut trees, electricity in restaurant only, good fish on menu. **E** *Lanta Riviera Bungalow*, 121 Moo 1, Saladan Koh Lanta. Bungalows with fan and attached shower, quiet and relaxed atmosphere and friendly staff, lovely clean beach. Recommended. **E** *Where Else*, 14 spacious bamboo and wooden bungalows with semi-outdoor bathrooms. Friendly owner, good views from the rooms on the southern side. The restaurant is known on the island for its Indian and vegetarian dishes as well as its Thai food. Recommended.

Ao Khlong Nin A-E *Lanta Miami*, T2284506. A/c and fan available. Family-run, all rooms come with attached bathrooms. Rooms are quite closely packed. Snorkelling organized from here. **B-C** *Lanta Coral Beach*, New bungalow resort. Concrete bungalows in rows in a garden. Rocky shore but with some areas where swimming is safe. Staff are not very friendly. Restaurant and tour desk. **C-E** *Lanta Nature Beach Resort*, good bungalows, friendly and helpful owners. One of the better places on this beach. Good discounts in the off season, reflected in the price range quoted here. **B (high)-D (low)** *Lanta Paradise*, T7230530. Not such a pleasant beach, all beds have mosquito nets and fans. Some new bungalows are behind the road away from the beach. Tour desk. Motorbike rental available. **D-E** *Dream Team*, good restaurant using their own home-grown produce, wooden huts with fans and night time electricity, lovely gardens but facing a rocky beach.

Ao Kantiang B-E *Lanta Marine Park Resort*, T3970793 A new resort set up high on the hill overlooking Ao Kantiang with great views of the bay from the bungalows in the front. Several styles of bungalows – the small bamboo bungalows set back from the view are the cheapest. The larger concrete bungalows with views from the balconies are the most expensive. Rooms are spacious and comfortable. The walk up to the bungalows will keep you fit! Free pick-up service from Saladan and taxi service for ฿35-40. Between Ao Kantiang and Ao Khlong Jaak is another very pleasant bay with white sands and a small stream. Here the only resort is the **C-E** *Same Same But Different*, 9 rooms built in amongst the trees on the bay with a restaurant and bar on the beach, and a rest area with hammocks swinging in the sea breezes. Nicely laid out with a bit of style, this does more than live up to its name. Same owner as the *Ruen Mai* restaurant in Krabi town (another location where not a tree has been felled!); if the restaurant is as good as *Ruen Mai*, Koh Lanta will be very well served. Recommended. **E** *Kan Tiang Bay View Resort*, 2 rows of basic bamboo bungalows with mosquito nets. Restaurant, tour desk, and motorbike rental. **E** *Seasun*, T7230497. Rather grotty concrete and some bamboo huts, one wooden bungalow up a 20-ft staircase with great views, very pretty and remote cove, not such good snorkelling, friendly Muslim owners.

Ao Khlong Jaak B-D *Waterfall Bay Resort*, T2284014, Krabi 612084. Adjacent to the national park, in a small but lovely bay with a couple of waterfalls within easy walking distance. Large A-frame bungalows, some with 2 storeys and attractive balconies, attached shower rooms. Very quiet and peaceful and close to the national park. The owner, Khun Areeya, has a strong conservation ethic and is an excellent cook (of both Indian and Thai food). She is happy to teach Thai cookery to anyone with an interest.

The staff is very friendly and extremely good with children – family-friendly place to stay. Open all year round, but it is best to book in advance from Oct to Mar. Boat trips are organised to nearby islands and other places of interest. **D-E** *Khlong Jaak Bungalows*, simple bamboo bungalow resort. Closed in the low season.

Eating

● on maps
Price codes: see inside front cover

All the guesthouses provide restaurants with similar menus; Thai and European food with lots of seafood and fruit. *Danny's*, southern end of Khlong Dao beach. Huge menu of seafood, Thai and international, Sun evening Thai buffets are very popular. In Sala Dan there are some small cafés. 3 restaurants overlook the bay between Lanta Yai and Lanta Noi (rather windy): *Seaview 1* (aka *Monkey in the Back*), slow service, good seafood, no electricity, cheap. *Seaview 2*, larger menu, Thai and seafood, friendly, cheap. *Swiss Bakery*, Sala Dan, good pastries and coffee. *Same Same but Different*, just down from Waterfall Bay, the owner runs the *Ruen Mai* restaurant in Krabi town. This is an excellent restaurant and reportedly the cook at *Same Same but Different* has been brought over from the *Ruen Mai*, so the food should be good! *Where Else*, cooks Indian and vegetarian as well as Thai food.

Bars *Reggae*, *First* and *Bongo*, Khlong Dao beach. *Sun Moon Music and Beer Bar*, *Dream Team* bungalows, Ao Khlong Nin.

Shopping Only basic supplies available in Sala Dan and Lanta (on southeast coast). *Minimart* on Khlong Dao beach open in high season.

Sport **Diving**: several schools in Sala Dan (some with German spoken); check equipment before signing on. *Atlantis*, *Aquarius Diving* and *Koh Lanta Diving Centre* are both to be found in Sala Dan. **Pool Tables**: in Sala Dan, opposite *Sea View 1*. **Snorkelling**: known locally as 'snorking'. Most guesthouses hire out equipment at about ฿30 per day, although the quality is varied.

Tour operators *Makaira Tour Centre*, 18 Moo 1 Sala Dan. *Sala Dan Travel Centre*, *O & M Travel*, *IC Travel*, are all in Sala Dan. Most bungalows can also make travel arrangements.

Transport **Local Long-tailed boats hire**: from bungalows for ฿600 per day. **Motorbike hire**: from bungalows for ฿250 per day or ฿40 per hour, or in Sala Dan. **Mountain bike hire**: from bungalows for ฿130 per day. **Pick-up trucks**: some ply the island, ฿100 to end of the island, others serve individual bungalows only. **NB** The laterite roads are rough.

Boat Boats leave from Sala Dan on the northern tip of the island, and from Lanta Pier on the southeast coast. Connections with Chao Fah Pier in Krabi, 2 hrs via Koh Jam (฿150). Departures vary, but usually one departure each day at 1300, Krabi to Lanta, 0900 and 1300 Lanta to Krabi. **NB** there is no ferry from Krabi to Lanta (and vice versa), in the wet season. Instead, a minibus runs from Chao Fah Pier and via 2 short car ferries across Lanta Noi and to Ban Sala Dan (2 hrs) (฿150). There are also boat connections with Ban Hua Hin, on southern tip of Koh Klang. Songthaews from Krabi go to Ban Hua Hin (฿25). In the high season, there is one boat a day from Phi Phi at 1300, 1 hr ฿150 one way. Guesthouse owners hassle mercilessly for your custom on this trip.

Directory **Banks** Siam City Bank Exchange in Sala Dan; you cant miss it, it's bright red. **Communications** Post Office: Lanta Pier. **Medical services** Health centre: in Sala Dan. Hospital: Lanta Pier. **Useful addresses** Police: Sala Dan.

Koh Jam

There are only three bungalow operations on the tiny island of Koh Jam. **E** *Joy Bungalow*, T01-7230502. 30 bungalows; good food, good location. Two newer, but not necessarily better, operations are: **E** *New Bungalows*, T01-4644230 which has simple wooden bungalows and a restaurant, and **D** *Andaman Bungalows*, T01-4646500 basic A-frame bungalows with tiled floors.

Boat The boat from Krabi to Koh Lanta goes via Koh Jam (see above) 1 hr 30 mins, ฿150. There are also connections with Koh Phi Phi and with Laem Kruat, on the mainland. **Transport**

Koh Bubu

Koh Bubu is a tiny island in the Lanta group of Koh Lanta Yai. There is one bungalow establishment here, with 13 thatched bungalows (**D-E**), restaurant and little else except sea and solitude. People who have stayed here report returning to the mainland completely relaxed and detached from the world they left behind.

Road and boat Regular vans from Krabi to Bo Muang village pier, then by boat to Samsan Pier on east coast of Lanta Yai (฿100), and finally on to Bubu by chartered **long-tailed boat** (฿150-200), contact *Thammachart*, Khong Kha Rd, Krabi. There is a free ferry service from Lanta Pier to Bubu (one a day). **Transport**

Koh Siboya

Koh Siboya is a small island with a population of about 1,000 people, most of whom are involved in rubber or fisheries. There is only one resort on the island so if you do plan on staying it is best to make arrangements for transportation after contacting their office in Krabi town or on the island. Bungalows are simple bamboo affairs set in spacious gardens near the sea. Bungalows vary in size and price (**D-E**). Private houses can also be rented (**B-C**). The resort has a very informative website with lots of pictures: http://members.home.net/siboya You can contact the resort on T01-2291415 or 075-612192.

Trang

Trang is an important port and commercial centre but is a fairly nondescript, Chinese town. In the years to come Trang will become an increasingly important jumping-off point for people heading to the exotic, coral islands just off the coast. It is famous for its char-grilled pork, sweet cakes and as the birthplace of Prime Minister Chuan Leekpai. *Phone code: 075*
Colour map 4, grid C4

The town was established as a trading centre in the first century AD, and flourished between the 7th and 12th centuries. Its importance rested on its role as a relay point for communications between the east coast of Thailand and Palembang (Srivijaya) in Sumatra. It was then known as Krung Thani and later as Trangkhapura, the 'City of Waves'. The name was shortened in the 19th century to Trang. During the Ayutthaya Period, the town was located at the mouth of the river and was a popular port of entry for Western visitors continuing north to Ayutthaya. Later, during King Mongkut's reign, the town was moved inland because of frequent flooding.

The arrival of the Teochew (Chinese) community in the latter half of the 19th century was a boon to the local economy which, until the introduction of rubber from Malaysia, was reliant on tin mining. Trang's rubber plantations were the first in Thailand (the first tree was planted just south of the city) and its former ruler, Phraya Rasdanupradit Mahitsara Phakdi, is credited with encouraging the spread of its cultivation. He also built the twisting road from Trang across the Banthat Range to Phattalung. There is a statue of him 1 km out of town on the Phattalung road. Rubber smallholdings and plantations are still the biggest money-earner in the region.

Trang has retained the atmosphere of a Chinese immigrant community with some good Chinese restaurants and several Chinese shrines. The **Kwan Tee Hun shrine**, dedicated to a bearded war god, is in Ban Bang Rok, 3 km north of Trang on Route 4. Clearly, to keep tourists in Trang for longer than it takes to catch a minibus to Pakmeng for the boat to Trang's offshore islands requires a sight or two. The **Trang Aquarium**, within the Rajamangala Institute, should now be open. **Prime Minister Chuan Leekpai's house** (ask locally for directions) has also become a pilgrimage spot of sorts and is open to visitors.

There is a temporary **tourist office** at the Railway Station and plans to build a TAT office. ■ *Best time to visit is between January and April, out of the monsoon season.*

Excursions **Beaches around Trang** Trang's embryonic tourism industry has so far escaped the hard sell of Phuket and Pattaya – excellent news for nature-lovers, reef-divers and explorers. The strip of coast running south from Pakmeng (38 km west from Trang) round to Kantang, boasts some of the south's best beaches.

Pakmeng and Chang Lang beaches are the most accessible – 40 km west of Trang town. The sea is poor here for swimming, but it's a nice place to walk. **Sleeping Pakmeng**: B-C *Pakmeng Resort*, T218940. Turn left after reaching the main seafront and continue on towards the national park. The resort is on the left and is well marked. Wooden bungalows with attached bathroom and fan, excellent restaurant. Newer air-conditioned bungalows have a bit more style about them and are slightly pricier. The resort backs onto the main *khlong* leading to the river. Motorbikes (฿250 per day) and bicycles (฿70 per day) for rent. B *Le Trang Resort*, T274027-8 F274029. A new bungalow resort just up from the pier. The restaurant is well known and serves good seafood. The bungalows are in a very pleasant garden with some seating. Well built, and well equipped but quite small for the price and there is no hot water. Sea canoes can be rented for ฿150 per hour and guides are available on request. There are mangroves and small islands along the shore so it is possible to use the canoes even in the monsoon season. The resort will also arrange camping on the nearby islands, complete with picnic and mobile phone should anything go wrong! Very enthusiastic owner. **D** *no name – look for the Mittweida sign*, T230200. Associated with the *Thai Jin Resort* in Trang municipality, the bungalows are behind a café near the many seafood stalls along Pak Meng beach. Simple bamboo rooms, very well-equipped and nicely decorated. **Chang Lang**: C *Chang Lang Resort*, well signposted and with a very grand entrance, the resort itself is rather run down. Adequate bungalows but nothing special for the price. D *Chang Lang Sea Sand Resort*, T213611 is on the main road to the national park. Unattractive concrete bungalows with sparse furnishings to say the very least. Not recommended. To the north, down the road from Sikao is **Hua Hin**, which also has a good beach and is famed for its *hoi tapao* – sweet-fleshed oysters. Unfortunately the oyster season climaxes in November – the peak of the wet season. Hua Hin Bay is dotted with limestone outcrop islets. Other beaches to the south include **Hat San**, **Hat Yong Ling**, **Hat Yao** and **Hat Chao Mai**; private ventures are not permitted at any of the beaches within the national park (ie Hat Chao Mai, Hat Yong Ling and Hat San). Hat Yao has a very good restaurant (**Mid-range**: *Hat Yao Seafood*) which is open-fronted and looks out onto the beach. **Sleeping**: **C-E** *Barn Chom Talay – Seaview Guest House*, dormitory room and bungalows all clean. The bungalows are nicely furnished. The daughter of the owners speaks excellent English. Also offer every type of tour including kayak rental, trips to the nearby caves, and boat tours to the islands. A pleasant out-of-the-way place to stay. Recommended. There are also impressive caves near the village, known for their layered curtain stalactites. The beaches and many of the offshore islands fall under the jurisdiction of the 230 sq km **Hat Chao Mai National Park**. Accommodation available at park headquarters (6 km outside Chao Mai); **D** bungalows; there is no restaurant here – you can buy food from a very small shop in Chao Mai village. Further south of Kantang, in Amphoe Palien, is Hat Samran. ■ *Getting there: taxis to Pakmeng, Chao Mai, Katang and Palien leave from outside Trang's Diamond Department Store, near the railway station.*

Khao Chong Forest Park 20 km from town, off the Trang-Phattalung road, supports one of the few remaining areas of tropical forest in the area and has two waterfalls (*Nam Tok Ton Yai* and *Nam Tok Ton Noi*), where government resthouses are available. ■ *Getting there: taxis leave from outside the Diamond Department Store, near the railway station (₿100) or get a local bus (from the bus station on Huay Yod Rd), bound for Phattalung or Hat Yai (₿10).*

Trang

To Thamrin Thara Hotel, Bus Terminal, Kwan Tee Hun Shrine & Nakhon Si Thammarat

Utmalaat Rd

Phattalung Rd

Khlong Huay Yong

Visetkul Rd

Huay Yod Rd

kao Rd

Saingaam Rd

Rachdamnern Rd

Taklang & Municipal Market
Talad Rd

Kantang Rd

Koh Mook Resort Office

Koh Hai Villa Travel Agency

Phraram VI Rd

Clock Tower

Visetkul Soi 1

Rusda Rd

THAI Office

Diamond Dept Store

Taxis to Krabi

Taxis to Katang, Chao Mai & Khao Chong Forest Park

Visetkul Rd

To Trang Plaza Hotel (2 km), Clarion MP Resort Hotel (15 km), Pattalung & hat Ya

Buses to Satun

To Satun

N

0 metres   50
0 yards   50

■ **Sleeping**
1 Koteng
2 Petch
3 Queen's
4 Thumrin
5 Trang
6 Wattana

Trang's Andaman Islands See page 317.

Trang place names

Chang Lang

หาดฉางหลาง

Khao Chong Forest Park

อุทยานป่าเขาช่อง

Pakmeng

ปากเหม่ง

Tours **High season only (October-April):** *Trang Travel*, for trips to Trang's Andaman Islands. The company runs a boat and offers day-long excursions for a minimum of four, visiting islands and reefs on request, for ฿500-600 (including lunch and snorkelling equipment).

Sleeping
■ *on maps*
Price codes: see inside front cover

Most of Trang's hotels are on Phraram VI Rd, between the clock tower and the railway station. More recently a number of high-rise luxury hotels have sprung up slightly further out of town. **A** *Thamrin Thara*, 69/8 Huay Yod Rd, T223223. 285 rooms. Considered to be the No 1 hotel in town. The double rooms are more expensive than twins. Service is generally unresponsive: catering to local bigwigs at the expense of other guests. The hotel seems to have infrastructure problems with the boiler breaking down on more than one occasion (and no discount for no hot water). Unimpressive. **A** *Trang Plaza*, 132 Phattalung Rd, T226-90210. 2 km out of town, 2 restaurants, swimming pool. **A-B** *Clarion MP Resort*, 184 Phattalung Rd, T214230, F211177. 15 km out of town, restaurant, swimming pool, tennis, gym, golf driving range, 250-odd rooms.

C *Thumrin*, Thumrin Square, T211011, F218057. Some a/c, restaurant, OK but some signs of disrepair. Abundant staff. **C** *Trang*, 134 Visetkul Rd (clock tower intersection), T218157, F218451. Some a/c, restaurant, large rooms, some with balconies. More expensive rooms have TV and hot water.

D *Koteng*, 77-79 Phraram VI Rd, T218622. Some a/c, restaurant, friendly owners. Reasonable rooms; probably the best of the cheaper places. **D** *Queen's*, Visetkul Rd, T218229, F210414. Some a/c, no restaurant, large hotel with average rooms and attached bathrooms, hot water and western toilet. Clean but uninspiring. **D-E** *Wattana*, 127/3-4 Phraram VI Rd, T218184. Reasonable rooms, more expensive ones have a/c and TV, all have attached bathroom, some with hot water and western toilet, restaurant. Unimpressive management. **E** *Petch*, T218002. Good value, large, cheap rooms, some have attached bathroom with squat toilet, restaurant, friendly.

Eating
● *on maps*
Price codes: see inside front cover

Trang's barbecued pork is delicious and one of the town's few claims to national fame. It is made from a traditional recipe brought here by the town's immigrant Chinese community and is usually served with dim sum. It is the speciality of several Chinese restaurants in town.

Thai Cheap: *Sritrang Bakery*, Phattalung Rd. Desserts are a speciality. *Trokpla Seafood*, Trokpla Soi, Rama VI Rd. Excellent Thai and Chinese food on the 3rd floor of *Diamond Department Store*.

Chinese Mid-range: *Thumrin Coffee Shop*, 99 Thumrin Square. Extensive menu. **Cheap**: *Jan Jan*, Thaklang Rd. Barbecued pork. *Ko Choi*, Wienkapang Rd. Also serves Thai. *Ko Lan*, Huai Yod Rd. Trang-style barbecued pork. *Koyao*, Huai Yod Rd. Vast menu.

International Cheap: *Hoa*, at the front of *Diamond Department Store*, coffee shop and bar. *Queen's Hotel restaurant*, Visetkul Rd. Good American breakfast. *Sin Oh Cha*, next to railway station (opposite *Diamond Department Store*), coffee shop.

Foodstalls Two night markets offer good food, one is on Visetkul Rd, north of clock tower, the other is in the square in front of the railway station.

October *Vegetarian Festival* (movable). 9-day-long festival in which a strict vegetarian diet is observed to purify the body. Mediums pierce their cheeks and tongues with spears and walk on hot coals. On the sixth day a procession makes its way around town, in which everyone dresses in traditional costumes. The same event occurs in Phuket. **Festivals**

Best buys include locally woven cotton and wickerwork and sponge cake! **Shopping**

Markets Thaklang and Municipal Markets are next door to each other in the centre of town, off Rachdamnern Rd; they are a good place to browse for local goods.

Snorkelling: equipment for hire from *Trang Travel*, Thumrin Square. **Sport**

Trang Travel, Thumrin Square, T219598/9, F218057. *KK Tour & Travel*, opposite the railway station, T211198. **Tour operators**

Local **Motorbike hire**: at corner of Municipal market on Rachdamnern Rd, ฿200 per day. **Transport**
828 km from Bangkok
317 km from Phuket
163 km from Hat Yai

Air The airport is 7 km from town. Daily connections on *THAI* with Bangkok 2 hrs 10 mins (฿2,005), connections to Bangkok only.

Train The station is at the end of Phraram VI Rd. 2 daily connections with Bangkok (15½ hrs) at 1344 and 1820.

Road **Bus**: buses to most places leave from the bus terminal 1 km out of town on the Huay Yat road (get there by , ฿7-10) – the exception are the buses to Satun which leave from the terminal on Rusda Rd. Buses to Satun leave from Jermpanya Rd. Overnight connections with Bangkok 12 hrs and regular connections with Satun (2 hrs), Hat Yai (2 hrs), Phuket (฿62), Krabi (฿30), Phattalung (฿15) and Nakhon Si Thammarat (฿30). **Shared taxi**: to Nakhon Si Thammarat and Surat Thani leave from Huai Yod Rd (near junction with Rachdamnern Rd), taxis to Krabi leave from the railway station, taxis to Phattalung and Hat Yai leave from Phattalung Rd (opposite the police station), and to Satun they leave from Jermpanya Rd. Phuket (฿150), Krabi (฿50), Nakhon Si Thammarat (฿60), Hat Yai (฿50), Satun (฿50), Phattalung (฿30).

International connections with Langkawi, Malaysia: 4 ferries daily from Satun and Langkawi Island (at 0845, 1200, 1530 and 1700). Get a local bus to Satun (they take 1 hr 10 mins and cost ฿200).

Airline offices *Thai*, 199 Visetkul Rd (not in the centre of town), T218066. **Banks** Banks are clustered along Phraram VI Rd. **Communications** General Post Office and Telegraph Office: Jermpanya Rd. **Directory**

Trang's Andaman Islands

Trang's Andaman Islands number 47 in total, spread out to the south of Koh Lanta. Few tourists – relatively speaking – visit the islands, although their beauty, rich birdlife, and the clear waters that surround them make future development highly likely. **NB** There are no ferries to Trang's Andaman Islands in the rainy season, although long-tailed boats can be taken by those with the money and the courage. It is only advisable, though, in calm seas – check the weather forecast service, T02-3994012/3 (nationwide). *Colour map 4, grid C3*

The Andaman Sea Coast

Trang's Andaman Islands

Koh Chuak	Koh Mook
เกาะเชือก	เกาะมุก
Koh Hai (Ngai)	Koh Talibong (Libong)
เกาะไหง	เกาะลิบง
Koh Kradan	Koh Waen
เกาะกระดาน	เกาะแหวน

Although **Koh Ngai (Hai)** forms the southernmost part of Krabi province, and is most easily reached from Pakmeng in Trang province, 16 km away, it is also possible to get there from Koh Phi Phi and Koh Lanta. This 5 sq km island is cloaked in jungle and fringed with glorious beaches. A coral reef sweeps down the eastern side, ending in two big rocks, between which rips a strong current – but the coral around these rocks is magnificent. Koh Ngai is used as the jumping-off point for trips to the other islands.

Koh Chuak and **Koh Waen** (between Koh Hai and Koh Mook) are also snorkellers' havens – the latter is the best reef for seafan corals.

According to local fishermen, a colony of mermaids lives off the east coast of Koh Mook

On the western side of **Koh Mook** is the **Emerald Cave** or Tham Morakot – known locally as Tham Nam – which can only be entered by boat (or fearless swimmers) at low tide, through a narrow opening. After the blackness of the 80-m-long passage it opens into daylight again at a circular pool of emerald water ringed with powdery white sand and a backdrop of precipitous cliffs. The cave was only discovered during a helicopter survey not very long ago and – as is the way with these things – is thought to have been a pirates' lair. **Be warned**, you can only leave the pool at low tide. The island's west coast has white beaches backed by high cliffs where swallows nest. There are also beautiful beaches on the east coast facing the craggy mainland.

Koh Kradan, most of which falls within the bounds of the Chao Mai National Park, is regarded as the most beautiful of Trang's islands, with splendid beaches and fine coral, particularly on the east side. Two Japanese warships sunk during the Second World War lie off the shore and are popular dive spots. The areas not encompassed by the National Park are a mixture of rubber smallholdings and coconut groves. The island – bar the park area – is privately owned having been bought by Mon Sakunmethanon in 1985 for ฿5 million.

Koh Talibong (Libong), which is part of the Petra Islands group to the south, is renowned for its oysters and birdlife. The Juhoi Cape and the eastern third of the island is a major stopping-off point for migratory birds, and in March and April the island is an ornithologist's El Dorado. Typical visitors, on their way back to northern latitudes, include brown-headed gulls, crab plovers, four species of terns, waders, curlews, godwits, redshanks, greenshanks, reef egrets and black-necked storks. From October to March the island is famed for its unique Hoi Chakteen oysters. The rare manatee (*Manatus senegalensis*) and the green turtle also inhabit the waters off the island. The best coral reef is off the southwest coast, directly opposite the *Libong Beach Resort*. Snorkelling equipment is available from the resort who also provide fishing gear. Libong's main town is Ban Hin Kao, where the daily ferry from Kantang docks. Motorcycle taxis take visitors along rough trails to the island's beaches and villages. There is one hotel on the island (see **Sleeping**) and no nightlife. The population is almost exclusively Muslim, and alcohol is not widely available.

Koh Sukorn (Muu), **Koh Petra**, **Koh Lao Lieng** (**Nua** and **Tai**) are also part of the Petra Islands group, off Palien, 47 km south of Trang and can be reached from there or Kantang. **Koh Sukorn** (locally known as Koh Muu – or Pig Island) is, rather ironically, inhabited by Muslims. Apart from its golden powder-sand beaches, its main claim to fame are the mouth-watering water melons that are grown here (March/April).

Koh Petra and **Koh Lao Lieng** have sheer cliffs which are the domain of the birds' nest collectors who risk life and limb for swiftlet saliva (see page 304). The islands have excellent sandy beaches on their east coasts and impressive reefs which are exposed at low tide.

Dolphins can often be seen offshore

January-April. The weather is unsuitable for island-hopping from May-December and although it is sometimes still possible to charter boats out of season, it can be expensive and risky: the seas are rough, the water is cloudy and you may be stranded by a squall.

Best time to visit

Koh Ngai B *Koh Ngai Resort*, southeastern corner of the island, with its own magnificent private beach. More up-market than *Koh Ngai Villa*, chalets have fans and private balconies, they can be booked through the Trang office, 205 Sam-Yaek Mohwith,

Sleeping & eating

The Andaman Sea Coast

Trang's Andaman Islands

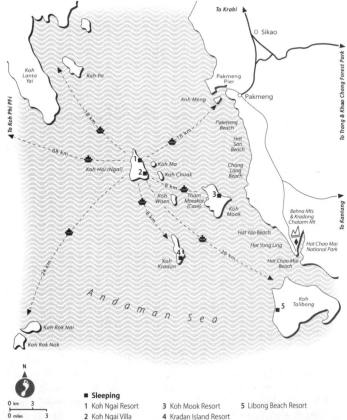

Sleeping
1 Koh Ngai Resort   3 Koh Mook Resort   5 Libong Beach Resort
2 Koh Ngai Villa   4 Kradan Island Resort

T210317 (or on the island T211045). See www.asiatravel.com/thailand/ prepaidhotels/kohngairesort/ **D** *Koh Ngai Villa* is half way up the eastern side of the island, facing the reef, contact Koh *Ngai Villa Travel Agency* in Trang, T210495. 15 grass-roofed chalets equipped with mosquito nets, restaurant, tents also available (฿150).

Koh Mook D-E *Koh Mook Resort*, only accommodation on the island, fantastic views (see map, page 319), office, 25/36 Sathani Rd, Trang, T211367.

Koh Kradan B-C *Kradan Island Resort*, only accommodation on the island, restaurant, rather expensive for the quality of accommodation provided (60 rooms). Recent visitors have been disappointed as the resort is run down with poor rooms at this price. However, the staff are friendly and enthusiastic and the island is wonderful. Tents are available for ฿150. Rooms can be booked at 25/36 Sathani Rd, T211367, Trang, or by phoning BT3920635, BF3911315. The Trang office also run a daily boat service to the island (฿240 return).

Koh Talibong (Libong) C *Libong Beach Resort*, Ban Lan Khao, T210013, or in Trang, T214676. Large open-fronted restaurant with about 15 basic bungalows set in a coconut grove facing onto a sandy beach, 5 km from the main town Ban Hin Khao, opened in 1993, the *Conservation of Wildlife Committee* on Libong Island also have a free guesthouse at Laem Juhol on the east coast, the guesthouse must be booked in advance, and food is not available, letters can be addressed to the secretary at the Libong Regional Department, PO Box 5, Kantang, Trang 92110 (T251932).

Koh Sukhorn south of Talibong **C** *Koh Sukhorn Resort*, T219679. 50 rooms.

Sport **Diving**: *Rainbow Divers*, in the *Koh Ngai Resort*, T211045, run by a German couple, they offer PADI courses and excursions around the island, open from mid-Nov until the end of Apr.

Transport **Boat** Boats leave from Pakmeng, about 25 km west of Trang. Mini-buses leave from the junction of Huay Yod and Kantang roads in Trang (฿30 one way). Boats from Pakmeng to Koh Hai 45 mins (฿150 one way, ฿1,000-฿1,500 day charter), that is boats are the same price for all 3 destinations; to Koh Mook 1 hr; to Koh Kradan 1½ hrs. *Kradan Island Resort* operates a hovercraft which takes a maximum of 5 people (฿600 return).

For Koh Talibong (Libong) it is cheaper and faster to take a taxi the 24 km from Trang to Kantang (฿10-15). From there a ferry leaves daily at 1200 for Koh Talibong's 'capital' of Ban Hin Khao. From there motorcycles take visitors the 5 km to the only hotel, the *Libong Beach Resort*. *Trang Travel*, opposite the *Thumrin Hotel* in Trang, also operates a boat which can be chartered to any of the islands. For those with less time on their hands, they offer day excursions (see **Tours**, Trang).

The islands can be reached from several small ports and fishing villages along the Trang coast, the main ones being Pakmeng and Kantang (24 km from Trang) – both ฿10 taxi ride from Trang – Chao Mai and Palien. It is also possible to charter boats with the Muslim fishermen who live on the islands.

Satun

Colour map 5, grid B2 Surrounded by mountains, Satun is cut off from the Malaysian Peninsula and the eastern side of the Kra Isthmus. Few tourists include Satun on their itinerary. Instead they make a bee-line for Ban Pak Bara 60 km or so north of town and catch a boat to the Turatao Islands (see page 322). But perhaps Satun deserves a few more visitors.

The province seems to have spent the last century searching for an identity separate from that of its neighbours. In the early years of this century it was administered as part of Kedah in Malaysia. In 1909, following a treaty between Thailand and Britain, it came under the authority of Phuket. Fifteen years later it found itself being administered from Nakhon Si Thammarat and it was not until 1932 that it managed to carve out an independent niche for itself when it was awarded provincial status by Bangkok.

The town is very Malay in feel and around two-thirds of the population are thought to be Muslim. The town's main mosque – the **Mesjid Bombang** – is a modern affair built in 1979 on Satunthani Road. More interesting perhaps are the preserved **Chinese shophouses** on Buriwanit Road. They are thought to be around 150 years old and fortunately the town's authorities slapped a preservation order on the buildings before they could be torn down to be replaced by something more hideous. **Ku Den's Mansion** on Satunthani Road also dates from the last century. It was originally the governor's residence but has been developed into the **Satun National Museum** (opened in May 2000).

Thale Ban National Park lies 40 km from Satun, bordering Malaysia, and was **Excursions** gazetted in 1980 after four years of wrangling and threats from local so-called *ithiphon muut,* or 'dark influences'. It is a comparatively small park, covering just over 100 sq km and in 1994 was visited by 14,000 people. How it got its name is the source of some dispute. Some people believe it is derived from the Malay words *loet roe ban,* meaning sinking ground; others that it is derived from the Thai word *thale,* meaning sea. The lake that lies at the core of the park covers some 30 ha, between two mountains, Khao Chin to the east at 720 m and Khao Wangpra to the west. A hiking trail leads from the park HQ to the summit of Khao Chin where it is possible to camp. (Tents available for hire from park HQ.) There are also waterfalls and caves; the most frequently visited waterfall is Ya Roi, situated 5 km north of the park HQ and accessible by vehicles. The falls here plunge through nine levels; at the fifth is a good pool for swimming. En route to Ya Roi is a modest cave: Ton Din. The park has a large bird population: hawks, hornbills, falcons and many migratory birds. Animal residents include dusky leaf monkeys, white-handed gibbon, lesser mousedeer, wild boar and, it is said, the Sumatran rhinoceros. Forest trails lead from the HQ and it is not unusual to see hornbills, langurs, macaques, even wild pigs. The round trip takes about four hours. Best time to visit: between December and April when rainfall in this wet area (2,662 mm per year) is at its least. **Sleeping** 10 bungalows for rent around the lake, sleeping between eight and 15. There is also a Thai restaurant and an information centre at the park HQ. **Camping**: tents available for hire from park HQ. ■ *Getting there: 37 km from Satun, 90 km from Hat Yai. Take Highway 4, 406 and 4184 to the park. By public transport catch a songthaew from Samantha Prasit Rd (by the pier) to Wang Prajan. From here there are occasional songthaews the last few kilometres, or take a motorcycle taxi.*

Charan Tour runs boat tours every day to the islands between October and **Tours** May. Lunch and snorkelling equipment are provided.

B-C *Sinkiat Thani*, Buri Wanit Rd, T721055, F721059. A hotel with a modicum of style, **Sleeping** large, well kept rooms and great views from the upper floors, Satun's No 1 hotel. Low-season discounts. **C** *Wangmai*, 43 Satunthani Rd, T711607. A/c, restaurant, a well-run place with good facilities and clean rooms, quite acceptable and well priced. **C-D** *Satunthani*, 90 Satunthani Rd, T711010. Some a/c, restaurant, OK but slow service. **E** *Rain Tong*, Samantha Prasit Rd (at the western end, by the river). Simple but clean rooms with attached bathrooms and cold-water showers.

Eating **Cheap**: *Kualuang*, Satuntanee Phiman. Best in a group of small Thai restaurants. *Banburee*, Buriwanit Rd. 1 of 2 places with English signs. Modern establishment situated behind the *Sinkiat Thani*. Thai food. *Suhana*, Buriwanit Rd. The other English-signed place on Buriwanit Rd, behind the mosque. Muslim food. *Smile*, round the corner from the *Wangmai Hotel* on Satuntanee Phiman Rd. Fast-food, budget prices. **The Baker's**, on Satuntanee Phiman, the main street into town, pastries, ice cream and soft drinks, budget. Pretty much opposite the Sinkiat Thani are several small restaurants serving Malay food and a *roti* shop selling banana, egg and plain *roti* in the mornings.

Foodstalls Night market with stalls serving Thai and Malay dishes on Satun Thani Soi 3. There is a plentiful supply of roadside food joints – particularly on Samantha Prasit Rd. All serve cheap rice and noodle dishes.

Entertainment **Cinema** On Satun Thani Rd, just past the *Satun Thani Hotel*. **Discos** The most popular disco in town is at the *Wangmai Hotel*.

Tour operators *Charan Tour*, 19/6 Satunthani Rd, T711453, F711982. *Satun Travel Ferry Service* (part of *Charan Tour*), Satunthani Rd, opposite *Wangmai Hotel*.

Transport *1,065 km from Bangkok* **Local** **Motorbike taxis**: from outside Thai Farmers Bank, near the market and from outside *Satunthani Hotel* on Satunthani Rd. **Road** **Bus**: overnight connections with Bangkok 15 hrs. Buses for Bangkok leave from Sarit Phuminaraot Rd. Regular connections with Hat Yai and Trang from opposite the wat on Buriwanit Rd. **Taxi**: Hat Yai from Bureevanith Rd, Trang from taxi rank next to Chinese temple. **Boat** It is possible to charter a boat from Satun to Koh Turatao, but it is a lot cheaper to bus it up to Ban Pak Bara and take one of the regular boats from there (see page 326).

Transport to Malaysia **Boat** Ferries leave from Satun and dock at one of 2 places, depending on the tide. If the tide is sufficiently high, boats arrive/leave from the jetty at the end of Samanta Prasit Rd. At low water boats dock at Tammalang Pier, south of Satun. Songthaews run to the pier from Buriwanit Rd. There are connections with Langkawi and Kuala Perlis. Daily ferries to Langkawi. Tickets can be purchased in advance from *Charan Tour*.

Directory **Banks** *Thai Military*, Buriwanit Rd (across from Hat Yai taxi rank on Buriwanit Rd). *Thai Farmers*, opposite the market. There are now branches of all the major banks, located on either Buriwanit or Satun Thani roads. **Communications** **Internet:** near the Sinkiat Hotel on Satunthani Rd is an e-café *Satun Cybernet* which offers internet connections for ฿30 per hour. **Post Office:** Samantha Prasit Rd (near Intersection with Satun Thani Rd). **Telephone Office:** attached to the GPO. **Useful Addresses** The new(ish) Immigration Office is at the end of Buriwanit Rd.

Turatao National Park and the Adang-Rawi Archipelago

Turatao National Park *Colour map 5, grid A1*

To Bu cliff, just behind the park headquarters on Ao Phante, has good views & is the spot for sunset romantics

Turatao was Thailand's first marine national park, created in 1974. It is made up of 51 islands, the main ones being Turatao, Adang, Rawi, Lipe, Klang, Dong and Lek. The park is divided into two main areas: the Turatao Archipelago and the Adang-Rawi Archipelago. This is one of Thailand's best preserved marine areas with excellent coral reefs, beaches and wildlife. Don't, though, expect luxurious living: this is for visitors who can do without mini-bars, watersports, satellite TV and air-conditioning.

The mountainous island of **Turatao** is the largest of the islands, 26 km long and 11 km wide and covering an area of 151 sq km. A mountainous spine runs north-south down the centre of the island, with its highest point reaching 708 m. The interior remains largely forested, cloaked in dense semi-evergreen rain forest. The main beaches are Ao Moh Lai, Hin Ngam, Ao Phante, Ao Chak and Ao Son, mostly on the west of the island which has long sweeps of sandy beach punctuated by headlands and areas of mangrove. Ao Son, for example, is a 3 km-long stretch of sand fringed with casuarina trees. (Much of the mangrove was cut for charcoal during the early 1960s before the national park was finally gazetted in 1974.) The prison at Ao Talo U-Dang, in the south, was established in 1936 and was once used as a concentration camp for Thailand's political prisoners; the graveyard, charcoal furnaces and a fish fermentation plant are still there. The other main camp was at Ao Talo Wao on the east side of the island and was used for high-security criminals. A road, built by inmates, connects the two camps. It is said that high-class political prisoners were segregated from the lowlier criminals, and the latter had to wait upon the former. During the Second World War, when communications were slow and difficult, the remoteness of the island meant that it was cut off from supplies of food. It is said that 700 out of the total prison population at that time of 3,000 died. In order to survive some of the guards and prisoners took to piracy – which was only qashed when British soldiers re-taking Malaya invaded the island in 1946. The prisons have been partially restored as historical monuments but there are no plans to reactivate them – today the only people living on the island are the park wardens.

Coconut plantations still exist on Turatao but the forests have barely been touched, providing a natural habitat for lemur, wild boar, macaques and mouse deer. Crocodiles are said to inhabit Khlong Phante and there is a large cave on the Choraka (crocodile) water system known as Crocodile Cave (bring a flashlight). There are also many species of birds on the islands, including colonies of swiftlets found in the numerous limestone caves – mainly on Koh Lo Tong (to the south of Turatao) and Koh Ta Kieng (to the northeast). Large tracts of mangrove forest are found here, especially along Khlong Phante Malacca on Turatao. The islands are also known for their trilobite fossils, 400 to 500 million years old, found not just on Turatao but all over the national park.

Many of the islands' caves have been used by pirates for centuries but some are still unexplored

The Andaman Sea Coast

Turatao National Park

While the waters around Turatao are home to four species of turtle – the Pacific Ridleys, green, hawksbill and leatherback – and dugongs, whales and dolphins are also occasionally seen, the sea is clearer further west in the waters of the Adang-Rawi archipelago (see below).

Turatao is just 4,800 m north of Malaysia's Langkawi Island, which, in contrast, is already a leading tourism destination. Both the Malaysian and Thai islands were traditionally pirates' lairs and Turatao and Langkawi were said to be cursed and hidden from the outside world for seven generations. The name Turatao is thought to be derived from a Malay word meaning mysterious. It was not until 1964 that the British Navy finally rid the area of its pirates, and its piratical associations may have helped protect the island and the waters around it from the sort of unwelcome attention paid to other areas.

Adang-Rawi place names

Koh Bulon
เกาะบุหลัน
Koh Bulon-Leh
เกาะบุหลันเล
Koh Hin Ngam
เกาะหินงาม
Koh Khai
เกาะไข่
Koh Lipe
เกาะหลีเป๊ะ

Adang-Rawi archipelago

Adang and **Rawi** lie 43 km west of Turatao and are the main islands in the archipelago of the same name. They offer a stark contrast to Turatao. While Turatao is composed of limestone and sandstone, the rugged hills of Adang and Rawi are granite. Adang's highest mountain rises to 703 m while Rawi's is 463 m in height. Koh Adang is almost entirely forested and there is a trail that leads up to the summit, for good views over Koh Lipe and the Andaman Sea. The main beaches on Adang are Khai, Laem Son, Ao Lo Lae Lae and Lo Lipa, and Sai Khao on Rawi.

Koh Lipe is a stunning island, a true tropical idyll

Koh Lipe is the flattest island in the group and has the largest settlement in the archipelago, of Chao Le fisherpeople (some 900 people), who were the original inhabitants of the islands. They have their own unique culture, language and peculiar architectural style. The Chao Le hold a traditional ceremony called *pla juk* twice a year. A miniature boat is built out of *rakam* and *teenped* wood by the villagers. Once the boat is completed, offerings are placed in it, and the Chao Le dance until dawn and then launch the boat out to sea, loaded with the village's communal bad luck. The prisoners originally incarcerated on Turatao have been moved to Koh Lipe where they now complete their sentences. It was only in 1940 that Koh Lipe officially became Thai territory – up to then it was none too clear whether the Chao Le here were putative Malaysians or Thais. Locals maintain that the Thai authorities encouraged them to plant coconut trees to show that they had settled, presumably on the basis that occupation is as good as ownership. Paths criss-cross this small island and the main beach here, unfortunately named Pattaya Beach, is miles more attractive than it more famous namesake to the east. Most accommodation in the Turatao archipelago is concentrated on Koh Lipe and, unusually for an island in a national park, the local Chao Le have been granted land ownership rights. Inevitably, though, these are being gradually taken up by powerful Bangkok-based interests. By early 2000 there were five resorts with a total of some 200 bungalows.

Koh Hin Ngam is southwest of Adang and is known for its strange-shaped stones found on the beaches. **Koh Khai** has white powdery sand beaches and some excellent diving.

Koh Bulon and **Koh Bulon-Leh** are less than 20 km north of Koh Turatao and about the same distance west of Ban Pak Bara. While they are part of the same archipelago as Turatao the islands are outside the boundaries of the Turatao National Park. The two islands have developed into quiet beach resorts with simple bungalow accommodation. There are a number of small fishing villages inhabited by so-called Sea Gypsies or Chao Le in the northern part of Koh Bulon-Leh. While development here is still low-key, land speculation began during the 1990s and investors are no doubt hoping that the island will develop.

Despite dynamite-fishing in some areas, the island waters still have reasonable coral, and provide some of the best **dive sites** in Thailand – particularly around the natural stone arch on Koh Khai. Adang Island has magnificent coral reefs.

Whales, dolphins & turtles are common here

November to April, coolest months are November and December. Park is officially closed May-October, but it is still possible to get there – services run providing the weather is OK. Bulon Leh island is accessible year round.

Best time to visit

For tours to Turatao, see Satun, page 321, *Tarutao Travel*, T781284, 781360 in La-Ngu town (on the way to Pak Bara Pier), and *Udom Tour* in Pak Bara itself (the office is round the back near the National Park's office – Khun Udom is a licensed tour guide, local to the area, and with a good knowledge of the islands, etc.) T01-8974765.

Tours

Accommodation is restricted to Koh Turatao, Koh Adang and and Koh Lipe. On the former two islands the accommodation is Forestry Department (ie government) run; Koh Lipe is the only island where the private sector has a presence. As a result it is on Koh Lipe where resorts are best.

Sleeping

Turatao Book through the National Parks' office in Bangkok BT5790529 or T074-711383 (the Pak Bara office). There is also a National Parks office at Ban Pak Bara pier. Accommodation is in the north and west of Turatao. *Tabag Bungalows*, on northern tip of Turatao, 2 rooms **B**, one room **C** - rooms accommodate 4 people. **D** *Bamboo house.* **F** per person *'Longhouse'* dormitory. **Camping**   Hired tent ฿60, *own tent* ฿10. Best spots for camping are on Ao Jak and Ao San.

Adang Accommodation is at Laem Son. *Bamboo longhouse* with 10 rooms, each accommodating 4 people at **F** per person. There is also a simple restaurant. The island essentially closes down during the rainy season.

Lipe Five bungalow operations (**B-D** are in enthusiastic competition. A few years ago these were mainly operated by the indigenous Chao Le, but more commercially astute outsiders are beginning to muscle in on the tourism industry. The accommodation is basic – it is best to check bungalows out before deciding where to stay. There are no telephones on the island, so advance booking is impossible.

Koh Bulon Leh

Bulon-Leh E-F *Pansand   Resort*, T7220279, or *First Andaman Travel*, in Trang, T218035, F211010. A-frame bungalow accommodation with attached bathrooms along with dormitories. Good watersports. They also organize camping, snorkelling and boat trips. There are also around 5 or 6 other, smaller bungalow operations on the island all in our **E-F** price categories.

Ban Pak Bara E-F *Andrew's* and a number of bungalow operations strung out along the beach (**E-F**). Some of these are moving a little up-market. The **D-E** *Diamond Beach* offers bungalows with sea views, and the **C** *Bara Resort* has a/c bungalows with hot water, also right on the beach. About 20-30 mins drive from Pak Bara Pier, near Langu town (free transportation is provided) is the **D** *Panyong Country Club Resort*, T781230, a grand name for quite a simple set-up – a new(ish) development with simple wooden bungalows and a restaurant in a garden overlooking Nipa palms, mangroves and some marshland. It's about 200-m walk to a beach on a shallow bay. The beach is nothing special although the views are nice, and the resort is quiet.

Camping *Charan Tours* can organize tent hire (see page 321).

Eating Guesthouses all offer food, but of the basic single-dish Thai variety with little choice. Fish is usually the best bet.

Koh Lipe The best restaurant on the island is run by Mrs Supenpit, who also has a few bungalows. Here seafood dishes are divine.

Sport **Snorkelling**: equipment for hire on Adang. Some of the best spots for coral in the park are: northwest of Koh Rang Nok, northwest of Turatao, southeast of Koh Rawi, around Koh Klang between Turatao and Adang, and off Koh Kra off Koh Lipe's east coast.

Transport Koh Turatao lies off the coast 30 km south of Ban Pak Bara; Koh Adang, Rawi and Lipe are another 40 km out into the Andaman Sea; while Koh Bulon-Leh is 20 km due west of Ban Pak Bara. Ferries leave and dock at Ban Pak Bara which is about 60 km north of Satun.

Local Boats: for hire from Turatao and Adang. ฿350 to go between the 2 islands. ฿200 to Crocodile Cave from Turatao.

Boat Ferries and boats for all the islands leave from Ban Pak Bara, 62 km north of Satun. Boats to **Koh Turatao** at 1030 and 1400 from Nov-May, 2 hrs (฿100 one way). They dock at Ao Phante Malaka on the island's west coast. The return leg from Turatao departs at 0900 and 1400. It is often too rough between May and Oct for ferries to operate, and the park is officially closed in any case. However boats can, in fact, be chartered at the discretion of their captains throughout the year (฿800 plus). Boats to **Koh Adang**, **Lipeh** and **Rawi** are less frequent. Ferries leave every Tue, Thu and Sat during the season at 1030 for these 3 islands. The ferries stop at Turatao on the way out and then continue on. Boats can also be chartered from Turatao. **Koh Bulon** is visited once a day by boat from Ban Pak Bara (฿100); the boat leaves at 1400 and takes 1½ hrs; Koh Bulon-Leh can only be reached by long-tail boat from Koh Bulon. Boats travel on from Koh Bulon to Koh Adang, Koh Turatao and Koh Lipe. Long-tailed boat charters from Ban Pak Bara to Koh Bulon cost ฿700-1000 per boat. **NB** Beware of travelling to any of these islands during bad weather; it is dangerous and a number of boats have foundered.

To get to Ban Pak Bara **Road Bus**: from the market in Satun, or from in front of Plaza Market, Hat Yai during the tourist season. Hat Yai is 158 km east of Ban Pak Bara. There are also regular buses from Trang (100 km north) to Ban Pak Bara. Buses from Satun, Ban Pak Bara connect with ferries. **Taxi**: to Langu (from Satun) and then a songthaew to Ban Pak Bara. There are also taxi connections with Trang. **Accommodation in Ban Pak Bara**: not really recommended except as a last resort but there are several guesthouses – mostly of the short-stay variety – strung out along the beach road. A much more salubrious alternative is the *Pak Nam Resort*, T074-781129, on Koh Kebang, a 15-min long-tailed taxi ride from Ban Pak Bara pier. The accommodation ranges from bungalows to A-frame huts, all with fan and attached bathroom. Excellent restaurant but the water here is dirty.

The Gulf of Thailand

7

The Gulf of Thailand

It is as one travels south through the provinces included in this section that Thailand's 'other' becomes apparent. Many southerners (or the 'Thai Pak Tai') are Muslim. Historically, they have identified – culturally and sometimes politically – with Malaysia and they speak a dialect which has more in common with Malay than with Thai. The countryside too becomes increasingly 'Malay' in the Far South; the vegetation is more tropical and rice paddies are replaced by rubber plantations. Villages are dominated by mosques rather than Buddhist wats and the pha sin *is replaced by the sarong. Even the cuisine is distinct from that of Central Thailand. Specialities include southern rice noodles,* kor lae *chicken and preserved fish-kidney curry.*

Surat Thani, the gateway to the islands of Koh Samui, Koh Phangan and Koh Tao, is still firmly part of Buddhist Thailand. At Chaiya, 50 km north of Surat Thani, is one of the most revered monasteries in the country dating back more than a millennium. The island of Samui developed in the 1980s from modest beginnings but is now one of Thailand's premier beach resorts. Budget travellers then paved the way to neighbouring Koh Phangan and from there to Koh Tao - the latter with a particularly good reputation for its diving.

Nakhon Si Thammarat is another Thai city with historical muscle and famous for its shadow puppetry, or nang thalung, *which is thought to have originated in Java. But Hat Yai and its sister city of Songkhla mark the beginning of Thailand's Far South. Few visitors make it down to Pattani, Narathiwat and Yala, the provinces of the 'other' Thailand, but there are good beaches and national parks, excellent food, and a character wholly different from the rest of the Kingdom.*

The East Coast: Chumphon to Phattalung

Just west of Chumphon the road south divides; Route 4 runs down the west coast of the peninsula, while Route 41 skirts inland down the east coast. Surat Thani, over 200 km south of Chumphon, is the departure point for Koh Samui and other islands in the Gulf of Thailand. About 50 km north of Surat Thani is the important historic town of Chaiya. Taking Route 41 south, Nakhon Si Thammarat (180 km) is another historic town associated with the Sumatran-based Srivijayan Empire. From here Route 403 traverses the peninsula to Trang, while Route 41 links up with Phattalung, nearly 900 km south of Bangkok.

Surat Thani

Phone code: 077
Colour map 4, grid A3

Surat Thani or 'City of the Good People' is a provincial capital and the jumping-off point for Koh Samui. During the 1970s, the Communist Party of Thailand was active in the area, the guerrillas being disillusioned ethnic Tais, not Malays as further south. Although the town has an interesting river front worth a visit, its main purpose serves as a transportation hub; either to Koh Samui, Koh Phangan or Koh Tao, or south to Krabi. **Suan Sattarana Park** lies south of town, on the river. Boats can be hired for trips on the river (฿200 for up to six people). The better journey is upstream. There is a big **Chinese temple** and an attractive old viharn in the compound of **Wat Sai**, both on Thi Lek Road, near the *Seree Hotel*. The town brightens up considerably during the *Chak Phra Festival* in September or October (see below).

The **tourist office**, *TAT*, 5 Talat Mai Rd, T288818, F282828, near *Wang Tai Hotel*, southwest of the town centre, is a good source of information for less-frequented sights in the province. Areas of responsibility are Surat Thani, Chumphon and Ranong.

Chaiya

Lying 50 km north of Surat Thani on Route 41, this city was an important outpost of the Sumatran-based Srivijayan Empire and dates from the late seventh century – making it one of the most ancient settlements in Thailand. Given the quantity of antiquities found in the area, some scholars have suggested that Chaiya may have been the capital of Srivijaya, rather than Palembang (Sumatra) as usually thought. Recent excavations in Sumatra however, seem to have confirmed Palembang as the capital. The Mahayana Buddhist empire of Srivijaya dominated Sumatra, the Malay Peninsula, and parts of Thailand and Java between the seventh and 13th centuries. It had cultural and commercial links with Dvaravati, Cambodia, north and south India and particularly Java. The syncretic art of this civilization clearly reveals these links. Many of the artefacts found in the area are now exhibited in the National Museum in Bangkok. Chaiya today is a pleasant, clean town with many old wooden houses.

Wat Phra
Boromthat
Chaiya

Two kilometres outside Chaiya, 1 km from the Chaiya railway station, stands **Wat Phra Boromthat Chaiya**, one of the most revered temples in Thailand. Within the wat compound, the central *chedi* is strongly reminiscent of the eighth-century *candis* of Central Java, square in plan with four porches and rising in tiers topped with miniature *chedis*. The *chedi* is constructed of brick and vegetable mortar and is thought to be 1,200 years old. Even though it was extensively restored in 1901 and again in 1930, its Srivijayan origins are still evident. A small **museum** nearby exhibits relics found in the vicinity which have not been 'acquired' by the National Museum in Bangkok. ■ *Wed-Sun, 0900-1200, 1300-1600 ₿20.* Another architectural link with Srivijaya can be seen at **Wat Kaeo**, which contains a recently restored sanctuary reminiscent of Cham structures of the ninth century (Hoa-lai type, South Vietnam), but again with Javanese overtones (with particular links to Candi Kalasan on the Prambanan Plain). Just outside Chaiya is the village of Poomriang, where

Chumphon & Surat Thani Provinces

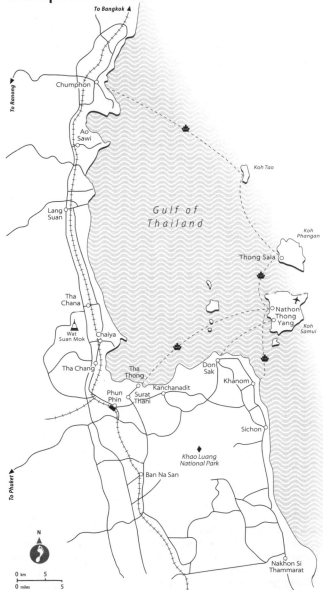

visitors can watch silk being woven. **Sleeping** There is just one hotel in Chaiya, the (**E**) *Udornlarb*, located near the market, T431123, just 11 large, clean rooms. ■ *Getting there: trains from Surat Thani's Phun Phin station northwards stop at Chaiya (40 mins). Regular buses from Surat Thani to Chaiya from Talat Kaset Nung (1). Regular songthaews ('taxis') from close to Talat Kaset Song (2) (฿30).*

Surat Thani place names

Chaiya
ไชยา

Wat Kaeo
วัดแก้ว

Wat Phra Boromthat Chaiya
วัดพระบรมธาตุไชยา

Wat Suan Mok
วัดสวนโมก

Wat Suan Mok
Courses for Westerners are run with the assistance of a number of foreign monks & novices

Also known as **Wat Suan Mokkh** or, in full, **Wat Suan Mokkhabalarama**, this popular forest Wat (*wat pa*) which has become an international Buddhist retreat, lies 50 km north of Surat Thani on Route 41. The monastery was founded by one of Thailand's most revered monks, the late Buddhadasa Bhikkhu, on a peaceful plot of land covering around 50 ha of fields and forest. Since he died in 1993 the monastery has been run by monks who have continued to teach his reformist philosophy of eschewing consumerism and promoting simplicity and purity. (Buddhadasa Bhikku developed and refined the study of Buddhist economics and he follows a long tradition in Thailand of scholar-monks.) Ten-day *anapanasati* meditation courses are held here beginning on the first day of each month; pick up a leaflet from Surat Thani's TAT office or telephone Khun Supit on BT4682857. Enrolment onto the course takes place on the last day of the month, on a first-come first-served basis and the full course costs ฿900. For those who are considering taking the course, bear in mind that students sleep on straw mats, are woken to a cacophony of animal noises at 0400, bathe in a communal pool, and are expected to help with chores around the monastery. But the course does include tasty rice and vegetable meals twice a day at 0800 and 1300. No alcohol, drugs or tobacco are permitted and the sexes tend to be segregated. If intending to visit the monastery or enrol on a course, it is worth bringing a torch and mosquito repellant (or buy these at the shop by the main entrance). ■ *Getting there: by bus from Talat Kaset Nung (1); the road passes the wat (1 hr). The town of Chaiya is closer to the monastery, so if arriving by train direct from Bangkok alight here and catch a songthaew to Wat Suon Mok.*

Monkey training centre

This is south of Surat Thani on Route 401, towards Nakhon Si Thammarat, 2 km off the main road. The only monkey capable of being trained to pick coconuts is the pig-tailed macaque (or *ling kung* in Thai). The male is usually trained, as the female is smaller and not so strong; strength is needed to break off the stem of the coconut. The training can start when the animals are eight months old. The course lasts three to five months, and when fully trained, the monkeys can pick as many as 800 coconuts in a day and will work for 12-15 years. "Working monkeys are very cheap – they cost no more than ฿10 a day but make millions of baht a year", Somphon Saekhow, founder of a coconut-collecting school. ■ *Getting there: take a songthaew or bus from Surat Thani heading towards Nakhon Si Thammarat, on Talat Mai Rd, which becomes Route 401. The turning to the centre is on the right-hand side, just over the Thathong Bridge, past a wat and school. The centre is 2 km down this road.* **NB** There were rumours that the centre was due to close down; check at the TAT office before leaving.

For some reason, it seems that all Surat Thani's hotel owners must have sat down over a few cases of Singhas and decided to name their hotels so as to confuse their guests. So, before venturing out into the night, make sure you know whether you are staying at the *Wang Tai*, the *Muang Tai*, the *Thai*, the *Thai Thani*, the *Siam Thani*, or the *Siam Thara*. The choice in our **D** category is enormous.

Sleeping
■ *on maps*
*Price codes: see
inside front cover*

A *Southern Star* (formerly the *Thanawat*), 253 Chonkasem Rd, T216414, F216427. The most luxurious hotel in the centre of town. The rooms are tastefully decorated and are well equipped with satellite TV and minibar. There are 3 restaurants, one on the 16th floor which commands great views over the city. For those looking for nightlife, the *Southern Star* is also home to the largest discotheque in the south. **A** *Wang Tai*, 1 Talat Mai Rd, T283020, F283020, BT2537947. A/c, restaurant, pool, top hotel in town (southwest of town centre).

C *Siam Thani*, 180 Surat-Phun Phin Rd, T273081, F282169. A/c, restaurant, pool, tennis. **C** *Siam Thara*, 1/144 Donnok Rd, T273740, F282169. A/c, restaurant. **C-D** *In Town Hotel*. Near the *Bandon Hotel*. The matter-of-fact name says it all: clean functional rooms, some a/c, with satellite TV and hot water. **C-D** *Lamphoo Bungalow*, Tapi River Island, T272495. Some a/c, restaurant, for a change of scene, this accommodation is a little more unusual. **C-D** *Tapi*, 100 Chonkasem Rd, T272675. Large clean rooms, some a/c, with large shower rooms. An improvement on others in this price bracket as the rooms have Thai TV, drinking water and hot water showers.

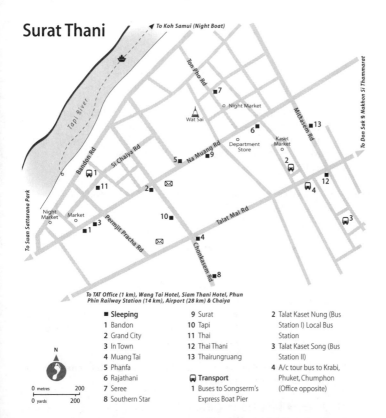

Surat Thani

To Koh Samui (Night Boat)

Tapi River · *Ton Pho Rd* · *Bandon Rd* · *Si Chaiya Rd* · *Na Muang Rd* · *Mittasem Rd* · *Permjit Pracha Rd* · *Chonkasem Rd* · *Talat Mai Rd*

To Don Sak & Nakhon Si Thammarat

To Suan Sattarana Park

Wat Sai · *Night Market* · *Department Store* · *Kaset Market* · *Night Market* · *Market*

To TAT Office (1 km), Wang Tai Hotel, Siam Thani Hotel, Phun Phin Railway Station (14 km), Airport (28 km) & Chaiya

N

0 metres 200
0 yards 200

The Gulf of Thailand

■ **Sleeping**	9 Surat	2 Talat Kaset Nung (Bus
1 Bandon	10 Tapi	Station I) Local Bus
2 Grand City	11 Thai	Station
3 In Town	12 Thai Thani	3 Talat Kaset Song (Bus
4 Muang Tai	13 Thairungruang	Station II)
5 Phanfa		4 A/c tour bus to Krabi,
6 Rajathani	🚌 **Transport**	Phuket, Chumphon
7 Seree	1 Buses to Songserm's	(Office opposite)
8 Southern Star	Express Boat Pier	

D *Thairungruang*, T286351, F286353. Some a/c, characterless hotel with dark, forbidding corridors but rooms are clean and have large windows. Attached shower rooms with western toilet. **D** *Grand City*, 428/6-10 Na Muang Rd, T272960. Very tatty hotel, fan cooled rooms with squat loos. Some a/c. Overpriced. **D** *Muang Tai*, 390-392 Talat Mai Rd, T272559. The large rooms could be cleaner but some are a/c and all have attached Western bathroom. **D** *Rajathani*, 293/96-99 Talat Kaset, T273584. Reasonably clean rooms, TV, some a/c, attached bathroom with squat toilet**. D** *Seree*, 2/2-5 Ton Pho Rd, T273193. The rooms are clean, but the décor is somewhat tasteless. Most have attached shower rooms with a western toilet. The cheapest is much dirtier and only has a squat toilet. Coffee shop. **D** *Thai Thani*, 442/306-8 Talat Mai Rd, T272977. Large, cleanish rooms with attached shower rooms, some a/c. **D** *Surat*, 496 Na Muang Rd, T272287. Overpriced hotel. The rooms are not particularly clean and the communal facilities are grotty. Some a/c. **D** *Bandon*, Na Muang Rd, T272167. Clean tiled rooms, some a/c, all with private shower rooms. Best value in town. **D** *Thai*, 24/4-6 Si Chaiya Rd, T272932. Large clean rooms, squat loos, management speaks no English. **E** *Phanfa*, 247/2-5 Namuang Rd, T272287. These large, cleanish rooms with attached shower rooms are the cheapest in town.

Eating
● *on maps*
Price codes: see inside front cover

Mid-range: *Suan Isaan*, near Donnok Rd, in a small *soi*. Large traditional Thai house, northeastern Thai food, menu in Thai but excellent food. Recommended. *Kampan*, Pakdee Rd, Thai. There is a good **bakery** next to the *Tapi Hotel* on Chonkasem Rd. **Cheap**: *J Home*, near corner of Chonkasem and Na Muang roads. A/c café, English menus. *Malisas*, in the Night Market, for coffee, beer, ice cream.

Foodstalls On Ton Pho Rd (delicious mussel omelettes near to intersection with Na Muang Rd). Plentiful supply of fruit and *kanom* stalls along the waterfront. Market next to the local bus terminal (Talat Kaset 1). Good **Night Market** on Na Muang Rd, and on Ton Pho Rd and vicinity, road down to Si Chaiya Rd from Na Muang Rd. **Breakfast**: Good European breakfast in little café opposite the pier.

Festivals

August *Rambutan Fair* (movable). **October-November** *Chak Phra Festival* (movable) marks the end of the 3-month Buddhist Rains Retreat and the return to earth of the Buddha. Processions of Buddha images and boat races on the Tapi River, in long boats manned by up to 50 oarsmen. Gifts are offered to monks as this is also *kathin*, celebrated across Buddhist Thailand.

Entertainment

Sports Massage: available at the *Seree Hotel* (฿80 per hour). **Swimming**: non-residents can use the pools at the *Wang Tai* or the *Siam Thani Hotel*.

Shopping

Department Stores *Jula Department Store*, Vithi That Rd. *Sahathai Department Store*, Na Muang Rd. **Jewellery** At shops near corner of Chonkasem and Na Muang roads.

Tour operators

Phantip, 442/24-25 Talat Mai Rd, T272230, opposite *Thai Thani Hotel*. *Songserm Travel Centre Co Ltd*, opposite night boat pier, T285124. *Samui Tour*, 326/12 Talat Mai Rd, T282352. *Samui Ferry Co*, T423026. *Ferry Phangan Co*, 10 Chonkasem Rd, T286461. Other agents organizing bus transport are to be found on Bandon, Chonkasem and Na Muang roads.

Transport
644 km S of Bangkok

Local Songthaews: known as 'taxis'. Suzuki vans, bus. **Motorbike hire**: shop next to *Samui Tours* on Talat Mai Rd (฿350-750 per day).

Air The airport is 27 km south of town on Phetkasem Rd, T200605. Twice daily connections with Bangkok on **THAI** (1 hr).

Train The station is at Phun Phin, 14 km west of Surat Thani (T311213) local buses go into town stopping at the Talat Kaset Nung (1) terminal. Regular connections with Hualamphong station, Bangkok (11-13 hrs). The 1830 train is the most convenient for catching a ferry to Koh Samui. Trains out of Phun Phin are often full: advance booking can be made at *Phantip* travel agency on Talat Mai Rd. *Songserm Travel Service*, Koh Samui also arrange reservations. Regular connections with Hua Hin, Trang, Yala, Hat Yai and Sungei Golok. Buses meet the train for the transfer to the various ferry terminals for Koh Samui, Phangan and Tao (see page 339). An international express leaves for Butterworth at 0155 (11 hrs) from where it continues on to Kuala Lumpur and Singapore.

Road Bus: the 2 stations in Surat Thani are within easy walking distance of one another – Talat Kaset Nung (1) is for local buses (for example Krabi) and Talat Kaset Song (2) for longer-distance journeys. **NB** Bus services are sometimes badly organized, with overbooked buses and combination tickets being no guarantee of follow-on services. A good supply of patience is sometimes required. Regular a/c connections with Southern bus terminal in Thonburi (Bangkok), 11 hrs; non-a/c connections with the new terminal on Phra Pinklao Rd (11 hrs). Also buses to Narathiwat (6 hrs), Trang (3 hrs), Phuket (6 hrs), Nakhon Si Thammarat (2½ hrs), Krabi (3½ hrs) and Hat Yai (5 hrs) and on to Kuala Lumpur and Singapore. Note that the border at Sungei Golok closes at 1700; not all buses (and despite protestations to the contrary) make it there before then so be prepared to spend a night in Sungei Golok. **Private tour companies** run bus services to/from Bangkok (10 hrs) (฿285-440) and Krabi 3-4 hrs (฿80) (see travel agents for listing). The advantage of taking a tour bus from here to Krabi is that they go all the way into Krabi town, to the Chao Fah Pier, rather than stopping at the bus station, out of town. Tour buses to Bangkok go from opposite the Phangan Ferry Office on Chonkasem Rd. **A/c minibus**: for some destinations there are very few buses but minibuses leave for most places regularly from the bus terminal and cost approximately 50% more than the a/c bus. **Taxi**: terminal next to bus terminal. Taxis to Trang 3 hrs (฿110), Nakhon 2 hrs (฿60), Krabi 2 hrs (฿150), Hat Yai 3½ hrs (฿150), Phuket 4 hrs (฿150), Phangnga 4 hrs (฿150).

Boat Hovercraft: a service leaves from Tha Thong Pier, 5 km from Surat Thani at 0730 and 1030, 1½ hrs (฿350), it docks at Na Thon Pier, Koh Samui. For more details on transport to and from Koh Samui, see page 339.

Directory

Airline offices *Thai*, 3/27-28 Karunrat Rd, T273710. **Banks** Several currency exchanges on Na Muang and Chonkasem roads. An exchange van operates from 0630-1800 across the street from the Koh Samui/Koh Phangan boat pier. **Communications** Main Post Office: near corner of Talat Mai and Chonkasem roads. **Branch Post Office**: on corner of Na Muang and Chonkasem roads (check letters are franked in your presence). **Telephone service**: for overseas calls on Don Nok Rd. **Medical services** *Bandon Hospital*, Na Muang Rd. **Useful addresses** Tourist Police: Na Muang Rd, T272095.

The Gulf of Thailand

Koh Samui

Phone code: 077
Colour map 4, grid A5

Koh Samui is the third largest of Thailand's islands, after Phuket and Koh Chang. Over the last decade tourism has exploded and now that it is accessible by air, the island is making the transition from a backpacker's haven to a sophisticated beach resort. Unlike Phuket, it does still cater for the budget traveller, with a great variety of bungalows scattered around its shores. The following sections have been organized by beach, beginning at Nathon (Samui's 'capital') and working clockwise around the island.

Ins and outs

Getting there Flying is the easiest and quickest option. It is relatively inexpensive and hassle free, landing you in the northeastern corner of the island after a flight from Bangkok of little more than an hour. The airport – really an airfield, with just a strip and a few airport buildings – is privately owned by Bangkok Airways. There are multiple daily connections with Bangkok and flights to U-Tapao (near Pattaya) and Phuket. There are also daily international connections with Singapore. The alternative to flying is to take a ferry. Most leave from one of Surat Thani's piers and the journey takes about 2 hrs. See page 341 for further details on the list of possibilities. Surat Thani can be reached either by bus from Bangkok or by train to Phun Phin, 14 km from Surat Thani. The alternative to travelling from Surat Thani is to catch the boat from Chumphon to Koh Tao, and from there to Koh Samui via Koh Phangan (see the map on page 331). But this is a much longer sea journey and only really makes sense if intending to stop off on Koh Tao.

Getting around Koh Samui is a large island – well over 20 km both long and wide. Beaches and hotels and guesthouses can be found on just about every stretch of coastline although the two most popular and developed beaches are both on the east coast, Chaweng and Lamai. The main town of Nathon, where most of the ferries dock, is on the west side of the island. A ring road follows the coast along the north, east and south sides of the island, but runs inland cutting off the southwestern corner. *Songthaews* run around the island during daylight hours and can be flagged down anywhere. The destination is displayed on the front. From dusk the service becomes increasingly intermittent. There are scores of places renting out motorbikes and jeeps but note that the accident rate on Koh Samui is horrendously high (see page 341).

There is no TAT representation on Koh Samui – the nearest **tourist office** is at 5 Talat Mai Road, Surat Thani, T288818. However, since Koh Samui is such a well-developed and popular tourist destination, stacks of information is available. Several tourist magazines are distributed free of charge: *Samui* (www.go-siam.com), *What's on Samui*, *Samui Guide* and *Samui Welcome* (samuiwelcom.com). Free maps include *Samui Guide Map*, *Green Map* and *Guide Map to Samui*. Pick them up from the Koh Samui information desk at Don Muang Airport, from Koh Samui Airport, or from hotel lobbies and shops across the island.

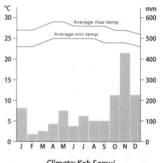

Climate: Koh Samui

The Gulf of Thailand

● ●

Sea, water and weather conditions on Koh Samui

March-October Light winds (averaging 5 knots), calm seas, the driest period of the year but downpours can still occur. Water visibility is good. This is the period of the southwest monsoon and though generally calm, Bophut and Mae Nam beaches can be windy, with choppy conditions offshore. Chaweng is normally calm even when Bophut and Mae Nam are rough.

October-February The northeast monsoon brings rain and stronger winds, averaging 10-15 knots but with gusts of 30 knots on some days. Sea conditions are sometimes rough and water visibility is generally poor although Koh Tao (see page 368) offers good year-round diving.

● ●

Sights

Koh Samui is the largest in an archipelago of 80 islands, six of which are inhabited. It is 25 km long and 21 km wide. About 40,000 people live here, many of whom are fishermen-turned hoteliers. The number of annual visitors is many times this figure. The first foreign tourists began stepping ashore on Samui in the mid-1960s and early 1970s. At that time there were no hotels, no electricity (except generator-supplied), no telephones, no surfaced roads – nothing, it seems, but an over-abundance of coconuts. This is still evident because, apart from tourism, the mainstay of the economy is coconuts; two million are exported to Bangkok each month. Monkeys are taught to scale the trees and pluck down the ripe nuts; even this traditional industry has cashed in on tourism – visitors can watch the monkeys at work and also visit the coconut fibre factory, about 5 km from the Hin Lad Waterfall. (A monkey training centre has been established outside Surat Thani, see page 332.)

The island's main attractions are its wonderful beaches; most people head straight there, where they remain until they leave. However, if boredom sets in, there are motorbikes or jeeps for hire to explore inland. Two-thirds of the island is forested and hilly with some impressive (in the wet season) waterfalls – **Hin Lad Waterfall** and wat are 3 km south of Nathon and can be reached from the town on foot, or by road 1 km off Route 4169. It's a 45-minute walk from the vehicle parking area. **Na Muang Waterfall**, in the centre of the island has a 30-m drop (and a good pool for swimming). *Songthaews* leave for the waterfall from Nathon. This being the only fall on the island which is accessible by paved road makes it overpopulated at weekends and holidays. The sign to **Samui Highland Park** is just before the 3-km marker, south of Nathon. From here, it is a two-hour climb to the highest ridge, through rubber plantations (the route can be confusing, so ask directions). There are good views of the south and west coasts from the top. The **Temple of the Big Buddha** sits on an island linked to the mainland by a short causeway, near Bophut Beach. This unremarkable, rather featureless modern seated image is 12 m high. In recent years, the site has been smartened up and made into a 'proper' tourist attraction; there are now 50 or so trinket stalls at the entrance and several foodstalls. It has become a popular spot on the motorbike touring trail. There is a '**Monkey Theatre**' just south of Bophut, which holds several shows daily, displaying Thai sword fighting and Thai dancing, followed by monkey baiting. All rather unpleasant and tacky. ■ *Overpriced at ฿150, and ฿50 for children, T245140.* There is a **Cultural Hall** and small museum near Ban Lamai and a group of phallic rock formations, known as **Grandfather and Grandmother Rocks** (or, less obtusely, the **Genital Rocks**), at the south end of Lamai Beach, with the usual array of touristy shops leading up to it. The signpost marks them 'Wonderful rocks'. The **Samui Butterfly Garden** is set on the side of the hill

The Gulf of Thailand

behind *Laem Set Inn*. It features a screened butterfly garden with a limited collection of butterflies, a display of (dead) insects, moths and butterflies, a few beehives, a hillside observatory, observation platforms for views of the coast, a glass-bottomed boat for viewing a coral reef and a restaurant. **NB** Their boats emit appalling fumes and could be considered a health hazard. They are in the process of building some bungalows here too. ■ *0930-1800, ₿50 (adult), ₿20 (child). T424020-2.*

Many of Koh Samui's inhabitants are not Thai, but Chinese from Hainan who settled on the island between 150 and 200 years ago. So far as most visitors are concerned, this little nugget of history will remain hidden; the Chinese across Thailand have assimilated to such a degree that they are almost invisible. However, evidence of this immigration of Hainanese can be seen reflected in the **traditional architecture** of the island. Houses, though they may also incorporate Indian, Thai and Khmer elements, are based on Hainanese prototypes. The use of fretwork to decorate balconies and windows; the tiled, pitched roofs; the decoration of the eaves – elements such as these make the older houses of Samui distinctive in Thai terms. The sadness is that it is unlikely that many will survive the next decade or two. They are being torn down to make way for more modern structures, or renovated and extended in such a way that their origins are obscured.

Koh Samui place names

Hin Lad Waterfall
น้ำตกหินลาด

Na Muang Waterfall
น้ำตกหน้าเมือง

Samui Highland Park
สมุยไฮแลนด์

Temple of the Big Buddha
วัดพระใหญ่

Best time to visit March to June is hot and fine with a good breeze and only the occasional thunderstorm. At this time of year good discounts can be had on accommodation. June to October is also sunny and hot, with short showers. The 'worst' time of year is October to February, when the monsoon breaks and rain is more frequent. Note, though, that even during this period daily hours of sunshine average 5-7 hours.

Essentials

Sleeping There are well over 300 registered bungalows and hotels providing over 6,000 rooms (with yet more under construction); the choice is overwhelming. For nightlife, the two most popular beaches are still Lamai and Chaweng, both on the east side of the island. They also have the longest stretches of uninterrupted beach, with good swimming and watersports. Mae Nam and Bophut, on the north shore, are also becoming popular, with good watersports. For a quieter scene, there are some remote bungalows down the west shore, although it is best to hire a vehicle, as many of them are off the main road. Some of these bungalows have their own generators, so electricity may only be available in the evenings. The advantage of staying on this side of the island is to see the spectacular sunsets. The list of places to stay is not comprehensive; bungalows survive on reputation and it is often best to stay somewhere which has been personally recommended. **NB** Accommodation prices tend to soar during the peak months. Bargain during the off-season; a reduction of up to 50% is possible.

Sport See each beach for details. **NB** Jet skis/propellor skis are a cause of loss of life and limb annually. Extreme caution is advised.

The easiest way to get to Koh Samui is by air. The overland journey can be rather arduous, with an overnight bus (or train) to Surat Thani, another bus to the ferry and then the crossing to the island, but is considerably cheaper. It is possible to buy 'combination' bus/ferry tickets from any travel agent in Khaosan Rd (Bangkok), prices vary so it's worth shopping around, they should cost about ฿260.

Local Hitching: is quite easy. **Motorbike and jeep hire**: cheaper from the town of Nathon than on the beaches. Jeep hire is ฿600-900 per day without insurance (see box, page 341 for cautions). **Motorbike taxis**: available from the port. **Songthaews**: the most common form of transport, *songthaews* visit all the island's beaches during daylight hours. Their final destination is usually written on the front of the vehicle and they stop anywhere (prices start at ฿20 per person). From Nathon, *songthaews* travel in a clockwise direction to Chaweng and anti-clockwise to Lamai. After 2100, *songthaews* are thin on the ground and expensive.

Air The airport is in the northeast of the island. This is a private airport, and **Bangkok Airways** is a private airline, which accounts for the grossly inflated airport departure tax (฿500 from Koh Samui, only ฿30 from Bangkok). *Airport facilities*: hotel reservation (**NB** this is owned by Bangkok Airways and attempts are made to divert clients to *Samui Palm Beach* – owned by the airline), reconfirmation of flights, restaurant. **Hertz** car rental, money changer. *Transport to town or beach*: a/c minibus to Bo Phut, Mae Nam, Chaweng, Choeng Mon, Lamai and Big Buddha. Again prices are enormously inflated, but Bangkok Airways have a monopoly. The alternative is to walk out onto

Transport
84 km NE of Surat Thani

The Gulf of Thailand

Koh Samui

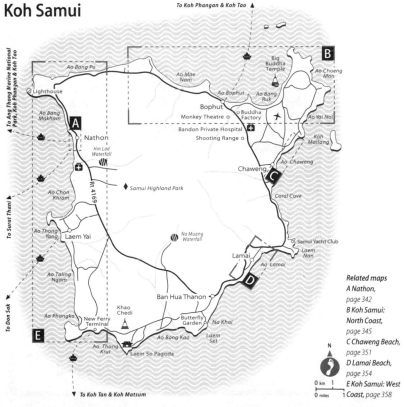

Related maps
A Nathon,
page 342
B Koh Samui:
North Coast,
page 345
C Chaweng Beach,
page 351
D Lamai Beach,
page 354
E Koh Samui: West
Coast, page 358

0 km   1
0 miles   1

The Gulf of Thailand

● ●

Road madness on Samui

By some measures, Thailand has the world's highest death rate on the roads. Koh Samui has the highest rate in Thailand and accidents, fatal and otherwise, are certainly horrifyingly common. There are several reasons for this state of affairs:

narrow roads
poorly maintained vehicles and machines
visitors unused to driving on the left
visitors unused to driving in Thailand
locals driving without lights
visitors driving drunk or on drugs

It means that visitors should be especially careful when driving on the island and also make sure that they test their motorbike (particularly) or car before completing a rental agreement. It is also advised that people ***do not leave their passports*** *as collateral. Should there be an accident, it leaves the renter of the vehicle at the mercy of its owner. For more details on driving in Thailand see page 34.*

● ●

the road, but it is a 1 km walk and tricky with luggage. Multiple daily connections with Bangkok, 1 hr 10 mins. **Bangkok Airways** also fly to Phuket twice a day, 50 mins, and to U-Tapao (Pattaya) and Krabi, once a day. BT2534014 (Bangkok) and T272610 (Koh Samui) for reservations. **THAI** flies to Surat Thani, 1 hr, with a connecting limousine and boat service (see Surat Thani entry).

Train From Bangkok's Hualamphong station to Phun Phin, outside Surat Thani, 10-12 hrs. The State Railway runs a rail/bus/ferry service from Bangkok to Koh Samui 18 hrs. This needs to be booked 2-3 days in advance. Note that it is not necessary to buy a combination ticket; buses from all the ferry companies meet trains to transfer passengers to the various ferry terminals.

Road Bus: to Surat Thani, from Bangkok's Southern bus terminal, a/c buses leave between 2000 and 2200, 12 hrs. See page 335 for further details.

Boat The listings below may seem confusing, but because of the number of tourists visiting Koh Samui, the transport system is well organized and it is difficult to go wrong. Options are:

1. *Songserm Travel* run 3 **express passenger boats** daily during the peak season (Nov-May), leaving Surat Thani 0730, 1200 and 1400, and leaving Koh Samui at 0730, 1230 and 1500, 2 hrs. These boats usually dock at Tha Thong Pier, 6 km east of Surat Thani and at Nathon Pier, on Koh Samui. To reach Tha Thong Pier, take a bus from Ban Don Rd, on the riverfront in Surat Thani. On leaving Koh Samui, a/c buses meet the 0730 express boat for transfers to Phuket, Krabi, Hat Yai and Penang. BT2529654 (Bangkok) for more information. **NB** *Songserm* tend to overload their boats and not provide sufficient lifejackets.

2. **The slow overnight boat** leaves from the pier in Surat Thani (otherwise known as Ban Don) at 2300, 6-7 hrs and docks at the pier in Nathon.

3. **The vehicle and passenger ferry** (known as the 'Express ferry') leaves from Don Sak, 60 km from Surat Thani. Travellers arriving by train at Phun Phin will be transferred to Don Sak. Buses from Surat Thani to Don Sak leave 1½ hrs before ferry departs either from *Samui Tour*, Talat Mai Rd or from *Phuntip Tour*, Talat Kaset I. The ferry docks at Tong Yang, south of Nathon. 8 ferries leave Samui and Surat Thani daily, more on

The Gulf of Thailand

public holidays and peak periods, 1½ hrs. T282352 in Surat Thani for more information. *Songthaews* run from Tong Yang to Nathon and the beaches. There is also a *Songserm* car ferry from the mainland port of Khanom which docks in downtown Nathon at the new dock there. If you are coming from Surat Thani, the only advantage this port has over Don Sak is the fact that they will take bookings for cars – a great advantage during peak periods.

Hovercraft: a service leaves from Tha Thong Pier, 5 km from Surat Thani at 0730 and 1030, 1½ hrs (฿350); it docks at Na Thon Pier, Koh Samui.

Directory   **Communications** **Internet** There are internet cafés in all the beach resort areas. **Telephone**: Calls are much cheaper if made at the post office. High street 'booths' are 3-4 times more expensive. International calls can also be made from many hotels and travel agents. **Medical services** Koh Samui has three hospitals. The Samui International Hospital in Chaweng, Bandon International Hospital in Bo Phut and a government-run hospital in Nathon. All three offer a 24-hr emergency clinic and the Samui International Hospital also has a dental clinic. Note that if someone is involved in a serious accident it is best to transport the injured person to the hospital; the ambulance service can be very slow. A reasonable level of English is spoken. **Useful addresses** **Tourist Police:** T421281 or T1699 for emergency.

Nathon

Phone code: 077
Colour map 4, grid A5

Nathon is Koh Samui's capital, where the ferry docks. It is a town geared to tourists, with travel agents, exchange booths, clothes stalls, bars, and restaurants supplying travellers' food. Nathon consists of three roads running parallel to the seafront, with two main roads at either end linking them together.

Excursions   **Ang Thong** (or 'Golden Basin') **Marine National Park** is made up of 40 islands lying northwest of Koh Samui, featuring limestone massifs, tropical rainforests and beaches. Particular features are **Mae Koh** (a beautiful beach) and **Thale Nai** (an emerald saltwater lake), both on **Koh Mae Koh** and **Koh Sam Sao**, which has a coral reef and a huge rock arch as well as a hill providing good views of the surrounding islands. The area is the major spawning ground of the short-bodied mackerel, a popular eating fish in Thailand. There is also good snorkelling (the main attraction), swimming and walking. The park's headquarters are on Koh Wua Talap. It is best to visit between late March and October, when visibility is at its best. **Sleeping** Available on Koh Wua Talap (T286025 or BT5790529), five guesthouses sleep 10-20 people each, ฿600-1,000 per guesthouse, tents available for rent (฿50). ■ *Getting there: daily tour from*

Nathon

To Chaweng & Airport

Dumrong Town Hall

Express Boats to Koh Phangan

Express & Night Boats to Surat Thani

Book Exchange
Stalls
Stalls
T-shirt Stalls

Restaurants
Angthong Rd

Palace

Dive Samui

Fresh Market

Bangkok Airways

Handicrafts
Hardware Market

Gulf of Thailand

N

0 metres   100
0 yards   100

● **Eating**
1 Bird in the Hand   4 Sunset House
2 Fountain   5 Tang's Bakery
3 RT Bakery

Related maps
Koh Samui, page 339

Nathon pier, leaving at about 0800 (฿240). *It is possible to leave the tour, stay on Koh Wua Talap and rejoin it several days later at no extra charge (make sure you tell the ferry driver which day you want to be picked up). The boat returns to Nathon at about 1700.*

Koh Phangan Passenger boats travel from Bophut Pier (north of the island) to Koh Phangan, leaving at about 0930, 40 minutes (see page 359).

Day trips to **Ang Thong Marine National Park** for snorkelling, fishing and diving leave Nathon at 0830 and return at 1700 (฿300). There are also day tours around the island (฿380, including lunch). Book with *Samui Holiday Tour*, 112/2 Chonvithi Road, T421043 or at *Highway Travel Booking*, 11/11 Taweraj Pakdi Road, T421285 (opposite the pier). *Songserm* organize day tours to Koh Phangan, two to three boats each day, 30 minutes (฿60). **Tours**

Few people stay in Nathon, for obvious reasons. **Sleeping**

C-D *Palace*, seafront road, T421079, F421080. A/c, clean, adequate and well- maintained rooms, hot water.

There are plenty of places to eat here, particularly good are the 'coffee shop' patisseries – there are a couple off the main road and some on the seafront. **Eating**

Thai Mid-range: *Koh Kaeo*, on seafront, best Thai food in Nathon. Good noodle and rice restaurant almost opposite the pier.

International Mid-range: *Fountain*, Angthong Rd. Italian proprietor (and food). Recommended. *Sunset House*, south end of town overlooking the sea, good Thai and international food. *Tang's*, near market at south end of main road, pizza, pasta, sandwiches and pastries. **Cheap**: *New York Deli and Grill*, near market at southern end of main road, pizza, seafood, pasta, breakfast, rather dirty. *RT Bakery*, corner of main road and Watana Rd. Excellent breakfasts, rolls and croissants. *Bird in the Hand*, north end of town, on east/west road remains popular. *El Pirata*, near *Bird in the Hand*, Spanish. *Golden Lion*, opposite *El Pirata*, European/seafood.

Seafood On seafront road.

Eden, main road. Open 1600-0300. There are a number of other bars near the *Bird in the Hand* restaurant, at north end of town. **Bars**

Tattoo artist: on southeast/west road. **Thai traditional massage**: at north end of seafront road. **Entertainment**

Nathon remains the centre for shopping on the island. It is worth a visit to browse through the stalls and take a walk down the main road, past the fresh market on the left and on down to the 'hardware' market on the right. The stalls provide the usual array of T-shirts, tapes, watches, handicrafts, etc. As usual, remember to bargain hard. The inner road – Angthong Rd – is worth walking down too. **Shopping**

Book Exchange On northern east/west road.

Handicrafts Several shops on the main east/west road to the south of town selling puppets, etc.

Shoemaker On the main east/west road to the south of town.

The Gulf of Thailand

Silk and jewellery shop On the seafront road.

Supermarket *Giant*, sells English, German and French newspapers as well as good range of European food.

T-shirt shop *Samui Seven Seas*, 2 shops on Angthong Rd, for the best designs on the island.

Sport　**Scuba diving**: there are a number of different dive schools on the island. *Swiss Dive Centre* (41 Na-Amphur Rd), *Matlang Divers* (67 Watana Rd), *Koh Samui Divers* (64 Nathon Pier) and *Pro Divers* all have shops in town, as well as having small offices on the various beaches. Most of the schools have English-speaking instructors. A 5-day PADI course should cost about ฿7,000-8,000. A 1-day trip for those with certification, including 2 dives and food, costs about ฿1,200-1,800, depending on the dive destination. A trip to one of the islands, 2 nights/3 days, for about 6 dives, will cost around ฿4,000. The best time for diving is Apr and the best water is to be found around Koh Tao, Tan, Matsum and the Marine Park. Visibility is obviously variable, depending on the weather. Most of the schools also organize advanced open-water courses, rescue and first aid. **Shooting range**: Route 4169 just south of Monkey Theatre, near the airport, open 0900-1800, T425370. **Thai boxing**: at north end of town.

Tour operators　There are many travel agents cluttered along the seafront (particularly around the pier) and main roads, providing air/train/bus bookings and reconfirmation of flights. For example, *Songserm*, 64/1-2 Nathon Pier, Chonvithi Rd, T420163 seems efficient; they organize joint train and express boat tickets from Bangkok, via Surat Thani and on to Koh Phangan.

Transport　**Local**　For details on local transport, see page 339. Motorbikes and jeeps can be hired in Nathon and *songthaews* travel from here to all the beaches – destinations written on the front of each vehicle. **Boat charter**: for visiting some of the islands in the Marine National Park, T425360 and ask for Khun Lek.

Directory　**Airline offices** *Bangkok Airways*, 72/1 Chonvithi Rd, T420133, F421297, or at the airport, T425012, F425010. **Banks** Exchange booths along the seafront and main roads. Open Mon-Sun, 0830-1700 or 1800. **Communications** Post Office: to the north of the pier, international telephone and poste restante service. **Medical services** Clinic and dentist: on main road in town. **Hospitals**: in the event of an accident *Bandon International Hospital* is the best hospital on the island. It is located near the airport, almost opposite the Shooting Range, T425382/245236, F425342, 24-hr emergency service. The government hospital outside Nathon is not well equipped to handle foreign tourists. *Doctor Pongsak* is probably the best doctor on the island (outside the hospitals), he is to be found at the *Lamai Clinic*, T424219, F424218, near the Boxing Stadium. His English is fluent. **Places of worship** Catholic Church: 0830 and 1830. **Useful addresses** British Consular representative at *Laem Set Inn*, T424393. **Immigration office:** on main road next to the police station. A 2-month tourist visa can be extended here by 30 days for ฿550. **Tourist police:** 3 km south of town T421245, just past turning to Hin Lad Waterfall.

Bang Bo

Sleeping　**C-D** *Sunbeam*, only bungalow here, quiet location, clean, friendly, private beach, some private bathrooms. Recommended.

Mae Nam

A quiet, clean beach, good for swimming and a good atmosphere. There is a post office, currency exchange and health centre here, as well as a bookshop for rental or exchange of books.

L *Santiburi*, 12/12 Moo 1 Tambon Mae Nam, T425031, F425040, santiburi @dusit.com (part of the Dusit group of hotels). A/c, restaurant, pool, superb new resort of beautifully furnished Thai-style villas and suites, watersports, sauna, tennis and squash courts, situated on a quiet stretch of beach so there's also some degree of privacy. **AL** *Seafan*, T/F421350. A/c, pool, restaurant, overpriced but lovely wooden bungalows on stilts, whirlpool, attractive gardens, watersports facilities. **A** *Chaiya Rai*, T425290, F425290. A/c, restaurant, pool, price includes breakfast, excellent service, large, clean and well-maintained bungalows. Recommended.

D *Co-Co Palm*, quiet, nice garden. Recommended. **D** *Naplarn*, off beach, big, clean rooms, own bathroom. Recommended. **D** *Palm Point Village*, T425095. 15 mins walk from Mae Nam village, this place has bungalows on the beach (quiet and peaceful here), the more expensive with attached showers (cold water) and balcony, good food, motorbikes for hire. Recommended. **D** *Rainbow*, bungalows close together, some private bathrooms. **D-E** *Home Bay*, T247241, quiet, rather scruffy, some private bathrooms. **D-E** *Tokoh*, average rooms, nice beach. **D-F** *Koseng II*, T425252 and T427106. Friendly and popular in ideal quiet location, excellent food, bungalows ranging from very basic to much more comfortable to suit all budgets. **E** *OK Village*, T427189, off the beach, restaurant, own bathroom. Recommended. **E** *Shady Shack*, T425392, restaurant, recently refurbished, clean, some private bathrooms, very friendly people, good value.

Chez Tom for French and Thai food. *Golden Dream*, east end of Mae Nam, for pizzas, pasta and Thai food in a traditional raised Thai house.

Local Motorbike hire: on the beach.

Bophut

Bophut is one of the few places on the island where there are still traditional wooden Samui houses with Chinese lettering above the doors side-by-side with modern tourist accommodation. Unsurprisingly, it has grown increasingly popular in the last few years and there are now currency exchanges, bookshops, restaurants and good watersports facilities, yet none of these has really spoilt the ambience. The beach itself is rather straight and lacks the sweeping expanse of Chaweng, or the quiet intimacy of Laem Set, yet the place maintains a friendly village atmosphere. A daily passenger boat leaves here for

Colour map 4, grid A5

Koh Samui north coast

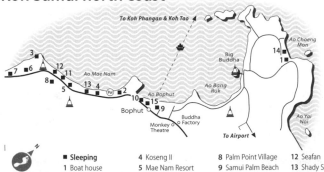

■ **Sleeping**
1 Boat house
2 Chaiya Rai
3 Home Bay
4 Koseng II
5 Mae Nam Resort
6 Naplarn
7 OK Village
8 Palm Point Village
9 Samui Palm Beach
10 Sandy Resort
11 Santiburi
12 Seafan
13 Shady Shack
14 White House
15 World

The Gulf of Thailand

Koh Phangan (Hat Rin West), at 1030 and 1530, 50 minutes (฿30), see page 359. There are no clubs in Bophut so the nightlife is less noisy (or less fun, depending on your viewpoint), than Chaweng or Lamai but the restaurant scene is popular and vibrant. For those in need of the club scene, there is a nightly taxi service from the various hotels into Chaweng and Lamai, leaving Bophut at 2000 and returning 0300-0400 (฿50).

Excursions   *Bophut Guesthouse* offers fishing, snorkelling and sightseeing charters.

Sleeping   **AL** *Euphoria*, 101/3 Bophut Bay, T425100, F425107, euphoria@loxinfo.co.th A/c, res-
■ *on maps*   taurant, pool. A rather impersonal hotel with 124 rooms in an unattractive 3-storey
Price codes: see   block. The facilities, however, are comprehensive and include tennis and squash courts,
inside front cover   a pool, a putting green and a variety of watersports. **A** *Samui Palm Beach*, 175/3
Thaveerat-Pakdee Rd, T425494 F425358, spbresot@samart.co.th Well-designed a/c
bungalows facing the sea and some cheaper accommodation with no sea view. There is
a good pool and an international and Thai restaurant. **A-B** *World*, T/F425355/427202,
world@sawadee.com Fan and a/c bungalows. The a/c accommodation is particularly
appealing, as the rooms are spacious and wood panelled. There is a large pool and a
beach restaurant that serves Thai and Western food.

B *The Lodge*, 91/1 Moo 1, Bophut, T425337, F425336. This small, appealing hotel has
a number of well-decorated a/c rooms, all of which have satellite TV, a minibar, and en
suite bathroom. While there is no restaurant, there is a bar that serves basic Western
food. **B** *Nara Garden* T425364, F425292. A/c, restaurant, small pool. This well-run
resort provides a U-shaped group of attractive rooms with decking walkways, good
discounts available, simple but clean and professionally run. **B** *Peace*, T425357,
F425343. Offers basic fan bungalows, with attached shower-room, to very nicely decorated a/c bungalows. The fan rooms are overpriced. There is a beachside restaurant
that serves Thai, international and seafood. **B-C** *Smile*, T425361, F425239. There is a
choice of either a/c, or fan bungalows. Both are kept quite clean, but they are small
and crammed far too close together. Large pool on the roadside, so a little public. The
fan accommodation is good value. Beachside restaurant (see **Eating**). **B-D** *New Boon*,
T421362. Some a/c, new but already scruffy, no hot water. **B-D** *Ziggy Stardust*,
T/F245354. These clean fan and a/c Thai-style bungalows are excellently laid out in a
mature tropical garden. The staff are helpful and friendly and there is a good
beachside restaurant (see **Eating**). Recommended. **C** *Sandy Resort*, 177/1 Bophut
Beach. T425353, F425325, sandy@sawadee.com Accommodation ranges from
fan-cooled bungalows to a/c rooms in a somewhat ugly 2-storey building. There are 2
restaurants, one of which is on the beach.

D *Salathai*, quiet and clean with fan rooms. Expensive restaurant (but good food).
D-F *Calm Beach Resort*, T425357, run down but quiet, no mosquito nets for cheapest
bungalows. **E-F** *Oasis*, near pier for boats to Hat Rin (Koh Phangan), rooms in private
house. **F** *Boon*, tiny wooden huts with Samui-style detailing. Shared washing facilities. Run by the shop on the opposite side of the road.

Eating   Unlike Chaweng and Lamai, Bophut is small enough to cater for the demand for sea-
● *on maps*   food without having to import produce from elsewhere. There are, therefore, a num-
Price codes: see   ber of restaurants that set up elaborate seafood displays. Inevitably, the choice on
inside front cover   offer varies from day to day.

Expensive: *La Sirene*, a delightful little restaurant that is run by a friendly Frenchman.
The seafood is fresh and locally caught, and the coffee is excellent. French and Thai
food offered. Recommended. **Expensive-mid-range**: *Bird in the Hand*, Thai and

The Gulf of Thailand

Western food in an attractive building that has good views across the bay. *Smile*, offers a wide variety of seafood. **Mid-range**: *Ziggy Stardust*, in one of the best positions on the beach with great views over to Big Buddha Beach. Thai and seafood.

Paris London Bar. A stylish bar that invites people to view the beautiful sunset with a cocktail. *Rasta Baby*. The loudest place on Bophut is towards the western end of the beach and out of earshot of most places. **Bars & clubs**

There are a number of shops along the main road of Bophut. There is a good bookshop, selling books in German, English and French, and a few shops selling gifts, clothes and produce from around Thailand, Laos and Cambodia. **Shopping**

Fishing: organized by *Bophut Guesthouse*. **Snorkelling**: organized by *Bophut Guesthouse*. **Watersports**: windsurfing and waterskiing (฿150), sailing (฿300) and jet skis (฿350-800). High speed 30-ft boat available from Bophut Pier. **Sport**

Local As with most of the more remote beaches on Samui, the *songthaews* that are allotted for the beach run rather infrequently. It is possible to charter them, and there are always motorcycle taxis around. **Transport**

Banks There are no major banks in Bophut, but there are several bank booths and tour agencies that change money. **Directory**

Big Buddha or Bang Ruk

A small bay which has become increasingly popular, despite being near the road. Accommodation is rather cramped and it also tends to be rather noisy, as the bungalows are squashed between the beach and the road. However, the beach is quiet and palm-fringed and the water is good between May and September, but gets choppy during October to February when it is unsuitable for swimming. See page 337 for details on the Big Buddha.

A-B *Farn Bay Resort*, T273920, F286276. Some a/c, restaurant, small pool, videos, breakfast included, hot water, tiled-roof bungalows on a small casuarina and palm tree plot, rather too close together, but well-run establishment, may be overpriced. **A-B** *Nara Lodge*, T421364, B2482094. A/c, restaurant, pool, tennis court, videos, some hot water, motel-style accommodation, US manager, popular with families. **C** *Ocean View*, T425439, ovsamui@yahoo.com Some a/c, concrete and wooden bungalows, some rather small. **C-D** *Beach House*, T245124, F245123. Some a/c and hot water, small restaurant, small operation on the beach, quite quaint but overpriced. **C-D** *Big Buddha Bungalows*, T425282. Some a/c, restaurant, large, comfortable rooms, good value, popular. **C-D** *Phongphetch Servotel*, T245100, F425148, this needs to be mentioned as an example of appallingly misplaced architectural design – it's a horror and should never have passed the regulators. **D** *Champ Bungalows*, some a/c, friendly, diving school. **D-E** *LA Resort*, some a/c, friendly staff, excellent food, clean, comfortable, good-value bungalows, very popular bar by the beach. Recommended. **E** *Kinaree*, small huts rather close together and very unfriendly, but good food. **E** *Sunset Song*, T421363, average rooms, private bathroom. **Sleeping**
■ *on maps*
*Price codes: see
inside front cover*

Crowded House, good food, pool table, video and bar. **Eating**

Diving: *Swiss Dive Resort*. **Sailing, fishing and snorkelling**: organized by *Asian Yacht Charter*. **Sport**

The Gulf of Thailand

Choeng Mon

At the northeasternmost part of the island, this is arguably the prettiest bay on Samui. The crescent of extremely fine white sand has an island at the most eastern end, attached to the mainland by a sandbar, traversible at low tide. While in places it is rocky underfoot in the centre of the bay, the sand continues well out to sea. The beach does not have any nightlife to speak of; everything grinds to a halt well before midnight. Prior to this, however, the restaurant scene is pretty lively, particularly in the centre of the beach where bamboo tables with oil lamps reach right down to the bonfires near the water's edge. Occasionally fire jugglers are hired to provide entertainment. The beach is most popular with couples and families.

Sleeping
■ *on maps*
Price codes: see inside front cover

L *Tongsai Bay*, western end, T425041, F425460, BT2619000, www.tongsaibay.co.th A/c, restaurant, pool. Attractive bungalows scattered across a hillside coconut plantation, and overlooking their own private bay. Watersports, tennis courts and gym. The best bungalows are the newer ones which are very appealing and well designed. The rooms in the older block near the swimming pool are rather public and less attractive. The hotel's USP is its open-air bathtubs. Food in the main restaurant is excellent, particularly the buffet breakfast which is stupendous. There are two further restaurants, one a beachside bar and café and a rather more sophisticated place for dinner (disappointing on our last visit). Overall an excellent place with friendly and professional management and staff. Recommended. **L** *The White House*, centre of the beach, 59/3 Moo 5, T245315, F245318, www.whitehouse.kohsamui.net Set in a delightful shady tropical garden, this is a small collection of large white houses with Thai-style architectural detailing. There's a small museum which residents may view on request in a traditional Ayutthayan wooden house which is over 70 years old. The hotel also has the standard pool, jacuzzi and restaurants. Overall, a highly refined place. Recommended.

AL *Boat House* (Imperial Group), eastern end, T425041, F425460, BT2619000, www.imperialhotels.com A/c, restaurant, pool, 34 converted teak rice barges make for unusual suites, 182 other rooms in 3-storey ranch-style-comes-to-Thailand blocks, with limited views, watersports available, boat-shaped pool adds to the theme-park feel of the place. **B-D** *Island View*, eastern end, 24/9 Moo 5, T245031, F425081. Some a/c in concrete bungalows, cheaper rooms are made of wood and have small verandah areas and squat loos. **B-E** *O Soleil*, T425232. Some a/c rooms with hot water. Even the cheapest rooms here are solidly built and bamboo lined with mosi-screens on the windows and attached (and clean) private shower rooms. Single rooms are available even more cheaply for solo travellers. Good restaurant. Recommended.

C *Chat Kaeo*, centre of the beach, some a/c. White concrete villas with roof terraces set back from the sea. Fan cooled huts are wooden and situated towards the seafront. Unfriendly staff and slightly overpriced. **C** *PS Villas*, towards the western end, T425160. Large wooden constructions with uninspired décor. A double and single bed in every room. Some a/c. **C-D** *Sun Sand*, just beyond the headland at the eastern end T425404, F421322. A/c, restaurant. The first bungalows on Choeng Mon, these well-spaced bungalows are spacious with solid wood floors, bamboo-lined walls and ceilings, and large windows on all sides facing the sea. On the hill overlooking the bay the bungalows are linked by winding wooden slatted walkways (it's a steep descent to the beach). The position at the end of the beach and the distance between the rooms also mean that it has more privacy than most.

Eating Choeng Mon is blessed with a number of excellent eateries. This is a selection of the best.

Mid-range: *Bong Go*, centre of the beach. Especially good as a night-time venue, as it is the best value of the restaurants in the centre of the beach. It also serves reasonably priced breakfasts. Recommended. *Honey Seafood Restaurant and Bar*, at the most easterly tip of the beach. Great seafood. Recommended. *Jeanys Kitchen*, eastern end. Very small, with only 2 tables but decorated in a homely manner and rather appealing. *Otto's Pub and Restaurant*, centre of the beach. Thai food and a Thai interpretation of pizza and pasta dishes. Also offers a range of alcoholic beverages. *Phayorm Park Restaurant and Shadows Restaurant and Bar*, centre of the beach. A range of Thai and Western dishes. **Cheap**: *O Soleil*, towards the western end. Offers the best value for money, particularly good is the curry fried rice. Recommended.

Local Car hire: Avis, *Imperial Tongsai*, T425015. **Songthaew**: Choeng Mon is off the main Samui road and *songthaews* officially designated to serve this beach may come only once an hour. There is a *songthaew* station at the far eastern side of the town, behind the beach. **Transport**

Chaweng

This is the biggest beach on the island, split into three areas – north, central and Chaweng Noi. **Chaweng Noi** is to the south, round a headland and has three of the most expensive hotels on the island. **Central Chaweng** is a vast sweep of sand with lovely water for swimming and a proliferation of bungalows, restaurants and bars. The town that has grown up here is entirely geared towards tourists and in recent years it has become swamped. Along the incredibly uneven track, there are dozens of Pattaya-like bars, discos, clubs, tourist agencies, and watersports facilities and for those trying to find a secluded spot, this area is best avoided. In comparison to the other beaches on the island it is very crowded.

Chaweng contains a rather jarring combination of international hotels and basic bungalows. This gives it an unusual feel, and enables visitors staying in US$150-a-night hotels to cross the road and have a full American breakfast for under US$2. Compared with Lamai, Chaweng is slightly more up-market and a little cleaner.

NB Many of the hotels, particularly those in the centre of the beach, are affected by the noise pollution coming from the discotheques, often until as late as five or six in the morning

L *Central Samui Beach Resort*, T230500, F422385, www.centralgroup.com An elegant, if expensive, low-rise Greek temple comes to the Orient-style block resort with good facilities. The accommodation is wood panelled and set in a palm grove. Large pool, health centre and a very good restaurant. **L** *Poppies*, T422419, F422420. A/c, restaurant, pool, following their success on Bali, *Poppies* have built on this tiny plot. Beautifully designed to maximize space, these Thai-style houses have open-air bathrooms (familiar to anyone who has visited Ubud, in Bali), and set in a tropical garden with water running through it. An excellent and very popular open air restaurant (see **Eating**), but small pool. Though very refined, it is overpriced for the facilities on offer. **Sleeping**
■ *on maps*
Price codes: see inside front cover

AL *Amari Palm Reef* (north end), T422015, F422394, palmreef@amari.com This hotel is built on two sides of the main road through Chaweng. The original part of the hotel is on the seaward side of the road. Rooms here are in blocks, in a garden compound. There is also a rather public swimming pool, right next to the beach. All slightly cramped. On the other side of the road are the newer Thai-style bungalows and duplexes. There is a quieter, more secluded pool here. Restaurant is average. Facilities include a tennis court, dive centre and massage. **AL** *Baan Samui Resort*,14/7 Moo 2, T230965, F422412, bansamui @loxinfo.co.th A rather awkward resort with an

The Gulf of Thailand

ugly 3-storey building at the front. The accommodation is clean and the facilities include a good pool and restaurant, but the Spanish stucco and tiling make it feel slightly out of place. There is no sense of Thai-ness and its overpriced. **AL** *Beachcomber*, 3/5 Moo 2, T422041, F422388, www.kohsamuinet/beachcomber A popular luxury resort, often frequented by tour groups. 60 rooms in a 3-storey block, children's pool and jacuzzi; this could be on a tropical beach resort anywhere in the world. **AL** *Blue Lagoon* northern end, T422037, F422401, www.kohsamuinet/ blue-lagoon A/c, international restaurant, large and attractive pool, well-designed accommodation with 60 rooms in 2-storey Thai-style blocks. Recommended. **AL** *Chaweng Regent*, 155/4 Chaweng Beach, T422008, F422222, cr22222 @loxinfo.co.th A/c, good restaurant (seafood speciality, Thai and European), large pool, 137 wooden Thai-style cottages linked by decking, rather close together, attractive but overpriced and rather big and impersonal, no shade by the pool. **AL** *Imperial* southern end, T422020, F422396. A/c, restaurant, saltwater and freshwater pools. The first 5-star hotel on the island, rooms are in a large 5-storey Tuscan style block. **AL** *Chaweng Buri Resort*, 14/6 Moo 2, T230349, F422466, info @chawengburi.com, www.chawengburi.com Reasonably attractive a/c bungalows set in a garden. There is a restaurant and a pool, but the place is rather anonymous. **AL-A** *The Fair House (The President Samui)*, 4/3 Moo 3, T422255, F422373, fairhouse@sawadee.com Some a/c, restaurant, pool. Down a lengthy track from the road. A variety of rooms in attractive garden setting. The more expensive rooms are light and airy, while the bungalows have privacy as they do not fall into the common trap of being packed together. The cheaper rooms, however, are a little tatty. Its main advantage is that it's right on the beach. **AL-C** *Samui Resotel* (previously *Munchies*), T422374, F422421, resotel@sawadee.com A wide range of accommodation from fan rooms to luxurious suites; all of them are well decorated. They are, predictably, too close to one another, but this place emerges as being better than most as it has a pleasant beachside restaurant and live music. **A** *Chaweng Cabana*, T422377, F42137. Not to be confused with *Samui Cabana*. This is yet another resort where the good a/c bungalows are constructed with little space to breathe. International restaurant and pool. **A** *Chaweng Resort*,T422247, F421378. A/c bungalows, decent pool and restaurant, attractive gardens. **A** *Coral Bay Resort*, T422223, F422392, north of Chaweng Beach (Yai Noi Bay). A/c, restaurant, pool, good a/c bungalows in a spacious setting. The beach is not good for swimming or sunbathing and it is very overpriced for the services provided. **A** *First*, T422327, F422243. As implied by its name, this was the first resort to appear on Chaweng Beach and the a/c bungalows are clean and nicely laid out. There is a restaurant, but no pool – a big minus when most other places in this price bracket do. **A** *The Princess Village*, northern end of beach, T422216, F422382, princess@sawadee.com Tries hard to disconnect the guests from the less-attractive side of Western culture, by deliberately not having televisions in the transplanted traditional Ayutthayan-style houses which are set in a strikingly attractive tropical garden. Unlike most places, the houses are not built too close together. It is the most unusual luxury resort along the beach and perhaps the most appealing. There is a good beachside restaurant. Recommended. **A** *Sans Souci Samui*, T422044, F422045. Small, personal resort with only 13 rooms set in a nice garden. **A** *Tradewinds*, T230602, F231247. A very appealing resort, as the 21 excellent bungalows are set out in an attractive part of the beach. As a result of its size, it is an intimate place and is relatively peaceful at night. There is a beachside bar and restaurant and a pool. **A** *Tropicana Beach*, T412408. Rather characterless resort with restaurant and pool, but good, clean rooms. **A** *Victorian*, Chaweng Noi Beach, T422011, F422111, BT4245392. Southern end, a/c, restaurant, small pool, 2/3-storey ugly 'Victorian' building, too many rooms in too small a space. **A** *Villa Flora*, T281535, BT2517646. A/c, restaurant, unattractive resort, split into two by a busy road, with 2 pools, one of which is far too public for comfort. Most of the accommodation is on the non-beach side of the road.

Chaweng Beach

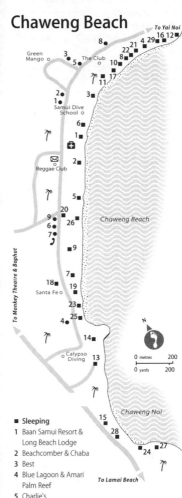

To Yai Noi

Green Mango

The Club

Samui Dive School

Reggae Club

Chaweng Beach

To Monkey Theatre & Bophut

Calypso Diving

0 metres 200
0 yards 200

Santa Fe

N

Chaweng Noi

To Lamai Beach

■ **Sleeping**
1 Baan Samui Resort & Long Beach Lodge
2 Beachcomber & Chaba
3 Best
4 Blue Lagoon & Amari Palm Reef
5 Charlie's
6 Chaweng Buri Resort
7 Chaweng Cabana
8 Chaweng Regent & The Island
9 Chaweng Resort
10 Chaweng Villa
11 Coconut Grove
12 Coral Bay Resort
13 Fair House
14 First
15 Imperial
16 Matlang Resort & Matlang Divers
17 Montien House
18 Parrot
19 Poppies & Joy
20 Princess Village & Village
21 Samui Cabana
22 Samui Natien

23 Samui Resotel
24 Samui Yacht Club
25 Sans Souci Samui
26 Tradewinds
27 Tropicana Beach
28 Victorian
29 Villa Flora

● **Eating**
1 Café Thai
2 Chez Andy
3 Crystal
4 Eden Seafood
5 La Taverna
6 Magic Light
7 Oriental Gallery
8 Rainbow
9 Wild Orchid & Chaweng Arcade

B *Blue Horizon Bungalows*, 210/Moo 4, T422426. A small place to stay with good clean bungalows. The a/c accommodation is better value than the fan rooms. Restaurant. **B** *Central Bay*, T422118, a huge new resort owned by *Central Department Store*, it's a miracle they don't contravene the height restrictions – or do they? **B** *Chaweng Villa*. T231123, F231124, www.kohsamui.net/ chawengvilla Each large, wood- floored, a/c bungalow has its own balcony. Those nearer the beach are more expensive. Beachside restaurant with BBQs each evening. Friendly management. **B** *The Island*, T424202. A/c, restaurant, north end of beach, some a/c, good restaurant, bathrooms, individual huts right on the beach, attractive garden, run by *farang*, bar open after 2200, ideal for 'trendy backpackers'. **B** *Montien House* northern end of beach, T422169. Some a/c, restaurant on the beach. Too many bungalows, but they are large and clean and laid out in a pleasant shady garden. For the services provided, however, it is overpriced. **B** *Samui Yacht Club*, T422225, F421378, south end of Chaweng, just before headland. A/c, restaurant, pool, traditional-style thatched attractive bungalows set in coconut plantation, fitness centre, private beach. **B** *Village*, T422216, F422382. Some a/c, restaurant, Thai-style bungalows, simpler version of the *Princess Village*, yet similarly attractive. **B-C** *Chaweng Gardens*, T422265, F422265. Some a/c, bungalows close together but well designed. **B-C** *Samui Natien Resort*, T422405, F422309, natien@loxinfo.co.th Accommodation ranges from fan cooled to a/c bungalows. Clean, but a little basic for the price. **B-D** *Best*. A very popular resort towards the north end of the beach with a large range of accommodation from basic guesthouse rooms to a/c hotel rooms – all attractively decorated. Pool and a rather expensive restaurant. **B-D** *Long Beach Lodge*, T/F422372. Some a/c, very large coconut- studded plot for so few bungalows (20), laid back and peaceful, bungalows are a reasonable size, a/c rooms good value. Recommended.

C-D *Matlang Resort*, T422172. Some a/c, restaurant, small brick bungalows with

The Gulf of Thailand

Related maps
Koh Samui, page 339
Nathon, page 342
Koh Samui:
North Coast, page 345
Lamai Beach, page 354
Koh Samui:
West Coast, page 358

rattan roofs, quite nice garden, secluded spot but rather dirty. **D** *Coconut Grove*. The wood and concrete bungalows are too close together once again and are rather bland. At the beach end of the resort there is *Plonkers Bar,* which succinctly describes the type of person that would choose to drink here. **D** *Lucky Mother* (north end), T230931, friendly, clean, excellent food, some private bathrooms. Recommended. **D** *Parrot*, T231221, F422347. Some a/c, 20 bungalows in wonderful overgrown jungle, on 'wrong' side of the road, but it's quiet and unusual. The rooms are well designed, spacious, comfortable and good value. There is no restaurant but there are plenty nearby. Friendly owner. Recommended. **D** *Samui Cabana*, T421405. Well-laid-out huts at the north end of the beach, some a/c. Good value. **D** *Tropic Tree Resort*, T230998. Basic rustic bungalows with fan, clean and right on the beach, good restaurant, friendly welcome. **D-E** *Charlie's*, T422343, F422482. Divided into 3 main compounds, each with separate restaurants, though the menu is the same. The accommodation is very simple, the cheapest being in clean fan-cooled wooden huts with thatched roofs. Shared washing facilities of variable cleanliness. No electricity between 1000 and 1800. This is certainly the place to stay if you are a first time solo traveller and need some reassurance as to how easy it is to meet people. **D-E** *Joy*, T421376, F421376. Attractive Spanish-style bungalows in mature colourful garden, rooms are small. A good cheap place to stay.

Eating
● *on maps*
Price codes: see inside front cover

Chaweng offers a range of international restaurants as well as plenty of seafood. **Expensive**: *Chez Andy Restaurant*, 164/2 Chaweng Beach Rd, T8916148. A popular grill house, though it is a little impersonal and expensive. *Eden*, attractive thatched pavilions, excellent seafood, rather tacky décor. *La Taverna* serves good range of Italian food, though the prices are inflated. *Magic Light*, near the Chaweng Arcade, a Swiss-owned restaurant serving a wide range of European cuisine as well as some Thai food, pizzas and seafood. Bakery attached. *Mama Roma*. T230649. Another Italian restaurant notable for its very good pizzas. *Poppies*, T422419, an excellent Thai and international restaurant, perhaps the best on the beach. *Spice Island*, T23500 ext 4950. Part of the *Central Samui Resort*. Sit either in the a/c or the relaxing beachside part of the restaurant and try good BBQ food and a wide range of excellent, and sophisticated, Thai dishes. *Tropic Tree Resort*, lovely restaurant on the beach.

Mid-range: *Café Thai*, 164/9 Chaweng Beach, T231096. Offers a wide range of good Thai and French food at reasonable prices. *Crystal Restaurant*. A wide choice of Thai food on offer. *Oriental Gallery*, T/F422200, a very atmospheric restaurant with books on Oriental and Southeast Asian art available to buy or simply read over a meal. Refined décor and elegant garden furniture associated with an exclusive antique shop. An oasis on a busy road. Recommended. *Wild Orchid*. Next to the *Oriental Gallery*. Specializes in more unusual Thai dishes. *Osteria*, T230057, Chaweng Arcade 1st Floor. Italian. *Caffé e Cucina*, opposite *OP Bungalows*. A new Pizzeria run by Angelo from Rome. Good Italian food, friendly and excellent value. Recommended. *The Island*, north end of beach, part of *The Island Hotel*, seafood, Thai, pasta and even Australian steaks and lamb. *Munchies*, popular seafood restaurant which spills onto the beach, live music. *Rainbow* (off the main drag, across the road from *Chaweng Villa* and *Montien House* at north end of beach), a restaurant which aims to serve good food without the usual tourist accompaniments of TV, video and music.

Bakery *Will Wait Bakery* T231152, for excellent pastries and breakfast.

Bars & nightclubs

Most of the bars are at the northern end of the strip. *The Reggae Club* is popular, as is *Santa Fe* and *The Cotton Club*. Other clubs on the strip include *Bananas*, *Eden*, *Green Mango* and *Mao*. *The Club* is a particularly good place, with good music, and no prostitutes. All are on the road parallel to the beach. *Black Cat* and *Green Mango* are also on the road parallel to the beach.

There is a wide range of shops along the beach road, where most things can be **Shopping** bought. Many places remain open until late. There are the usual array of tourist shops, beachware, T-shirts, jewellery, handicrafts. *Sawang Optical*, 168/5 Chaweng Beach Rd, for a large range of frames and a professional service. *Sawang Watch*, 168/5 Chaweng Beach Rd, for range of Swatch watches.

Diving: *Koh Samui Divers*, T421465, are to be found on the beach. *Matlang Divers* **Sports** are at *Matlang Resort*. *Samui International Diving School* is at the Malibu Beach Club, T422386/413050, F231242, info@planet-scuba.net *Calypso Diving*, southern end of beach, T422437, info@calypso-diving.com **Snorkelling**: masks and fins can be hired from most bungalows. **Speedboats**: can be rented for ฿1,200 per hour. **Watersports**: include windsurfing, catamaran sailing (฿440 per hour), waterskiing (฿200 per session), jet skis (฿400 per hour), jet scooters (฿400 per hour), parasailing (฿400 per 10 minutes fly). *Chaweng Cabana* has good watersports. Many luxury hotels offer such services.

There are dozens of these along Chaweng Beach Rd. **Tour operators**

Local Car hire: Avis, *Imperial Hotel*, T422020. **Minibus**: there is an a/c minibus that **Transport** leaves from the northern end of the beach and goes to the airport, 6 times a day (฿40). **Motorbike taxis**: Motorcycle taxis will take you anywhere for a price. Rough costs are: to Lamai ฿100, Bophut ฿80, Choeng Mon ฿130, airport ฿130 and waterfall ฿15.

Banks Money-changing facilities are strung out all along Chaweng Beach Rd. The bank booths **Directory** are worth seeking out for their substantially lower rates of commission. **Medical services** Clinic: There are a couple of clinics along the road and the Samui International Clinic is nearby. German and English spoken. As it is a private clinic, the service provided is pricey. One on road into Chaweng from Route 4169, one near the *Thai Restaurant*. **Places of worship** Catholic Church: on the main road. Service at 1030.

Between Chaweng and Lamai

There is not much beach along this stretch of coast but some snorkelling off the rocky shore. **Sleeping A Samui Yacht Club**, T422225, F422400. A/c, restaurant, pool, health centre, children's room, peaceful bay, small pool but good-sized bungalows, mature jungled garden, good value. **A Coral Cave Chalet**, T422260, F422496. A/c, restaurant, small pool, lovely chalets on hillside, linked by decking walkways, steps down to very small private beach with little sand but some snorkelling offshore, well run tropical ambience. Recommended. **B Silver Beach**, T422478, F422479, a/c, restaurant, 20 clean but quite basic rooms, rather close together, lovely little bay, quiet, relaxing atmosphere with friendly management.

Snorkelling is best at Coral Cove, between Chaweng & Lamai or at Yai Noi, North of Chaweng

Lamai

Koh Samui's 'second' beach is 5 km long and has a large assortment of accommodation. Much of the lower grade accommodation is so bad that it has not been included in this listing. Rates are similar to Chaweng, but the supporting 'tourist village' has developed rapidly and is somewhat dishevelled looking. However, the beach itself is still nice. The renowned **'grandmother'** (*Hinyai* and *Hinta*) and **'grandfather'** rocks are to be found just south of here (signpost to 'Wonderful rocks').

The first edition of the *Greater Samui Magazine* in 1995 attempted to paint Lamai as some sort of traditional village getaway with nightlife attachments when the editors wrote: "This second most popular of Samui's beaches offers a combination of plentiful accommodation, nightlife and picturesque village scenes ... Visitors are charmed by the open market and the old monastery". Such a vision of Lamai is really stretching credulity a little too far. Depending who you talk to, or who you are, this is either a rather tawdry, down-market Pattaya, or an idiosyncratic, slightly hip and colourful Hua Hin. It is not particularly peaceful; nor could it be described as picturesque. It can be a lot of fun though, and some people love it.

Tours Companies along the main road parallel to the beach, for trips around the islands, fishing and snorkelling.

Sleeping **AL-A** *The Pavilion*, T424420, F424029.
■ *on maps*
Price codes: see
inside front cover
52 large, round, a/c bamboo and wood huts with verandahs and comfortable teak chairs. There is an attractive small pool, a gift shop, tour information and a restaurant serving Thai and Western food. **A** *Aloha*, T424418, F424419, www.sawadee.com.samui/aloha Well-designed a/c rooms in this relaxing resort. There is a good pool and the restaurant offers a wide range of good seafood, though it is not locally caught. Tours can be booked here. **A** *P&P Resort*. The bungalows are well appointed and the ones nearer the beach more expensive. There is a good restaurant, with a large choice of seafood. **A** *Royal Blue Lagoon*, T424086, F424195. Not to be confused with the other 2 *Blue Lagoons*, this is the first and the best. A family-run affair, the accommodation is in attractive Thai-style bungalows set in lush gardens in a striking position on Laem Nan headland at the northern end of Lamai. There is a private beach and a freshwater pool. The restaurant (see **Eating**) is one of the most appealing on the island, as it has stunning views of Lamai Bay. Recommended. **A** *Samui Laguna Resort*, T424215, F424371. A/c rooms are in an ugly 3-storey block, but there are some pleasant a/c wood and concrete bungalows, each with a verandah. Small pool.

Related maps
Koh Samui, page 339
Nathon, page 342
Koh Samui:
North Coast, page 345
Chaweng Beach,
page 351
Koh Samui:
West Coast, page 358

A *Samui Park Resort*, T/F424008. A/c, restaurant with good views, pool. The rooms are clean and spacious but they are in a rather ugly 3-storey block; popular with Thais. **A-B** *Galaxy Resort*, 124/61 Moo 3. T424441. The teak bungalows are too close together for comfort and while

Lamai Beach

To Chaweng Beach

Ban Lamai Cultural Hall
Easy Divers
Clinic
Clinic
Bars
Lamai Beach
Lamai Morning Market
Rt 4169
Doi Thai
Pongpanrat Rd
Shops
Tourist
Shops
Hinyai & Hinta Rocks
To Butterfly Garden & Namuang Waterfall

N

0 metres 200
0 yards 200

■ **Sleeping**
1 Aloha
2 Coconut Beach
3 Galaxy
4 Lamai Coconut Resort
5 Lamai Inn 99
6 Magic Resort
7 Marina Villa
8 Pavilion

9 Platuna
10 Rocky
11 Rose Garden
12 Royal Blue Lagoon
13 Samui Laguna Resort
14 Samui Park Resort
15 Samui Residence
16 Sea Breeze
17 Sea Garden
18 Spa Resort
19 Suan Thale
20 Wanchai Villa
21 Weekender Bungalows
22 Weekender Resort
23 Whitesand

The Gulf of Thailand

they are clean and fully equipped, the décor is somewhat reminiscent of the seventies. **A-B** *Weekender Resort*, T424429, F424011. This pleasant resort has 3 types of accommodation, in a/c bungalows, an ugly 3-storey block, and Thai-style houses. All of them are good and clean, but they do tend to get swamped by tour groups.

B-C *Marina Villa* T424426. The reasonably furnished, fan and a/c huts on stilts are far too close together to create a relaxed atmosphere. **B-D** *Rocky* T418367, F418366, rockie@surat.loxinfo.co.th This is another long-time resort dating from around 1980. Each of the bungalows has a verandah. The well-placed restaurant commands beautiful views. Videos shown nightly. **B-D** *Sea Breeze*,124/3 Moo 3, T424258. One of the oldest places on the island. The accommodation ranges from basic fan rooms to comfortable a/c bungalows with hot water. The restaurant serves Thai and Western food at reasonable prices and the staff are very friendly. **C** *Lamai Coconut Resort*, next to the *Weekender Resort*, T232169. The a/c bungalows are basic, but nevertheless attractively decorated and the management are friendly. The restaurant serves a range of Thai food (**3**). **C** *Lamai Inn 99*, T424427. Rather dull rooms. Some a/c and some with fridge and TV. Thai restaurant. **C-D** *Rose Garden* northern end, T424115. Some a/c bungalows with shower-rooms attached. Rather badly laid out in a rose garden that has seen better days. Restaurant. **C-D** *Samui Residence*, large peaceful plot (for Lamai), with good-sized bungalows – less regimented than most and therefore more attractive, rustic feel, plot leads down to beach. The bungalows, some a/c, are good and clean. **C-E** *Coconut Beach*, T434209, shabby, some attached bathrooms. **C-E** *Spa Resort*, T230855, F424126, www.surat.loxinfo.co.th/-thespa As far as health resorts go this is excellent as the services provided are very good value and the staff are very welcoming. Run by an American and his Thai wife, with sauna, steam room and excellent bungalows with attached bathrooms.

D *Magic Resort*, T424229, no a/c, twin row of small bungalows, some thatched, on long thin plot running down to the beach, very average. **D** *Platuna*, T424138. More expensive rooms have bathrooms attached, no hot water, fan, 10 solidly built bungalows, rather crammed onto a small plot next to a canal, good restaurant attached, quiet end of Lamai. **D** *Sea Garden Bungalows*, T424238. A small resort with just a handful of huts in a coconut grove that leads down to the beach. A bit too central to be quiet but appealing nevertheless. Bikes for hire. **D** *Weekender Bungalows*, T424417. Not the same management as the more up-market *Weekender Resort* opposite, simple cheap bungalows behind a supermarket run by the same woman, on inland side of road, stuffy and no breeze, so can be very hot. **D-E** *Suan Thale*, T424230. Some a/c, restaurant, rooms in bungalow 'blocks', largish plot, reasonable rooms with a bit more atmosphere than most. **E** *Animal House*, average rooms, attached bathroom. **E** *Green Banana*, Laem Nan headland, north of Lamai, very small A-frame huts and some larger bungalows in a large plot, quiet and peaceful spot, away from the nightlife of Lamai. **E** *Whitesand*, T424298, large, clean bungalows on beachfront, attached bathroom. **E-F** *Wanchai Villa*, T424296, 3 km south of Lamai. Rather out of the way but motorbikes available for hire, simple bungalows, shared facilities, very friendly owners and the restaurant serves excellent food, quiet and good value.

There are several seafood restaurants along the Lamai beach road offering a wide choice such as the *L'Auberge* and the *Rimklong*. Prices vary enormously and there is nowhere particularly good and cheap. Below is a just a selection of the better places to eat.

Eating
● *on maps*
Price codes: see
inside front cover

International cuisine Widely available along the road parallel to the beach in restaurants such as *Il Tempo*. **Expensive**: *Sala Thai* T233180. Serves good Thai food, seafood, steaks and Italian. It is, however, far too expensive. *Papas*, a popular restaurant serving pasta and Thai food, and is particularly well known for its steaks. *The Spa*.

Serves a wide range of vegetarian and Thai food, though it is expensive. *Rimklong*, *L'Auberge*, *Toms Bakery* and *Milan*. A popular breakfast joint is the *Will Wait Bakery*, with delicious pastries and croissant.

Bars Most are located down the *sois* which link the main road and the beach. *Flamingo Mix* (large dancefloor), and *Time Spaceadrome*.

Entertainment **Buffalo fighting** In the stadium at the north end (ask at hotel for date of next fight).

Massage On the beach.

Spa The *Spa Resort*, T230855, F424126, www.spasamui.com, offers 'exotic rejuvenation', anything from Herbal Steam Room to a 'Liver Flush Fast', prices seem quite reasonable, they are to be found next to the *Weekender Villa* at the north end of the beach.

Videos At many of the bungalows.

Shopping Jewellery, beachware and clothing boutiques along the main road, attractive sarongs in little boutique at entrance to *Thai House Inn*.

Sports **Diving**: *Matlang Divers* are based at *Aloha*. *Swiss Dive Centre* are at *Weekender*. *Pro Divers* is based at *Rocky Bungalows*. *Easy Divers*, near *Lamai Resort* (north end of beach), T231190, F424244, www.thaidive.com German, English and Swedish spoken. **Fishing**: T231190, tackle for rent or sale. **Snooker club**. **Watersports**: waterskiing (฿300), jet skis, windsurfing, parasailing (฿500), snorkelling at southern end of the beach. **Thai boxing**: classes available.

Tour operators Companies along the main road organize ticket reservations.

Transport **Local** **Jeep and motorbike hire**: widely available. **Songthaews**: to Nathon (฿15).

Directory **Banks** Currency exchanges are to be found along the main road parallel to the beach. **Communications** Post Office: south end of main road. **Medical services** *Lamai Clinic*, T424219, F424218, near the Boxing Stadium. Doctor Pongsak here is excellent and speaks fluent English.

The South Coast

The small beaches that line the south coast from Ban Hua Thanon west to Thong Krut are quieter and less developed, with only a handful of hotels and bungalows.

Ban Hua Thanon Ban Hua Thanon is an attractive rambling village with wooden shophouses and *kwaytio* stalls – and the only Muslim community on Koh Samui. The forebears of the inhabitants come from Pattani in Thailand's far south. The village is quiet and rarely visited by tourists. North of the village are a couple of restaurants – one seafood, one northeastern Thai.

Na Khai **A** *Samui Orchid*, T424017, F424019, a/c, restaurant, large pool, some older bungalows and a new three-floor 'apartment' block, secluded resort amongst coconut grove, rocky beach, off the beaten track. **B-D** *Samui Maria Resort*, T433394, F424024, some a/c, basic restaurant, large pool, snooker and outdoor multi-gym, concrete a/c bungalows built in regimental line, featureless resort with bare garden, basic rooms and dirty beach. **E** *Cosy Resort*, about 12 small bamboo bungalows in a rather tatty coconut grove, very basic rooms with nets and shower rooms, rather dirty but lots of space on the compound, very quiet place to stay, dirty beach (bought by *Samui Maria Resort*, who will be expanding); **E** *Hi He Resort*, T424340, next to *Cosy*, five very basic bungalows in a quiet, peaceful coconut grove, Mr He speaks English and has been trained at Wat Po in the art of acupuncture. Mrs He is a good cook.

AL-A *Laem Set Inn*, 110 Mu 2, Hua Thanon, T424393, F424394, www.laemset.com Some a/c, restaurant, pool. This is an exclusive, secluded resort in an attractive compound, with a range of accommodation, run by an Englishman. Several private a/c 'suites' with small pools attached, all commanding beautiful views of the South China Sea; many of the buildings are reconstructed wooden Samui houses. A more recent addition is a brick-built villa with several well-designed (but small) rooms, and adjoining bunk-bed rooms. All rooms are more expensive than comparable accommodation elsewhere on the island, but the owner believes his set-up is unique, providing a very different experience to the big, rather sterile alternatives in this price bracket. Room rate includes use of mountain bikes, kayaks pedal boats, masks and snorkels. This is an ideal place for families, with day nursery and baby-sitting facilities (hourly rates charged), children's and toddler's playground. The food is excellent and well priced (lunchtime meals are popular with non-residents). The staff are delightful and offer a homely welcome. Cookery courses are held in May and Sep in custom-built training kitchens at the Inn. Jeep for rent. Reccommended. **AL** *The Butterfly Garden*,T424020. The rooms are decorated in an elegant Japanese style, and very well equipped. Nevertheless, they are crammed far too closely together in the tropical garden setting. The international restaurant has an unimaginative menu, the snorkelling equipment is expensive to hire. Too expensive for the services on offer. Price includes American breakfast.

Laem Set

A quiet but not very attractive beach. **D** *Waikiki*, average rooms. **E** *River Garden*, T424035, attached bathroom. Between Bang Kao and Thong Krut, the Laem So Pagoda overlooks the sea. It has recently been smartened up and is worth visiting if you're passing. It houses the remains of a monk, whose diocese included the Hainanese community on Koh Tan.

Bang Kao

Ferries go daily from Thong Krut to Koh Tan and Koh Matsum and there are several tour companies here who organize fishing and snorkelling trips, T423117. There is an excellent Thai restaurant here. It has no name in English but is recognizable by the red mailbox outside the front. It has some of the best genuine Thai food on the island. **E** *Thong Krut Bungalow*, rather close to the road but very quiet, friendly and unspoilt. Recommended.

Thong Krut

This island lies due south of Thong Krut and is about 3 km long and 2 km wide. It was first colonized by Hainanese; there is a Chinese cemetery with those first colonizers' graves on the island. There are three small villages and four bungalow developments on the island which, though undeveloped, is not blessed with spotless beaches and crystal-clear waters – as one might suppose. Still, it is quiet and just about away from it all. **E** *Tan Village Bungalow*, T9684131. Rather bare compound studded with bungalows within a stone's throw of the sea. **E** *Koh Tan Resort*, T233342. Large bungalows on the beach, with clean attached shower rooms, some attempt at a garden, the owner is rather camp but the accommodation is good value.

Koh Tan

This is a sorry sight – all the coconut trees have been stripped by a beetle, leaving a desolate landscape of bare tree trunks. The Butterfly Garden have opened bungalows here, but it's not really worth the visit. The *Laem Set Inn* organize barbecues, but the place is full of dumped rubbish and not very appealing.

Koh Matsum

The west coast

Like the south coast, the western coastline south of Nathon is undeveloped, with secluded coves and beautiful sunsets. Phangka, near the southwest tip of the island has good snorkelling in the quiet waters of a small bay; Thong Yang, further north, is an isolated strip of beach, relatively untouched by the frantic developments underway elsewhere. The vehicle ferry from Don Sak, on the mainland, docks here. Chon Khram is the last bay before Nathon.

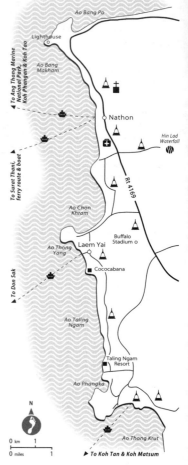

Koh Samui west coast

Sleeping **L-AL** *Ban Taling Ngam Resort*, T423019. A/c, restaurants, 2 pools, in an isolated position, built on the side of the hill, Thai-style houses spill down to the shore, very plush but somehow rather out of place here, the suites, tennis courts and one of the pools and restaurant are down by the beach – a steep climb down, or for the less energetic, there are buggies provided. The beach is disappointing, with dirty water and the lower pool is small for the size of the resort.

Phangka **D** *Cococabana*, T423174, north of Phangka, just before vehicle ferry. Friendly, quiet, some bathrooms. **D-E** *Pearl Bay*. Some attached bathrooms. **D-E** *Sea Gull* T423091. Some attached bathrooms. **E** *Emerald Cove*. Clean, attached bathrooms. Recommended. **F** *Gems House* T423006. Clean, attached bathroom. Recommended.

Related maps
Koh Samui, page 339
Nathon, page 342
Chaweng Beach, page 351
Koh Samui: North Coast, page 345
Lamai Beach, page 354

Chon Khram   **B-E** *International*, T423366. Some a/c, range of bungalows, some hot water. **D-E** *Lipa Lodge*, friendly.

Koh Phangan

Koh Phangan (pronounced Pa-ngan), is Koh Samui's younger sister and is at an earlier stage in the tourist development cycle. Bungalows are generally basic and tourist facilities less extensive. Fishing and coconut production remain mainstays of the economy, and villages still have a traditional air – although tourism is now by far the island's largest single industry.

Phone code: 077
Colour map 4, grid A5

Ins and outs

There is no airport on Koh Phangan and everyone arrives by boat. There are daily ferries from Don Sak Pier and Bandon near Surat Thani on the mainland (a 4-6-hr journey, depending on the service) and also from the larger, neighbouring island of Koh Samui. The quickest way to Koh Phangan is to fly from Bangkok to Koh Samui (see page 339) and then to catch one of the express boats from Samui to Koh Phangan (a 40-min journey). This saves on the long bus or train journey south from the capital. Alternatively, it is possible to fly to Surat Thani. If also intending to travel to Koh Tao then it may make sense to catch a boat from Chumphon to Koh Tao; there are regular ferries between Koh Tao and Koh Phangnan (1½ hrs).

Getting there

Koh Phangan stretches 15 km north to south and 10 km east to west. The main settlement is Thong Sala and there is a limited network of poor roads and tracks served by *songthaews*. For off-the-road beaches it is often easiest to travel by long-tailed boat. Motorbikes are available for hire and so too are mountain bikes. In many instances walking is the best option.

Getting around

The island

The pace of development on the island has been extremely rapid. The number of bungalows increased from a mere eight in 1983 to 23 by 1986, while between 1989 and 1990 the number rose from 94 to 146. In 1994, 167,764 tourists visited Koh Phangan, about 60% of these being overseas visitors. In 1993 the five-storey *Phangan Central Hotel* opened in Thongsala marking the arrival of big money on the island. Though still relatively unspoilt, more and more travellers are passing Koh Phangan by and continuing on to the next, and yet more geographically remote island of Koh Tao.

These tropical islands that fringe the coast are liable to change more rapidly than any other tourist destination in Thailand

The main village of Koh Phangan is the port of **Thong Sala** where most boats from Koh Samui, Surat Thani, and Koh Tao dock. Thong Sala has a branch of the Siam City Bank, telephone and fax facilities, a post office and telegraph service (poste restante), travel and tour agents, a small supermarket, dive shops, photo processing, motorbike hire, and a second-hand bookstore. The greatest concentration of bungalows is at Hat Rin on the southern 'foot' of the island-and the place where the infamous Full Moon Parties are held.

Sights

Koh Phangan offers 'natural' sights such as waterfalls, forests, coral, and viewpoints but little of historical or cultural interest. The best way to explore the island is on foot, following one of the many tracks that link the various villages and beaches, which cannot be negotiated by *songthaew* or (sometimes) by motorbike. Most roads are unpaved and poor, although improvement work is underway (as it has been for many years!). Even the longest hike is an easy day's walk.

It is a good idea to buy one of the maps of the island available in town

The Gulf of Thailand

Waterfalls **Phaeng Waterfall** is to be found in the interior of the island, about 4½ km from Thong Sala and 2 km from the village of Maduawan. The walk east to Hat Sadet runs parallel to a river along which are three waterfalls and the carved initials of several Thai kings who visited here, including King Chulalongkorn (Rama V) who was so enamoured that he reportedly came here on 10 occasions between 1888 and 1909, and the present King Bhumibol (Rama IX) in 1962. These can be reached on foot or on mountain bikes. Other waterfalls include **Ta Luang** and **Wang Sai** in the northwest corner, **Paradise** in the north (and near the *Paradise Resort*), and **Thaan Prawet** and **Wung Thong** in the northeast corner. The highest point is **Khao Ra** (627 m). A path runs to the summit although visitors have reported that the trail is indistinct and a guide is necessary. Outside Ban Tai, on the coast and to the east of Thong Sala, is **Wat Khao Tum** and the **Vipassana Meditation Centre**. There are views from the hill-top wat to Samui and the Ang Thong Islands. Ten-day meditation courses are held every month with 20-day courses and three-month retreats also available (all in English). All-in fees are ฿1,600 for ten days. Write to: Wat Khao Tum, Koh Phangan, Surat Thani, Thailand, for more information. It is possible to walk on a trail from Hat Rin up the east coast to Hat Sadet and then on to Thong Nai Pan, where four-wheel drive vehicles offer a daily service to Thong Sala, depending on the weather (฿60).

Koh Phangan

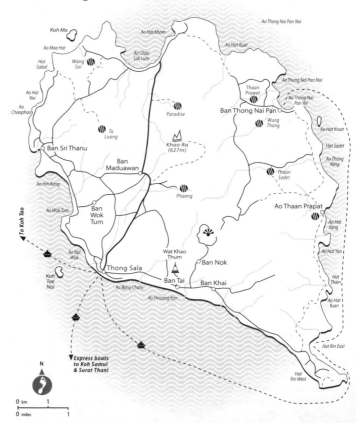

Full Moon Parties

The Full Moon Parties, which have been going since 1990, are now accompanied by Half and Black Moon Parties ... oh, and of course, Saturday Night Parties. On Full Moon night, if you are not planning to party till dawn, it is advisable to stay elsewhere, unless you feel you can sleep to the boom of the bass from the beach. Up to 10,000 people turn up on Hat Rin East every month to dance and watch the jugglers, fire eaters and fireworks displays.

Tips for the party

Be aware that the musical choice is restricted to techno, trance, drum and bass, dance and reggae. Don't bring valuables with you; if safety deposit boxes are an option at your bungalows it is worth leaving your passport and credit cards there, otherwise secrete them in a discrete place in your bungalow.

Do not eat or drink anything that is offered by strangers.

Don't take drugs. It's not worth the risk. At almost every party plain clothes policemen take a number of Westerners down to the jail from where they will only be released on bail if they can pay the ฿50,000 fine. Otherwise they will be held for five to six weeks prior to trial.

Follow the above advice and you should have a fantastic time.

Except for Hat Rin, the beaches are uncrowded although not quite as beautiful as those on Koh Samui. The water is good for snorkelling, particularly during the dry season when clarity is at its best.

Excursions Boats leave from Thong Sala for the Ang Thong Marine National Park (see page 343).

Sleeping
■ *on maps*
Price codes: see inside front cover

Besides the *Phangan Central Hotel* in Thong Sala, there are no big hotels. It is also worth noting that many of the bungalows are without frills; that is they have neither fans or attached shower rooms. Still, they are mainly located right on the seafront, so they receive they sea breezes and not having standing water in your room means you get fewer mosquitoes. In addition, communal facilities tend to be more frequently cleaned. In general, expect to pay in our **F** range for a hut with shared bathroom, **D-E** for a bungalow with private bathroom. The higher of the price ranges given for most of the accommodation indicates an attached bathroom. Hat Rin is more expensive than other beaches. During the high season (Dec-Feb and Jul-Sep), prices are 50% higher than in the low season: bargain if bungalows seem empty. The bungalows are listed below in order, running anti-clockwise round the island from the capital, Thong Sala.

Thong Sala (pronounced Tong-sala) **AL-A** *Phangan Central Hotel*, T377068, F377032. The only five-star hotel on the island. Some a/c rooms overlooking the sea, opened in 1993, this 5-storey hotel offers TVs and fridges. **B-C** *Phangan Chai Hotel*, 45/65 Mu 1, T377068, F377032. Price varies with the view – the more expensive look out on to the sea, the others on to the garden. All are a/c, with a fridge, shower and a western toilet. The choice of décor, however, leaves something to be desired. **D** *Kao Guest House*, 210/9-10 Thongsala-Chaloklum Rd, T238061. Some a/c, travel agency attached. Main door is locked at 2300. **D** *Buakhao Inn*, some a/c, A very small hotel. **D** *Blackhouse*. Another very small guesthouse. **E** *Sea Mew*. Behind the windy wood and thatch frontage of the restaurant is a concrete terrace of very clean, well-maintained tiled rooms, each with a mattress on the floor and a good fan. Squat toilet and shower room attached. **E** *Shady Nook*. A guesthouse with just 3 rooms, clean, comfortable but basic, useful if taking the early morning ferry.

The Gulf of Thailand

From Thong Sala to Ban Tai: Bang Charu and Hinsong Kon This stretch of beach is unpopular with visitors due to its proximity to Thong Sala and as a result accommodation is good value. The beach shelves gently and is good for children, but the water is a little murky. Bungalows are well spread out and quiet: **B-C** *First Villa*, T/F377225, firstvilla@kohphangan.com, kohphangan.com/firstvilla Garishly decorated but clean a/c and fan rooms along the beach front in a pleasant tropical garden. Overpriced. **D-F** *Charm Beach Resort*. The bungalows are well laid out and the most expensive are a/c. The cheap rooms, which are bamboo and thatch huts, are particularly good value, but often full. The restaurant serves Thai and European food. **E-F** *Phangan Villa*, T377083. Rooms with or without attached bathroom. Free horse riding. **F** *Liberty Bungalows*, T238171. Very quiet as the owner doesn't solicit custom at the pier. Clean and comfortable rooms with attached shower rooms.

From Ban Tai to Ban Khai and just beyond Some snorkelling, good swimming, generally quiet and secluded. The beach may not be so good as at Hat Rin, but this is more than made up for by cheaper accommodation and less noise. **B-F** *Chokana Resort*, T238085. A huge choice of rooms, from basic huts with an outside shower, to very smart, rather glamorous, round a/c bungalows. **E** *Mac's Bay Resort*, a very popular spot with basic huts. Food available. Slightly better than most, well run and clean. The more expensive rooms are large and have attached shower rooms. There is a restaurant with a wide menu and nightly videos. Money exchange and an international collect-call service. **E-F** *Triangle Lodge*, F421263. Some rooms beginning to look slightly dilapidated, but they all have hammocks and access to a western toilet. The restaurant is appealing as it has a wide and imaginative menu with tasty interpretations of Western dishes and the staff are friendly. **D-E** *Dream Land Bungalow*. The 2 cheaper rooms are made of wood and have hammocks, while the villas are rather small and not particularly appealing. Nightly BBQ on the beach, and the restaurant offers Thai food. **E** *Phangan Lodge*, T01-2701075. This very laid back place has unusual and brightly coloured triangular huts. **E-F** *Bantai Beach*. The cheapest rooms have no fan, while the most expensive are board huts on the beach and have attached shower rooms. The restaurant serves cheap food. **E-F** *Lee's Garden*, T238150, basic huts set in a garden, good food, quiet, well-run.

THE place for parties, noise & activity (full moon parties are particularly popular, see box page 361

Hat Rin is at the southeastern tip of Koh Phangan. The best, and most popular beaches are to be found here, with some good snorkelling. It also has the greatest concentration of bungalows which are packed close together (except on the hillsides). A hair-raising, twisting, winding road has been built from Thongsala along which *songthaew* drivers either turn up their music really loud, or toot their horns every 5 seconds to warn oncoming drivers. The more restful alternative is to catch a boat here – boats run from both Thong Sala and Ban Khai to Hat Rin. A boat leaves Hat Rin for Thong Sala at about 1030, 45 minutes (฿40), where it meets up with boats to Koh Samui and Surat Thani. The 'East' beach is more attractive – it is cleaned every morning and there are waves. The 'West' beach is dirtier and is almost non-existent at high tide; accommodation is slightly cheaper here. The two beaches are less than 10 minutes walk apart and are both wonderfully quiet until about 1300, as most people are sleeping off the night's excesses. At night the noise from generators and the bars can be overpowering.

Hat Rin West On the whole the accommodation here is rather unappealing but it is cheaper than in Hat Rin East. The restaurants also have a habit of closing down in the off season. However, this isn't really a problem as it's only a few minutes to the centre of Hat Rin where there is plenty of choice. The bungalows from *Sun Beach* to *Rainbow Bungalows* are on the worst stretch of the beach with rotting and vandalized accommodation due to a chronic lack of attention. Expect to be charged over the odds (**E**) for a grotty little hut. **C-F** *Family House*, this recently upgraded place has accommodation ranging from basic huts to a/c bungalows. **D-E** *Charung Bungalow*, simple bungalows with attached shower room and fan. They also have 24-hr electricity. Hammocks in front of every room. Restaurant has Thai cushions and mats on the floor. **D-E** *Friendly*, clean, and with a higher standard than most. **D-E** *Palm Beach*, some bungalows with attached shower rooms, on the side of the small headland which is less affected by litter, popular. **D-F** *Crystal Palace*. Still one of the crummier options. While the bungalows themselves are fine and those near the front are flower bedecked, the site itself looks like a bomb's hit it. Litter has gathered on this part of the beach, thanks to a rocky outcrop which stops it being washed further down the beach. No effort is made to keep the actual grounds clean either. **E** *Hatrin Village*, fan, own shower and toilet, hammocks. **E** *Neptune*, probably the best kept of the bungalows in Hat Rin West – not that there is masses of competition. The huts are bamboo, some with thatched roofs and there is a fairly pleasant stretch of beach immediately in front.

A-D *Pha-ngan Bay Shore Resort*, T7250661. Cheapest rooms have shared washing facilities, the most expensive are a/c and kept very clean. Films are shown nightly. Hammocks on the verandahs of some rooms. **B-E** *Sea View Hat Rin Resort* , T01-7250599. Huge range of rooms from very simple huts with shared washing facilities, to a/c bungalows with 2 double beds. **C-E** *Palita Lodge*, T01-2135445. All rooms are fan cooled and the cheapest have shared shower rooms. The restaurant is given over to a food festival every full moon when a wide range of Thai food is available. They also provide travel services. **D** *Mountain View Resort*. On the hillside at the most northerly end of the beach, overlooking the bay. All the bungalows have attached shower rooms with squat loos and fans. Restaurant and rather appealing bar. **D** *Paradise*, T01-7250661. The originators of the full moon party, the management of this set up run, what are now, slightly tatty bungalows with attached shower rooms. But on the plus side, these are set in a pleasant garden and can accommodate up to 4 people in 2 double beds. **D-E** *Serenity*. Some rooms with attached shower rooms. As the name suggests this is one of the more peaceful locations in Hat Rin with rooms perched on rocks just the other side of the cape. **D-E** *Tommy's Resort*, T01-2293327. Some bungalows have attached shower rooms. Those without are tatty board constructions crammed in behind the others.

Hat Rin East

E *Haad Tien Resort*, T01-2293919, koh phangan.com/haadtien/ There is no road access to this peaceful resort which is 15 mins from Hat Rin by boat. The wood and bamboo bungalows all have attached shower rooms and verandah areas. **E-F** *Sanctuary*. A quiet and appealing little place, only accessible by boat.

Hat Thien to Thaan Sadet

This is a relatively quiet double bay (Noi and Yai) with fine white-sand beaches and excellent snorkelling; it is said to have been Rama V's favourite beach on the island. The journey by truck from Thong Sala takes almost an hour and the road is very muddy in the rainy season, but it does take you through untouched jungle and so is quite an experience. It is also possible to get a boat from Hat Rin here. **A-B** *Panviman Resort*, T377048, F377154, kohphangan.com/panviman.html Mediterranean-style villas or large, airy rooms in the hotel block. Their taxi service will collect you from the pier at Thong Sala. Impressively huge thatch-roofed restaurant. **C-F** *White Sand*. Offers a range of accommodation, but the cheapest huts are particularly good value. The food is tasty and very reasonably priced, and the staff are friendly. Recommended.

Thong Nai Pan

C-F *Nice Beach Bungalows*. The cheapest rooms do not have a fan or a shower room. The most expensive are large, concrete and tiled bungalows with western toilets, but they are rather unappealing. Motorbikes and jeeps are available for rent. Restaurant.

Thong Nai Pan Noi

The Gulf of Thailand

Thong Nai
Pan Yai
E *Star Huts*. By far the largest, and certainly the most popular place on the beach. The bamboo huts with thatched roofs are attractive, though built too close together. The good restaurant serves Thai and Western food (cheap). It is well managed and efforts are made to keep the beach clean. The owner does not appreciate guests indulging in the use of illicit substances. Good information about the island available. Recommended. **D-E** *Tong Ta Pong*. A range of wooden bungalows set either on a hillside, or on the beach. Some have attached shower rooms.The restaurant has an almost Mediterranean feel with its terracotta floor tiles and mosaics. The food is also good and very reasonably priced. **E** *Central Cottage*, T238447. Attractive bamboo huts with wood shutters and thatched roofs. They have a tiled shower room, a western toilet, and a verandah. The restaurant offers Thai food (cheap).

Hat Kuat
5 km northwest of Thong Nai Pan, Hat Kuat it is even more isolated, with a beautiful beach. However, standards have fallen in recent years and bungalows are not as well maintained as they used to be. It has also developed a reputation for being a bit of an English ghetto. To get there take a taxi boat from Chao Lok Lum; the journey lasts about 10 mins. **E-F** *Bottle Beach*, wooden bungalows under coconut palms, very peaceful. **E-F** *OD Bungalows*, northern end, bungalows built perched on boulders, with bamboo walkways, superb views and sunsets, basic.

Chao Lok Lum
This is a deep, sheltered bay on Koh Phangan's north coast. There is now an excellent road from Thong Sala to here, daily *songthaews* leave the pier at Thong Sala at 1230, 20 mins (₿50), or by taxi (₿70 per person). It is gradually developing into a quiet, comparatively refined, beach resort area. In the village of Ban Chao Lok Lum, there are bikes and diving equipment for rent. **E** *Paradise*, inland from the coast, very friendly with swimming at a nearby waterfall. Recommended. **E** *Wattana Resort*, the larger rooms have balconies on 2 sides with hammocks and mosquito screens. The cheaper rooms are large, but very basic, though they have mosquito nets. **F** *Try Thong*, attached shower, friendly management, good food, quiet.

Hat Salad &
Ao Mae Hat
This is one of the most peaceful parts of the island and has the cheapest accommodation. **D-F** *Island View Cabana*. One of the oldest places on the island, it is set in a particularly wide part of the beach where a sand bar stretches out to an offshore island which provides good snorkelling. The accommodation is in fairly simple huts, some of which have attached shower rooms with western toilets. The restaurant has a wide menu and serves good, cheap food, and there is a pool table (₿60 per hour). This is a well-organized place and popular. Recommended. **E-F** *Crystal Island*. There are 12 bungalows here set on a hill overlooking Ban Maehat and the more expensive have attached shower rooms. **F** *My Way Bungalows*. Bamboo bungalows with thatched roofs and hammocks, but no fan. The electricity stops at 2300. Clean, tiled communal shower room. The restaurant serves good, cheap Thai cuisine. **F** *Salad Huts*. Bamboo huts with hammocks. The communal facilities are clean, but the restaurant is overpriced. Electricity until 2200. **F** *Maehat Bungalows*. The more expensive rooms have attached shower rooms. The communal facilities are clean. Friendly management. Electricity between 1800 and midnight. **F** *Maehaad Bay Resort*. A variety of accommodation, crowded in together. Very small bamboo and thatch huts, and the slightly larger ones are concrete. **F** *Wang Sai Resort*. In a beautiful setting behind a stream feeding into the sea, the 18 attractive bungalows, some of which are perched on boulders, are clean and well maintained, though from most it is not possible to see the sea. Snorkelling equipment is available to hire, and there is a book exchange. The restaurant serves Thai and Western food (cheap). Electricity from 1800 until 2300.

Hat Yao
An attractive, clean beach on the west coast with good swimming and snorkelling. 20 mins by *songthaew* from Thong Sala. Bungalows are spread out and quiet. **D-E** *Sea*

Board Bungalows. The accommodation is board-lined and has mosquito screens, with attached tiled shower rooms and western toilets. There is a travel agent attached with overseas call facility. Good snorkelling equipment for hire. Restaurant. **F** *Sandy Bay*. Some rooms have attached shower rooms. The bungalows are kept clean and all have verandah areas with hammocks. It has the best restaurant on the beach which mainly serves Thai food (cheap). Recommended. **B-E** *Hat Yao*. Accommodation ranges from basic huts to a/c bungalows. All have attached tiled shower rooms with western toilets. There are hammocks in front of every room. **F** *Blue Coral*. Very basic bungalows without fans, though some have a shower. The restaurant offers Thai and Western food (cheap). **E** *Ibiza*. A strange, and rather unfriendly atmosphere pervades this establishment. **F** *Benja Waan Bungalows*. There are only 10 bamboo huts with thatched roofs here, some without fans. Each is set on a hillside and overlooks the bay and has a hammock. The restaurant serves Thai and Western food (cheap). **C-D** *Dream Hill Bungalows*. Rather drab bungalows lined with grey board, but each has its own verandah with great views. The restaurant serves a wide range of food at reasonable prices, snorkelling equipment is available for hire, and there is an overseas call facility. **D-F** *Silver Beach*. A rather haphazard range of materials has been used to build these bungalows. They all have tiled shower rooms and fans, though with a squat toilet. The restaurant serves Thai and Western food (cheap).

Ao Chaophao **E** *Great Bay Resort*. Rather characterless bungalows with attached shower rooms. Restaurant offering Thai and Western food. **E** *Haad Chaophao*. Bungalows set in pleasant garden, with attached shower rooms. Restaurant offering Thai and *farang* food. Electricity until midnight. **E** *Seaflower*. Prices vary with distance from the beach. Run by a Canadian-Thai couple, this offers well-laid-out wooden bungalows, with high peaked thatched roofs set in a mature, shady garden. The management run camping expeditions and organize snorkelling (their equipment is free for guests), fishing, cliff diving and caving trips. Restaurant with an interesting menu. Recommended. **E** *Seethanu Bungalow*. Basic fan bungalows, some with attached shower rooms. The restaurant has attractive Thai cushions and mats and offers good Thai food. **E** *Jungle Huts*. 2 rows of large and airy huts made of board, timber and thatch with attached shower rooms. On the large verandahs there are hammocks. Restaurant specializes in cocktails, of which they have 38 varieties.

Ao Sri Thanu This is a long but rather narrow strip of sand. 15 mins by *songthaew* from Thong Sala. It is a peaceful spot to spend a few days. Behind the beach is a freshwater lake fringed by pine trees which is ideal for swimming. **D-E** *Laem Son*. Family-run bungalows, the more expensive of which have western loos and attached shower rooms. **D-E** *Loyfa Bungalows*. There is a range bungalows on the sunset side of the hillside overlooking Ao Sri Thanu. Most have hammocks. **E** *Laem Son Bay Bungalows*. Family-run establishment with fan bungalows of varying size along the beach front. Signs request that guests should eat at their restaurant which offers Thai and some Western food (cheap). 24-hr electricity. **F** *Nantakarn Resort*. Well-maintained concrete bungalows. Free use of snorkelling equipment. Good food and great shakes. **F** *Seaview Rainbow*. Small resort with wooden huts with attached shower rooms; fan cooled.

Ban Wok Tum North of Thong Sala and south of Ban Sri Thanu; the beaches here are average and swimming is poor because the seabed shelves gently. Accommodation is good value: **E** *Siripun*, south of Wok Tum, popular bungalows, fans, swimming ok; **E-F** *Charn*; **E-F** *Lipstick*, north of Wok Tum, quiet location, rocky swimming, some fans in rooms. **F** *Chuenjit Garden*, positioned above the beach, good food. **F** *Cookies*, basic. **F** *Kiet*, excellent food, average bungalows but good value on beach, Italian-managed. **F** *OK*, friendly, short distance off the beach.

Ao Hin Kong to Ao Nai Wok   North of Thong Sala and south of Ban Sri Thanu; the beaches here aren't particularly striking and swimming is difficult as the seabed shelves so gently. Accommodation is correspondingly good value. **C-E** *Siripun*. All rooms have attached shower rooms, some are a/c. They range from small bamboo huts to large concrete villas. **D-E** *Sea Scene*. The more expensive rooms are characterless concrete bungalows. However the cheapest rooms are charming, solidly built wood and bamboo constructions with thatched roofs, a verandah area and hammocks. **E** *Darin*. The fairly large bungalows are lined up along the seafront. They have bamboo weave walls and thatched roofs, roomy verandahs, and tiled shower rooms are attached to some of them. **E-F** *Bounty Bungalows*. Clean and attractive board huts with tiled shower rooms. Snorkelling gear available. Does not yet have 24-hr electricity. **E-F** *Cookies*. Very attractive bamboo bungalows set in a pleasant garden. Those without attached shower rooms are particularly good value with their seafront location and verandahs with hammocks screened by large boulders. Less private are the communal showers which are open topped and in clear view of the bungalow on the hill behind. The helpings at the restaurant are slightly thin (cheap). **E-F** *Lipstick Cabana*. A friendly, family-run establishment, the simple huts have attached shower rooms but no fans. They are set in a shady garden with views over the tidal Ao Hin Kong. **E-F** *OK Bungalows*, T84280. Set in a shady garden, fairly large but basic bamboo bungalows, some of which have attached shower rooms.

Eating   Most visitors eat at their bungalows and some serve excellent, and cheap, seafood. Most of the cheaper bungalows serve standard meals of rice and noodles. However there are also increasing numbers of restaurants and cafés in virtually every village and hamlet. Word-of-mouth recommendations are the best guide; new ones are opening all the time, and old ones deteriorate. **Cheap**: *Mr Chin* at Thong Sala Pier sells good food.

Bars   In Hat Rin and Thong Sala. Nightlife starts around 2200.

Entertainment   **Traditional massage**   At most beaches (฿60-80 per hour).

Videos   At some of the bars or guesthouses.

Shopping   **Batik art and paintings**   The biggest range is available from *Thongsala Batik*, 79/10-12 Thong Sala Town, T/F238401.

Sport   **Diving**: For the trained diver, the west coast offers the best diving with hard coral reefs at depths up to about 20 m. There are also some islets which offer small walls, soft coral and filter corals along with large shoals of fish. Dive trips are also available to further sites such as Koh Wao Yai in the north of the Ang Thong Marine National Park, or Hin Bai (Sail Rock). Here the dives are deeper. *Chang Diving School* are based on Hat Rin East. They do courses and trips on a daily basis. T01-8213127, F377028, kohphangan.com/ChangDiving   *Phangan Divers* are also based in Hat Rin, near the pier on the west side, T01-9584857. *Chaloklum Diving School* is based in Chao Lok Lum Village or contactable through *Wang Sai Resort*. *NAS German Diving School*, PO Box 13, Thong Sala (behind *Phangan Central Hotel*), T377136. *NAS* offers PADI certificated courses as well as canoe rental and snorkelling trips. **Snorkelling**: There is coral to found off most beaches, except for those on the east coast. Particularly good are those in Mae Hat where corals are just a few meters below the surface. **Fishing**: *Ang Thong Island Tours*, Thong Sala. **Gym and Thai boxing**: *Haadrin Jungle Gym*, www://kohphangan.com   A fully equipped gym run by a Canadian and a Kiwi offering Thai boxing courses as well as aerobics, yoga and other training and courses. At Thong Sala, boxers from Bangkok and elsewhere fight every 2-3 weeks, especially on holidays. ฿50 and ฿100 tickets.

Mr Chin, Thong Sala Pier, T377010, F377039. *Songserm Travel Co*, 35/1 Talat Thong **Tour operators**
Sala, T377045.

Local The roads remain poor on Phangan. There is a concrete road from Thong Sala **Transport**
to Ban Khai but the stretch from Ban Khai to Hat Rin is hilly and impassable for anything but a 4-wheel drive vehicle during the rainy season. **Boat**: long-tailed boats take
passengers from Thong Sala and Ban Kai piers to Hat Rin, Thong Nai Pan, Hat Yao and
Hat Kuat. Expect to pay about ฿150 per person from Thong Sala to Thong Nai Pan –
bargain hard. Boat charter is about ฿500. **Motorcycle hire**: in Thong Sala and from
the more popular beaches. Some of the guesthouses also hire out motorbikes. Expect
to pay ฿150 per day upwards. **Songthaews**: run from the pier to any of the bays
served by road. A trip to Hat Rin is ฿50, to Thong Nai Pan, ฿80. The cost to the other
bays depends on how many people are going with you. **Mountain Bikes**: the most
appealing area in which to ride bikes is in the south and west of the island, which are
fairly flat. Well-maintained imported bikes can be hired from the *Phangan Batik Shop*
in Thong Sala for ฿160 per day. They also provide a local bike trail map. Open 1000 to
2000. **Walking**: is the best way to see the island.

Train The State Railways of Thailand run a train/bus/ferry service to Koh Phangan
from Bangkok's Hualamphong Station (฿459-489).

Boat All boats dock at the pier at Thong Sala.

1. A ferry leaves daily from Don Sak Pier, Surat Thani, at 0915, 3¾ hrs (฿105-125). Buses
leave Surat Thani at 0745 to take passengers to Don Sak Pier. The night boat leaves Koh
Phangan for Surat Thani at 2100. A night boat leaves from the pier at Bandon, Surat
Thani at 2300 (and from Phangan at 2100), 6 hrs (฿70-90). Day boats depart from Koh
Phangan at 0615 and 1230 (4 hrs). Contact Ferry Phangan, on corner of Bandon and
Chonkasem roads in Surat Thani, T286461, or in Thong Sala, Phangan, T377028.

2. An express boat leaves twice a day from Don Sak Pier, Surat Thani, at 0730 and
1330 (and from Phangan at 0615 and 1300), 3¼ hrs (฿145). Buses from Surat Thani,
from the airport, and from Phun Phin Railway Station connect with these boats.

From Nathon on Koh Samui, express boats leave at 1000 and 1600 (and from Phangan
to Samui at 0615, 1230 and 1600), 40 mins (฿60). A boat also leaves from Bophut, on
Samui and lands at Hat Rin East, 1 hr (฿50). From Hat Rin Pier to Bophut, boats leave at
0930, 1130 and 1430. *Songserm* ferries link Koh Phangan with Koh Tao, departing
daily at 1000 and 1230 (leaving Koh Tao at 0900) 1½ hrs (฿150). From Koh Tao there
are ferries to Chumphon (see page 374).

Banks *Siam City Bank* (currency exchange centre), south end of Thong Sala, open 0830-1800. **Directory**
There is a currency exchange on Hat Rin. There is as yet no ATM machine on the island but major
credit cards can be used to withdraw money at the bank. **Communications** Internet *Phangan
Batik Internet Service* is in Thong Sala. They charge ฿4 per minute with a minimum time of 15 mins.
International telephone and fax service: Thong Sala. **Post Office:** at the far eastern end of the
sea front road. The post office is open 0830-1630, Mon-Fri and until 1230 on Sat. **Medical
services** The main hospital is 3 km north towards Ban Hin Kong but there are also a number of
smaller clinics in Hat Rin and Thong Sala. **Useful addresses Police:** 2 km down the road from
Thong Sala towards Chao Lok Lum.

The Gulf of Thailand

Koh Tao

Phone code: 077 but numbers prefixed by '01' are mobile phones & will not require this code.
Colour map 3, grid C3

The name Koh Tao, literally translated as turtle island, relates to the shape of the island rather than to the wildlife in the surrounding seas. While your chances of spotting a turtle may be slim, the waters around Koh Tao are still reputed to offer some of the best diving and snorkelling sites in the Gulf of Thailand. Bleaching of the coral through exposure to unusually high water temperatures and storm damage in 1997 means the shallow coral beds are less spectacular than in the past, but they are still swarming with large and brightly coloured fish and their habitat is expected to recover.

Avoid bringing any plastic bottles or tin cans to the island as these are very difficult to dispose of

The easy accessibility of interesting marine life at depths available to beginners, the fairly gentle currents and the relatively low costs all contribute to making Koh Tao a particularly good place to learn to dive. The presence of giant manta rays and whale sharks (plankton feeders which can reach 6 m in length) means that even more experienced divers will find something of interest here. With these attractions in its favour, Koh Tao's reputation as a good, low-cost dive centre has grown rapidly, and in the space of just 10 years the island has made the transition from out-of-the-way backwater to mainstream destination. Improved transport links with the mainland have also made the island more accessible to the short-stay tourist, and so it is no surprise that the former economic mainstay of coconuts has now been eclipsed by the still-expanding tourist trade. Already, the number of rooms for tourists outnumbers the Thais resident on the island. Sensibly, though, as on Koh Samui, there are height restrictions on new buildings and this, in conjunction with the poor infrastructure, means the 'palm tree horizon' has not yet been blotted by multi-storey monstrosities.

While most people come here for the swimming, snorkelling and diving – as well as beach life in general – the fact that most paths are vehicle-unfriendly makes the island walker-friendly and there are some good trails to explore. Land-based wildlife includes monitor lizards, fruit bats and various non-venomous snakes. If planning to go on walks it is worth purchasing V Honsombud's *Guide Map of Koh Phangan & Koh Tao*.

Excursions **Koh Nang Yuan** lies off the northwest coast of Koh Tao and is surrounded by crystal clear water. Once a detention centre for political prisoners, the three islands that make up this mini-archipelago are surrounded by wonderful coral and are linked by sandbars at low tide. There is one bungalow complex, the **C-D** *Koh Nangyuan Dive Resort,* T2295085, F2295212, marion@kscl15.th.com

Snorkelling trips around the island Taxi boats around the island cost around ฿200 per person for a day trip with stops for snorkelling. ■ *Getting there: there is a daily boat at 1030 (฿60) from Ban Hat Sai Ri. A return boat leaves Koh Nangyuan at 1530.*

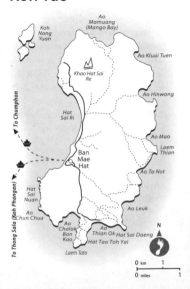

Koh Tao

Related map
Ban Mae Hat, page 370

• •
Koh Tao place names

Ban Mae Hat

บ้านแม่หาด

Hat Sai Ri

หาดทรายรี

Koh Nang Yuan

เกาะนางยวน
• •

Sleeping

■ *on maps*
Price codes: see
inside front cover

The densest areas of accommodation are Hat Sai Ri and Chalok Ban Kao. These offer some degree of nightlife and easy access to the dive schools. On the other hand, if you are looking for a greater sense of remoteness, the other bays are more secluded. This has largely been due to the poor quality of the roads which makes them considerably more difficult to reach without a bit of a trek or the use of taxi boats.

Despite the rapid rate of bungalow construction it remains difficult for non-divers to find empty, cheap accommodation unassisted during the high season. If you don't want to risk having to hike around with a heavy backpack for several hours in search of free rooms, the simplest option is to follow a tout from the pier. You can always move out the following day, but try and book the next place in advance. Alternatively, make your way straight to one of the more remote bays where places are often less booked out, but be warned that if they are full you may have to walk further to locate a final resting place. If diving, you should head straight for the dive shops around the pier where they will find you a place to stay in affiliated accommodation – often at a subsidised rate on the days when you are diving.

Twenty-four hour electricity is the exception rather than the rule on Koh Tao, although the relevant authorities are now beginning to make noises about bringing in a more comprehensive service. While being sent off to your room with just an oil lamp and glorious silence from the television adds to the romance of the place for many people, for those staying a shorter time, the lack of a fan overnight, particularly in the warmer months, can be rather trying.

The other unusual point about accommodation in Koh Tao is the early check out times. These reflect the need to free up rooms for those arriving on the early boats from the mainland. Finally, it is not unknown for guests to be evicted from their bungalows if they have not been spending enough in the restaurant so it is worth enquiring if there is a minimum expenditure before checking in. Most guesthouses have restaurants attached to them, but see also listings under 'Eating' on page 373.

Around Ban Mae Hat (west coast) This is the beach either side of the harbour with easiest access to the facilities in town.

To the south of the pier **A-D** *Sensi Paradise* T2293645. A great range of rooms, the cheapest of which are very overpriced having neither fans nor private shower rooms. Nor are they particularly attractive. At the other end of the price range, however, the buildings are very sensitively designed wooden affairs with traditional Thai architectural features. The garden in which it is set is also richly planted and the small bay behind the resort is truly idyllic. They also operate an environmental policy. **B-D** *Koh Tao Royal Resort*. Smart, well-maintained wood and bamboo bungalows. Some a/c. Friendly staff and a lively restaurant. 24-hr electricity. **D-E** *CL Bungalows*. Simple bamboo huts with thatched roofs. Those set back from the beach are the smallest and cheapest and have shared toilet and shower facilities. Those on the beach are larger, with roomy verandahs. 24-hr electricity.

To the north of the pier **B-C** *Beach Club* T01-2101808. Very attractive, airy rooms with high bamboo-lined ceilings, some with a/c. Recommended. **C** *Crystal* T2294643, F2293828. Cement bungalows with rather garish décor but clean and tiled bathrooms. In high season reserved exclusively for divers.

Hat Sai Ri (west coast) The longest stretch of uninterrupted beach on the island. **B** *Sunset Buri Resort*, T377171. Swimming pool. Only the most expensive rooms have a/c. Offers a good deal on snorkelling equipment. The restaurant serves rather meagre helpings. **B-D** *AC Resort*, T377197. Well-maintained bungalows on the 'wrong' side of the road with mosquito screens on the windows and nets over the beds. Tiled shower rooms, fan, verandah and 24-hr electricity. **C-D** *SB Cabana*. Fan-cooled chalet-style huts with a sea front restaurant. **C-D** *Seashell Resort*, T01-2293152. Attractive wood and bamboo huts with spacious verandahs. Travel agency attached. Roasted rice with shrimp and pineapple is reportedly among the best dishes at the restaurant. Plans to build some a/c rooms. **C-E** *O-Chai*. Same management as *Pranee's*. The cheapest rooms don't have fans, the largest are very smart wooden chalets. Electricity until midnight.

D *AC Two Resort*. On the landward side of the road, private shower room, fan, verandah and 24-hr electricity. **D** *Bow Thong Beach*. The last place on the beach and well-spaced bungalows, so quite private and quieter than most. Squat loos only. Electricity until midnight. **D** *Pranee's Bungalows*. A small resort with wooden bungalows set in a coconut grove. Snorkelling gear and kayaks for hire. 24-hr electricity. **D** *Sai Ree Huts*, T01-2293152. Bamboo weave and timber bungalows with hammocks and a swing on the beach. **D** *Sairee Cottage*. A well-established resort with the more expensive rooms situated on the beach front. Relaxed and friendly with a volleyball net in the garden. Western loos in all rooms, spacious verandahs. The restaurant serves reasonably priced food and does cheap cocktails. **D** *Simple Life Villa*. A mixture of concrete and wooden bungalows. Electricity cut off at midnight. **D-E** *Blue Wind*. Small and friendly set up. The cheaper rooms have shared shower rooms. Basic wood bungalows nestled in a beautiful mature garden. Recommended. **D-E** *New Way*. Peaceful, calming atmosphere. Basic wooden huts with palm frond roofs. Very reasonably priced restaurant with a number of tasty vegetarian dishes on the menu. Recommended. **D-E** *Suthep*, F377196. Run by an English-Thai couple, the cats have gone but the restaurant has been refurbished and produces excellent, tasty Thai and Western dishes. Films at the restaurant at 2000 every night. Library hires out a good range of books for ฿20 a day. Small bar on the beach serves drinks at cheaper rates at sunset. **D-F** *Ban's Diving Resort*, T01-2293181. In peak season the accommodation in this large resort is reserved exclusively for divers. More rooms are being added some of which will be a/c (and slightly more expensive). 24-hr electricity.

E-F *Queen Resort, Tommy's Dive Resort* and *View Cliff*. Owned by the same family and offering identical deals and prices. A mixture of clean concrete, wood and bamboo huts, some a/c, allied to the *VL Dive* school. Cheapest rooms are in *Tommy's Resort*, above the office. **F** *Scuba Junction*, T377169. Has just 6 newly built bungalows, exclusively for the use of divers. Shared shower room.

Related map
Koh Tao, page 368

Ban Mae Hat

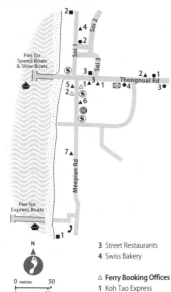

0 metres   50
0 yards   50

■ Sleeping
1 Beach Club
2 Sensi Paradise
3 Crystal & Dive School

● Eating
1 Farango
2 Far Out Cafe

3 Street Restaurants
4 Swiss Bakery

△ Ferry Booking Offices
1 Koh Tao Express
2 Speed boats

▲ Dive Schools
1 Buddha View
2 Carabao
3 Koh Tao Divers
4 Master Divers
5 Nangyuan
6 Scuba Junction
7 Sea Rover

The Gulf of Thailand

Environmental problems on Koh Tao

The lack of a decent waste disposal system is threatening the sustainability of Koh Tao's promotional image as an example of a pristine tropical island getaway. While recycling of plastic bottles does occur, the refund to the bottle collector of just ฿3 per kilo makes it so uneconomic to transport them to the plant on the mainland that it is not widely practised. Instead bottles are burnt or dumped in the sea. For this reason some resorts only provide glass bottles – and where they do not, it may be worth requesting them, if only to bring home the fact that there is a demand for glass over plastic. Rubbish is also accumulating on beaches which are not privately owned. Sadly, although the diving schools promote their environmental credentials, they have as yet failed to organize regular,

systematic clearance of the beaches, either by hired labour or by dive students in return for discounts on their courses, as goes on elsewhere.

The water shortage is another major problem. There is no surface water on Koh Tao. The sudden growth in population on the island has lead to excessive ground water extraction for shower and toilet facilities and pumping is now at a rate significantly higher than that of replenishment. As a result, the water-table has dropped markedly in recent years. If demand continues to escalate there is an imminent danger that salt water incursion will occur, contaminating the fresh water supplies. For this reason, several bungalows have signs in their shower facilities reminding guests not to be wasteful of water.

Cliff at the northern end of Sai Ri Beach D-F *CFT*. Views over to Koh Nang Yuan, rather isolated and very quiet. Very cheap rooms with shared shower facilities. Electricity until midnight. **E** *Golden Cape*. Small and very basic huts with thatched roofs. Mainly inhabited by long-term residents. Restaurant with views over the hillside. **E** *Silver Cliff*. Several rooms have great views out to sea. No fans in the cheaper room and tank and bucket rather than shower facilities. Hammocks on all verandahs. Slightly pricey food and with a sign reading 'Please eat here'. **F** *Sun Lord* This guesthouse is only accessible by an unconvincing track through the jungle. Nevertheless, it commands fantastic views and the cheapest rooms made of bamboo and without shower room are perched precariously on huge granite boulders. Beneath them there is good coral, perfect for snorkelling. **E-F** *Sun Sea*. Cheaper rooms have clean shared shower rooms with squat loos. Most room have great views out to sea. Signs request your patronage at mealtimes. **F** *Eden*. Shared shower rooms and no fan. Very laid back. Set in a tropical garden on the landward side of the main road. Electricity until midnight. Some rooms with Western loos.

Ao Mamuang (north coast) No tracks or roads lead to this bay so it remains solely accessible by boat. **F** *Coral Cove*, peaceful and well managed. Recommended. **F** *Mango Bay*. Secluded.

Ao Hinwong (east coast) A very peaceful bay with no beach to speak of but you can swim off the rocks. A taxi from the pier (฿50) will normally stop 1 km short of the bay itself from where the road deteriorates making it difficult for vehicles to pass. The accommodation consists of very simple huts with shared washing facilities and no electricity in the rooms. **F** *Green Tree Resort*. All rooms have shared toilet facilities. For ฿100 the resort will provide you with snorkelling gear whenever it is required for the duration of your stay. **F** *Hin Wong Bungalows*. Well spaced and clean wooden huts with verandahs overlooking the sea. Plenty of windows to let in the sea breeze, reasonably priced restaurant, snorkelling equipment for hire, friendly staff.

Ao Mao and Laem Thian (east coast) **F** *Laem Thian*. **F** *Sunrise*.

Ao Ta Not (east coast) A poor road serves the bay but vehicles brave the conditions to pick up guests from the ferry. **C-E** *Ta Not Bay Resort*, T01-9704703. Cheaper rooms have shared shower rooms, electricity until midnight. **C-F** *Poseidon*, T01-2294495, F377196. Cheaper rooms with shared shower rooms. Overseas call service. Taxis leave the resort twice a day for the pier (฿50). Electricity until 0600. **D-E** *Mountain Reef Resort*. A family-run resort which will take guests out fishing for their dinner. Taxi boats to the pier can be arranged here costing ฿50 (around 30 mins). **E** *Bamboo Huts*. Simple bamboo and thatch huts.

Ao Leuk (east coast) This beach shelves more steeply than most of the others around Koh Tao and so is good for swimming and has some of the best snorkelling on the island. This does mean groups visit from elsewhere, but on the whole this is a very quiet beach. Both the establishments here are very small and simple and neither have fans in the rooms. **D-E** *Leuk Bungalows*. Simple wood bungalows. Cheaper rooms have shared shower rooms. You can get a boat to the pier from here for ฿100, restaurant. **E** *Nice Moon*, F01-2293828. Just a couple of hundred metres south of the beach itself on cliffs overlooking the bay. Snorkelling equipment is free to guests. Kiet who runs the place in conjunction with his mother is friendly and informative and the restaurant serves delicious Thai food. Recommended.

Hat Taa Toh Yai (south coast) Easy access from Chalok Ban Kao. **C-E** *Tah Toh Lagoon Resort*, T01-2294486. Very good deals available for divers and in high season the resort is reserved exclusively for their use. The cheapest rooms for non-divers are those above the office which have fans, although the electricity only runs until midnight. Some 'luxury' bungalows have been added recently.

Ao Thian Ok (south coast) **E** *Rocky Bungalows*, only bungalows in bay. Basic but well spaced out and friendly with reasonably priced food.

Ao Chalok Ban Kao (south coast) This large bay has the highest concentration of diving resorts. **A** *Ko Tao Cottage Dive Resort* T377198, F01-7250751. The first up-market resort on the island. **C-D** *Laemklong*. Wooden huts on stilts with good views out to sea from roomy verandahs. Squat loos, electricity until midnight. Travel agency attached offering the normal services. **D** *Porn Resort*, T377744. Spacious rooms in either wood or concrete. Both are rather unusual, with the rooms of concrete including sections of massive granite boulders as part of the walls and the rooms of wood having bathroom walls made of glass bottles set in concrete giving a rather quaint stained glass effect. Recommended. **D** *Sunshine*. Attractive wood bungalows lined with bamboo weave with tiled bathrooms and western loos. Electricity until 0200. **D** *Sunshine 1*. Bad value for money, no water, very noisy restaurant and rude staff. **D-F** *Big Bubble Dive Resort*. Don't be confused by the separate signs for *Taraporn Bar and Restaurant, Haraporn Bungalows* and *View Point Bungalows* – they all operate as a whole. The large bamboo and thatch rooms are clean and pleasant with great views, the cheapest have shared shower rooms. Particularly good bargains available for those diving with the school. Recommended. **E** *Big Fish Dive Resort*, T377832, www.bigfishresort.com Accommodation is reserved solely for divers during high season. Electricity until 0600. Large, clean wooden bungalows with squat loos. **F** *Carabao Dive Resort*, T/F377898. Rather scruffy board huts, some with fans. The shared washing facilities are clean but very basic having only squat loos and tank and bucket showers. Electricity until midnight. Free for open-water certificate students. **F** *Buddha View Dive Resort*, 45 Moo 3, T2294693, F2293948. Clean, well-maintained painted timber, bamboo or thatch bungalows with mosquito screens on the windows and verandahs, or rooms in a rather characterless hotel block all with 24-hr electricity. A/c class rooms. Free water skiing for divers.

Hat Sai Nuan Really a series of small beaches but widely known by their collective name. **D-E** *Siam Cookies*. Attractive bamboo huts. Rooms don't have fans. Cheaper rooms share very clean and well-maintained shower rooms. **D-F** *Char Bungalows*. Friendly family-run bungalows in which the cheapest rooms have shared shower rooms and no fans. Electricity until 2300. Snorkelling equipment is free to guests. Squat loos. **E-F** *Taa Thong Bungalows*. On the headland so views of the sea on both sides. Simple wood and bamboo huts with large verandahs, well placed to make the most of sea breezes. Recommended.

Around Ban Mae Hat (west coast) Mid-range: *Farango* Thongnual Rd, an Italian restaurant which serves excellent pizzas. Now offers a delivery service. *Swiss Bakery* Thongnual Rd. Makes western-style bread. **Cheap**: *Far Out Café*, Thongnual Soi 2. Small friendly café serving a decent breakfast and a wide range of sandwiches. *Pon Bakery*, next to *Sairee Cottage*, rye, granary and sour dough bread sold.

Eating
● *on maps*
Price codes: see
inside front cover

Cliff at the northern end of Sai Ri Beach Expensive-mid-range: *DD Hut Seafood Restaurant*. Films shown nightly. *Gelmo Bistro*, opposite the *Blue Wind Bakery*. An up-market (ish) place for more sophisticated soirées. **Mid-range**: *Flower Restaurant*, centre of the beach. Quieter alternative to *ACs*, allied to *AC Two*. *Suthep Restaurant*, centre of the beach. Western specials served every 3rd day. Does great mashed potato, also toad in the hole, and Marmite sandwiches. Popular with long-term Western residents on the island. Good value. Stops serving at 2200. **Mid-range-cheap**: *AC Seafood*, centre of the beach. Large complex with impressive fresh seafood displays. **Cheap**: *New Way Restaurant*, towards the northern end of the beach. Very good Thai food at reasonable prices and cheap drinks. Has a number of tasty vegetarian dishes on the menu. Recommended. *Blue Wind Bakery*, towards the northern end of the beach. Specializes in breads and desserts and does reasonable sandwiches. Now also offers fresh pasta including stuffed speciality pastas with basil, sun-dried tomato and mushroom-fillings. Upstairs, videos are shown at around 1930 if requested.

Ao Ta Not (east coast) Mid-range: *Poseidon*.A good range of vegetarian dishes on the menu.

Ao Chalok Ban Kao (south coast) Mid-range: *New Heaven*, rather a climb, at the top of the hill. A bit pricey but very good food. Only open in the evenings. *Taraporn Bar & Restaurant*, across the slatted walkway at the most westerly end of the beach. There are hammocks and cushions and mat floor seating at this restaurant on stilts above the sea. A great venue. *Sunshine Dive School*, has a BBQ evening buffet every night with baked potatoes, garlic bread, calamari, kebabs, salad and some rice dishes. **Cheap**: *Viewpoint Restaurant*, beyond the *Bubble Dive Resort* at the eastern end of the beach. Wide menu of Thai and some Western food. Also perched just above the sea. A very laid back restaurant serving very reasonably priced food in comparison to most others on the beach.

At night the bars on Sai Ri Beach do quite a brisk trade. *Acs* is probably the most developed club here. The ambience at *Venus* (Sai Ri Beach) is more intimate. It is on a smaller scale and the owners have deliberately avoided using imported building materials. On the other main beach on the island (Ao Chalok Ban Kao), the *Museum Bar* is the main night spot. A number of smaller bars are also growing up on both these beaches. *The Watering Hole*, Sai Rai Beach. Wooden bar, very sociable, some food, good ambience and live music from time to time. *Babaloo*, Ao Chalok Ban Kao. Excellent bar set in the rocks and decorated with sculptures, open from 2100.

Bars & clubs

Meditation Retreat Centres *Two View* runs yoga courses, fasting and colonic irrigation and does past life sessions. On top of the prices for the courses you have to pay ฿50 a night

Entertainment

The Gulf of Thailand

for a basic hut; alternatively you can opt to sleep in the nearby caves if you have your own sleeping mat and bag. ■ *Getting there: the retreat is a 1 hr hike off the main road (from where it is clearly signed), along a steep but clearly marked track. It is best to start out in the early morning.* 5-day courses based in *New Way Bungalows* (Hat Sai Ri) are run most weeks on the subject of *Tian Chi Kung* by an Australian teacher who trained in China.

Shopping   **Unwanted possessions**   *Mr J* has a well-signed shop to the south of the pier which buys and sells second-hand goods from books to boots. He also accepts used batteries which he recycles.

Sport   **Diving** is big on Koh Tao with the number of dive shops now exceeding well over 20. All
Diving is possible all   dive schools have come to an arrangement where they charge exactly the same amount
year round on Koh Tao   for an open water course (฿7,800). What varies are the sizes of the groups and the additional perks you will receive such as a free dive or free or subsidised accommodation. A discover scuba dive is about (฿800) and a fun dive for qualified divers is (฿600). All schools will accept credit card payment. If you are considering diving but want to watch the divers in action before making the investment, many of the dive schools are prepared to take you out to dive sites with their groups. You only pay for the snorkelling equipment. **Snorkelling equipment hire:** many of the guesthouses hire out their own equipment, but this is frequently of low quality. The most reliable gear is that hired from the dive shops. You generally pay (฿50) for the mask and snorkel and a further (฿50) for fins.

Transport   **Local   Kayak hire**: ฿150 per hour from *Seashell Resort*. ฿300 per day from *Pranee's*
59 km N of Koh Samui   *Bungalows*. ฿250 per day or ฿80 per hour from *Laemklong Bungalows* on Ao Chalok
47 km N of Koh   Kao. **Bicycle hire:** at the northern end of Sairee Beach a former dive instructor has set
Phangan   up shop offering mountain bikes for ฿150 per day from the back of her bungalow. **Motorbike hire:** ฿200 per day from *Seashell Resort* and *Pranee's Bungalows*. **NB** Unless you are a very experienced dirt bike rider this is not really an advisable form of transport as reaching any of the isolated bays involves going along very narrow, twisting, bumpy trails. **Long-tailed boats**: link the beaches, ฿20-50. **Songthaews**: during daylight hours cost ฿20 to anywhere on the island. After dark, ฿100.

Boats   There is an overnight boat to Surat Thani which leaves at 0800 and arrives at around 2000 the following morning. (฿250). The speed boat to Chumphon costs ฿400, the express boat ฿300 and the slow night boat ฿200. The speed boat to Koh Phangan costs ฿300, the express boat ฿200 and the slow boat ฿150. The speed boat to Koh Samui is ฿400, the express boat ฿300 and the slow boat ฿200. There are also boats to Koh Tao running from the places listed above. In the monsoon season it is worth leaving a couple of spare days to get back on to the mainland as boats are occasionally cancelled. It is really only worth booking all-in-one (boat, bus and train) tickets on Thai holidays and during the high season.

Directory   **Banks**   The only bank booth is the *Siam Commercial* at the end of the pier which is open Mon-Fri 1100-1400. It will not accept money transfers but does change travellers cheques with the lowest commission on the island. Two money changers in Ban Mae Hat offer visa advances but demand a heavy 7% commission. They are open from 0900-2000. Some dive shops will also sometimes provide cash back on credit cards for an additional 5%. **Communications Internet:** *Scuba Junction* offers the facility to send messages but it is apparently less keen to let you read those which have been sent to your account. *Koh Tao Cottages* will let you read your incoming mail for ฿50 and send replies for an additional ฿50 (for 15 mins). *Banana Rock*, on Ao Chalok Ban Kao, offers email at ฿1 per minute. **Overseas telephone** facilities are easily available on Sai Ri Beach, Ao Chalok Ban Kao and Ban Mae Hat. If you are on Tanot Bay you will have to go to *Poseidon Bungalows*. There are no telephone connections (bar mobile) from the other bays. Telephone calls are expensive. **NB** The phone lines on Koh Tao remain temperamental and are liable to go down at any time. **Post Office:** Thongnual Rd, straight up from the pier.

Nakhon Si Thammarat

Nakhon Si Thammarat ('the Glorious city of the Dead' or Nagara Sri   *Phone code: 075*
Dhammaraja, 'the city of the Sacred Dharma Kings'), has masqueraded under   *Colour map 4, grid B5*
many different aliases: Marco Polo referred to it as Lo-Kag, the Portuguese called
it Ligor – thought to have been its original name – while to the Chinese it was
Tung Ma-ling. Today, it is the second biggest city in the south and most people
know it simply as Nakhon, or Nakhon Si.

Ins and outs

Nakhon, as it is locally known, although it may not be a very popular tourist destina-   **Getting there**
tion is a provincial capital and therefore well connected. There is an airport north of
town with daily flights to Bangkok. Nakhon lies on the main north-south railway line
linking Bangkok with points south and the station is within easy walking distance of
the town centre. The main bus station is about 1 km west of town, with connections
to Bangkok and most destinations in the south. There are also minibus and share taxi
services to many destinations in the south.

The centre of Nakhon is comparatively compact, and navigable on foot. But for sights   **Getting around**
on the edge of town – like Wat Phra Mahathat – it is necessary to catch a public
songthaew, or a *saamlor* or motorcycle taxi. The *songthaew* is the cheapest option.The
tourist office, *TAT*, is at Sanam Na Muang, Rachdamnern Rd, T346516. The staff here
produce a helpful pamphlet and hand out sheets of information on latest bus and taxi
prices. A useful first stop. ■*Mon-Sun, 0830-1630.* (Close by is the unremarkable city pillar or *lak muang* contained within a concrete monstrosity.)

History

Nakhon has links with both the Dvaravati and Srivijayan empires. Archaeological artefacts from the area indicate that the province figured prominently
as a centre of both Hinduism and Mahayana Buddhism from the third century. There has been some discussion whether the distinctive art produced
here should warrant a separate label (the School of Nakhon Si Thammarat) or
whether it was merely an outlier, albeit an innovative one, of Srivijaya. Buddhist monks from Nakhon are supposed to have propagated religion throughout the country perhaps even influencing the development of Buddhism in
Sukhothai, Thailand's former great kingdom. The city is surrounded by rich
agricultural land, and has been a rice exporter for centuries.

Nakhon was at its most powerful and important during King
Thammasokarat's reign in the 13th century, when it was busily trading with
south India and Ceylon. But as Sukhothai and then Ayutthaya grew in influence, the city went into a gradual decline. During the 17th century, King
Narai's principal concubine banished the bright young poet, Si Phrat, to
Nakhon. Here he continued to compose risqué rhymes about the women of
the governor's court. His youthful impertinence lost him his head.

Nakhon used to have the dubious honour of being regarded as one of the
crime capitals of Thailand – a position it had held, apparently, since the 13th
century. Locals maintain that the city has now cleaned up its act and Nakhon is
probably best known today for its prawn farms (see box, page 402) and
nielloware industry (see page). The shop where the industry started some 50
years ago still stands on Sitama Road and production techniques are demonstrated on Si Thammasok I Road. Elsewhere, other than in a few handicraft

The Gulf of Thailand

● ●

Nakhon Si Thammarat names

Khanom beach	Nai Phlao beach
หาดขนอม	หาดนายเพลา
Khao Luang National Park	Wat Phra Mahathat
อุทยานแห่งชาติเขาหลวง	วัดพระมหาธาตุ
Khao Wang Thong Cave	Wat Wang Tawan Tok
ถ้ำเขาวังทอง	วัดวังตะวันตก

● ●

shops on Tha Chang Road, nielloware is a rather illusive commodity, although the National Museum has some examples on display.

Sights

Wat Phra Mahathat A 2 km-long wall formerly enclosed the old city and its wats – only a couple of fragments of this remain (the most impressive section is opposite the town jail on Rachdamnern Road). Wat Phra Mahathat, 2 km south of town on Rachdamnern Road, is the oldest temple in town and the biggest in South Thailand – as well as being one of the region's most important. The wat dates from 757 AD, and was originally a Srivijayan Mahayana Buddhist shrine. The 77 m-high stupa, *Phra Boromathat* – a copy of the Mahathupa in Ceylon – was built early in the 13th century to hold relics of the Buddha from Ceylon. However, the wat underwent extensive restoration in the Ayutthayan Period and endured further alterations in 1990. The *chedi's* square base, its voluptuous body and towering spire are all Ceylonese-inspired. Below the spire is a small square platform decorated with bas-reliefs in gold of monks circumambulating (*pradaksina*) the monument. The spire itself is said to be topped with 962 kg of gold, while the base is surrounded by small stupas. The covered cloisters at its base contain many recently restored Buddha images all in the image of subduing Mara. Also here is the *Vihara Bodhi Langka*, a jumbled treasure-trove of a museum. It contains a large collection of archaeological artefacts, donated jewellery, bodhi trees, Buddhas, and a collection of sixth to 13th-century Dvaravati sculpture – some of the latter are particularly fine. The mural at the bottom of the stairs tells the story of the early life of the Buddha, while the doorway at the top is decorated with figures of Vishnu and Phrom dating from the Sukhothai Period. ■ *The cloisters are open Mon-Sun 0830-1200 and 1300-1630. ฿5.*

Phra Viharn Luang The nearby Phra Viharn Luang (to the left of the main entrance to the stupa) is an impressive building – with an intricately painted and decorated ceiling – dating from the 18th century. The best time to visit the monastery is in October during the Tenth Lunar Month Festival when Wat Mahathat becomes a hive of activity: foodstalls, travelling cinemas, shadow-puppet masters, the local mafia, businessmen in their Mercedes, monks, and handicraft sellers all set up shop – making the wat endlessly interesting.

Puppet workshop Not far from Wat Mahathat is the puppet workshop of Nakhon's most famous *nang thalung* master – Khun Suchart Subsin. His workshop is signposted off the main road near the Chinese temple (hard to miss) and as well as giving shows (see **Entertainment**) and selling examples of his work starting at ฿50 or so for a simple elephant the compound itself is interesting and peaceful with craftsmen hammering out puppets under thatched awnings.

Returning to the main road, and wishing for a change from Theravada Buddhist Thailand, this Chinese Pagoda offers a respite. Magnificent dragons claw their way up the pillars and inside, wafted by incense, are various unidentifiable Chinese gods, Bodhisattvas and demons. ■ *Getting there: it's a 2-km hike out to the monastery; blue songthaews constantly ply the road to the monastery and back (฿4).*

Saan Chao Mae Thap Thim Chinese Pagoda

Nakhon Si Thammarat

To Airport, Surat Thani
Thaksin Hotel & Khanom

Neramit Rd

To Pak Nakhon

Chamroen Withi Rd

Wat Wang
Tawan Tok

Yommarat Rd

Rachdamnern Rd

Share Taxi
Terminal

Market

Karom Rd

Tha Chang Rd

Si Prat Rd

Pol

Lak Muang
(City Pillar)

Handicraft
Shops

Sanam
Na Muang

Khlong Na Muang

A

Prison

Old City
Wall

Khlong To Wang

Si Thammarat Rd

Semamuang
Temple

Hor Phra
Narai

Hor Phra
Isuan

Si Thammasok Rd

Rachdamnern Rd

Chapel of Phra
Buddha Sihing

Clocktower

Saan Chao Mae Thap Thim
Chinese Temple

Tachee Rd   Phaanyom Rd

Mangkut Rd

Suchart Subsin's
Puppet Workshop

N

0 metres   100
0 yards   100

Wat Phra Mahathat
& Phra Viharn Luang

Wat Na Phra
Boromthat

To National Museum

Also on Rachdamnern Road, about 700 m or so beyond Wat Mahathat, the Nakhon branch of the National Museum is one of the town's most worthwhile sights. The impressive collection includes many interesting Indian-influenced pieces as well as rare pieces from the Dvaravati and later Ayutthaya Periods. Some exhibits are labelled in English. The section on art in South Thailand explains and charts the development of the unusual local Phra Phutthasihing (or Buddha Sihing) style of Buddha image, which was popular locally in the 16th century. Also in this section is the oldest Vishnu statue in Southeast Asian art (holding a conch shell on his hip) dating from the fifth century. The museum has sections on folk arts and crafts and local everyday implements. To the right of the entrance hall, in the prehistory section, stand two large Dongson bronze kettle drums – two of only 12 found in the country. The one decorated with four ornamental frogs is the biggest ever found in Thailand. ■ *Wed-Sun, 0900-1200, 1300-1600, ฿10. Getting there: the museum is a long 2-km walk from most of the hotels; catch one of the numerous blue songthaews running along Rachdamnern Rd and ask for 'Pipitipan Nakhon Si Thammarat' (฿4).*

The Nakhon Si Thammarat National Museum

Back in the centre of town is Wat Wang Tawan Tok, across Rachdamnern Road from the bookshop. It has, at the far side of its sprawling compound, a southern Thai-style wooden house, built between 1888 and 1901. Originally the house (which is really three houses in one) was constructed without nails – it has since been poorly repaired using them. The door panels, window frames and gables, all rather weather-beaten now, were once intricately carved but it is still infinitely

Wat Wang Tawan Tok

Related maps A Nakhon Si Thammarat centre, page 379

The Gulf of Thailand

more appealing than the concrete shophouses going up all over Thailand.

Chapel of Phra Buddha Sihing   The Chapel of Phra Buddha Sihing, sandwiched between two large provincial office buildings just before Rachdamnern Road splits in two, may contain one of Thailand's most important Buddha images. During the 13th century an image, magically created, was shipped to Thailand from Ceylon (hence the name – Sihing for the Sinhalese people). The Nakhon statue, like the other two images that claim to be the Phra Buddha Sihing (one in Bangkok, see page 86, and one in Chiang Mai, Northern Thailand), is not Ceylonese in style at all; it conforms with the Thai style of the peninsular.

Hindu temples   There are two 13th-14th-century Hindu temples in the city, along Rachdamnern Road. The first is **Hor Phra Isuan**, next to the Semamuang Temple, housing an image of Siva, the destroyer. Opposite is **Hor Phra Narai** which once contained images of Vishnu, now in the city museum.

Market   A worthwhile early morning walk is west across the bridge along Karom Road to the **Morning Market** (about 1 km). This gets going early, but by 0630 or 0700 it is feverish with activity. It is almost entirely a fresh food market.

Thai Traditional Medicine Centre   On the outskirts of the city, after Wat Mahathat is the small Wat Mechai. While the temple is fairly ordinary, at one end of the temple grounds is a recently established centre for traditional medicine, including massage. If you want a traditional massage, the cost is about ฿120 per hour (if you'd like longer you will need to say first). You can also take a course in massage, paying by the hour, and learn more about traditional herbal medicine (there is a small garden of medicinal plants at the front).

Essentials

Sleeping
on maps
Price codes: see
inside front cover

Although recent additions and upgrades have improved the standard of accommodation in Nakhon it must still have some of the grimmest hotels in Thailand. At the top level, it is well served with a decent 5-star hotel, and the middle range now has a couple of hotels worthy of a mention, but as for the rest, there is little to choose between them.

A *Twin Lotus Hotel* (used to be the Southern BM), on the outskirts of the town centre, opened in 1995, 410 a/c rooms with TV and minibars, and a reasonably sized swimming pool, fitness centre, etc. The usual services expected for a 5-star hotel for what is quite a reasonable price (including a good buffet-style breakfast). A well-run and well-maintained hotel, and the staff are friendly, but the hotel is too large to offer a personal service. **B-C** *Grand Park Hotel*, 1204/79 Pak Nakhon Rd, T317666-73 F317674. Opposite the Nakhon Garden Inn – a bit of a block architecturally, it doesn't really live up to its grand name, but clean, adequate rooms, centrally located, with lots of parking. A/c hot water, TV, mini-bar. One of the better hotels in this category. **B-C** *Taksin*, 1584/23 Si Prat Rd, T342790, F342794. A/c, another pretty mediocre hotel – even gruesome. Hideous block, kitsch rooms, massage parlour, karaoke bar and disco for those in need.

C-D *Montien*, 1509/40 Yommarat Rd, T341908, F345561. Some a/c, from the outside this looks like a combination fire and health hazard, inside the rooms may come as a pleasant surprise by comparison, with attached bathrooms and western toilets, and more expensive ones with TV and hot water – but it is still pretty grim. **C-D** *Thai*, 1375 Rachdamnern Rd, T341509, F344858. Some a/c, restaurant, formerly the best hotel in a rather mediocre bunch, it still has the advantage of a central location over the

Nakhon Si Thammarat centre

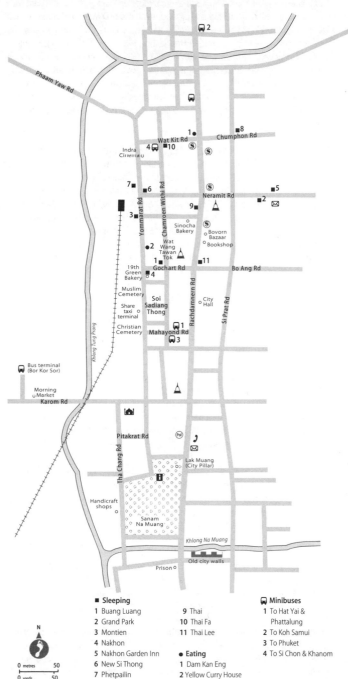

■ Sleeping

1 Buang Luang
2 Grand Park
3 Montien
4 Nakhon
5 Nakhon Garden Inn
6 New Si Thong
7 Phetpailin
8 Taksin

9 Thai
10 Thai Fa
11 Thai Lee

● Eating

1 Dam Kan Eng
2 Yellow Curry House
(Kaeng San)

🚐 Minibuses

1 To Hat Yai &
Phattalung
2 To Koh Samui
3 To Phuket
4 To Si Chon & Khanom

*Related maps
A Nakhon Si
Thammarat,
page 377*

newcomer, *Twin Lotus Hotel*, but otherwise there is little to recommend it, the front part is cheaper while the rear annex is a touch more up-market, still pretty grim with requisite karaoke bar, ancient massage parlour and disco. **D** *Nakhon Garden Inn*, 1/4 Pak Nakhon Rd, T344831, F342926. A/c, restaurant, friendly staff, one of the nicest mid-range places to stay – a rustic feel for Nakhon, with two brick buildings on either side of a large garden compound with clean rooms and hot water. The rooms have been nicely decorated in keeping with the rustic feel – rather dark, but good value and something a bit different from most of the places in the city centre. The rooms come with coupons for a 50% discount for breakfast. Souvenirs from Khiriwong (tie-dye clothing in natural dyes) and Cha-ouad district (basketry) are sold at the front desk. Recommended.

D-E *Bua Luang*, 1487/19 Sai Luang Muang, Chamroen Withi Rd, T341518, F342977. Some a/c, large clean rooms, popular with businessmen. **D-E** *Nakhon Hotel*, 1477/5 Yommarat Rd, T356318. Some a/c, the best of the Chinese-style hotels in this category, more expensive rooms come with a/c, hot water and TV. **D-E** *Phetpailin*, 1835/38-39 Yommarat Rd, T341896, F343943. Some a/c, right by the railway station, over 100 rooms in this ugly block, the sort of hotel where men clean out their ears in the lobby with surgical equipment. **D-E** *Sakol Hotel*, on Pak Nakhon Rd, just after the turn in to the road. The sign is in Thai only, but the hotel is very easy to find. It is a large pale blue building that looks a little like a school, set back a couple of hundred metres from the road, and lying behind a large green wooden house in a garden (incidentally, this house is about a 100 years old and gives a good idea of a traditional urban home of a wealthy family of the time). Although very simply furnished, and with the most basic of bathrooms (but there are sit-down toilets), *Sakol Hotel* looks good for its 50 or so years! Both ceiling fan and a/c are available. The rooms upstairs are better than those on the ground floor as they have a private balcony on the way out to the bathroom. Very friendly management. **E** *Thai Lee*, 1128 Rachdamnern Rd, T356948. Large, bright, clean rooms with fan and attached bathroom (western toilet), friendly management, best-value accommodation in the lower end of the market. **E-F** *New Si Thong*, 1547/2-3 Yommarat Rd, T356702. Much like the *Thai Fa*, a Chinese hotel with bare very functional rooms, sometimes dirty. **E-F** *Thai Fa*, 1751 Chamroen Withi Rd, T356727. Chinese-style hotel, bare rooms but reasonably clean, and a good size with attached bathrooms (squat toilet), though not very private as the top metre of the partition is wire mesh only.

Eating
● *on maps*
Price codes: see inside front cover

Prawns are Nakhon's speciality – farms abound in the area. Good seafood (including saltwater prawns) at reasonable prices is served in most of the town's restaurants. Roadside stalls sometimes sell a Nakhon speciality: small prawns in their shells, deep fried in a spicy batter and served as a sort of prawn pattie. The *Bovorn* Bazaar in the centre of town off Rachdamnern Rd is a good place to start in any hunt for food: it has restaurants, stalls, a bakery, a bar and a coffee shop.

Thai Expensive: *Rim Nam*, Jaturong Ratsami Rd. This restaurant is reputedly the best place for southern curries and seafood. It is about 2 km out of town. **Expensive-mid-range**: *Lakorn*, at the back of Bovorn Bazaar off Rachdamnern Rd. Only restaurant in Nakhon with an Indian rubber tree growing through the middle of it, pleasant eating spot, with open verandahs, art work, wicker chairs and a reasonable line in seafood dishes. Recommended. **Mid-range**: *Dam Kan Eng*, intersection of Wat Kit and Rachdamnern roads. Very good Sino-Thai restaurant which locals believe serve some of the best food in town, seafood is especially good. *Dang Ah*, 74 Rachdamnern Rd. Excellent sea-fresh tandoori prawns, also serves Chinese. Recommended. *Pak Nakhon*, 10 km out of town on Pak Nakhon Rd. Highly recommended for seafood, also serves Chinese. *Yellow Curry House*, 1467 Yommarat Rd. This place is recommended by the local culinary élite, seafood specialities and also some oddities (to the western palate), like red ants.

International Mid-range: *Hao Coffee Shop*, in Bovorn Bazaar, off Rachdamnern Rd. Attempt at creating some ambience: charmingly decorated with antiques and assorted oddities. *A & A Restaurant*, a/c restaurant just down the road from the Nakhorn Garden Inn and marked with flags boasting fresh coffee. Serves Thai-style toasted bread with jam, marmalade, condensed milk, sugar, etc, excellent fresh coffee, and very tasty Thai food. They also do western breakfasts for a very reasonable price. Try the *Kuay Tioaw Si Khrong Moo* (pork rib noodle soup) and the fried minced chicken noodles. At the front of the shop you can buy herbal products from the Khiriwong village, including a mangosteen soap and shampoo!

Bakeries Nakhon has tens of bakeries, some of them really very good. *Ligos*, on corner of Rachdamnern Rd and Bovorn Bazaar, has a good selection of pastries and doughnuts; perhaps even better is *Sinocha* (sign only in Thai), down the narrow alleyway by the *Thai Hotel*. It sells danish pastries, doughnuts and more sickly concoctions as well as a good range of dim sum. Recommended. Another a/c bakery is the *19th Green* on Yommarat Rd which does a good line in gaudy cakes. *A & A Restaurant*, on Pak Nakhon Rd has some excellent cookies of various kinds and serves bread, steamed or toasted, with jam, marmalade, condensed milk, etc. *Nom Sod and Bakery*, at the front of Bovorn Bazaar, has a sign in Thai only, but is pretty easy to spot right at the front, a/c and serving fresh milk, Thai-style toast and steamed bread with jam, condensed milk, etc.

Foodstalls *Nam Cha Rim Tang* is a stall in the *Bovorn Bazaar*, which sets up in the early evening and produces exceedingly good banana rotis. Lining Rachdamnern Rd, along the wall of the playing fields for nearly a kilometre (up to *Dang Ah* restaurant) there are countless stalls selling *som tam*, a chilli-hot papaya salad from Thailand's northeastern region usually served with BBQ chicken or *kai yaang*.

Bars *Rock Bar and Grill*, Bovorn Bazaar, Rachdamnern Rd. A western-style open-air bar with cold beer and a small menu.

Entertainment **Shadow plays** Most of the plays relate tales from the Ramakien (see page 87) and the *jataka* tales. Narrators sing in ear-piercing falsetto accompanied by a band comprised of *tab* (drums), *pi* (flute), *mong* (bass gong), *saw* (fiddle) and *ching* (miniature cymbals). There are 2 sizes of puppets. *Nang yai* (large puppets) which may be 2 m tall, and *nang lek* (small puppets) (see page). Shows and demonstrations of how the puppets are made can be seen at the workshop of Suchart Subsin, 110/18 Si Thammasok *Soi* 3 (take the road opposite Wat Phra Mahathat, turn left – there's a small pond at the top of the *soi* where Suchart Subsin is signposted – and walk 50 m), T346394. This group have undertaken several royal performances.

Festivals **February** *Hae Pha Khun That* (20th-29th) 3 day event when homage is paid to locally enshrined relics of the Buddha.

September-October *Tenth Lunar Month Festival* (movable). A 10-day celebration, the climax of which is the colourful procession down Rachdamnern Rd to Wat Phra Mahathat; *Chak Phra Pak Tai* (movable) centred around Wat Mahathat, includes performances of *nang thalung* (shadow plays) and *lakhon* (classical dance). This is a southern Thai festival also held in Songkhla and Surat Thani.

The Gulf of Thailand

Shopping   Nakhon is the centre of the South Thai handicrafts industry. Nielloware, *yan liphao* basketry (woven from strands of vine of the same name), shadow puppets, Thai silk brocades and *pak yok* weaving are local specialities.

Books   *Suun Nangsuu Nakhon*, Rachdamnern Rd close to *Bovorn Bazaar* has a small selection of English books plus articles on the surrounding area and sells day-old English-language newspapers.

Clothes   An array of cheap clothes stalls down the alleyway behind the *Thai Hotel*.

Handicrafts   Shops on Tha Chang Rd, notably the *Thai Handicraft Centre* (in the lime green tradition at wooden house on the far side of the road behind the tourist office), *Nabin House* and *Manat Shop*. With the exception of the *Thai Handicraft Centre* silverware predominates. Odds and ends can also be picked up in the market in front of Wat Phra Mahathat.

Nielloware   Original shop on Chakrapetch Rd. A few handicraft shops on Tha Chang Rd also sell it.

Shadow puppets   From the craftsmen at *Suchart House*, Si Thammasok Rd, Soi 3 (see above) and stalls around Wat Phra Mahathat.

Yan liphao   Best at *Tha Rua Village*, 10 km out of town on Route 408 or shops on Tha Chang Rd.

Sports   **Thai boxing**: every Sun 2100 in the stadium, Rachdamnern Rd. ฿40.

Transport   **Local   Songthaew**: from one end of town to the other (฿4). **Saamlor**: the old pedal
800 km S of Bangkok   *saamlor* is still in evidence though it is gradually being pushed out by the noisier and more frightening **motorcycle taxi** of which there seem to be hundreds.

Air   Airport lies north of town. Connections with Bangkok (daily), 1 hr 55 mins.

Train   Station on Yommarat Rd. Overnight connections with Bangkok. Most southbound trains stop at the junction of Khao Chum Thong, 30 km west of Nakhon, from where one must take a bus or taxi. Two trains go into Nakhon itself, the Rapid No 47, which leaves Bangkok's Hualamphong station at 1735 and arrives at Nakhon the next day at 0840, and the Express No 15, which leaves Bangkok at 1915 and arrives at 0930.

Road   Bus: the bus station (*bor kor sor*) for non-a/c connections is about 1 km out of town over the bridge on Karom Rd, west of the mosque. Most people pick up a bus as it works its way through town though. The TAT office produces a useful sheet giving the latest information on bus and share taxi fares and times. Overnight connections with Bangkok's Southern bus terminal 12 hrs. Regular connections with Krabi (3 hrs), Surat Thani (2½-3 hrs), Hat Yai (3½ hrs), Phuket (7 hrs), Trang (3 hrs), Phattalung, Songkhla and with other southern towns. A number of **minibus** services are also operating to destinations in the south including Hat Yai, Phuket, Krabi, Trang and Surat Thani. They tend to be marginally quicker and slightly more expensive than a/c coaches. See the map for locations but check beforehand as their 'patches' seem to change from time to time. **Share taxi**: as in Malaysia, this is a popular way of travelling long distance in the south. The share taxi terminal is on Yommarat Rd. Prices are fixed (they are listed on a board at the terminal) and most large centres in the south are served from here including Hat Yai, Phuket, Krabi, Trang, Surat Thani, Phattalung and Songkhla.

Airline offices *THAI*, 1612 Rachdamnern Rd, T342491 and T343874. **Banks** *Bangkok*, 1747 **Directory**
Rachdamnern Rd. *Bank of Ayudhya*, 1366/1-3 Rachdamnern Rd. *Thai Farmers*, 1360
Rachdamnern Rd. *Siam Commercial*, 1166 Rachdamnern Rd. **Communications** Internet:
Internet cafés can be found opposite the *Twin Lotus Hotel* and in the area around Bovorn Bazaar.
Post Office: Rachdamnern Rd (opposite the police station). There is also a small post office
opposite the *Nakhon Garden Inn* on Pak Nakhon Rd. **Telephone office:** attached to the post office
on Rachdamnern Rd, overseas calls available.

Beaches north of Nakhon Si Thammarat

Beaches around Nakhon are unattractive, with filthy water. But 80 km north,
near Khanom district, there are some secluded stretches of shoreline:
Khanom beach (2 km from the village), **Nai Phlao beach** nearby, and a couple of other bays opening up to development. This area is predominantly visited by Thai tourists. The recent economic crisis has seriously affected the
tourism business in this area with quite a few of the older operations looking
very run-down. Newer operations seem also to be targeting western tourists

Beaches north of Nakhon Si Thammarat

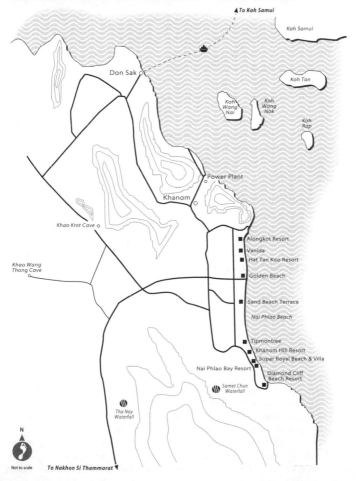

The Gulf of Thailand

who are beginning to look towards the mainland in this area for reasonably priced peace and quiet, and convenience they have failed to find in Samui.

Sleeping **A-B** *Khanom Golden Beach Hotel*, T326690, F529225, khanom@nksrat.ksc.co.th Hotel block with pool and all amenities (snooker room, children's room), tour desk, restaurant, and rental of windsurf boards, sailing dinghies, bicycles, etc. Friendly and professional staff. Rooms are rather characterless but clean and comfortable. The larger suites (prices not listed here) are very spacious and well equipped. The honeymoon suite (completely pink) comes with chaise longue and heart-shaped pillows! Also offer tours to the Southern Archipelago National Park. **A-B** *Supar Royal Beach Hotel*, T529039, hotel block under same management as the *Supar Villa*. Clean rooms, tiled floors, every room has a view of the sea but the rooms are generally pretty characterless. **A-C** *Alongkot Resort*, T529119, boring layout with tacky rooms and overpriced, and for those who like heavy industry there is an industrial port just down to the right! ors, every room has a view of the sea but the rooms are generally pretty characterless. **A-C** *Nai Phlao Bay Resort*, T529039. A/c, restaurant, large resort, quite pricey for what it is. Impersonal service. **B-C** *Khanab Nam Diamond Cliff Resort*, T529144. A/c, restaurant, pool, no hot water. A good location with views over the bay, cottage-style accommodation, but very run-down and with generally unfriendly staff. No beach access. The restaurant is exorbitantly expensive given the quality and quantity of food. **B-C** *Khanom Hill Resort*, overlooking the bay, fairly standard bungalows. A/c and fan available. The views are obscured by the large, private, Thai-style holiday home which occupies the prime place in the grounds. **B-C** *Supar Villa*, T529237. A/c, restaurant. **B-D** *Sand Beach Terrace Resort*, Huge range of clean, well-maintained rooms, some with a/c and some with fan, including some 'house-style' accommodation with several rooms for rent separately or as a set. Friendly staff, good-value food, including western-style breakfasts. Nicely laid out grounds with places to sit on the beach. Gently sloping and safe swimming beach. Recommended. **C** *GB Resort*, T529253, A-frame bungalows on the beach with mature trees providing plenty of shade. A/c rooms come with hot water and a fridge. Tiny bathrooms. **C** *Tipmontree Resort*, T528147, large comfortable bungalows with basic amenities on pretty beach front. Laid-back, friendly staff. **C** *Vanida Resort*, T326329, Spacious rooms, very basic bathrooms, TV (Thai channels only). Okay. **C-D** *Had Tan Koo Resort*, T529039, Bungalow accommodation, quite old but well kept and clean. Fan only. ■ *Getting there: regular buses from Nakhon (฿20), a/c micro buses (฿60) leave from Wat Kit Rd, near the Thai Fa Hotel (see map, page 379). The beaches are situated about 8 km off the main road; turn at the 80-km marker.*

Khao Luang National Park

Colour map 4, grid A4 Lying less than 10 km west of Nakhon, the Khao Luang National Park is named after Khao Luang, a peak of 1,835 m – the highest in the south. Within the boundaries of the mountainous, 570-sq-km national park are three waterfalls. **Karom Waterfall** which lies 30 km from Nakhon, off Route 4015, has a great location with views over the lowlands. There is a Visitors Centre here. Also here are cool forest trails and fast-flowing streams. The park is said to support small populations of tiger, leopard and elephant, although many naturalists believe they are on the verge of extinction here. ■ *Getting there: take a bus to Lansaka (then walk 3 km to falls) or charter a minibus direct.* **Phrom Lok Waterfall** is about 25 km from Nakhon, off Route 4132. ■ *Getting there: take a minibus from Nakhon and motorbike taxis can be hired for ฿10 for the last very pleasant 8-km trip to the falls.* However, the most spectacular of the waterfalls is **Krung Ching** – 'waterfall of a hundred thousand raindrops' – 70 km out of town, and a 4-km walk from the park's accommodation. The 1,835-m climb up **Khao Luang** starts from Khiriwong village, 23 km from Nakhon, off Route 4015. The mountain is the highest in South Thailand and part of the Nakhon Si Thammarat range, running from Koh Samui south through Surat Thani to Satun. The scenic village, surrounded by forest, was partially destroyed by mudslides in 1988 – an event which led to the introduction of a nationwide logging ban at the beginning of 1989. The climb takes three days and is very steep in parts, with over 60° slopes. If you plan on doing this walk on your own, there is no accommodation, so it is necessary to carry your own equipment and food. Dr Buncha Pongpanit, the owner of *Saun Sangsan Nakhon Bookstore*, Rachdamnern Road (close to Bovern Bazaar) will sometimes organize climbs for tourists. The villagers at Khiriwong village can organise trips up the mountain, but do not speak English. Alternatively, TVS-REST (T02-6910437-9, F02-6902796), a Thai not-for-profit involved in community development, offers tours and visits to Khiriwong village, with activities and accommodation at the village and with treks into the forest. See www.ecotour.in.th/indexen.html The tour leaves from Bangkok and costs ฿3,600. Tours to Krung Ching waterfall, including white-water rafting, and other tours in the province can be organised at: *Krung Ching Tours* and other tour companies in the city of Nakhon Sri Thammarat. ■ *Getting there: Mazda songthaews leave Nakhon for Kiriwong every 15 mins or so (฿15).*

Khao Wang Thong Cave

One of the less-publicized sights in the Nakhon area is Khao Wang Thong cave. It lies 100 km north of town, 11 km off Route 4142. The cave is on the south side of the middle peak of three limestone mountains near Ban Khao Wang Thong in Khanom district. Villagers and a group of Nakhon conservationists saved the cave from a dolomite mining company in 1990. The entrance is past the cave keeper's house, 15 minutes' walk uphill from the village. A few tight squeezes and a short ladder climb are rewarded by some of Thailand's most spectacular cave formations. Its four spacious chambers – one of which has been dubbed 'the throne hall' – are sumptuously decorated with gleaming white curtain stalactites. It is presently maintained by groups of local villagers and plans are afoot to install a lighting system. Until then, it is advisable to bring a strong flashlight. ■ *Getting there: by chartered songthaew, around ฿800 per day.*

Khao Nan National Park

Just North of Khao Luang National Park is the new Khao Nan National Park. At 1,430 m, Khao Nan Yai is not as high as Khao Luang, but is still tall enough to support cloud forest on its summit. The national park has a beautiful waterfall near its entrance, lush forests, waterfalls and caves. One cave, **Tham Hong**, has a waterfall inside it and is well worth visiting, and fairly easily accessible but you'll need a flashlight. Treks to the top of Khao Nan Yai taking 3-4 days are organised by the Forestry Department staff. You should call the Forestry Department in Bangkok at least a couple of days in advance, and to date they cannot offer English-speaking guides, so you would need to go with a Thai speaker. The treks go to the top of Khao Nan where you can camp out in cloud forest. Temperatures at the top are always cool and there is a wide variety of ferns and mosses in the understorey of the forest. Khao Nan and Khao Luang are also known for Pa Pra – a deciduous tree which loses its leaves during the dry season (February to April) with the leaves first changing colour to a brilliant red. ■ *Getting there: take the main route up to Khanom beyond Ta Sala and turn left down the road – there are signposts to the Sunantar Waterfall and the National Park.*

The Gulf of Thailand

Phattalung

Phone code: 074
Colour map 4, grid C5

The 'town of the hollow hill,' is so named because of the cave systems in its limestone hills (Khao Hua Taek to the west and Khao Ok Thalu to the east). In fact the town enjoys a rather beautiful position surrounded by rugged, tree-clothed, limestone outcrops (although one is being insensitively quarried for road-building material leaving a vivid scar visible for miles around).

But Phattalung's main claim to fame is as the place where *nang thalung*, Thai shadow plays, originated; records mention them as far back as the 15th century. *Nang* means leather and *thalung* probably derives from Phattalung. That said, *nang thalung* was almost certainly not 'invented' in Thailand: it is thought to have reached Siam from Java (where *wayang kulit* have been shadow dancing for centuries), possibly via Cambodia. The more popular Thai *khon* dances developed from it, supplanting the *nang thalung* everywhere except in the south. Performances of this traditional form of theatre can still be seen in Phattalung (only during festivals) and in Nakhon Si Thammarat. Performances begin around midnight – emphasizing the artform's links with the spirit world – and end at about 0400.

Phattalung is a very quiet provincial capital. Perhaps being sandwiched between Hat Yai to the south and Nakhon Si Thammarat to the north – two of Thailand's largest cities – has drained it of its commercial life blood. Anyway, here there are no a/c shopping malls, no glitzy hotels – even karaoke bars are pretty thin on the ground. It's easy to explore on foot. The tourist office, on Ramet Road (near the intersection with Kanasan Road), is not really a tourist office, but more like a handicraft shop which provides limited information.

Phattalung

■ Sleeping
1 Hor Fah
2 Phattalung
3 Phattalung Thai

🚍 Transport
1 Buses to Thale Noi & Nakhon Si Thammarat
2 Songthaews to Thale Noi
3 Buses to Hat Yai (a/c)

Sights

Wat Kuhasawan, to the west side of town on the road to Tha Miram, is associated with a large cave, **Tham Kuhasawan**, containing images of monks and the Buddha. Steps lead around the cave to the top of the mountain, from where there is a good view of the surrounding countryside. On the second set of steps is a statue to commemorate a hermit who lived in the cave. **Tham Malai Cave** is 3 km north of Phattalung – take a boat from behind the railway station to get there.

Excursions

Wat Wang is 6 km east of the town, on the road to Lam Pam, and is thought to be several hundred years old. The original *chedi* lies in front of the wat, while the closed *bot* contains unrestored murals dating back 200 years. ■ *Getting there: motorbike taxis (฿20 return) from outside the post office or a songthaew from the same spot.*

Wang Kao and **Wang Mai**, the Old and New palaces respectively, lie about 8 km east of Phattalung in Tambon Lam Pam. Originally there were four palaces (the third and fourth being the Suan Dok and Central palaces), but two fell into disrepair and their sites have been redeveloped. The Old and New palaces however have been extensively restored by the Fine Arts Department, the work beginning in 1988. The buildings were constructed between 1866 and 1868 and became the residences of Phraya Apaiborirak, after whom the road from town towards the palaces is named (it is Rame-Apaiborirak Road). The structures consist of a number of traditional raised wooden houses, roofed with unglazed terracotta tiles, and linked together into a single living unit. ■ *Getting there: by songthaew or motorcycle taxi from outside the Post Office.*

Lam Pam is the nearest 'coastal' village, situated on the **Thale Sap Songkhla**, an unspectacular and highly toxic inland sea – swimming is not advisable (see page 398). But from the beach stalls at sunset (which serve simple seafood), it is peaceful, verging on the picturesque. **Sleeping D** *Lam Pam Resort*, T611486. Good restaurant, chalets, near the lake, are very clean and have mosquito screens, no hot water or fans, raft trips on the lake. ■ *Getting there: songthaew (฿5) or motorbike taxis (฿10) from outside the Post Office.*

The **Thale Noi Waterbird Sanctuary** is 39 km northeast of Phattalung at the northernmost end of the Thale Sap Songkhla, where the water is fresh (towards its southern end it is saline). The sanctuary supports nearly 200 species of bird (100 of which are waterfowl) and becomes an ornithological paradise between January and April when the migrants stop here. The best way to see the birdlife (jacanas, crakes, egrets, teal ...) is by hiring a boat to venture along the waterways (฿150 per hour). There is a viewing platform on the lake and several hundred families live in stilted houses along its shores. **Sleeping D** *Forestry Department* bungalow on the lake. ■ *Getting there: the turn-off for the sanctuary is 20 km north of Phattalung along Route 41. Here turn right onto Route 4187 (it is signposted), for another 19 km. Songthaews leave from close to the train station off Nivat Rd for Thale Noi (see map).*

Sleeping

Phattalung's handful of hotels have improved considerably over the last few years and 2 at least offer clean and functional rooms. The only catch is that hotels here charge almost twice as much for rooms with 2 beds as they do for those with a double bed. **C-D** *Hor Fah*, 28-30 Khuha-Sawan Rd, T611645, F613380. Some a/c, 6-storey

■ *on maps*
Price codes: see inside front cover

The Gulf of Thailand

hotel with good views from the upper rooms, the rooms are fine, surprisingly good in fact given first lobby impressions – clean and bright – but perhaps a little overpriced. **C-D** *Phattalung Thai Hotel*, 14/1-5 Dissara-Sakharin Rd, T611636. Some a/c, very reasonable rooms, clean with good bathrooms and showers, friendly management, marginally the better bet in this category. **E-F** *Phattalung Hotel*, Ramet Rd (opposite Thai Farmers Bank). Hard to spot and best missed, a grim place but the cheapest rooms in town.

Eating **Thai Cheap**: *Klert Beer*, 6/4 Dissara-Sakharin, just down from *Thai Hotel*. Phattalung's best attempt at ambience, simple but good menu – including seafood.

Out of town Cheap: *Lam Pam Resort*, Lam Pam, good menu with lots of seafood.

Ice cream *Boom*, in front of the railway station, for sundaes and cold drinks. **Foodstalls** Perhaps the best place to eat in town is from one of the stalls that set up near and in the *Pian Plaza*, on Pian Yin Dii Rd.

Shopping **Books** English-language newspapers available from the store opposite the *Pian Plaza* on Pian Yin Dii Rd.

Transport **Local Motorbike taxis** (฿10) and **songthaews** from Ramet Rd, next to the post office.

888 km from Bangkok
110 km from Hat Yai

Train Station between the canal and Nivat Rd. Overnight connections with Bangkok, 15 hrs and regular connections with all stops on Bangkok-Butterworth route, Sungei Golok 5 hrs, Hat Yai 1 hr 20 mins, Yala 3 hrs 20 mins and Surat Thani 4 hrs.

Road Bus: buses leave from between the market place and the railway station. Overnight connections with Bangkok 12 hrs; also connections with Nakhon Si Thammarat 3 hrs, Hat Yai 1½ hrs and other southern towns. **Share taxi**: for Nakhon Si Thammarat leave from the road in front of the train station, 2½ hrs, ฿50. There are also share taxis to Trang.

Directory **Banks** *Bangkok Bank*, Ramet Rd. *Thai Farmers*, Ramet Rd (main road through town). **Communications** **Post Office:** off Ramet Rd, not far from the railway station.

Sister cities – Hat Yai and Songkhla

Although Hat Yai is by far the biggest town in Songkhla province, Songkhla has a much longer history and used to be one of the wealthiest towns in the South (arguably it still may be). Hat Yai was actually founded in the 1930s as a market town with free market facilities provided for traders. The founder's aim was to establish a key commercial centre, and in that he has definitely succeeded. Ironically, much of the money used to set up businesses in Hat Yai was borrowed from the wealthy families of Nakhon Nai and Nakhon Nok streets in Songkhla. To show the difference between old and new money, the tale told by Songkhla residents is that while the Hat Yai business people drove their Mercedes to Songkhla to borrow money, Songkhla residents rode the public buses to collect the interest.

The Far South

The largest town in the south is the thriving commercial settlement of Hat Yai, 950 km south of Bangkok. Most of the tourists who visit the city come from Malaysia and Singapore, largely on shopping and massage or S&M trips. In 1998 the TAT estimated that 90% of foreign tourists to the Far South came from Malaysia. Songkhla, just 30-odd km away, is the provincial capital but is much quieter and less commercialized than its brash and brazen sister settlement to the west. From here Route 42 links up with Pattani (103 km) and Narathiwat (197 km), both Thai towns with distinct 'Malay' overtones. South of Pattani is Yala (35 km), while west of Songkhla on Route 4 and Route 406 is Satun (125 km). The islands of the Turatao National Park can be reached from Ban Pak Bara, north of Satun.

Hat Yai

Hat Yai has become a 'rest and relaxation' centre for Malaysians and Singaporeans. Many come for the shopping, and Hat Yai has a seemingly inexhaustible supply of gold shops and air-conditioned shopping centres. It must also be admitted – although the TAT office tries desperately to counter these slurs against Hat Yai's probity – that many Malaysians come to sample the city's 'barbershop' and ancient massage industries. For all its sins, Hat Yai is the unofficial capital of the south and the region's largest city with around 150,000 inhabitants. The local tourist office is doing its best to change the city's image to a more wholesome one. In this it may be fighting a losing battle.

Phone code: 074
Colour map 4, grid C6

The Gulf of Thailand

Ins and outs

Getting there

Hat Yai is the South's largest city and lies nearly 1,000 km south of Bangkok. The airport is 12 km from town and there are regular domestic connections with Bangkok and Phuket and international flights to Singapore and Kuala Lumpur. The train station is on the western edge of the city centre. There are connections with Bangkok and destinations to the south including Butterworth and Kuala Lumpur (Malaysia), and Singapore. The main bus terminal has a rather inconvenient out-of-town location but there are also many tour bus companies with centrally situated offices. Buses of all levels of luxury travel to Bangkok, destinations in the south, and even to towns in the north like Chiang Mai. Because so many visitors to Hat Yai are from south of the border, buses to destinations in Malaysia and Singapore are also very frequent. For connections to Hat Yai's sister town of Songkhla catch one of the striped green buses that leave from the clock tower every 7 mins through the day.

Getting around   Hat Yai is a large and busy city. *Songthaews* provide the main form of local public transport along with a good number of *tuk-tuks* and taxis. There are also several car hire outlets in town.

The **tourist office**, *TAT*, 1/1 Soi 2, Niphat Uthit 3 Rd, T243747, F245986, covers the Songkhla, Hat Yai and Satun area. The office is 30 m off Niphat Uthit 3 Rd. Grit Wattanapruek is very helpful and keen but he does have his work cut out for him – with respect to Hat Yai at least.

Sights

On the plus side, Hat Yai does have numerous, excellent restaurants to choose from, and some of the best Chinese and Malay food to be had in Thailand. But beyond its cuisine and one or two good clubs and bars, there is little to love in Hat Yai.

Hat Yai's paucity of anything culturally interesting is exemplified by **Wat Hat Yai Nai**, which, for the town's top sight, is mediocre. The wat is 3 km west of Hat Yai, off Phetkasem Road (before U-Taphao Bridge), and houses the world's third longest reclining Buddha (35 m tip to toe) – *Phra Phuttah-atmongkol*. This spectacularly hideous statue now resides in a massive new concrete viharn. It is occasionally possible to climb inside the Buddha for an inspection of his lungs, but the temple authorities now seem to have restricted access to this breathtaking pleasure. At the exit to the compound, next to a merry-go-round of 10 rotating monks, a jaunty banner reads: 'May the triple gems always be with you'. *Songthaews* running past the wat leave from the *hor nalikaa* (clock tower) on Phetkasem Road (฿5).

For those who really want to scrape the sights barrel there is an amusing **Chinese temple** on Niphat Uthit 3 Road, just north of the *Hat Yai Central Hotel*. **Wat Lian Kao Ko** is jauntily painted in bright colours and outside its gates on the pavement sit ladies selling wild birds that visitors can buy and set free to accumulate merit. It is scarcely significant in any artistic or architectural sense, but the vast incense sticks and the doors painted with giant and fearsome warriors are entertaining. Another promoted sight is **bullfighting** (see **Sports**).

Excursions

Ton Nga Chang are cascades which lie 24 km west of town along Route 4, best seen from October to December. ■ *Getting there: take a songthaew from the stop on Montri Rd.*

Tham Khao Rup Chang   10 km from Padang Besar (on the Thai/Malaysian border) consists of three large caverns featuring stalactites and stalagmites. An associated wat, Wat Tham Khao Rup Chang, is also here.

Essentials

Sleeping   Hat Yai has a huge collection of hotels – around 100 – and there are new ones spring-
■ *on maps*   ing up all the time. Recently built establishments tend to be much cleaner, and are
Price codes: see   often good value for money. The town's hotel industry has a symbiotic relationship
inside front cover   with its booming 'hairdressing' industry. For those venturing into barbershop country in pursuit of a room for the night, there is a general rule of thumb: if a TV costs an extra ฿200, it's likely there are pornographic films on the in-house video. The distinction between 'Thai Traditional Massage' (ubiquitous throughout Thailand) and 'Ancient Massage' (ubiquitous throughout Hat Yai and the south) should also be noted. Ancient masseuses usually belong to the oldest profession. Many of them are located

around Tanrattanakorn and Phaduangpakdi roads. Hotels with clocks showing Malaysian or Singapore time in the lobbies cater for Malaysian and Singaporean clientele. Those with garish and ugly grandfather clocks indicate a Sino-Thai commercial interest in the establishment. Not far away, on the other side of the fetid *khlong* however, is Boss Square around which there are a number of smart, clean hotels and

Hat Yai

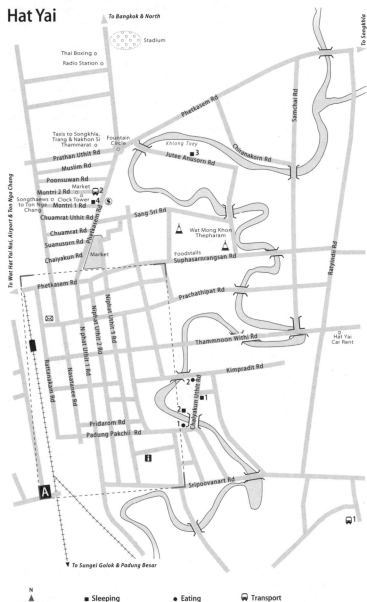

N

0 metres 200
0 yards 200

■ **Sleeping**
1 Daiichi
2 Garden Home
3 JB
4 Sorrasilp Guesthouse

● **Eating**
1 Isan Garden
2 Seafood Court

🚌 **Transport**
1 City terminal
2 Buses to Songkhla, Phattalung, Nakhon Si Thammarat, Pattani, Yala etc

Related map
Hat Yai detail,
page 393

restaurants. Where Hat Yai gets poor marks on the accommodation stakes is in regard to its budget accommodation which is limited, almost uniformly characterless, and often grubby.

A-AL *Central Sukhontha*, 3 Sanehanusorn Rd, T352222, F352223, CENTEL @ksc.th.com A/c, restaurant, pool, this place is run by the *Central Department Store* chain and is attached to their Hat Yai branch. One of the most luxurious places to stay in the city with a business centre and gym. **A** *JB*, 99 Jutee-Anusorn Rd, T234300, F234328. A/c, restaurant, pool, health club, tennis courts and 400-odd rooms, the Ritz of Hat Yai, but not central, situated about 1½ km north of the town centre. **A-B** *BP Grand Tower*, 74 Sanehanusorn Rd, T239051, F239767. A/c, restaurant, pool, a large new addition to Hat Yai's hotels. Across the road is its even more up-market sister hotel the *BP Grand Suite*, (T355155, F354528). **A-B** *Daiichi*, 29 Chaiyakun Uthit 4 Rd, T230724, F231315. A/c, restaurant, enormous, glitzy hotel, catering for conventions, small but smart rooms, reasonable value for money. **A-B** *Grand Plaza*, 24/1 Sanehanusorn Rd, T234340, F230050. A/c, restaurant, pool, better than many in town and recently expanded and given a new frontage to trick people into thinking it's a 1990s construction, older rooms are cheaper. **A-B** *Regency*, 23 Prachathipat Rd, T234400, F234102. A/c, restaurants, a notch above many of the other hotels in price and facilities but even so can't throw off the impression that it's just another very ordinary Hat Yai hostel with plastic trees in the lobby and an over-enthusiastic use of marble.

B *Asian*, 55 Niphat Uthit Rd, T353400, F234890. A/c, yet another addition to Hat Yai's mid-range hotels, has the advantage of being new, so rooms are in good condition, the staff are keen, and the décor is not too overwhelming. **B** *Diamond Plaza*, 62 Niphat Uthit 3 Rd, T230130, F239824. A/c, restaurant, this was the best hotel in this bracket in Hat Yai, but while it has declined in quality other new and better hotels have opened. It is now rather down-at-heel and overpriced given the competition, but still quite acceptable – and it has a pool. **B** *Florida*, 8 Sripoovanart Rd, at the southern end of Niphat Uthit 2 Rd, T234555, F234553. A/c, restaurant, situated on a large plot of land, average rooms and with the usual array of facilities including a club with local talent on show (vocal) and an ancient massage parlour. **B** *Hat Yai Central*, 180-181 Niphat Uthit 3 Rd, T230000, F230990. Another Hat Yai hotel almost indistinguishable from every other, it has the requisite karaoke bar, massage parlour (rather amusingly named the *Tum Rub Massage*), and snooker club, and 250 acceptable but scarcely memorable rooms. **B** *Hat Yai Rama*, 9/5 Sripoonvanart Rd, T230222, F234560. A/c, restaurant, this is one of the kitschest hotels in Hat Yai, which for Hat Yai is saying a great deal. The *Slubpetch* restaurant could do with being rechristened but the hotel is quite good value and the staff, apparently realizing that if they don't try no one will stay, are friendly and welcoming. **B** *Kosit*, 199 Niphat Uthit Rd, T234366, F232365. A/c, restaurant, club with crooners, massage, barber shop plus 200 rooms which were clearly decorated by someone who was either just beginning their career or who lacked any intuitive feel for the art of interior design. **B** *Lee Gardens*, 1 Lee Pattana Rd, T234422, F251888. A/c, restaurant, currently the best of the places in the competitive ฿600-900 price bracket, newly refurbished, rooms are cheaper in the old wing which dates back to the mid-1980s but even there the rooms have been well maintained and are surprisingly pleasant. **B** *Lee Gardens Plaza*, 29 Prachatipat Rd, T261111, F353555. A/c, restaurant, pool, health centre (under development). A large hotel which feels like it mostly caters to tours. Rooms don't feel very cosy, but the bathrooms are well designed and the hotel provides all the amenities one would expect for the price. 2 non-smoking floors are provided. Great views from the upper levels (especially the larger suites which have a wall of windows), but rather impersonal service. Like the *Central Sukhontha* (opposite) it is located above a shopping mall. Part of the Lee Gardens Group. **B** *Siam City*, 25-35 Niphat Uthit 2 Rd, T353111,

F231060. A/c, restaurant, snooker club, karaoke bar, massage parlour, a new place with 200 rooms, central location and reasonable rooms and at the time of writing comparatively clean and glitzy. Character and charm? Forget it. **B** *VL Hotel*, 1-7 Niphat Uthit Rd, T352201, F352210. A/c, mid-range hotel, much like all the others. **B-C** *Indra*,

Hat Yai detail

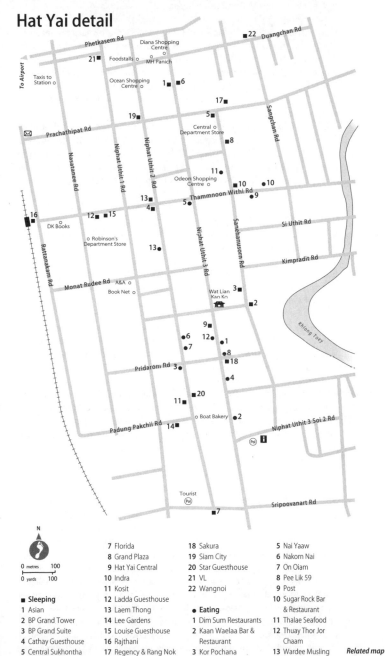

The Gulf of Thailand

N

0 metres 100
0 yards 100

■ **Sleeping**
1 Asian
2 BP Grand Tower
3 BP Grand Suite
4 Cathay Guesthouse
5 Central Sukhontha
6 Diamond Plaza

7 Florida
8 Grand Plaza
9 Hat Yai Central
10 Indra
11 Kosit
12 Ladda Guesthouse
13 Laem Thong
14 Lee Gardens
15 Louise Guesthouse
16 Rajthani
17 Regency & Rang Nok
Restaurant

18 Sakura
19 Siam City
20 Star Guesthouse
21 VL
22 Wangnoi

● **Eating**
1 Dim Sum Restaurants
2 Kaan Waelaa Bar &
Restaurant
3 Kor Pochana
4 Mae Thip

5 Nai Yaaw
6 Nakorn Nai
7 On Oiam
8 Pee Lik 59
9 Post
10 Sugar Rock Bar
& Restaurant
11 Thalae Seafood
12 Thuay Thor Jor
Chaam
13 Wardee Musling

Related map
Hat Yai, page 391

94 Thammnoon Withi Rd, T245896. Some a/c, one of Hat Yai's more venerable establishments, now given a coat of lime green paint, rooms could do with some improvement too, lacklustre but central and perhaps the finest bevy of sequined crooners in Southern Thailand. **B-C** *Sakura*, 185/1 Niphat Uthit 3 Rd, T246688, F235936. A/c, restaurant, clean, reasonable and very popular.

C *Garden Home*, 51/2 Hoi Mook Rd, T234444, F232283. A/c, restaurant (sometimes), plush and well looked after modern hotel, built around waterfall garden. Rooms at the front have small balconies, all are well appointed and excellent value for money. The only downside is that this modest stab at Rome-comes-to-the-jungle overlooks a canal with scarcely a thing alive in it. Recommended. **C** *Rajthani*, 1 Thammnoon Withi Rd, T231020. A/c, restaurant, station hotel, so convenient for transit stop-overs although rooms are average. There is a small steam locomotive outside the front. **C-D** *Laem Thong*, 46 Thammnoon Withi Rd, T244433, F237574. Some a/c, clean old Chinese hotel, fan rooms are particularly good value. Recommended. **D-E** *Ladda Guesthouse*, 13-15 Thammnoon Withi Rd, T220233. Some a/c, convenient for station, rooms are small but very clean with good attached bathrooms, well run, the best place in this bracket. Recommended. **D-E** *Louise Guesthouse*, 21-23 Thammnoon Withi Rd, T220966, F232259. A/c, convenient for station, close to the *Ladda Guesthouse* and almost as good, clean rooms keenly priced. Recommended. **D-E** *Sorrasilp*, 251/7-8 Phetkasem Rd, T232635. Some a/c, reasonable place right by the *hor nalikaa* or clock tower, so great for picking up an early morning bus. **D-E** *Wangnoi*, 114/1 Sangchan Rd, T245729. A/c, clean, good value, but short on windows.

E *Star Guesthouse*, Niphat Uthit Rd (opposite the *Kosit Hotel*), situated above a tour company and run by a Sino-Thai family, rooms are dark and grubby, consider it in a crisis. **E-F** *Cathay Guesthouse*, corner of Thammnoon Withi and Niphat Uthit 2 roads, T243815. Centrally located and well run with friendly management although it could not be said that operating-theatre levels of cleanliness are achieved. Even so, it has become one of the busiest travellers' places to stay with good information and services for those on a tight budget. Rooms are a little dingy but have attached squat loos, it is situated above a tour company's offices, dorm beds available.

Eating
• *on maps*
Price codes: see inside front cover

Hat Yai's saving grace is its cuisine. There are excellent Chinese, Malay and Thai restaurants. The city is particularly noted for its seafood (including shark's fin) and birds' nests. Many of the restaurants exist to meet the culinary predilections of the thousands of visitors from south of the border. Snacking from the roadside stalls is an entertaining way to dine – everything from saté to deep fried battered sea crabs in their shells (*bu thalae thort*).

Thai Expensive-mid-range: *Thuay Thor Jor Chaam*, Niphat Uthit 3 Rd (just south from *Hat Yai Central Hotel*). Clean a/c restaurant serving fried rice, chicken rice, noodles, plus speciality coffees. **Mid-range**: *Isan Garden*, Padungpakdee Rd (opposite *Ambassador Hotel*). Isan food in open-air restaurant next to the stinking *khlong*. *Kor Pochana*, Niphat Uthit 2 Rd. Really excellent Chinese/Thai restaurant – very popular so grab a table while you can. *Nai Yaaw*, corner of Thammnoon Withi and Niphat Uthit 3 roads. Very popular Sino-Thai restaurant, it may look rather chaotic but the food is tremendous. *Pee Lik 59*, across from *Sakura Hotel* on junction of Niyomrat Rd and Niphat Uthit 3 Rd. Barbecued seafood in a large (and very popular) open-air restaurant. Recommended. **Mid-range-cheap** *Mae Thip*, 187-188 Niphat Uthit 3 Rd. Clean and airy place with good Thai food as well as some Malay favourites like saté, succulent BBQ seafood available. Recommended. **Cheap**: *A&A*, Niphat Uthit 2 Rd (on intersection with Pridarom Rd). Good little 'hawker centre' with Sino-Thai favourites as well as some Malay dishes including *rojak penang*, clean. *On Oiam*, 186 Niphat

Uthit 2 Rd. Simple restaurant selling very good (and firey) Thai curries in clean surroundings, the dishes are displayed and customers point and select. Recommended.

International Expensive-mid-range *Post Restaurant*, Thammnoon Withi Rd
(opposite the *Indra Hotel*). A *farang* hangout, a/c, wicker chairs, steaks, salads and
sandwiches, cold beer, some Thai food and laser discs. **Mid-range**: *Sometime*, *Hat Yai
Garden Home Hotel*, 51/2 Hoi Mook Rd. Reasonably priced menu with a good selection
of seafood. *Sugar Rock*, 114 Thammnoon Withi Rd (30 m east from the *Indra Hotel*).
A/c restaurant with music, steaks, salads and sandwiches, also serves breakfast,
draught beer available. **Cheap**: *Boat Bakery*, 190/11 Niphat Uthit 2. Cakes, ice creams
and soft drinks, breakfasts also served. *Nakorn Nai*, 167 Niphat Uthit 2. Good breakfasts, salads, sandwiches, pasta and pizza as well as a reasonable selection of Thai food
in an attractive setting.

Chinese Very expensive-expensive *Rang Nok*, Prachathipat Rd (close to the
Regency Hotel). Specializing in bird's nest and shark's fin dishes, also other seafood
dishes. **Expensive-mid-range** *Thalae/Seafood*, Sanehanusorn Rd (not far from the
Indra Hotel in the *Pahurat Shopping Centre*). This little open-air place serves excellent
seafood – lobster, crab and tiger prawns, shark's fin – the name is only in Thai and Chinese but it is worth checking out.

Malay There is a concentration of restaurants serving Malay (Muslim) food to the
hordes of Malaysians who come to Hat Yai on Niphat Uthit 2 Rd, especially between
Pridarom and Thammnoon Withi roads. Recommended is *Wardee Musling Restoran*
at 121 Niphat Uthit 2 Rd (just south of Thammnoon Withi Rd), which serves excellent
rojak and *rotis*.

Dim Sum *Dim sum* or Chinese 'dumplings' are good in Hat Yai. There is a row of dim
sum shops north of the *Sakura Hotel* on Niphat Uthit 3 Rd.

Fast food *KFC* and *Dunkin' Donuts* in the *Diana Shopping Centre* on the corners of
Niphat Uthit 3 and Duangchan roads. There is another branch of *KFC*, as well as a
Burger King and a *Mister Donut* in *Robinson's Department Store* on Nasathani Rd.

Foodstalls Suphasarnrangsan Rd, Chee Kim Yong Complex, Hat Yai municipal market.
There is a good little group of stalls operating on the corner of Duangchan and Niphat
Uthit 2 roads, serving simple Sino-Thai dishes like *khao muu daeng* (red pork and rice),
khao man kai (chicken and rice), and *khao naa pet* (duck and rice). The newly opened
Robinson's Department Store on Nasathani Rd has an a/c food court. For cheap(ish) sea-
food try the open-air food court just over the pungent *khlong* on Kimpradit Rd.

Kaan Waelaa, Niphat Uthit 3 Rd (a little north from the TAT office). Looks rather like an **Bars &**
antique shop and the sign is only in Thai, live music in the evenings and some food, **nightclubs**
atmospheric. The *Post Restaurant* on Thammnoon Withi Rd (opposite the *Indra
Hotel*) is also a popular watering hole with *farangs*, it has draught beer, laser discs,
shows football and serves food. *Grand Laser House*, *Grand Plaza Hotel*, 24/1
Sanehanusarn Rd. Popular with Hat Yai's young and active.

Disco *New York Club*, *Manhattan Palace*, 29 Lamai Songkroh 4 Rd. *Royal*, 106
Prachathipat Rd.

Nightclubs In many of the major hotels, such as the *Nora*, *Lee Gardens*, *Emperor*,
Kosit. There are karaoke bars on every street and 'sexy shows' in several hotels and
hairdressing outlets.

The Gulf of Thailand

Entertainment **Cinema** With English-speaking soundproof-rooms – *Plaza* on Phetkasem Rd, *Chalerm Thai* on Suphasarnrangsan Rd and *Diana 2* in the *Diana Department Store* on Niphat Uthit 3 Rd.

Shopping The principal shopping areas are concentrated around Niphat Uthit 1, 2 and 3 roads, Sanehanusorn Rd and the Plaza Market. The narrow *sois* between these roads are packed with stalls. As the main reason why Malaysians and Singaporeans come here is to shop, the city is rather overloaded with gold and jewellery shops and shopping centres.

Batik A good place for batik and other textiles and some made-up garments is *MH Panich* on Duangchan Rd.

Books *Praevittaya Bookshop*, 124/1 Niphat Uthit 3. Regional and international English-language magazines available. *DK Books*, 2/4-5 Thammnoon Withi Rd, west end, for English-language books, maps and magazines; there is also a book department on the top floor of the *Central Department Store* on Sanehanusorn Rd. *Book Net*, Niphat Uthit 2 (opposite Thai Airways), English-language newspapers and some – mostly travel – books.

Gold and jewellery Acres of them on Thammnoon Withi Rd.

Markets The main market area is at the southern end of Phetkasem Rd – piles of clothes, fruit, leather goods, batik, torches, toys, etc.

Shopping centres and department stores *Diana Shopping Centre*, Duangchan and Niphat Uthit 3 roads. *Central Department Store*, Sanehanusorn Rd. *Odeon Shopping Centre*, Thammnoon Withi Rd. *Robinson's Department Store*, Nasathani Rd. *Ocean Shopping Town*, Niphat Uthit 3 Rd.

Sport **Bullfights**: held once a month, on the first Sat of the month (contact TAT for information). Fights (and gambling), take place continuously from 0900 to 1600. The local tourist office recommend that visitors check the venue with them as it changes from time to time. Recently fights were being held near the Nern Khua Thong Garden, about 8-9 km from town en route to the airport. To get there, take a *songthaew* from the *hor nalikaa* (clock tower) on Phetkasem Rd. ■ ฿100-200. **Golf**: the best course near Hat Yai is the *Hat Yai Exclusive Golf Course*. They have an office in town at 120 Jutee Anusorn Rd (opposite the *JB Hotel*), T/F234921, T243179, green fees are ฿600 for 18 holes, Mon-Fri, ฿800 on Sat and Sun with a discount after 1530. Clubs (฿300), shoes (฿100) and caddies (฿150) all available. *Kho Hong Golf Course*, 4 km northeast of town on Route 407, 9 holes. Green fees ฿200 Mon-Fri, ฿400 Sat and Sun, caddy fee ฿50, T211500-3 ext 549 for reservations. **Thai boxing**: competitions held every Sat from 1400-1700, just north of the sports stadium on Niphat Songkhroh Rd. ■฿30-40.

Tour operators There are scores of tour and travel agents mostly operating tours to Songkhla and surrounding sights. Most are concentrated along Niphat Uthit 1, 2 and 3 roads and on Thammnoon Withi Rd.

Transport **Local Car hire**: Hat Yai Car Rent, 189 Thammnoon Withi Rd (opposite *Nora Hotel*), T234591. **Avis**, Ground Floor, *Dusit JB Hotel*, 99 Jutee-Anusorn Rd, T234300. **Jutee Car Rent**, 59/2 Jutee-Anusorn Rd, T239447. Cheapest car rental in town with prices starting at around ฿1,500. **Share taxis**: for Songkhla and Satun the taxi stand is on Prathan Uthit Rd, between the *President Hotel* and the *Siam Nakharind Department Store* (฿20 per person during the day, ฿25 at night, 7 people per taxi). **Tuk-tuks** and **songthaews** around town cost ฿5-10, bargain for longer distances. Just flag one down and say where you are going.

933 km from Bangkok
480 km from Phuket
209 km from Nakhon Si Thammarat
290 km from Sungei Golok

Air Hat Yai airport is 12 km west of town (T244145, 244521). *Transport to town*: Thai Airways operate a minibus to and from their office on Niphat Uthit 2 Rd (฿50). Taxis operating on a voucher system cost ฿180 to Hat Yai or ฿250 to Songkhla. *Songthaews* run past the airport and terminate at the *hor nalikaa* (clock tower) on Phetkasem Rd. There is a tourist information desk at the airport (not always manned), as well as a Post Office and restaurant. Regular daily connections with Bangkok 1 hr 25 mins and Phuket 40 mins on THAI. At the airport there is a notice with a checklist of identifying characteristics of a 'hippy'. For reference, they are: 1. A person who wears just a singlet without underwear; 2. A person who wears skirts that are not respectable; 3. A person who wears any type of slippers or wooden sandals except when these are part of a national costume; 4. A person who wears silk pants that do not look respectable; 5. A person who has long hair that appears untidy and dirty; 6. A person who is dressed in an impure and dirty-looking manner. In theory, anyone with any of these characteristics can be prevented from entering the country.

Train Station on Ratakan Rd. Overnight connections with Bangkok, 16-19 hrs. Regular connections with Phattalung, Yala, Sungei Golok and Surat Thani.

Road Bus: the main a/c bus terminal is inconveniently located some way out of town to the northeast on Shotikun Rd. Partly as a result, most people book tickets through one of the many private tour companies concentrated along Niphat Uthit 2 and 3 roads. Non-a/c buses to most destinations in the south including Pattani, Yala, Nakhon Si Thammarat, Krabi, Surat Thani, etc can be picked up at the municipal market on Montri I and Phetkasem roads, better known as the *hor nalikaa* or clock tower which is within walking distance of the town centre. For Songkhla, green striped buses (no 1871) leave every 7 mins from the clock tower, 0600-1930 (฿9). They can also be flagged down on their way out of town. Overnight connections with Bangkok 14 hrs. Also regular connections with Phuket 6 hrs, Krabi 4 hrs, Koh Samui (including ferry), Nakhon Si Thammarat 2 hrs, Satun 1 hr, Sungei Golok 4 hrs, Surat Thani 4 hrs, Songkhla 30 mins. A/c **tour buses** and **mini vans** operated by private tour companies run to destinations in southern Thailand (Phuket, Krabi, Surat Thani), to Bangkok, and to Northern Thailand. There are also combined bus/boat tickets available to Koh Samui and Koh Phangan. Many of the companies have offices on Niphat Uthit 2 and Niphat Uthit 3 roads. **Taxi**: see map for positions of taxi ranks.

Air Daily connections with Singapore (1 hr 20 mins) on **THAI** and **Silk Air**. Regular connections with Kuala Lumpur on **MAS** and **Silk Air**. **Train** Daily connections with Padang Besar (on the Malaysian border), Butterworth, 4 hrs, Kuala Lumpur and Singapore. **Road Bus**: there are several travel agencies on Niphat Uthit 2 and 3 roads offering packages by bus south to Butterworth, Kuala Lumpur, Langkawi, Singapore and elsewhere on the Malay Peninsular, most going via Padang Besar. For long-distance journeys south it is more comfortable to take the bus to Padang Besar, 1 hr and change on to the train south down the west coast of Peninsular Malaysia and on to Singapore (see above). But there are through buses to Butterworth (for Penang), Kuala Lumpur 13 hrs and Singapore 17 hrs. There are also Malaysian shared taxis from Padang Besar. **Taxi**: to Penang leave from the railway station. **Taxi agents** include: *Asia Tours*, 85 Niphat Uthit 2 Rd, T232147. *Magic Tour*, 93/1 Niphat Uthit 2 Rd (*Cathay Hotel*), T234535. **Transport to Malaysia & Singapore**

Airline offices *SilkAir*, Chaiyong Building, 7-15 Jutee Uthit Rd, T238901, F238903. *THAI*, 166/4 Niphat Uthit 2 Rd, T245851. *MAS*, Lee Garden Hotel, Thammnoon Withi Rd, T243729. **Banks** There are multitudes of banks and money changers in Hat Yai, many on Niphat Uthit 1 Rd and Niphat Uthit 3 Rd. *Thai Farmers*, 188 Phetkasem Rd. *Bangkok*, 37 Niphat Uthit 2 Rd, open until 1900 or 2000. Large hotels have money changers. **Communications** Post Office: the GPO is on Niphat Songkroh Rd, some way from the centre of town going north towards the stadium; there is **Directory**

also a more convenient branch office on Rattakarn Rd. **Telephone centre:** Phangnga Rd. Numerous shops offer IDD services. The main telephone office is by the GPO on Niphat Songkhroh Rd, some distance from the centre. **Medical services** *Hat Yai Hospital*, Rattakarn Rd, T243016. **Useful addresses Immigration:** Nasathanee Rd. **Police:** T243021/243333 or T1699. **Tourist Police:** 1/1 Soi 2, Niphat Uthit 3, T246733. Also tourist police office on Sripoonvanart, just set back from the road down an alley and 50 m or so from the *Florida Hotel*, and a tourist police booth on Sanehanusorn Rd, near the *Meridian Shopping Centre*.

Songkhla

Phone code: 074
Colour map 4, grid C6

Songkhla, known historically as Singora, is situated on a spit of land between the Gulf of Thailand and the mouth of a huge lake – the Thale Sap Songkhla. This is Thailand's largest – and probably most polluted – body of inland water – 80 km long and 20 km wide. Although it is a freshwater lake, the water is quite salty closer to the Gulf. The lake used to be a fertile fishing ground but catches are now small due to extensive dumping of effluent.

Ins and outs

Getting there Songkhla is off the main transport routes – although it is not too difficult to get here. The rail line was closed some years ago and the nearest airport is at Hat Yai, about 40 km west. But there are direct buses to Bangkok and some other destinations in the south and the transport hub of Hat Yai is also very well connected, with buses leaving for the city every 7 mins through the day.

Getting around Songkhla is a small and pedestrian-friendly town. There are also public *songthaews* which scoot around town and visit outlying destinations.

History

The city's early history is as murky as its lake, but like Nakhon Si Thammarat, it was incorporated into the Srivijayan Empire (eighth to 13th century). Unfortunately, little remains of this period apart from a number of small Srivijayan bronze images unearthed at nearby Sating Phra. Songkhla was mentioned in 1769 when a Chinese merchant, Yienghoa, petitioned the king for licences to collect birds' nests from Koh Siand and Koh Ha in the east of the province. The present city was built in 1836 by Phraya Vichian Khiri, the governor of Songkhla during the reign of Rama III. Later, Chinese immigrants flooded into South Thailand hoping to make their fortunes from tin mining. Their descendants settled in Songkhla, and the town retains its Chinese atmosphere. Songkhla is the provincial capital, although its sister city Hat Yai is the main commercial centre. There is a sizeable expatriate population here, mainly oil-workers servicing the offshore platforms in the gulf.

Sights

Waterfront Although the port is unsuitable for big ships and has gone into decline, the **waterfront** on the inland sea side still bustles with activity as fishermen unload their catch in the early morning and evenings. Fish – fresh, frozen, fermented and sun-dried – is one of Songkhla's major exports. The fish-packing factories along the road to Hat Yai bear malodorous witness to the scale of the fish industry. The town itself is a mixture of Chinese, Malay and Thai styles. The town's oldest thoroughfare is Nakhon Nai Road where many old Southern-style Chinese shophouses still stand.

The town is surrounded on three sides by water, but swimming is only possible (or advisable) on the seaward side. The focal point of the main beach, Laem Samila (or Samila Beach), is a pouting bronze mermaid, opposite the *BP Samila Hotel*. Further up the peninsula is Son On Beach, lined with seafood restaurants. The two offshore islands, Koh Nu and Koh Maew (Mouse and Cat Island respectively) are both uninhabited.

Most visitors to the province of Songkhla stay in Hat Yai rather than Songkhla. Yet Songkhla is a much nicer town. There is more to see, it is more attractive with its Sino-Thai architecture and less frenetic atmosphere, and the accommodation, especially at the lower end, is better. With beaches within walking distance and a coastal feel, Songkhla is the better option for anyone who is not too bothered about shopping, sharks' fin soup, or massage parlours (for which Hat Yai wins hands down).

Wat Matchimawat (also called **Wat Klang**), a little way south of the centre of town on Saiburi Road, is 400 years old and the largest temple in Songkhla. The **Partsee Museum** within the complex has a chaotic display of disparate items: from human skulls to Buddha statues, stuffed snakes and coins. Nothing is labelled and the museum is badly lit. ■ *Wed-Sun 0900-1700*. The *bot* is said to contain some interesting 19th-century frescoes, representing the arrival of European navigators in the South China Sea, although it is usually locked. On Nang Ngam Road, not far from Wat Matchimawat stands the **city pillar** (*lak muang*).

Wat Matchimawat & Partsee Museum

Songkhla

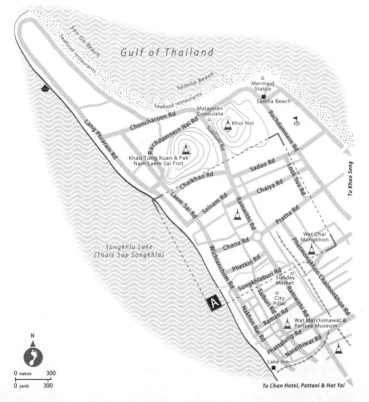

The Gulf of Thailand

The mouse, dogs, cat, garuda, Emperor, crystal and the poor man from Songkhla with the fantastic vegetables

The islands off Samila Beach (Cat and Mouse Island) have a fairy tale associated with them. The story goes that one day a poor, but virtuous, honest, generous, and hard-working (aren't they all?), young man who lived in Songkhla returned from work with some vegetables. He stopped by a pond, put on his pakhama (a multi-purpose cotton cloth worn by men) and went for a swim. After his swim he forgot his pakhama which he had left to dry. Shortly afterwards, a Krut – the mythical garuda – flew past and seeing the pakhama, and thinking it was a snake, attacked the cloth and flew off with it. The poor young man was very sad when he returned to find his pakhama gone for this, and his sarong, was all he had to wear.

However, late that night, a handsome stranger came and knocked on the door of his simple house. He had brought back the pakhama which he had taken by mistake. The poor young man was very polite and welcomed the stranger into his house and gave him breakfast. The stranger saw the young man's poverty and appreciated his generosity and gave him a gift of a magic crystal which could grant any wish the man made. The poor young man accepted the gift very graciously and humbly and simply wished that his vegetables would grow quickly and beautifully.

This wish was quickly granted and the following day the young man was greeted by the sight of a lush garden full of the most beautiful vegetables. From that day on the young man harvested his vegetables and shared them with his neighbours, and because he always wished for good luck, prosperity and happiness for everybody, soon the whole community was thriving.

Now, there is always a dark side to every fairy tale and in this instance it was the Emperor of China who had come to hear of this magic crystal and determined that he must have it. In order to avoid a war with Thailand he sent a clever mouse to fetch the crystal. This the mouse did with little trouble and the Emperor of China was greatly pleased. However, when the Krut heard about the loss of the crystal he immediately returned it to the young man in Songkhla.

On learning that the crystal had been returned to its owner in Songkhla the Emperor of China was furious and set forth a great fleet to capture the crystal. However, again to avoid war, first he sent the mouse to steal the crystal. But this time the mouse was not so lucky. The little rodent made so much noise scratching and scampering while he stole the crystal that the young man's dogs (Tangkuan and Noi) began to bark and the young man's cat chased after the mouse. As the mouse tried to escape to the Emperor of China's ships the dogs blocked its way back to the mainland and the cat blocked its way to the ships.

All this noise attracted the attention of the Krut as he flew near by. He looked down and saw the misery caused by his gift. So to stop all this nonsense he turned the dogs into Khao Tankuang and Khao Noi, the mouse into Mouse Island (Koh Noo) and the cat into Cat Island (Koh Maew). And the young man was left to deal with his problems on his own!

The telling of this story has been adapted from Thai Tales: Folktales of Thailand *Retold by Supaporn Vathanaprida and edited by Margaret Read MacDonald (published in 1994 by Libraries Unlimited).*

Wat Chai Mongkhon The other main wat in Songkhla is Wat Chai Mongkhon, known for its Buddha relic from Ceylon, which is buried somewhere in the main golden *chedi*. In front of the *chedi* is the monastery's unusual squat viharn. Although the doors are often locked, it is usually possible to peek through the windows to see the wat's pride and joy: a reclining Buddha protected behind a glass screen.

The Gulf of Thailand

Songkhla place names

Chana

จะนะ

Folklore Museum

พิพิธภัณฑ์ศิลปพื้นบ้าน

Khu Khut Waterfowl Park

อุทยานนกน้ำคูขุด

Thale Sap Songkhla

ทะเลสาบสงขลา

Wat Pakho

วัดพะโค๊ะ

Songkhla National Museum The Songkhla branch of the National Museum is housed in an 1870's Sino-Thai-style building, built as a private residence for the influential Phraya Sunthranuraksa family. Phraya Sunthranuraksa was governor of Nakhon Si Thammarat province in the latter years of the 19th century. After decades of neglect when it was used for various government tasks, the building was renovated in 1977 and converted into a museum. It is situated between Rong Muang and Chana roads with the main entrance on Wichianchom Road. On the ground floor there is a good prehistory section including a collection of primitive jewellery along with bronze cannon, swords and spears, a whale skeleton and various assorted pieces of farm equipment. Archaeological investigations have shown the Songkhla area to have been a thriving commercial centre for centuries and some of the eighth- and ninth-century finds are exhibited in the museum along with Tang Dynasty ceramics from the seventh to 10th centuries. Upstairs is a large collection of southern religious art (including some rare Srivijayan pieces), as well as furniture (including King Mongkut's bed) and various household items. The museum is a joy partly because of the charming building with its airy rooms, balconies, flaking plaster work and polished wooden upper floors, and partly because of the highly eclectic collection that it contains. The museum staff have even provided some informative material in English which is more than can be said of many provincial museums in Thailand. ■ *Wed-Sun, 0900-1200, 1300-1600, ฿10.*

The old city wall Opposite the museum on Chana Road are some remains of the **city wall**, built in 1839 by Phraya Vichian Khiri, then governor of Songkhla. A little way east of here is a modest, traditional Thai stilt house. This was the birth place of Songkhla's most famous son – the 16th Prime Minister of Thailand, Prem Tinsulanond. In many ways he was the architect of Thailand's 'miracle', bringing political and economic stability to a country which had been chronically unstable. A picture of the eminent man – who is still alive and very influential, being perhaps the King's favourite politician – stands at the top of the wooden stairs. Prem's legacy is also recorded in concrete in the **Tinsulanond Bridge** which completes the road link up the east coast, spanning the Thale Sap via Koh Yo; it was completed in 1986 and is 2.6 km long.

Docks Although it is not billed as a sight by the TAT, the **docks** just to the west of the museum and old city walls are well worth a wander. Here trawlers unload their catches and stock up with ice before putting to sea once more. Burnished and finely muscled men, many sporting tattoos to ward off bad luck and evil spirits, make the boats ready, while children play and dogs fight. The fish stocks in the inland sea – the Thale Sap – have been much depleted by over-fishing and pollution (which is all too evident). Although most trawler captains still fish the Gulf of Thailand, some are now going south to Indonesian waters, even relocating to the Andaman Sea (especially Ranong) on the west side of the peninsula in their search for fish.

The Gulf of Thailand

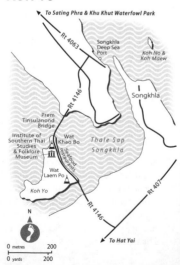

Making a killing from the tiger prawn

The coastline north from Sating Phra and Ranot is one of Thailand's major prawn farming areas. The paddy fields have been dug out, aerators have been installed and beginning in the early 1980s the farmers of the area began to take out large loans to get into the lucrative business of farming tiger prawns. Environmentally the effects have sometimes been disastrous. The protective mangroves and nipa palms were uprooted to make more space for prawns and in so doing destroyed the breeding grounds for many fish and crustacea as well as promoting erosion along the exposed shoreline. The water from the ponds polluted nearby ricelands and viral infections often killed the prawns that farmers had invested so much money in raising. In recent years the government has been researching and promoting more sustainable prawn aquaculture.

Khao Noi & Khao Tung Kuan The north end of the peninsula is dominated by two hills. On the top of **Khao Noi** there is an old *chedi* and a small topiary garden affording panoramic views of the town. **Khao Tung Kuan**, to the west of Khao Noi, is littered with shrines which were restored during the reign of Rama IV. The *chedi* at the top of the hill was built by King Mongkut in 1866. **Pak Nam Laem Sai Fort** is on the side of the hill, on Laem Sai Road. It dates from the early 19th century.

Excursions

Koh Yo Koh Yo is a small island near the outlet of Songkhla's interior 'sea', the Thale Sap Songkhla. Or it was an island until the **Tinsulanond Bridge** (really more of an elevated causeway) was completed which uses the island as a convenient staging post. Koh Yo is still well worth visiting though. At its southern end, and visible from the highway, is the attractive **Wat Laem Po**. Travelling north, the eastern shoreline is dotted with seafood restaurants while at the northern end of the island is the **Institute of Southern Thai Studies** with its excellent little **Folklore Museum** (or *Khatichon Wittaya Museum*). It has a permanent exhibition of southern arts and culture and also mounts occasional shadow play shows. The museum has a reasonable collection of books and other material on southern Thai culture. Apparently it is possible to stay at the Institute, but it should be borne in mind that the gates to the Institute are closed at 1700 and it could be pretty lonely up on the hill ■ *Mon-Sun, 0830-1700, ฿50, T311187-8*. Also on the northern end of the island is Koh Yo's second monastery, **Wat Khao Bo**. The cages which float just offshore are used to raise and fatten sea bass. An added attraction of Koh Yo is the island's small cotton weaving industry. *Phaa Khao Yo* are woven from cotton on traditional looms and available from the market on the island either in lengths or made up into shirts and skirts. The local

Koh Yo

To Sating Phra & Khu Khut Waterfowl Park

Rt 4063

Songkhla Deep Sea Port

Koh No & Koh Maew

Rt 4146

Songkhla

Prem Tinsulanond Bridge

Institute of Southern Thai Studies & Folklore Museum

Wat Khao Bo

Thale Sap Songkhla

Seafood Restaurants

Wat Laem Po

Koh Yo

Rt 407

Rt 4146

N

To Hat Yai

0 metres   200
0 yards   200

Tambon Council for Koh Yo has engaged in some small-scale and culturally focused tourism. Visit their office to rent a bicycle and obtain a map and you can take a cultural cycling tour of the island. The map is excellent, giving deatils of restaurants around the island as well as some of the island sights. Eight sites are marked with signposts giving some information about what you can see there. Sites include an old house, a woman's weaving group (complete with looms), and a fruit orchard. The southernmost route around the island is a very pleasant cycling route, albeit without a proper trail, passing several lovely old Koh Yo-style houses, complete with terracotta tiles, along the island coast. The Tambon Council can also organise boat trips around the island. For further information email: kohyaw@hotmail.com or look at http://www.thai.to/web/kohyaw The staff at the Tambon Council office are very friendly, but English is not particularly strong. **Sleeping** Most places providing accommodation on Koh Yo will quote hourly as opposed to nightly rates and are generally not to be recommended. ■ *Getting there: although the island is accessible by road the best way to get here is by boat from the market wharf in town.*

This lies 3 km south of town, in Khao Seng. It was set up as an information and development centre for the coastal fisheries. It is possible to visit the laboratories and hatcheries as well as the fish museum (T311895 to arrange visit). Khao Seng itself is a muslim fishing village, known for its hand-painted boats (*kor lae*). ■ *Getting there: songthaew (฿10).* **National Institute of Coastal Aquaculture**

Up the hill from the National Institute of Coastal Aquaculture is a small wat with steps leading to the very top of the hill. There is a figurine of a hermit on the left-hand side as you walk to the top. At the top of the hill there is a lovely view across the bay towards the beach and plenty of places to clamber about. Right near the sea, there is a large boulder (usually fixed with white cotton thread blessed by monks) perched on the edge of a huge rock and from here derives the name *khao seng*, or 900,000. The story goes that underneath this boulder there are 900,000 pieces of gold ready for the taking of anyone who can push the boulder off into the sea. You have to clamber about a bit to get to the boulder, but it's always worth giving it a push! **Khao Seng Rock**

Thirty kilometres from Songkhla, north of the district town of Sating Phra the **Khu Khut Waterfowl Park** has a huge migratory bird population between December and April; over 140 species have been recorded. The park is comparatively small, covering around 500 sq km but the park office is well organized and has pamphlets and organizes boat outings. The best time to visit is early in the morning. ■ *Getting there: boats can be hired from Khu Khut village (฿100-200). Regular buses from Songkhla to Sating Phra and from there a motorcycle taxi.* **Khu Khut Waterfowl Park**

About 10 km north of Khu Khut (half way between Sating Phra and Ranot), on the lake, this wat is better known for its legend than its architecture, although it has a reclining Buddha and some murals. The story: once upon a time Luang Pho Thuat, an abbot, was kidnapped by pirates while crossing the lake. Their boat ran into a violent squall and the abbot and his captors, stranded mid-journey, ran out of food and fresh water. The venerated Luang Pho Thuat saved the day by turning the saltwater lake into drinking water. The pirates were so impressed that, duly quenched, they released him. A statue of the holy man stands in the complex. ■ *Getting there: same buses as to Khu Khut Waterfowl Park (฿12).* **Wat Pakho**

Thirty-three kilometres south of Songkhla, Chana stages singing competitions for its captive dove population between January and July. The competitions **Chana** are taken very seriously and good avine singers sell for large sums. Dove cages are hung from 8 m-high poles and their singing judged for pitch, melody and volume. ■ *Getting there: bus 1881.*

Essentials

Sleeping
■ *on maps*
Price codes: see
inside front cover

Unlike its sister city Hat Yai, Songkhla has a good selection of budget accommodation, generally well maintained, clean and friendly. It does not have the multitudes of mid-range places to stay which throng Hat Yai, but in many respects even here Songkhla offers a better deal.

A *BP Samila Beach Hotel*, Samila Beach, T440222 F440442. Located right on the beach front and with a large free-form pool, this is Songkhla's top hotel. Operated by the BP Group (from Hat Yai), with comfortable rooms and lovely views over the sea. The pool is open to the public (for ฿60 per day for an adult) and fortunately, is large enough to take the crowds of children in the afternoons and at weekends. **A** *Hat Kaeo Princess*, 5 km north of town, towards Khu Khut Waterfowl Park, on the Sathingphra Strait, T331059, F331058. A/c, restaurant, pool, situated on a lagoon, rooms and bungalows available, recently taken over by the Dusit group. **A** *The Pavilion*, 17 Pratha Rd, T441850, F323716. A/c, restaurant, used to be Songkhla's most sophisticated hotel and it does have more élan than most places in Hat Yai, but now out-competed by the newer, better-equipped and better-positioned *BP Samila Beach Hotel*. It has the requisite karaoke bar and snooker club but these are low key and generally restrained, central location, well run, and not too

Songkhla detail

■ Sleeping
1 Amsterdam Guesthouse
2 Arom Guesthouse
3 Choke Dee
4 Holland House
5 Narai
6 Pavilion
7 Queen Hotel
8 Royal Crown
9 Sansabai
10 Songkhla
11 Sooksomboon II

● Eating
1 Jazz Pub & Restaurant
2 Kuaytiaw
3 Raan Phonphun
4 Sip Muun

0 metres 200
0 yards 200

large. **A-B** *Green World Palace*, 99 Samakkeesuk Rd, just off Saiburi Soi 7, T437900-8 F437899. Well equipped and reasonably priced with good views over the lake from the west side. The top floor is a bit more pricey and also has views of the sea. A/c, pool, minibar, well-run with friendly staff. Popular with long-staying oil workers. Karaoke, etc, but very low-key. The pool is crowded out with children in the evenings and at weekends. Sometimes gives promotional rates of half the standard rates. Out of the centre, but the hotel offers free transport to and from anywhere in the town. **B** *Royal Crown Hotel*, 38 Sai Ngam Rd, T312174, F321027. A/c, restaurant, a nice, little hotel down a quiet road with comfortable rooms and enthusiastic staff, but looking rather tired.

C *Lake Inn*, 301-303 Nakhon Nok Rd, T314823, F314843. A/c, restaurant, refurbished in 1991 and well appointed, the more expensive front rooms (recommended) have great views of the lake, looking out over the wharf where the fishing boats put in. **C** *Songkhla Palace*, Rachaphat Institute, Songkhla, T443013. A/c, clean, well maintained. This hotel is owned and operated by the Rachaphat Institute partly to provide training opportunities for students majoring in tourism. Very reliable, but located well outside the main part of town and somewhat lonely at night. **C-D** *Nang Ngam Hotel*, 42 Nang Ngam Rd, T313913 or 01-8481162. Right in the heart of the old Chinese part of town on one of the best eating streets in Songkhla this newly, and tastefully, renovated hotel is more than half a century old. Rooms have been decorated in keeping with the style of the hotel, but with a/c. Sadly, upstairs the owner has used carpets rather than opt for the more traditional polished wood. All rooms have shared bathrooms but these are spotless and well equipped. Nice details throughout, including a small garden in a courtyard. Without a doubt the star in the firmament at this price range (discounts for long lets are also available). The hotel also offers tours of the city in a plush *tuk-tuk*. Recommended. **C-D** *Queen*, 20 Saiburi Rd, T311138, F313252. A/c, a rather characterless place and certainly no match for the other hotels and guesthouses in town, cheaper rooms have no windows. **C-D** *Sansabai*, 1 Phetkiri Rd, T311106. Some a/c, clean, but overpriced. **D** *Abritus Guesthouse*, 28/16 Ramwithi Rd, T326047, abritus_th @yahoo.com Centrally located within walking distance of the Pavilion and the sea (a longish walk), family-operated by a Bulgarian family and very friendly. Clean. Must be popular as it has been full at every visit! Serve good breakfasts with fresh coffee. Recommended. **D** *Chan*, 469 Saiburi Rd, T311903. Some a/c, restaurant, south of town. **D** *Sooksomboon II*, 14-18 Saiburi Rd, T323808. Some a/c, restaurant, old hotel with wooden and tile flooring and fan-cooled rooms, and a plush new a/c annex, excellent value, with spotless, spacious, very comfortable rooms. Recommended.

E *Amsterdam Guesthouse*, 15/3 Rong Muang Rd, T314890. The best of the cheaper places to stay, clean and bright rooms, well maintained with attractive sitting area on the ground floor, quiet and attractive, as the name suggests, it is run by a Dutch woman. Recommended. **E** *Choke Dee*, 14/19 Wichianchom Rd, T311158. A/c, restaurant, refurbished in 1991 and well appointed, the more expensive front rooms (recommended) have great views of the lake, looking out over the wharf where the fishing boats put in. **E** *Holland House*, 27 Rong Muang Rd. Rooms in a small, wooden house, previously a private residence, well maintained and quite acceptable. **E** *Narai*, 14 Chaikhao Rd, T311078. Rooms basic but clean and large, only a few with attached bath, small, friendly, family-run hotel on the north side of town in a quiet leafy area and overlooked by Khao Tung Kuan, peaceful and relaxing place to spend a few days. **E** *Songkhla Hotel*, 68-70 Wichianchom Rd. Rooms are light and airy and generally pretty clean, the hotel is on a busy road so it can be noisy, but the house is a traditional one with wooden floors and some character. **E-F** *Arom Guesthouse*, Rong Muang Rd. Next door to the rather more popular *Amsterdam Guesthouse*, this place, though, has cheaper dormitory beds (**F**) and bicycles and motorcycles for rent.

The Gulf of Thailand

Eating
● on maps
Price codes: see
inside front cover

Expensive-mid-range: *Chay Khao*, Nang Ngam Rd, just along from *E&P's Bakery* bakery products are more Thai-style than in *E&P's* and only serves instant coffee. Does western-style breakfasts and serves alcohol and some basic Thai meals throughout the day. A very nice renovation and pleasant decor in a pale yellow and cream bringing out the details of this lovely wooden building. Friendly management. *Chinatown*, Nang Ngam Rd, a stylish renovation in the old Chinese part of town serving very tasty Thai food. The main restaurant is a/c, but you can also sit out in a garden at the back. Recommended. *Jazz Pub and Restaurant*, Pratha Rd (opposite the *Pavilion Hotel*). A/c restaurant and bar patronized by the *farangs* who live in Songkhla. *Raan Phonphun*, Srisuda Rd. A/c Thai restaurant serving good spicy salads, *laap* (minced meat, Isan style), fish like *plaa chon* and frog).

Mid-range: *Isan*, Srisuda Rd. The name of this little restaurant serving spicy northeastern Thai food is not in English but it is opposite the *Paradise Beer Garden* and is worth visiting if you like chillis. **Mid-range-cheap**: *Aray*, corner of Srisuda and Chaiya roads. Ice creams and some other simple dishes. *Open Bakery*, Pratha Rd (at intersection with Srisuda Rd). Cakes and sandwiches served in an open-air cafeteria-style restaurant, cakes are rather sickly but OK for a coffee and rest. *Sip Muun*, Wichianchom Rd (10 m north of the *Songkhla Hotel*). This is a very well-run, open-air Thai restaurant (the name, which is not in English, means Ten Thousand), with good Thai salads and seafood, all freshly cooked out front. Recommended. *E&P's Bakery*, Nang Ngam Rd, the best of three in terms of coffee and bakeries. A/c, excellent fresh coffee (best in Songkhla), and very good cakes (especially the baked cheesecake and the apple pie). Open from 1100 to 2100. Recommended.

Cheap: *Kuaytiaw*, intersection of Nakhon Nai and Songkhlaburi roads. Some of the best noodles in town served on the ground floor of this old Sino-Thai house. Recommended.

Seafood A string of restaurants on Son On Beach all offer excellent fresh seafood. There is another group of seafood restaurants on Samila Beach.

Traditional Chinese Food Nang Ngam Rd has a plethora of old Chinese restaurants serving excellent traditional favourites. Hainanese chicken (*khao man kai*), red pork (*khao moo daeng*), various noodle soups, and rice porridge and there is one shop that sells some of the best *jok* with pork in Thailand – just ask for the jok shop it is so well known no one will have any problem pointing you in the right direction – only open in the morning. Another excellent restaurant has no sign in English – it's about halfway down the Nang Ngam section with the *Nang Ngam Hotel* but on the other side and has lots of old wooden chairs and tables and ceiling fans (it's also usually full which is another indicator of the quality of the food). The *tom yam haeng* is excellent and something a little different.

Foodstalls The main concentration is around the Post Office on Wichianchom Rd. Foodstalls also set up on Samila Beach, and in the area in front of the old train station. An unusual place to find a foodstall is in the grounds to the Chinese school on Nang Ngam Rd. The stall is set up with tables under the stage used for Chinese theatre. Needless to say eating under the stage isn't really an option for anyone over 5 ft 5 ins, and there are also seats 'outside'. The stall has been operating in the same place for over 80 years with the recipes passed on from mother to daughter. They are now on to their third generation. Excellent pork meatballs which you can have with soup, or separate in a bowl with a sauce, chicken (you might want to indicate if you don't want the feet, etc). Recommended.

Bars There are a number of watering holes down quiet Srisuda Rd which has become something of a *farang* enclave. *Auntie's Bar* is an a/c place with some food, the *Paradise Beer Garden* a little further north really speaks for itself while the *Lucky Pub*, at the corner of Chaiya Rd is a noisier place to drink. Turning east onto Sai Ngam Rd are 2 small open-air bars, very popular with oil workers, the *Jungle Bar* and *Parlang*. *Laguna Terrace*, *Lake Inn*, 301 Nakhon Nok Rd. Roof-top bar, good views.

September-October *Chinese Lunar Festival* (movable), Thais of Chinese origin make offerings to the moon or Queen of the Heavens. Festivities include lion and dragon dances, lantern processions, folk entertainment.

Festivals

The main shopping areas are along Nakhon Nai and Nang Ngam roads.

Shopping

Markets Central Market, on Nakhon Nai Rd, opposite the Post Office. Sunday market near the main bus and taxi stand.

Textiles Songkhla is known for *phaa kaw yor* woven cotton, made on Koh Yo in the middle of the lake. Available in shops along Nang Ngam and Nakhon Nai roads.

Golf: *Songkhla Golf Course*, 9-hole beachside course next to the *Samila Hotel*. Clubs for hire. Green fees, ฿100. **Watersports**: *Watersports Centre* on Samila Beach, near the golf course, hires out rowing boats, paddle boats, speedboats and jet skis.

Sports

Piya Tours, 51 Platha Rd, T313770.

Tour operators

Local Songthaews: ฿5 around town. There are always several around the bus station.

Transport
950 km S of Bangkok, 30 km from Hat Yai

Air Nearest airport at Hat Yai (see page 396). **Train** Nearest station is at Hat Yai (see page 397). The rail line to Songkhla is now overgrown and the old station reeks of urine – though it still stands near the centre of town. **Road Bus**: buses for Hat Yai leave every 10 mins or so from Saiburi Rd, opposite Wat Chaeng (฿9). Overnight connections with Bangkok, 13 hrs. Regular connections with Nakhon Si Thammarat, 2½ hrs. **Taxi**: share taxis to Songkhla leave from Wichianchom Rd. **Boat** Ferries across the lake leave from Lang Phraram Rd, north of town. There is a boat which travels to Bangkok, 14 hrs.

Banks *Bangkok Bank* and *Bank of Ayutthaya* are on Wichianchom Rd, near the market. The *Thai Farmers Bank* at the intersection of Chana and Ramwithi roads has an exchange desk. *Thai Military* on corner of Nakhon Nok and Ramwithi roads. **Communications** Post Office: opposite the market on Wichianchom Rd, nearby telephone office for international calls. **Embassies & consulates** *Malaysian Consulate*, 4 Sukhum Rd, T311062. **Medical services** 161 Ramwithi Rd, T311494. **Useful addresses** Police: there is a small police box on Wichianchom Rd, near the post office and market.

Directory

Pattani

Pattani province, once a semi-autonomous Malay-speaking sultanate, and an important trading port in Southeast Asia since well before the sixteenth century, is the heartland of Malay-Muslim South Thailand – although there are a lot of Thai-speaking Muslims here too. Unlike the Chinese, the Malays of South Thailand are not recent immigrants. Their descendants settled on the lower Kra Isthmus centuries ago, yet they have never willingly assimilated into modern Thailand. Few have found their way into local or central government and school children prefer to drop out after primary education rather than continue their studies in the Thai medium.

Phone code: 073
Colour map 6, grid A2

Pattani is strongly Muslim and the big mosque, **Matsayit Klang**, is a key place of interest. It is quite a beautiful mosque, located on Yarang Road, 200 m from the bus stop and is considered to be the central mosque for the three provinces of Narathiwat, Pattani and Yala. Worth a visit is the **Chao Mae Lim Kor Niew Shrine**. Centred around a cashew nut tree (apparently moved from the site where Chao Mae Lim Kor Niew hanged herself), and around figures of this tragic figure (now revered as a goddess) carved out of cashew nut wood this shrine is a major focus of pilgrimage for Malaysian, Thai and Singaporean ethnic Chinese. Fairly gaudy and mostly modern, it is the major tourist location for Pattani's current tourism market. Ceremonies to pay respect to the goddess are held every year during the 3rd month of the lunar calendar (about two weeks after Chinese New Year). During this time the main statue of the goddess is paraded around the streets. The street in which the shrine is located is the oldest in the town of Pattani and contains some lovely examples of Sino-Thai architecture. If you walk down towards the river, there is also a pleasant walk along the river front where there are also some beautiful examples of traditional architecture and picturesque sights of boats on the river. There is also an interesting Chinese clan house **Muun Nithi Chao Ong Sua**. In any case, Pattani is a very picturesque town, particularly along the river, where the **harbour** is choked with gaily painted fishing vessels including the *ko-lae* for which Pattani is famous.

Excursions For excursions from Pattani, see page 410.

Sleeping For a provincial capital, Pattani is remarkably devoid of hotels and guesthouses. There is just one up-market hotel – the *CS Pattani*. That said, this has to be one of the nicest (if not THE nicest) of this class of hotel in the whole of this part of the southern region of Thailand.

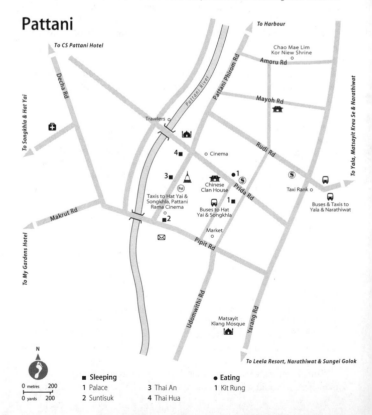

Pattani

■ **Sleeping**
1 Palace
2 Suntisuk
3 Thai An
4 Thai Hua

● **Eating**
1 Kit Rung

Muslims in a Buddhist world

The far south of Thailand is more Muslim than Buddhist and successive governments' failure to integrate the Muslim population into the mainstream has created animosity – and fuelled a long-running separatist movement. In the early 1970s a separatist group, the United Pattani Freedom Movement (bankrolled by Colonel Gadaffi), sprang up in defiance of heavy-handed Thai bureaucracy. A decade later their rebellion had all but died out, but the seeds of alienation remain today. In recent years the King has tried to make Muslims feel more a part of

the Thai nation – by presenting awards for Koranic studies and meeting with Muslim leaders. However, Malay Muslims remain unenthusiastic celebrants of water festivals and other Buddhist holidays which dominate the Thai calendar. At the end of 1997 a bomb damaged the bridge over the Pattani River and two weeks later another bomb was planted at a police station, injuring three officers. Right at the end of December a fire broke out at a school in the province. In each instance, Muslim separatists were thought to have been at work.

B *CS Pattani Hotel*, 299 M4, Nongjik Rd, a little out of town on the same road as the Provincial Hall. T335093-4, F331620, cspatani@cscoms.com Established by a 4th generation wealthy business Chinese-Pattani family and associated with the sports club and restaurant next door (all facilities are available to guests including badminton courts, two pools, sauna, etc). The *CS Pattani* has been designed and is operated with love and care. The friendly, western-educated, owner and manager is frequently on hand to welcome guests. Rooms are spacious and well designed (the corner doubles are beautiful with lots of light), and suites are very spacious. Twins are cheaper than the doubles. All the amenities you could ask for and some extra details to leave you feeling very well-cared for (including tea and coffee-making facilities, excellent mattresses and great big beds). The design of the hotel draws much from the southern heritage – staff are dressed in traditional southern-style uniforms, and southern music is softly played in the elevators and corridors! The details even extend to the excellent buffet breakfast included in the price where different local specialities are served every day along with the usual western and Asian favourites. Extremely well run, this hotel makes every guest feel welcome even when it is swamped with local and international bigwigs! Highly recommended. Incidentally a small point of interest for this hotel is that the basement has apparently been colonised by swiftlets of the edible-nest species. This is considered to be a very good omen and is also quite a lucrative side business. Dark and slightly damp, the basement must resemble a cave to the swiftlets. **B-D** *My Gardens*, 8/28 Charoenpradit Rd, west of town, T348933, F348200. Some a/c, restaurant, a good hotel with clean and spacious rooms – it is about 1 km out of town though. **C** *Leela Resort*, 52 km south of Pattani (10 km from Chana), T7120144. Some a/c. **D-E** *Palace Hotel*, 190 Prida Rd (behind the *Chong Ar Restaurant*), T349039. Some a/c, the closest thing Pattani has to luxury in the centre of town, large attached restaurant, rooms are OK. **E** *Suntisuk*, 1/16 Pipit Rd, T349122. The best of the cheaper Chinese hotels, attached bathrooms, some rooms with TV, friendly owner and central. **E** *Thai An*, 67 Pattani Phirom Rd, T348267. Basic.

Thai Mid-range: *Diana* (opposite *My Gardens Hotel*), opens 1800, seafood speciality. *River*, Rong-Ang Rd (road straight down from clock tower to the river). Set on a bend in the river, very picturesque, excellent Thai menu. Recommended by locals. **Cheap**: *Black Coffee*, on the roundabout by the clock tower. Good selection of coffees, menu in Thai. *Kit Rung*, Prida Rd (next to the Bangkok Bank).   **Eating**

Splitting the birds' nests

A curiosity on the same street as the Mae Lim Ko Nieow shrine in Pattani is a Chinese shophouse with two clear entrance ways. The house has been divided through a feud over the lucrative dividends from collecting birds' nests. Apparently, the swiftlets that produce edible nests have been nesting in this house for a couple of generations, and collection of the nests produces a very considerable income (up to ฿400,000 baht per month!). A family feud at the current generation has resulted in the house being physically divided. Only the level with the birds' nests is left complete and there is only one staircase up to this level. Every month the two sides of the family make an appointment to meet and collect the nests together – this being the only way they feel confident of not being cheated.

Chinese Mid-range: *Chong Ar*, 190 Prida Rd. Large selection of dishes at this large restaurant attached to the *Palace Hotel*. *Pailin* (*My Gardens Hotel* restaurant), also serves seafood. **Pornthip**, 9/38 Watanatham Rd, T348123. Large fancy restaurant with a huge menu with all the expensive specialities, prices quoted are for parties of 6-10, so no need to panic, open 1000-0200.

Foodstalls There is a row of good *kuaytiaw* shops on Pipit Rd not far from the bridge.

Entertainment Music *Black Coffee*, by the clock tower, band in the evenings. *Pornthip*, live Chinese pop band.

Sports Golf: there is a golf driving range around 3 km out of town on the road to Hat Yai/Songkhla.

Festivals March *Chao Mae Lim Kornaeo* (2nd weekend) fire-walking festival.

Transport Local Songthaews: ฿5 around town.

1,149 km from Bangkok
115 km from Hat Yai
105 km from Songkhla

Air There is a THAI office in town, and an airport about 15 km out of town on the way to Hat Yai and Songkhla but in 1999 THAI were still operating no service, having suspended it in 1994. **Road Bus**: buses leave from the intersection of Rudi/Ramkomud/Yarang roads. Overnight connections with Bangkok's Southern bus terminal on Pinklao-Nakhon Chaisi Rd, 15 hrs. Regular connections with Narathiwat and Hat Yai. **Taxis**: most taxis leave from stands near the bus stops on Yarang Rd, taxis to Hat Yai leave from near the bridge.

Directory Airline offices *THAI*, 8 Prida Rd, T394149. **Banks** Bank with currency exchange on Rudi Rd, not far from intersection with Yarang Rd. *Bangkok Bank*, corner of Prida and Udomwithi roads. **Communications Internet:** Several cafés and computer shops on the road leading up the Prince of Songkhla University, Pattani campus. **Post Office:** Pipit Rd (not far from the bridge).

Excursions from Pattani

Matsayit Kreu Se The oldest mosque in the area, Matsayit Kreu Se lies 8 km east of Pattani, on Route 42 in the village of Ban Kreu Se. The mosque was built in 1578 by Lim To Khieng, a Chinese immigrant who married a local Pattani woman and converted to Islam. His betrothal was not received enthusiastically by his family, and on hearing the news his sister travelled from China to dissuade him and encourage him to return to the fold. Unable to persuade him to return, it is reported that his sister (Chao Mae Lim Kor Niew) hanged herself from a cashew nut tree but not before cursing the mosque so that it could never be completed (a shrine to the tragic figure is in town – see above). Its brick walls and arches are still standing in a well-tended garden and the mosque is in use today. Locals say that after 400 years, plans are afoot to finish its construction, but would-be contractors risk being struck by lightning: this is said to be the fate awaiting those who try. Though the story is quaint the mosque is unremarkable. ■ *Getting there: bus to Narathiwat.*

Yarang Ancient Town

Located in Tambon Wat of Yarang district, Yarang Ancient Town is believed to be the site of the ancient city of Lankasuka which is referred to in trading documents of the period. This major archaeological site of the South consists of at least two sites in Ban Wat and Ban Prawae townships. Occupation at the larger and more important settlement at Ban Wat dates back to the 6th-8th centuries. Unfortunately, the Fine Arts Department has only a limited budget and there is not as much interpretation of the information available on this site as one might wish. Many of the artefacts found here have been moved to the Songkhla National Museum, some are also to be found in the museum at the Prince of Songkhla University campus in Pattani. ■ *Getting there: bus to Yarang and songthaew or motorcycle taxi to the old town (muang borahn).*

Wat Chang Hai Rasburanaram

This is another temple with an ancient legend and a venerable past. Apparently the temple was established when Governor Gaemdam of Saiburi wanted to build a city for his sister, Jehsiti. He made a wish and sent off two elephants to find a suitably propitious location for the new city followed by the Governor, his sister and their entourage. The elephants came to the spot where Wat Chang Hai is located (hence the name *chang hai* or bestowed by elephants) and circled the area three times. Unfortunately, the setting didn't please Jehsiti and another site was eventually chosen and named Pattani (originally at Krue Se). However, on the Governor's return he passed the place the elephants chose and decided to build a temple. After his return to Saiburi, he invited Somdej Prakoh, or Luang Pu Thuad (of Wat Pakho fame in Songkhla) to be the abbot of this new temple. Before Luang Pu Tuad passed away at Saiburi, he gave instructions that he be cremated at Chang Hai temple. A stupa was subsequently built here to enshrine his remains. This is considered a major site of pilgrimage for southern Buddhists and is the venue where annual rituals are carried out to bless the remains of this most revered southern monk. Most of the temple buildings are fairly new, but the *Wat Chang Hai Vocational Training Centre* is quite interesting and a good place to look for local handicrafts. ■ *Getting there: take route from Pattani to Khok Pho district. The turn-off to the temple is about 30 km from Pattani and then a further 1 km up the road.*

Wat Chang Hai Vocational Training Centre just down the road from the Chang Hai temple was set up by a former governor of Pattani in response to suggestions from Her Majesty the Queen. Local people are trained in the production of handicrafts and arts such as silk-weaving, basketry, embroidery, the manufacture of *kris*, engraving of the *kris hilt*, and the manufacture of *korlae* boats and miniature boats. All these can be purchased at the centre and on occasion you can see them being made there too. Unfortunately, this centre has not taken off as a major tourist destination and the stock and number of activities being carried out at any one time varies enormously. ■ *Getting there: take route 409 to Khok Pho district. The turn-off to the temple is about 30 km from Pattani and then little way up the road to Wat Chang Hai.*

Paseyawor Village

About 50 km from the provincial town and some 2 km from Saiburi District. Paseyawor Village is known for the production of the colourful *korlae* boats.

The Gulf of Thailand

Racing of the boats is held annually in the village. Although similar to the boats of *Ban Thon* in Narathiwat province, apparently the *korlae* boats of Pattani are distinct in their design and decoration. You'd need to have a pretty finely tuned sense of design and decoration to spot this at first glance though! ■ *Getting there: take a local bus to Saiburi district and a songthaew to Paseyawor Village.*

Sai Khao National Park Sai Khao National Park is located in Kohk Pho district, about 33 km from Pattani off Route 409 between Pattani and Yala. The route to the waterfall is well signposted, about 6 km down the turn-off to Wat Huai Ngoh. A popular recreational spot on the weekends, the visitors centre is located near the waterfall – a lovely cascade, 40 m in height, with 10 levels. There are several other waterfalls in the 110-sq-km park. There are some forestry department bungalows available for rent. The Forestry Department runs treks into the park from February to July every year providing camping gear and a (Thai-speaking) guide. T431344 (during working hours). ■ *Getting there: take the route 409 between Pattani and Yala and follow the signs to the national park. Alternatively, take a songthaew from Khok Pho town on Route 409.*

Folk Studies Museum The Folk Studies Museum (*Pipitapan katichonwittaya*) is in the grounds of the Prince of Songkhla University Pattani Campus. There are actually two museums. The first, in the temple-like building, contains a mixed collection of artefacts donated to the museum by a famous monk (things used by the monk are held on the first floor up the stairs). Of most interest are the pieces of traditional Pattani cloth which has not been woven for about a century. Unfortunately there are almost no labels in either English or Thai anywhere in the museum and the only explanatory information on the fabric is in a Thai pamphlet. Behind this museum is the modern building housing the folk studies collection. Not the best of these types of collections in the South (the Institute of Folk Studies in Songkhla province is more extensive and better laid out) but there are some lovely pictures of the traditional Malay-style houses of this part of the South. Unfortunately these are about the only exhibits with no English labels at all! The museum also contains a Chinese gravestone believed to be the oldest in Southeast Asia and demonstrating the long links between Pattani's port and the Chinese trading communities in this area. ■ *Getting there: songthaews and taxis, ask for 'mahawitiyalai songkhla-nakarin' and then for the 'pipitipan' when you get into the grounds.*

Beaches
There are some lovely beaches all along the coast from the north near Songkhla down to Saiburi district

Laem Ta Chee, Ta Chee peninsular, lies just beyond Pattani town and can be reached by boat taxi from the pier in the town, or by driving the 30 km along its length (it might be possible to negotiate with a *songthaew* driver to take you there, but otherwise self-drive is pretty much the only option). No accommodation to date, and not a huge amount to do, but this is still an interesting viewpoint for the sea and the mainland.

It should be borne in mind that the deep south is not the place for stripping off to sunbathe. Most local visitors will be dressed in at least a T-shirt and shorts when they enter the water; anything less would be regarded as deeply shocking and indecent. **Rachadapisek** lies around 13 km west of town. Stalls are set up under the casuarina trees and at weekends demurely attired locals frolic carefully. About the same distance east of town is **Talo Kapo Beach** – more a fishing village than a resort, but the beach is OK and there are various vendors and stall keepers, especially at weekends. **Khae Khae Beach** is one of the prettiest beaches along the coast, with yellow sand and some lovely rock formations in a small bay with a hilly backdrop, about 30 km to the south of the main town. A local favourite is **Wasukri Beach** about 80 km from Pattani town on highway 42. This is a long stretch of white sand with casuarina trees and a gently sloping beach good for swimming. Gradually, small bungalow operations are setting up along the coast north and south of Pattani – most of these cater to middle-class Thais, with air-conditioning, a small restaurant, etc. Prices are mostly in the **B-D** range. As individual bungalow operations are somewhat isolated from anything else, this may be a better option for those with their own transport rather than for travellers dependent on local buses. If you do want to take local transport, most beaches to the north (and bungalow operations) can be reached by taking the Pattani-Songkhla bus or the Pattani-Hat Yai bus and getting off when you see a sign to a bungalow.

Narathiwat

Narathiwat is an Islamic stronghold and has one of the biggest mosques in southern Thailand. There is also a **Muslim fishing village – Ban Thon** just beyond the market to the north of the town, where they still use the brightly painted *kor lae* – traditional fishing boats with curved bows and tails. Today the *kor lae* is an endangered species: diesel-powered Darwinism dictates that long-tails do it better. Across the bridge from the Muslim village is a pleasant beach area known as of Hat Narathat, rather like Samila Beach at Songkhla. There are several small outdoor restaurants serving seafood and it is a popular spot with locals and visiting Malaysians.

Phone code: 073
Coloured map 6, grid A3

The town's two main **mosques** are a contrast in architectural styles. At the northern edge of town, close to the Muslim fishing village, is a new mosque built in modern style, while in the centre of town, near the clock tower, is the wooden **Mesjid Klang** or Central Mosque built over 100 years ago. No prizes for guessing which is the more appealing.

While the Communist Party of Thailand may have become part of Thailand's history, there is another nasty little conflict which continues. The Pattani National Liberation Organization or PULO, along with its off-shoot New PULO, continue to battle for the independence of this slice of Thailand. In September 1993, PULO guerrillas ambushed a train in Narathiwat province, killing one Thai student and injuring nine other passengers. There have also been a spate of arson attacks, most recently in 1998 when New PULO (it was assumed), blew up some earth-moving equipment. While for many Thais Narathiwat conjures up images of Muslim extremists the town is, in fact, remarkably peaceful and relaxed with a pleasant walk along the river and some interesting old houses on the street at the riverfront.

Wat Khao Kong is 6 km southwest of town. The centre piece of this monastery is a 25 m-high seated golden (but bronze) Buddha image (Phra Buddha Taksin Ming Mongkol) – making it the largest seated image in Thailand – built on a small hill. It is more than 15 m from knee to knee and decorated with gold mosaic tiles. ■ *Getting there: songthaew (₿5).*

Excursions

Taksin Palace is the Royal Summer Palace on Manao Bay, 8 km south of Narathiwat, off the main Narathiwat-Tak Bai Road. The palace is worth a visit for its beautifully kept gardens right on the coast. There is also a small zoo here, and a handicraft centre under the SUPPORT project (an income-generation project under the patronage of Her Majesty the Queen). Products in the handicraft centre may seem a little on the pricey side when compared with similar products to be found around Thailand, but the quality of the workmanship is truly excellent. The palace itself is modern and not of great interest. ■ *Mon-Sun, 0800-1200, 1300-1630 except when the King or Queen are in residence (usually between Aug and Sep). Getting there: songthaew (₿8).*

The Gulf of Thailand

Hala Bala Wildlife Sanctuary lies adjacent to one of the larger forested areas in Malaysia and covers parts of Narathiwat and Yala province. The proximity to forests in Malaysia means that although covering only a small area, it is exceptionally rich in plant and animal species. Several hornbills, including the rhinoceros

Narathiwat place names

Taksin Palace

พระตำหนักทักษิณราชนิเวศน์

Wat Khao Kong

วัดเขากง

hornbill can be found in this sanctuary. Access to Hala Bala can be either from Betong district in Yala or Waeng district in Narathiwat. Prospective visitors interested in going to the sanctuary to study the wildlife there (eg birdwatchers) are requested to contact the sanctuary office in advance (Hala Bala Wildlife Sanctuary, PO Box 3, Amphur Waeng, Narathiwat 96120).

The **Sirindhorn Peat Swamp Forest Nature Study and Research Centre** is located on the way to Sungei Golok from Tak Bai and is located at the edge of one of the few remaining areas of freshwater peat forest (Pa Pru) in Thailand. Bird species found in the forest include Malaysian blue flycatcher, rufous-tailed shama, red-crowned barbet and the rare garnet pitta. The small mouse deer can also be seen on occasion. An English-language handbook is available at the centre providing information on the history and ecology of the forest. A board walk nature trail has been laid out through the forest with the entrance just behind the visitors centre. Various nature interpretation signs have been posted along the trail and there is a tower which bird watchers can use for observation purposes. ■ *0800-1600, T01-7150159. Getting there: from Sungei Golok on Route 4057 to Tak Bai, at Km 5 turn at the Chawanant intersection, head along this route for approximately 5 km and you will reach the centre.*

Talo Mano or Wadi Al-Hussein Mosque a beautiful wooden mosque in Amphur Ba Jo, is known in places as the '200-year-old mosque' or the '300-year-old mosque'. Some literature gives the date of foundation as AD 1624, while others argue it was built in AD 1769. The entire building was built without the use of nails or screws. The design and decoration of the mosque incorporates Chinese-, Malay- and Thai-style reliefs carved in wood. ■ *Getting there: take Route 42 from Narathiwat to Pattani, and take the exit for Ban Beu Ra Ngair.*

Beaches There are several good beaches and a handful of resorts between Narathiwat and Tak Bai. Few Westerners stop off in these places – they are mostly used by Malaysians. The beaches are deserted and safe for swimming, although it's not the cleanest stretch of sand in Thailand. **Sleeping C-D** *Panon Resort*, T514749, 3 km from Taksin Palace (signposted off the main road). This resort has beach-front chalets, a golf driving range (of all things!), and large gardenc. A/c, restaurant, concrete bungalows and chalets, cheaper motel-style rooms a bit like factory units. ■ *Getting there: songthaew (฿10).*

Ao Manao (or Lime Bay) is another stretch of beach, this with a national parks office, considered to be the most beautiful in the area by most natives of Narathiwat. It is a long bay with yellow sand, lined with casuarinas and some picturesque rocks at each end. **Sleeping C-D** *Ao Manao Resort*, small bungalows and rooms in a hotel block. Plain but adequate. No hot water in any of the rooms. Fan and a/c. ■ *Getting there: songthaew (฿10).* The bay is about 3 km out of the provincial town off the route south to Tak Bai.

Most of the hotels are strung out along and just off Pichit Bamrung Rd. **B** *Royal Princess Narathiwat*, 228 Pichit Bamrung Rd, T515041, F515040, rsvnctr @dusit.com This 117-room hotel opened in 1997. Plush carpets and solid doors herald your entry into sumptuous if predictable rooms. The service is good and the price (in the off season, at the low end of our banding) is superb. There is a pleasant pool, which can also be used by non-residents. **C** *Tanyong*, 16/1 Sophaphisai Rd, T511477, F511834. A/c, restaurant, once the best hotel in town, the Tanyong hasn't yet adjusted to the idea of competition, clean and well appointed but overpriced and rather noisy. The snooker club, disco and massage parlour give the game away. **C-D** *Ban Burong*, T511027. A pleasant building on the river, only 3 rooms – apparently all with views. The owner runs a visa extension service for people spending more than a couple of months in Thailand. Canoes, bicycles and motorbikes are available for rent. Just opposite is a small bakery that does various plain and creamy cakes, ice cream, cold drinks, *salapao* (delicious), and some very nice 'butterscotch' buns – well priced too!

Sleeping
■ *on maps*
Price codes: see inside front cover

Narathiwat

To Taksin Palace & Tak Bai (30 km)

D *Pacific*, 42/1-2 Warakhamphiphit Rd, T511076. Some a/c, restaurant, cheerless rooms but good value. **D-E** *Rex*, 6/1-2 Chamroonnara Rd, T511134, F511190. A/c, restaurant, clean, airy and well-kept rooms. **D-E** *Yaowarat*, 131 Pichit Bamrung Rd, T511148, F511320. A/c, Chinese-run and characteristically clean, tidy – and rather characterless. **E** *Cathay*, 275 Pupha Pakdi Rd, T511014. Another Chinese warehouse-like hotel, lazy management, lacklustre but adequate rooms. **E** *Narathiwat*, 341 Pupha Pakdi Rd, T511063. Attractive wooden building on waterfront, shared bathrooms with Asian toilets. Building has charm but rooms are dreary. **E-F** *Bang Nara*, 274 Pupha Pakdi Rd, T511036. Clean and large rooms.

Thai Expensive-mid-range: *Mangkornthong*, Chinese and Thai on the river with plenty of seafood. Popular with local business people. Good views and plentiful servings of well-cooked food. **Cheap**: *Boonthong*, 55 Sophapisai Rd. *Run Thai*, Satilraya Rd. *Chittawat*, opposite the *Cathay Hotel* on Pupha Pakdi Rd. More of a bakery with a sitting area, but good for light snacks and refreshments. *Makanan Islam*, Pichit Bamrung Rd. Muslim delicacies, quite cheap but nothing extravagant.

International Mid-range: *Nida Foodland*, Sophapisai Rd. Chinese. *Rimnam*, 3 km down Tak Bai Rd, T511559. The town's most sophisticated restaurant patronized by the high society of Narathiwat, it's a longish hike out of

Eating
● *on maps*
Price codes: see inside front covert

The Gulf of Thailand

town on the road south, but worth the trouble, seafood and curries. **Cheap**: *Smerp*, opposite *Yaowarat* on Chamroonnara Rd. Foremost ice creams and cold drinks. *Tanyong Hotel*, 16/1 Sophapisai Rd. Set-meal rates, huge restaurant, band at night.

Seafood Line of scruffy seafood stalls along the beach just to the north of town. **Mid-range**: *Bang Nara*, Tak Bai Rd (by the bridge). A little out of town, but excellent seafood and views over the mosquito-infested river. **Cheap**: *Nasir*, Pichit Bamrung Rd. Also serves Thai and Malay food.

Festivals May *Jao Mae To-Mo Fair.*

September *Narathiwat Fair* (3rd week), *Kor lae* boat racing takes place on the Bang Nara River. Dove cooing contests and sale of local produce.

Sport **Swimming**: non-residents can use the pool at the *Royal Princess Narathiwat*, 228 Pichit Bamrung Rd.

Transport **Local Songthaews and motorbike taxis** from opposite the market.

1,315 km from Bangkok

Air Airport north of town. **THAI** operate a minibus for passengers to and from their office in the centre of town. Daily connections with Bangkok via Phuket.

Road Bus: buses leave from near the Muslim fishing village and from Pichit Bamrung Rd. Overnight connections with Bangkok 17 hrs. Regular connections with Hat Yai, Pattani, Yala and Sungei Golok. **Taxi**: from Pichit Bamrung Rd.

Directory **Airline offices** *Thai*, 322-324 Phupha Pakdi Rd, T511161. **Banks** *Thai Farmers*, Phupha Pakdi Rd, beyond Thai Airlines office. There are also branches of other major banks in the centre of town. **Communications** Internet: computer shops providing internet services can be found in the shophouses just across from the *Royal Princess Hotel* (friendly owner who speaks some English and can give information about places to visit in Narathiwat), and down Jitpatima Rd. **Post Office:** Pichit Bamrung Rd (south of the clock tower). **Telephone Office:** international calls can be placed at the telephone office attached to the GPO on Pichit Bamrung Rd.

Tak Bai and Ta Ba

Colour map 6, grid B3

Tak Bai is the first village on the road south from Narathiwat; its major attraction is **Wat Chonthala Singh**, the last bastion of Thai Buddhist culture before the Malaysian border. When Malaya's British colonial administration laid claim to the former Thai provinces that are now the states of Perlis and Kedah (to the west), at the beginning of the century, they had their eyes on Narathiwat too. Rama V defiantly built this strategically important wat to stake Siam's territorial claim to the area.

Within its sprawling compound are a collection of sadly dilapidated wooden buildings in the beautiful and distinctive southern style. The monks, workmen and everyone else in and around the wat enclave speak Thai – nearly everyone else in Tak Bai speaks Malay. The wat is signposted off the road in Tak Bai (to get there, go straight through the market and turn left) and sits in a picturesque spot on the riverbank. Just down from the temple is a wooden walkway which leads out to Koh Yao – a small island with some fishing villages. This area has been settled for over a hundred years. A peaceful place for a stroll with attractive views.

Peculiar to this region is the longkorn, a golf-ball-sized fruit

Two kilometres down the road from Tak Bai is the small port town of **Ta Ba**, where passenger and car ferries ply the river to and from Malaysia. Ta Ba has an exciting, colourful **market**, with what must be some of the juiciest, tastiest fruit in Southeast Asia – particularly during the mango and durian seasons.

All the hotels are on the road to Narathiwat, about 1 km from the port of Ta Ba.   **Sleeping**

Taba Plaza, 7/20 Takbai-Taba Rd, T581234. A/c, restaurant. **C** *Takbai Lagoon Resort*, 311/2 Moo 7 Tambon Che Hey (signposted on main road), T581478, tlagoon @cscoms.com A/c, restaurant, same price as *Taba Plaza*, but better. Canoes and bicycles for rent here. **C C-D** *Masaya Resort*, 58/7 Muangmai Rd, T581125. Some a/c, restaurant, clean and best of the 3. **D** *Pornphet*, 58/22 Takbai Rd, T581331. Some a/c, restaurant. Off the main road. Now looking slightly jaded, but its OK if you want to stay in Tak Bai.

Taba Tours, Takbai-Taba Rd (next to *Taba Plaza Hotel*); express bus and train tickets   **Tour operators**
(from Sungei Golok).

Road   Bus: buses leave from pier by Ta Ba market and pick up passengers in Tak Bai. Reg-   **Transport**
ular connections with Narathiwat and Sungei Golok. **Taxi**: from pier by Ta Ba market.   *39 km from Narathiwat*

Ta Ba is a little-used but speedy crossing-point between Thailand and Malaysia, as taxi   **Transport to**
and bus stands on both sides are adjacent to the ferry. The disadvantage is that Ta Ba   **Malaysia**
is not well connected with other towns in Thailand, although it is easy enough to get
to Sungei Golok (just 32 km to the west) for the train north.

Boat The border is open Mon-Sun 0700-1600 (Thai time). Passenger ferry crossing
from next to Ta Ba market and bus stop. If crossing with a car it is necessary to go
through the customs section in a large compound next door. Regular crossings from
Ta Ba to Pengkalan Kubor, Malaysia. On the Malaysian side, there are regular buses
from Pengkalan Kubor to Kota Bahru.

Banks Bank next to the *Taba Plaza Hotel* with exchange facilities. *Krung Thai* in Tak Bai and *Thai*   **Directory**
Military Bank in Ta Ba.

Yala

Yala is the capital of the only landlocked province on the Kra Isthmus. Con-   **Sights**
spicuously prosperous, much of its wealth has been built on the rubber indus-   *Phone code: 073*
try. The town has a bit of a split personality. South of the railway line it feels   *Colour map 6, grid A2*
very Chinese. The buildings show southern-Chinese influences, particularly
in their roof styles, the hotels are run by Sino-Thais, and many of the restaurants serve Chinese food – and, like the shops, use Chinese as well as Thai characters in their names. North of the railway line, on Sirias Road, is the notably
muslim **Central Mosque** – a modern brick-and-concrete affair – as well as
Malay-style houses (sadly, though, being demolished with enthusiasm), Muslim food, demure women in headscarves, and men in sarongs and wearing the
white skull cap indicating they have made the Haj to Mecca.
    Wat Phutaphoom on Pipitpakdi Road has a highly visible, albeit unremark-
able, standing Buddha in its extensive grounds. Not far away on Phutphumvithi
Road is the Chinese **Mair Lim Niao** temple. **Chuang Phuak Park**, to the north
of the railway station, is a popular spot with locals, offering a large man-made
lake with boats for hire. Founded as a provincial capital in 1933, the city is well
laid out with broad avenues and leafy parks and has received the accolade of
being voted the 'cleanest city in Thailand' on several occasions.

The Gulf of Thailand

Excursions Travelling south from Hat Yai or Songkhla towards Yala and Pattani, the change from 'Buddhist' Thailand to 'Muslim' Thailand is very evident. Pigs make an exit while goats begin to make an appearance nibbling away at the verges; wats give way to village mosques; houses become more Malay with their tiled roofs and fretwork barge boards, while caged song birds hang in the verandahs; and the extravagant flares and bell bottoms of the cities of the north are replaced by the sarong and headscarf.

Yala place names

Bang Lang Dam

เขื่อนบางลาง

Than To National Park

อุทยานแห่งชาติธารโต

Bang Lang Dam lies 12 km off the Yala-Betong road, 10 km south of Ban Nang Sata. The road twists up through the hills to two small villages, Ban Santi 1 and 2 on the far side of the lake. There is a very picturesque drive overlooking the lake, which is dotted with tiny islands. **Than To National Park** is another 3 km further down the Yala-Betong Road. **Sleeping** E Bungalows by the lake, run by the Electricity Generating Authority of Thailand (EGAT), T213699, reservations essential as it is a popular venue for conferences; the road to the bungalows is to the right up a very steep hill just after the entrance barrier, restaurant, pool and tennis courts. ■ *Getting there: songthaew from the railway station.*

Wat Khuha (also known as **Wat Khuha Phimuk** or, popularly, **Wat Naa Tham**) – one of the most important monuments in the south – is signposted off the Yala-Hat Yai road (Route 409 to the provincial town of Yaha), 8 km northwest of town on the left-hand side. It is around a kilometre walk to the cave temple from the main road – the limestone outcrop gives the game away. A small museum by the entrance to the **cave temple** exhibits some of the Srivijayan finds from the area: votive tablets, manuscripts and small bronze figures. Wat Khuha was assumed by archaeologists to have been an important religious centre in the south during the Srivijaya Period from the seventh to 13th century. The 25-m reclining Buddha – Phra Phutthasaiyat – is in the main cave sanctuary of this pleasant cave temple. Its sprawling interior is dramatically lit by shafts of light. The statue has been restored and is believed to have an older Bodhisattva figure inside. The original image dates from 757 AD, and was commissioned by the Srivijayan King of Palembang (Sumatra). There are a couple of other cave temples to explore nearby – take the path along the bottom of the rock face. The caves are huge and well illuminated but not especially interesting. There are several other caves in the area including **Tham Sumphao Thong**, signposted in Thai off the road about 3 km back towards the city. Notable here are, reportedly, a collection of Srivijayan murals although murals in their original state (that is untouched-up) would never have survived this long. ■ *Getting there: songthaew from the railway station.*

Ban Sakai, home to some of Thailand's few remaining so-styled 'hunter-gatherers' (they scarcely count as such today) is accessible from Yala but really only by hired vehicle (see page 423 for more details).

Sleeping
■ *on maps*
Price codes: see inside front cover

B *Chang Lee*, Sirirot Rd, T211223, F211773. A/c, restaurant, 16-storey hotel and Yala's pride and joy – although it is hard to see why. It opened in 1995 and while Yala's great and good may congregate here – and the rooms are very comfortable – service is slow and unenthusiastic. This is surpsiring because just a few years ago the staff seemed to be bubbling over with pride that they were working in such a cosmopolitan place. Now they are thin on the ground and seemingly keen to avoid contact with guests! **B-C** *Yala Rama*, 21 Sribamrung Rd, T212563, F214532. A/c, restaurant, until 1995 this was the best hotel in town, rooms are comfortable, with satellite TV and are very well priced, facilities include the requisite disco, Karaoke bar, massage parlour and snooker club. Although it's been eclipsed by the *Chang Lee* as Yala's No 1 spot, it is still very acceptable, a lot cheaper and friendly.

D-E *Cola Hotel*, Kotchasani 1 Rd, T212208. Some a/c, rather a dingy place with what seems like a regular turn around of short-stay customers. **D-E** *Saensuk*, *Muang Thong* and *Metro*, Ratakit Rd. Three Chinese hotels with very little to choose between them, in fact they seem to be competing in a cunning look-like-your-neighbour competition. Reasonable food served downstairs in each, average rooms bordering on the grubby upstairs. How you find the rooms seems to depend on the day of the week or the month of the year but the *Metro* got our vote at the last visit. **D-E** *Sri Yala*, 16-22 Chaicharat Rd, T212170. Some a/c, restaurant. Fair rooms but the prices are not competitive. **D-E** *Thepwimarn*, 31-37 Sribamrung Rd, T212400. Some a/c, restaurant, basic and rambling, rooms are fine and it is probably the best place to stay at this price. It is not, however, a palace of deity nor pleasant as territory heavenly, as they claim, although for wishful thinking the management deserve top marks.

E *Hua Ann*, Sirirot Rd, T212989. A classic Chinese hotel with 40-odd rooms, feels more like a converted warehouse than a hotel, rooms are OK with attached bathrooms. Popular with travelling salesmen, which just about sums it up – a bed for the night, nothing more, the management, though, appealingly bill their hotel as the hotel 'which makes you feel at home but with a service which makes you feel like a king'! **E-F** *Aun Aun Hotel*, 32-36 Pipitpakdi Rd, T212216. Typical Chinese affair, sombre but clean rooms. Good for budget travellers. **E-F** *Phan Far Hotel*, Sirirot Rd, right next door to *Hua Ann* and very similar in price and standard – nothing to choose between them. **E-F** *Daan Naman*,

Yala centre

Sleeping	8 Phan Far	2 Fast Food Joint
1 Aun Aun	9 Saensuk	3 Luuk Ket
2 Chang Lee	10 Sri Yala	4 Seafood Restaurant
3 Cola	11 Thepwimarn	
4 Daan Naman	12 Yala Rama	🚌 Transport
5 Hua Ann		1 To Hat Yai
6 Metro	● Eating	2 To Pattani
7 Muang Thong	1 Ai Hiang	3 Bus Station

The Gulf of Thailand

Phutphumvithi Rd. Central location and a rather fetching lime green colour scheme, but otherwise nothing to recommended it – except price perhaps.

Eating
● *on maps*
Price codes: see inside front cover

Expensive-cheap: *Ai Hiang* (name only in Thai and Chinese), corner of Phutphumvithi and Kotchasani 3 roads. Excellent little Chinese restaurant, it looks very average, but the food is good and prepared and cooked in a bank of woks for all to see. Recommended. **Mid-range**: *Luuk Ket*, Pipitpakdi Rd. A/c restaurant, good for ice creams and a cool off, also serves regular Thai dishes like fried rice of mediocre quality. *Yala Rama Coffee Shop*, 21 Sribamrung Rd. Reasonable Thai buffet and international food. *Unnamed seafood restaurant* (see map for location), seafood cooked before you in this open, corner side restaurant. *Thai fast-food joint* (see map for location), burgers, chicken, etc – a Western incursion, virtually the only gastronomic one in the town.

Entertainment

Wild West, Rotfai Rd. Folk music in the evenings.

Festivals

February *Chinese New Year* (movable) celebrated enthusiastically by Yala's large population of Sino-Thais.

March *Dove competition* (1st weekend), and ASEAN competition, with exhibitions.

May/June *Yala city pillar* celebrations (movable) in honour of the town's guardian spirit, Jao Paw Lak Muang. Traditional southern Thai entertainment such as shadow puppet performances. A great time to be in the city if you are interested in southern Thai culture.

Shopping

Books *Bookshop*, Sribamrung Rd (close to the *Yala Rama Hotel*), sells mostly Thai-language books but does also carry English-language newspapers.

Transport
1,153 km from Bangkok
178 km from Hat Yai

Air There is no airport at Yala – the nearest is outside Pattani. However, there is a **Thai Airways** office in town, on Pipitpakdi Rd. **Train** Station on northeast side of town. Overnight connections with Bangkok and other stops north. Also regular connections with Hat Yai and Sungei Golok.

Road Bus: Pattani buses leave from Pattani Rd on the far side of the railway track. Buses to all other destinations leave from the mini *bor kor sor* just southeast of the railway station, not far from the *Yala Rama Hotel*. Regular connections with Bangkok 16 hrs, Hat Yai 3 hrs, Songkhla 3 hrs, Pattani 2 hrs, Phetburi, Prachuap Khiri Khan, Phattalung, and Sungei Golok. Betong buses (mini Mercedes) leave mornings only. No buses to Narathiwat. **Taxi**: from along the road in front of the railway station – ask for the exact spot. **Share taxis** to Betong, Pattani, Hat Yai, and Songkhla each laying claim to a different piece of pavement.

Directory

Airline offices *THAI*, Pipitpakdi Rd (close to Bangkok Bank of Commerce). **Banks** *Bangkok Bank of Commerce*, Pipitpakdi Rd. *First Bangkok City Bank*, Pipitpakdi Rd. *Thai Military Bank*, Sirirot Rd. **Communications** Post Office: Sirirot Rd (100 m south of the *Chang Lee Hotel*). **Telephone Office:** international calls can be made from the Post Office on Sirirot Rd, or from the Telecom Office about 1-2 km out on Pipitpakdi Rd.

The Gulf of Thailand

Betong

After the magnificent mountain drive from Yala which winds up through dramatic limestone hills, Betong is a disappointing, ugly town, full of barbershops, massage parlours and hotels catering for Malaysians on cross-border weekends and 'business trips'. The only reason to come here is to leave it – to cross the border; it is a dreary town.

Phone code: 073
Colour map 6, grid B1

Until 1990, when Chin Peng's Communist Party of Malaya came out of the jungle and the rebels laid down their arms, Betong's forested hills concealed his HQ and acted as the base for guerrillas heading south down the peninsula. Joint Malaysian-Thai army patrols regularly mounted search-and-destroy missions against the CPM base, known ominously as 'Target One'. The Communists made this as difficult as possible by seeding trails with anti-personnel mines, which they are now being made to clear in joint Thai-Malaysian-CPM operations. Now that this subversive excitement is history, Betong's only claim to fame – other than its sex industry – is an **enormous postbox** which is said to be the biggest in the world, but is actually disappointingly diminutive.

Betong Hot Springs are situated 10 km from town; drive 3 km north on the road to Yala and then turn right onto a dirt track for a further 7 km. The big steaming pool is rather dirty, although the smaller pool is cleaner. The springs are in a pleasant setting surrounded by hills. There are several stalls catering mainly for elderly Chinese tour groups hoping for a cure or second lease of life.
■ *Getting there: hire a saamlor from Betong (฿100 upwards).*

Excursions

Highland Friendship Village (Pityamit One) is 10 km up the road from the hot springs and is a former jungle base camp belonging to the Marxist-Leninist faction of the Communist Party of Malaya, which fought the Malaysian and Thai armies from here for nearly 30 years (see box). Even the intelligence services of both armies were unaware of the existence of the camp until after the communists laid down their arms in 1989. At the entrance, there is now a 4 m-high statue of four white doves in the middle of a fountain. (This is the emblem of the

The Gulf of Thailand

Betong

To Hot Springs, Highland Friendship Village, Ban Sakai & Yala

Sukhayang Rd

Veeraphan Rd

Rattanasatien Rd

Penthouse Resort

Saritdech Rd

New
Tesachinda Rd

Tanta Veera Rd

To Wat Phutthathiwat & Hospital

Customs
Immigration

Soi Fah-unrung

Fa Un Rong

Chantarothai Rd

Jirajinda Rd

Samon Ta Rat Rd

Rattanakit Rd

To border (8 km)

Sukhayang Rd

Clock Tower

Sri Betong
Khong Kha

Chayachaowalit Rd

Merlin

Fortuna

Pakdidamrong Rd

Amarit Rd

Thammawithi Rd

Public Park

N

Not to scale

Pityamit One: from guerrilla camp to holiday camp

The Malayan Emergency was one of the few insurgencies which the Communists lost. But their shelling, ambushes, bombings and assassinations cost the lives of more than 10,000 soldiers and civilians over 40 years. The Emergency started just after the Second World War. At its peak, tens of thousands of Commonwealth troops were pitted against an estimated 3,500 Communists – most of whom were Chinese – in the Malayan jungle. Newly independent Malaysia pronounced the Emergency officially over in 1960. They had the Communists on the run. The guerrillas fled across Malaysia's jungled frontier into south Thailand – but once ensconced there, they held out for another 30 years against both the Malaysian and Thai armies.

Most of their secret camps were never found. The Communists had laced the border itself with booby trap devices and regularly launched attacks and ambushes across the border. The people on the frontline of the war were the residents of the Malaysian border town of Pengkalan Hulu (formerly Keroh), which means 'forward base'. Many atrocities were committed in and around the town, which was still under curfew until well into the 1980s. The Communists also made themselves unpopular in Thailand, where they demanded protection money from local businesses around Betong. They never surrendered, but finally, in 1989, they reached what was known as "an honourable settlement" with the Malaysian and Thai governments, bringing to an end one of the world's longest-running insurgencies. Realizing that most of the former guerrillas would be unwilling to return to their homeland, King Bhumipol of Thailand offered them land around their former camps and built

them houses. One of those camps, Pityamit I, has now opened to the public for the first time. Like others in the vicinity, nobody knew it was there until recently.

Having laid down their Kalashnikovs, former revolutionaries now take tourists round their old jungle stronghold. Some sell herbal medicine and soft drinks to the tourists; others have become vegetable farmers at the Highland Friendship Cooperative (the camp's new name). The trees which once afforded them thick cover from helicopter gunships have been chopped down and the steep hillsides have been planted out. About 1,200 former fighters have now settled into their new lives but few have any regrets about their old ones as members of the Communist Party of Malaya's pro-Moscow splinter group. "Money is important," one of them told a visiting journalist. "Without it you can't do anything." They are happy to regail tourists with tales of the jungle. Some have been living in it since 1948. Although they admit that Communism worldwide appears to have failed, they urge those who are prepared to listen not to jump to hasty conclusions: "The final decisions should be up to our sons and grandsons."

About 100 former Communists have returned to booming modern Malaysia. They are in detention under the country's Internal Security Act in Taiping, where in the words of their comrades across the border, they are being "rehabilitated" and "brain-washed". In Kuala Lumpur, few people stop to think of the Emergency years; they seem like ancient history now because things have moved so fast. But if it's all been partially forgotten, the Communists themselves have not been forgiven as the scars still run deep.

village – the former guerrillas themselves refer to them as 'peace pigeons'; literature from one Betong hotel misguidedly refers to the statue as 'a seagull memorial'). The camp's residents sell souvenirs to tourists and host guided tours of the old jungle camp itself, which is a 10-minute walk up the hillside to the right of the main entrance. Exhibits are carefully labelled; they include uniforms and other regalia and memorabilia of the former People's Liberation Army of Malaya. Camp facilities are on show – including the kitchen area which had an ingenious

•••••••••••••••••••••••

Betong place names

Ban Sakai

บ้านซาไก

Betong Hot Springs

น้ำพุร้อนเบตง

•••••••••••••••••••••••

flue, constructed so as to suck up the smoke and embers and release them on the other side of the hill enabling the camp's location to remain a secret. The pride of the camp, however, is its network of subterranean tunnels in which the comrades once sheltered from Malaysian mortars and Thai patrols. They took 50 cadres three months to dig, working round the clock in shifts. There are eating and sleeping areas and a radio communications room 10 m underground. Other nearby camps had similar tunnel systems, but they have not yet been opened to the public as their environs are still strewn with boobytraps. **Sleeping** *Friendship Resort*, Pityamit One, fan, food available at hot springs, clean little white rooms in two modern bungalows on hillside overlooking village, modestly furnished but a pleasant alternative to staying in Betong. ■ *Getting there: as with hot springs, hire saamlor/taxi from Betong (฿150-200).*

Ban Sakai is home to a community of formerly semi-nomadic Sakai 'aboriginals'. Turn left near a bridge off the main Betong-Yala road between the Km 66 and Km 67 markers. The road follows the river up the valley for 4 km; Ban Sakai is signposted from the main village. In Malaysia, the Sakai are called *orang asli* (indigenous man); the Thais are less polite, referring to them as *ngao* – or 'rambutans', as the fruit has a not dissimilar hairstyle. This is one of the few remaining groups of Sakai in Thailand, although they are largely settled now. Most work as tappers in the local rubber holdings. ■ *Getting there: take Yala buses and walk 4 km from the main road.*

Although most of Betong's hotels cater for the sex industry, a number of more sophisticated hotels have recently opened, the best of which is the *Merlin*. Prices are mainly quoted in Malaysian ringgit. **B** *Merlin*, 33 Chayachaowalit Rd, T230222, F231357. A/c, restaurant, pool, superb value for money, very high standard of rooms with wide range of facilities including fitness centre, snooker club, sauna and disco. Recommended. **B** *Penthouse Resort*, 68/1 Rattanasatien Rd, T231501, F230879. A/c, restaurant, smaller rooms than *Merlin*, but well-kept in lush garden surrounds, good range of facilities. **B-D** *Sri Betong*, Thammwithi Rd, T230188. 3 buildings with different rates (newest rooms are most expensive). Rates are also divided into Fri-Sat and Sun-Thu. Notwithstanding the feeling that this hotel has more than its fair share of short-stay visitors, it has decent rooms. **C-D** *Cathay*, 17-21 Chantarothai Rd, T230999. A/c, restaurant, formerly top hotel in town, newly spruced up to keep pace with recent arrivals, reasonably clean, spacious rooms, facilities include barber shop and disco, ticketing agent. Good value. **C-D** *Khong Kha*, 1 Thammwithi Rd, T230441. Some a/c, restaurant, poor. **D** *Fortuna*, 50-58 Pakdidamrong Rd, T231180. A/c, restaurant, reasonable value, best of lower bracket. **E** *Fa Un Rong*, 113/1-2 Chantarothai Rd, T231403. Another hotel which is passable but where Malaysians enjoying Thai womanhood are common. A sign on the desk warns that only condom users are well served.

Sleeping
■ *on maps*
Price codes: see inside front cover

Chinese Several restaurants around town. **Cheap**: *New Restaurant*, on the road in front of the clock tower, is the best, standard Chinese fare, serves dim sum for breakfast. Plenty more restaurants along Sukhayang Rd.

Eating

Malay and Chinese stalls Behind the *Cathay Hotel*.

Transport **Road Bus**: daily connection with Yala from the road in front of the clock tower. **Taxi**: to Yala, 4 hrs from the road in front of the clock tower.

Transport to The border post is 8 km out of town but it is only a short stroll across to Malaysia and
Malaysia there are plenty of taxis waiting the other side. It is marked by an old boundary stone emblazoned with a quaint colonial map of Malaya.

Road Taxi: from Betong to the border post (฿80 for the whole taxi) or *saamlor* (฿10). From the Malaysian side of the border post to Keroh (M$1). From Keroh to Sungai Petani (M$25).

Directory **Banks** *Thai Farmers* and *Thai Military* opposite Esso station. Other banks are to be found on Sukhayang Rd and around the clock tower

Sungei Golok

Phone code: 073
Colour map 6, grid B3
This border town is the jumping-off point for the east coast of Malaysia and is another unattractive southern Thai town catering for Malaysian 'business travellers'. The border crossing connects with Rantau Panjang. The *Tourist centre service*, Asia 18 Rd, next to immigration post on the bridge, T612126, F615230, covers the areas of Narathiwat, Yala and Pattani. They are helpful, with plenty of maps and information.

Sungei Golok

■ Sleeping			● Eating
1 City	4 Intertower	7 Tara Regent	1 Angel Bakery
2 Genting	5 Marina	8 Valentine	2 Ramli
3 Grand Garden	6 Plaza	9 Venice Palace	

0 metres 50
0 yards 50

Most of the hotels are around Charoenkhet Rd. Many are used by Malaysians on short **Sleeping** stays. Hotels accept Thai baht or Malaysian ringgit.

B *Genting*, 250 Asia 18 Rd, T613231, F611259. A/c, restaurant, featureless block, good-sized pool. Very good value and well run. **B** *Grand Garden*, 66 Soi 3 Prachawiwat Rd, T613600. A/c, restaurant, small pool with waterfall, featureless rooms. **B-C** *Marina*, 173 Charoenkhet Soi 3, T613881, F613385. A/c, restaurant, pool. The cheaper rooms are well priced, clean and presentable.

C *City*, 28-32 Sariwong Rd, T613521. Rambling, unsightly block, fair rooms, well kept. Central location in town. **C** *Intertower*, 160-166 Prachawiwat Rd, T612700, F613400. A/c, restaurant. Fair rooms but dull. **C** *Tara Regent*, 45 Charoenkhet Soi Phuthon, T611801, F613385. Some a/c, restaurant. Rooms are a bit dingy but tidy; not as good value as others in this price bracket. **C** *Venice Palace*, 22 Cheunmanka Rd, T613700, F612418. Friendly staff, a/c rooms have hot water and are clean and smart. Good value at this price. **C-D** *Plaza*, 2 Thetpathom Rd, T611875, F613402. Interesting lime green colour scheme in the rooms but otherwise, superb. Clean rooms with hot water, TV, fridge and a/c. Very good value. Well used by tours and business groups. **D** *Valentine*, 2/1 Waman Amnoey Rd, T611229, F611929. Some a/c, rooms are OK but no hot water. Hospitable welcome.

There is a plethora of other hotels in the **D-E** brackets. None of them is anything special, some are easier to spot than others. Rooms have no mod cons. It is worth paying an extra ฿100-200 and get a decent (if uninspired) room.

Angel Bakery, Waman Amnoey Rd (opposite *Valentine Hotel*). Good sweet pastries **Eating** and other snacks. Ramli Restaurant, *Charoenkhet Soi 3, Muslim cuisine*. There are plenty of other roadside places to eat.

Malaysian batik Available in shops all around town. **Shopping**

Local Motorcycle taxi: from town over the border (฿10-20). **Transport**
1,220 km from Bangkok

Train Station on Asia 18 Rd (the road to the border). Overnight connections with Bangkok. Connections to Yala, Hat Yai, Phattalung, Nakhon Si Thammarat. **Road Bus**: station on Bussayapan Rd (near *An An Hotel*). Overnight connections with Bangkok 18 hrs. Regular connections with Surat Thani 10 hrs, Hat Yai 4 hrs, Narathiwat 1 hr. **Taxi**: Tak Bai, Narathiwat, Pattani, Yala, Hat Yai.

Border open Mon-Sun, 0500-1700 Thai time. This is the main crossing-point on the **Transport to** east side of the peninsula, as Sungei Golok is well connected with other towns by train **Malaysia** and bus (฿40 by train to Hat Yai). But the bus stop and railway station in Sungei Golok are at least 1 km from Golok Bridge (the crossing-point), so it is necessary to hire a motorbike or trishaw to go from the railway station or bus stop across the bridge.

Road Bus: Rantau Panjang's bus stand is 1 km from Golok Bridge. Regular connections with Kota Bahru. **Taxi**: taxi stand in Rantau Panjang is opposite Golok Bridge. **Share taxis** to almost anywhere in Malaysia including Kota Bahru, Kuala Lumpur, Butterworth and Alor Star.

Communications Post Office: off Bussayapan Rd. **Directory**

The Gulf of Thailand

Background

8

Background

History

Prehistory

Research since the end of the Second World War has shown Thailand to be a 'hearth' –
or core area – in Southeast Asian prehistory. Discoveries at archaeological sites such as
Ban Chiang in the northeast, Non Nok Tha in the north, and Ban Kao (see page) in the
west have revealed evidence of early agriculture (possibly, 7000 BC) – particularly rice
cultivation – pottery (3500 BC) and metallurgy (2500 BC). Although heated argument
over the significance and the dating of the finds continues, there is no doubt that
important technologies were being developed and disseminated from an early date.
These finds have altered the view of this part of the world from being a 'receptacle' for
outside influences to being an area of innovation in its own right.

   Today, the population of Thailand is made up of Tai-speaking peoples. For long it
has been thought that the Tai migrated from southern China about 2,000 years ago,
filtering down the valleys and along the river courses that cut north-south down the
country. These migrants settled in the valleys of North Thailand, on the Khorat Plateau,
and in parts of the lower Chao Phraya basin. Even at this early date there was a clear
division between hill and lowland people. The lowland Tai mastered the art of wet rice
cultivation, supporting large populations and enabling powerful states and impressive
civilizations to evolve. In the highlands, people worked with the forest, living in small
itinerant groups, eking out a living through shifting cultivation or hunting and
gathering. In exchange for metal implements, salt and pottery, the hill peoples would
trade natural forest products: honey, resins such as lac, wild animal skins, ivory and
herbs. Even today, lowland 'civilized' Thais view the forest (*pa*) as a wild place (*thuan*),
inhabited by spirits and hill peoples. This is reflected in the words used to denote
'civilized' lowland Thais   *Khon Muang*, People of the Town   and 'barbaric' upland
people – *Khon Pa*, People of the Forest.

Mon, Srivijayan and Khmer influences

Before the Tais emerged as the dominant force in the 13th century, Thailand was
dominated by Mon and Khmer peoples. The Mon kingdom of Dvaravati was centred
close to Bangkok, with cities at modern-day Uthong and Nakhon Pathom. Dvaravati
relics have also been found in the north and northeast, along what are presumed to
have been the trade routes between Burma east to Cambodia, north to Chiang Mai
and northeast to the Khorat Plateau and Laos. The Dvaravati Kingdom lasted from
the sixth to the 11th century. Only the tiny Mon kingdom of Haripunjaya, with its
capital at Lamphun in the north, managed to survive annexation by the powerful
Khmer Empire and remained independent until the 13th century.

Dvaravati

The powerful Srivijayan Empire, with its capital at Palembang in Sumatra, extended
its control over South Thailand from the seventh to the 13th century. Inscriptions
and sculptures dating from the Srivijayan period have been found near the modern
Thai towns of Chaiya and Sating Phra in Surat Thani and Songkhla provinces. They
reveal an eclectic mixture of Indian, Javanese, Mon and Khmer artistic influences,
and incorporate both Hindu and Mahayana Buddhist iconography. Probably the
best examples of what little remains of Srivijayan architecture in Thailand are Phra
Boromthat and a sanctuary at Wat Kaeo, both in Chaiya (see page 330).

Srivijaya

The Khmer Of all the external empires to impinge on Thailand before the rise of the Tai, the most influential was the Khmer. Thailand lay on the fringes of the Angkorian Kingdom, but nonetheless many Thai towns are Khmer in origin: That Phanom, Sakhon Nakhon, and Phimai in the northeast; Lopburi, Suphanburi and Ratburi in the lower central plain; and Phitsanulok, Sawankhalok and Sukhothai in the upper central plain.

The Tai

The Tai did not begin to exert their dominance over modern Thailand until the 12th to 13th centuries. By then they had taken control of Lamphun in the north, founded Chiang Mai, established the Sukhothai Kingdom in the Yom River valley, and gained control of the southern peninsula. From the 13th century onwards, the history of Thailand becomes a history of the Tai people.

An important unit of organization among the Tai was the *muang*. Today, *muang* is usually translated as 'town'. But it means much more than this, and to an extent defies translation. The *muang* was a unit of control, and denoted those people who came under the sway of a *chao* or lord. In a region where people were scarce but land was abundant, the key to power was to control manpower, and thereby to turn forest into riceland. At the beginning of the 13th century, some Tai lords began to extend their control over neighbouring *muang*, forging kingdoms of considerable power. In this way, the Tai began to make a history of their own, rather than merely to be a part of history.

Sukhothai

At the point where the rivers of the north spill out onto the wide and fertile Central Plains, a second Thai kingdom was evolving during the 13th century: the Sukhothai Kingdom. Its most famous king was **Ramkhamhaeng** (?1279-1298) or 'Rama the Brave' who gained his name, so it is said, after defeating an enemy general in single-handed elephant combat at the age of 19. When Ramkhamhaeng ascended to the throne in 1275, Sukhothai was a relatively small kingdom occupying part of the upper Central Plain. When he died in 1298, extensive swathes of land came under the King of Sukhothai's control, and only King Mengrai of Lanna and King Ngam Muang of Phayao could be regarded as his equals. But King Ramkhamhaeng is remembered as much for his artistic achievements as for his raw power. Under Khmer tutelage, he is said to have devised the Thai writing system and also made a number of administrative reforms. The inscription No 1 from his reign is regarded as the first work of Thai literature, and contains the famous line:

'Nai naam mii plaa, nai naa mii khao' – 'in the water there are fish, in the fields there is rice'.

Although the Kingdom of Sukhothai owed a significant cultural and artistic debt to the Khmers, by the 13th century the Tais of Sukhothai were beginning to explore and develop their own interpretations of politics, art and life. The Kingdom promoted Theravada Buddhism, sponsoring missionary monks to spread the word. For many Thais today, the Sukhothai period – which lasted a mere 200 years – represents the apogée, the finest flowering of Thai brilliance.

Ayutthaya

From the 14th century In the middle of the 14th century, Sukhothai's influence began to be challenged by another Thai kingdom, Ayutthaya. Located over 300 km south on the Chao Phraya River, Ayutthaya was the successor to the Mon kingdom of Lavo (Lopburi). It seems that from the 11th century, Tais began to settle in the area and were peacefully incorporated into the Mon state where they gradually gained influence. Finally, in 1350, a Tai lord took control of the area and founded a new capital at the confluence of the Pa Sak, Lopburi and Chao Phraya rivers. He called the city Ayutthaya – after the sacred town of Ayodhya in the Hindu epic, the *Ramayana*. This kingdom would subsequently be known as Siam. From 1350, Ayutthaya began to extend its power south as far as Nakhon Si Thammarat, and east to Cambodia, raiding Angkor in the late 14th century and taking the city in 1432.

During the Ayutthayan period, the basis of Thai common law was introduced by King Ramathibodi (1351-69), who drew upon the Indian Code of Manu, while the powerful King Boromtrailokant (1448-88) centralized the administration of his huge kingdom and introduced various other civil, economic and military reforms. Perhaps the most important was the *sakdi naa* system in which an individual's social position was related to the size of his landholdings. The heir apparent controlled 16,000 ha, the highest official, 1,600 ha, the lowest commoner, 4 ha. A code of conduct for royalty was also introduced, with punishments again linked to position: princes of high rank who had violated the law were to be bound by gold fetters, those of lower rank by silver. The execution of a member of the royal family was, it has been said, carried out by placing them in a sack and either beating them to death with scented sandalwood clubs or having them trampled by white elephants. Even kicking a palace door would, in theory, lead to the amputation of the offending foot.

By King Boromtrailokant's reign, Ayutthaya had extended its control over 500,000 sq km, and the capital had a population of 150,000. Although the art of Ayutthaya is not as 'pure' as that of Sukhothai, the city impressed 16th- and 17th-century European visitors. Perhaps it was the tiger and elephant fights which excited the Europeans so much. The elephants (regarded as noble and representing the state) were expected to win by tossing the tiger (regarded as wild and representing disorder) repeatedly into the air. The fact that the tigers were often tied to a stake or attacked by several elephants at once must have lengthened the odds against them. Despite the undoubted might of Ayutthaya and the absolute power that lay within each monarch's grasp, kings were not, in the main, able to name their successors. Blood was not an effective guarantee to kingship and a strong competitor could easily usurp a rival even though he might – on paper – have a better claim to the throne. As a result, the history of Ayutthaya is peppered with court intrigues, bloody succession struggles, and rival claims.

From the 16th through to the 18th centuries

During this period, the fortunes of the Ayutthayan Kingdom were bound up with those of Burma. Over a 220-year period, the Burmese invaded on no less than six occasions. The first time was in 1548 when the Burmese king of Pegu, Tabengshweti encircled the capital. King Mahachakrapat only survived the ensuing battle when one of his wives drove her elephant in front of an approaching warrior. Elephants figured heavily in war and diplomacy during the Ayutthayan period: Tabengshweti justified his invasion by pointing out that he had no white elephants, the holiest of beasts (the Buddha's last reincarnation before his enlightenment was as a white elephant). The Ayutthayan king meanwhile had a whole stable of them, and was not willing to part with even one. Although this attack failed, in 1569, King Bayinnaung mounted another invasion and plundered the city, making Ayutthaya a vassal state. When the Burmese withdrew to Pegu, they left a ravaged countryside, devoid of people, and large areas of riceland returned to scrub and forest. But a mere 15 years later Prince Naresuan re-established Thai sovereignty and began to lay the foundations for a new golden age in which Ayutthaya would be more powerful and prosperous than ever before.

The 17th century

The 17th century saw a period of intense commercial contact with the Dutch, English and French. In 1608, Ayutthaya sent a diplomatic mission to the Netherlands and in 1664 a trading treaty was concluded with the Dutch. Even as early as the 17th century,

Background

Thailand had a flourishing prostitution industry. In the 1680s an official was given a monopoly of prostitution in the capital; he used 600 women to generate considerable state revenues.

The 18th century The height of Ayutthaya's power and glory is often associated with the reign of King Boromkot (literally, 'the King in the urn [awaiting cremation]', as he was the last sovereign to be honoured in this way). Boromkot ruled from 1733 to 1758 and he fulfilled many of the imagined pre-requisites of a great king: he promoted Buddhism and ruled effectively over a vast swathe of territory. But, in retrospect, signs of imperial senility were beginning to materialize even as Ayutthaya's glory was approaching its zenith. In particular, King Boromkot's sons began to exert their ambitions. Prince Senaphithak, the eldest, went so far as to have some of the king's officials flogged; in retaliation, one of the aggrieved officials revealed that the prince had been having an affair with one of Boromkot's three queens. He admitted to the liaison and was flogged to death along with his lover.

The feud with Burma was renewed in 1760 and Ayutthaya finally fell in 1767. The city was too damaged to be renovated for a second time, and the focus of the Thai state moved southwards once again – to Thonburi, and from there to Bangkok.

Bangkok and the Rattanakosin period

After the sacking of Ayutthaya, **General Taksin** moved the capital 74 km south to Thonburi, on the other bank of the Chao Pharaya River from modern-day Bangkok. Taksin's original name was Sin. Proving himself an adept administrator, he was appointed Lord of Tak (a city in the upper Central Plain), or Phraya Tak. Hence his name Tak-sin. From Thonburi, Taksin successfully fought successive Burmese invasions, until the stress caused his mental health to deteriorate to the extent that he was forced to abdicate in 1782. A European visitor wrote in a letter that "He [Taksin] passed all his time in prayer, fasting, and meditation, in order by these means to be able to fly through the air". He became madder by the month and on 6 April 1782, a group of rebels marched on Thonburi, captured the king and asked one of Taksin's generals, Chao Phya Chakri, to assume the throne. The day that Chao Phya Chakri became King Ramatobodi, 6 April, remains a public holiday in Thailand – Chakri Day – and marks the beginning of the current Chakri Dynasty. Worried about the continuing Burmese threat, Rama I (as Chao Phya Chakri is known) moved his capital to the opposite, and safer, bank of the Chao Phraya River, founded Bangkok and began the process of consolidating his kingdom. By the end of the century, the Burmese threat had dissipated, and the Siamese were once again in a position to lead the Tai world.

19th century During **Rama II**'s reign (1809-24), a new threat emerged to replace the Burmese: that of the Europeans. In 1821, the English East India Company sent John Crawfurd as an envoy to Siam to open up trading relations. Although the king and his court remained unreservedly opposed to unfettered trade, Crawfurd's visit served to impress upon those more prescient Siamese where the challenges of the 19th century would lie.

Rama II's death and succession illustrates the dangers inherent in having a claim to the throne of Siam, even in the 19th century. The court chronicles record that in 1824 Prince Mongkut was ordained as a monk because the death of a royal white elephant indicated it was an 'ill-omened time'. Historians believe that Rama II, realizing his death was imminent, wished to protect the young prince by bundling him off to a monastery, where the robes of a monk might protect him from court intrigues.

Rama III's reign (1824-51) saw an invasion by an army led by the Lao King Anou. In 1827, Anou took Nakhon Ratchasima on the edge of the Central Plain and was within striking distance of Bangkok before being defeated. After their victory, the Siamese marched on Vientiane, plundering the city and subjugating the surrounding countryside. In 1829, King Anou himself was captured and transported to Bangkok, where he was displayed to the public in a cage. Anou died shortly after this humiliation – some say of shame, others say of self-administered poison. Before he died he is said to have laid a curse on the Chakri dynasty, swearing that never again would a Chakri king set foot on Lao soil. None has, and when the present king Bhumibol attended the opening of the Thai-Lao Friendship Bridge over the Mekong in 1994, he did so from a sand bar in the middle of the river. There were also ructions at the court in Bangkok: in 1848 Prince Rakrannaret was found guilty of bribery and corruption and, just for good measure, homosexuality and treason as well. Rama III had him beaten to death with sandalwood clubs, in time-honoured Thai fashion.

The 19th century was a dangerous time for Siam. Southeast Asia was being methodically divided between Britain, France and Holland as they scrambled for colonial territories. The same fate might have befallen Siam, had it not been blessed with two brilliant kings: King Mongkut (Rama IV 1851-68) and King Chulalongkorn (Rama V 1868-1910).

Mongkut was a brilliant scholar. He learnt English and Latin and when he sat his oral Pali examination performed brilliantly. Indeed, his 27 years in a monastery allowed him to study the religious texts to such depth that he concluded that all Siamese ordinations were invalid. He established a new sect based upon the stricter Mon teachings, an order which became known as the *Thammayutika* or 'Ordering Adhering to the Dharma'. To distinguish themselves from those 'fallen' monks who made up most of the Sangha, they wore their robes with both shoulders covered.

But Mongkut was not an other-wordly monk with scholarly inclinations. He was a rational, pragmatic man who well appreciated the economic and military might of the Europeans. He recognized that if his kingdom was to survive he would have to accept and acquiesce to the colonial powers, rather than try to resist them. He did not accede to the throne until he was 47, and it is said that during his monastic studies he came to realize that if China, the Middle Kingdom, had to bow to Western pressure, then he would have to do the same.

He set about modernizing his country along with the support of other modern-thinking princes. He established a modern ship-building industry, trained his troops in European methods and studied Western medicine. Most importantly, in 1855, he signed the **Bowring Treaty** with Britain, giving British merchants access to the Siamese market and setting in train a process of agricultural commercialization and the clearing of the vast Central Plains for rice cultivation. Mongkut's meeting with Bowring illustrates the lengths to which he went to meet the West on its own terms: he received the British envoy and offered him port and cigars from his own hand, an unheard of action in Thai circles.

Unfortunately, in the West, Mongkut is not known for the skilful diplomacy which kept at bay expansionist nations considerably more powerful than his own, but for his characterization in the film *The King and I* (in which he is played by Yul Brynner). Poorly adapted from Anna Leonowens's own distorted accounts of her period as governess in the Siamese court, both the book and the film offend the Thai people. According to contemporary accounts, Mrs Leonowens was a bad-tempered lady obviously given to flights of fantasy. She never became a trusted confidant of King Mongkut who scarcely needed her limited skills and there is certainly no evidence to indicate that he was attracted to her sexually. It appears that she was plain in appearance.

King Mongkut died on 1 October 1868 and was succeeded by his 15 year-old son **Chulalongkorn**. However for the next decade a regent controlled affairs of state and it was not until 1873, when Chulalongkorn was crowned for a second time, that he could begin to mould the country according to his own vision. The young king quickly showed himself to be a reformer like his father – for in essence Mongkut had only just begun the process of modernization. Chulalongkorn set about updating the monarchy by establishing ministries and ending the practise of prostration. He also accelerated the process of economic development by constructing roads, railways, schools and hospitals. The opium trade was regulated, court procedures streamlined and slavery finally completely abolished in 1905. Although a number of princes were sent abroad to study – Prince Rajebuidirekrit went to Oxford – Chulalongkorn had to also rely on foreign advisors to help him undertake these reforms. In total he employed 549 foreigners – the largest number being British, but also Dutch, Germans, French and Belgians. Chulalongkorn even held fancy dress parties at New Year and visited Europe twice.

These reforms were not introduced without difficulty. The *Hua Boran* – or 'The Ancients' as the King derogatorily called them – strongly resisted the changes and in late December 1874 Prince Wichaichan attempted to take the Royal Palace and usurp the king. The plot was thwarted at the last possible moment, but it impressed upon Chulalongkorn that reform could only come slowly. Realizing he had run ahead of many of his subjects in his zeal for change, he reversed some of his earlier reforms, and toned-down others. Nevertheless, Siam remained on the path of modernization – albeit progressing at a rather slower pace. As during Mongkut's reign, Chulalongkorn also managed to keep the colonial powers at bay. Although the king himself played a large part in placating the Europeans by skilful diplomacy and by presenting an image of urbane sophistication, he was helped in this respect by a brilliant minister of foreign affairs, Prince Devawongse (1858-1923), who controlled Siam's foreign relations for 38 years.

The fundamental weakness of the Siamese state in the face of the European powers was illustrated in the dispute with France over Laos. Despite attempts by Prince Devawongse to manufacture a compromise, the French forced Siam to cede Laos to France in 1893 and to pay compensation – even though they had little claim to the territory. As it is said, power grows out of the barrel of a gun, and Chulalongkorn could not compete with France in military might. After this humiliating climb down, the king essentially retired from public life, broken in spirit and health. In 1909, the British chipped away at more of Siam's territory, gaining rights of suzerainty over the Malay states of Kelantan, Terengganu, Kedah and Perlis. King Chulalongkorn died on 24 October 1910, sending the whole nation into deep and genuine mourning.

The 20th century The kings that were to follow Mongkut and Chulalongkorn could not have been expected to have had such illustrious, brilliant reigns. Absolute kingship was becoming increasingly incompatible with the demands of the modern world, and the kings of Thailand were resisting the inevitable. Rama VI, **King Vajiravudh** (1910-25), was educated at Oxford and Sandhurst Military Academy and seemed well prepared for kingship. However he squandered much of the wealth built up by Chulalongkorn and ruled in a rather heavy-handed, uncoordinated style. He did try to inculcate a sense of 'nation' with his slogan 'nation, religion, king', but seemed more interested in Western theatre and literature than in guiding Siam through a difficult period in its history. He died at the age of only 44, leaving an empty treasury.

Like his older brother, **King Prajadhipok** (Rama VII 1925-35), was educated in Europe: at Eton, the Woolwich Military Academy and at the Ecole Supérieure de Guerre in France. But he never expected to become king and was thrust onto the throne at a time of great strain. Certainly, he was more careful with the resources that his treasury had to offer, but could do little to prevent the country being seriously affected by the Great Depression of the 1930s. The price of rice, the country's principal export, declined by two-thirds and over the same two-year period (1930-32) land values in Bangkok fell by 80%. The economy was in crisis and the government appeared to have no idea how to cope. The people, both the peasantry and the middle class, were dissatisfied by the course of events and with their declining economic position. But neither group was sufficiently united to mount a threat to the King and his government. Nevertheless, Prajadhipok was worried: there was a prophesy linked to Rama I's younger sister Princess Narinthewi which predicted that the Chakri Dynasty would survive for 150 years, and end on 6 April 1932.

The date itself passed without incident, but just 12 weeks later, on 24 June, a clique of soldiers and civilians staged a **coup d'état** while the king was holidaying at the seaside resort of Hua Hin. This episode is often called the Revolution of 1932, but it was not in any sense a revolution involving a large rump of the people. It was orchestrated by a small élite, essentially for the élite. The king accepted the terms offered to him, writing:

The Revolution of 1932

> *"I have received the letter in which you invite me to return to Bangkok as a constitutional monarch. For the sake of peace; and in order to save useless bloodshed; to avoid confusion and loss to the country; and, more, because I have already considered making this change myself, I am willing to cooperate in the establishment of a constitution under which I am willing to serve."*

However, King Prajadhipok had great difficulty adapting to his lesser role and, falling out with the military, he abdicated in favour of his young nephew, Prince Ananda Mahidol in 1935. The Prince at the time was only 10 years old, and at school in Switzerland, so the newly created National Assembly appointed two princes to act as regents. From this point until after the Second World War the monarchy was only partially operative. Ananda was out of the country for most of the time, and the civilian government took centre stage. Ananda was not to physically reoccupy the throne until December 1945 and just six months later he was found dead in bed, a bullet through his head. The circumstances behind his death have never been satisfactorily explained and it remains a subject on which Thais are not openly permitted to speculate. Books investigating the death are still banned in Thailand.

While the monarchy receded from view, the civilian government was going through the intrigues and power struggles which were to become such a feature of the future politics of the country. The two key men at this time were the army officer Phibun Songkhram, and the left-wing idealist lawyer Pridi Panomyong. Between them they managed to dominate Thai politics until 1957.

When **Prime Minister Pridi Panomyong** tried to introduce a socialist economic programme in 1933, pushing for the state control of the means of production, he was forced into exile in Europe. This is often seen as the beginning of the tradition of authoritarian, right-wing rule in Thailand, although to be fair, Pridi's vision of economic and political reform was poorly thought through and rather romantic. Nonetheless, with Pridi in Paris – at least for a while – it gave the more conservative elements in the government the chance to promulgate an anti-communist law, and thereby to usher in a period of ultra-nationalism. Anti-Chinese propaganda became more shrill, with some government positions being reserved for ethnic Tais. In 1938 the populist writer Luang Wichit compared the Chinese in Siam with the Jews in Germany, and thought that Hitler's policies might be worth considering for his own country.

This shift in policy can be linked to the influence of one man: **Luang Phibun Songkhram**. Born of humble parents in 1897, he worked his way up through the army ranks and then into politics. He became Prime Minister in 1938 and his enduring influence makes him the most significant figure in 20th-century Thai politics. Under his direction, Siam became more militaristic, xenophobic, as well as 'religiously' nationalistic, avidly pursuing the reconversion of Siamese Christians back to Buddhism. As if to underline these developments, in 1939, Siam adopted a new name: Thailand. Phibun justified this change on the grounds that it would indicate that the country was controlled by Thais and not by the Chinese or any other group.

Second World   During the Second World War, Phibun Songkhram sided with the Japanese who he
War & Post-War   felt sure would win. He saw the war as an opportunity to take back some of the
Thailand   territories lost to the French (particularly) and the British. In 1940, Thai forces
invaded Laos and Western Cambodia. A year later, the Japanese used the Kingdom
as a launching pad for their assaults on the British in Malaya and Burma. Thailand
had little choice but to declare war on the Allies and to agree a military alliance with
Japan in December 1941. As allies of the Japanese, Phibun's ambassadors were
instructed to declare war on Britain and the United States. However, the ambassador
in Washington, Seni Pramoj, refused to deliver the declaration (he considered it
illegal) and Thailand never formally declared war on the US. In Thailand itself Pridi,
who had returned as regent to the young monarch King Ananda, helped to
organize the Thai resistance – the Free Thai Movement. They received help from the
US Office of Strategic Services (OSS) and the British Force 136, and also from many
Thais. As the tide of the war turned in favour of the allies, so Prime Minister Phibun
was forced to resign. He spent a short time in gaol in Japan, but was allowed to
return to Thailand in 1947.

 After the war, Seni Pramoj, Thailand's ambassador in the US, became Prime
Minister. He was soon followed by Pridi Panomyong as Prime Minister who had
gathered a good deal of support due to the role he played during the conflict.
However, in 1946 King Ananda was mysteriously found shot dead in his royal
apartments and Pridi was implicated in a plot. He was forced to resign, so enabling
Phibun to become Prime Minister once again – a post he kept until 1957. Phibun's
fervent anti-Communism quickly gained support in the US, who contributed
generous amounts of aid as the country became a front-line state in the battle
against the 'red tide' which seemed to be engulfing Asia. Phibun's closest brush with
death occurred in June 1951. He was leading a ceremony on board a dredge, the
Manhattan, when he was taken prisoner during a military coup and transferred to
the Thai navy flagship the *Sri Ayutthaya*. The airforce and army stayed loyal to
Phibun, and planes bombed the ship. As it sank, the Prime Minister was able to swim
to safety. The attempted coup resulted in 1,200 dead – mostly civilians. For the navy,
it has meant that ever since it has been treated as the junior member of the armed
forces, receiving far less resources than the army and airforce.

 Prime Minister Phibun Songkhram was deposed following a coup d'état in 1957,
and was replaced by **General Sarit Thanarat**. General Sarit established the National
Economic Development Board (now the National Economic and Social Development
Board) and introduced Thailand's first five-year national development plan in 1961. He
was a tough, uncompromising leader and following his death in 1963 was replaced by
another General – **Thanom Kitticachorn**. With the war in Indochina escalating,
Thanom allowed US planes to be based in Thailand from where they flew bombing
sorties over the Lao panhandle and Vietnam. In 1969 a general election was held,
which Thanom won, but as the political situation in Thailand deteriorated, so Prime
Minister Thanom declared martial law. However, unlike his predecessors Sarit and
Phibun, Thanom could not count on the loyalty of all elements within the armed
forces and although he tried to take the strongman – or *nak laeng* – approach, his
administration always had a frailty about it. In addition, historian David Wyatt argues
that developments in Thai society – particularly an emergent middle class and an
increasingly combative body of students – made controlling the country from the
centre rather harder than it had been over the previous decades.

 It was Thailand's students who precipitated probably the single most tumultuous
event since the Revolution of 1932. The student body felt that Thanom had
back-tracked and restricted the evolution of a more open political system in the
country. In June 1973 they began to demonstrate against the government, printing
highly critical pamphlets and calling for the resignation of Thanom. A series of
demonstrations, often centred on Sanaam Luang near the radical Thammasat

University and the Grand Palace, brought crowds of up to 500,000 onto the streets. During the demonstrations, Thanom lost the support of the army: the Commander-in-Chief, General Krit Sivara, was unwilling to send his troops out to quell the disturbances while Thanom, apparently, was quite willing to kill thousands if necessary. With the army unwilling to confront the students, and with the king – crucially – also apparently siding with Thanom's army opponents, he was forced to resign from the premiership, and fled the country.

The '**October revolution**' ushered in a period of **turbulent democratic government** in Thailand, the first such period in the country's history. It was an exciting time: radical scholars could openly speak and publish, students could challenge the establishment, labour unions could organize and demonstrate, and leftist politicians could make their views known. But it was also a period of political instability. While there had been just five prime ministers between 1948 and 1973, the three years following 1973 saw the rapid coming and going of another four: Sanya Dharmasakti (October 1973-February 1975), Seni Pramoj (February-March 1975), Kukrit Pramoj (March 1975-January 1976) and Seni Pramoj (April-October 1976). This instability was reinforced by the feeling among the middle classes that the students were pushing things too far. The fall of Vietnam, Cambodia and Laos to Communism left many Thais wondering whether they would be the next 'domino' to topple. This gave an opening for rightist groups to garner support, and anti-Communist organizations like the Red Gaurs and the Village Scouts gained in influence and began, with the support and connivance of the police, to harrass and sometimes to murder left-wingers. "Violence, vituperation, and incivility", as Wyatt writes, "were now a part of public life as they never had been before in Thailand".

This was the background that led the army to feel impelled to step in once again. However the trigger for the **appalling events of October 1976** was the return of former Prime Minister Thanom from exile, who joined the sangha and became a monk. Installed in a Bangkok monastery, Thanom was visited by members of the royal family. The students took this as royal recognition of a man who had led the country into violence and to the edge of civil war. Demonstrations broke out in Bangkok, again centred on Sanaam Luang and the nearby Democracy Monument. This time, though, the students were not able to face down the forces of the Right. Newspapers printed pictures apparently showing the Crown Prince being burnt in effigy by students at Thammasat, and right-wing groups, along with the police and the army, advanced on the university on 6 October. Details of the hours that followed are hazy. However it seems clear that an orgy of killing ensued. With the situation rapidly deteriorating, the army stepped in and imposed martial law. Tanin Kraivixien was installed as Prime Minister, to be replaced the following year by Kriangsak Chomanan.

The 1976 massacre was a shot in the army for the **Communist Party of Thailand (CPT)**. Left-wing intellectuals and many students, feeling that they could no longer influence events through the political system, fled to the jungle and joined the CPT. The victories of the Communists in neighbouring Indochina also reinforced the sense that ultimately the CPT would emerge victorious. By the late 1970s the ranks of the party had swelled to around 14,000 armed guerrillas who controlled large areas of the northeast, north and south. However, with the ascendancy of Prem Tinsulanond to the premiership in 1980 and a rapidly changing global political environment, the CPT fragmented and quickly lost support. Its leaders were divided between support for China and the Cambodian Khmers Rouges on the one hand, and the Soviet Union and Vietnam on the other. When the government announced an amnesty in 1980, many of the students who had fled into the forests and hills following the riots of 1973, returned to mainstream politics, exhausted and disenchanted with revolutionary life. In true Thai style, they were largely forgiven and reintegrated into society. But those who died on Sanaam Luang and in the streets leading off it have never been acknowledged and in many cases their parents were never informed that they had been killed. Nor were they allowed to collect their children's bodies.

Prem Tinsulanond presided over the most stable period in Thai politics since the end of the Second World War. He finally resigned in 1988, and by then Thailand – or so most people thought – was beginning to outgrow the habit of military intervention in civilian politics. Chatichai Choonhaven replaced Prem after general elections in 1988, by which time the country was felt to be more stable and economically prosperous than at any time in recent memory. During his reign, the present King Bhumibol has played a crucial role in maintaining social stability while the political system has been in turmoil. He is highly revered by his subjects, and has considerable power to change the course of events. There are essentially two views on the role of the king in contemporary Thailand. The general view is that he has influence far beyond that which his constitutional position strictly permits but that he is careful not to over-exercise that power and only intervenes at times of crisis. The king, in short, is his own man and acts in the best interests of the Thai people. The alternative view is that after his coronation, influential courtiers and generals tried to diminish the power of the king by making him a semi-divine figurehead and surrounding him in protocol. The king became a tool used by right-wing dictators and the army to justify their authoritarian ways.

Modern Thailand

From Bangkok's high-rise offices and glitzy hotels it is all too easy to forget that in 1992 the Thai army fired on unarmed demonstrators protesting against General Suchinda Kraprayoon's military dictatorship. Well over 100 students and others were killed. Parliamentary democracy in Thailand is new and fragile and not only have there been 16 constitutions inflicted on the people of Thailand since 1932, but these have been interspersed with 18 coup d'états.

While the events of the early 1990s are, in a sense, already history they are worth recounting because they illustrate the tension that has always existed between the military and civilian politicians. They also show the delicate balancing act between anarchy and authoritarianism which is a recurring motif in the Kingdom's political development.

A political vignette: Thailand in 1991-92 In February 1991, **General Suchinda Kraprayoon** staged a bloodless coup d'état and ousted the democratically elected government of Prime Minister Chatichai Choonhavan. (Thailand has now had 17 coups or attempted coups since 1945, and over the 67 years since the original coup of 1932, army strongmen have been in power for no less than 49 years.) Suchinda claimed that he acted because of the extreme corruption associated with Chatichai's administration. Most Thais took him at his word, happy that a manifestly corrupt government had been removed from power. Suchinda then created an army-dominated National Peacekeeping Council but asked the civilian **Anand Panyarachun** to act as caretaker prime minister. In appointing Anand, Suchinda was hoping to gain the support of ordinary Thais worried about a return to military government. But, while Anand was doing a fine job running the country, opposition politicians were becoming increasingly concerned about the army's intentions. Two former army generals-turned-politicians (another recurring theme), Chamlong Srimuang and Chaovalit Yongchaiyut, tried to prevent Suchinda's attempts to cement the army's power by forging a pro-military constitution. In November 1991, 100,000 people gathered in Bangkok to protest against the constitution which would allow an unelected person to become prime minister and give the army the power to appoint 270 members in the Senate, the upper house. It is said Suchinda visited a Buddhist shrine in the

The oldest industry: prostitution in Thailand

Embarrassingly for many Thais, their country is synonymous in many foreigners' minds with prostitution and sex tourism, and now with AIDS. That prostitution is big business cannot be denied: various estimates put the numbers of women employed in the industry at between 120,000 and two million in some 60,000 brothels. Estimating the numbers of commercial sex workers (CSWs) is difficult, but a survey by the Thai Red Cross and Mahidol University plumped for a figure at the lower end of this range – between 120,000 and 200,000.

Despite the ubiquitousness of the prostitute in Thai life, the government has often appeared blind to the scale of the industry. This is clear in one official estimate of the numbers of prostitutes and brothels in the Kingdom: 67,067 and 5,754 respectively. Part of the problem is admitting to the problem in a society where these things are usually left unsaid. As US-based Thai author Somtow Sucharitkul explained: "The main difference between American and Thai sexuality is that in America you can only talk about it but can't do it, but in Thailand you can't talk about it, you can only do it."

southern Thai town of Nakhon Si Thammarat just after the rally to ask the guardian spirit's advice over the growing opposition. After setting off 5,000 firecrackers, he was told that unless he accepted the opposition's demands he would face a 'fateful event'.

The spirit's prediction turned out to be tragically correct. In the elections of March 1992, there was no clear winner. After much debate, a coalition of pro-military parties asked Narong Wongwan, the leader of the airforce-backed Sammakhi Tham Party, to become prime minister. But when allegations surfaced that Narong had been involved in drug trafficking, and that he had been denied a visa to visit the US, his candidacy was withdrawn. With no other obvious candidate, Suchinda – who had earlier made a public promise that he would not become prime minister – was offered the job. The unelected Suchinda tearfully agreed, and he became Premier on the 7 April.

Chamlong Srimuang took this as his cue to call his supporters onto the streets to resist what he viewed as the army's imposition of itself on the Thai people. In the elections, his Palang Dharma Party had won 32 out of the 35 seats in Bangkok. On 4 May he announced he was going on hunger strike. Tens of thousands of people crowded into the streets around the Parliament buildings and then onto Sanaam Luang, near the Grand Palace. Suchinda tried to suppress coverage of the **demonstrations**, but failed. The ruling coalition agreed to a constitutional amendment that would ensure any future prime minister would have to be elected. Chamlong ended his fast on 9 May and asked his supporters to go home. The people of Thailand then waited for Suchinda to do as he promised. It quickly became clear that he had no intention of stepping down.

On Sunday 17 May, tens of thousands of demonstrators took to the streets once again to try and force Suchinda into honouring the agreement. Like the demonstrations of 1973, the focus of discontent was the area around Sanaam Luang and the Democracy Monument in the heart of the capital and like his predecessor Thanom, who was Prime Minister in 1973, Suchinda called in the army to clear the streets. Scores of people were killed as the army opened fire (after the confrontation, 52 bodies were recovered, although 163 people are still listed as missing by relatives). When demonstrators fled into the Royal Hotel, the army followed to drag them out and herd them off to gaol. Television audiences in the West were treated to pictures of a brutal, blood-soaked Land of Smiles.

Three days after the confrontation between the army and the demonstrators, **King Bhumibol** ordered both Suchinda and opposition leader Chamlong – who had to be released from gaol for the meeting – to his palace. There, television cameras were waiting to witness Suchinda's global, public humiliation. He and

Chamlong prostrated themselves on the floor while the king lectured them, asking rhetorically: "What is the use of victory when the winner stands on wreckage?" Immediately afterwards, the army and the demonstrators withdrew from the streets. On the Friday, Suchinda offered his resignation to the King and on Saturday, less than one week after the killing began, Suchinda Kraprayoon fled the country. In a televised address, Suchinda accepted responsibility for the deaths.

Although it is sometimes hard for outsiders to understand, the Thai army has traditionally seen its role as 'protector' of the people against the excesses of corrupt civilian politicians, rather than the other way around. Politicians are seen to be irredeemably selfish, with an interest only in the size of their bank balances and the army has been 'forced' to step in on several occasions to 'protect the people'. There is no doubt that many poorer Thais, especially those in rural areas, have sympathy with this view. As one Thai academic said to the *Financial Times* in 1992, most rural MPs are simply "hoodlums in suits".

Politics since the massacre of May 1992 After the riots of May 1992, and General Suchinda's (and by association, the army's) humiliating climb-down, Anand Panyarachun was appointed interim prime minister for a second spell. New elections were set for 13 September. The Thai media characterized the elections of September as a contest between 'angel' (pro-democracy) and 'devil' (pro-military) parties. The comparatively angelic Democrat Party won the largest number of seats and its leader, **Chuan Leekpai**, was **appointed 1992's fourth prime minister** on 23 September, after he had managed to piece together a bare majority. Chuan, a mild-mannered Southerner from a poor background – his father was a fish vendor in Trang – gained his law degree while living as a novice monk in a monastery. Chuan's administration continued where the Anand II government had left off, taking further small steps to ensure that a repeat performance of the May massacre could not occur.

Chuan's government lasted a little over 2½ years, making it the longest-serving elected government in Thai history – which says something about their longevity. It finally fell over a land scandal and elections were called for 2 July 1995.

The Chart Thai Party led by 62-year-old **Banharn Silpa-Archa** won the election – or at least the largest number of seats – to the dismay of many in Bangkok. Following the election, Banharn formed a coalition government of seven parties controlling 233 seats in the 391-seat parliament. Banharn's Chart Thai was closely associated with the military junta led by General Suchinda. Banharn never enjoyed particularly good relations with the press. They were dismayed when he won the election in 1995, and continued to characterize him as a old-style pork-barrel politician winning support with money rather than ideas, and his government as irredeemably sleazy, taking kick-backs whenever possible and corrupt to the core. Two Chart Thai candidates in the elections were even accused of involvement in the narcotics trade. At the beginning of **1996**, the Bangkok-based English-language daily *The Nation* boldly stated that "the only way for 1996 to be a good year is for the Banharn government to go". That this didn't happen was partly because Banharn enjoyed the support of many poorer people up-country.

But the one element in the Thai political system which no politician can ever ignore is the King, and in late summer 1995 Banharn's government found itself explicitly criticized by the palace when the King highlighted government failures to address Bangkok's infrastructural mess and its shortcomings in dealing with serious flooding. Ministers, the King said, only "talk, talk, talk and argue, argue, argue".

In the middle of September 1996, as a parliamentary vote of no confidence loomed, the babel of voices calling for his resignation reached a crescendo. Businessmen, influential civil servants including four former Bank of Thailand governors, opposition politicians (of course), even his own daughter, were asking that he step down. Particularly worrying was a slow down in the economy which many analysts linked to

Banharn's administration, and few people believed he – as a country hick – was in a position to tackle. The three-day no confidence debate led Banharn to announce on 21 September 1996 that he would resign as prime minister and he asked the King to dissolve parliament and called elections for 17 November.

The **elections of 17 November 1996** were close, with **Chaovalit Yongchaiyudh's** New Aspirations Party (NAP) just managing to win the largest number of seats and after the usual bickering and horse-trading he managed to stitch together a six-party coalition controlling 221 seats in the 393-seat House of Representatives. Chaovalit was an old-style patronage politician who depended on his links with the army and on handing out lucrative concessions to his supporters. "Transparency", as Democrat MP Surin Pitsuwan was quoted as saying in August 1996, "is not in his dictionary". People in Bangkok – and especially the middle-class intelligentsia and many foreign investors – had hoped that the Democrats would win the most seats, giving Chuan Leekpai a second stab at the premiership.

Chaovalit was, in a sense, unlucky to take over the reins of government when he did. Economic conditions were a cause for concern in the country in late 1996, but no one – scholar or pundit – predicted the economic meltdown that was just a few months away. He appointed the well-respected Amnuay Virawan as Finance Minister. But the collapse of the baht, the Bangkok stock market, the property and finance sectors, and a haemorrhaging loss of domestic and international confidence created conditions that were impossible to manage. Even so, his performance was hardly memorable. As *The Economist* tartly put it, "he dithered when decisions were needed, bumbled when clear words might have helped, and smiled benignly while the economy got worse". The central bank spent a staggering US$10 bn trying to defend the baht's peg to the US$ and interest rates were raised to 1,300% for offshore borrowers in an ultimately futile attempt to keep the speculators at bay. The baht was allowed to float on 2 July, ending 13 years during which it had been pegged to the US$. Two cabinet reshuffles during August did little to stem the criticism of Chaovalit and his administration and on 7 November, **Chaovalit resigned** as Prime Minister after less than a year in power.

In retrospect, the mid-1990s may turn out to be a **watershed in contemporary Thailand's history**. On 18 July 1995 the Princess Mother (the King's mother) died. After the King she was probably the most revered person in the country. Born a commoner and trained as a nurse she married a prince. Her funeral in 1996 was a grandiose affair and her death has been likened to that of Britain's Princess Diana. Even Bangkok's massage parlours closed as a mark of respect. 1996 also saw the 50th anniversary of King Bhumibol's accession to the throne and the country threw a massive party to celebrate the event. The celebrations were as much a mark of Thailand's coming of age as of the King's golden jubilee. No expense was spared by the newly self-confident Tiger Thailand. Both events – the Princess Mother's funeral and the King's jubilee – were, for those so inclined, omens. The night before the funeral there was an unseasonable rain storm; and during the procession of royal boats on the Chao Phraya it also poured. The King's boat was washed off course and had to be rescued by the navy. As it turned out, 1996 was the last year when money was no object.

Following Chaovalit's resignation, Chuan Leekpai, leader of the Democrat Party, stitched together a new seven-party, 208-person coalition and became prime minister. Given the talk of military intervention a few months earlier, it was a relief to many that Thailand had achieved a peaceful change of government. The key question, however, was whether Chuan could do any better than Chaovalit, particularly given the mixed make-up of his coalition government. Chuan and his finance minister, Tarrin Nimmanahaeminda – the year's fourth – vigorously implemented the IMF's rescue package and even managed to negotiate a slight loosening of the terms of the package.

The Chuan II administration

The economic crisis enabled a coterie of young, reform-minded politicians to gain high office like urbane, US-educated foreign minister Surin Pitsuwan. Fed up with coups and corruption, and backed by an increasingly assertive middle class, these politicians are committed to change. As Chuan's special assistant Bunaraj Smutharaks explained to journalist Michael Vatikiotis, "If we don't seize this opportunity to instigate change, the future generations will see this [economic] crisis as a lost opportunity" (FEER, 30.6.98).

Under Chuan's leadership, Thailand became a role model for the IMF and foreign investors applauded the government's attempts to put things in order. The difficulty that Chuan faced throughout his second period as premier was that what began as just an economic 'blip' took far longer to work itself out – and in particular to have an impact on Thailand's poor. Particularly galling for Chuan must have been those who argued that he, the poorest prime minister in Thailand's history, was anti-poor. As this book went to press Thailand was waiting for an election.

Thailand and the 21st century

As Thailand entered the 21st century and the Third Millennium the country was also, rather shakily, recovering from the deepest contraction of the economy since the 1930s. The fact that most Thais are more comfortable thinking of the year AD 2000 as 2543 BE (or Buddhist Era) could not detract from the realization that a Rubicon has been crossed.

Until July 1997, everything was hunky dory in Thailand. Or that, at least, is what the World Bank and most businessmen and pundits thought. The Kingdom's economy was expanding at close to double-digit rates and the country was being showered with strings of congratulatory epithets. It was a 'miracle' economy, an Asian 'tiger' or 'dragon' ready to pounce on an unsuspecting world. Thailand has become the 'Cinderella' of Southeast Asia – a beautiful woman long disguised beneath shabby clothes – and academics and journalists were writing books with glowing titles like *Thailand's Boom* (1996), *Thailand's turn: profile of a new dragon* (1992) and *Thailand's macro-economic miracle* (1996). Wealth was growing, poverty falling and Bangkok was chock-full of designer shops meeting the consumer needs of a growing – and increasingly hedonistic – middle class.

Then everything went horribly wrong. The local currency, the baht, went into free-fall, the stockmarket crashed, unemployment more than doubled, and the economy contracted. Bankrupt businessmen, the nouveau pauvre, cashed in their Mercedes, and minor wives were put on strict spending diets. Almost overnight apparently prescient commentators, who had remained strangely silent during the years of growth, were offering their own interpretations of Thailand's fall from economic grace. A distinct whiff of schadenfreude filled the air. Epithet writers went back to their computers and came up with titles like the 'Asian contagion', the 'Asian mirage', 'Frozen miracles' and 'Tigers lose their grip'. In Thailand itself, locals began to talk of the *Thaitanic* as it sank faster than the doomed liner.

Notwithstanding the slowdown associated with the economic crisis, the rapid pace of change has brought with it social, economic and environmental tensions and conflicts. Bangkok is overstretched, its transport system on the verge of collapse, and around one million people live in slum conditions in the captial. Deforestation is such that the government felt impelled to impose a nationwide logging ban at the beginning of 1989 and national parks are poached and encroached. In the poor Northeastern region, incomes have stagnated, causing social tensions to become more acute and millions to migrate to the capital each dry season in a desperate search for work. In the Central Plains, the country's rice bowl, land is now so scarce that some households are being forced to give up farming altogether. While in the

North, AIDS has cut a scythe of death through some villages where scarcely a household has not been touched by the disease.

In the 1970s some scholars suggested that the country could be encapsulated by reference to the 'four Rs': rice, rivers, religion and royalty. Today computer parts, jewellery and garments all exceed rice in terms of export value. Highways have replaced rivers as arteries of communication and religion has become so commercialized that Thais have coined a word to describe it: *Buddhapanich*. Only the King has stood head and shoulders above the fray, the one thread of continuity in a country changing and reinventing itself with bewildering speed.

'Traditional' Thai life is becoming the stuff of history as modernity engulfs people and places. But just as the recent past becomes sepia-tinted, so the future becomes less compelling. Even before the crisis, some economists worried that Thailand's miracle had run its course. The country's green movement laments the environmental costs of economic growth, and sociologists highlight the wasted youth, the drug culture, and the underclass as evidence of the corrosive social effects of modernization. Tourism has brought its own problems – 80% of freshwater wells in the Phi Phi National Park are contaminated because of the sheer numbers using the island's limited services. Some educated Thais also blame tourists for the explosion of the sex industry, and the proliferation of AIDS (see page 55). Where Thailand is headed as it continues its roller coaster ride is as much a mystery as a challenge.

Religion

The Thai census records that 94% of the population is Buddhist. In Thailand's case, this means Theravada Buddhism, also known as Hinayana Buddhism. Of the other 6% of the population, 3.9% are Muslim (living predominantly in the south of the country), 1.7% Confucianist (mostly Sino-Thais living in Bangkok), and 0.6% Christian (mostly hill tribe people living in the north). Though the king is designated the protector of all religions, the constitution stipulates that he must be a Buddhist.

Theravada Buddhism was introduced into Southeast Asia in the 13th century, when monks trained in Ceylon (Sri Lanka) returned actively to spread the word. As a universal and a popular religion it quickly gained converts and spread rapidly amongst the Tai. Theravada Buddhism, from the Pali word *thera* ('elders'), means the 'way of the elders' and is distinct from the dominant Buddhism practiced in India, Mahayana Buddhism or the 'Greater Vehicle'. The sacred language of Theravada Buddhism is Pali rather than Sanskrit, Bodhisattvas (future Buddhas) are not given much attention, and emphasis is placed upon a precise and 'fundamental' interpretation of the Buddha's teachings, as they were originally recorded.

Theravada Buddhism

Buddhism, as it is practiced in Thailand, is not the 'other-worldly' religion of Western conception. Ultimate salvation – enlightenment, or *nirvana* – is a distant goal for most people. Thai Buddhists pursue the Law of Karma, the reduction of suffering. Meritorious acts are undertaken and demeritorious ones avoided so that life, and more particularly future life, might be improved. Outside many wats it is common to see caged birds or turtles being sold: these are purchased and set free, and in this way the liberator gains merit. 'Karma' (act or deed, from Pali, *kamma*) is often thought in the West to mean 'fate'. It does not. It is true that previous karma determines a person's position in society, but there is still room for individual action – and a person is ultimately responsible for that action. It is the law of cause and effect.

It is important to draw a distinction between 'academic' Buddhism, as it tends to be understood in the West, and 'popular' Buddhism, as it is practiced in Thailand. In Thailand, Buddhism is a 'syncretic' religion: it incorporates elements of Brahmanism,

The Thai Wat

Wats are usually separated from the secular world by **two walls**. Between these outer and inner walls are found the **monks quarters** or dormitories (kutis), perhaps a **bell tower** (hor rakang) that is used to toll the hours and to warn of danger and, in larger complexes, schools and other administrative buildings. Traditionally the kutis were placed on the south side of the wat. It was believed that if the monks slept directly in front of the principal Buddha image they would die young; if they slept to the left they would become ill; and if they slept behind it there would be discord in the community of monks. This section of the compound is known as the sanghavasa or sanghawat (ie for the Sangha, the monkhood).

The inner wall, which in bigger wats often takes the form of a **gallery** or cloister (phra rabieng) lined with Buddha images, represents the division between the worldly and the holy, the sacred and the profane. It is used as a quiet place for meditation. This part of the wat compound is known as the buddhavasa or phutthawat (ie for the Buddha). Within the inner courtyard, the holiest building is the **ordination hall** or ubosoth, often shortened to just **bot**. This building is reserved for monks only. It is built on consecrated ground, and has a ring of eight stone tablets or boundary markers (bai sema), sometimes contained in mini-pavilions, arranged around it at the cardinal and subcardinal points. These bai sema are shaped like stylized leaves of the bodhi tree, and often carved with representations of Vishnu, Siva, Brahma or Indra, or of nagas. Buried in the ground beneath the bai sema are luuk nimit – stone spheres – and sometimes gold and jewellery. The bai sema mark the limit of earthly power – within the stones, not even a king can issue orders.

The bot is characteristically a large, rectangular building with high walls and multiple sloping roofs covered in glazed clay tiles (or wood tiles, in the north). At each end of the roof are chofaa, or 'bunches of sky', which represent garuda grasping two nagas in its talons. Inside, often through elaborately carved and inlaid doors, is a Buddha image. There may also be numerous subsidiary images. The inside walls of the bot may be decorated with murals depicting the Jataka tales or scenes

Wat Suwannaram (Bangkok)

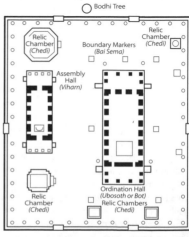

Library (Hor Trai)

Bell Tower (Hor Ramang)

Monks Quarters (Kutis)

Relic Chamber (Chedi)

N

0 metres 10
0 yards 11

Bodhi Tree

Relic Chamber (Chedi)

Relic Chamber (Chedi)

Boundary Markers (Bai Sema)

Assembly Hall (Viharn)

Ordination Hall (Ubosoth or Bot)

Relic Chambers (Chedi)

from Buddhist and Hindu cosmology. Like the Buddha image, these murals are meant to serve as meditation aids. It is customary for pilgrims to remove their shoes on entering any Buddhist building (or private house for that matter) although in state ceremonies, officials in uniform are not required to do so.

The other main building within the inner courtyard is the **assembly hall** or **viharn**, but not all wats have one, and some may have more than one. Architecturally this is often indistinguishable from the bot. It contains the wat's principal Buddha images. The main difference between the bot and viharn is that the latter does not stand on consecrated ground, and can be identified by the absence of any bai sema – stone tablets – set around it. The viharn is for general use and unlike the bot is rarely locked. Both bot and viharn are supposed to face water, because the Buddha himself was facing a river when he achieved enlightenment under the bodhi tree. If there is no natural body of water, the monks may dig a pond. In the late Ayutthayan period, the curved lines of the bot and viharn were designed to symbolize a boat.

Also found in the inner courtyard may be a number of other structures. Among the more common are **chedis**, bell-shaped **relic chambers** with tapering spires. In larger wats these can be built on a massive scale (such as the one at Nakhon Pathom, see page 112), and contain holy relics of the Buddha himself. More often, chedis are smaller affairs containing the ashes of royalty, monks or pious lay people. A rarer Khmer architectural feature sometimes found in Thai wats is the **prang**, also a relic chamber (see page). The best known of these angular corn-cob-shaped towers is the one at Wat Arun in Bangkok (see page).

Another rarer feature is the **library** or scripture repository (hor trai), usually a small, tall-sided building where the Buddhist scriptures can be stored safely, high off the ground. Salas are open-sided **rest pavilions** which can be found anywhere in the wat compound; the sala kan parian or **study hall** is the largest and most impressive of these and is almost like a bot or viharn without walls. Here the monks say their prayers at noon.

animism and ancestor worship. Amulets are worn to protect against harm and are often sold in temple compounds (see page 89). Brahmanistic 'spirit' houses can be found outside most buildings. In the countryside, farmers have what they consider to be a healthy regard for the spirits (phi) and demons that inhabit the rivers, trees and forests. Astrologers are widely consulted by urban and rural dwellers alike. Even former prime minister Chaovalit Yongchaiyudh employed a monk to knock his head with a wooden mallet for good luck. It is these aspects of Thai Buddhism which help to provide worldly assurance, and they are perceived to be complementary, not in contradiction, with Buddhist teachings. But Thai Buddhism is not homogeneous. There are deep scriptural and practical divisions between 'progressive' monks and the sangha (the monkhood) hierarchy, for example.

Islam

While Thailand is often portrayed as a 'Buddhist Kingdom', the provinces of the far south are majority Muslim. This is because these provinces have, historically, come under the cultural influence of the former sultanates of the Malay peninsula.

Background

In Siddhartha's footsteps: a short history of Buddhism

Buddhism was founded by Siddhartha Gautama, a prince of the Sakya tribe of Nepal, who probably lived between 563 and 483 BC. He achieved enlightenment and the word buddha means 'fully enlightened one', or 'one who has woken up'. Siddhartha Gautama is known by a number of titles. In the west, he is usually referred to as The Buddha, ie the historic Buddha (but not just Buddha); more common in Southeast Asia is the title Sakyamuni, or Sage of the Sakyas (referring to his tribal origins).

Over the centuries, the life of the Buddha has become part legend, and the Jataka tales which recount his various lives are colourful and convoluted. But, central to any Buddhist's belief is that he was born under a sal tree, that he achieved enlightenment under a bodhi tree in the Bodh Gaya Gardens, that he preached the First Sermon at Sarnath, and that he died at Kusinagara (all in India or Nepal).

The Buddda was born at Lumbini (in present-day Nepal), as Queen Maya was on her way to her parents' home. She had had a very auspicious dream before the child's birth of being impregnated by an elephant, whereupon a sage prophesied that Siddhartha would become either a great king or a great spiritual leader. His father, being keen that the first option of the prophesy be fulfilled, brought him up in all the princely skills – at which Siddhartha excelled – and ensured that he only saw beautiful things, not the harsher elements of life.

Despite his father's efforts Siddhartha saw four things while travelling between palaces – a helpless old man, a very sick man, a corpse being carried by lamenting relatives, and an ascetic, calm and serene as he begged for food. The young prince renounced his princely origins and left home to study under a series of spiritual teachers. He finally discovered the path to enlightenment at the Bodh Gaya Gardens in India. He then proclaimed his thoughts to a small group of disciples at Sarnath, near Benares, and continued to preach and attract followers until he died at the age of 81 at Kusinagara.

In the First Sermon at the deer park in Sarnath, the Buddha preached the Four Truths, which are still considered the root of Buddhist belief and practical experience: suffering exists; there is a cause of suffering; suffering can be ended; and to end suffering it is necessary to follow the 'Noble Eightfold Path' – namely, right speech, livelihood, action, effort, mindfulness, concentration, opinion and intention.

Soon after the Buddha began preaching, a monastic order – the Sangha – was established. As the monkhood evolved in India, it also began to fragment into different sects. An important change was the belief that the Buddha was transcendent: he had never been born, nor had he died; he had always existed and his life on earth had been mere illusion. The emergence of these new concepts helped to turn what up until then was an ethical code of conduct, into a religion. It eventually led to the appearance of a new Buddhist movement, Mahayana Buddhism which split from the more traditional Theravada 'sect'.

Despite the division of Buddhism into two sects, the central tenets of the religion are common to both: specifically, the principles pertaining to the Four Noble Truths, the Noble Eightfold Path, the Dependent Origination, the Law of Karma, and nirvana. In addition, the principles of non-violence and tolerance are also embraced by both sects. In essence, the differences between the two are of emphasis and interpretation. Theravada Buddhism is strictly based on the original Pali Canon, while the Mahayana tradition stems from later Sanskrit texts. Mahayana Buddhism also allows a broader and more varied interpretation of the doctrine. Other important differences are that while the Thervada tradition is more 'intellectual' and self-obsessed, with an emphasis upon the attaining of wisdom and insight for oneself, Mahayana Buddhism stresses devotion and compassion towards others.

The practice of Islam: living by the Prophet

Islam is an Arabic word meaning 'submission to God'. As Muslims often point out, it is not just a religion but a total way of life. The main Islamic scripture is the Koran or Quran, the name being taken from the Arabic al-qur'an or 'the recitation'. The Koran is divided into 114 sura, or 'units'. Most scholars are agreed that the Koran was partially written by the Prophet Mohammad. In addition to the Koran there are the hadiths, from the Arabic word hadith meaning 'story', which tell of the Prophet's life and works. These represent the second most important body of scriptures.

The practice of Islam is based upon five central tenets, known as the Pillars of Islam: Shahada (profession of faith), Salat (worship), Zakat (charity), saum (fasting) and Haj (pilgrimage). The mosque is the centre of religious activity. The two most important mosque officials are the imam – or leader – and the khatib or preacher – who delivers the Friday sermon.

The **Shahada** is the confession, and lies at the core of any Muslim's faith. It involves reciting, sincerely, two statements: 'There is no god, but God', and 'Mohammad is the Messenger [Prophet] of God'. A Muslim will do this at every **Salat**. This is the daily prayer ritual which is performed five times a day, at sunrise, midday, mid-afternoon, sunset and at night. There is also the important Friday noon worship. The Salat is performed by a Muslim bowing and then prostrating himself in the direction of Mecca (in Malaysian kiblat, in Arabic qibla). In hotel rooms throughout there is nearly always a little arrow, painted on the ceiling – or sometimes inside a wardrobe – indicating the direction of Mecca and labelled kiblat. The faithful are called to worship by a mosque official. Beforehand, a worshipper must wash to ensure ritual purity. The Friday midday service is performed in the mosque and includes a sermon given by the khatib.

A third essential element of Islam is **Zakat** – charity or alms-giving. A Muslim is supposed to give up his 'surplus' (according to the Koran); through time this took on the form of a tax levied according to the wealth of the family. In Thailand there is no official Zakat as there is in Saudi Arabia, but good Muslims are expected to contribute a tithe to the Muslim community.

The fourth pillar of Islam is **saum** or fasting. The daytime month-long fast of Ramadan is a time of contemplation, worship and piety – the Islamic equivalent of lent. Muslims are expected to read one-thirtieth of the Koran each night. Muslims who are ill or on a journey have dispensation from fasting, but otherwise they are only permitted to eat during the night until "so much of the dawn appears that a white thread can be distinguished from a black one".

The **Haj** or Pilgrimmage to the holy city of Mecca in Saudi Arabia is required of all Muslims once in their lifetime if they can afford to make the journey and are physically able to. It is restricted to a certain time of the year, beginning on the eighth day of the Muslim month of Dhu-l-Hijja. Men who have been on the Haj are given the title Haji, and women hajjah.

The Koran also advises on a number of other practices and customs, in particular the prohibitions on usury, the eating of pork, the taking of alcohol, and gambling. In Thailand, these are not strictly interpreted. Islamic banking laws have not been introduced, and drinking is fairly widespread – although not in all areas. There is quite a powerful Islamic revival in Malaysia and Brunei and some scholars and commentators identify the beginnings of a similar trend in Thailand. But while the use of the veil is becoming de rigueur in Brunei and increasingly in Malaysia it is still only rarely encountered in Thailand. The Koran says nothing about the need for women to veil, although it does stress the necessity of women dressing modestly.

Land and environment

Geography Thailand covers an area of 500,000 sq km (about the size of France) and had a population in 1998 of 61.5 million growing at 1½% each year. It shares its borders with Myanmar (Burma), Laos, Cambodia and Malaysia.

Climate Thailand lies within the humid tropics and remains hot throughout the year. Mean temperatures vary between 24°C in the far north to 29°C in the central region, while rainfall ranges from 1,200 mm in parts of the northeast to over 4,000 mm in some parts of the south (eg Ranong) and east (eg Khlong Yai, Chantaburi). Far more important than these mean annual figures are seasonal fluctuations in rainfall and, to a lesser extent, temperature. With the exception of the southern isthmus, which receives rainfall throughout the year, Thailand has a dry season which stretches from November to April corresponding with the period of the northeast monsoon, and a wet season from May to October, corresponding with the southwest monsoon.

The dry season can be divided into two, cool and hot. The cool season extends from December to February and the hot season from March to June when temperatures may exceed 40°C before the cooling rains arrive towards the end of the period.

Hot Season March to May, dry with temperatures 27°C-35°C, but sometimes in the 40s for extended periods.

Wet or rainy season June to October, wet with lower temperatures (due to the cooling effect of the rain and increased cloud cover) 24°C-32°C, but higher humidity.

Cool season November to February, when conditions are at their most pleasant, with little rain and temperatures ranging from 18°C-32°C.

Seasons in the South Similar weather to that of the Malay peninsula with hot, humid and sunny weather most of the year. Chance of rain at any time, although more likely during the period of the two monsoons, May-October (particularly on west side of the peninsula) and November-April (particularly on east coast).

Marine life Thailand's coastline abuts onto both the Indian Ocean (Andaman Sea) and the South China Sea (Gulf of Thailand) and therefore has marine flora and fauna characteristic of both regions. In the Gulf, 850 species of open-water fish have been identified including tuna, of which Thailand is the world's largest exporter (although most are now caught outside Thailand's waters). In the Andaman Sea, game fish such as blue and black marlin, barracuda, sailfish and various sharks are all present.

Among sea mammals, Thailand's shores provide nesting sites for four species of **sea turtle**: the huge leatherback, green, Ridley's and the hawksbill turtle. The hawksbill is now very rare, while a fifth species, the loggerhead turtle, has disappeared from Thailand's shores and waters. Other marine mammals include several species of sea snake (see above), the saltwater crocodile (which may now be extinct), three species of dolphin, and the dugong or sea cow.

Coral reefs probably contain a richer profusion of life than any other ecosystem – even exceeding the tropical rainforest in terms of species diversity. Those in Thailand's Andaman Sea are among the finest in the region – and maritime parks like the Surin and Similan islands have been gazetted to help protect these delicate habitats. Although the country's reefs remain under-researched, 210 species of hard coral and 108 coral reef fish have so far been identified in the Andaman Sea. Literally tens of thousands of other marine organisms including soft corals, crustacea, echinoderms and worms would have to be added to this list to build up a true picture of the ecosystem's diversity.

But like the rest of Thailand's natural heritage, life under the sea is also threatened. Collin Piprell and Ashley J Boyd vividly recount this story in their book *Thailand's coral reefs: nature under threat* (Bangkok: White Lotus). Some reefs have been virtually wiped out by human depradations – for example that off Koh Larn near Pattaya. Fish stocks in the Gulf of Thailand are seriously depleted and the destruction of mangroves along both the eastern and western seaboards has seriously eroded the main breeding grounds for many fish. Untreated effluent and raw sewage are dumped into the Gulf and because it is an almost enclosed body of water this tends to become concentrated. Marine biologists have identified some instances of sex-changes in shellfish communities – apparently because of the build-up of toxic compounds.

It has to be acknowledged that although tourism in some areas of Thailand has an interest in maintaining the sanctity of the marine environment, it has also been a major cause of destruction. Anchors, rubbish and sewerage, the thrashing fins of novice divers, and the selfish grabbing hands of collectors of shells, all contribute to the gradual erosion of the habitat that tourists come to experience. Other sources of destruction have less or nothing to do with tourism: the accumulation of toxic chemicals, Thailand's voracious fishermen, cyanide and dynamite fishing, the trade in aquarium fish, and the collection and sale of certain species for their use in traditional Chinese medicines. The Kingdom is, for example, the world's largest exporter of seahorses. Around 15 tonnes of the dried creatures are exported each year, mostly to Taiwan and Hong Kong where their crushed bodies are believed to be an aphrodisiac and a cure for certain respiratory ailments. Like the Kingdom's forests, there are fears that within a decade there might be little left for the discerning diver to enjoy.

National Parks

In 1961 Khao Yai became Thailand's first national park – although King Ramkhamhaeng of Sukhothai created a royal reserve in the 13th century, and the grounds of Buddhist wats have always provided havens for wildlife. By the end of 1995 there were 81 parks covering over 41,000 sq km spread throughout the kingdom, encompassing all the principal ecological zones - and more have been gazetted since. Including Thailand's 35 wildlife sanctuaries (which cover another 29,000 sq km), and 48 non-hunting areas, nearly 15% of Thailand's land area is protected in some way.

National park facilities

Most national parks have a park office with wardens (often not English-speaking), bungalows and dormitories for hire, camping grounds, and trails (not always well marked). Bungalows in the more popular parks are often booked-up, so advance booking is recommended. For reservations contact: Reservation Office, National Parks Division, Royal Forestry Department, Phanhonyothin Road, Bangkhen, Bangkok BT5794842/5790529/5614292; or telephone park offices given in the relevant sections of this guide.

Background

Footnotes

9

452

Footnotes

Glossary

A

Amitabha
the Buddha of the Past
(see *Avalokitsvara*)

Amphoe
district; administrative division below
the province

Amulet
protective medallion

Ao
bay

Arhat
a person who has perfected himself;
images of former monks are sometimes
carved into *arhat*

Avadana
Buddhist narrative, telling of the deeds
of saintly souls

Avalokitsvara
also known as Amitabha and
Lokeshvara, the name literally means
'World Lord'; he is the compassionate
male Bodhisattva, the saviour of
Mahayana Buddhism and represents
the central force of creation in the
universe; usually portrayed with a lotus
and water flask

B

Bai sema
boundary stones marking consecrated
ground around a Buddhist bot

Ban
village; shortened from *muban*

Baray
man-made lake or reservoir

Batik
a form of resist dyeing

Bhikku
Buddhist monk

Bodhi
the tree under which the Buddha
achieved enlightenment (*Ficus religiosa*)

Bodhisattva
a future Buddha. In Mahayana
Buddhism, someone who has attained
enlightenment, but who postpones
nirvana to help others reach it.

Bot
Buddhist ordination hall, of rectangular
plan, identifiable by the boundary
stones placed around it; an abbreviation
of *ubosoth*

Brahma
the Creator, one of the gods of the Hindu
trinity, usually represented with four
faces, and often mounted on a *hamsa*

Brahmin
a Hindu priest

Bun
to make merit

C

Caryatid
elephants, often used as buttressing
decorations

Celadon
pottery ware with blue/green to grey
glaze

Chakri
the current royal dynasty in Thailand.
They have reigned since 1782

Champa
rival empire of the Khmers, of Hindu
culture, based in present-day Vietnam

Changwat
province

Chao
title for Lao and Thai kings

Chat
honorific umbrella or royal multi-tiered
parasol

Chedi
from the Sanskrit *cetiya* (Pali, *caitya*)
meaning memorial. Usually a religious
monument (often bell-shaped)
containing relics of the Buddha or other

holy remains. Used interchangeably
with stupa
Chofa
'sky tassel' on the roof of wat buildings
CPT
Communist Party of Thailand

Deva
a Hindu-derived male god
Devata
a Hindu-derived goddess
Dharma
the Buddhist law
Dipterocarp
family of trees (Dipterocarpaceae)
characteristic of Southeast Asia's forests
Dvarapala
guardian figure, usually placed at the
entrance to a temple

Farang
Westerner

Ganesh
elephant-headed son of Siva
Garuda
mythical divine bird, with predatory
beak and claws, and human body; the
king of birds, enemy of *naga* and mount
of Vishnu
Gautama
the historic Buddha
Geomancy
the art of divination by lines and figures
Gopura
crowned or covered gate, entrance to a
religious area

Hamsa
sacred goose, Brahma's mount; in
Buddhism it represents the flight of the
doctrine
Hang yaaw
long-tailed boat, used on canals
Harmika
box-like part of a Burmese stupa that
often acts as a reliquary casket

Hat
beach
Hinayana
'Lesser Vehicle', major Buddhist sect in
Southeast Asia, usually termed
Theravada Buddhism
Hong
swan
Hor kong
a pavilion built on stilts where the
monastery drum is kept
Hor takang
bell tower
Hor tray/trai
library where manuscripts are stored in
a Thai monastery
Hti
'umbrella' surmounting Burmese
temples, often encrusted with jewels

Ikat
tie-dyeing method of patterning cloth
Indra
the Vedic god of the heavens, weather
and war; usually mounted on a
three-headed elephant

Jataka(s)
the birth stories of the Buddha; they
normally number 547; the last ten are the
most important

Kala (makara)
literally, 'death' or 'black'; a demon
ordered to consume itself; often
sculpted with grinning face and bulging
eyes over entrances to act as a door
guardian; also known as *kirtamukha*
Kathin/krathin
a one-month period during the eighth
lunar month when lay people present
new robes and other gifts to monks
Ketumula
flame-like motif above the Buddha head
Khao
mountain
Khlong
canal

Khruang
amulet
Kinaree
half-human, half-bird, usually depicted
as a heavenly musician
Kirtamukha
see kala
Koh
island
Koutdi
see kuti
Krating
wild bull, most commonly seen on
bottles of *Red Bull* (Krating Daeng)
stimulant drink
Krishna
incarnation of Vishnu
Kuti
living quarters of Buddhist monks in a
monastery complex

Laem
cape (as in bay)
Lak muang
city pillar
Lakhon
traditional Thai classical music
Laterite
bright red tropical soil/stone
commonly used in construction of
Khmer monuments
Linga
phallic symbol and one of the forms of
Siva. Embedded in a pedastal shaped to
allow drainage of lustral water poured
over it, the *linga* typically has a
succession of cross sections: from
square at the base through octagonal to
round. These symbolise, in order, the
trinity of Brahma, Vishnu and Siva
Lintel
a load-bearing stone spanning a
doorway; often heavily carved
Lokeshvara
see *Avalokitsvara*

Mahabharata
a Hindu epic text written about 2,000
years ago

Mahayana
'Greater Vehicle', major Buddhist sect
Maitreya
the future Buddha
Makara
a mythological aquatic reptile,
somewhat like a crocodile and
sometimes with an elephant's trunk;
often found along with the *kala* framing
doorways
Mandala
a focus for meditation; a representation
of the cosmos
Mara
personification of evil and tempter of
the Buddha
Matmii
Northeastern Thai cotton *ikat*
Meru
sacred or cosmic mountain at the centre
of the world in Hindu-Buddhist
cosmology; home of the gods
Mon
race and kingdom of southern Burma
and central Thailand from 7th-11th
century
Mondop
from the sanskrit, *mandapa*. A
cube-shaped building, often topped
with a cone-like structure, used to
contain an object of worship like a
footprint of the Buddha
Muang
'town' in Thai, but also sometimes
'municipality' or 'district'
Muban
village, usually shortened to ban
Mudra
symbolic gesture of the hands of the
Buddha

Naga
benevolent mythical water serpent,
enemy of Garuda
Naga makara
fusion of *naga* and *makara*
Nalagiri
the elephant let loose to attack the
Buddha, who calmed him
Namtok
waterfall

Footnotes

456

Nandi/nandin
bull, mount of Siva
Nang thalung
shadow play/puppets
Nikhom
resettlement village
Nirvana
release from the cycle of suffering in
Buddhist belief; 'enlightenment'

Pa kama
Lao men's all-purpose cloth usually
woven with checked pattern
paddy/padi
unhulled rice
Pali
the sacred language of Theravada
Buddhism
Parvati
consort of Siva
Pha sin
tubular piece of cloth, similar to sarong
Phi
spirit
Phnom/phanom
Khmer for hill/mountain
Phra sinh
see *pha sin*
Pradaksina
pilgrims' clockwise circumambulation of
holy structure
Prah
sacred
Prang
form of stupa built in Khmer style,
shaped like a corncob
Prasada
stepped pyramid (see *prasat*)
Prasat
residence of a king or of the gods
(sanctuary tower), from the Indian
prasada

Quan Am
Chinese goddess (Kuan-yin) of mercy

Rai
unit of measurement, 1ha = 6.25rai
Rama
incarnation of Vishnu, hero of the Indian
epic, the *Ramayana*
Ramakien
Thai version of the *Ramayana*
Ramayana
Hindu romantic epic, known as
Ramakien in Thailand

Saamlor
three-wheeled bicycle taxi
Sakyamuni
the historic Buddha
Sal
the Indian sal tree (*Shorea robusta*), under
which the historic Buddha was born
Sala
open pavilion
Sangha
the Buddhist order of monks
Sawankhalok
type of ceramic
Singha
mythical guardian lion
Siva
the Destroyer, one of the three gods of
the Hindu trinity; the sacred linga was
worshipped as a symbol of Siva
Sofa
see *dok sofa*
Songthaew
'two rows': pick-up truck with benches
along either side
Sravasti
the miracle at Sravasti when the Buddha
subdues the heretics in front of a
mango tree
Stele
inscribed stone panel
Stucco
plaster, often heavily moulded
Stupa
chedi

Footnotes

T

Talaat
market
Tambon
a commune of villages
Tam bun
see *bun*
Tavatimsa
heaven of the 33 gods at the summit of Mount Meru
Tazaungs
small pavilions found within Burmese temple complexes
Tham
cave
Thanon
street
That
shrine housing Buddhist relics, a spire or dome-like edifice commemorating the Buddha's life or the funerary temple for royalty; peculiar to parts of Northeastern Thailand as well as Laos
Thein
Burmese ordination hall
Theravada
'Way of the Elders'; major Buddhist sect also known as Hinayana Buddhism ('Lesser Vehicle')
Traiphum
the three worlds of Buddhist cosmology – heaven, hell and earth
Trimurti
the Hindu trinity of gods: Brahma, the Creator, Vishnu the Preserver and Siva the Destroyer
Tripitaka
Theravada Buddhism's Pali canon
Tuk-tuk
motorised three-wheeled taxi
Tukata
doll

U

Ubosoth
see *bot*
Urna
the dot or curl on the Buddha's forehead, one of the distinctive physical marks of the Enlightened One

Usnisa
the Buddha's top knot or 'wisdom bump', one of the physical marks of the Enlightened One

V

Vahana
'vehicle', a mythical beast, upon which a *deva* or god rides
Viharn
from Sanskrit *vihara*, an assembly hall in a Buddhist monastery; may contain Buddha images and is similar in style to the bot
Vishnu
the Protector, one of the gods of the Hindu trinity, generally with four arms holding a disc, conch shell, ball and club

W

Wai
Thai greeting, with hands held together at chin height as if in prayer
Wat
Buddhist 'monastery' with religious and other buildings

Words & phrases

Thai is a tonal language with five tones: mid tone (no mark), high tone (ˊ), low tone (ˋ), falling tone (ˆ), and rising tone (ˇ). Tones are used to distinguish between words which are otherwise the same. For example, 'see' pronounced with a low tone means 'four'; with a rising tone, it means 'colour'. Thai is not written in Roman script but using an alphabet derived from Khmer. The Romanization given below is only intended to help in pronouncing Thai words. There is no accepted method of Romanization and some of the sounds in Thai cannot be accurately reproduced using Roman script.

Polite particles

At the end of sentences males use the polite particle 'krúp', and females, 'kâ' or 'ká'.

Learning Thai

The list of words and phrases below is only very rudimentary. For anyone serious about learning Thai it is best to buy a dedicated Thai language text book or to enrol on a Thai course. Recommended among the various 'teach yourself Thai' books is: Somsong Buasai and David Smyth's (1990) *Thai in a Week*, Hodder & Stoughton: London. A useful mini-dictionary is the Hugo *Thai phrase book* (1990). For those interested in learning to read and write Thai, the best 'teach yourself' course is the *Linguaphone* course.

General words & phrases

Yes/no
   chái/mâi chái, or: *krúp(kâ)/mâi krúp(kâ)*
Thank you/no thank you
   kòrp-kOOn/mâi ao kòrp-kOOn
Hello, good morning, goodbye
   sa-wùt dee krúp(kâ)
What is your name? My name is...
   Koon chêu a-rai krúp (kâ)? Pŏm chêu...
Excuse me, sorry!
   kŏr-tôht krúp(kâ)
Can/do you speak English?
   KOON pôot pah-săh ung-grìt
a little, a bit *nít-nòy*
Where's the... *yòo têe-năi...*
How much is... *tâo-rài...*
Pardon? *a-rai ná?*
I don't understand
   pŏm (chún) mâi kao jái
How are you? Not very well
   sa-bai dee mái? Mâi sa-bai

At hotels

What is the charge each night?
   kâh hôrng wun la tâo-rài?
Is the room air conditioned?
   hôrng dtìt air rěu bplào?
Can I see the room first please?
   kŏr doo hôrng gòrn dâi mái?
Does the room have hot water?
   hôrng mii náhm rórn mái?
Does the room have a bathroom?
   hôrng mii hôrng náhm mái?
Can I have the bill please?
   kŏr bin nòy dâi mái?

Travelling

Where is the train station?
   sa-tăhn-nee rót fai yòo têe-năi?
Where is the bus station?
   sa-tăhn-nee rót may yòo têe-năi?
How much to go to...?
   bpai...tâo-rài?
That's expensive
   pairng bpai nòy
What time does the bus/train leave for...?
   rót may/rót fai bpai...òrk gèe mohng?
Is it far? *glai mái?*
Turn left/turn right
   lée-o sái / lée-o kwăh
Go straight on
   ler-ee bpai èek
It's straight ahead
   yòo dtrong nâh

At restaurants

Can I see a menu?
   kŏr doo may-noo nòy?
Can I have...?/ I would like...? *Kŏr...*
Is it very (hot) spicy?
   pèt mâhk mái?
I am hungry *pŏm (chún) hěw*
Breakfast *ah-hăhn cháo*
Lunch *ah-hăhn glanhg wun*

Time & days

in the morning	*dtorn cháo*
in the afternoon	*dtorn bài*
in the evening	*dtorn yen*
today	*wun née*
tomorrow	*prÔOng née*
yesterday	*mêu-a wahn née*
Monday	*wun jun*
Tuesday	*wun ung-kahn*
Wednesday	*wun pÓOt*
Thursday	*wun pá-réu-hùt*
Friday	*wun sÒOk*
Saturday	*wun săo*
Sunday	*wun ah-tít*

Numbers

1	*nèung*
2	*sŏrng*
3	*săhm*
4	*sèe*
5	*hâa*
6	*hòk*
7	*jèt*
8	*bpàirt*
9	*gâo*
10	*sìp*
11	*sìp-et*
12	*sìp-sŏrng...etc*
20	*yêe-sìp*
21	*yêe-sìp-et*
22	*yêe-sìp-sŏrng...etc*
30	*săhm-sìp*
100	*(nèung) róy*
101	*(nèung) róy-nèung*
150	*(nèung) róy-hâh-sìp*
200	*sŏrng róy...etc*
1,000	*(nèung) pun*
10,000	*mèun*
100,000	*săirn*
1,000,000	*láhn*

Basic vocabulary

airport	*sa-năhm bin*
bank	*ta-nah-kahn*
bathroom	*hôrng náhm*
beach	*hàht*
beautiful	*sŏo-ay*
big	*yài*
boat	*reu-a*
bus	*rót may*
bus station	*sa-tăh-nee rót may*
buy	*séu*

chemist	*ráhn kai yah*
clean	*sa-àht*
closed	*bpìt*
cold	*yen*
day	*wun*
delicious	*a-ròy*
dirty	*sòk-ga-bpròk*
doctor	*mor*
eat	*gin (kâo)*
embassy	*sa-tăhn tôot*
excellent	*yêe-um*
expensive	*pairng*
food	*ah-hăhn*
fruit	*pŏn-la-mái*
hospital	*rohng pa-yah-bahn*
hot (temp)	*rórn*
hot (spicy)	*pèt*
hotel	*rôhng rairm*
island	*gòr*
market	*dta-làht*
medicine	*yah*
open	*bpèrt*
police	*dtum-ròo-ut*
police station	*sa-tăh-nee dtum-ròo-ut*
post office	*bprai-sa-nee*
restaurant	*ráhn ah-hăhn*
road	*thanon*
room	*hôrng*
shop	*ráhn*
sick (ill)	*mâi sa-bai*
silk	*măi*
small	*lék*
stop	*yÒOt*
taxi	*táirk-sêe*
that	*nún*
this	*née*
ticket	*dtŏo-a*
toilet	*hôrng náhm*
town	*meu-ung*
train station	*sa-tăh-nee rót fai*
very	*mâhk*
water	*náhm*
what	*a-rai*

Food glossary

a-haan food
ba-mii egg noodles
bia beer
chaa tea
check bin bill/cheque
chorn spoon
jaan plate
gaeng curry
gaeng chud soup
kaafae (ron) coffee (hot)
kaew glass
kai chicken
kap klaem snacks to be eaten when drinking
kwaytio noodle soup, white noodles
khaaw niaw sticky rice
khaaw tom rice gruel
khaaw/khao rice
khai egg
khai dao fried egg
khai khon scrambled egg
khanom sweet, dessert or cake
khanom cake cake
khanom pang bread
khanom pang ping toast
khing ginger
khuan scramble
khuat bottle
kin to eat
kleua salt
krueng kieng side dishes
kung shrimp
lao liquor
man root vegetable
man farang potatoes
manaaw lemon
mekong Thai whisky

mit knife
muu pork
nam chaa tea
nam kheng ice
nam kuat bottled water
nam manaaw soda lime soda
nam plaa fish sauce
nam plaa prik fish sauce with chilli
nam plaaw plain water
nam som orange juice
nam taan sugar
nam tom boiled water
nom milk
nua meat (usually beef)
phak vegetables
phat to stir fry
phet hot (chilli)
phon lamai fruit
pla fish
poo crab
priaw sour
priaw waan sweet and sour
prik hot chilli
raan a-haan restaurant
ratnaa in gravy
rawn hot (temperature)
sa-te satay
sorm fork
talaat market
thao mai luai morning glory
thua nut/bean
tom to boil
tort to deep fry
waan sweet
yam salad
yen cold

Fares and timetables

Average distances and flying time on domestic routes

ROUTE	DISTANCES (km)	FLYING TIME (outbound)
From Bangkok to:		
Hat Yai	776	1 hour 25 minutes
Nakhon Si Thammarat	611	1 hour 55 minutes
Phuket	693	1 hour 15 minutes
Trang	720	2 hours 5 minutes
Surat Thani	555	1 hour 5 minutes
From Nakhon Si Thammarat to:		
Surat Thani	117	35 minutes
From Phuket to:		
Hat Yai (ATR)	265	44 / 55 minutes
Surat Thani	146	35 minutes
Trang	160	40 minutes
Narathiwat	419	1 hour 15 minutes
From Surat Thani to:		
Nakhon Si Thammarat	117	35 minutes

Footnotes

Sample domestic air fares

ROUTE	FARE (baht)*	ROUTE	FARE (baht)*
Thai Airways		**Bangkok Airways**	
Bangkok to:		**Bangkok to:**	
Hat Yai	2,885	Ranong	2,280
Nakhon Si Thammarat	2,305	Koh Samui	3,150
Narathiwat (via Phuket)	3,220	**Samui to:**	
Phuket	2,570	Phuket	1,530
Surat Thani	2,325	**U-Tapao (Pattaya) to:**	
Trang	2,575	Koh Samui	1,890
Phuket to:			
Hat Yai	1,180	**Angel Air**	
Narathiwat	1,425		
		Bangkok to:	
		Phuket	2,000

* late 2000 fares quoted, one-way economy (return fares are double)

State railways of Thailand: sample routes and fares

ROUTE	HOURS	DISTANCE (km)	FARE (Baht) 1st Class	2nd Class	3rd Class
Bangkok east to:					
Chonburi	2¾ hours	108			23
Pattaya	3¾ hours	155			31
Bangkok south to:					
Nakhon Pathom	1½ hours	64	60	31	14
Kanchanaburi	2½ hours	133	123	64	28
Phetburi	3 hours	167	153	78	34
Hua Hin	4 hours 10 minutes	229	202	102	44
Prachuap Khiri Khan	5 hours	318	272	135	58
Chumphon	7 hours 45 minutes	485	394	190	82
Surat Thani	11 hours	651	519	248	107
Trang	15 hours	845	660	311	135
Nakhon Si Thammarat	15 hours	832	652	308	133
Phatthalung	15 hours	862	675	318	137
Hat Yai	16 hours	945	734	345	149
Yala		1,055	815	382	165
Sungei Golok		1,159	893	417	180

Buses in Thailand:
sample routes and fares

ROUTE	DISTANCE (km)	HOURS	VIP	FARE A/C	Non-A/C
Bangkok south to:					
Nakhon Pathom	56	1	-	28	15
Phetburi	160	2	-	-	51
Hua Hin	201	3½	-	92	61
Chumphon	500	7	268	190	136
Surat Thani	668	11	350	285	158
Nakhon Si Thammarat	800	12	640	410	230
Phangnga	879	15	625	401	224
Phuket	891	14	570	378	254
Krabi	867	14	655	421	234
Trang	862	14	685	439	246
Hat Yai	954	15	625	428	289
Songkhla	1,004	16	500	425	286
Yala	1,153	16	865	555	310
Sungei Golok	1,266	18	-	533	282
Bangkok east to:					
Chonburi	80	-	-	47	26
Pattaya	136	-	-	66	37
Ban Phe	196	-	-	90	50
Chantaburi	239	-	-	129	92
Trat	317	-	-	158	113

Note:

1. Times are for travelling by a/c bus; non-a/c buses are slower

2. Note that fares may have increased and they also vary between services (for example, there is more than one type of a/c service).

3. VIP coaches have fewer seats (just 8 rows) and seats that can recline further; VIP coaches are not available on all routes and most travel on overnight journeys only.

Footnotes

464

Shorts

Index

Footnotes

Footnotes

Maps

Will you help us?

We try as hard as we can to make each Footprint Handbook as up-to-date and accurate as possible but, of course, things always change. Many people write to us - with corrections, new information, or simply comments.

If you want to let us know about an experience or adventure - hair-raising or mundane, good or bad, exciting or boring or simply something rather special - we would be delighted to hear from you. Please give us as precise information as possible, quoting the edition number (you'll find it on the front cover) and page number of the Handbook you are using.

Your help will be greatly appreciated, especially by other travellers. In return we will send you details about our special guidebook offer.

email Footprint at:
bbea1_online@footprintbooks.com

or write to:
Elizabeth Taylor
Footprint Handbooks
6 Riverside Court
Lower Bristol Road
Bath BA2 3DZ
UK

Footprint travel list

Footprint publish travel guides to over 120 countries worldwide. Each guide is packed with practical, concise and colourful information for everybody from first-time travellers to travel aficionados . The list is growing fast and current titles are noted below. For further information check out the website **www.footprintbooks.com**

Andalucía Handbook
Argentina Handbook
Bali & the Eastern Isles Hbk*
Bangkok & the Beaches Hbk*
Bolivia Handbook
Brazil Handbook
Cambodia Handbook
Caribbean Islands Handbook
Chile Handbook
Colombia Handbook
Cuba Handbook
Dominican Republic Handbook*
East Africa Handbook
Ecuador & Galápagos Handbook
Egypt Handbook Handbook
Goa Handbook
India Handbook
Indian Himalaya Handbook*
Indonesia Handbook
Ireland Handbook
Israel Handbook
Jordan Handbook*
Jordan, Syria & Lebanon Hbk
Laos Handbook
Libya Handbook*
Malaysia Handbook
Myanmar Handbook
Mexico Handbook
Mexico & Central America Hbk
Morocco Handbook
Namibia Handbook
Nepal Handbook
Pakistan Handbook

Peru Handbook
Rio de Janeiro Handbook*
Scotland Handbook
Singapore Handbook
South Africa Handbook
South American Handbook
South India Handbook*
Sri Lanka Handbook
Sumatra Handbook
Thailand Handbook
Tibet Handbook
Tunisia Handbook
Venezuela Handbook
Vietnam Handbook

* available autumn 2000

In the pipeline – Turkey, London, Kenya, Rajasthan, Scotland Highlands & Islands, Syria & Lebanon

Also available from Footprint
Traveller's Handbook
Traveller's Healthbook

Available at all good bookshops

What the papers say

"Who should pack the Footprint guides – travellers who want to escape the crowd."
The Observer

"Footprint can be depended on for accurate travel information and for imparting a deep sense of respect for the lands and people they cover."
World News

"Footprint Handbooks, the best of the best."
Le Monde, Paris

"The guides for intelligent, independently minded souls of any age or budget."
Indie Traveller

"Intelligently written, amazingly accurate and bang up-to-date. Footprint have combined nearly 80 years' experience with a stunning new format to bring us guidebooks that leave the competition standing."
John Pilkington, writer and broadcaster

Footnotes

Mail order
Available worldwide in bookshops and on-line. Footprint travel guides can also be ordered directly from us in Bath, via our website **www.footprintbooks.com** or from the address on the imprint page of this book.

BTS Skytrain

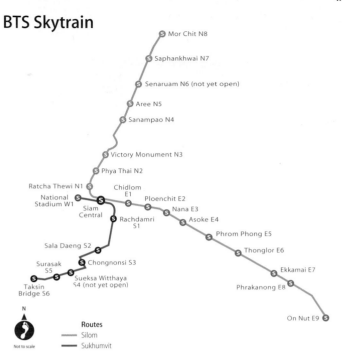

	Narathiwat	Yala	Pattani	Songkhla	Hat Yai	Phattalung	Trang	Nakhon Si Thammarat	Krabi	Phuket	Phangnga	Surat Thani	Ranong	Prachuap Khiri Khan	Phetburi	Kanchanaburi	Nakhon Pathom
Yala	128																
Pattani	92	35															
Songkhla	194	128	99														
Hat Yai	197	132	103	26													
Phattalung	299	234	205	121	95												
Trang	355	288	280	176	148	56											
Nakhon Si Thammarat	360	295	266	161	187	99	123										
Krabi	491	425	396	313	285	193	131	233									
Phuket	671	606	577	494	466	370	312	336	176								
Phangnga	581	515	486	403	375	283	221	245	86	87							
Surat Thani	503	437	408	304	329	238	226	134	211	287	196						
Ranong	725	659	630	525	506	415	403	356	296	300	226	219					
Prachuap Khiri Khan	869	804	775	670	653	580	548	500	534	582	506	364	288				
Phetburi	1026	961	932	827	810	716	705	658	691	740	666	521	445	158			
Kanchanaburi	1164	1096	1069	964	947	854	842	795	828	877	803	658	582	295	144		
Nakhon Pathom	1124	1058	1029	925	907	814	802	755	788	837	763	618	542	255	96	85	
Bangkok	1149	1064	1055	950	933	840	828	780	814	862	788	644	588	281	123	128	56

South and West Thailand, distances between provincial capitals (Km)

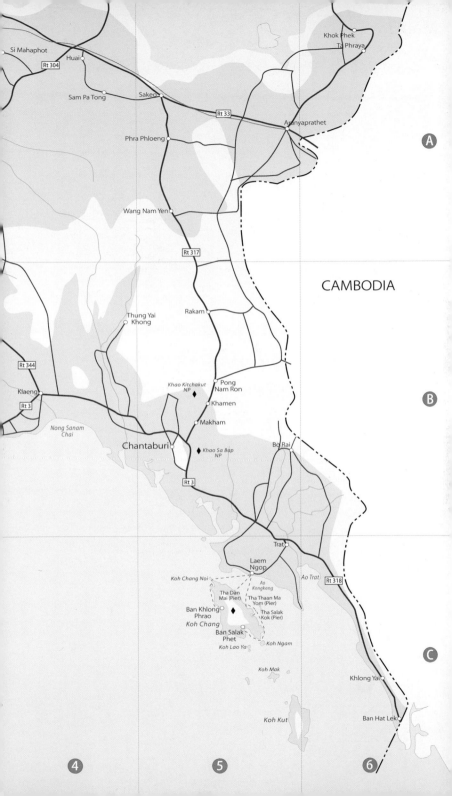

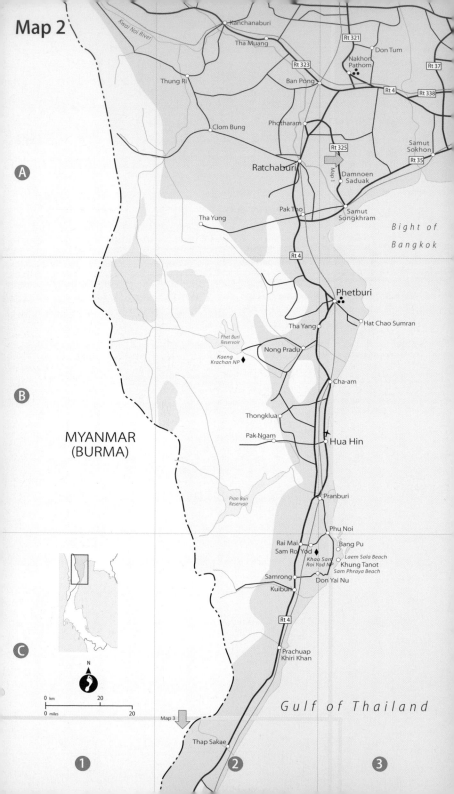

Map 3

MYANMAR
(BURMA)

Gulf of Thailand

Thap Sakae

Map 2

Bang Saphan

Koh Wiang

Mai Sombun

Rt 4

Pathiu

Tha Sae

Ao Bang
Saphan

Hin Dang

Chumphon

Pak Nam

Kra Buri

Ao Sawi

Khao Thaiu

Ao Sawi

Rt 4

Kawthoung

Ranong

Lang
Suan

Phato

Rt 41

Khuan

Nam Sai

Isthmus of Kra

Ban Mae
Hat

Koh Tao

Chong Tao

Koh Phangan

Map 4

Tha Chana

Ang Thong
Marine NP

Tong Sala

Chong Phangan

Wat Suan
Mok

Koh Ang Tong

Bophut

Chaiya

Koh Phaluai

Nathon

Tong Yang

Koh Samui

Koh Katen

Ao Ban Don

Koh Nok
Ta Phao

Chong Samui

Tha Chang

Don Suak

Khanom

Tha
Thong

Kanchanadit

Surat
Thani

Rt 401

Phun Phin

Krut

Rt 41

Chieo Lan
Reservoir

A

B

C

1

2

3

N

0 km 20

0 miles 20

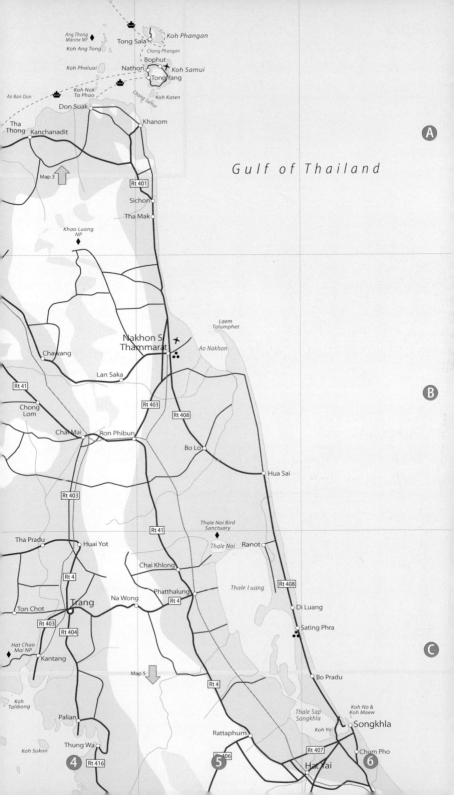

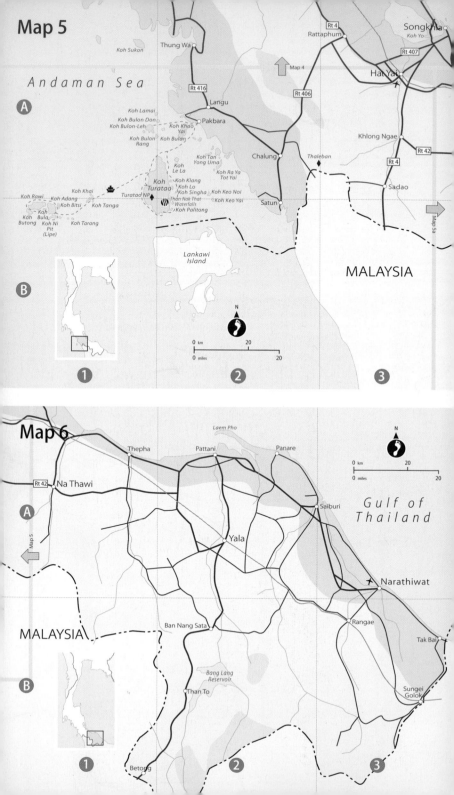

Acknowledgements

The authors would like to thank everyone for their contributions to this edition of **Bangkok and the Beaches Handbook**. We are especially grateful to Patrick Gilbert for his continued and entertaining updates.

There are also many people who have written to us with their comments, suggestions and updates. We are grateful to:

Vesa Frantsila, Finland; Mickolci Antal, Hungary; Doug Hardin, Thailand; Ian Hamilton, Thailand; V Rasten, Norway; Malousch Köhler, The Netherlands; Miskolci Antal, Hungary; Stasse Vervacke and Stephanie Pascal, Belgium; Jasmine Saville, UK; Noah Shepherd, Thailand; Caroline Broadfoot, UK; David Parry, Thailand; Maryvonne Rosseneu, Belgium; Alfred Molon; Michael Kolat, Thailand; SC Kam, Singapore; Francesca Seghetti; Dirk Singer, UK; Jeremy Krantz; Chris Mosley and Meg Fearns, UK; Olivier Meyer, Thailand; Professor Stefano Magistretti, London; Scott Brown, UK; Wendy Kinsman, Koh Phangan, Thailand; Janthana and Christian Braendli, Switzerland.

Joshua Eliot and Janie Bickersteth

Joshua Eliot has a long-standing interest in Asia. He was born in India, brought up in Hong Kong and spent a year living in a small town in northeast Thailand in the early 1980s. Since then he has visited the country two or three times a year. He has written academic and children's books about the country and advised businessmen, given radio broadcasts and lectured on cruise liners.

Janie Bickersteth first visited Thailand in 1980. She has since returned on numerous occasions to research and write about the country. As an artist, Jane has a particular interest in the material cultures of Thailand, and especially the Khmer art and architecture of the northeastern region.

Sophia Buranakul and Natapon Buranakul

Sophia Buranakul is British but has been living in Thailand off and on since 1991 and speaks Thai fluently. She has travelled extensively throughout the south of Thailand with her family, and is currently working to promote more sustainable forms of tourism in the Krabi area.

Natapon Buranakul was born in Songkhla in the south of Thailand, but spent most of his childhood in the US. Since he returned to Thailand in 1994 he has been working for various environmental organizations.